A PEOPLE AND A NATION

Brief Edition

A **P**EOPLE AND A **N**ATION

A History of the United States
Volume 2   Since 1865

Brief Seventh Edition

Mary Beth Norton
Cornell University

David M. Katzman
University of Kansas

David W. Blight
Yale University

Howard P. Chudacoff
Brown University

Fredrik Logevall
Cornell University

Beth Bailey
Temple University

Thomas G. Paterson
University of Connecticut

William M. Tuttle, Jr.
University of Kansas

Houghton Mifflin Company   Boston New York

Publisher: Charles Hartford
Sponsoring Editor: Sally Constable
Senior Development Editor: Jeffrey Greene
Editorial Assistant: Arianne Vanni
Senior Project Editor: Bob Greiner
Editorial Assistant: Katherine Leahey
Senior Art and Design Coordinator: Jill Haber Atkins
Senior Photo Editor: Jennifer Meyer Dare
Composition Buyer: Chuck Dutton
Manufacturing Buyer: Florence Cadran
Senior Marketing Manager: Sandra McGuire

Cover Image: Colin Bootman, Secure, 1998. Oil on board. Private Collection / Bridgeman Art Library.

Printed in the U.S.A.

Library of Congress Catalog Number: 2005926283

Instructor's exam copy:
ISBN 13: 978-0-618-73027-8
ISBN 10: 0-618-73027-3

For orders, use student text ISBNs:
ISBN 13: 978-0-618-61152-2
ISBN 10: 0-618-61152-5

2 3 4 5 6 7 8 9-VH-09 08 07 06

Brief Contents

Maps *xi*

Figures *xi*

Tables *xi*

Preface to the Brief Seventh Edition *xiii*

Preface to the Full-Length Seventh Edition *xvi*

16 Reconstruction: An Unfinished Revolution, 1865–1877 *279*

17 The Development of the West, 1877–1900 *299*

18 The Machine Age, 1877–1920 *317*

19 The Vitality and Turmoil of Urban Life, 1877–1920 *337*

20 Gilded Age Politics, 1877–1900 *358*

21 The Progressive Era, 1895–1920 *376*

22 The Quest for Empire, 1865–1914 *396*

23 Americans in the Great War, 1914–1920 *415*

24 The New Era, 1920–1929 *434*

25 The Great Depression and the New Deal, 1929–1941 *453*

26 Peaceseekers and Warmakers: Americans in the World, 1920–1941 *474*

27 The Second World War at Home and Abroad, 1941–1945 *492*

28 The Cold War and American Globalism, 1945–1961 *511*

29 America at Midcentury, 1945–1960 *532*

30 The Tumultuous Sixties, 1960–1968 *553*

31 Continuing Divisions and New Limits, 1969–1980 *574*

32 Conservatism Revived, 1980–1992 *595*

33 Global Bridges in the New Millennium: America Since 1992 *615*

Appendix *A-1*

Index *I-1*

CONTENTS

MAPS   *xi*

FIGURES   *xi*

TABLES   *xi*

PREFACE TO THE BRIEF SEVENTH EDITION   *xiii*

PREFACE TO THE FULL-LENGTH SEVENTH EDITION   *xvi*

16 Reconstruction: An Unfinished Revolution, 1865–1877   *279*

Wartime Reconstruction   *281*

The Meanings of Freedom   *282*

Johnson's Reconstruction Plan   *284*

The Congressional Reconstruction Plan   *286*

Reconstruction Politics in the South   *289*

Reconstruction Reversed   *292*

LINKS TO THE WORLD: **The Grants' Tour of the World**   *294*

Summary   *297*

LEGACY FOR A PEOPLE AND A NATION: **The Fourteenth Amendment**   *297*

17 The Development of the West, 1877–1900   *299*

The Economic Activities of Native Peoples   *301*

The Transformation of Native Cultures   *302*

The Extraction of Natural Resources   *306*

Irrigation and Transportation   *309*

Farming the Plains   *310*

LINKS TO THE WORLD: **The Australian Frontier**   *311*

The Ranching Frontier   *314*

Summary   *315*

LEGACY FOR A PEOPLE AND A NATION: **The West and Rugged Individualism**   *316*

18 The Machine Age, 1877–1920   *317*

Technology and the Triumph of Industrialism   *319*

LINKS TO THE WORLD: **The Atlantic Cable**   *321*

Mechanization and the Changing Status of Labor   *324*

Labor Violence and the Union Movement   *326*

Standards of Living   *329*

The Corporate Consolidation Movement   *333*

The Gospel of Wealth and Its Critics   *334*

Summary   *335*

LEGACY FOR A PEOPLE AND A NATION: **Industrialism, Smoke, and Pollution Control**   *336*

19 The Vitality and Turmoil of Urban Life, 1877–1920   *337*

Growth of the Modern City   *338*

Urban Neighborhoods   *343*

Living Conditions in the Inner City   *345*

Managing the City   *347*

Family Life   *350*

The New Leisure and Mass Culture   *352*

LINKS TO THE WORLD: **Japanese Baseball**   *354*

Summary   *357*

LEGACY FOR A PEOPLE AND A NATION: **Ethnic Food**   *357*

20 Gilded Age Politics, 1877–1900 *358*

The Nature of Party Politics   *360*
Issues of Legislation   *360*
LINKS TO THE WORLD: Missionaries   *361*
The Presidency Restrengthened   *364*
Discrimination, Disfranchisement, Response   *365*
Agrarian Unrest and Populism   *367*
The Depression and Protests of the 1890s   *370*
The Silver Crusade and the Election of 1896   *372*
Summary   *374*
LEGACY FOR A PEOPLE AND A NATION: Interpreting a Fairy Tale   *374*

21 The Progressive Era, 1895–1920 *376*

The Varied Progressive Impulse   *378*
Governmental and Legislative Reform   *381*
LINKS TO THE WORLD: Russian Temperance   *382*
New Ideas in Social Institutions   *383*
Challenges to Racial and Sexual Discrimination   *385*
Theodore Roosevelt and the Revival of the Presidency   *388*
Woodrow Wilson and the Extension of Reform   *392*
Summary   *394*
LEGACY FOR A PEOPLE AND A NATION: Margaret Sanger, Planned Parenthood, and the Birth-Control Controversy   *394*

22 The Quest for Empire, 1865–1914 *396*

Imperial Dreams   *398*
Ambitions and Strategies   *402*

Crises in the 1890s: Hawai'i, Venezuela, and Cuba   *403*
The Spanish-American War and the Debate over Empire   *405*
Asian Encounters: War in the Philippines, Diplomacy in China   *407*
LINKS TO THE WORLD: The U.S. System of Education in the Philippines   *408*
TR's World   *410*
Summary   *413*
LEGACY FOR A PEOPLE AND A NATION: The Status of Puerto Rico   *414*

23 Americans in the Great War, 1914–1920 *415*

Precarious Neutrality   *417*
The Decision for War   *418*
Winning the War   *420*
Mobilizing the Home Front   *423*
LINKS TO THE WORLD: The Influenza Pandemic of 1918   *424*
Civil Liberties Under Challenge   *427*
Red Scare, Red Summer   *428*
The Defeat of Peace   *429*
Summary   *432*
LEGACY FOR A PEOPLE AND A NATION: Freedom of Speech and the ACLU   *432*

24 The New Era, 1920–1929 *434*

Big Business Triumphant   *435*
Politics and Government   *436*
Materialism Unbound   *438*
Cities, Migrants, and Suburbs   *440*
New Rhythms of Everyday Life   *441*
LINKS TO THE WORLD: Pan American Airways   *442*
Lines of Defense   *445*
The Age of Play   *448*

Cultural Currents   *449*

The Election of 1928 and the End of the New Era   *450*

Summary   *451*

LEGACY FOR A PEOPLE AND A NATION: Intercollegiate Athletics   *452*

25 The Great Depression and the New Deal, 1929–1941   *453*

Hoover and Hard Times: 1929–1933   *455*

Franklin D. Roosevelt and the Launching of the New Deal   *459*

Political Pressure and the Second New Deal   *461*

Labor   *466*

Federal Power and the Nationalization of Culture   *467*

LINKS TO THE WORLD: The 1936 Olympic Games   *469*

The Limits of the New Deal   *470*

Summary   *472*

LEGACY FOR A PEOPLE AND A NATION: Social Security   *473*

26 Peaceseekers and Warmakers: Americans in the World, 1920–1941   *474*

Searching for Peace and Order in the 1920s   *476*

The World Economy, Cultural Expansion, and Great Depression   *477*

U.S. Dominance in Latin America   *480*

The Course to War in Europe   *481*

Japan, China, and a New Order in Asia   *483*

U.S. Entry into World War II   *484*

LINKS TO THE WORLD: Radio News   *487*

Summary   *490*

LEGACY FOR A PEOPLE AND A NATION: Presidential Deception of the Public   *490*

27 The Second World War at Home and Abroad, 1941–1945   *492*

The United States at War   *494*

The Production Front and American Workers   *496*

Life on the Home Front   *498*

The Limits of American Ideals   *500*

LINKS TO THE WORLD: War Brides   *501*

Life in the Military   *504*

Winning the War   *505*

Summary   *509*

LEGACY FOR A PEOPLE AND A NATION: Atomic Waste   *510*

28 The Cold War and American Globalism, 1945–1961   *511*

From Allies to Adversaries   *513*

Containment in Action   *517*

The Cold War in Asia   *519*

The Korean War   *520*

Unrelenting Cold War   *522*

LINKS TO THE WORLD: The People-to-People Campaign   *524*

The Struggle for the Third World   *525*

Summary   *530*

LEGACY FOR A PEOPLE AND A NATION: The National Security State   *531*

29 America at Midcentury, 1945–1960   *532*

Shaping Postwar America   *534*

Domestic Politics in the Cold War Era   *536*

Cold War Fears and Anticommunism   *538*

The Struggle for Civil Rights   *540*

Creating a Middle-Class Nation   *543*

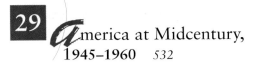

Men, Women, and Youth at Midcentury   *545*

   LINKS TO THE WORLD: Barbie   *548*

The Limits of the Middle-Class Nation   *549*

Summary   *551*

LEGACY FOR A PEOPLE AND A NATION: The Pledge of Allegiance   *551*

30 *T*he Tumultuous Sixties, 1960–1968   *553*

Kennedy and the Cold War   *555*

Marching for Freedom   *557*

Liberalism and the Great Society   *560*

Johnson and Vietnam   *563*

A Nation Divided   *567*

1968   *570*

   LINKS TO THE WORLD: The British Invasion   *571*

Summary   *572*

LEGACY FOR A PEOPLE AND A NATION: The Immigration Act of 1965   *573*

31 *C*ontinuing Divisions and New Limits, 1969–1980   *574*

The New Politics of Identity   *576*

The Women's Movement and Gay Liberation   *578*

The End in Vietnam   *580*

Nixon, Kissinger, and the World   *582*

Presidential Politics and the Crisis of Leadership   *583*

   LINKS TO THE WORLD: OPEC and the 1973 Oil Embargo   *584*

Economic Crisis   *587*

An Era of Cultural Transformation   *590*

Renewed Cold War and Middle East Crisis   *591*

Summary   *593*

LEGACY FOR A PEOPLE AND A NATION: Human Rights   *594*

32 *C*onservatism Revived, 1980–1992   *595*

Reagan and the Conservative Resurgence   *597*

"Reaganomics"   *599*

Reagan and the World   *601*

   LINKS TO THE WORLD: CNN   *602*

A Polarized People: American Society in the 1980s   *606*

The End of the Cold War and Global Disorder   *610*

Summary   *613*

LEGACY FOR A PEOPLE AND A NATION: The Americans with Disabilities Act   *614*

33 *G*lobal Bridges in the New Millennium: AMERICA SINCE 1992   *615*

Social Strains and New Political Directions   *617*

"The New Economy" and Globalization   *619*

Paradoxes of Prosperity   *623*

September 11 and the War on Terrorism   *626*

Americans in the New Millennium   *630*

   LINKS TO THE WORLD: The Global AIDS Epidemic   *634*

Summary   *636*

LEGACY FOR A PEOPLE AND A NATION: The Internet   *636*

APPENDIX   *A-1*

Documents   *A-1*

   Declaration of Independence in Congress, July 4, 1776   *A-1*

   Constitution of the United States of America and Amendments   *A-2*

Presidential Elections   *A-12*

Presidents and Vice Presidents   *A-17*

Justices of the Supreme Court   *A-19*

INDEX   *I-1*

SPECIAL FEATURES

Maps

16.1 The Reconstruction *288*
16.2 Presidential Election of 1876 and the Compromise of 1877 *296*
17.1 The Development and Natural Resources of the West *306*
18.1 Industrial Production, 1919 *320*
19.1 Urbanization, 1880 and 1920 *340*
21.1 Woman Suffrage Before 1920 *389*
22.1 Imperialism in Asia: Turn of the Century *409*
22.2 U.S. Hegemony in the Caribbean and Latin America *411*
23.1 American Troops at the Western Front, 1918 *423*
26.1 Japanese Expansion Before Pearl Harbor *485*
26.2 The German Advance, 1939–1942 *486*
27.1 The Pacific War *495*
27.2 The Allies on the Offensive in Europe, 1942–1945 *506*
28.1 Divided Europe *518*
28.2 The Rise of the Third World: Newly Independent Nations Since 1943 *526*
30.1 Southeast Asia and the Vietnam War *565*
31.1 The Continued Shift to the Sunbelt in the 1970s and 1980s *589*
32.1 The United States in the Caribbean and Central America *605*
33.1 The Middle East *629*
33.2 Mapping America's Diversity *631*

Figures

18.1 Distribution of Occupational Categories Among Employed Men and Women, 1880–1920 *325*
22.1 The Rise of U.S. Economic Power in the World *400*
24.1 Changing Dimensions of Paid Female Labor, 1910–1930 *444*
24.2 Sources of Immigration, 1907 and 1927 *447*
25.1 The Economy Before and After the New Deal, 1929–1941 *463*
26.1 The United States in the World Economy *478*
29.1 Birth Rate, 1945–1964 *535*
29.2 Marital Distribution of the Female Labor Force, 1944–1970 *546*
32.1 While the Rich Got Richer in the 1980s, the Poor Got Poorer *603*
32.2 Poverty in America by Race, 1974–1990 *608*
33.1 The Changing American Family *632*

Tables

18.1 American Living Standards, 1890–1910 *330*
24.1 Consumerism in the 1920s *439*
25.1 New Deal Achievement *462*
30.1 Great Society Achievement, 1964–1966 *562*
33.1 U.S. Military Personnel on Active Duty in Foreign Countries, 2001 *635*

PREFACE TO THE BRIEF SEVENTH EDITION

Creation of the Brief Edition

More than two decades have passed since the publication of the first brief edition of *A People and a Nation*. In that initial brief edition, as well as each subsequent one, the intent was to preserve the uniqueness and integrity of the complete work while condensing it. This Brief Seventh Edition once again reflects the scholarship, readability, and comprehensiveness of the full-length version. It also maintains the integration of social, cultural, political, economic, and foreign relations history that has been a hallmark of *A People and a Nation*.

The authors collectively mourn the death of William J. Brophy, who prepared the brief text for the previous six editions. His successors, though, have worked closely with us, ensuring that the changes in content and organization incorporated in the full-length Seventh Edition were retained in the condensation. The authors attained reductions by paring down details rather than deleting entire sections. The Brief Seventh Edition thus contains fewer statistics, fewer quotations, and fewer examples than the unabridged version. A sufficient number of quotations and examples were retained, however, to maintain the richness in style created by the authors.

The Brief Seventh Edition is available in both one- and two-volume formats. The two-volume format is divided as follows: Volume 1 contains Chapters 1 through 16, beginning with a discussion of three cultures—American, African, and European—that intersected during the exploration and colonization of the New World, and ending with a discussion of the Reconstruction era. Volume 2 contains Chapters 16 through 33, beginning its coverage at Reconstruction and extending the history of the American people to the present. The chapter on Reconstruction appears in both volumes to provide greater flexibility in matching a volume to the historical span covered by a specific course.

Changes in This Edition

While the preface to the full-length Seventh Edition elaborates on specific content changes, we note here that the authors paid increased attention to the following: ethnic and religious diversity in the United States; the environment and technology; the domestic, political, economic, and social impact of the nation's wars; and popular culture. The discussion of the relationship between America and the rest of the world from the colonial period to the present has been expanded throughout the book, as is exemplified in a feature now appearing in each chapter, "Links to the World." These emphases and the complete reorganization of the post-1960 chapters, as well as the updated scholarship on which they are based, are retained in the Brief Seventh Edition.

Although each author feels answerable for the whole of *A People and a Nation*, we take primary responsibility for particular chapters: Mary Beth Norton, Chapters 1–8; David M. Katzman, Chapters 9–12; David Blight, Chapters 13–16; Howard P. Chudacoff, Chapters 17–21 and 24; Fredrik Logevall, Chapters 22, 23, 26, 28, and shared responsibility for 30–33; Beth Bailey, Chapters 25, 27, 29, and shared responsibility for 30–33.

Teaching and Learning Aids

These supplements have been created with the diverse needs of today's students and instructors in mind.

For the Instructor

■ The **Online Teaching Center** (http://college.hmco.com/pic/nortonbrief7e) includes PowerPoint slides of hundreds of maps, images, and other media related to each chapter in the book as well as web links and questions for use with Personal Response Systems. Instructors have access to 100 interactive maps and over 500 primary sources to use for assignments. In addition, there is an Instructor's Resource Manual that can aid in encouraging classroom discussions or constructively enhance a class presentation.

■ A **Class Prep CD-ROM** contains a computerized test bank prepared by George Warren of Central Piedmont Community College that includes search functions that allow instructors to design tests thematically by entering keywords. This CD contains the maps and images that are on the Online Teaching Center web site.

■ The **Blackboard/WebCT CD** provides instructors who want to offer all or part of their entire course online with much of the fundamental material for their course, including graded homework questions organized by topic. From this base, instructors can customize the course to meet their needs.

■ **Eduspace** provides the ability for instructors to create part or all of their courses online, using the widely recognized tools of Blackboard Learning System and content from Houghton Mifflin. Instructors can quickly and easily assign homework exercises, quizzes and tests, tutorials, and supplementary study materials and can modify or add content of their own. A powerful grade book in Eduspace allows instructors to monitor student progress and easily tabulate grades.

■ The **Houghton Mifflin U.S. History Transparency Set, Volumes I and II**, is a set of standard U.S. history transparencies, taken from illustrations and maps in the Houghton Mifflin survey texts. It includes 150 full-color maps.

■ **BiblioBase for U.S. History** is a database of hundreds of primary source documents—including speeches, essays, travel accounts, government documents, and memoirs—covering U.S. history from the fifteenth century to the present. This comprehensive database enables you to create a customized course pack of primary sources to complement any U.S. history text. You can search for documents by period, region, approach, theme, and type and then view the documents in their entirety before choosing your course pack selections.

■ The **Rand McNally Atlas of American History** is offered for packaging with the textbook. Please contact your sales representative for additional information.

For the Student

■ The **Online Study Center** (http://college.hmco.com/pic/nortonbrief7e) is a student web site that includes a wide array of interactive study content such as pre-class quizzes, ACE Practice Tests, vocabulary-building exercises, identification exercises, and interactive map activities, among other resources. This web site also contains the same primary sources and interactive maps that are on the Online Teaching Center.

■ **Icons** in the text direct students to interactive maps, primary sources, and ACE Practice Test questions.

Acknowledgments

For essential assistance in the preparation of this abridged edition, we are grateful to Jan Fitter and Debra Michals.

Author teams rely on review panels to help create and execute successful revision plans. For the revision of this Brief Seventh Edition, we were guided by the many historians whose thoughtful insights and recommendations helped us with the preparation of the full-length Seventh Edition. Their names appear in the preface to that edition that follows.

Finally, we want to thank the many people who have contributed their thoughts and labors to this work, especially the talented staff at Houghton Mifflin.

For the authors,
Mary Beth Norton,
Coordinating Author

PREFACE TO THE FULL-LENGTH SEVENTH EDITION

Some readers might think that a book entering its seventh edition would be little changed from the previous version. Nothing could be further from the truth. In this seventh edition, *A People and a Nation* has undergone major revisions, while still retaining the narrative strength and focus that characterized its earlier editions and made it so popular with students and teachers alike. In the years since the publication of the sixth edition, new documents have been uncovered, new interpretations advanced, and new themes (especially globalization) have come to the forefront of American historical scholarship. The authors—including two new members of our team—have worked diligently to incorporate those findings into this text.

Like other teachers and students, we are always re-creating our past, restructuring our memory, rediscovering the personalities and events that have influenced us, injured us, and bedeviled us. This book represents our continuing rediscovery of America's history—its diverse people and the nation they created and have nurtured. As this book demonstrates, there are many different Americans and many different memories. We have sought to present all of them, in both triumph and tragedy, in both division and unity.

About *A People and a Nation*

A People and a Nation, first published in 1982, was the first major textbook in the United States to fully integrate social and political history. Since the outset, the authors have been determined to tell the story of *all* the people of the United States. This book's hallmark has been its melding of social and political history, its movement beyond history's common focus on public figures and events to examine the daily life of America's people. All editions of the book have stressed the interaction of public policy and personal experience, the relationship between domestic concerns and foreign affairs, the various manifestations of popular culture, and the multiple origins of America and Americans. We have consistently built our narrative on a firm foundation in primary sources—on both well-known and obscure letters, diaries, public documents, oral histories, and artifacts of material culture. We have long challenged readers to think about the meaning of American history, not just to memorize facts. Both students and instructors have repeatedly told us how much they appreciate and enjoy our approach to the past.

As has been true since the first edition, each chapter opens with a dramatic vignette focusing on an individual or a group of people. These vignettes develop key questions, which then frame the chapters in succinct introductions and summaries. Numerous maps, tables, graphs, and charts provide readers with the necessary geographical and statistical context for observations in the text. Carefully selected illustrations—many of them unique to this book—offer readers visual insight into the topics under discussion, especially because the authors have written the captions. In this edition, as in all previous ones, we have sought to incorporate up-to-date scholarship, readability, a clear structure, critical thinking, and instructive illustrative material on every page.

What's New in This Edition

Planning for the seventh edition began at a two-day authors' meeting at the Houghton Mifflin headquarters in Boston. There we discussed the most recent scholarship in the field, the reviews of the sixth edition solicited from instructors, and the findings of our own continuing research. For this edition, we added two new colleagues, who experienced the intellectual exhilaration and rigor of such an authors' meeting for the first time. Beth Bailey, who has written acclaimed works on sexuality and popular culture in modern America, now writes the chapters and sections dealing with domestic matters after the 1920s. Fredrik Logevall, whose scholarship on the Vietnam War has won international recognition, now writes all the chapters and sections on foreign policy since the Civil War. These new authors have substantially reworked and reorganized the post-1945 chapters, in ways outlined below.

This seventh edition enhances the global perspective on American history that has characterized the book since its first edition. From the "Atlantic world" context of European colonies in North and South America to the discussion of international terrorism, the authors have incorporated the most recent globally oriented scholarship throughout the volume. We have worked to strengthen our treatment of the diversity of America's people by examining differences within the broad ethnic categories commonly employed and by paying greater attention to immigration, cultural and intellectual infusions from around the world, and America's growing religious diversity. At the same time, we have more fully integrated the discussion of such diversity into our narrative, so as not to artificially isolate any group from the mainstream. Treatments of environmental history and the history of technology have both been expanded. Finally, we have streamlined the useful chronologies that appear near the beginning of each chapter.

As always, the authors reexamined every sentence, interpretation, map, chart, illustration, and caption, refining the narrative, presenting new examples, and bringing to the text the latest findings of scholars in many areas of history, anthropology, sociology, and political science. More than a quarter of the chapter-opening vignettes are new, as is also true of the popular "Legacy" features introduced in the sixth edition.

To students who question the relevance of historical study, the legacies offer compelling and timely answers. Those brief essays, which follow the chapter summaries, explore the historical roots of contemporary topics. New subjects of legacies include the "self-made man" ideal, states' rights, reparations for slavery, Planned Parenthood, the Social Security system, the concern for human rights, and the Americans with Disabilities Act.

New "Links to the World"

In keeping with the emphasis on globalization in this edition, and building on the long-standing strength of this text in the history of American foreign relations, we have introduced a new feature in each chapter: "Links to the World." Examining both inward and outward ties between America (and Americans) and the rest of the world, the "Links" appear at appropriate places in each chapter to explore specific topics at considerable length. Tightly constructed essays detail the often little-known connections between developments here and abroad. The topics range broadly over economic, political, social, technological, medical, and cultural history, vividly demonstrating that the geographical region that is now the United States has never lived in isolation from other peoples and countries. Examples include the impact of American maize (corn) on the rest of the world, the introduction of coffee and tea into the American colonies, the discovery of gold in California, proposals to annex Cuba, baseball in Japan, Pan American Airways, the influenza pandemic of 1918, the 1936 Olympics, Barbie dolls, CNN, and the AIDS epidemic. Each "Link" highlights global interconnections with unusual and lively examples that will both intrigue and inform students.

Themes in This Book

Several themes and questions stand out in our continuing effort to integrate political, social, and cultural history. We study the many ways Americans have defined themselves—gender, race, class, region, ethnicity, religion, sexual orientation—and the many subjects that have reflected their multidimensional experiences. We highlight the remarkably diverse everyday lives of the American people—in cities and on farms and ranches, in factories and in corporate headquarters, in neighborhoods and in legislatures, in love relationships and in hate groups, in recreation and in work, in the classroom and in military uniform, in secret national security conferences and in public foreign relations debates, in church and in voluntary associations, in polluted environments and in conservation areas. We pay particular attention to lifestyles, diet and dress, family life and structure, labor conditions, gender roles, migration and mobility, childbearing, and child rearing. We explore how Americans have entertained and informed themselves by discussing their music, sports, theater, print media, film, radio, television, graphic arts, and literature, in both "high" culture and popular culture. We study how technology has influenced Americans' lives, such as through the internal combustion engine and the computer.

Americans' personal lives have always interacted with the public realm of politics and government. To understand how Americans have sought to protect their different ways of life and to work out solutions to thorny problems, we emphasize their expectations of governments at the local, state, and federal levels; governments' role in providing answers; the lobbying of interest groups; the campaigns and outcomes of elections; and the hierarchy of power in any period. Because the United States has long been a major participant in world affairs, we explore America's participation in wars, interventions in other nations, empire-building, immigration patterns, images of foreign peoples, cross-national cultural ties, and international economic trends.

Section-by-Section Changes in This Edition

Mary Beth Norton, who had primary responsibility for Chapters 1 through 8 and served as coordinating author, expanded coverage of ancient North America (the Anasazi and Mississippians); Brazil, the Caribbean islands, and Nova Scotia; witchcraft, especially the 1692 Salem crisis; migration to the colonies from England, Ireland, and Germany; the trade in African and Indian slaves and the impact of that trade on African and Native American societies; the trans-Appalachian west in peace and war; and slavery and gradual emancipation after the Revolution. She also reorganized Chapter 3 to consolidate related materials on politics and the imperial context, and extensively revised and expanded Chapter 6 to reflect recent scholarship. There are new sections on the West during the revolutionary era and on the experiences of ordinary Americans in wartime, both in and out of the military.

David M. Katzman, with responsibility for Chapters 9 through 12, has continued (as in the sixth edition) to sharpen the chronological flow in these chapters. He has broadened the discussion of political culture and emerging partisanship in the young republic, reflecting the current rethinking of politics at that time. He has expanded coverage of religious life and the links between religion and social and political reform. The discussions of families, immigrant lives (especially the Irish), and African American identity, culture, and communities have all been completely revised. Throughout, there is greater attention paid to technology, global ties, and popular culture.

David W. Blight, who had primary responsibility for Chapters 13 through 16, enhanced the discussion of women and gender throughout these chapters. He also added material on the lives of freed people, before, during, and after the Civil War; the impact of the Fugitive Slave Law; the West in the Civil War and Reconstruction eras; and the home front during wartime. He revised the interpretation of the Denmark Vesey slave rebellion and increased coverage of the Underground Railroad, and of the role of the Mormons and westward expansion in the slavery crisis. In Chapter 15, he developed new sections on how the Civil War shaped the future of Indians in the far West, as well as the conflict's significance abroad, especially in England.

Howard P. Chudacoff, responsible for Chapters 17 through 21 and 24, has increased the coverage of technology throughout his chapters, adding discussions of farming technology, the machine tool industry, technological education in universities, birth-control devices, and the automobile. He has included new material on the environment as well, expanding his discussion of such topics as water supply and sewage disposal, the unanticipated effects of national parks, and the conservation movement. Topics related to ethnicity—including anti-Chinese violence and exclusion laws, Mexican immigration, and holiday celebrations by ethnic groups—also receive increased attention. He has reconfigured portions of Chapters 18, 19, and 21 to clarify the narrative.

Fredrik Logevall, with primary responsibility for Chapters 22, 23, 26, and 28, worked to internationalize the treatment of America's foreign relations by giving greater attention to the perspectives of nations with which we interacted, and by examining the foreign policy aims of such leaders as Joseph Stalin, especially in Chapters 23 and 26. He significantly expanded the coverage of U.S. relations with the Middle East, showing the increasing importance of America's dealings with that region during the past four decades. He has also brought a sense of contingency to the narrative of American foreign relations, suggesting that matters might have turned out quite differently at various key junctures had policymakers reached different decisions. He made major changes in Chapter 28 (formerly Chapter 29), creating greater thematic unity and incorporating much new scholarship on the Cold War and relations with China and the Soviet Union. Throughout, Logevall builds on the excellent foundation laid by Thomas G. Paterson, who wrote these and the post-1960 foreign policy chapters in the previous six editions of this textbook, and who also served as the coordinating author for all six of those editions.

Beth Bailey, primarily responsible for Chapters 25, 27, and 29, integrated the experiences and actions of various groups into the main narrative while still focusing on the diversity of the American people in the modern era. In general, she enhanced coverage of the South and West (especially Latinos and Mexican immigrants in the Southwest) and added material on gender, sexuality, and popular culture. Throughout these chapters she placed Americans' fears about their nation's future in an international context. In Chapter 25, she strengthened the discussion of New Deal policies, showing how assumptions about race and gender structured these important social programs. Chapter 27 has a stronger chronological framework, as well as new treatments of culture and daily life during WWII, in combat and on the home front. Chapter 29 (formerly Chapter 28) has been extensively revised, assessing the myriad transformations of American society and culture in the 1950s, with particular attention to race, labor, masculinity, McCarthyism, and the impact of new federal policies. Bailey's work updates the domestic policy chapters written superbly in the previous six editions by William M. Tuttle, Jr.

Post-1960 Chapters

Bailey and Logevall shared responsibility for the new Chapters 30 through 33. In these completely revamped chapters, domestic and foreign topics are discussed in tandem rather than separately, demonstrating the extensive linkages between them. The two authors collaborated closely to create a fresh and lively, comprehensive, chronologically based narrative that places events in the United States in their appropriate international setting. The coverage of foreign relations includes increased attention to the Middle East and to the motivations of America's allies and opponents alike. The treatment of the Vietnam War now draws on Logevall's own scholarship, just as the discussion of recent popular culture and sexuality is based on Bailey's original research. Increased attention is given to the civil rights movement, the rise of second- and third-wave feminism, new patterns of immigration, and the growth of grassroots conservatism.

Teaching and Learning Aids

The supplements listed here accompany this Seventh Edition of *A People and a Nation.* They have been created with the diverse needs of today's students and instructors in mind, with extensive print and non-print resources available.

We are proud to announce the ***History Companion,*** your new primary source for history technology solutions. The *History Companion* has three components: the ***Instructor Companion,*** the ***Student Study Companion,*** and the ***Student Research Companion.*** Each of these components is described below: the *Instructor Companion* under instructor resources, and the *Student Research Companion* and *Student Study Companion* under student resources.

For the Instructor:
■ The ***Instructor Companion*** is an easily searchable CD-ROM that makes hundreds of historical images and maps instantly accessible in PowerPoint format.

Each image is accompanied by notes that place it in its proper historical context and tips for ways it can be presented in the classroom. With this edition of *A People and a Nation*, this CD also includes a wealth of additional resources, including testing, lecture, and course planning tools. A computerized test bank is included complete with search functions, which allows instructors to design tests thematically by entering keywords to bring up particular questions. An Instructor's Resource Guide is also included that can aid in encouraging classroom discussions or constructively enhance a class presentation. This CD is free to instructors with the adoption of this Houghton Mifflin textbook.

- A print **Test Bank**, prepared by George Warren of Central Piedmont Community College, also accompanies the text and contains many multiple choice, identification, geography, and essay questions for use in creating exams.

- In addition, a series of **PowerPoint** slides, created by Barney Rickman of Valdosta State University, is included to assist in instruction and discussion of key topics and material.

- The **Blackboard/WebCT Basic CD** provides instructors who want to offer all or part of their entire course online with much of the fundamental material for their course. From this base, instructors can customize the course to meet their needs.

- **The Houghton Mifflin U.S. History Transparency Set, Volumes I and II,** is a set of standard U.S. history transparencies, taken from illustrations and maps in the Houghton Mifflin survey texts. It includes 150 full-color maps.

- **BiblioBase for U.S. History** is a database of hundreds of primary source documents—including speeches, essays, travel accounts, government documents, and memoirs—covering U.S. history from the fifteenth century to the present. This comprehensive database enables you to create a customized course pack of primary sources to complement any U.S. history text. You can search for documents by period, region, approach, theme, and type and then view the documents in their entirety before choosing your course pack selections.

- The **Rand McNally Atlas of American History** is offered for packaging with the textbook. Please contact your sales representative for additional information.

For the Student:
The **Houghton Mifflin History Companion** for *A People and a Nation,* Seventh Edition, has two student components.

- The *Student Study Companion* is a free online study guide that contains ACE self-tests, flashcards, timelines, chronology exercises, graphic organizer exercises, map exercises, text feature exercises, web links, and Internet exercises. These study tools will help your students to be more successful.

- The *Student Research Companion* is a free Internet-based tool with 100 interactive maps and 500 primary sources. The primary sources include headnotes that provide pertinent background information, and both the maps and the primary sources include questions that students can answer and e-mail to their instructors.

■ **Study Guide Volumes I and II,** by George Warren, offers students learning objectives, vocabulary exercises, identification suggestions, skill-building activities, multiple choice questions, essay questions, and map exercises in two volumes.

■ **American Ethnic Identities: Online Activities**
By using examples throughout American history, these informative and lively activities will broaden your understanding of the different ethnic groups that make up the United States.

Acknowledgments

The authors would like to thank the following persons for their assistance with the preparation of this edition: Shawn Alexander, David Anthony Tyeeme Clark, Mike Ezra, David Farber, Max Bailey/Farber, Steve Jacobson, Andrea Katzman, Eric Katzman, Julee Katzman, Theo Katzman, Ariela Katzman-Jacobson, Elieza Katzman-Jacobson, Iris Jane Katzman, Sharyn Brooks Katzman, Danyel Logevall, Chester Pach, Cheryl Ragar, Ann Schofield, Daniel Williams, and Norman Yetman.

At each stage of this revision, a sizable panel of historian reviewers read drafts of our chapters. Their suggestions, corrections, and pleas helped guide us through this momentous revision. We could not include all of their recommendations, but the book is better for our having heeded most of their advice. We heartily thank:

Marynita Anderson, *Nassau Community College*
Erica R. Armstrong, *University of Delaware*
Jim Barrett, *University of Illinois at Urbana-Champaign*
Virginia R. Boynton, *Western Illinois University*
Robert Cottrell, *California State University, Chico*
Bruce Dierenfield, *Canisius College*
Lisa Lindquist Dorr, *University of Alabama*
Latricia E. Gill-Brown, *Pensacola Junior College*
Melanie Gustafson, *University of Vermont*
Jorge Iber, *Texas Tech University*
Anthony E. Kaye, *Pennsylvania State University, University Park*
Carol A. Keller, *San Antonio College*
Kathleen Kennedy, *Western Washington University*
Anne Klejment, *University of St. Thomas*
Carolyn J. Lawes, *Old Dominion University*
Patrick K. Moore, *University of West Florida*
Jared Orsi, *Colorado State University*
Chester Pach, *Ohio University*
Marie Jenkins Schwartz, *University of Rhode Island*
Erik R. Seeman, *SUNY-Buffalo*

Sayuri G. Shimizu, *Michigan State University*
Manisha Sinha, *University of Massachusetts, Amherst*
Evelyn Sterne, *University of Rhode Island*
Benson Tong, *Wichita State University*
Michael M. Topp, *University of Texas, El Paso*

The authors once again thank the extraordinary Houghton Mifflin people who designed, edited, produced, and nourished this book. Their high standards and acute attention to both general structure and fine detail are cherished in the publishing industry. Many thanks, then, to Jean Woy, editor-in-chief; Sally Constable, sponsoring editor; Ann Hofstra Grogg, freelance development editor; Bob Greiner, senior project editor; Sandra McGuire, senior marketing manager; Henry Rachlin, senior designer; Carol Merrigan, senior production/design coordinator; Marie Barnes, senior manufacturing coordinator; Pembroke Herbert, photo researcher; Charlotte Miller, art editor; and Kisha Mitchell and Trinity Peacock-Broyles, editorial assistants.

RECONSTRUCTION: AN UNFINISHED REVOLUTION 1865–1877

*A*fter a prolonged Union bombardment, the lower half of Charleston, South Carolina, the seedbed of secession, lay burning and in ruin when most of the white population evacuated on February 18, 1865. Among the first Union troops to enter Charleston was the Twenty-first U.S. Colored Regiment, which received the surrender of the city from its mayor. In symbolic celebrations, black Charlestonians, most of whom were former slaves, proclaimed their freedom and announced their rebirth.

Still, in Charleston, as elsewhere, death demanded attention. During the final year of the war, the Confederates had converted the planters' Race Course, a horseracing track, into a prison, where Union soldiers were kept in terrible conditions without shelter. The 257 who died of exposure and disease were buried in a mass grave behind the judges' stand. After the fall of the city, Charleston's blacks organized to create a proper burial ground for the Union dead. During April, more than twenty black workmen reinterred the dead in marked graves.

Then, on the morning of May 1, 1865, a procession of ten thousand people marched around the planters' Race Course, led by three thousand children carrying armloads of roses and singing "John Brown's Body." They were followed by black women and men, members of black and white Union regiments, and white missionaries and teachers. All who could fit assembled at the gravesite; five black ministers read from Scripture, and a black children's choir sang. When the ceremony ended, the large crowd retired to the Race Course for speeches, picnics, and military festivities.

The war was over in Charleston, and "Decoration Day"—now Memorial Day, the day to remember the war dead and decorate their graves—had been founded by African Americans. Black people had created an American tradition. In their vision, they were creating the Independence Day of a Second American Revolution.

Wartime Reconstruction

The Meanings of Freedom

Johnson's Reconstruction Plan

The Congressional Reconstruction Plan

Reconstruction Politics in the South

Reconstruction Reversed

LINKS TO THE WORLD
The Grants' Tour of the World

LEGACY FOR A PEOPLE AND A NATION
The Fourteenth Amendment

Online Study Center
This icon will direct you to interactive map and primary source activities on the website
http://college.hmco.com/pic/nortonbrief7e

C H R O N O L O G Y

1865 • Johnson begins rapid and lenient Reconstruction
• Confederate leaders regain power
• White southern governments pass restrictive black codes
• Congress refuses to seat southern representatives
• Thirteenth Amendment ratified, abolishing slavery

1866 • Congress passes Civil Rights Act and renewal of Freedmen's Bureau over Johnson's veto
• Congress approves Fourteenth Amendment
• Most southern states reject Fourteenth Amendment
• In *Ex parte Milligan* the Supreme Court reasserts its influence

1867 • Congress passes Reconstruction Acts and Tenure of Office Act
• Seward arranges purchase of Alaska
• Constitutional conventions called in southern states

1868 • House impeaches Johnson; Senate acquits him
• Most southern states readmitted to the Union under Radical plan
• Fourteenth Amendment ratified
• Grant elected president

1869 • Congress approves Fifteenth Amendment (ratified in 1870)

1871 • Congress passes second Enforcement Act and Ku Klux Klan Act

1872 • Amnesty Act frees almost all remaining Confederates from restrictions on holding office
• Grant reelected

1873 • *Slaughter-House* cases limit power of Fourteenth Amendment
• Panic of 1873 leads to widespread unemployment and labor strife

1874 • Democrats win majority in House of Representatives

1875 • Several Grant appointees indicted for corruption
• Congress passes weak Civil Rights Act
• Democratic Party increases control of southern states with white supremacy campaigns

1876 • *U.S. v. Cruikshank* further weakens Fourteenth Amendment
• Presidential election disputed

1877 • Congress elects Hayes president
• "Home rule" returns to three remaining southern states not yet controlled by Democrats; Reconstruction considered over

Reconstruction would bring revolutionary circumstances, but revolutions can go backward. The Civil War and its aftermath wrought unprecedented changes in American society, law, and politics, but the underlying realities of economic power, racism, and judicial conservatism limited Reconstruction's revolutionary potential.

Nowhere was the turmoil of Reconstruction more evident than in national politics. Lincoln's successor, Andrew Johnson, fought bitterly with Congress over the shaping of Reconstruction policies. Though a southerner, Johnson had always been a foe of the South's wealthy planters, and his first acts as president suggested that he would be tough on "traitors." Before the end of 1865, however, Johnson's policies changed direction. Jefferson Davis stayed in prison for two years, but Johnson quickly pardoned other rebel leaders and allowed them to occupy high offices. He also ordered the return of plantations to their original owners.

Johnson imagined a lenient and rapid "restoration" of the South to the Union rather than the fundamental "reconstruction" that Republican congressmen favored. Between 1866 and 1868, the president and the Republican leadership in Congress engaged in a bitter power struggle over how to put the United States back together again. Before it ended, Congress had impeached the president, enfranchised the freedmen, and given them a role in reconstructing the South. The nation also adopted the Fourteenth and Fifteenth Amendments. But little was done to open the doors of economic opportunity to black southerners. Moreover, by 1869, the Ku Klux Klan employed extensive terror to thwart Reconstruction and undermine black freedom.

As the 1870s advanced, industrial growth accelerated, creating new opportunities and priorities. The West, with its seemingly limitless potential and its wars against Indians, drew American resources and consciousness like never before. Political corruption became a nationwide scandal, bribery a way of doing business.

Thus, Reconstruction became a revolution eclipsed. White southerners' desire to take back control of their states and of race relations overwhelmed the national interest in stopping them. But Reconstruction left enduring legacies the nation has struggled with ever since. ■

Wartime Reconstruction

*R*econstruction of the Union was an issue as early as 1863. The very idea of Reconstruction raised many questions: How would the nation be restored and southern states and leaders treated? What was the constitutional basis for readmission of states to the Union? More specifically, four vexing problems compelled early thinking and would haunt the Reconstruction era. One, who would rule in the South once it was defeated? Two, who would rule in the federal government: Congress or the president? Three, what were the dimensions of black freedom, and what rights under law would the freedmen

enjoy? And four, would Reconstruction be a preservation of the old republic or a second revolution, a reinvention of a new republic?

Online Study Center Improve Your Grade
Interactive Map: The Reconstruction

Abraham Lincoln had never been antisouthern. In his Second Inaugural Address, he had promised

LINCOLN'S 10 PERCENT PLAN

"malice toward none; with charity for all" as Americans strove to "bind up the nation's wounds." Lincoln planned early for a swift and moderate Reconstruction process. In his "Proclamation of Amnesty and Reconstruction," issued in December 1863, he proposed to replace majority rule with "loyal rule" as a means of reconstructing southern state governments. He proposed pardoning all ex-Confederates except the highest-ranking military and civilian officers. As soon as 10 percent of the voting population in the 1860 election in a given state had taken an oath and established a government, the new state would be recognized. Lincoln did not consult Congress in these plans, and "loyal" assemblies (known as "Lincoln governments") were created in Louisiana, Tennessee, and Arkansas in 1864, states largely occupied by Union troops.

Congress responded with great hostility to Lincoln's moves to readmit southern states in what

CONGRESS AND THE WADE-DAVIS BILL

seemed such a premature manner. Many Radical Republicans considered the 10 percent plan a "mere mockery" of democracy. Thaddeus Stevens of Pennsylvania advocated a "conquered provinces" theory, and Charles Sumner of Massachusetts employed an argument of "state suicide." Both contended that by seceding, southern states had destroyed their status as states. They therefore must be treated as "conquered foreign lands" and revert to the status of "unorganized territories" before Congress could entertain any process of readmission.

In July 1864, the Wade-Davis bill, named for its sponsors, Senator Benjamin Wade of Ohio and Congressman Henry W. Davis of Maryland, emerged from Congress with three specific conditions for southern readmission: one, it demanded a "majority" of white male citizens participating in the creation of a new government; two, to vote or be a delegate to constitutional conventions, men had to take an "iron-clad" oath (declaring they had never aided the Confederate war effort); and three, all officers above the rank of lieutenant and all civil officials in the Confederacy would be disfranchised and deemed "not a citizen of the United States." Lincoln pocket-vetoed the bill and announced that he would not be inflexibly committed to any "one plan" of Reconstruction.

This exchange came during Grant's bloody campaign in Virginia against Lee, when the outcome of the war and Lincoln's reelection were still in doubt. Radical members of his own party, indeed, were organizing a dump-Lincoln campaign for the 1864 election. What emerged in 1864–1865 was a clear-cut debate and a potential constitutional crisis. Lincoln saw Reconstruction as a means of weakening the Confederacy and winning the war; the Radicals saw it as a longer-term transformation of the political and racial order of the country.

In early 1865, Congress and Lincoln joined in two important measures that recognized slavery's centrality to the war. On January 31, with strong administration backing, Congress passed the Thirteenth Amendment, which had two provisions: it abolished involuntary servitude everywhere in the United States, and it declared that Congress shall have power to enforce this outcome by "appropriate legislation."

THIRTEENTH AMENDMENT

The Thirteenth Amendment had emerged from a long congressional debate and considerable petitioning and public advocacy. One of the first and most remarkable petitions for a constitutional amendment abolishing slavery was submitted early in 1864 by Elizabeth Cady Stanton, Susan B. Anthony, and the Women's Loyal National League. Women throughout the Union accumulated thousands of signatures, even venturing into staunchly pro-Confederate regions of Kentucky and Missouri to secure supporters. It was a long road from the Emancipation Proclamation to the Thirteenth Amendment, but the logic of winning the war by crushing slavery, and of securing a new beginning for the nation that so many had now died to save, won the day.

Potentially as significant, on March 3, 1865, Congress created the Bureau of Refugees, Freedmen, and Abandoned Lands—the Freedmen's Bureau, an unprecedented agency of social uplift, necessitated by the ravages of the war. In the mere four years of its existence, the Freedmen's Bureau supplied food and medical services, built over

FREEDMEN'S BUREAU

four thousand schools and some colleges, negotiated several hundred thousand employment contracts between freedmen and their former masters, and tried to manage confiscated land.

The Bureau would be a controversial aspect of Reconstruction, both within the South, where whites generally hated it, and within the federal government, where politicians divided over its constitutionality. The war had forced into the open an eternal question of republics: What are the social welfare obligations of the state toward its people, and what do people owe their governments in return?

The Meanings of Freedom

Entering life after slavery with hope and circumspection, freed men and women tried to gain as much as they could from their new circumstances. Often the changes they valued the most were personal: alterations in location, employer, or living arrangements.

Online Study Center **Improve Your Grade**
Primary Source: Black Testimony on the Aftermath of Enslavement

For America's former slaves, Reconstruction had one paramount meaning: a chance to explore freedom.

THE FEEL OF FREEDOM

Former slaves remembered singing far into the night after federal troops, who confirmed rumors of their emancipation, reached their plantations. The slaves on a Texas plantation shouted for joy, their leader proclaiming, "We is free—no more whippings and beatings." One man recalled that he and others "started on the move," either to search for family members or just to exercise the human right of mobility.

Many freed men and women reacted more cautiously and shrewdly, taking care to test the boundaries of their new condition. "After the war was over," explained one man, "we was afraid to move. Just like terrapins or turtles after emancipation. Just stick our heads out to see how the land lay." As slaves they had learned to expect hostility from white people, and they did not presume it would instantly disappear. Life in freedom might still be a matter of what was allowed, not what was right. One sign of

■ *The Armed Slave,* William Sprang, oil on canvas, c. 1865. This remarkable painting depicts an African American veteran soldier, musket with fixed bayonet leaning against the wall, cigar in hand indicating a new life of safety and leisure, reading a book to demonstrate his embrace of education and freedom. The man's visage leaves the impression of satisfaction and dignity.   (Courtesy of The Civil War Library and Underground Railroad Museum of Philadelphia)

their caution was the way freedpeople evaluated potential employers, wandering in search of better circumstances. A majority of blacks eventually settled as agricultural workers back on their former farms or plantations. But they relocated their houses and did their utmost to control the conditions of their labor.

Throughout the South, former slaves devoted themselves to reuniting their families, separated during slavery or by dislocation during the war. With only shreds of information to guide them, thousands of freedpeople embarked on odysseys in search of a husband,

REUNION OF AFRICAN AMERICAN FAMILIES

wife, child, or parent. Some succeeded in their quest, sometimes almost miraculously. Others never found their loved ones.

Husbands and wives who had belonged to different masters established homes together for the first time, and, as they had under slavery, parents asserted the right to raise their own children. A mother bristled when her old master claimed a right to whip her children. She informed him that "he warn't goin' to brush none of her chilluns no more." The freed men and women were too much at risk to act recklessly, but as one man put it, they were tired of punishment and "sure didn't take no more foolishment off of white folks."

To avoid contact with overbearing whites who were used to supervising them, blacks abandoned the slave quarters and fanned out to distant corners of the land they worked. Some described moving "across the creek" or building a "saplin house . . . back in the woods." Others established small all-black settlements that still exist today along the back roads of the South.

BLACKS' SEARCH FOR INDEPENDENCE

In addition to a fair employer, what freed men and women most wanted was the ownership of land. Land represented self-sufficiency and a chance to gain compensation for generations of bondage. In February 1865 General Sherman ordered 400,000 acres in the Sea Islands region set aside for the exclusive settlement of the freedpeople. But President Johnson ordered them removed in October and returned the land to its original owners under army enforcement.

FREEDPEOPLE'S DESIRE FOR LAND

Most members of both political parties opposed genuine land redistribution to the freedmen. Even northern reformers showed little sympathy for black aspirations. The former Sea Island slaves wanted to establish small, self-sufficient farms. Northern soldiers, officials, and missionaries insisted that they grow cotton, emphasizing profit, cash crops, and the values of competitive capitalism.

"The Yankees preach nothing but cotton, cotton" complained one Sea Island black. "We wants land," wrote another, but tax officials "make the lots too big, and cut we out." Indeed, the U.S. government sold thousands of acres in the Sea Islands, 90 percent of which went to wealthy investors from the North.

Ex-slaves reached out for valuable things in life that had been denied them, including education. Blacks of all ages hungered for the knowledge in books that had been permitted only to whites. With freedom, they started schools and filled classrooms. On log seats and dirt floors, freed men and women studied their letters in old almanacs and discarded dictionaries. Young children brought infants to school with them, and adults attended at night or after "the crops were laid by."

THE BLACK EMBRACE OF EDUCATION

The federal government and northern reformers of both races assisted this pursuit of education through Freedmen's Bureau schools and others founded by private northern philanthropy. More than 600,000 African Americans were enrolled in elementary school by 1877.

Blacks and their white allies also saw the need for colleges and universities to train teachers, ministers, and professionals for leadership. The American Missionary Association founded seven colleges, including Fisk and Atlanta Universities, between 1866 and 1869. The Freedmen's Bureau helped to establish Howard University in Washington, D.C., and northern religious groups supported dozens of seminaries and teachers' colleges.

During Reconstruction, African American leaders often were highly educated individuals; many were from the prewar elite of free people of color and often blood relatives of wealthy whites; some planters had given their mulatto children an outstanding education. Francis Cardozo, who held various offices in South Carolina, had attended universities in Scotland and England. The two black senators from Mississippi, Blanche K. Bruce and Hiram Revels, possessed privileged educations. These men and many self-educated former slaves brought to political office not only fervor but useful experience.

Freed from the restrictions and regulations of slavery, blacks could build their own institutions as they saw fit. The secret churches of slavery came into the open; throughout the South, ex-slaves "started a brush arbor," which was "a sort of . . . shelter with leaves for a roof," but the freed men and women worshiped in it enthusiastically. Within a few years, however, independent branches of the Methodist and

GROWTH OF BLACK CHURCHES

Baptist denominations had attracted the great majority of black Christians in the South.

The desire to gain as much independence as possible also shaped the former slaves' economic arrangements. Since most of them lacked the money to buy land, they preferred the next best thing: renting the land they worked. But the South had a cash-poor economy with few sources of credit. Therefore, black farmers and white landowners turned to sharecropping, a system in which farmers kept part of their crop and gave the rest to the landowner while living on his property. The landlord or a merchant "furnished" food and supplies needed before the harvest. Although landowners tried to set the laborers' share at a low level, black farmers had some bargaining power, at least at first. Sharecroppers would hold out, or move and try to switch employers from one year to another. As the system matured during the 1870s and 1880s, most sharecroppers worked "on halves"— half for the owner and half for themselves.

RISE OF THE SHARECROPPING SYSTEM

The sharecropping system originated as a desirable compromise. It eased landowners' problems with cash and credit and provided them a permanent, dependent labor force; blacks accepted it because it gave them more freedom from daily supervision. Instead of working in the hated gangs under a white overseer, as in slavery, they farmed their own plot of land in family groups. But sharecropping later proved to be a disaster. Owners and merchants developed a monopoly of control over the agricultural economy, and sharecroppers found themselves riveted into ever-increasing debt. Moreover, southern farmers concentrated on cotton, and cotton prices began a long decline.

Johnson's Reconstruction Plan

*W*hen Reconstruction began under President Andrew Johnson, many former slaveowners, as well as northern Radicals, had reason to believe that he would deal sternly with the South. Throughout his career in Tennessee, he had criticized the wealthy planters and championed the small farmers. When one Radical suggested the exile or execution of ten or twelve leading rebels to set an example, Johnson replied, "How are you going to pick out so small a number?"

Like his martyred predecessor, Johnson followed a path in antebellum politics from obscurity to power.

ANDREW JOHNSON OF TENNESSEE

With no formal education, he became a tailor's apprentice. But from 1829, while in his early twenties, he held nearly every office in Tennessee politics, including two terms as governor, and he was a U.S. senator by 1857. Although elected as a southern Democrat, Johnson was the only senator from a seceded state who refused to follow his state out of the Union. Lincoln appointed him war governor of Tennessee in 1862, hence, his symbolic place on the ticket in the president's bid for reelection in 1864.

Although a staunch Unionist, Johnson was also an ardent states' rightist. And while he vehemently opposed secession, he advocated limited government. His philosophy toward Reconstruction may be summed up in the slogan he adopted: "The Constitution as it is, and the Union as it was."

Through 1865, Johnson alone controlled Reconstruction policy, for Congress recessed shortly before he became president and did not reconvene until December. In the following eight months, Johnson put into operation his own plan, forming new state governments in the South by using his power to grant pardons.

Although never a planter, Johnson had owned house slaves. He accepted emancipation as a result of

JOHNSON'S RACIAL VIEWS

the war, but he did not favor black civil and political rights and was a thoroughgoing white supremacist. Johnson believed that black suffrage could never be imposed on a southern state by the federal government, and that set him on a collision course with the Radicals. In perhaps the most blatantly racist official statement ever delivered by an American president, Johnson declared in his annual message of 1867 that blacks possessed less "capacity for government than any other race of people."

Such racial views had an enduring effect on Johnson's policies. Where whites were concerned, however, Johnson seemed to be pursuing changes in class relations. He proposed rules that would keep the wealthy planter class at least temporarily out of power.

White southerners were required to swear an oath of loyalty as a condition of gaining amnesty or

JOHNSON'S PARDON POLICY

pardon, but Johnson barred several categories of people from taking the oath: former federal officials, high-ranking Confederate officers, and political leaders or graduates of West Point or Annapolis who had joined or aided the Confederacy. To this list Johnson added another important group: all ex-Confederates whose taxable property was worth more than $20,000. These individuals had to apply personally to the president for pardon and restoration of their political rights. It thus appeared that the leadership class of the Old South would be removed from power.

Johnson appointed provisional governors who began the Reconstruction process by calling constitutional conventions. The delegates chosen for these conventions had to draft new constitutions that eliminated slavery and invalidated secession. After ratification of these constitutions, new governments could be elected, and the states would be restored to the Union with full congressional representation. But only those southerners who had taken the oath of amnesty and been eligible to vote on the day the state seceded could participate in this process. Thus, unpardoned whites and former slaves were not eligible.

If Johnson intended to strip the old elite of its power, he did not hold to his plan. Surprisingly, he

PRESIDENTIAL RECONSTRUCTION

started pardoning aristocrats and leading rebels. These pardons, plus the rapid return of planters' abandoned lands, restored the old elite to power.

Why did Johnson allow the planters to regain power? In part, he was determined to implement a rapid Reconstruction to deny the Radicals the opportunity for the more thorough racial and political changes they desired in the South. Johnson also needed southern support in the 1866 elections. Hence, he declared Reconstruction complete only eight months after Appomattox, and in December 1865 many Confederate leaders, including the vice president of the Confederacy, traveled to Washington to claim seats in the U.S. Congress.

The election of such prominent rebels troubled many northerners. So did other results of Johnson's

BLACK CODES

program. Some of the state conventions were slow to repudiate secession; others admitted only grudgingly that slavery was dead. Furthermore, to define the status of freed men and women and control their labor, some legislatures merely revised large sections of the slave codes by substituting the word *freedmen* for *slaves*. The new black codes compelled the former slaves to carry passes, observe a curfew, live in housing provided by a landowner, and give up hope of entering many desirable occupations. Stiff vagrancy laws and restrictive labor contracts bound freedpeople to plantations.

It seemed to northerners that the South was intent on returning African Americans to servility. Thus, the Republican majority in Congress decided to call a halt to the results of Johnson's plan. On reconvening, the House and Senate considered the credentials of the newly elected southern representatives and decided not to admit them. Instead, they bluntly challenged the president's authority and established a joint committee to investigate a new direction for Reconstruction.

The Congressional Reconstruction Plan

*N*orthern congressmen were hardly unified, but they did not doubt their right to shape Reconstruction policy. The Constitution mentioned neither secession nor reunion, but it gave Congress the primary role in the admission of states. Moreover, the Constitution declared that the United States shall guarantee to each state a republican form of government. This provision, legislators believed, gave them the authority to devise policies for Reconstruction.

They soon found that other constitutional questions affected their policies. What, for example, had rebellion done to the relationship between southern states and the Union? Lincoln had always insisted that states could not secede—they had engaged in an "insurrection"—and that the Union remained intact. Not even Andrew Johnson, however, accepted the southern position that state governments of the Confederacy could simply reenter the nation. Congressmen who favored vigorous Reconstruction measures argued that the war had broken the Union and that the South was subject to the victor's will. Moderate congressmen held that the states had forfeited their rights through rebellion and thus had come under congressional supervision.

These theories mirrored the diversity of Congress itself. Northern Democrats denounced any idea of racial equality and supported John-

THE RADICALS son's policies. Conservative Republicans favored a limited federal role in

Reconstruction. The Radical Republicans wanted to transform the South. Although a minority in their party, they had the advantage of clearly defined goals. They believed it was essential to democratize the South, establish public education, and ensure the rights of freedpeople. They favored black suffrage, supported some land confiscation and redistribution, and were willing to exclude the South from the Union for several years if necessary to achieve their goals. A large group of moderate Republicans did not want to go as far as the Radicals but opposed Johnson's leniency.

Ironically, Johnson and the Democrats sabotaged the possibility of a conservative coalition. They refused to cooperate with conservative or moderate Republicans and insisted that Reconstruction was over, that the new state governments were legitimate, and that southern representatives should be admitted to Congress. Among the Republicans, the Radicals' influence grew in proportion to Johnson's intransigence.

Trying to work with Johnson, Republicans believed a compromise had been reached in the spring of 1866. Under its terms, Johnson

CONGRESS VS. JOHNSON would agree to two modifications of his program: extension of the life of the Freedmen's Bureau for another year and passage of a civil rights bill to counteract the black codes. This bill would force southern courts to practice equality before the law by allowing federal judges to remove from state courts cases in which blacks were treated unfairly. Its provisions applied to public, not private, acts of discrimination. The civil rights bill of 1866 was the first statutory definition of the rights of American citizens.

Johnson destroyed the compromise by vetoing both bills (they later became law when Congress overrode the president's veto). All hope of presidential-congressional cooperation was now dead. In 1866 newspapers reported daily violations of blacks' rights in the South and carried alarming accounts of antiblack violence. In Memphis, for instance, forty blacks were killed and twelve schools burned by white mobs. Such violence convinced Republicans, and the northern public, that more needed to be done. A new Republican plan took the form of the Fourteenth Amendment to the Constitution, forged out of a compromise between radical and conservative elements of the party.

Of the four parts of the Fourteenth Amendment, the first would have the greatest legal significance in

FOURTEENTH AMENDMENT

later years. It conferred citizenship on the freedmen and prohibited states from abridging their constitutional "privileges and immunities." It also barred any state from taking a person's life, liberty, or property "without due process of law" and from denying "equal protection of the laws." These resounding phrases became powerful guarantees of African Americans' and all other citizens' civil rights in the twentieth century.

Nearly universal agreement emerged among Republicans on the amendment's second and third provisions. The second declared the Confederate debt null and void and guaranteed the war debt of the United States. The third provision barred Confederate leaders from holding state and federal office. Only Congress, by a two-thirds vote of each house, could remove the penalty.

The fourth part of the amendment dealt with representation and embodied the compromises that produced the document. Emancipation made every former slave a full person rather than three-fifths of a person, which would increase southern representation. Thus, the postwar South stood to gain power in Congress, and if white southerners did not allow blacks to vote, former secessionists would derive the political benefit from emancipation. So Republicans determined that if a southern state did not grant black men the vote, its representation would be reduced proportionally. This compromise avoided a direct enactment of black suffrage but would deliver future black voters to the Republican Party.

The Fourteenth Amendment specified for the first time that voters were "male," but it ignored female citizens, black and white. For this reason, it provoked a strong reaction from the women's rights movement. Prominent leaders such as Elizabeth Cady Stanton and Susan B. Anthony ended their alliance with abolitionists and fought more determinedly for themselves. Thus, the amendment infused new life into the women's rights movement and caused considerable strife among old allies.

In 1866 the major question in Reconstruction politics was how the public would respond to the congressional initiative. Johnson did his best to block the Fourteenth Amendment in both North and South. Condemning Congress for

THE SOUTH'S AND JOHNSON'S DEFIANCE, 1866

its refusal to seat southern representatives, the president urged state legislatures in the South to vote against ratification. Every southern legislature except Tennessee's rejected the amendment by a wide margin.

To present his case to northerners, Johnson boarded a special train for a "swing around the circle" that carried his message into the Northeast, the Midwest, and then back to Washington. In city after city, he criticized the Republicans in a ranting, undignified style. Increasingly audiences rejected his views and hooted and jeered at him.

The elections of 1866 were a resounding victory for Republicans in Congress. Radicals and moderates whom Johnson had denounced won reelection by large margins, and the Republican majority grew to two-thirds of both houses of Congress. The North had spoken clearly: Johnson's policies were prematurely giving the advantage to rebels and traitors. Thus, Republican congressional leaders won a mandate to pursue their Reconstruction plan.

After some embittered debate, Congress passed the First Reconstruction Act in March 1867. This plan, under which the southern states were readmitted to the Union, incorporated only a part of the Radical program. Union generals, commanding small garrisons of troops and charged with supervising all elections, assumed control in five military districts in the South (see Map 16.1). Confederate leaders designated in the Fourteenth Amendment were barred from voting until new state constitutions were ratified. The act guaranteed freedmen the right to vote in elections for state constitutional conventions and in subsequent elections. In addition, each southern state was required to ratify the Fourteenth Amendment, ratify its new constitution by majority vote, and submit it to Congress for approval. The Second, Third, and Fourth Reconstruction Acts, passed between March 1867 and March 1868, provided the details of operation for voter registration boards, the adoption of constitutions, and the administration of "good faith" oaths on the part of white southerners.

RECONSTRUCTION ACTS OF 1867–1868

In the words of one historian, the Radicals succeeded in "clipping Johnson's wings." But they had hoped Congress could do much more. Thaddeus Stevens, for example, argued that economic opportunity

FAILURE OF LAND REDISTRIBUTION

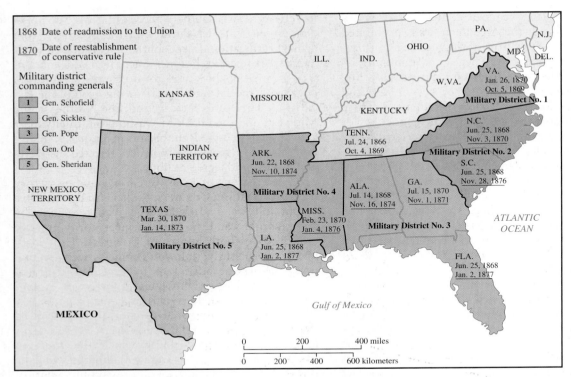

Map 16.1   The Reconstruction

This map shows the five military districts established when Congress passed the Reconstruction Act of 1867. As the dates within each state indicate, conservative Democratic forces quickly regained control of government in four southern states. So-called Radical Reconstruction was curtailed in most of the others as factions within the weakened Republican Party began to cooperate with conservative Democrats.

was essential to the freedmen. Stevens therefore drew up a plan for extensive confiscation and redistribution of land. Only one-tenth of the land affected by his plan was earmarked for freedmen, in forty-acre plots. The rest was to be sold to generate money for Union veterans' pensions, compensation to loyal southerners for damaged property, and payment of the federal debt.

But plans for property redistribution were unpopular measures, and virtually all failed. Northerners were accustomed to a limited role for government, and the business community staunchly opposed any interference with private property rights, even for former Confederates.

Congress's quarrels with Johnson grew more bitter. To restrict Johnson's influence and safeguard its plan, Congress passed a number of controversial laws. First, it limited Johnson's power over the army by requiring the president to issue military orders through the General of the Army, Ulysses S. Grant, who could not be dismissed without the Senate's consent. Then Congress passed the Tenure of Office Act, which gave the Senate power to approve changes in the president's cabinet. Designed to protect Secretary of War Edwin M. Stanton, who sympathized with the Radicals, this law violated the tradition that a president controlled ap-

CONSTITUTIONAL CRISIS

pointments to his own cabinet. These measures, as well as each of the Reconstruction Acts, were passed by a two-thirds override of presidential vetoes.

Johnson took several belligerent steps of his own. He issued orders to military commanders in the South limiting their powers and increasing the powers of the civil governments he had created in 1865. Then he removed military officers who were conscientiously enforcing Congress's new law, preferring commanders who allowed disqualified Confederates to vote. Finally, he tried to remove Secretary of War Stanton. With that attempt the confrontation reached its climax.

Twice in 1867, the House Judiciary Committee had considered impeachment of Johnson, rejecting

IMPEACHMENT OF PRESIDENT JOHNSON

the idea once and then having its recommendation by a 5-to-4 vote decisively defeated by the House. After Johnson tried to remove Stanton, a third attempt to impeach the president carried easily in early 1868. The indictment concentrated on his violation of the Tenure of Office Act, though many modern scholars regard his efforts to impede enforcement of the Reconstruction Act of 1867 as a far more serious offense.

Johnson's trial in the Senate began promptly and lasted more than three months. The prosecution attempted to prove that Johnson was guilty of "high crimes and misdemeanors." But they also argued that the trial was a means to judge Johnson's performance, not a judicial determination of guilt or innocence. The Senate ultimately rejected such reasoning, which could have made removal from office a political weapon against any chief executive who disagreed with Congress. Although a majority of senators voted to convict Johnson, the prosecution fell one vote short of the necessary two-thirds majority. Johnson remained in office, politically weakened and with only a few months left in his term.

In the 1868 presidential election Ulysses S. Grant, running as a Republican, defeated Horatio Seymour,

ELECTION OF 1868

a New York Democrat. Grant was not a Radical, but his platform supported congressional Reconstruction and endorsed black suffrage in the South. (Significantly, Republicans stopped short of endorsing it in the North.) The Democrats vigorously denounced Reconstruction.

Participating in their first presidential election ever on a wide scale, blacks voted en masse for General Grant.

In office Grant acted as an administrator of Reconstruction but not as its enthusiastic advocate. He vacillated in his dealings with the southern states, sometimes defending Republican regimes and sometimes currying favor with Democrats. On occasion Grant called out federal troops to stop violence or enforce acts of Congress. But he never imposed a true military occupation on the South. The later legend of "military rule," so important to southern claims of victimization during Reconstruction, was steeped in myth.

In 1869, in an effort to write democratic principles into the Constitution, the Radicals passed the

FIFTEENTH AMENDMENT

Fifteenth Amendment. This measure forbade states to deny the right to vote "on account of race, color, or previous condition of servitude." Such wording did not guarantee the right to vote. It deliberately left states free to restrict suffrage on other grounds so that northern states could continue to deny suffrage to women and certain groups of men—Chinese immigrants, illiterates, and those too poor to pay poll taxes. Although several states outside the South refused to ratify, three-fourths of the states approved the measure, and the Fifteenth Amendment became law in 1870.

With passage of the Fifteenth Amendment, many Americans, especially supportive northerners, considered Reconstruction essentially completed. "Let us have done with Reconstruction," pleaded the *New York Tribune* in April 1870. "The country is tired and sick of it. . . . Let us have Peace!"

Reconstruction Politics in the South

*F*rom the start, Reconstruction encountered the resistance of white southerners. In the black codes and in private attitudes, many whites stubbornly opposed emancipation, and the former planter class proved especially unbending. In 1866 a Georgia newspaper frankly observed that "most of the white citizens believe that the institution of slavery was right, and . . . they will believe that the condition, which comes nearest to slavery, that can now be established will be the best."

Fearing loss of control over their slaves, some planters attempted to postpone freedom by denying or misrepresenting events. Former

WHITE RESISTANCE

slaves reported that their owners "didn't tell them it was freedom" or "wouldn't let [them] go." To hold onto their workers, some landowners claimed control over black children and used guardianship and apprentice laws to bind black families to the plantation. Whites also blocked blacks from acquiring land. After President Johnson encouraged the South to resist congressional Reconstruction, some white conservatives worked hard to capture the new state governments, while others boycotted the polls in an attempt to defeat Congress's plans.

Very few black men stayed away from the polls. Enthusiastically and hopefully, they voted Republi-

BLACK VOTERS AND THE SOUTHERN REPUBLICAN PARTY

can. Most agreed with one man who felt he should "stick to the end with the party that freed me." Illiteracy did not prohibit blacks (or uneducated whites) from making intelligent choices. A Mississippi black testified that he and his friends had no difficulty selecting the Republican ballot. "We stood around and watched," he explained. "We saw D. Sledge vote; he owned half the county. We knowed he voted Democratic so we voted the other ticket so it would be Republican."

Thanks to a large black turnout and the restrictions on prominent Confederates, a new southern Republican Party came to power in the constitutional conventions of 1868–1870. Republican delegates consisted of a sizable contingent of blacks (265 out of the total of just over 1,000 delegates throughout the South), some northerners who had moved to the South, and native southern whites who favored change. The new constitutions were more democratic. They eliminated property qualifications for voting and holding office, and they turned many appointed offices into elective posts. They provided for public schools and institutions to care for the mentally ill, the blind, the deaf, the destitute, and the orphaned.

The conventions broadened women's rights in property holding and divorce. Usually the goal was not to make women equal to men but to provide relief to thousands of suffering debtors. In families left

■ Thomas Nast, in this 1868 cartoon, pictured the combination of forces that threatened the success of Reconstruction: southern opposition and the greed, partisanship, and racism of northern interests.
(Library of Congress)

poverty stricken by the war and weighed down by debt, it was usually the husband who had contracted the debts. Thus giving women legal control over their own property provided some protection to their families. The goal of some delegates, however, was to elevate women with the right to vote.

Under these new constitutions, the southern states elected Republican-controlled governments.

TRIUMPH OF REPUBLICAN GOVERNMENTS

For the first time, the ranks of state legislators in 1868 included some black southerners. But in most states, whites were in the majority, and former slaveowners controlled the best land and other sources of economic power. James Lynch, a leading black politician from Mississippi, explained why African Americans shunned the "folly" of disfranchisement of ex-Confederates. Unlike northerners who "can leave when it becomes too uncomfortable," landless former slaves "must be in friendly relations with the great body of the whites in the state."

Far from being vindictive toward the race that had enslaved them, most southern blacks treated leading rebels with generosity and appealed to white southerners to adopt a spirit of fairness and cooperation. In this way, the South's Republican Party condemned itself to defeat if white voters would not cooperate. Within a few years, Republicans were reduced to the embarrassment of making futile appeals to whites while ignoring the claims of their strongest supporters, blacks. But for a time, some propertied whites accepted congressional Reconstruction as a reality and declared themselves willing to compete under the new rules. All sides found an area of agreement in economic policies.

Reflecting northern ideals and southern necessity, the Reconstruction governments enthusiastically promoted industry. Reconstruction *INDUSTRIALIZATION* legislatures encouraged investment with loans, subsidies, and exemptions from taxation for periods up to ten years. The southern railroad system was rebuilt and expanded, and coal and iron mining made possible steel plants in Birmingham, Alabama. Between 1860 and 1880, the number of manufacturing establishments in the South nearly doubled. This emphasis on big business, however, produced higher state debts and taxes, drew money away from schools and other programs, and multiplied possibilities for corruption.

Policies appealing to African American voters never went beyond equality before the law. In fact, the whites who controlled the southern *REPUBLICANS* Republican Party were reluctant to *AND RACIAL* allow blacks a share of offices pro- *EQUALITY* portionate to their electoral strength. Aware of their weakness, black leaders did not push very far for revolutionary economic or social change. In every southern state, they led efforts to establish public schools, although they did not press for integrated facilities.

Economic progress was uppermost in the minds of most freedpeople. Black southerners needed land, and much land did fall into state hands for nonpay-

ment of taxes and was offered for sale in small lots. But most freedmen had too little cash to bid against investors or speculators. Any widespread redistribution of land had to arise from Congress, which never supported such action. The lack of genuine land redistribution remained the significant lost opportunity of Reconstruction.

Within a few years, as centrists in both parties met with failure, white hostility to congressional Reconstruction began to dominate. *MYTH OF* Taking the offensive, conservatives *"NEGRO RULE"* charged that the South had been turned over to ignorant blacks and deplored "black domination," which became a rallying cry for a return to white supremacy.

Such inflammatory propaganda was part of the growing myth of "Negro rule." African Americans participated in politics but hardly dominated or controlled events. They were a majority in only two out of ten state constitution–writing conventions (transplanted northerners were a majority in one). In the state legislatures, only in the lower house in South Carolina did blacks ever constitute a majority; among officeholders, their numbers generally were far fewer than their proportion in the population. Sixteen blacks won seats in Congress before Reconstruction was over, but none was ever elected governor. Only eighteen served in a high state office such as lieutenant governor, treasurer, superintendent of education, or secretary of state. However, elected officials, such as Robert Smalls in South Carolina, labored tirelessly for cheaper land prices, better health care, access to schools, and the enforcement of civil rights for their people.

Conservatives also assailed the allies of black Republicans. Their propaganda denounced whites from the North as "carpetbaggers," greedy *CARPETBAGGERS* crooks planning to pour stolen tax *AND SCALAWAGS* revenues into their sturdy luggage made of carpet material. In fact, most northerners who settled in the South had come seeking business opportunities, as schoolteachers, or to find a warmer climate and never entered politics. Those who did enter politics generally wanted to democratize the South and introduce northern ways, such as industry, public education, and the spirit of enterprise.

Conservatives also coined the term *scalawag* to discredit any native white southerner who cooperated with the Republicans. A substantial number did so. Most scalawags were yeoman farmers, men from mountain areas and nonslaveholding districts who saw that they could benefit from the education and opportunities promoted by Republicans. Banding together with freedmen, they pursued common class interests and hoped to make headway against the power of long-dominant planters. A majority of scalawags, however, did not support racial equality. The black-white coalition was thus vulnerable on the race issue.

Taxation was a major problem for the Reconstruction governments. Republicans wanted to main-

TAX POLICY AND CORRUPTION AS POLITICAL WEDGES

tain prewar services, repair the war's destruction, stimulate industry, and support important new ventures such as public schools. But the Civil War had destroyed much of the South's tax base. Thus, an increase in taxes was necessary even to maintain traditional services, and new ventures required still higher taxes. Republican tax policies aroused strong opposition, especially among yeomen.

Corruption was another serious charge levied against the Republicans. Unfortunately, it often was true. Many carpetbaggers and black politicians engaged in fraudulent schemes, sold their votes, or padded expenses, taking part in what scholars recognize was a nationwide surge of corruption. Corruption carried no party label, but the Democrats successfully pinned the blame on unqualified blacks and greedy carpetbaggers among southern Republicans.

All these problems hurt the Republicans, but in many southern states the deathblow came through vi-

KU KLUX KLAN

olence. The Ku Klux Klan began in Tennessee in 1866; it spread through the South and rapidly evolved into a terrorist organization. Violence against African Americans occurred from the first days of Reconstruction but became far more organized and purposeful after 1867. Klansmen sought to frustrate Reconstruction and keep the freedmen in subjection. Nighttime harassment, whippings, beatings, rapes, and murder became common, and terrorism dominated some counties and regions.

The Klan's main purpose was political. Lawless nightriders targeted active Republicans. Leading white and black Republicans were killed in several states. After freedmen who worked for a South Carolina scalawag started voting, terrorists visited the planta-

tion and, in the words of one victim, "whipped every nigger man they could lay their hands on." Klansmen also attacked Union League clubs—Republican organizations that mobilized the black vote—and schoolteachers who aided the freedmen.

Klan violence was not a spontaneous outburst of racism; very specific social forces shaped and directed it. In North Carolina, for example, the sites of the worst Klan violence were Alamance and Caswell Counties. There, slim Republican majorities rested on cooperation between black voters and white yeomen, who together had ousted officials long entrenched in power. The wealthy and powerful men who had lost their accustomed political control then organized a deliberate campaign of terror. The campaign of intimidation and murder weakened the Republican coalition and restored a Democratic majority.

Klan violence injured Republicans across the South. One in ten of the black leaders who had been delegates to the 1867–1868 state constitutional conventions was attacked, seven fatally. A single attack on Alabama Republicans in the town of Eutaw left four blacks dead and fifty-four wounded. According to historian Eric Foner, the Klan "made it virtually impossible for Republicans to campaign or vote in large parts of Georgia."

Thus, a combination of difficult fiscal problems, Republican mistakes, racial hostility, and terror

FAILURE OF RECONSTRUCTION

brought down the Republican regimes. In most southern states, "Radical Reconstruction" lasted only a few years (see Map 16.1). The most enduring failure of Reconstruction, however, was not political; it was that Reconstruction failed to alter the South's social structure or its distribution of wealth and power. Without land of their own, freedpeople were at the mercy of white landowners. Armed only with the ballot, they had little chance to effect significant changes.

Reconstruction Reversed

*N*ortherners had always been more interested in suppressing rebellion than in aiding southern blacks, and by the early 1870s the North's commitment to bringing about change in the South weakened. In one southern state after another, Democrats regained control. And for one of only a few times in American history, violence and terror emerged as a tactic in normal politics.

In 1870 and 1871, the violent campaigns of the Ku Klux Klan forced Congress to pass two Enforce-

POLITICAL IMPLICATIONS OF KLAN TERRORISM

ment Acts and an anti-Klan law. These laws made actions by individuals against the civil and political rights of others a federal criminal offense for the first time. They also provided for election supervisors and permitted martial law and suspension of the writ of habeas corpus to combat murders, beatings, and threats by the Klan. Federal prosecutors used the laws rather selectively. In 1872 and 1873, Mississippi and the Carolinas saw many prosecutions, but in other states where violence flourished, the laws were virtually ignored. Southern juries sometimes refused to convict Klansmen.

Some conservative but influential Republicans opposed the anti-Klan laws. Rejecting other Republicans' arguments that the Thirteenth, Fourteenth, and Fifteenth Amendments had made the federal government the protector of citizens' rights, these dissenters echoed an old Democratic charge that Congress was infringing on states' rights. This opposition foreshadowed a more general revolt within Republican ranks in 1872.

Disenchanted with Reconstruction, a group calling itself the Liberal Republicans bolted the party in

LIBERAL REPUBLICAN REVOLT

1872 and nominated Horace Greeley, the well-known editor of the *New York Tribune,* for president. The Liberal Republicans were a varied group, including civil service reformers, foes of corruption, and advocates of a lower tariff. Normally such disparate elements would not cooperate, but two popular and widespread attitudes united them: distaste for federal intervention in the South and an elitist desire to let market forces and the "best men" determine events, in both the South and Washington. The Democrats also gave their nomination to Greeley in 1872. The combination was not enough to defeat Grant, who won reelection, but it reinforced Grant's desire to avoid confrontation with white southerners.

Dissatisfaction with Grant's administration grew during his second term. Strong-willed but politically naive, Grant made a series of poor appointments. His secretary of war, his private secretary, and officials in the Treasury and Navy Departments were involved in

bribery or tax-cheating scandals. Instead of exposing the corruption, Grant defended the culprits. In 1874, as Grant's popularity and his party's prestige declined, the Democrats recaptured the House of Representatives.

The effect of Democratic gains in Congress was to weaken legislative resolve on southern issues. Already,

A GENERAL AMNESTY

in 1872, Congress had adopted a sweeping Amnesty Act, which pardoned most of the remaining rebels, lifting the political disabilities of the Fourteenth Amendment, and left only five hundred barred from political office. In 1875 Congress passed a Civil Rights Act purporting to guarantee black people equal accommodations in public places, such as inns and theaters, but the bill was watered down and contained no effective provisions for enforcement. And by 1876, the Democrats had regained control in all but three southern states. Meanwhile, new concerns were capturing the public's attention.

Both industrialization and immigration were surging, hastening the pace of change in national life.

RECONCILIATION AND INDUSTRIAL EXPANSION

Within only eight years, postwar industrial production increased by an impressive 75 percent. For the first time, nonagricultural workers outnumbered farmers, and only Britain's industrial output was greater than that of the United States. Lured by employment prospects in the expanding economy, 3 million immigrants entered the country between 1865 and 1873.

Then the Panic of 1873 ushered in over five years of economic contraction. Three million people lost their jobs, and the clash between labor and capital became the major issue of the day. Class attitudes diverged, especially in large cities. Debtors and the unemployed sought easy-money policies to spur economic expansion. Businessmen, disturbed by the widespread strikes and industrial violence that accompanied the panic, fiercely defended property rights and demanded "sound money" policies. The chasm between farmers and workers and wealthy industrialists grew ever wider.

Nowhere did the new complexity and violence of American race relations play out so vividly as in the

THE WEST, RACE, AND RECONSTRUCTION

West. Across the West, the federal government pursued a policy of containment against Native Americans. In California, where white

The Grants' Tour of the World

On May 17, 1877, two weeks after his presidency ended, Ulysses S. Grant and his wife, Julia, embarked from Philadelphia on a grand tour of the world that would last twenty-six months. Portrayed as a private vacation, the trip was a very public affair. The small entourage included John Russell Young, a reporter for the *New York Herald* who recorded the journeys in the two-volume illustrated *Around the World with General Grant*.

The Grants spent many months in England attending a bewildering array of banquets, one with Queen Victoria. In Newcastle, thousands of workingmen conducted a massive parade in Grant's honor. Grant was viewed as a warrior statesman, the savior of the American nation, the liberator of slaves, and a celebrity—a measure of the American presence on the world stage. On the European continent, the pattern continued as every royal or republican head of state hosted the Grants.

The Grants next went to Egypt, where they rode donkeys into remote villages along the Nile. They traveled by train to the Indian Ocean and embarked for India. They encountered British imperialism in full flower in Bombay and that of the French in Saigon. Northward in Asia, the grand excursion went to China and Japan. In Canton, Grant passed before an assemblage of young men who, according to a reporter, "looked upon the barbarian with . . . contempt in their expression, very much as our young men in New York would regard Sitting Bull or Red Cloud."

"I am both homesick and dread going home," Grant wrote in April 1879. Sailing across the Pacific, the Grants landed in San Francisco in late June. The former president would spend his final years a war hero and a national symbol. No American president would again establish such personal links to the world until Woodrow Wilson at the end of World War I.

On their tour of the world, Ulysses and Julia Grant sat here with companions and guides in front of the Great Hypostyle Hall at the Temple of Amon-Ra in Karnak in Luxor, Egypt, 1878. The Grants' extraordinary tour included many such photo opportunities, often depicting the plebeian American president, and now world celebrity, in exotic places with unusual people. (Library of Congress)

farmers and ranchers often forced Indians into captive labor, some civilians practiced a more violent form of "Indian hunting." By 1880, thirty years of such violence left an estimated 4,500 California Indians dead at the hands of white settlers.

In Texas and the Southwest, the rhetoric of national expansion still deemed Mexicans and other mixed-race Hispanics to be debased, "lazy," and incapable of self-government. And in California and other states of the Far West, thousands of Chinese immigrants became the victims of brutal violence. Few whites had objected to the Chinese who did the dangerous work of building railroads through the Rocky Mountains. But when the Chinese began to compete for urban, industrial jobs, great conflict emerged. Anticoolie clubs appeared in California in the 1870s, seeking laws against Chinese labor and organizing vigilante attacks on Chinese workers and the factories that employed them. Western politicians sought white votes by pandering to prejudice, and in 1879 the new California constitution denied the vote to Chinese.

During Reconstruction, America was undergoing what one historian has called a "reconstruction" of the very idea of "race" itself. And as it did so, tumbling into some of the darkest years of American race relations, the turbulence of the expanding West reinforced a resurgent white supremacy, a new nationalism, and the reconciliation of North and South.

Following the Civil War, pressure for expansion reemerged, and in 1867 Secretary of State William H.

FOREIGN EXPANSION — Seward arranged the purchase of Alaska from the Russian government. Opponents ridiculed Seward's $7.2 million venture, but he convinced important congressmen of Alaska's economic potential, and other lawmakers favored the dawning of friendship with Russia.

Also in 1867 the United States took control of the Midway Islands, a thousand miles northwest of Hawai'i. And in 1870 President Grant tried unsuccessfully to annex the Dominican Republic.

Meanwhile, the Supreme Court played its part in the northern retreat from Reconstruction. During the

JUDICIAL RETREAT FROM RECONSTRUCTION — Civil War, the Court had been cautious and inactive. Reaction to the *Dred Scott* decision (1857) had been so violent, and the Union's wartime emergency so great, that the Court avoided interference with government actions. In 1866, however, *Ex parte Milligan* reached the Court.

Lambdin P. Milligan of Indiana had plotted to free Confederate prisoners of war and overthrow state governments. For these acts, a military court sentenced Milligan, a civilian, to death. Milligan claimed that he had a right to a civil trial. The Supreme Court declared that military trials were illegal when civil courts were open and functioning, and its language indicated that the Court intended to reassert its authority.

In the 1870s the Court successfully renewed its challenge to Congress's actions when it narrowed the meaning and effectiveness of the Fourteenth Amendment. The *Slaughter-House* cases (1873) began in 1869, when the Louisiana legislature granted one company a monopoly on the slaughtering of livestock in New Orleans. Rival butchers in the city promptly sued. Their attorney argued that the Fourteenth Amendment had revolutionized the constitutional system by bringing individual rights under federal protection. This argument articulated an original goal of the Republican Party: to nationalize civil rights and guard them from state interference.

The Court rejected the argument and thus dealt a stunning blow to the scope and vitality of the Fourteenth Amendment. State citizenship and national citizenship were separate, the Court declared. National citizenship involved only matters such as the right to travel freely from state to state and to use the nation's navigable waters, and only these narrow rights were protected by the Fourteenth Amendment.

The Supreme Court also concluded that the butchers who sued had not been deprived of their rights or property in violation of the amendment's due-process clause. The Court's majority declared that the framers of the recent amendments had not intended to "destroy" the federal system, in which the states exercised "powers for domestic and local government, including the regulation of civil rights." Thus, the justices severely limited the amendment's potential for securing and protecting the rights of black citizens—its original intent.

The next day the Court decided *Bradwell v. Illinois,* a case in which Myra Bradwell, a female attorney, had been denied the right to practice law in Illinois on account of her gender. Pointing to the Fourteenth Amendment, Bradwell's attorneys contended that the state had unconstitutionally abridged her "privileges and immunities" as a citizen. The Supreme Court rejected her claim, alluding to women's traditional role in the home.

In 1876 the Court weakened the Reconstruction era amendments even further by emasculating the enforcement clause of the Fourteenth Amendment and revealing deficiencies inherent in the Fifteenth Amendment. In *U.S. v. Cruikshank* the Court overruled the conviction under the 1870 Enforcement Act of Louisiana whites who had attacked a meeting of blacks and conspired to deprive them of their rights. The justices ruled that the Fourteenth Amendment did not give the federal government power to act against these whites. The duty of protecting citizens' equal rights, the Court said, "rests alone with the States." Such judicial conservatism had a profound impact down through the next century, blunting the revolutionary potential in the Civil War amendments.

The 1876 presidential election confirmed that the nation was increasingly focused on economic issues and that the North was no longer willing to pursue the goals of Reconstruction. Samuel J. Tilden, the Democratic governor of New York, ran strongly in the South and needed only one more electoral vote to triumph over Rutherford B. Hayes, the Republican nominee. Nineteen electoral votes from Louisiana, South Carolina, and Florida (the only southern states yet "unredeemed" by Democratic rule) were disputed; both Democrats and Republicans claimed to have won in those states despite fraud committed by their opponents. One vote from Oregon was undecided because of a technicality (see Map 16.2).

DISPUTED ELECTION OF 1876 AND THE COMPROMISE OF 1877

To resolve this unprecedented situation Congress established a fifteen-member electoral commission, with membership to be balanced between Democrats and Republicans. Since the Republicans held the majority in Congress, they prevailed 8 to 7 on every attempt to count the returns, along strict party lines. Hayes would become president if Congress accepted the commission's findings.

Congressional acceptance was not certain, and many citizens worried that the nation had entered a major constitutional crisis and would slip once again into civil war. The crisis was resolved when Democrats acquiesced in the election of Hayes based on a

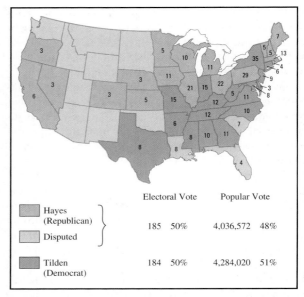

	Electoral Vote		Popular Vote	
Hayes (Republican)	185	50%	4,036,572	48%
Disputed				
Tilden (Democrat)	184	50%	4,284,020	51%

Map 16.2   Presidential Election of 1876 and the Compromise of 1877

In 1876 a combination of solid southern support and Democratic gains in the North gave Samuel Tilden the majority of popular votes, but Rutherford B. Hayes won the disputed election in the electoral college, after a deal satisfied Democratic wishes for an end to Reconstruction.

"deal" cut in a Washington hotel between Hayes's supporters and southerners who wanted federal aid to railroads, internal improvements, federal patronage, and removal of troops from southern states. Northern and southern Democrats simply decided they could not win and did not contest the election of a Republican who was not going to continue Reconstruction. Thus, Hayes became president.

Southern Democrats rejoiced, but African Americans grieved over the betrayal of their hopes for equality. To many of these people, the only hope lay outside the South. Thus, from South Carolina, Louisiana, Mississippi, and other southern states, thousands gathered up their possessions and migrated to Kansas. They were called Exodusters, disappointed people still searching for their share in the American dream. Even in Kansas they met disillusionment as the wel-

BETRAYAL OF BLACK RIGHTS

come extended by the state's governor soon gave way to hostility among many whites.

Blacks now had to weigh their options, which were not much wider than they had ever been. Frederick Douglass looked back on fifteen years of unparalleled change for his people and worried about the hold of white supremacy on America's historical memory: "If war among the whites brought peace and liberty to the blacks, what will peace among the whites bring?" Douglass's question would echo down through American political culture for decades.

Summary *Online Study Center* ACE the Test

*R*econstruction left a contradictory record. It was an era of tragic aspirations and failures, but also of unprecedented legal, political, and social change. The Union victory brought about an increase in federal power, stronger nationalism, sweeping federal intervention in the southern states, and landmark amendments to the Constitution. But northern commitment to make these changes endure had eroded, and the revolution remained unfinished.

The North embraced emancipation, black suffrage, and constitutional alterations strengthening the central government. But it did so to defeat the rebellion and secure the peace. As the pressure of these crises declined, strong underlying continuities emerged and placed their mark on Reconstruction. The American people and the courts maintained a preference for state authority and a distrust of federal power. The ideology of free labor dictated that property should be respected and that individuals should be self-reliant. Racism endured and transformed into the even more virulent forms of Klan terror. Concern for the human rights of African Americans was strongest when their plight threatened to undermine the interests of whites, and reform frequently had less appeal than moneymaking in an individualistic, enterprising society.

In the wake of the Civil War, Americans faced two profound tasks: the achievement of healing and the dispensing of justice. Both had to occur, but they never developed in historical balance. Making sectional reunion compatible with black freedom and equality overwhelmed the imagination in American political culture, and the nation still faced much of this dilemma more than a century later.

LEGACY FOR A PEOPLE AND A NATION
The Fourteenth Amendment

Before the Civil War, no definition of civil rights existed in America. Reconstruction legislation, especially the Fourteenth Amendment, changed that forever. Approved by Congress in 1866, the Fourteenth Amendment enshrined in the Constitution the ideas of birthright citizenship and equal rights. The Fourteenth Amendment was designed to secure and protect the rights of the freedpeople. But over time, the "equal protection of the law" clause has been used at times to support the rights of states, cities, corporations, immigrants, women, religious organizations, gays and lesbians, students, and labor unions. It has advanced both tolerance and intolerance, affirmative action and anti-affirmative-action programs. It provides the legal wellspring for the generations-old civil rights movement in the United States.

The amendment as originally written required individuals to pursue grievances through private litigation, alleging state denial of a claimed federal right. At first, the Supreme Court interpreted it conservatively, especially on racial matters, and by 1900, the idea of color-blind liberty in America was devastated by Jim Crow laws, disfranchisement, and unpunished mob violence.

But Progressive reformers used the equal-protection clause to advocate government support of health, union organizing, municipal housing, and the protection of woman and child laborers. In the 1920s and 1930s, a judicial defense of civil liberties and free speech took hold. The Supreme Court expanded the amendment's guarantee of equality by a series of decisions upholding the rights of immigrant groups to resist "forced Americanization," especially Catholics in their creation of parochial schools. And from its inception in

1910, the National Association for the Advancement of Colored People waged a long campaign to reveal the inequality of racial segregation in schooling and every other kind of public facility. Led by Charles Houston and Thurgood Marshall, this epic legal battle culminated in the *Brown v. Board of Education* desegregation decision of 1954. In the Civil Rights Act of 1964, the equal-protection tradition was reenshrined into American law. Since 1964, Americans have lived in a society where the Fourteenth Amendment's legacy is the engine of expanded liberty for women and all minorities, as well as a political battleground for defining the nature and limits of human equality, and for redistributing justice long denied.

THE DEVELOPMENT OF THE WEST 1877–1900

*I*n 1893 young historian Frederick Jackson Turner delivered a stunning lecture at the Columbian Exposition in Chicago. In it, Turner expounded a theory that would preoccupy the textbooks for several generations. Titled "The Significance of the Frontier in American History," the paper argued that the existence of "free land, its continuous recession, and the advancement of American settlement westward" had created a distinctively American spirit of democracy and egalitarianism. The conquest of a succession of frontier Wests explained American progress and character.

Across the street, the folk character Buffalo Bill Cody staged two performances daily of an extravaganza, "The Wild West," dramatizing his version of the conquest of frontiers. Where Turner described a relatively peaceful settlement of empty land, Cody portrayed violent conquest of territory occupied by savage Indians. Turner's heroes were farmers who tamed the wilderness with plows. Buffalo Bill's heroes were rugged scouts who defeated Indians with firepower. Turner used images of wagon trains and wheat fields to argue that the frontier fashioned a new, progressive race. Cody depicted the West as a place of brutal aggression and heroic victory.

Despite exaggerations and inaccuracies, both Turner and Cody were correct to some degree. The American West inspired progress and witnessed the domination of one group over another and over the environment. Both men believed that by the 1890s, the frontier era had ended. Over time, Turner's theory was abandoned (even by Turner himself) as too simplistic, and Buffalo Bill was relegated to the gallery of rogues and showmen. Still, their versions of the West persist in the romance of American history, partially obscuring the complex truth of western development in the late nineteenth century.

Much of the West was never empty, however, and its inhabitants used its resources in different ways. On the Plains, for example, Pawnee Indians planted crops in the spring, left their fields in summer to hunt buffalo, then returned for harvesting. They sometimes battled with Cheyennes and

The Economic Activities of Native Peoples

The Transformation of Native Cultures

The Extraction of Natural Resources

Irrigation and Transportation

Farming the Plains

LINKS TO THE WORLD
The Australian Frontier

The Ranching Frontier

LEGACY FOR A PEOPLE AND A NATION
The West and Rugged Individualism

Online Study Center
This icon will direct you to interactive map and primary source activities on the website http://college.hmco.com/pic/nortonbrief7e

CHRONOLOGY

1862 • Homestead Act grants free land to citizens who live on and improve the land
   • Morrill Land Grant Act gives states public land to finance agricultural and industrial colleges

1864 • Chivington's militia massacres Black Kettle's Cheyennes at Sand Creek

1869 • First transcontinental railroad completed, with connection at Promontory Point, Utah

1872 • Yellowstone becomes first national park

1873 • Barbed wire invented, enabling western farmers to enclose and protect fields cheaply

1876 • Sioux annihilate Custer's federal troops at Little Big Horn

1877 • Nez Percé Indians under Young Joseph surrender to U.S. troops

1878 • Timber and Stone Act allows citizens to buy timberland cheaply but also enables large companies to acquire huge tracts of forest land

1879 • Carlisle School for Indians established in Pennsylvania

1880–81 • Manypenny's *Our Indian Wards* and Jackson's *A Century of Dishonor* influence public conscience about poor government treatment of Indians

1881 • Shootout at OK Corral between Clantons and Earps

1881–82 • Chinese Exclusion Acts prohibit Chinese immigration to the United States

1883 • National time zones standardized

1884 • U.S. Supreme Court first defines Indians as wards under government protection

1887 • Dawes Severalty Act ends communal ownership of Indian lands and grants land allotments to individual Native American families
   • Hatch Act provides for agricultural experiment stations in every state
   • California passes law permitting farmers to organize into districts

1886–88 • Devastating winters on Plains destroys countless livestock and forces farmers into economic hardship

1890 • Final suppression of Plains Indians by U.S. Army at Wounded Knee
   • Census Bureau announces closing of the frontier
   • Yosemite National Park established

1892 • Muir helps found Sierra Club

1893 • Turner presents "frontier thesis" at Columbian Exposition

1896 • Rural Free Delivery made available

1902 • Newlands Reclamation Act passed

Arapahos over access to hunting grounds. For Pawnees, concepts of private property and profit had little meaning.

To white Americans, however, the expanses of land and water should be used for economic gain. They excavated the earth for valuable minerals, felled forests for construction, linked markets with railroads, and dammed rivers and plowed soil with crop machines. Their goal: opening markets nationally and internationally through corporate big business. As they transformed the landscape, the triumph of market economies transformed the nation.

By 1870, the West spanned from the Mississippi River to the Pacific Ocean and consisted of several regions of varying economic potential. Abundant rainfall along the northern Pacific coast fed huge forests. California's woodlands and grasslands provided fertile valleys for vegetable fields and orange groves. Eastward, the deserts and plateaus from the Cascades and Sierra Nevada to the Rocky Mountains contained gold, silver, and other buried minerals. East of the Rockies, the Great Plains could support grain crops and livestock with its semiarid western side of few trees and tough buffalo grass and eastern sector of ample rainfall and tall grasses.

The West had long been the scene of great migrations. Before contact with whites, Indian peoples had moved around the region, warring, trading, and negotiating with each other as they searched for food and shelter. In parts of the Southwest, Native Americans built towns, farms, and ranches. After the Civil War, white migration overwhelmed the native peoples, swelling the population between 1870 and 1890 from 7 million to nearly 17 million.

The West's abundance of exploitable land and raw materials filled white Americans with faith that anyone eager and persistent enough could succeed. This confidence rested on a belief that white people were somehow special and asserted itself at the expense of people of color, the poor, and the environment. By 1890 farms, ranches, mines, towns, and cities could be found in almost every corner of the present-day continental United States. Though of symbolic importance, the fading of the frontier had little impact on people's behavior. As long as vast stretches of land remained unsettled, pioneers who failed in one locale merely tried again somewhere else. A surplus of seemingly uninhabited land led Americans to believe they would always have a second chance. This belief, more than Turner's theory of frontier democracy or Cody's heroic reenactments, left a deep imprint on the American character. ■

The Economic Activities of Native Peoples

Historians once defined the American frontier as "the edge of the unused," implying, as Turner had, that the frontier was barren before whites arrived. Scholars now recognize that Native Americans settled and developed the West for centuries before others migrated there. Nevertheless, almost all native economic systems weakened in the late nineteenth century.

Western Indian cultures varied. Some Indians lived in permanent settlements; others were nomadic.

SUBSISTENCE CULTURES

Still, most Indians engaged in and were affected by the large-scale flow of goods, culture, language, and disease carried by migrating groups. Indian economies were based to differing degrees on four activities: crop growing; livestock raising; hunting, fishing, and gathering; and trading and raiding. Corn was the most common crop; sheep and horses, acquired from Spanish colonizers and from other Indians, were the livestock; and buffalo (American bison) were the primary prey of hunts. Indians raided one another for food, tools, hides, and horses, which they then traded with other Indians and whites. Indians sought a balanced economic system, subsisting on crops when a buffalo hunt failed and hunting buffalo, trading livestock, or stealing food and horses in a raid when crops failed.

For Indians on the Great Plains, life focused on the buffalo. They cooked and preserved buffalo meat; fashioned hides into clothing, shoes, and blankets; used sinew for thread and bowstrings; and carved tools from bones and horns. Buffalo were so valuable that the village-dwelling Pawnees and nomadic Lakotas often struggled over access to herds. To feed their herds, Plains Indians periodically set fire to tall-grass prairies, which burned away dead plants and facilitated the growth of new grass so horses could feed all summer.

In the Southwest, Indians herded sheep, goats, and horses. Old Man Hat, a Navajo, explained, "The herd is money. . . . You know that you have some good clothing; the sheep gave you that. And you've just eaten different kinds of food; the sheep gave that food to you. Everything comes from the sheep." He was not speaking of money in a business sense, but rather in terms of status and security. Like many other Indians, the Navajos emphasized generosity and distrusted private property. Within the family, sharing was expected; outside the family, gifts and reciprocity governed relationships. Southwestern Indians too altered the environment, building elaborate irrigation systems to maximize use of scarce water supplies.

What buffalo were to the Plains Indians and sheep were to Southwestern Indians, salmon were to Indians of the Northwest. Before the mid-nineteenth century, the Columbia River and its tributaries supported the densest population of native peoples in North America. The Clatsops, Klamathets, and S'Klallam applied their technology of stream diversion, platform construction over the water, and special baskets to better harvest fish.

On the Plains and areas of the Southwest, this native world began to dissolve after 1850 when whites competed with Indians over natural resources. Perceiving buffalo and Indians as hindrances, whites endeavored to eliminate both. Railroads sponsored buffalo hunts in which eastern sportsmen shot at the bulky targets from slow-moving trains. The army refused to enforce treaties that reserved hunting grounds for exclusive Indian use.

SLAUGHTER OF BUFFALO

What neither Indians nor whites realized was that a combination of circumstances doomed the buffalo before the slaughter of the late 1800s. Indians depleted herds by increasing their kills to trade with whites and other Indians. Also, in generally dry years in the 1840s and 1850s, Indians moved to more fertile river basins, thereby pushing the bison out of important grazing territory to face starvation. Whites too settled in basin areas, further forcing buffalo away. At the same time, lethal animal diseases such as anthrax and brucellosis, brought in by white-owned livestock, decimated buffalo, already weakened by malnutrition and drought. Increased numbers of horses, oxen, and sheep owned by white newcomers and some Indians devoured grasses that buffalo required. The mass killing after 1850 struck the final blow. By the 1880s, only a few hundred remained of the 25 million bison estimated on the Plains in 1820.

In the Northwest, salmon suffered a similar fate. White commercial fishermen and canneries moved into the Columbia and Willamette River valleys during the 1860s and 1870s, and by the 1880s had greatly

DECLINE OF SALMON

diminished the salmon runs. Numerous salmon running upriver to spawn were being caught before they laid their eggs, preventing the fish supply from replenishing. By the twentieth century, the construction of dams on the river and its tributaries further impeded salmon reproduction. The government protected Indian fishing rights, and hatcheries helped restore some of the fish supply, but the need for electrical power from dams, combined with overfishing and pollution, curtailed the salmon supply.

The Transformation of Native Cultures

Buffalo slaughter and salmon reduction undermined Indian subsistence, but human demography also contributed. Throughout the nineteenth century, white migrants were overwhelmingly young, single males in their twenties and thirties, the age when they were most prone to violence. In 1870 white men outnumbered white women by three to two in California, two to one in Colorado, and two to one in Dakota Territory. The whites whom Indians were most likely to come into contact with first were explorers, traders, trappers, soldiers, prospectors, and cowboys—almost all of whom possessed guns and had few qualms about using them against animals and humans who got in their way.

Moreover, these men subscribed to prevailing attitudes that Indians were primitive, lazy, devious, and cruel. Such contempt made exploiting and killing native peoples easier, further "justified" by claims of preempting threats to life and property. When Indians raided white settlements, they sometimes mutilated bodies, burned buildings, and kidnapped women, acts that were embellished in campfire stories and popular fiction—reinforcing images of Indians as savages. In saloons, men boasted about fighting Indians and showed off trophies of scalps and other body parts taken from victims.

Indian warriors were also young, armed, and prone to violence and similarly boasted of fighting white interlopers. But Indian communities contained large groups of women and children, making native bands less mobile and therefore vulnerable to attack. They also were vulnerable to the bad habits of the bachelor white society, bingeing on whiskey and prostitution. The syphilis and gonorrhea that Indian men contracted from Indian women infected by whites killed many and impaired reproduction, a consequence that their population, already declining from smallpox and other white diseases, could not afford. Thus, the age and gender structure of the white frontier population, combined with racial contempt, threatened Indian existence in the West further.

Government policy reinforced efforts to remove Indians. North American native peoples were organized

LACK OF NATIVE UNITY

not into tribes, as whites believed, but rather into bands and confederacies. Two hundred distinct languages and dialects separated these groups, making it difficult for Indians to unite against white invaders. Although a language group could be defined as a tribe, separate bands and clans had their own leaders, and seldom did a tribal chief hold widespread power. Moreover, bands usually spent more time quarreling among themselves than with white settlers.

After the Treaty of Greenville in 1795, American officials regarded Indian tribes as nations with which

TERRITORIAL TREATIES

they could make pacts, ensuring peace and defining land boundaries. But the U.S. government did not understand that a chief who agreed to a treaty did not speak for everyone and that the group might not abide by it. Moreover, whites seldom accepted treaties as guarantees of Indians' future land rights. In the Northwest, whites considered treaties protecting Indians' fishing rights on the Columbia River as nuisances and ousted Indians from the best locations. On the Plains, whites settled wherever they wished, typically commandeering choice farmlands.

From the 1860s to the 1880s, the federal government tried to force western Indians onto reservations

RESERVATION POLICY

under the guise of "civilizing" them. Reservations usually consisted of those areas of a group's previous territory that were least desirable to whites. In exchange, the government promised protection from white encroachment along with food, clothing, and other necessities.

The reservation policy helped make way for the market economy. Early on, trade had benefited both Indians and whites equally. Indians acquired clothing, guns, and horses in return for furs, jewelry, and sometimes military assistance to whites against other Indians. Over time, however, Indians became more dependent, and whites increasingly dictated trade. For example, white traders persuaded Navajo weavers in the Southwest to produce heavy rugs for eastern customers and to adapt colors and designs to boost sales. Meanwhile, Navajos raised fewer crops and were forced to buy food. Soon they were selling land and labor to whites, and their dependency made it easier to force them onto reservations.

Indians had no voice concerning their own affairs on reservations. Supreme Court decisions in 1884 and 1886 defined them as wards (falling, like helpless children, under government protection) and denied them the right to become U.S. citizens. Thus, they were unprotected by the Fourteenth and Fifteenth Amendments, which had extended citizenship to African Americans. Second, pressure from white farmers, miners, and herders who sought Indian lands made it difficult for the government to preserve reservations intact. Third, the government ignored native history, even combining on the same reservation Indian bands that habitually warred against each other. Rather than serving as civilizing communities, reservations weakened Indian life.

Not all Indians succumbed to market forces and reservation restrictions. Pawnees in the Midwest, for

NATIVE RESISTANCE AND INDIAN WARS

example, resisted disadvantageous deals. Some Native Americans preserved their cultures even as they became dependent on whites. Pawnees left their Nebraska homelands for a reservation in the hope that they could hunt buffalo and grow corn their way.

Online Study Center Improve Your Grade
   Interactive Map:
      Major Indian-White Clashes in the West

Whites responded to western Indian defiance with military aggression. In 1864, for example, in the Sand Creek region of Colorado, a militia led by Methodist minister John Chivington attacked a Cheyenne band under Black Kettle, killing almost every Indian. In 1877 four detachments of troops, aided by Crow and Cheyenne scouts, chased 800 Nez Percé Indians in the Northwest, finally killing many before one of their leaders, Young Joseph, surrendered.

The most infamous Indian battle occurred in June 1876 when 2,500 Lakotas led by Chiefs Rain-in-the-Face, Sitting Bull, and Crazy Horse annihilated

256 government troops led by the rash General Geoerge A. Custer near the Little Big Horn River in southern Montana. Though Indians demonstrated military skill, supply shortages and relentless pursuit by U.S. soldiers eventually overwhelmed Indian resistance. Native Americans were not so much conquered as they were harassed and starved into submission.

In the 1870s and 1880s, officials and reformers sought peaceful means of dealing with Native Americans.

REFORM OF INDIAN POLICY

Instead of battling Indians, whites would "civilize" them through landholding and education. The U.S. government pressured Indians to abandon their traditional cultures and adopt values of the American work ethic: ambition, thrift, and materialism. Other forces argued for sympathetic—and sometimes patronizing—

treatment. Reform treatises, such as George Manypenny's *Our Indian Wards* (1880) and Helen Hunt Jackson's *A Century of Dishonor* (1881), and unfavorable comparison with Canada's more sympathetic management of Indian affairs aroused the American conscience.

In the United States, the two most active Indian reform organizations were the Women's National Indian Association (WNIA) and the Indian Rights Association (IRA). The WNIA, composed mainly of white women using domestic skills to help needy people, urged gradual assimilation of Indians. The influential IRA, which had few Native American members, supported Indian citizenship and landholding. Most reformers believed Indians were culturally inferior and could succeed economically only by embracing middle-class values of diligence and education.

■ Plains Indians did not write books or letters as whites did, but they did tell stories and spread news through art. They painted scenes on hides and notebooks to represent events such as this one, which depicts the Indians' annihilation of General George A. Custer's soldiers at Little Big Horn in 1876.

(National Anthropological Archives, Smithsonian Institution [72-3934])

Reformers particularly deplored Indians' sexual division of labor. Women seemed to do all the work—tending crops, raising children, cooking, curing hides, making tools and clothes—while being servile to men, who hunted but were otherwise idle. WNIA, IRA, and others wanted Indian men to bear more responsibilities, treat Indian women respectfully, and resemble male heads of white middle-class households. But when Indian men and women adopted the model of white society, Indian women lost much of the economic independence and power over daily life that they once had.

In 1887 Congress reversed its reservation policy and passed the Dawes Severalty Act, which achieved the reformers' goal of ending community-owned property in favor of individual family land grants. The government held that land in trust for twenty-five years, so families could not sell their allotments. The law also awarded citizenship to those accepting allotments (a 1906 act of Congress delayed citizenship for those Indians who had not yet taken their allotment). And it entitled the government to sell unallocated land to whites. Undergirding the Dawes Act was the belief that private property would more easily integrate Indians into the larger society. Officials also believed that Indians would abandon their "barbaric" habits more quickly if their children were educated away from the reservations.

DAWES SEVERALTY ACT

The Dawes Act reflected a Euro-American and Christian worldview that a society of families headed by men was most desirable. Professional educators similarly saw schools as tools to create a patriotic, industrious citizenry. In 1879, educators established the Carlisle School in Pennsylvania as the flagship of the government's Indian school system based on the Hampton Institute founded ten years earlier in Virginia to educate newly freed slaves. Boarding schools imposed white-defined sex roles: boys were taught farming and carpentry, while girls learned sewing, cleaning, and cooking.

With active resistance suppressed, Lakotas and other groups turned to the Ghost Dance as a spiritual means of preserving culture. The Ghost Dance involved movement in a circle until the dancers reached a trancelike state and envisioned dead

GHOST DANCE

ancestors. Involving several days of dancing and meditation, the Ghost Dance expressed a messianic vision of a day when buffalo would return to the Plains and all elements of white civilization, including guns and whiskey, would be buried.

Ghost Dancers forswore violence, but as the religion spread, government agents worried about the possibility of renewed Indian uprisings. Charging that the cult was anti-Christian, they arrested Ghost Dancers. Late in 1890, the government sent Custer's former regiment, the Seventh Cavalry, to detain Lakotas moving toward Pine Ridge, South Dakota. Although the Indians were starving, the army assumed they were armed for revolt. Overtaking the band at Wounded Knee Creek, the troops massacred an estimated three hundred men, women, and children in the snow.

The Dawes Act effectively accomplished what whites wanted and Indians feared: it reduced native control over land. Between 1887 and the 1930s, Indian landholdings dwindled from 138 million acres to 52 million. Land-grabbing whites were particularly cruel to the Ojibwas of the northern plains. In 1906 Senator Moses E. Clapp of Minnesota attached a rider to an Indian appropriations bill declaring that mixed-blood adults were "competent" (meaning educated in white ways) enough to sell their land without the Dawes Act's twenty-five-year waiting period. When the bill became law, speculators duped many Ojibwas into signing away their land in return for counterfeit money and worthless merchandise. The Ojibwas lost more than half their original holdings and were ruined economically.

LOSING THE WEST

Ultimately, political and ecological crises overwhelmed most western Indian groups. Buffalo extinction, enemy raids, and disease, in addition to white military force, weakened subsistence culture so that Native Americans had no alternative but to yield their lands to market-oriented whites. Believing their culture superior, whites determined to transform Indians into successful farmers by teaching them the value of private property, educating them in American ideals, and eradicating their "backward" languages, lifestyles, and religions. Indians tried to retain their culture, but by century's end, they had lost control of the land and faced increasing pressure to shed their group identity.

The Extraction of Natural Resources

*U*nlike Indians, who used natural resources primarily for subsistence and small-scale trading, most whites who migrated to the West and the Great Plains saw the vast territory as an untapped source of wealth (see Map 17.1). Extracting its rich resources advanced settlement, created new markets at home and abroad, and fueled revolutions in transportation, agriculture, and industry across the United States. At the same time, extraction of nature's wealth led to environmental

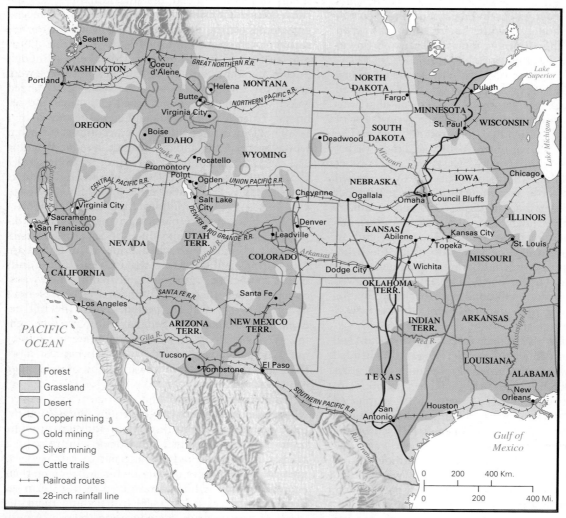

Map 17.1   The Development and Natural Resources of the West

By 1890, mining, lumbering, and cattle ranching had penetrated many areas west of the Mississippi River, and railroads had linked together the western economy. These characteristics, along with the spread of agriculture, contributed to the Census Bureau's announcement in 1890 that the frontier had disappeared; yet as the map shows, large areas remained undeveloped.

wastefulness and fed habits of racial and sexual oppression.

In the mid-1800s, the mining frontier advanced rapidly, drawing thousands of people to Nevada, Idaho, Montana, Utah, and Colorado in search of gold, silver, timber, and copper. California's gold rush populated the thriving state with over 300,000 people by 1860 and furnished many of the miners moving on to nearby states in search of riches. Others followed traditional routes, moving from the East to the West.

MINING AND
LUMBERING

Prospectors climbed mountains and trekked across deserts in search of precious metals. They shot game for food and financed their explorations by convincing merchants to advance credit for equipment in return for a share of the as-yet-undiscovered lode. Unlucky prospectors whose credit ran out took jobs and saved up for another search.

Digging for and transporting minerals was expensive, so prospectors who discovered veins sold their claims to large mining syndicates such as the Anaconda Copper Company. Financed by eastern capital, these companies brought in engineers, heavy machinery, railroad lines, and work crews, making mining as corporate as eastern manufacturing. Although discoveries of gold and silver first drew attention to the West, mining companies usually exploited equally lucrative lead, zinc, tin, quartz, and copper.

Midwest and southern lumber companies headed west, spurred by the demand for the rich timber resources there and the depletion of forests at home. The Timber and Stone Act of 1878 sought to stimulate settlement in California, Nevada, Oregon, and Washington, by allowing private citizens to buy, at low prices, 160-acre plots "valuable chiefly for timber." Lumber companies grabbed millions of these acres by hiring seamen from waterfront boarding houses to register private claims to timberland and then transfer those claims to the companies. By 1900 most of the 3.5 million acres believed to be sold to private citizens in truth belonged to corporations.

At the same time, oil companies were beginning to drill in the Southwest. In 1900 most of the nation's petroleum came from the Appalachians and the Midwest, but rich oil reserves had been discovered in southern California and eastern Texas. Although oil and kerosene were still used mostly for lubrication and lighting, Southwest oil would become a vital new fuel source.

The West became a rich multiracial society, comprising Native Americans, native-born white migrants, Hispanics, African Americans, and Asians. A crescent borderland from western Texas through New Mexico and Arizona to northern California supported Hispanic ranchers and sheepherders, descendants of the early Spanish settlers. In New Mexico, Spaniards mixed with Indians to form a *mestizo* population. Throughout the Southwest, Mexican immigrants moved into American territory to find work. Some returned to Mexico seasonally; others stayed.

A COMPLEX
POPULATION

Before federal law excluded them in 1881 and 1882, 200,000 Chinese immigrants—mostly young, single males—came to the United States, building communities in California, Oregon, and Washington. The state's fertile fields and citrus groves demanded a huge migrant work force, and by the 1870s, Chinese composed half of California's agricultural laborers.

Japanese, Mexican, and European immigrants also moved around, working in mining and agricultural communities. The region consequently developed its own migrant economy, with workers relocating as they took short-term jobs.

African Americans tended to congregate in the West, many of them "Exodusters" who inhabited all-black towns. Nicodemus, Kansas, for example, was founded in 1877 by African American migrants from Lexington, Kentucky, and grew to six hundred residents within two years, surviving challenging times with the aid of food, firewood, and staples from nearby Osage Indians.

Although unmarried men numerically dominated the frontier, some white women also came to find fortune. But they usually accompanied a husband or father and seldom prospected themselves. With their labor as a resource, many women earned money cooking, laundering, and in some cases working in houses of prostitution. In the Northwest, they worked in canneries, cleaning and salting fish.

For white settlers, race became a vital means of controlling labor and social relations. They usually identified four nonwhite races, all ascribed with demeaning characteristics: Indians, Mexicans (including

SIGNIFICANCE
OF RACE

Mexican Americans and immigrants), "Mongolians" (referring to Chinese), and "Negroes." Through these categories, whites imposed racial distinctions on people who, with the possible exception of African Americans, had never considered themselves to be a "race" and then deemed them permanently inferior. In 1878, for example, a federal judge in California ruled that Chinese could not become U.S. citizens because they were not "white persons."

Racial minorities occupied the bottom half of a two-tiered labor system and encountered prejudice as whites sought to reserve the West's riches for themselves. Whites dominated the top tier of managerial and skilled labor positions, while Irish, Chinese, and Mexicans held unskilled jobs in mines, railroad construction, and as agricultural and domestic laborers. Indians barely participated in the labor system at all. Anti-Chinese violence erupted during hard times. When the Union Pacific Railroad tried to replace white workers with lower-waged Chinese in Rock Springs, Wyoming, in 1885, whites burned down the Chinese part of town and killed twenty-eight. Mexicans, many of whom had been the original landowners, saw their property claims ignored or stolen by whites. In California, many Mexicans moved to cities, where they could get only unskilled, low-paying jobs.

Because so many white male migrants were single, intermarriage with Mexican and Indian women was common. Such intermarriage was acceptable for white men, but not for white women, especially with Asian immigrants. Most miscegenation laws passed by western legislatures were intended to prevent Chinese and Japanese men from marrying white women.

Protestant missions had long sponsored benevolent activities abroad, such as in China, and had aided the settlement of Oregon in the 1840s. But in the mid-nineteenth century, a number of women broke away from male-dominated organizations and established missionary societies in the United States. In the West, they built homes to rescue women—unmarried mothers, Mormons, Indians, and Chinese—who they believed had fallen prey to men lacking Christian virtue.

Questions about natural resources caught Americans between a desire for progress and a fear of spoiling the land. After the Civil War, people eager to protect the natural landscape organized a conservation movement. Sports hunters, concerned about loss of wildlife, lobbied state legislatures

CONSERVATION MOVEMENT

to regulate commercial hunting. Artists and tourists in 1864 persuaded Congress to preserve the beautiful Yosemite Valley by granting it to California for public use. In 1872 Congress designated the Yellowstone River region in Wyoming as the first national park. And in 1891, conservationists, led by naturalist John Muir, pressured Congress to authorize President Benjamin Harrison to create forest reserves—public lands protected from private-interest cutting. Despite Muir's activism and efforts by the Sierra Club (which Muir helped found in 1892) and corporations supporting rational resource development, opposition was loudest in the West, where people remained eager to exploit nature's bounty. Moreover, national parks induced some spoiling of the land they intended to preserve, as tourist services necessitated the building of roads, hotels, restaurants, and sewers in the wilderness.

Online Study Center
Improve Your Grade
Primary Source:
John Muir on the Dominion of Nature

Development of mining and forest regions brought western territories to the threshold of statehood (see Map 17.1). In 1889 Republicans seeking to solidify control of Congress passed a bill granting statehood to North Dakota, South Dakota, Washington, and Montana. Wyoming and Idaho, which allowed women to vote, were admitted the next year. Congress denied statehood to Utah until 1896, awaiting assurances from the Mormons, a majority of the territory's population and leaders, that they would abandon polygamy.

ADMISSION OF NEW STATES

Mining towns and lumber camps spiced American folklore and fostered a go-getter optimism that distinguished the American spirit. The lawlessness of places such as Deadwood in Dakota Territory and Tombstone in Arizona Territory gave the West notoriety and romance. Cowboys especially captivated popular imagination in the United States and Europe.

Arizona's mining towns, with their free-flowing cash and loose law enforcement, attracted gamblers, thieves, and opportunists who came to stand for the Wild West. Near Tombstone, the infamous Clanton family and their partner, John Ringgold (known as Johnny Ringo), engaged in smuggling and cattle rustling. The Earp brothers—Wyatt, Jim, Morgan, Virgil, and Warren—and their friends William ("Bat")

Masterson and John Henry ("Doc") Holliday operated on both sides of the law as gunmen, gamblers, and politicians. A feud between the Clantons and Earps climaxed on October 26, 1881, in a shootout at the OK Corral, where three Clantons were killed and Holliday and Morgan Earp were wounded.

Mark Twain, Bret Harte, and other writers captured for posterity the drama of western life, and characters like Buffalo Bill, Annie Oakley, Wild Bill Hickok, Poker Alice, and Bedrock Tom became folk heroes. But in reality, most miners and lumbermen worked long hours, often for corporations rather than as rugged individuals, and they had little time or money for gambling, carousing, or gunfights. Women worked hard too, as teachers, laundresses, storekeepers, and housewives. Only a few were sharpshooters or dance-hall queens. For most, western life was a matter of survival.

Irrigation and Transportation

*W*estern economic development is the story of how public and private interests used technology and organization to develop the region's river basins and make the land agriculturally productive. For centuries, Indians had irrigated southwestern lands for subsistence farming. When the Spanish arrived, they irrigated farms in southwest Texas, New Mexico, and California. Later they channeled water to the California mission communities of San Diego and Los Angeles. The first Americans of northern European ancestry to practice extensive irrigation were the Mormons. Arriving in Utah in 1847, they diverted streams and rivers into networks of canals, enabling them to farm the hard-baked soil. By 1890 Utah boasted over 263,000 irrigated acres, supporting more than 200,000 people.

Irrigation in Colorado and California raised controversies over rights to the precious streams that flowed through the West. Americans

RIGHTS TO WATER

had inherited the English common-law principle of riparian rights, which held that the stream itself belonged to God; those who lived near it could take water as needed but were not to diminish the river. Intended to protect nature, this principle discouraged economic development by prohibiting property owners from damming or diverting water at the expense of neighbors along the banks.

Westerners, taking cues from eastern Americans who had diverted waterways to power mills, asserted the doctrine of prior appropriation: water, like other natural resources, existed to serve human needs, so anyone intending a "reasonable" (economically productive) use of river water should have the right to appropriation. The courts generally agreed.

Under appropriation, those who dammed and diverted water often reduced its flow downstream. People disadvantaged by it could protect their interests by either suing or establishing a public authority to regulate water use. Thus, in 1879 Colorado created several water divisions. In 1890 Wyoming added a constitutional provision declaring that the state's rivers were public property subject to state supervision.

California maintained a mixed legal system that upheld riparianism while allowing for some appropriation. This system disadvantaged irrigators, who sought to change state law. In 1887 the legislature passed a bill permitting farmers to organize into districts that would construct and operate irrigation projects. An irrigation district could use its public authority to purchase water rights, seize private property for irrigation canals, and finance projects through taxation or by issuing bonds. As a result, California became the nation's leader in irrigated acreage, with more than 1 million irrigated acres by 1890, making it the most profitable agricultural state in the country.

Still, the federal government owned most of western lands in the 1890s. Prodded by land-hungry

NEWLANDS RECLAMATION ACT

developers, states claimed that they could make these lands profitable through reclamation and subsequent irrigation. Congress generally refused to transfer the land because of potential controversies. If one state sponsored irrigation, who would regulate waterways that flowed through more than one state? If, for example, California controlled the Truckee River, which flowed westward to the Nevada border, how would Nevadans ensure that California would give them sufficient water? Only the federal government, it seemed, could regulate regional water development.

In 1902, after years of debates, Congress passed the Newlands Reclamation Act. This allowed the federal government to sell western public lands to individuals in parcels of under 160 acres and to use the proceeds to finance irrigation. Often seen as sensitive to natural-resource conservation, the Newlands

Reclamation Act in fact represented a decision by the federal government to aid the agricultural and general economic development of the West.

Between 1865 and 1890, railroad construction grew from 35,000 to 200,000 miles, mostly west of the Mississippi River (see Map 17.1).

RAILROAD
CONSTRUCTION

By 1900, the United States contained one-third of all railroad track in the world. The Central Pacific imported seven thousand Chinese to build its tracks; the Union Pacific used mainly the Irish. Workers lived in shacks and tents that were dismantled, loaded on flatcars, and relocated every 60 miles or so. After 1880, railroads helped to boost the steel industry by switching from iron to steel rails. Railroad expansion also spawned related industries, including coal production, passenger- and freight-car manufacture, and depot construction. Transporting people and freight, lines such as the Union Pacific and Southern Pacific accelerated the growth of western hubs such as Omaha, Kansas City, Cheyenne, Los Angeles, Portland, and Seattle.

Railroads received some of the largest government subsidies in American history. Executives argued that because railroads were a public benefit, the government should give them land from the public domain, which they could sell to finance construction. During the Civil War, Congress, dominated by business-minded Republicans, was sympathetic, granting over 180 million acres to railroad corporations, mostly for interstate routes. Railroads funded construction by using the land as security for bonds or by selling it. State legislators, many of whom had financial interests in a railroad's success, granted an additional 50 million acres. Cities and towns also assisted, usually through loans or by purchasing railroad bonds or stocks.

RAILROAD
SUBSIDIES

Without public help, few railroads could have prospered sufficiently to attract private investment, yet such aid was not always voluntary. Localities that could not or would not pay suffered. The Southern Pacific, for example, threatened to bypass Los Angeles unless the city paid a bonus and built a depot. Some laborers and farmers fought subsidies, arguing that companies like Southern Pacific would become too powerful. Many communities boomed, however, as railroads helped attract investment into the West and drew farmers into the market economy.

The growth of railroads required technological and organizational reforms. By the late 1880s, almost all lines had adopted standard-gauge rails allowing their tracks to connect. Air brakes, automatic car couplers, standardized handholds on freight cars, and other devices made rail transportation safer and more efficient. The need for gradings, tunnels, and bridges spurred the growth of the engineering profession. Organizational advances included systems for coordinating passenger and freight schedules and the adoption of uniform freight classification.

STANDARD
GAUGE;
STANDARD TIME

Railroads also altered conceptions of time and space. First, instead of expressing distance in miles, people began to refer to the time it took to travel from place to place. Second, railroad scheduling required nationwide standardization of time. Before railroads, local church bells and clocks struck noon when the sun was directly overhead, and people set clocks accordingly. But because the sun was not overhead at the same moment everywhere, time varied by place. Boston's clocks differed from New York's by almost twelve minutes. By 1880 there were nearly fifty different standards. In 1883 the railroads, without authority from Congress, agreed to establish four standard time zones that would regularize the country. Railroad time became national time.

Farming the Plains

*W*estern agriculture in the late nineteenth century yielded two notable achievements: the transformation of arid prairies into crop-producing land and the transformation of agriculture into big business via mechanization, transportation, and scientific cultivation. The climate and terrain of the Great Plains presented formidable challenges. Technological innovation and the mechanization enabled farmers to feed the burgeoning population and turned the United States into the world's breadbasket.

During the 1870s and 1880s, thousands of hopeful farmers streamed into the Great Plains region, cultivating more land in states such as Kansas, Nebraska, and Texas than in the entire country during the previous 250 years. The number of

SETTLEMENT OF
THE PLAINS

The Australian Frontier

Australia, founded like the United States as a European colony, bred a frontier society that paralleled the American experience in its mining development, folk society, and treatment of indigenous people. Australia experienced a gold rush two years after the United States in 1851, and large-scale mining companies quickly moved into its western regions to extract lucrative mineral deposits.

A promise of mineral wealth lured thousands of immigrants, primarily males, to Australia in the late nineteenth century, many from China. As in the United States, anti-Chinese riots erupted, and beginning in 1854 Australia passed laws restricting Chinese immigration. When the country became an independent British federation in 1901, it implemented a strict liter-acy test that eliminated Chinese immigration for over fifty years.

While Australians lauded "white men," they considered native peoples, whom they called "Aborigines," to be savages. Christian missionaries viewed natives as pagans and tried to convert them. In 1869 the government of Victoria passed the Aborigine Protection Act, encouraging the removal of native children from their families to learn European customs in white schools. Aborigines tried in their own ways to adapt or, if they had light skin, sometimes reported themselves as white for the census. In the end, Australians resorted to reservations. Like the Americans, Australians could not find a place for Aborigines in a land of opportunity for whites.

Much like the American counterpart, the Australian frontier was populated by natives before Anglo colonists arrived. The Aborigines, as the Australian natives were called, lived in villages and used their own culture to adapt to the environment. This photo shows a native camp in the Maloga reserve. (National Library of Australia)

farms tripled from 2 million to over 6 million between 1860 and 1910. Several states opened offices in the East to lure migrants westward. Land-rich railroads aggressively advertised cheap land, arranged credit, and offered reduced fares. Railroad agents—often former immigrants—traveled to Denmark, Sweden, Germany, and other European nations to recruit settlers.

Most families migrated because opportunities in the West seemed to promise a better existence. Railroad expansion enabled farmers to ship produce to market, and the construction of grain elevators eased storage problems. Worldwide and national population growth fueled demand for farm products, and the prospects for commercial agriculture became increasingly favorable.

Farm life was harder than advertisements and railroad agents suggested. Migrants often encountered scarcities of essentials they had once taken for granted. The open prairies contained little lumber, so families

HARDSHIP ON THE PLAINS

built houses of sod and burned buffalo dung for heat. Water was often scarce too. Few families were wealthy enough to buy land near a stream that did not dry up in summer. Machinery for drilling wells was expensive, as were windmills for drawing water to the surface.

The weather was especially formidable. The climate between the Missouri River and the Rocky Mountains divides along a line running from Minnesota southwest through Oklahoma, then south, bisecting Texas. West of this line, annual rainfall averages less than twenty-eight inches, not enough for most crops, and even that rain was never certain.

Weather was unpredictable. In summer, weeks of heat and parching winds suddenly gave way to violent storms that washed away crops and property. Winter blizzards piled up mountainous snowdrifts that halted outdoor movement. Melting snow swelled streams, and floods threatened millions of acres. In the fall, a rainless week turned dry grasslands into

■ Posing in front of their sod house, this proud Nebraska family displays the seriousness that derived from their hard lives on the Great Plains. Although bushes and other growth appear in the background, the absence of trees is notable.   (Nebraska State Historical Society, Solomon D. Butcher Collection)

tinder, and the slightest spark could ignite a raging prairie fire. Although early Plains settlers were optimistic about a wet-weather cycle, the climate changed abruptly in 1886, beginning a four-year drought that drove many off the land.

Nature could be cruel even under good conditions. Weather that was favorable for crops was also good for breeding insects. In the 1870s and 1880s, swarms of grasshoppers devoured everything: plants, tree bark, and clothes. As one farmer lamented, the "hoppers left behind nothing but the mortgage."

Settlers also braved isolation. New England and European farmers lived in villages, traveling daily to

SOCIAL ISOLATION

nearby fields. In the Plains, the Far West, and the South, peculiarities of land division compelled rural dwellers to live far apart. The Homestead Act of 1862 and other measures offered cheap or free plots to people who would reside on and improve their property. Because most small farmers' plots were rectangles of about 160 acres, at most four families could live close by, but only if they congregated around the shared four-corner intersection. In practice, farm families lived back from their boundary lines with at least a half-mile separating farmhouses.

Letters that Ed Donnell, a young Nebraska homesteader, wrote to his family in Missouri reveal how circumstances could dull optimism. In fall 1885, Donnell rejoiced to his mother: "I like Nebr first rate. . . . I have saw a pretty tuff time a part of the time since I have been out here, but I started out to get a home and I was determined to win or die in the attempt. . . . Have got a good crop of corn, a floor in my house and got it ceiled overhead." A year and a half later, Donnell's dreams were dissolving, and still a bachelor, he was beginning to look elsewhere. He wrote to his brother, "If I sell I am going west and grow up with the country." By fall, conditions had worsened. Donnell lamented, "We have been having wet weather for 3 weeks. . . . My health has been so poor this summer. . . . If I can sell I will . . . move to town for I can get $40 a month working in a grist mill and I would not be exposed to the weather." Thousands shared Donnell's hardships and cityward migration, fueling late-nineteenth-century urban growth (see Chapter 19).

By 1900 two developments brought rural settlers into closer contact with modern consumer society

MAIL-ORDER COMPANIES AND RURAL FREE DELIVERY

(though people in sparsely settled regions west of the 28-inch-rainfall line remained isolated for several more decades). First, mail-order companies such as Montgomery Ward and Sears, Roebuck made new products available to almost everyone by the 1870s and 1880s. Ward and Sears were outlets for sociability as well. Letters from customers to Mr. Ward reported family news and sought advice on needs from gifts to childcare. A Washington man wrote, "As you advertise everything for sale that a person wants, I thought I would write you, as I am in need of a wife, and see what you could do for me."

Second, after farmers petitioned Congress for extension of the postal service, the government in 1896 widely expanded the Rural Free Delivery (RFD) it had begun in West Virginia. Farmers who previously had to pick up mail in town could receive letters, newspapers, and catalogues in roadside mailboxes almost daily. In 1913 the postal service inaugurated parcel post, reducing the cost of package delivery.

Expanded use of machinery drove the agricultural revolution. When the Civil War drew men away

MECHANIZATION OF AGRICULTURE

from farms in the upper Mississippi River valley, the women and older men who remained behind began using reapers and other mechanical implements. After the war, continued demand and high prices encouraged farmers to depend more on machines, and inventors developed new grain implements. Seeders, combines, binders, mowers, and rotary plows improved grain growing in the 1870s and 1880s. The centrifugal cream separator, patented in 1879, aided dairy farming by speeding the skimming of cream from milk.

For centuries, grain farmers could plant only as much as could be harvested by hand. Machines—driven first by animals and then by steam—significantly increased productivity. Before mechanization, a farmer could harvest about 7.5 acres of wheat; with an automatic binder that cut and bundled the grain, he could harvest 135 acres. Machines facilitated farming other crops as well.

Congress and scientists worked to improve existing crops and develop new ones. The 1862 Morrill Land

LEGISLATIVE AND SCIENTIFIC AIDS

Grant Act gave states federal lands to finance agricultural research and development. New state universities were established in Wisconsin, Illinois, Minnesota, California, and other states. A second Morrill Act in 1890 aided more schools, including some black colleges. The Hatch Act of 1887 provided for agricultural experiment stations in every state, further encouraging farming science and technology.

Science also enabled farmers to use the soil more efficiently. Researchers developed dry farming, a plowing and harrowing technique that minimized evaporation. Botanists perfected varieties of "hard" wheat whose seeds could withstand northern winters. Agriculturists also adapted new varieties of alfalfa from Mongolia, corn from North Africa, and rice from Asia. George Washington Carver, a son of slaves who became a chemist and taught at Alabama's Tuskegee Institute, created new products from peanuts, soybeans, sweet potatoes, and cotton wastes and developed industrial applications from agricultural products. Other scientists developed means of combating plant and animal diseases. Science and technology helped American farming expand productivity in the market economy.

The Ranching Frontier

Commercial farming ran headlong into one of the region's most romantic industries—ranching. Beginning in the sixteenth century, Spanish landholders raised cattle in Mexico and what would become the American Southwest. They employed Indian and Mexican cowboys, known as *vaqueros*, to tend herds and round up free-roaming cattle. American immigrant ranchers moving into Texas and California in the early nineteenth century hired *vaqueros* to train them in roping, branding, horse training, and saddle making. By the 1860s, cattle raising became increasingly profitable as population growth boosted beef demand and railroads simplified food transportation. By 1870 drovers were herding thousands of Texas cattle northward to Kansas, Missouri, and Wyoming (see Map 17.1). At the northern terminus—usually Abilene, Dodge City, or Cheyenne—the cattle were sold or loaded onto trains bound for Chicago and St. Louis slaughterhouses.

The long drive gave rise to romantic lore of bellowing cattle, buckskin-clad cowboys, and smoky campfires. But trekking over 1,000 miles for months made cattle sinewy and tough, and herds were sometimes shot at for trespassing on Indian and farmers' land. When ranchers discovered that crossing Texas longhorns with Hereford and Angus breeds produced animals better able to survive northern winters, cattle raising expanded northward. Between 1860 and 1880, the cattle population of Kansas, Nebraska, Colorado, Wyoming, Montana, and the Dakotas increased from 130,000 to 4.5 million, crowding out already declining buffalo.

Cattle raisers kept costs down through open-range ranching. It worked like this: ranchers would buy a few acres bordering a stream, and then let their herds graze on adjacent public domain land that no one wanted because it lacked water access. This way, a cattle raiser could use thousands of acres while owning considerably less. Neighboring ranchers often formed associations and allowed their herds to graze together, burning a brand into their animals' hide for identification. But as cattle production rose to meet demand, cattle began to overrun the range, making it difficult for ranchers to control the land.

THE OPEN RANGE

Meanwhile, sheepherders from California and New Mexico also were using the public domain, sparking territorial clashes. Ranchers complained that sheep ruined grassland by eating down to the roots and that cattle refused to graze where sheep had been. Cowboys and sheepherders sometimes resorted to violence rather than settle disagreements in court, where a judge might discover that both were using public land illegally.

More important, the farming frontier generated new land demands. Lacking sufficient timber and stone for fencing, western settlers could not easily mark their property. Tensions flared when farmers accused cattle ranchers of letting herds trespass on cropland and when herders charged that farmers should fence their property.

The solution was barbed wire. Invented in 1873 by Joseph F. Glidden, a DeKalb, Illinois, farmer, this inexpensive and mass-produced fencing consisted of two wires held in place by sharp spurs twisted around them. It enabled Plains homesteaders to protect their farms from grazing cattle. It also ended open-range ranching and made roundups unnecessary because it enclosed private land that had been used ille-

BARBED WIRE

■ A group of cowboys prepare for a roundup. Note the presence of African Americans, who, along with Mexicans, made up one-fourth of all cowboys. Although they rarely became trail bosses or ranch owners, black cowboys enjoyed an independence on the trails that was unavailable to them on tenant farms and city streets.   (Nebraska State Historical Society)

gally for grazing. Likewise, the development of the round silo for storing and making feed (silage) enabled cattle raisers to feed herds without grazing.

By 1890 big businesses were taking over the cattle industry and applying scientific methods of breeding and feeding. Similarly, big corporations used technology to squeeze larger returns from meatpacking. All parts of a cow had uses: its hide became leather, and about half was salable meat. Meatpackers' largest profits came from livestock byproducts: blood for fertilizer, hooves for glue, fat for candles and soap, and the rest for sausages. But cattle processing polluted the environment, as meatpackers and leather tanners dumped what they could not sell into rivers and streams. By the late nineteenth century, the Chicago River created such a powerful stench that residents became sick.

RANCHING AS BIG BUSINESS

The environment contributed to changes in ranching. The brutal winters of 1886–1888 destroyed 90 percent of some herds and drove small ranchers out of business. Cowboys formed labor organizations and went on strike for higher pay. The myth of the cowboy's freedom and individualism lived on, but ranching quickly became a corporate business.

Summary   *Online Study Center* ACE the Test

The land of the American West exerted a lasting influence on the complex mix of people who settled it. Living mostly in small groups, Indians, the original inhabitants, depended heavily on delicate resources such as buffalo herds and salmon runs. When they came into contact with commerce-minded Euro-Americans, their resistance to the market economy, diseases, and violence that whites brought into the West failed.

Migrants discovered a reciprocal relationship between human activities and the environment too. Miners, timber cutters, farmers, and builders extracted raw minerals for eastern factories, used irrigation and mechanization to yield agricultural abundance, filled pastures with cattle and sheep to expand food sources, and constructed railroads to tie the nation together. But the environment exerted its own power through climate, insects and predators, undesirable plant growths, and impenetrable barriers to agriculture.

The West's settlers employed force, violence, and greed that sustained discrimination within a multiracial society, left many farmers feeling cheated, provoked contests over water and pastures, and sacrificed environmental balance for market profits. The region's raw materials and agricultural products improved living standards and hastened the industrial progress of the Machine Age, but not without costs.

LEGACY FOR A PEOPLE AND A NATION
The West and Rugged Individualism

Though born in New York State, Theodore Roosevelt, twenty-sixth president of the United States, thought of himself as a westerner. In 1884, at age twenty-five, he moved to Dakota Territory to ranch. In the West, Roosevelt believed, he developed "rugged individualism," an ability to conquer challenges through strength and fortitude. He once wrote that he "knew toil and hardship . . . but we felt the beat of hardy life in our veins, and ours was the glory of work and the joy of living."

Americans have long shared Roosevelt's fascination with the West. They have popularized western settings and characters in movies and on television. The film *Cimarron* (1930) was one of the first to win an Academy Award, and *Gunsmoke* held the record as one of the longest-running television series (1955–1975). Movie star John Wayne epitomized the rugged westerner in dozens of films. From *The Virginian,* published in 1902, to the recent novels of Larry McMurtry, Americans have made books about the West bestsellers. In many, a lone individual, usually male and white, overcomes danger and hardship through solitary effort.

Western reality, however, is far different from the myth of rugged individualism. Migrants traveled on railroads built with government subsidies, acquired land cheaply from the federal government under the Homestead and Timber and Stone Acts, depended on the army to remove Indians, and cut forests and diverted rivers with federal support. More recently, western politicians who oppose big government have received votes from constituents who depend on federal farm subsidies and price supports, free or subsidized water, and government-financed relief from droughts, floods, and tornadoes.

The West could not have been settled and developed without both individualism *and* government assistance—what might be called "rugged cooperation." Here was the West's true legacy.

*T*HE MACHINE AGE 1877–1920

*I*n 1911, iron molders at the Watertown Arsenal, a government weapons factory near Boston, went on strike after a worker was fired. Joseph Cooney had objected to having his work timed by an efficiency expert with a stopwatch, and the molders knew they soon would be given new work routines. Iron molders union president John Frey explained, "The workman believes when he goes on strike that he is defending his job." The molders felt a property right to their labor—that jobs could not be changed or taken away without their consent.

The army officers who ran the factory, however, believed they owned the molders' labor and that output was "one-half what it should be." To increase production, managers had installed an incentive-pay system, but when that failed, they hired Dwight Merrick, an expert in the new field of "scientific management," to time workers and speed up performance.

The day Merrick began his time study, a molder named Perkins secretly timed the same task. Merrick reported that the job should take twenty-four minutes; Perkins found that to do the job right required fifty minutes. That evening, the molders discussed how they should respond to the discrepancy between Merrick's report and their own. Cooney argued for resisting scientific management; the workers drew up a petition and were ready to walk out.

Eventually the molders and their bosses reached a compromise, but this incident reveals a consequence of the industrialization that made many new products available in the late 1800s. To increase production, factories and machines divided work into minute, repetitive tasks, organized by timetables. Workers who had long thought themselves skilled now struggled to avoid becoming slaves to machines. Defenders of the new system devised theories to justify it, while laborers tried to combat what they thought were demoralizing abuses of power.

In the mid-nineteenth century, an industrial revolution swept through parts of the United States, and improved mechanization triggered a second round in the late 1800s and early 1900s. Three technological developments

Technology and the Triumph of Industrialism

LINKS TO THE WORLD
The Atlantic Cable

Mechanization and the Changing Status of Labor

Labor Violence and the Union Movement

Standards of Living

The Corporate Consolidation Movement

The Gospel of Wealth and Its Critics

LEGACY FOR A PEOPLE AND A NATION
Industrialization, Smoke, and Pollution Control

Online Study Center
This icon will direct you to interactive map and primary source activities on the website http://college.hmco.com/pic/nortonbrief7e

C H R O N O L O G Y

1869 • Knights of Labor founded

1873–78 • Economic decline

1876 • Bonsack invents machine for rolling cigarettes

1877 • Widespread railroad strikes protest wage cuts

1878 • Edison Electric Light Company founded

1879 • George's *Progress and Poverty* argues against economic inequality

1881 • First federal trademark law begins spread of brand names

1882 • Standard Oil Trust formed

1884–85 • Economic decline

1886 • Haymarket riot in Chicago protests police brutality against labor demonstrators
 • American Federation of Labor (AFL) founded

1890 • Sherman Anti-Trust Act outlaws "combinations in restraint of trade"

1892 • Homestead (Pennsylvania) steelworkers strike against Carnegie Steel Company

1893–97 • Economic depression causes high unemployment and business failures

1894 • Workers at Pullman Palace Car Company strike

1895 • *U.S. v. E. C. Knight Co.* limits Congress's power to regulate manufacturing

1896 • *Holden v. Hardy* upholds law regulating miners' work hours

1898 • Taylor promotes scientific management as efficiency measure in industry

1901–03 • U.S. Steel Corporation founded
 • E. I. du Pont de Nemours and Company reorganized
 • Ford Motor Company founded

1903 • Women's Trade Union League founded

1905 • *Lochner v. New York* overturns law limiting bakery workers' work hours and limits labor protection laws
 • Industrial Workers of the World (IWW) founded

1908 • *Muller v. Oregon* upholds law limiting women to ten-hour workday
 • First Ford Model T built

1911 • Triangle Shirtwaist Company fire in New York City leaves 146 workers dead

1913 • Ford begins moving assembly line

1919 • Telephone operator unions strike in New England

propelled this latter stage: the harnessing of electricity, the internal combustion engine, and new applications in the use of chemicals. Steam engines' limitations generated demand for a new power source—electricity. The railroads' mechanization spurred progress in automobile manufacture. And the textile industry's experiments with dyes, bleaches, and cleaning agents advanced chemical research.

In 1860 only one-fourth of the American labor force worked in manufacturing and transportation;

by 1900, over half did so. As the twentieth century dawned, the United States was the world's largest producer of raw materials and food and the most productive industrial nation (see Map 18.1). From 1880 to 1920, labor-saving machines boosted productivity. Innovations in business organization and marketing also fueled the drive for profits.

Between 1877 and 1920, a new consumer society took shape as goods that had once been accessible to a few became available to many. Products such as canned foods and machine-made clothing became common. Industrialism furthered the extraction of natural resources and the expansion of agriculture. These processes brought together people, the environment, and technology in ways that were both constructive and destructive. ■

Technology and the Triumph of Industrialism

*I*n 1876 Thomas A. Edison and his associates set up a laboratory in a wooden shed in Menlo Park, New Jersey. There they intended to turn out "a minor invention every ten days and a big thing every six months or so." Edison envisioned his lab as an invention factory, where creative people pooled ideas to fashion marketable products, under a systematic work ethic. But, Edison believed, if Americans wanted new products, they had to organize and work purposefully toward progress.

To many, the machine symbolized opportunity. The patent system, created by the Constitution to "promote the Progress of science and useful Arts," reveals American mechanical inventiveness. Between 1790 and 1860, the U.S. Patent Office granted a total of 36,000 patents. Between 1860 and 1930, it registered 1.5 million. Inventions in fields such as electricity, internal combustion, and industrial chemistry often sprang from the marriage of technology and business organization.

Most of Edison's more than one thousand inventions used electricity to transmit light, sound, and images. Perhaps his biggest "big thing"

BIRTH OF THE ELECTRICAL INDUSTRY

began in 1878 when the Edison Electric Light Company embarked on a search for a cheap, efficient means of indoor lighting. After tedious experiments, Edison perfected an incandescent bulb. He also devised a system of power generation and distribution to provide electricity conveniently to a large number of customers.

Edison's system of direct current could transmit electric power only a mile or two, losing voltage the farther it was transmitted. Inventor George Westing-

house solved the problem. He purchased European patent rights to generators that used alternating current and transformers that reduced high-voltage power to lower voltage levels, thus making long-distance transmission more efficient.

Other entrepreneurs used new business practices to market Edison's and Westinghouse's technological breakthroughs. Samuel Insull, Edison's private secretary, organized Edison power plants nationwide, amassing an electric utility empire. In the late 1880s and early 1890s financiers Henry Villard and J. P. Morgan bought up patents in electric lighting and merged small equipment-manufacturing companies into the General Electric Company. Westinghouse Electric and General Electric established research laboratories to create electrical products for everyday use.

Independent inventors continued to develop and attempt to sell their handiwork and patents—sometimes successfully, other times not—to manufacturers. Granville T. Woods, an engineer sometimes called the "black Edison," patented thirty-five devices vital to electronics and communications. Most were sold to companies such as General Electric, including an automatic circuit breaker, an electromagnetic brake, and instruments to aid communications between railroad trains.

European engineers made early innovations in the technology of the internal-combustion engine, which

HENRY FORD AND THE AUTOMOBILE INDUSTRY

powers a piston by a series of explosions within a confined space. Major progress occurred in Germany in 1885, when Gottlieb Daimler built a high-speed internal-combustion engine driven by vaporized gasoline.

In the 1890s Henry Ford, an electrical engineer in Detroit's Edison Company and one of America's most visionary manufacturers, experimented with powering a vehicle using Daimler's gasoline-burning engine. Applying organizational genius to this invention, Ford spawned a massive industry.

Ford had a scheme as well as a product, declaring in 1909, "I am going to democratize the automobile. When I'm through, everybody will be able to afford one." Ford planned to mass-produce thousands of identical cars. Ford engineers set up assembly lines that drastically reduced the time and cost of production. Instead of performing numerous tasks, each worker handled only one, performed repeatedly.

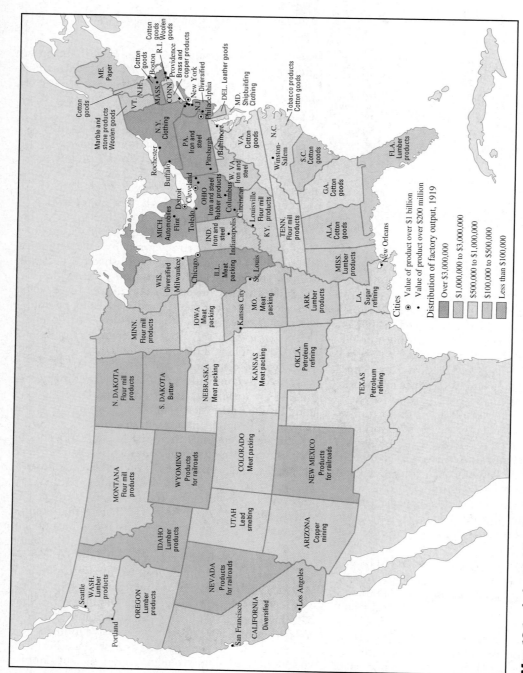

Map 18.1 Industrial Production, 1919

By the early twentieth century, each state could boast of at least one kind of industrial production. Although the value of goods produced was still highest in the Northeast, states like Minnesota and California had impressive dollar values of outputs.   (Source: Data from U.S. Bureau of the Census, *Fourteenth Census of the United States,* 1920, Vol. IX, *Manufacturing* [Washington, D.C.: U.S. Government Printing Office, 1921].)

The Atlantic Cable

During the late nineteenth century, as American manufacturers expanded their markets overseas, their ability to communicate with customers and investors improved as a result of telegraph cable beneath the Atlantic Ocean. The telegraph was an American invention, and Cyrus Field, who came up with the idea of laying cable across the Atlantic, was an American. Yet most of the engineers and capitalists involved were British. In 1851 a British company laid the world's first successful undersea telegraph cable from Dover, England, to Calais, France, proving that an insulated wire could carry signals underwater. This inspired British and American businessmen to attempt a larger project across the Atlantic.

The first efforts failed, but in 1866 a British ship, funded by British investors, successfully laid a telegraph wire that operated without interruption. Thereafter, England and the United States grew more closely linked in their diplomatic relations, and citizens of both nations developed greater concern for each other. When American president James Garfield was assassinated in 1881, the news traveled almost instantly to Great Britain, and Britons mourned the death profusely.

Financially savvy individuals experienced welcome benefits as a result of the cable's link. Rapid availability of stock quotes caused the businesses of the New York and London stock exchanges to boom. Newspaper readers enjoyed learning about events on the other side of the ocean the next day instead of a week later. By 1902 underwater cables circled the globe. The age of global telecommunications had begun.

Laid by British ships across the ocean in 1866, the Atlantic cable linked the United States with England and continental Europe so that telegraph communications could be sent and received much more swiftly than ever before. Now Europeans and Americans could exchange news about politics, business, and military movements almost instantly, whereas previously such information could take a week or more to travel from one country to another. (Library of Congress)

■ The assembly line broke the production process down into simple tasks that individual workers could efficiently repeat hour after hour. Here, assembly-line workers at the Ford plant in Highland Park, Michigan, outside Detroit, are installing pistons in engines of the Model T around 1914.   (From the Collections of The Henry Ford Museum and Greenfield Village)

The Ford Motor Company began operation in 1903. In 1908 Ford rolled out the Model T and sold 10,000. In 1913 the company's first full assembly line began producing automobiles outside Detroit, and the next year, 248,000 Fords were sold. Rising automobile production created more jobs, higher earnings, and greater profits in related industries such as oil, paint, rubber, and glass, which necessitated increased resources from the West and abroad. The internal-combustion engine led to the manufacture of trucks, buses, and, ultimately, airplanes. These industries, as well as many others, would not have been possible without precision machine tools creating standardized parts.

By 1914 many Ford cars cost $490, about one-fourth of their price a decade earlier, but that was still too expensive for many workers, who earned at best $2 a day. That year, Ford tried to spur productivity, reduce labor turnover, head off unionization, and better enable his workers to buy cars through his Five-Dollar-Day plan—a combination of wages and profit sharing.

The du Pont family similarly transformed the chemical industry. In 1902, fearing antitrust prosecution for the company's near-monopoly of the explosives industry, three cousins, Alfred, Coleman, and Pierre, took over E. I. du Pont de Nemours and Company and broadened into fertilizers, dyes, and other chemical products. In 1911 du Pont scientists and engineers in the nation's first research laboratory adapted cellulose to the production of new materials such as photographic film, rubber, lacquer, textile fibers, and plastics; the innovation wrought a significant transformation in consumer products. Du Pont

THE DU PONTS AND THE CHEMICAL INDUSTRY

research into dyestuffs aided the pharmaceutical industry, and the company pioneered methods of management, accounting, and reinvestment of earnings, contributing to efficient production, better recordkeeping, and higher profits.

The South's two major staple crops, tobacco and cotton, propelled it into the machine age. Before

TECHNOLOGY AND SOUTHERN INDUSTRY

the 1870s, Americans used tobacco mainly for snuff, cigars, and chewing. But in 1876 James Bonsack, an eighteen-year-old Virginian, invented a cigarette-rolling machine. Sales soared when James B. Duke of North Carolina began marketing cigarettes with free samples, trading cards, and billboards. By 1900 his American Tobacco Company was a nationwide business, employing Jewish immigrant cigar makers who trained laborers to mass-produce cigarettes. Cigarette factories in southern cities employed black and white workers (including women), though in segregated work rooms.

New technology helped relocate the textile industry to the South. Factories with electric looms were more efficient than New England's water-powered mills, and local investors built them in small towns along the Carolina Piedmont and wherever else cheap labor was available. Women and children earned 50 cents for twelve or more hours a day—about half the wages of northern workers. New textile machinery needed fewer workers with fewer skills, and electric lighting expanded the hours of production.

By 1900 the South had more than four hundred textile mills, with 4 million total spindles. Many companies built villages around their mills, where they controlled housing, stores, schools, and churches. Owners also banned criticism of the company and squelched union organization.

Northern and European capitalists financed other southern industries. Between 1890 and 1900, northern lumber syndicates moved into pine forests of the Gulf states, boosting production 500 percent. During the 1880s, northern investors developed southern iron and steel manufacturing, much of it in Birmingham, Alabama. With few exceptions, the South lacked technological innovations that had enabled northern industries to compete with other industrializing nations. Nevertheless, southern boosters heralded the emergence of a New South. In reality, that New South would not emerge until after the First World War.

Machines broadly altered American life. Telephones and typewriters made face-to-face communi-

CONSEQUENCES OF TECHNOLOGY

cation less important and facilitated correspondence and recordkeeping in the growing insurance, banking, and advertising firms. Electric sewing machines mass-produced clothing. Refrigeration enabled the preservation and shipment of meat, fruit, vegetables, and dairy products. Cash registers and adding machines revamped accounting and created new clerical jobs. At the same time, American universities established programs in engineering.

Profits resulted from higher production at lower costs. As technological innovations made large-scale production more economical, owners replaced small factories with larger ones. Between 1850 and 1900, the average capital investment in a manufacturing firm increased from $700,000 to $1.9 million. Only large companies could afford complex machines. And large companies received discounts for buying raw materials and shipping in bulk—advantages that economists call "economies of scale."

Profitability also depended on how production was organized. Where once workers controlled how a product was made, by the 1890s engineers and managers with specialized knowledge planned every task to increase output. By standardizing production, they diminished workers' skills, boosting profits at the expense of worker independence.

The most influential advocate of efficient production was Frederick W. Taylor. As foreman and

FREDERICK W. TAYLOR AND EFFICIENCY

engineer for the Midvale Steel Company in the 1880s, Taylor concluded that companies could best reduce costs and increase profits by applying scientific studies of "how quickly the various kinds of work . . . ought to be done." This meant producing more for lower cost per unit, usually by eliminating unnecessary workers.

In 1898 Taylor took his stopwatch to the Bethlehem Steel Company in Pennsylvania to illustrate his principles of scientific management. His experiments involved studying workers and devising "a series of motions which can be made quickest and best." For shoveling ore, Taylor designed fifteen kinds of shovels and prescribed the proper motions for each. He reduced a crew of 600 men to 140. Soon other companies began applying Taylor's theories.

As a result, time, as much as quality, became the measure of acceptable work, and science rather than experience determined the ways of doing things. As elements of the assembly line, employees feared that they were becoming another interchangeable part.

Mechanization and the Changing Status of Labor

B y 1900, the status of labor had shifted dramatically. Technological innovation and assembly-line production created new jobs, but because most machines were labor saving, fewer workers could produce more in less time. Instead of producers, the working class now consisted mainly of employees who worked for hire. Producers had been paid based on the quality of what they produced; now, employees received wages for time spent on the job.

As mass production subdivided manufacturing into smaller, specialized tasks, workers became like machines. They no longer decided when to begin and end the workday, and what tools and techniques to use. Production experts regulated them. As a Massachusetts factory operative testified in 1879, "During working hours the men are not allowed to speak to each other . . . on pain of instant discharge. Men are hired to watch and patrol the shop."

MASS PRODUCTION

Workers struggled to retain independence. Artisans such as cigar makers, glass workers, and coopers (barrel makers), caught in the transition from hand labor to machine production, fought to preserve their work customs, such as appointing a fellow worker to read a newspaper aloud while they worked. Immigrants in factories tried to persuade foremen to hire their relatives and friends, thus preserving on-the-job family and village ties.

Employers, concerned with efficiency and productivity, supported temperance and moral-reform societies to combat immoderate drinking and debauchery. Ford Motor Company required workers to satisfy its behavior code before becoming eligible for the profit-sharing segment of the Five-Dollar-Day plan. To increase worker incentives, some employers established piecework rates, paying per item produced rather than an hourly wage. Efforts to increase productivity were intended to make workers as docile as the machines they operated.

As machines reduced the need for skilled workers, employers cut labor costs by hiring women and children for low-skill, low-wage jobs. Between 1880 and 1900, employed women soared from 2.6 million to 8.6 million. The proportion of women in domestic service (maids, cooks, laundresses)—the most common and lowest-paid form of female employment—dropped as jobs opened in other sectors (see Figure 18.1). In manufacturing, women usually held menial positions in textile mills and food-processing plants that paid them as little as $1.56 for seventy hours of labor. (Unskilled men received $7.00 to $10.00 for a similar workweek.) Although the number of female factory hands tripled between 1880 and 1900, the proportion of women workers remained about the same.

RESTRUCTURING OF THE WORK FORCE

General expansion of the clerical and retail sectors caused the numbers and percentages of women who were typists, bookkeepers, and sales clerks to skyrocket. New inventions such as the typewriter, cash register, and adding machine simplified tasks that were formerly done by men. By 1920 women filled nearly half of all clerical jobs; in 1880 only 4 percent in these jobs had been women. Although they were paid low wages, women were attracted to sales jobs because of the respectability, pleasant surroundings, and contact with affluent customers that such positions offered. Nevertheless, sex discrimination pervaded the clerical sector. In department stores, only men were cashiers; women were seldom given responsibility for billing or counting money. Women held some low-level supervisory positions, but males dominated the managerial ranks.

Meanwhile, the number of children in nonagricultural occupations tripled between 1870 and 1900. In 1890 over 18 percent of all children between ages ten and fifteen were gainfully employed, with large numbers in textile and shoe factories. Mechanization created numerous light tasks, such as running errands and helping machine operators, that children could handle cheaply. Conditions were especially hard for child laborers in the South, where mill owners induced struggling white sharecroppers and tenant farmers to contract their children to factories at miserably low wages.

Several states, especially in the Northeast, passed laws specifying minimum ages and maximum hours for child labor. But statutes regulated only firms operating within state borders, making it easy for large companies to circumvent them. Enforcing age requirements proved difficult because many parents, needing the income, lied about their children's ages. After 1900, state laws and automation, along with compulsory school attendance laws, began to reduce the number of children employed in manufacturing. After 1910 Progressive era reformers sought federal legislation to control child labor (see Chapter 21).

INDUSTRIAL ACCIDENTS

Repetitive tasks using high-speed machinery dulled concentration, and the slightest mistake could cause serious injury. Industrial accidents rose steadily before 1920, killing or maiming hundreds of thousands of people annually. In 1913, after factory owners had installed safety devices, 25,000 people died in industrial mishaps, and 1 million were injured. There was

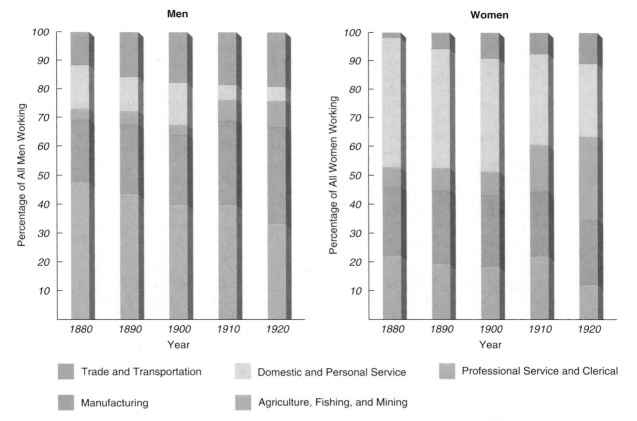

Men

Women

Trade and Transportation

Domestic and Personal Service

Professional Service and Clerical

Manufacturing

Agriculture, Fishing, and Mining

Figure 18.1 Distribution of Occupational Categories Among Employed Men and Women, 1880–1920

The changing lengths of the bar segments of each part of this graph represent trends in male and female employment. Over the forty years covered by this graph, the agriculture, fishing, and mining segment for men and the domestic service segment for women declined the most, while notable increases occurred in manufacturing for men and services (especially store clerks and teachers) for women.   (Source: U.S. Bureau of the Census, *Census of the United States, 1880, 1890, 1900, 1910, 1920* [Washington, D.C.: U.S. Government Printing Office].)

no disability insurance to replace lost income, and families suffered acutely.

The most notorious tragedy was a fire at New York City's Triangle Shirtwaist Company in 1911, which killed 146 workers, most of them teenage Jewish immigrant women trapped in locked workrooms. Despite public clamor for safety regulations, free-market views hampered passage of legislation, and employers denied responsibility for their employees' well-being.

Low wages compounded the suffering. Many employers believed that wage rates should be set by supply and demand. In theory, because *"Iron Law of Wages"* employers competed for labor, workers would receive the highest wages an employer could afford. In reality, employers could pay as little as workers were willing to accept.

Courts regularly denied labor the right to organize and bargain collectively on grounds that wages should be individually negotiated between employee and employer. Wage earners felt trapped. A factory worker told Congress in 1879, "The market is glutted . . . and the pay is cut down; our tasks are increased, and if we remonstrate, we are told our places can be filled."

Despite reform laws regulating working conditions, the Supreme Court limited such legislation by narrowly defining which jobs *Court Rulings on Labor Reform* were dangerous and which workers needed protection. In *Holden v. Hardy* (1896), the Court upheld regulating working hours of miners because overly long hours increased potential injuries. In *Lochner v. New York* (1905), however, the Court voided a law limiting bakery workers to a sixty-hour week and ten-hour day. It ruled that baking was not a dangerous enough occupation to justify restricting workers' right to sell their labor freely. Such restriction, according to the Court, violated the Fourteenth Amendment's guarantee that no state could "deprive any person of life, liberty, or property without due process of law."

In *Muller v. Oregon* (1908), the Court used a different rationale to uphold limiting women to a ten-hour workday in laundries. It set aside its *Lochner* argument to assert that a woman's well-being "becomes an object of public interest and care in order to preserve the strength and vigor of the race." The case represented a victory for labor reformers, who had sought government regulation of hours and working conditions. But based on *Muller*, later laws barred women from occupations such as printing and transportation that required heavy lifting, long hours, or night work, thus further confining women to low-paying, dead-end jobs.

Labor Violence and the Union Movement

*a*nxiety over the loss of independence via mechanization and a desire for better wages, hours, and working conditions pushed more workers into unions. Because trade unions dating back to the early 1800s restricted membership to skilled workers in particular crafts, their influence was limited. The National Labor Union, founded in 1866, claimed 640,000 members from a variety of industries but collapsed during the hard times of the 1870s.

In the economic slump following the Panic of 1873, which lasted until 1878, railroad managers cut wages, increased workloads, and *Railroad Strikes of 1877* laid off workers, especially union members. Workers responded with strikes and riots. The year 1877 marked a crisis for labor. In July unionized railroad workers organized a series of strikes to protest wage cuts. Violence spread from Pennsylvania and West Virginia to the Midwest, Texas, and California. State militia companies, organized and commanded by employers, broke up picket lines and fired into threatening crowds. Factory workers, wives, and merchants aided the strikers, and railroads enlisted strikebreakers to replace union men.

Pittsburgh saw the worst violence: on July 21 state troops bayoneted and fired on rock-throwing demonstrators, killing ten and wounding others. The infuriated mob drove troops into a roundhouse and set fires that destroyed 39 buildings, 104 engines, and 1,245 freight and passenger cars. The next day, the troops shot their way out and killed twenty more citizens before fleeing. After a month, President Rutherford B. Hayes sent in federal soldiers—the first significant use of the army in U.S. history to quell labor unrest.

The only broad-based labor organization to survive that depression was the Knights of Labor.

KNIGHTS OF LABOR

Founded in 1869 by Philadelphia garment cutters, the Knights began recruiting other workers in the 1870s. In 1879 Terence V. Powderly, a machinist and the mayor of Scranton, Pennsylvania, was elected grand master. Under his guidance, Knights membership grew, peaking at 730,000 in 1886. Knights welcomed unskilled and semiskilled workers, including women, immigrants, and African Americans.

The Knights sought a workers' alliance that offered an alternative to profit-oriented industrial capitalism. They believed they could eliminate labor and management conflict by establishing a cooperative society in which laborers owned the industries in which they worked. The goal, argued Powderly, was to "eventually make every man his own master— every man his own employer." The cooperative idea, attractive in the abstract, was unattainable because employers could outcompete laborers who might try to establish their own businesses. Strikes might achieve immediate goals, but Powderly and other leaders argued that strikes diverted attention from the long-term goal of a cooperative society and that workers lost more by striking than they won.

Some Knights, however, did support militant action. In 1886 railroad magnate Jay Gould refused to negotiate when Knights demanded higher wages and union recognition from Southwest Railroad. A strike began in Texas and spread to Kansas, Missouri, and Arkansas. As violence increased, Powderly met with Gould and called off the strike, hoping to reach a settlement. But Gould again rejected concessions, and the Knights gave in. Upset by Powderly's compromise, militant craft unions deserted the Knights. Membership dwindled, although the union made a brief attempt to unite with Populists in the 1890s (see Chapter 20). Craft unions replaced the Knights' broad-based but often vague appeal, and dreams of labor unity faded.

Meanwhile, several groups calling for an eight-hour workday generated the largest spontaneous labor demonstration in the country's history.

HAYMARKET RIOT

On May 1, 1886, in Chicago, over 100,000 workers turned out, including radical anarchists. In Europe, labor radicals had made May 1 a day of demonstration, and Chicago police, fearing that European radicals were transplanting their tradition of violence to the United States, mobilized against them. The day passed calmly, but two days later, police stormed an area near the McCormick reaper factory and broke up a battle between striking unionists and nonunion strikebreakers, killing two unionists and wounding several others.

The next evening, labor groups protested police brutality at Haymarket Square, near downtown Chicago. As police approached, a bomb exploded, killing seven and injuring sixty-seven. Authorities made mass arrests, and a court convicted eight anarchists of the bombing, despite questionable evidence. Four were executed, and one committed suicide in prison. The remaining three were pardoned in 1893 by Illinois governor John P. Altgeld.

Online Study Center
Improve Your Grade
Primary Source: Haymarket Trials

The Haymarket bombing, like the 1877 railroad strikes, drew attention to labor's growing discontent and heightened fear of radicalism. The participation of anarchists and socialists, many of them foreign born, heightened urgency that law and order act swiftly to prevent social turmoil. Private Chicago donors helped establish a military base at Fort Sheridan and the Great Lakes Naval Training Station. Elsewhere, governments strengthened police forces. Employer associations countered labor militancy by drawing up blacklists of union activists whom they would not employ and by hiring private detectives to suppress strikes.

The American Federation of Labor (AFL), founded in 1886, emerged from the upheavals as the major workers' organization. An al-

AMERICAN FEDERATION OF LABOR

liance of national craft unions, the AFL had about 140,000 members, most of them skilled workers. Led by Samuel Gompers, a pragmatic immigrant who headed the Cigar Makers' Union, the AFL pressed for higher wages, shorter hours, and the right to bargain collectively. In contrast to the Knights, the AFL accepted the industrial system and worked to improve conditions within it. It avoided party politics, adhering to Gompers's dictum to support labor's friends and oppose its enemies, regardless of party.

AFL membership grew to 1 million by 1901 and 2.5 million by 1917, when it represented 111 national unions and 27,000 local unions. Member unions tried to protect skilled workers by organizing by craft rather than by workplace and had little interest in recruiting unskilled workers or women. Of 6.3 million employed women in 1910, fewer than 2 percent belonged to unions. Male unionists rationalized women's exclusion by insisting that women should not be employed. According to one labor leader, "The mental and physical makeup of woman is in revolt against wage service. She is competing with the man who is her father or husband or is to become her husband." Mostly, unionists worried that because women were paid less than men, their own wages would be lowered or their jobs given to cheaper female laborers.

Organized labor also excluded most immigrant and African American workers, fearing that they would depress wages. Some trade unions welcomed skilled immigrants, but only the more radical unions had explicit policies of accepting immigrants and blacks. Blacks were prominent in the coal miners' union and were partially unionized in trades such as construction, barbering, and dock work, which had large numbers of African American workers. But they could belong only to segregated local unions in the South.

Online Study Center **Improve Your Grade**
Interactive Map: Percent of Foreign-Born Whites and Native Whites of Foreign or Mixed Parentage in Total Populations, by Counties, 1910

The AFL and the labor movement suffered setbacks in the early 1890s, when labor violence stirred
HOMESTEAD STRIKE public fears. In July 1892, the AFL-affiliated Amalgamated Association of Iron and Steelworkers went on strike against pay cuts in Homestead, Pennsylvania. Henry C. Frick, president of Carnegie Steel Company, then closed the plant. Shortly after, Frick tried to protect the plant by hiring three hundred guards from the Pinkerton Detective Agency and floating them in by barge under cover of darkness. Lying in wait, angry workers attacked and routed the guards. State troops intervened, and after five months, the strikers gave in. By then, public opinion had turned against the union.

In 1894 workers at the Pullman Palace (railroad
PULLMAN STRIKE passenger) Car Company walked out over exploitative policies at the company town near Chicago. The paternalistic George Pullman provided everything for the twelve thousand residents of the so-called model town named after him. His company owned and controlled all land and buildings, the school, the bank, and the water and gas systems. It paid wages, fixed rents, and spied on disgruntled employees.

One thing Pullman would not do was negotiate with workers. When hard times hit in 1893, Pullman protected profits by cutting wages 25 to 40 percent while holding firm on rents and prices. Hard-pressed workers sent a committee to Pullman to protest. He reacted by firing three members of the committee. When enraged workers called a strike, Pullman closed the factory. The railway union, led by Eugene V. Debs, refused to handle Pullman cars attached to any trains. The railroad owners' association then enlisted aid from U.S. Attorney General Richard Olney, a former railroad attorney, who obtained a court injunction to prevent the union from "obstructing the railways and holding up the mails." President Grover Cleveland ordered federal troops to Chicago. Within a month, strikers gave in, and Debs was jailed for defying the injunction. The Supreme Court upheld Debs's six-month sentence, arguing that the federal government had the power to remove obstacles to interstate commerce.

Colorado miners engaged in several bitter strikes. In 1905 they helped form a new, radical labor organi-
IWW zation, the Industrial Workers of the World (IWW). The IWW strove like the Knights to unite all laborers, including the unskilled and African Americans. Its motto was "An injury to one is an injury to all." But the "Wobblies," as IWW members were known, exceeded the Knights by espousing violence and sabotage.

Embracing the rhetoric of class conflict and socialism, Wobblies believed workers should seize and run the nation's industries. "Mother" Jones, an Illinois coalfield union organizer; Elizabeth Gurley Flynn, a fiery orator known as the "Joan of Arc of the labor movement"; and William D. (Big Bill) Haywood, the brawny, one-eyed founder of the Western Federation of Miners, led a series of strikes. Although the Wobblies' anticapitalist goals and aggressive tactics attracted publicity, union membership never exceeded 150,000. The organization collapsed during the First World War when federal prosecution sent many of its leaders to jail and local police forces violently harassed IWW members.

Although excluded from the general union movement, female workers had formed their own labor as-

WOMEN
UNIONISTS

sociations. Some, such as the 1860s Collar Laundry Union of Troy, New York, had successfully struck for higher wages. The "Uprising of the 20,000" in New York City, a 1909 strike by male and female immigrant members of the International Ladies Garment Workers Union (ILGWU), was one of the country's largest strikes. Female trade-union membership swelled during the 1910s, but men monopolized national trade-union leadership.

Women did dominate one union: the Telephone Operators' Department of the International Brotherhood of Electrical Workers. Organized in Montana and San Francisco early in the twentieth century, the union spread throughout the Bell system, the nation's monopolistic telephone company and single largest employer of women. To promote solidarity among their mostly young members, union leaders organized dances, excursions, and bazaars, as well as educational programs. The union resisted scientific management and increased supervision. In 1919 several militant union branches paralyzed phone service in five New England states, but the union collapsed after a failed strike there in 1923.

The first women's organization promoting interests of laboring women was the Women's Trade Union League (WTUL), founded in 1903 and patterned after a similar organization in England. The WTUL sought workplace protective legislation and reduced hours for female workers, sponsored educational activities, and campaigned for women's suffrage. It helped telephone operators organize, and in 1909 it supported the ILGWU's massive strike against New York City sweatshops. Initially the union's highest offices were held by sympathetic middle-class women, but control shifted in the 1910s to working-class leaders, notably Agnes Nestor, a glove maker, and Rose Schneiderman, a cap maker. The WTUL advocated opening apprenticeship programs to women and training female workers for leadership. It served as a vital link between the labor and women's movements into the 1920s.

Despite the visibility of struggles in the second half of the nineteenth century, only a small fraction of

THE EXPERIENCE
OF WAGE WORK

American workers belonged to unions. In 1900 about 1 million out of a total of 27.6 million workers

were unionized. By 1920, union membership had grown to 5 million, just 13 percent of the work force. Unionization was strong in construction trades, transportation, communications, and, to a lesser extent, manufacturing. For many workers, getting and holding a job took priority over wages and hours. Job instability and the seasonal nature of work seriously hindered union-organizing efforts. Few companies employed workers year-round; most hired laborers during peak seasons and laid them off during slack periods.

The millions of men, women, and children who were not unionized tried to cope with pressures of the machine age. Many native-born and immigrant workers turned to fraternal societies such as the Polish Roman Catholic Union and the Jewish B'nai B'rith. Widespread by the early twentieth century, these organizations provided life insurance, sickness benefits, and funeral expenses for small contributions.

The machine age had mixed benefits. Industrial wages rose between 1877 and 1914, boosting purchasing power and creating a mass market for standardized goods. Yet in 1900, most employees worked sixty hours a week at wages averaging 20 cents an hour for skilled work and 10 cents an hour for unskilled. Even as wages rose, living costs increased even faster.

Standards of Living

*T*he expansion of railroad, postal, and telephone service drew even isolated communities into the consumer-oriented society. American ingenuity combined with mass production and marketing to make available myriad goods that previously had not existed or had been the province of the wealthy. The new material well-being blended Americans of differing status into consumer communities and accentuated differences between those who could afford goods and services and those who could not.

If a society's affluence can be measured by the conversion of luxuries into commonplace articles, the

COMMONPLACE
LUXURIES

United States was indeed becoming affluent from 1880 and 1920. By 1899, manufactured goods and perishable foodstuffs had become increasingly available. That year Americans bought 2 billion machine-produced cigarettes and 151,000 pairs of silk stockings, consumed oranges at the rate of 100 crates for every 1,000 people, and spent an average of 63 cents per person on soap. In 1921 Americans smoked 43 billion cigarettes (403 per person), bought 217 million pairs of silk stockings, ate 248 crates of oranges per 1,000 people, and spent $1.40 on soap.

Data for the period also show that incomes rose broadly, spawning massive fortunes and creating a new industrial elite. By 1920, the richest 5 percent of the population received almost one-fourth of all earned income. Incomes also rose among the growing middle class. Average pay for clerical workers rose 36 percent between 1890 and 1910 (see Table 18.1). At the turn of the century, federal employees averaged $1,072 a year (between $20,000 and $25,000 in modern dollars). The middle class could afford relatively comfortable housing. A six- or seven-room house cost around $3,000 to buy (about $85,000 to $90,000 in current dollars) and from $15 to $20 per month ($450 to $550 in current dollars) to rent.

TABLE 18.1

American Living Standards, 1890–1910

	1890	1910
Income and earnings		
Annual income		
Clerical worker	$848	$1,156
Public school teacher	256	492
Industrial worker	486	630
Farm laborer	233	336
Hourly wage		
Soft-coal miner	0.18[a]	0.21
Iron worker	0.17[a]	0.23
Shoe worker	0.14[a]	0.19
Paper worker	0.12[a]	0.17
Labor statistics		
Number of people in labor force	28.5 million	41.7 million[b]
Average workweek in manufacturing	60 hours	51 hours

a. 1892
b. 1920

Although industrial wages increased, jobs were not always secure, and workers had to expend a disproportionate sum on necessities. Annual wages of factory workers rose about 30 percent, from $486 in 1890 (about $12,000 to $14,000 in modern dollars) to $630 in 1910 (about $15,000 to $17,000 in current dollars). In industries with large female work forces, hourly rates remained lower than in male-dominated industries. Nevertheless, as Table 18.1 shows, most wages moved upward.

Wage increases mean little, however, if living costs rise as fast or faster. The weekly cost of living for a typical family of four rose over

COST OF LIVING 47 percent between 1889 and 1913. Goods that cost $6.78 in 1889 increased, after a slight dip in the mid-1890s, to $10.00 by 1913. In few working-class occupations did income rise as fast as cost of living.

How could working-class Americans afford goods and services? Many could not. The daughter of a textile worker, recalling her school days, described how "some of the kids would bring bars of chocolate, others an orange. . . . I suppose they were richer than a family like ours. My father used to buy a bag of candy and a bag of peanuts every payday. . . . And that's all we'd have until the next payday."

Still, a family could raise its income and partake modestly in consumer society by sending children and women to work outside the home.

SUPPLEMENTS TO Where a father might earn $600 a
FAMILY INCOME   year, wages of other family members might lift total family income to $800 or $900. Many also rented rooms to boarders, yielding up to $200 a year and providing housewives with vital economic roles. Workers were thus able to improve their living standards, but not without sacrifices.

More than ever before, American workers existed within a wage economy. Between 1890 and 1920, the labor force increased by 50 percent, from 28 million workers to 42 million. These figures represent a change in the nature of work as much as an increase in the number of available jobs. Most Americans, male and female, had always worked. In the rural society of the nineteenth century, women and children performed the crucial jobs of cooking, cleaning, planting, and harvesting—labor typically absent from employment figures. As the nation industrialized and the agricultural sector declined, wage labor became more common. The proportion of Americans who worked probably did not increase markedly. What was new was the increase in paid employment, making purchases of consumer goods and services more affordable.

Medical advances, better diets, and improved housing sharply reduced death rates and extended life.

HIGHER LIFE EXPECTANCY Between 1900 and 1920, life expectancy rose by six years, and the death rate dropped 24 percent. Notable declines occurred in deaths from typhoid, diphtheria, influenza (except for a harsh pandemic in 1918 and 1919), tuberculosis, and intestinal ailments. There were, however, significantly more deaths from cancer, diabetes, and heart disease, afflictions of an aging population and of new environmental factors such as smoke and chemical pollution. Homicides and automobile-related deaths, too, increased dramatically.

Not only were luxuries more available, but upward mobility seemed more accessible as well. Public education, aided by new school construction and laws requiring children to stay in school to age fourteen, equipped young people to achieve a higher living standard than their parents'. The creation of managerial and sales jobs in service industries helped counter downward mobility when mechanization pushed skilled workers out of their crafts. And mass-produced goods made life more convenient for all workers.

The toilet stood at the vanguard of a revolution in American lifestyles. The chain-pull washdown

FLUSH TOILETS water closet, invented in England around 1870, reached the United States in the 1880s. Shortly after 1900, the flush toilet appeared. Before 1880, only luxury hotels and estates had private indoor bathrooms. By the 1890s, the germ theory of disease had raised fears about carelessly disposed human waste as a source of infection and water contamination. Americans began including water closets in middle-class urban houses. By the 1920s, they were prevalent in working-class homes too. Edward and Clarence Scott, who produced white tissue in perforated rolls, provided Americans a more convenient form of toilet paper than the rough paper they had previously used. Bodily functions took on an unpleasant image, and the home bathroom became a place of utmost privacy.

Before the mid-nineteenth century, Americans typically ate only foods that were in season. Drying, smoking, and salting could preserve meat

PROCESSED AND PRESERVED FOODS for a short time, but the availability of fresh meat and fresh milk was limited. A French inventor developed the cooking-and-sealing process of canning around 1810, and in the 1850s, an American man named Gail Borden devised a means of condensing and preserving milk. Availability of canned goods and condensed milk increased during the 1860s. By the 1880s, inventors had fashioned machines to peel fruits and vegetables, process salmon, and mass-produce cans from tin plate. Now, people everywhere could readily consume tomatoes, milk, oysters, and other alternatives to previously monotonous diets.

Other inventions broadened Americans' diets. Growing urban populations sparked demand for more produce. Railroad refrigerator cars enabled growers and meatpackers to ship perishables greater distances and preserve them for longer periods. By the 1890s, northern city dwellers could enjoy southern and western strawberries, grapes, and tomatoes for several months. Home iceboxes enabled middle-class families to store perishables.

The availability of new foods also inspired health reformers to correct the American diet. In the 1870s

DIETARY REFORM John H. Kellogg, a nutritionist and manager of the Western Health Reform Institute in Battle Creek, Michigan, began serving patients new health foods, including peanut butter and wheat flakes. Several years later, his brother, William K. Kellogg, invented corn flakes, and Charles W. Post introduced Grape-Nuts, replacing eggs, potatoes, and meat with ready-to-eat cereal. Growing numbers of published cookbooks and cooking schools reflected heightened interest in food and its possibilities for health and enjoyment.

As in the past, the poorest people still consumed cheap foods, heavy in starches and carbohydrates, and could seldom afford meat. Now, though, many could purchase previously unavailable fruits, vegetables, and dairy products. Workers spent almost half of a breadwinner's wages on food, but they never suffered the malnutrition that plagued other developing nations.

Before 1850, nearly all Americans wore clothes made at home or by seamstresses and tailors, depending on social status. Then in the 1850s, the sewing machine, invented in Europe but refined by Americans Elias Howe Jr. and Isaac M. Singer, came into use in clothing and shoe manufacture. By 1890 annual retail sales of machine-made garments reached $1.5 billion. Mass production enabled manufacturers to turn out quality apparel at relatively low cost and to standardize sizes. By 1900, only the poorest families could not afford "ready-to-wear" clothes. Tailors and seamstresses were relegated to repair work. Many women continued to make clothing at home, but commercial dress patterns injected another form of standardization into everyday life.

READY-MADE CLOTHING

As women became more active outside the home, dress designers began emphasizing comfort. In the 1890s, sleeves and skirt hemlines receded, and high-boned collars disappeared. Women began wearing tailored blouses called shirtwaists. Designers used less fabric; by the 1920s a dress required three yards of material instead of ten.

Men's clothes too became lightweight. Before 1900, men in the middle class and well-off working classes would have owned two suits—one for Sundays and special occasions and one for everyday. After 1900, manufacturers began to produce garments from fabrics of different weights for different seasons. Men replaced derbies with felt hats and stiff collars with soft ones; somber, dark-blue serge gave way to lighter shades and more intricate weaves.

Department and chain stores helped to create and serve this new consumerism. Between 1865 and 1900, Macy's in New York, Wanamaker's in Philadelphia, Marshall Field in Chicago, and Rich's in Atlanta became urban landmarks. Previously, working classes had bought goods in stores with limited inventories, and wealthier people patronized fancy shops; price, quality of goods, and social custom discouraged each from the other's establishments. Now, department stores, with their open displays, offered not only a wide variety but also home deliveries, exchange policies, and charge accounts.

DEPARTMENT AND CHAIN STORES

Meanwhile, the Great Atlantic Tea Company, founded in 1859, became the first grocery chain. Renamed the Great Atlantic and Pacific Tea Company in 1869 (and known as A&P), the stores bought in volume and sold to the public at low prices. By 1915, there were eighteen hundred A&P stores, and twelve thousand more over the next ten years.

In 1881 Congress passed a trademark law enabling producers to register and protect brand names. Thousands of companies registered products as varied as Hires Root Beer and Carter's Little Liver Pills. Advertising agencies—a service industry pioneered by N. W. Ayer & Son of Philadelphia—in turn offered expert advice to companies seeking to cultivate brand loyalty. In 1865 retailers spent about $9.5 million on advertising; that sum reached $95 million

ADVERTISING

■ Advertising, which developed into a powerful medium in the late nineteenth century, used explicit and implicit domestic images to reinforce a wife's role as homemaker. This ad implies that a devoted wife lovingly assumes tasks such as sewing and mending clothing, guided into her role by a strong and superior husband.   (Library of Congress)

by 1900 and nearly $500 million by 1919. Newspapers served as the prime instrument for advertising. More than ever before, people read newspapers to find out what was for sale as well as what was happening.

Outdoor billboards and electrical signs were also important advertising organs. Signs in railroad and subway stations and billboards on city buildings and alongside roads promoted national products such as Gillette razors, Kodak cameras, and Wrigley chewing gum. In the mid-1890s, electricity made lighted billboards more dynamic and appealing. The flashing electric signs on New York City's Broadway gave the street its label "the Great White Way."

The Corporate Consolidation Movement

*N*either new products nor new marketing techniques could mask unsettling factors in the American economy. The huge capital investment in new technology meant that factories had to operate at near capacity to recover costs. But the more manufacturers produced, the more they had to sell, which meant reducing prices. To compensate for price drops, they expanded production and often cut wages. To expand, they borrowed money. And to repay loans, they had to produce and sell even more. This spiraling process strangled small firms and thrust workers into constant uncertainty.

In this environment, optimism could dissolve at the hint that debtors could not meet their obligations. Financial panics afflicted the economy during every decade in the late nineteenth century. Economic declines that began in 1873, 1884, and 1893 lingered for several years. Some business leaders blamed overproduction; others pointed to underconsumption; still others blamed lax credit and investment practices. Either way, businesspeople sought to combat these boom-and-bust business cycles, often through centralized forms of business organization, notably corporations, pools, trusts, and holding companies.

Industrialists never questioned the capitalist system and embraced the incorporation laws adopted by states in the early 1800s to spur commerce and industry. Under such laws, anyone could start a company

RISE OF CORPORATIONS

and raise money by selling stock to investors. Stockholders shared in profits without personal risk because laws limited their liability for company debts to the amount of their investment. And responsibility for a firm's day-to-day operation rested with its managers.

By 1900 two-thirds of all goods manufactured in the United States were produced by corporations such as General Electric and the American Tobacco Company. In the 1880s and 1890s, the Supreme Court ruled that corporations, like individuals, are protected by the Fourteenth Amendment. That is, states could not deny corporations equal protection under the law and could not deprive them of rights or property without due process of law. Such rulings insulated corporations against government interference.

As downward business cycles threatened profits, corporations sought greater economic concentration. Between the late 1880s and early 1900s, business consolidation produced massive conglomerates that have since dominated the economy. At first, such alliances were informal, consisting of cooperative agreements, called pools, among firms manufacturing the same product or offering the same service. Competing companies tried to control the market by agreeing how much each should produce and sharing profits. Used by railroads, steel producers, and whiskey distillers, pools depended on members' honesty. But during slow periods, pool members secretly reduced prices or sold more than the agreed quota. The strategy was already fading by the time the Interstate Commerce Act of 1887 outlawed pools among railroads (discussed in Chapter 20).

POOLS

John D. Rockefeller, boss of Standard Oil, called pools undependable. In 1879 his lawyer, Samuel Dodd, devised another means of market domination. Because state laws prohibited one corporation from holding stock in another corporation, Dodd adapted an old device called a trust, a legal arrangement whereby a responsible individual would manage the financial affairs of a person unable to handle them alone. Dodd reasoned that one company could control an industry by luring stockholders of smaller companies to cede their stock "in trust" to the larger company's board of trustees. This allowed Rockefeller to achieve horizontal integration—the acquisition of several similar companies—of the profitable petroleum industry in 1882 by combining his

TRUSTS

Standard Oil Company of Ohio with other refineries he bought up.

In 1888 New Jersey adopted laws allowing corporations chartered there to own property in other states

HOLDING COMPANIES

and stock in other corporations. This facilitated creation of the holding company, which owned a partial or complete interest in other companies. Holding companies could merge their assets (buildings, equipment, inventory, and cash) as well as their management. Rockefeller's holding company, Standard Oil of New Jersey, merged forty refining companies. By 1898 Standard Oil refined 84 percent of all oil produced in the nation, controlled most pipelines, and engaged in natural-gas production and ownership of oil-producing properties.

To dominate their markets, many holding companies sought control over all aspects of their operations, including raw materials, manufacturing, and distribution. A model of such vertical integration was Gustavus Swift's meat-processing operation. During the 1880s, Swift invested in livestock, slaughterhouses, refrigerator cars, and marketing to ensure profits from the sale of his beef at prices he could control.

Mergers provided order and profits. Between 1889 and 1903, three hundred combinations were formed, most of them trusts and holding companies. The most spectacular was U.S. Steel Corporation, financed by J. P. Morgan in 1901. Made up of iron-ore properties, freight carriers, wire mills, and other firms, it was capitalized at over $1.4 billion. In 1896 fewer than a dozen corporations were worth over $10 million; by 1903 three hundred were worth that much, and seventeen had assets exceeding $100 million. These huge companies ruthlessly put thousands of competitors out of business.

The merger movement created a new species of businessman, whose vocation was financial organiz-

FINANCIERS

ing. Shrewd operators sought opportunities for combination, formed a holding company, and then persuaded producers to sell their firms to the new company. These financiers raised money by selling stock and borrowing from banks. Investment bankers like J. P. Morgan and Jacob Schiff piloted the merger movement, inspiring awe with their financial power.

Growth of corporations in the late nineteenth century turned stock and bond exchanges into hubs of activity. In 1886 trading on the New York Stock Exchange passed 1 million shares a day. By 1914, the number of industrial stocks traded reached 511, compared with 145 in 1869. Between 1870 and 1900, foreign investment in American companies rose from $1.5 billion to $3.5 billion. Assets of savings banks, concentrated in the Northeast and West Coast, rose by 700 percent between 1875 and 1897, to a total of $2.2 billion. States loosened regulations to enable banks to invest in railroads and industrial enterprises.

The Gospel of Wealth and Its Critics

usiness leaders used corporate consolidation to minimize competition, and justified their tactics through the doctrine of Social Darwinism. Social Darwinism loosely grafted Charles Darwin's theory of the survival of the fittest onto laissez faire, the doctrine that government should not interfere in private economic affairs. Social Darwinists reasoned that in an unconstrained economy, power and wealth would flow naturally to the most capable people. In this view, monopolies represented the natural accumulation of economic power by those best suited for wielding it.

Social Darwinists believed that wealth carried moral responsibilities. Steel baron Andrew Carnegie asserted "the Gospel of Wealth": that as guardians of society's wealth, he and other industrialists had a duty to serve society. Over his lifetime, Carnegie donated more than $350 million to libraries, schools, peace initiatives, and the arts. Such philanthropy, however, also enabled benefactors to define what was necessary for society; it did not translate into paying workers decent wages.

Leaders in the corporate consolidation movement extolled individual initiative but also pressed

GOVERNMENT ASSISTANCE TO BUSINESS

for government assistance. While denouncing efforts to legislate maximum working hours or factory conditions as interference, they lobbied forcefully and successfully for subsidies, loans, and tax relief to encourage business growth. Grants to railroads (see

Chapter 17) were one form of such assistance. When Congress imposed high tariffs on foreign goods such as kerosene, steel rails, woolen goods, and tin plate, American producers could raise prices on theirs to just under what comparable foreign goods would sell. Industrialists argued that tariff protection encouraged the development of new products and enterprises. But tariffs also forced consumers to pay artificially high prices.

Critics charged that trusts and other forms of big business stifled opportunity and originated from greed.

DISSENTING VOICES Such charges by farmers, workers, and intellectuals reflected an ardent fear of monopoly—the domination of an economic activity (such as oil refining) by one powerful company (such as Standard Oil). Those who feared monopoly believed that large corporations fixed prices, exploited workers by cutting wages, destroyed opportunity by crushing small businesses, and threatened democracy by corrupting politicians—all of which was not only unnatural, they said, but immoral.

By the mid-1880s, a number of intellectuals began to challenge Social Darwinism and laissez-faire economics. In *Dynamic Sociology* (1883), sociologist Lester Ward argued that a system guaranteeing survival only to the fittest was wasteful and brutal. Instead, Ward reasoned, cooperative activity fostered by government intervention was moral. Economists Richard Ely, John R. Commons, and Edward Bemis agreed that natural forces should be harnessed for the public good.

Others more directly questioned why the United States had so many poor people while a few became fabulously wealthy. Henry George was a San Francisco printer and writer who had fallen into poverty during the depression of the 1870s. He believed that inequality stemmed from the ability of a few to profit from rising land values, which made speculators rich simply because of increased demand for living and working space, especially in cities. To prevent profiteering, George proposed replacing all taxes with a "single tax" on the "unearned increment"—the rise in property values caused by increased demand rather than owners' improvements. Argued forcefully in *Progress and Poverty* (1879), this popular scheme almost won George the mayoralty of New York City in 1886.

Several states took steps to prohibit monopolies and regulate business. By 1900, fifteen states, mostly

ANTITRUST LEGISLATION in the agricultural South and West, had constitutional provisions outlawing trusts, and twenty-seven had laws forbidding pools. But state governments lacked staff and judicial support for an effective attack on big business, and corporations found ways to evade restrictions.

Congress moved hesitantly toward national legislation but in 1890 passed the Sherman Anti-Trust Act. Introduced by Senator John Sherman of Ohio, the law made illegal "every contract, combination in the form of trust or otherwise, or conspiracy in the restraint of trade." Those found guilty faced fines and jail terms, and those wronged by illegal combinations could sue for triple damages. However, the law, watered down by pro-business eastern senators, was left purposely vague. It did not clearly define "restraint of trade" and consigned interpretation of its provisions to the sometimes business-friendly courts.

Judges used the law's vagueness to blur distinctions between reasonable and unreasonable restraints of trade. When in 1895 the federal government prosecuted the so-called Sugar Trust for owning 98 percent of the nation's sugar-refining capacity, eight of nine Supreme Court justices ruled in *U.S. v. E. C. Knight Co.* that control of manufacturing did not necessarily mean control of trade. According to the Court, the Constitution empowered Congress to regulate interstate commerce, but not manufacturing.

Between 1890 and 1900, the federal government prosecuted only eighteen cases under the Sherman Anti-Trust Act. Ironically, the act equipped the government to break up labor unions: courts that did not consider monopolistic production a restraint on trade willingly applied antitrust provisions to boycotts encouraged by striking unions.

Summary *Online Study Center* ACE the Test

*M*echanization and new inventions thrust the United States into the vanguard of industrial nations and immeasurably altered daily life between 1877 and 1920. But aggressive consolidation changed the nature of work from individual activity by skilled producers to mass production by wage earners. Laborers fought to retain control of their work and struggled to develop unions. The outpouring of products created a mass society based on consumerism and dominated by technology and the communications media.

The problems of enforcing the Sherman Anti-Trust Act reflected the uneven distribution of power. Corporations consolidated to control resources, production, and politics. Laborers and reformers had numbers and ideas but lacked influence. In factories and homes, some people celebrated the industrial transformation while others struggled with the dilemma of industrialism: whether a system based on ever-greater profits was the best way to fulfill the nation's democratic destiny.

Industrial expansion proved impossible to stop, because so many powerful and ordinary people were benefiting from it. Moreover, waves of people pouring into the nation's cities increasingly provided both workers and consumers for America's expanding productive capacity.

LEGACY FOR A PEOPLE AND A NATION
Industrialization, Smoke, and Pollution Control

Coal fueled the steel mills and iron foundries of America's industrial era. Skies over cities such as Pittsburgh and St. Louis became clogged with choking pollution from factories, coal-burning railroads, steamboats, and home furnaces. The heaviest smoke came from burning soft, bituminous coal, which is cheaper and more plentiful than cleaner-burning anthracite coal. Prior to the First World War, the United States used four times as much bituminous coal as anthracite coal. New chemical plants began spewing other pollutants into the air as well.

Many Americans assumed that air was a free resource and accepted air pollution as a necessary nuisance. But others began campaigns to curb the worst pollution. By 1900, doctors reported a link between coal smoke and respiratory diseases such as bronchitis and pneumonia. Women's groups and health reformers argued that air contamination undermined efforts to keep cities clean. As early as 1881, Chicago and a few other cities passed anti-smoke legislation and hired smoke inspectors, but courts often declared such laws unconstitutional, and judges were reluctant to enforce regulations that remained on the books.

As the twentieth century advanced, air pollution from coal decreased as technological innovations reduced smoke output. By midcentury, many industries had converted to natural gas and petroleum, but governments refrained from emissions control because industries and citizens were reluctant to pay any added costs. And automobile emissions were creating pollution problems that may have seemed more innocuous but were just as dangerous.

In the late 1960s, air pollution became the defining issue of the new environmental reform movement. The Clean Air Act amendment of 1970 recognized for the first time that pollution was a national problem subject to federal authority. That act and subsequent legislation established air quality standards and prompted states and cities to pass laws. Since then, business interests and environmentalists have scuffled over regulations, often bouncing air pollution between health and cleanliness, on one hand, and economic progress, convenience, and jobs, on the other. Thus, an unwanted legacy of industrial progress—air pollution—remains unresolved.

THE VITALITY AND TURMOIL OF URBAN LIFE 1877–1920

Rahel Gollop grew up in a shtetl, a Jewish village in western Russia. Her father, facing anti-Jewish pogroms (violent persecutions by Russian officials), left his family in 1890 to find a better life. Arrested by Russian soldiers, he escaped to Germany and found passage on a steamship bound for New York City. After two and a half years in the United States, he had saved enough to bring the rest of the family to America.

Rahel's first impression of New York was awe. "I looked with wonder at the tall houses, the paved streets, the street lamps," she recalled. "I thought these things true only of America." But the Gollops' landlady, an immigrant who had arrived years earlier, gave Rahel a dose of reality. Rahel wrote:

> When we praised our new homeland, that landlady smiled a queer smile. "Life here is not all that it appears to the 'green horn' (new immigrant)," she said. ". . . where you used to live. You had your own house, and most of the food came from the garden. Here you will have to pay for everything; the rent!" she sighed, "for every grain of barley."

To help out, Rahel, only twelve years old, worked in a garment sweatshop. She witnessed—and experienced—many of the travails suffered by immigrants, including the beating of eastern European Jews on election night and the harassment of street vendors by drunken nativists. Like other immigrants, Rahel sought security with her own kind, rarely mingling with strangers.

Gradually Rahel broke away. She learned to read English and acquired an education. Rejecting the man whom her parents had selected for her husband, she married a grocer and became a writer. She published her autobiography in 1918 and died in 1925 at the age of forty-five, possibly of suicide.

Though it ended tragically, Rahel Gollop's story illustrates many themes characterizing American urban life in the late nineteenth and early twentieth centuries. Where to live, where to work, how to support the family, the

Growth of the Modern City

Urban Neighborhoods

Living Conditions in the Inner City

Managing the City

Family Life

The New Leisure and Mass Culture

LINKS TO THE WORLD
Japanese Baseball

LEGACY FOR A PEOPLE AND A NATION
Ethnic Food

Online Study Center
This icon will direct you to interactive map and primary source activities on the website
http://college.hmco.com/pic/nortonbrief7e

C H R O N O L O G Y

1867 • First law regulating tenements passes, in New York State

1870 • One-fourth of Americans live in cities

1876 • National League of Professional Baseball Clubs founded

1880s • "New" immigrants from eastern and southern Europe begin to arrive in large numbers

1883 • Brooklyn Bridge completed
• Pulitzer buys *New York World* and creates a major vehicle for yellow journalism

1885 • Safety bicycle invented

1886 • First settlement house opens, in New York City

1889 • Edison invents the motion picture and viewing device

1890s • Electric trolleys replace horse-drawn mass transit

1893 • Columbian Exposition opens in Chicago

1895 • Hearst buys the *New York Journal,* another major popular yellow-journalism newspaper

1898 • Race riot erupts in Wilmington, North Carolina

1900–10 • Immigration reaches peak
• Vaudeville rises in popularity

1903 • Boston beats Pittsburgh in first baseball World Series

1905 • Intercollegiate Athletic Association, forerunner of the National College Athletic Association (NCAA), is formed and restructures the rules of football

1915 • Griffith directs *Birth of a Nation,* one of the first major technically sophisticated movies

1920 • Majority (51.2 percent) of Americans live in cities

---

cash-based economy, ethnic consciousness and bigotry, the quest for independence and respectability—these made cities places of hope, frustration, comfort, and conflict.

Not until the 1880s did the United States become an urban nation. The technological innovations of the late nineteenth century fueled widespread economic and geographical expansion that funneled millions of people into cities. By 1920, a majority of Americans (51.2 percent) lived in cities (settlements with more than 2,500 people) for the first time.

Online Study Center **Improve Your Grade**
Interactive Map: Urbanization, 1880 and 1929

Cities served as marketplaces and forums, bringing together the people, resources, and ideas responsible for changes in neighborhoods, politics, commerce, and leisure. By 1900, a network of cities spanned every section of the country. Some people relished the opportunities cities offered; others found them disquieting. Either way, cities had become central to American life. ■

Growth of the Modern City

In the late nineteenth century, cities became the main arenas for industrial growth. As labor, transportation, and communication hubs, cities supplied everything factories needed. Capital accumulated by mercantile enterprises fed industrial investment. Residents also acted as consumers for new products. The further industrialization advanced, the more opportunities it created for jobs and investment. Increased opportunities drew more people to cities; as workers and as consumers, they fueled yet more industrialization.

Within cities, industrial product specialization gradually became common. Mass production of cloth-

INDUSTRIAL
DEVELOPMENT

ing concentrated in New York, shoes in Philadelphia, textiles in New England cities. Other cities processed products from surrounding agricultural regions: flour in Minneapolis, cottonseed oil in Memphis, beef and pork in Chicago. Still others processed natural resources: gold and copper in Denver, fish and lumber in Seattle, coal and iron in Pittsburgh and Birmingham, oil in Houston and Los Angeles. Such activities made cities a magnet for people in search of employment.

Urban and industrial growth freed the United States from dependence on European capital and goods. By 1900, urban development helped convert America from a debtor agricultural nation into an industrial, financial, and exporting power.

At the same time, the compact city of the early nineteenth century, where residences mingled among shops, factories, and warehouses, expanded. No longer did different social groups live close together. Instead, cities subdivided into distinct districts: working-class and ethnic neighborhoods, downtown, and a ring of suburbs. Two forces were responsible for this: mass transportation, which propelled people and enterprises outward, and economic change, which drew human and material resources inward.

Mass transportation moved people faster and farther. By the 1870s, horse-drawn vehicles began shar-

MECHANIZATION
OF MASS
TRANSPORTATION

ing city streets with motor-driven conveyances. At first, commuter railroads carried commuters to and from outlying communities; then cable cars did the job. In the 1890s, electric-powered streetcars began replacing horse cars and cable cars. Between 1890 and 1902, total electrified track grew from 1,300 to 22,000 miles. In Boston, New York, and Philadelphia, transit firms dug underground subway tunnels to avoid traffic congestion. Subways and elevated railroads were expensive, appearing in only the few cities with enough riders to ensure profits.

Mass transit created a commuting public. Those who could afford the fare—usually 5 cents—could

URBAN SPRAWL

live beyond the crowded central city and travel there for work, shopping, and entertainment. Working-class families, who needed every cent, found streetcars unaffordable. But the growing middle class could escape to quiet, tree-lined neighborhoods on the outskirts. Real-estate development boomed around city borders. Between 1890 and 1920, for example, developers in the Chicago area opened 800,000 new lots—enough to house at least three times the city's 1890 population.

When consumers moved outward, companies followed, with business centers emerging near trolley lines and railway stations. Branches of department stores and banks joined groceries, theaters, taverns, and shops to create neighborhood shopping centers. Meanwhile, the urban core became a work zone, where tall buildings loomed over streets clogged with people, horses, and vehicles.

Between 1870 and 1920, the number of Americans living in cities increased from 10 million to 54

POPULATION
GROWTH

million. During this period, the number of cities with more than 100,000 people swelled from fifteen to sixty-eight; the number with more than 500,000 rose from two to twelve (see Map 19.1).

American urban growth came from the annexation of bordering land and net migration (excess of in-migrants over out-migrants). The most notable such enlargement occurred in 1898 when New York City, formerly only Manhattan and the Bronx, merged with Brooklyn, Staten Island, and part of Queens and doubled to 3 million people. Suburbs often desired annexation for the schools, water, fire protection, and sewer systems that cities could provide. In the 1880s, Chicago, Minneapolis, and Los Angeles incorporated hundreds of undeveloped square miles into their borders to accommodate future residential growth.

In-migration from the countryside and immigration from abroad made by far the greatest contribu-

URBAN
IN-MIGRATION

tion to urban population growth. Urban newcomers arrived from two major sources: the American countryside and Europe. Smaller numbers of immigrants also came from Asia, Canada, and Latin America.

Rural populations declined as urban populations burgeoned. Low crop prices and high debts drove white farmers toward opportunities that cities seemed to offer. Such migration peopled major cities such as Detroit, Chicago, and San Francisco but also secondary cities such as Indianapolis, Salt Lake City, Nashville,

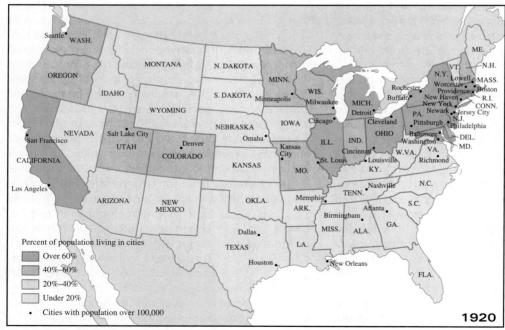

Map 19.1   Urbanization, 1880 and 1920

In 1880 the vast majority of states were heavily rural. By 1920, only a few had less than 20 percent of their population living in cities.

and San Diego. Despair drove farm boys to cities, but for every four men who migrated cityward, five women did the same, often to escape unhappy home life or to enjoy the independence that urban employment offered.

In the 1880s and 1890s, thousands of rural African Americans also moved cityward, seeking better employment and fleeing crop liens, ravages of the boll weevil on cotton crops, racial violence, and political oppression. Though black migration accelerated after 1915, thirty-two cities already had more than ten thousand black residents by 1900. Because few factories would employ African Americans, most found jobs in the service sector—cleaning, cooking, and driving. Since service jobs were traditionally female, black women outnumbered black men in cities. In the South, African Americans migrating from the countryside became an important source of unskilled labor in growing cities. By 1900 almost 40 percent of the total population of Atlanta, Georgia, and Charlotte, North Carolina, were blacks.

In the West, Latino migrants followed a similar pattern. They took unskilled construction and grading jobs previously held by Chinese laborers who had been driven from southern California cities. In some Texas cities, native Mexicans (called *Tejanos*) held most of the unskilled jobs. In places such as Los Angeles, males often left home for long periods to take temporary agricultural jobs, leaving behind female heads of household.

Foreign immigrants fled villages and cities in Europe, Asia, Canada, and Latin America for the United States. Many wanted only to earn enough money to return home and live in greater comfort. For every hundred foreigners who came to the United States, thirty ultimately left. Still, most of the 26 million immigrants arriving between 1870 and 1920 remained, settling largely in cities, where they helped reshape American culture.

FOREIGN IMMIGRATION

Population pressures, land redistribution, and industrialization induced millions of peasants, small farmers, and craftsmen to leave Europe and Asia for Canada, Australia, Brazil, and Argentina, as well as the United States. Religious persecution, too, particularly the merciless pogroms that Jews suffered in eastern Europe, also forced people to escape across the Atlantic.

THE NEW IMMIGRATION

Immigrants from northern and western Europe had long made the United States their main destination, but after 1880, economic and demographic changes propelled immigrants from other regions. Two-thirds of newcomers in the 1880s came from Germany, England, Ireland, and Scandinavia; between 1900 and 1909, two-thirds came from Italy, Austria-Hungary, and Russia. By 1910, arrivals from Mexico outnumbered arrivals from Ireland, and numerous Japanese had moved to the West Coast and Hawai'i. Foreign-born blacks, chiefly from the West Indies, also came.

Many long-settled Americans feared these so-called new immigrants, whose customs, Catholic and Jewish faiths, and poverty made them seem especially alien. Unlike earlier arrivals from Great Britain and Ireland, new immigrants did not speak English and typically worked in low-skilled occupations. Family connections aided both old and new immigrants. New arrivals usually knew where to go and how to get there from relatives who had already immigrated. Workers often helped kin obtain jobs, and family members pooled resources to improve their standard of living.

In-migrants and immigrants rarely stayed put. Each year millions of families packed up and moved.

GEOGRAPHIC AND SOCIAL MOBILITY

More than half the families residing in a city at any one time were gone ten years later. Even within a city, it was not uncommon for a family to live at three or more addresses over a ten-year period. One in every three or four families moved every year (compared to one in five today).

Migration offered one path to improved opportunity; occupational change offered another. An advance up the employment hierarchy was mostly available to white males. Thousands of businesses were needed to supply goods and services to burgeoning urban populations, and as corporations grew and centralized operations, they required new managerial personnel. Knowledge of accounting could qualify one for white-collar jobs with higher incomes than manual labor. And an aspiring merchant could open a saloon or shop for a few hundred dollars.

Although advancement occurred often, only a very few could accumulate large fortunes. The vast majority of the era's wealthiest businessmen began their careers with distinct advantages: American birth, Protestant religion, superior education, and relatively

■ The Caribbean as well as Europe sent immigrants to the United States. Proud and confident on arrival from their homeland of Guadeloupe, these women perhaps were unprepared for the double disadvantage they faced as both blacks and foreigners. (William Williams Papers, Manuscripts & Archives Division, The New York Public Library, Astor, Lenox and Tilden Foundations)

affluent parents. Yet considerable movement occurred along the road from poverty to moderate success, from manual to nonmanual jobs.

Rates of upward occupational mobility were slow but steady between 1870 and 1920. In fast-growing cities such as Atlanta, Los Angeles, and Omaha, approximately one in five white manual workers rose to white-collar or owner's positions within ten years. In older cities such as Boston and Philadelphia, upward mobility averaged closer to one in six workers in ten years. Some men slipped from a higher to lower rung on the occupational ladder, but rates of upward movement usually doubled those of downward movement.

What constitutes a better job, however, depends on one's definition of improvement. People with traditions of pride in manual skills considered nonmanual jobs demeaning and discouraged their children from them. As one Italian tailor explained, "I learned the tailoring business in the old country. Over here, in America, I never have trouble finding a job. . . . I want that my oldest boy learn my trade because I tell him that you could always make at least enough for the family."

Many manual workers sought security rather than mobility, preferring a steady wage to the risks of ownership. Failure rates were high among small proprietors in working-class neighborhoods because the low incomes of their customers made business uncertain.

Many women held paying jobs, but the chief means to improve their status was by marrying men with wealth or potential. Laws limited what women could inherit; educational institutions blocked their training in professions such as medicine and law; and prevailing assumptions attributed higher aptitude for manual skills and business to men. Assigned to lowest-paying occupations by prejudice, African Americans, American Indians, Mexican Americans, and Asian Americans could make even fewer gains.

A person might also achieve social mobility by acquiring property, not an easy task. Banks and savings-and-loan institutions had strict lending practices, and mortgage loans carried high interest rates and short repayment periods. Nevertheless, many families were able to amass enough savings for down payments on homes. Ownership rates varied regionally—higher in western cities, lower in eastern cities—but 36 percent of all urban American families owned their homes in 1900, the highest homeownership rate of any western nation except for Denmark, Norway, and Sweden.

Thus, while cities frustrated the hopes of some, they offered opportunities to others. The possibilities for upward mobility seemed to temper people's dissatisfaction with the frustrations of city life. For every story of rags to riches, a multitude of small triumphs mixed with disappointment occurred. Although the gap between the very rich and the very poor widened, the expanding economies of American cities created room for those in between.

Online Study Center Improve Your Grade
   Primary Source: Theory of the Leisure Class

Urban Neighborhoods

*a*merican cities were characterized by collections of subcommunities where people, most of whom had migrated from somewhere else, coped with daily challenges to their cultures. Rather than yield completely to assimilation, migrants and immigrants interacted with the urban environment to retain their identity while altering both their outlook and the social structure of cities themselves.

In their new surroundings, immigrants first anchored their lives to what they knew best: their culture.

CULTURAL RETENTION AND CHANGE

Old World customs persisted in immigrant districts. Orthodox Jewish men from eastern Europe grew earlocks, women wore wigs, and children attended afternoon religious training. Newcomers re-created mutual aid societies they had known in their homelands. For example, Japanese transferred *ken* societies, which organized social celebrations and relief services, and Chinese used loan associations, called *whey,* to help members acquire businesses. Chinese also transplanted associations called *fongs,* which rented apartments for homeless members, and *tongs,* which were secret aid societies that often acted as gangs extorting protection money from businesses. Southern Italians transplanted the system whereby a *padrone* (boss) found jobs for unskilled workers by negotiating with—and receiving a payoff from—an employer.

In industrial cities such as Chicago, Philadelphia, and Detroit, European immigrants initially clustered

URBAN BORDERLANDS

in inner-city neighborhoods where low-skill jobs and cheap housing were most available. These were typically multiethnic neighborhoods, places historians have called "urban borderlands," where people of diverse backgrounds coexisted. Even within districts identified with a certain group, such as Little Italy, Jewtown, Polonia, or Greektown, rapid mobility constantly undermined residential homogeneity as new inhabitants moved in and older ones left. Despite increasing ethnic mixes, businesses and institutions, such as the bakeries, and churches—operated by and for one ethnic group—gave a neighborhood its identity.

Some ethnic groups often tried to exclude outsiders from their neighborhoods. For example, Italians, Jews, and Poles deliberately maintained separate religious, linguistic, and cultural lifestyles. For such groups, neighborhoods acted as havens until individuals were ready to move into the majority society.

But these borderland experiences often dissolved. The expansion of mass transportation and factories enticed people to relocate, where they interspersed with families of their own socioeconomic class but not necessarily of their own ethnicity. European immigrants did encounter prejudice, such as the exclusion of Jews from certain neighborhoods, professions, and clubs, but discrimination was rarely complete. For people of color, however—African Americans, Asians, and Mexicans—discrimination made the borderlands increasingly less multiethnic over time.

Where small numbers of African Americans may have lived near or among whites in the eighteenth and

RACIAL SEGREGATION IN CITIES

early nineteenth centuries, by the late nineteenth century, rigid racial discrimination forced them into highly segregated areas later labeled ghettos. By 1920 in Chicago, Detroit, Cleveland, and other cities, two-thirds or more of the total African American population inhabited only 10 percent of the residential area. The only way blacks could relieve overcrowding was to expand residential borders into surrounding, previously white neighborhoods, a process often resulting in harassment and attacks by white residents who feared that black neighbors would cause property values to decline.

African Americans nurtured cultural institutions to ease urban life: shops, schools, clubs, theaters, dance halls, newspapers, and saloons. Churches, particularly the Baptist and African Methodist Episcopal (AME) branches of Protestantism, were especially influential. Pittsburgh boasted twenty-eight such churches in the early 1900s, and membership in Cincinnati's black Baptist churches doubled between 1870 and 1900. Black religious activity dominated urban local life and represented cooperation across class and regional lines.

Asians encountered similar isolation. Although Chinese immigrants often preferred to live apart from Anglos in the Chinatowns of San Francisco, Los Angeles, and New York City, where they created their own business, government, and protective institutions, Anglos made every effort to keep them separated. Using the slogan "The Chinese must go," Irish immigrant Dennis Kearney and his followers intimidated San Francisco employers into refusing to hire Chinese and drove hundreds of Asians out of the city. San Francisco's government prohibited Chinese laundries from locating in white neighborhoods and banned the wearing of queues, the traditional Chinese hair braid. In 1882 Congress passed the Chinese Exclusion Act, which suspended Chinese immigration and prohib-

ited naturalization of those Chinese already residing in the United States. And in 1892, Congress approved the Geary Act, which extended immigration restriction and required Chinese Americans to carry certificates of residence issued by the Treasury Department. It was upheld by the U.S. Supreme Court in 1893. Similarly prevented from becoming U.S. citizens, Japanese immigrants, called *Issei,* developed separate communities.

Mexicans in southwestern cities experienced more complex residential patterns. In places such as Los

MEXICAN BARRIOS

Angeles, Santa Barbara, and Tucson, Mexicans had been the original inhabitants, and Anglos were migrants who pushed Mexicans out, where they became increasingly isolated in adjoining districts called *barrios.* Frequently real-estate covenants reinforced this trend as property owners pledged not to sell homes to Mexicans (or to African Americans, or to Jews). Instead, they were confined to segregated areas away from the central-city multiethnic borderlands that housed European immigrants.

Immigrants struggled to maintain their native languages and customs. But English, taught in schools and

CULTURAL ADAPTATION

needed on the job, soon penetrated nearly every community. Foreigners fashioned homeland garments from American fabrics. Italians went to American doctors but still carried traditional amulets to ward off evil spirits. Music especially revealed adaptations. Polka bands blended American and Polish folk music; once dominated by violins, bands added accordions, clarinets, and trumpets so they could play louder. Mexican ballads acquired new themes that described border crossing and hardships in the United States.

The influx of so many immigrants between 1870 and 1920 transformed the United States from a basically Protestant nation into a diverse collection of Protestants, Catholics, Orthodox Christians, Jews, Buddhists, and Muslims. Newcomers from Italy, Hungary, Polish lands, and Slovakia joined Irish and Germans to boost the proportion of Catholics in many cities. German and Russian immigrants gave New York City one of the largest Jewish populations in the world.

Many Catholics and Jews tried to accommodate their faiths to the new environment. Catholic and

Jewish leaders from earlier immigrant groups supported liberalizing trends—use of English in sermons, phasing out of Old World rituals such as saints' feasts, and a preference for public over religious schools.

Newcomers usually resisted and held on to familiar practices, whether the folk Catholicism of southern Italy or the Orthodox Judaism of eastern Europe. Despite church attempts to make American Catholicism more uniform, bishops acceded to pressures from predominantly Polish congregations for Polish priests. Eastern European Jews, convinced that Reform Judaism sacrificed too much to American ways, established the Conservative branch, which retained traditional ritual but abolished the segregation of women in synagogues and allowed English prayers.

The cities nurtured rich cultural variety: American folk music and literature, Italian and Mexican cuisine, Irish comedy, Yiddish theater, African American jazz and dance, and much more. Newcomers changed their environment as much as they were changed by it.

Living Conditions in the Inner City

The central sections of American cities were plagued by poverty, disease, crime, and other unpleasant conditions that occur when large numbers of people live close together. City dwellers coped as best they could, and technology, private enterprise, and public authority achieved some remarkable successes.

In spite of massive construction in the 1880s and early 1900s, population growth outpaced housing supplies. Lack of inexpensive housing especially afflicted working-class families who, because of low wages, had to rent their living quarters. As cities grew, landlords took advantage of shortages by splitting up existing buildings to house more people, constructing multiple-unit tenements, and hiking rents. Low-income families adapted to high costs and short supply by sharing space and expenses. A one-family apartment was often occupied by up to three families or by a single family plus several boarders.

INNER-CITY HOUSING

The result was unprecedented crowding. In 1890 New York City's immigrant-packed Lower East Side, where the Gollop family lived, averaged 702 people per acre, one of the highest population densities in the world. Inside, conditions were harsh. The largest rooms were barely ten feet wide, and interior rooms lacked windows or opened onto narrow shafts that bred vermin and rotten odors. Few buildings had indoor plumbing; the only source of heat was dangerous, polluting coal-burning stoves.

Housing problems sparked widespread reform campaigns. New York State took the lead by applying light, ventilation, and safety codes for new tenement buildings with laws passed in 1867, 1879, and 1901. A few reformers, such as journalist Jacob Riis and humanitarian Lawrence Veiller, advocated "model tenements," with more spacious rooms and better facilities for low-income families. Model tenements meant lower profits, a sacrifice few landlords were willing to make. Both reformers and public officials opposed government financing, fearing that it might undermine private enterprise. Still, new housing codes and regulatory commissions strengthened the power of local government to oversee construction.

HOUSING REFORM

Technology radically changed home life. Advanced systems of central heating (furnaces), artificial lighting, and modern indoor plumbing created a new kind of consumption, first for middle-class households and later for most others. Whereas formerly families bought coal or chopped wood for cooking and heating, made candles, and hauled bath water, they increasingly connected to outside pipes and wires for gas, electricity, and water. Moreover, these utilities helped create new attitudes about privacy. Middle-class bedrooms and bathrooms became comfortable private retreats, while indoor plumbing replaced the unpleasant experiences of the outhouse.

NEW HOME TECHNOLOGY

Better housing for the poor came later, but scientific and technological advances enabled the nation to live better. By the 1880s, doctors had begun to accept the theory that microorganisms (germs) cause disease. Cities developed more efficient water purification and sewage disposal, which helped to control dread diseases such as cholera, typhoid fever, and diphtheria.

■ Inner-city dwellers used not only indoor space as efficiently as possible but also what little outdoor space was available to them. Scores of families living in this cramped block of six-story tenements in New York strung clotheslines behind the buildings. Notice that there is virtually no space between buildings, so only rooms at the front and back received daylight and fresh air.   (Library of Congress)

Meanwhile, street paving, modernized firefighting equipment, and electric street lighting spread rapidly across urban America. Steel-frame construction, which relies on a metal skeleton rather than masonry walls, made possible the erection of skyscrapers—and thus more efficient vertical use of scarce urban land. Electric elevators and steam-heating systems serviced these buildings. Steel-cable suspension bridges, developed by John A. Roebling and epitomized by his Brooklyn Bridge (completed in 1883), linked metropolitan sections more closely.

None of these improvements, however, lightened the burden of poverty. Since colonial days, Americans have disagreed about public responsibility for poor relief. According to **POVERTY RELIEF** traditional beliefs, still widespread by the early twentieth century, anyone could escape poverty through hard work and clean living; indigence was linked to moral weakness. Some people feared that granting aid to the poor encouraged them to rely on public support rather than their own efforts. As poverty increased, this attitude hardened, and city governments discontinued direct grants of food, fuel, and clothing to needy families. Instead, cities provided relief in return for work on public projects and sent special cases to state-run almshouses, orphanages, and homes for the blind, deaf, and mentally ill.

Between 1877 and 1892, philanthropists in ninety-two cities formed Charity Organization Societies to make social welfare (like business) more efficient by merging disparate charity groups into coordinated units. Believing poverty to be caused by defects such as alcoholism and laziness, members of these organizations visited the poor to determine if they were "deserving" and encourage them to be thriftier and more virtuous.

Close observation of the poor, however, prompted some humanitarians to conclude that people's environments, not their shortcomings, caused poverty. They believed poverty would be reduced by improving housing, education, sanitation, and job opportunities. This fueled campaigns for building codes, factory regulations, and public health measures in the Progressive era of the early twentieth century (covered in Chapter 21). Still, most middle- and upper-class Americans continued to endorse the creed that only the unfit were poor and that poverty relief should be tolerated but never encouraged.

Crime and disorder, as much as crowding and poverty, nurtured fears that cities and their slums threatened the nation. While homi-

CRIME AND VIOLENCE

cide rates declined in other industrialized nations, America's rose alarmingly, from 25 murders per million people in 1881 to 107 per million in 1898. Pickpockets, swindlers, and burglars roamed every city. Urban outlaws, such as Rufus Minor, acquired as much notoriety as western desperadoes. Short, stocky, and bald, Minor resembled a shy clerk, but one police chief labeled him "one of the smartest bank sneaks in America." Minor was implicated in bank heists in New York City, Cleveland, Detroit, Providence, Philadelphia, Albany, Boston, and Baltimore—all between 1878 and 1882.

In reality, urban crime may simply have become more visible rather than more prevalent. To be sure, concentrations of wealth and the mingling of different peoples provided opportunities for larceny, vice, and assault. But urban lawlessness probably did not exceed that of backwoods mining camps and southern plantations. Nativists were quick to blame immigrants for crime, but the criminal rogues' gallery included native-born Americans as well as foreigners.

The cityward movement of African Americans especially sparked white violence, and as the twentieth century dawned, a series of race riots spread across the nation. In 1898 citizens of Wilmington, North Carolina, resenting African Americans' involvement in local politics, rioted and killed dozens of blacks, ex-

pelled black officeholders, and instituted voting restrictions. An influx of African American unskilled laborers and strikebreakers into East St. Louis, Illinois, heightened racial tensions, and violence erupted in 1917 when blacks fired back at a car whose occupants they believed had shot into their homes. When whites discovered that the blacks had mistakenly killed two policemen in the car, a riot erupted, ending only after nine whites and thirty-nine blacks had been killed and over three hundred buildings destroyed. Domestic violence, muggings, and gang fights also made cities turbulent.

Managing the City

Burgeoning populations and business expansion created urgent needs for sewers, police and fire protection, schools, parks, and other services. Such needs strained municipal resources and city governments beyond their capacities. Legislative and administrative responsibilities for health, public works, and poverty relief were typically scattered among a mayor, city council, and independent boards. Philadelphia at one time had thirty different boards, plus a mayor and council. Also, state governments often interfered in local matters, appointing board members and limiting cities' abilities to levy taxes and borrow money.

Finding sources of clean water and a way to dispose of waste became increasingly urgent challenges.

WATER SUPPLY AND SEWAGE DISPOSAL

Earlier in the nineteenth century, urban households used privies (outdoor toilets) to dispose of human excrement, and factories dumped untreated sewage into nearby rivers, lakes, and bays. By the late nineteenth century, the installation of sewer systems and flush toilets, plus use of water as a coolant in factories, overwhelmed waterways and contaminated drinking water sources. The stench of rivers was often unbearable, and pollution bred disease. Memphis and New York experienced yellow-fever epidemics in the 1870s and 1880s, and typhoid fever threatened many cities.

Acceptance in the 1880s of the germ theory of disease prompted cities to reduce chances that human waste and other pollutants would endanger water supplies. Some states prohibited discharge of raw sewage into rivers and streams, and a few cities began the expensive process of chemically treating sewage. Gradually, water managers installed mechanical filters, and cities, led by Jersey City, began purifying water supplies by adding chlorine. These efforts dramatically reduced death rates from typhoid fever.

But waste disposal remained a thorny problem. Experts in 1900 estimated that every New Yorker generated annually some 160 pounds of garbage (food and bones), 1,200 pounds of ashes (from stoves and furnaces), and 100 pounds of rubbish (shoes, furniture, and other discarded items). Solid waste from factories and businesses included tons of scrap metal, wood, and other materials. Each of the estimated 3.5 million horses in American cities in 1900 dropped about 20 pounds of manure and a gallon of urine daily—a serious environmental problem. By the twentieth century, such debris were health and safety hazards.

Citizen groups, led by women's organizations, began discussing the dilemma in the 1880s and 1890s,

URBAN ENGINEERS

and by the turn of the century, urban governments hired sanitary engineers to develop garbage collection and disposal systems, mostly in incinerators and landfills. The American engineering profession developed new systems and standards of worldwide significance in such areas as street lighting, bridge and street construction, fire protection, and other urban needs that required technological creativity. Elected officials came to depend on the expertise of engineers in supervising urban expansion. Insulated within bureaucratic agencies and party politics, engineers made some of the most lasting contributions to urban management.

After the mid-nineteenth century, urban dwellers increasingly depended on professional police to protect life and property, but law en-

LAW ENFORCEMENT

forcement became controversial as various groups differed about how laws should be enforced. Ethnic and racial minorities were more likely to be arrested, and police officers applied the law less harshly to members of their own ethnic groups as well as to those offering bribes.

Often poorly trained and prone to corruption, police officers were caught between demands for swift and severe action on one hand and leniency on the other. As urban society diversified, some people clamored for crackdowns on drunkenness, gambling, and prostitution, while others objected to the violation of civil liberties. Achieving balance between criminal law and individual freedom grew increasingly difficult.

Out of the apparent confusion surrounding urban management arose political machines, organi-

POLITICAL MACHINES

zations whose main goals were the rewards—money, influence, and prestige—of getting and keeping power. Machine politicians routinely used fraud and bribery to further their ends. But they also provided relief, security, and services to voters who kept them in power.

Machines bred leaders, called bosses, who catered to urban working classes and especially to new immigrant voters, who provided their power base. Most bosses had immigrant backgrounds and had grown up in the inner city; they knew their constituents' needs firsthand and secured their loyalty by tending to problems of everyday life. In return for votes, bosses provided jobs, built parks and bathhouses, distributed food and clothing to the needy, and helped when someone ran afoul of the law. Pittsburgh's Christopher Magee gave his city a zoo and a hospital. Brooklyn's Hugh McLaughlin provided free burial services. Never before had public leaders assumed such responsibility for people in need. Bosses attended weddings and wakes, joined clubs, and held open house in saloons where neighborhood folk could speak to them personally. According to George Washington Plunkitt, a neighborhood boss in New York City, "As a rule [the boss] has no business or occupation other than politics. He plays politics every day and night . . . and his headquarters bears the inscription, 'Never closed.'"

To finance their activities, bosses exchanged favors for votes and money. Power over local government enabled machines to control who received public contracts, utility and streetcar franchises, and city jobs. Recipients of these favors were expected to repay the machine with a portion of their profits or salaries and to cast supporting votes on election day. Critics called this process graft; bosses called it gratitude.

Bosses such as Philadelphia's "Duke" Vare, Kansas City's Tom Pendergast, and New York's Richard Croker lived like kings, though their official incomes were slim. Yet machines were rarely as dictatorial or corrupt as critics charged. Rather, several machines, like businesses, evolved into highly organized political structures, such as New York's Tammany Hall organization (named after a society that originally began as a patriotic and fraternal club), that wedded public accomplishments with personal gain. The system rested on a popular base and was held together by loyalty and service. But most machines were coalitions of smaller organizations that derived power directly from inner-city neighborhoods. Machine-led governments constructed urban infrastructures—public buildings, sewer systems, schools, bridges, and mass-transit lines—and expanded urban services—police, firefighting, and public health departments.

Machine politics, however, was not always fair. Racial minorities and new immigrant groups such as Italians and Poles received only token jobs and nominal favors, if any. And bribes and kickbacks made machine projects and services costly to taxpayers. Cities could not ordinarily raise enough revenue for their construction projects from taxes and fees, so they financed expansion with loans from the public in the form of municipal bonds—which caused public debts and taxes to soar. In addition, payoffs from gambling, prostitution, and illicit liquor traffic became important sources of machine revenue. But bosses were no more guilty of discrimination and self-interest than were business leaders who exploited workers, spoiled the landscape, and manipulated government in pursuit of profits.

Many middle- and upper-class Americans feared that immigrant-based political machines menaced

CIVIC REFORM

democracy and wasted municipal finances. Anxious over the poverty, crowding, and disorder that accompanied city growth and convinced that urban services were making taxes too high, civic reformers organized to elect more responsible leaders.

Business-minded reformers believed government should run like a company. Thus, they advocated reducing city budgets, making public employees work more efficiently, and cutting taxes.

To implement business principles in government, civic reformers supported structural changes such as city-manager and commission forms of government, which would place administration in the hands of experts rather than politicians, and nonpartisan, city-wide rather than neighborhood-based election of officials. The reformers' goal was to weaken bosses' power bases in the neighborhoods.

A few reform mayors addressed social problems too. Hazen S. Pingree of Detroit, Samuel "Golden Rule" Jones of Toledo, and Tom Johnson of Cleveland worked to provide jobs to poor people, reduce charges by transit and utility companies, and promote governmental responsibility for the welfare of all citizens. They also supported public ownership of gas, electric, and telephone companies, quasi-socialist reforms that alienated their business allies. Civic reformers achieved some successes but rarely held office for very long.

Driven to improve as well as manage society, social reformers—mostly young and middle class—

SOCIAL REFORM

sought to solve urban problems. Housing reformers pressed local governments for building codes ensuring safety in tenements. Educational reformers pressed to use public schools to prepare immigrant children for citizenship by teaching them American values.

Perhaps the most ambitious urban reform movement was the settlement house. Located in inner-city neighborhoods and run mostly by young, middle-class women who lived and worked among the poor to bridge the gulf between social classes, settlements sponsored programs for better education, jobs, and housing. The first American settlement, patterned after London's Toynbee Hall, opened in New York City in 1886, and others quickly appeared across the country. Early settlement leaders included Jane Addams, founder of Hull House in Chicago in 1889 and one of the country's most influential women, and Florence Kelley, who pioneered laws protecting consumers and working women.

Their efforts to involve national and local governments in the solution of social problems put settlements in the vanguard of the Progressive era, when a reform spirit swept the nation. Moreover, settlement-house programs created new professional opportunities for women in social work, public health, and child welfare. These professions enabled female reformers to wield influence over social policy and make valuable contributions to national as well as inner-city life.

Still, the settlement-house movement was segregated. Middle-class white women lobbied for government programs to aid mostly white immigrant and native-born working classes. Black women reformers, excluded from white settlements, raised funds from private donors and promoted racial advancement by founding schools, old-age homes, and hospitals, as well as protecting black women from sexual exploitation. Their ranks included Jane Hunter, who founded a home for unmarried black working women in Cleveland in 1911 and inspired the establishment of similar homes in other cities.

Male reformers joined female activists' improvement efforts with their own City Beautiful campaign.

THE CITY BEAUTIFUL MOVEMENT Inspired by the Columbian Exposition of 1893, a dazzling world's fair held in Chicago, architects and planners aimed to redesign the urban landscape. City Beautiful advocates built civic centers, parks, and boulevards that would make cities economically efficient as well as beautiful, with projects in Chicago, San Francisco, and Washington, D.C., in the early 1900s. Yet neither government nor private businesses could finance large-scale projects, and planners disagreed among themselves and with social reformers over whether beautification would truly solve urban problems.

Urban reformers wanted to save cities, but they often failed to recognize the diversity of people and opinions about reform. To civic reformers, appointing government workers based on civil service exams rather than party loyalty meant progress, but to working-class men, civil service signified reduced employment opportunities. Moral reformers believed that restricting the sale of alcohol would prevent working-class breadwinners from squandering wages, but immigrants saw it as interference. Planners saw new streets and buildings as modern necessities, but such structures often displaced the poor. Well-meaning humanitarians criticized immigrant mothers for the way they dressed, did housework, and raised children, without recognition of their limited finances. Thus, urban reform merged idealism with naiveté and insensitivity.

Family Life

*U*rbanization and industrialization put strains on family life. New institutions—schools, social clubs, political organizations, unions—increasingly competed with the family to provide nurture, education, and security. Clergy and journalists warned that the growing separation between home and work, rising divorce rates, the entrance of women into the work force, and loss of parental control over children spelled peril for home and family. Yet the family remained a cushion in an uncertain world.

Since colonial times, most American households (75 to 80 percent) have consisted of nuclear families—

FAMILY AND HOUSEHOLD STRUCTURES usually a married couple, with or without children. About 15 to 20 percent of households have consisted of extended families—usually a married couple, with or without children, plus one or more relatives. About 5 percent of households have consisted of people living alone or in boarding houses and hotels. Despite slight variations, this pattern held relatively constant among ethnic, racial, and socioeconomic groups.

Several factors explain this pattern. Because immigrants tended to be young, the American population as a whole was young. In 1880 the median age was under twenty-one, and by 1920 it was still only twenty-five. (Median age at present is about thirty-three.) Moreover, in 1900 the death rate among people aged forty-five to sixty-four was double what it is today. Only 4 percent of the population was over sixty-five, versus about 13 percent today. Thus, few families could form extended three-generation households, and fewer children than today had living grandparents. Migration split up families, and the ideal of homeownership encouraged nuclear household organization.

Most of Europe and North America experienced falling birth rates in the nineteenth century. In 1880

DECLINING BIRTH RATES the birth rate was 40 live births per 1,000 people in the United States; by 1900 it had dropped to 32; by 1920 to 28. Although fertility was higher among blacks, immigrants, and rural people, birth rates of all groups fell. Several factors explain this decline.

First, the United States was becoming an urban nation, and birth rates are historically lower in cities than in rural areas. On farms, each child born represented an addition to the family work force. In the wage-based urban economy, children could not contribute significantly to the family income for many years, so a new child represented another mouth to feed. Second, infant mortality fell as diet and medical care improved, and families did not have to bear many children to ensure that some would survive. Third, awareness that smaller families meant improved quality of life seems to have stimulated decisions to limit family size—either by abstaining from sex during the wife's fertile period or through contraception and abortion. Families with three or four children instead of six or eight became the norm. Birth-control technology—diaphragms and condoms—had been used for centuries, but in this era, new materials made devices more convenient and dependable.

The process of leaving home to work altered household composition. Middle- and working-class families commonly took in boarders for additional income. Immigrants such as Rahel Gollop often lodged with relatives and fellow villagers until they could establish themselves. By 1900, as many as 50 percent of city residents had lived either as, or with, boarders at some point during their lifetime. Housing reformers charged that boarding caused overcrowding and loss of privacy.

BOARDING

For people on the move, boarding was a transitional stage, providing a quasi-family environment until they set up their own households. Especially in communities where housing was expensive or scarce, newlyweds sometimes lived temporarily with one spouse's parents. Families also took in widowed parents or unmarried siblings.

At a time when welfare agencies were rare, the family was the institution to which people could turn in times of need. Relatives often resided nearby and aided one another with childcare, meals, shopping, advice, and consolation. They also obtained jobs for each other. According to one new arrival, "After two days my brother took me to the shop he was working in and his boss saw me and he gave me the job."

But obligations of kinship were not always welcome. Immigrant families pressured last-born children to stay at home to care for aging parents, a practice that stifled opportunities for education, marriage, and economic independence. Tensions also developed when immigrant parents and American-born children clashed over the abandonment of Old World ways or the amount of wages children should contribute to the household. Nevertheless, kinship helped people cope with the stresses of urban-industrial society.

Large numbers of city dwellers were unmarried. In 1890 almost 42 percent of adult American men and 37 percent of women were single, almost twice as high as in 1960 but slightly lower than today. About half still lived with parents, but others inhabited rented rooms. Mostly young, these men and women constituted a separate subculture that supported institutions like dance halls, saloons, cafés, and the Young Men's Christian Association (YMCA) and Young Women's Christian Association (YWCA).

UNMARRIED PEOPLE

Some unmarried people were part of the homosexual populations in large cities like New York, San Francisco, and Boston. Though numbers are difficult to estimate, gay men had their own subculture of clubs, restaurants, coffeehouses, theaters, and support networks. A number of same-sex couples, especially women, formed lasting marital-type relationships, sometimes called "Boston marriages." People in this subculture were categorized more by how they acted—men acting like women, women acting like men—than by who their sexual partners were. The term *homosexual* was not used. Men who dressed and acted like women were called "fairies." Gay women remained largely hidden, and a visible lesbian subculture was rare until the 1920s.

Before the late nineteenth century, stages of life were less distinct than they are today. Childhood, for instance, had been regarded as a period during which young people prepared for adulthood by gradually assuming more responsibilities. The subdivisions of youth—toddlers, schoolchildren, teenagers, and the like—were not recognized. Because married couples had more children over a longer time span, active parenthood occupied most of adult life. Older children who cared for younger siblings might begin parenting even before reaching adulthood. And older people were not isolated from other age groups.

STAGES OF LIFE

In the late nineteenth century, demographic and social changes altered these patterns. Decreasing birth rates shortened the period of parental responsibility, so more middle-aged couples experienced an "empty nest" once their children grew up and left home. Longer life expectancy and a tendency by employers to force aged workers to retire separated the old from the young. As states passed compulsory school-attendance laws in the 1870s and 1880s, childhood and adolescence became distinct from adulthood. People's roles in school, in the family, on the job, and in the community came to be determined by age more than any other characteristic.

Thus, by 1900, new institutions were assuming tasks formerly performed by the family. Schools made education a community responsibility. Employment agencies, personnel offices, and labor unions were taking responsibility for employee recruitment and job security. Age-based peer groups exerted greater influence over people's values and activities. Migration and divorce seemed to be splitting families apart. Yet kinship remained a dependable though not always appreciated institution.

An emphasis on family togetherness became especially visible at holiday celebrations. Middle-class

HOLIDAY CELEBRATIONS

moralists helped make Thanksgiving, Christmas, and Easter special times for family reunion and child-centered activities. Birthdays too took on an increasingly festive quality as a milestone for measuring the age-related norms that accompanied life stages. In 1914 President Woodrow Wilson signed a proclamation designating the second Sunday in May as Mother's Day, capping a six-year campaign by schoolteacher Anna Jarvis, who believed grown children were neglecting their mothers. Ethnic and racial groups adapted national celebrations to their cultures, preparing special ethnic foods, and engaging in unique ceremonies. For many, holiday celebrations were a testimony to the vitality of family life.

The New Leisure and Mass Culture

*O*n December 2, 1889, as workers paraded through Worcester, Massachusetts, seeking shorter working hours, a group of carpenters hoisted a banner proclaiming, "Eight Hours for Work, Eight Hours for Rest, Eight Hours for What We Will." That last phrase laid claim to a segment of daily life belonging to the individual. Increasingly, leisure activities filled this time.

By the late 1800s, technology had become truly time-saving. Mechanization and assembly-line production cut the average manufacturing

INCREASE IN LEISURE TIME

workweek from sixty-six hours in 1860 to sixty in 1890 and forty-seven in 1920, which meant shorter workdays and freer weekends. White-collar employees spent eight to ten hours a day on the job and often worked only half a day or not at all on weekends. As the economy changed, more Americans engaged in a variety of diversions, and a substantial segment of the economy provided for—and profited from—leisure.

After the Civil War, amusement became a commercial activity. Production of games, toys, and musical instruments expanded. Improvements in printing and paper production and the rise of manufacturers such as Milton Bradley and Parker Brothers increased the popularity of board games. Significantly, the content of board games shifted from moral lessons to topics involving transportation, finance, and sports. Also, by the 1890s, middle-class families were buying mass-produced pianos and sheet music that made singing of popular songs a common form of home entertainment. The vanguard of new leisure pursuits, however, was sports. Formerly a fashionable indulgence of elites, organized sports became a favored pastime of all classes.

The most popular organized sport was baseball. Derived from older bat, ball, and base-circling games,

BASEBALL

baseball was formalized in 1845 by the Knickerbocker Club of New York. By 1860 at least fifty baseball clubs existed. The National League of Professional Baseball Clubs, founded in 1876, gave the sport a stable, businesslike structure. As early as 1867 a "color line" excluded black players from professional teams. By the 1880s professional baseball was big business. In 1903 the National League and competing American League (formed in 1901) began a World Series between their championship teams. The Boston Red Sox beat the Pittsburgh Pirates in that first series.

Baseball appealed mostly to men. But croquet, which also swept the nation, attracted both sexes.

CROQUET AND CYCLING

Middle- and upper-class people held croquet parties and night contests that increased opportunities for social contact between the sexes.

■ Amusement centers such as Luna Park, at Coney Island in New York City, became common and appealing features of the new leisure culture. One of the most popular Coney Island attractions was a ride called Shooting the Chutes, which resembled modern giant water slides. In 1904 Luna Park staged an outrageous stunt when an elephant slid down the chute. It survived, apparently unfazed.   (Picture Research Consultants and Archives)

Meanwhile, cycling achieved popularity rivaling that of baseball, especially after 1885, when the cumbersome velocipede, with its huge front wheel and tall seat, gave way to safety bicycles with pneumatic tires and wheels of identical size. By 1900 Americans owned 10 million bicycles, and clubs petitioned state governments to build more paved roads. Organized cycle races brought international fame to professional riders such as Major Taylor, an African American. Moreover, the bicycle helped free women from constraints of Victorian fashions. In order to ride the dropped-frame female models, women had to wear divided skirts and simple undergarments. As the 1900 census declared, "Few articles . . . have created so great a revolution in social conditions as the bicycle."

American football, as an intercollegiate competition, mostly attracted players and spectators wealthy enough to have access to higher education. By the late nineteenth cen-

FOOTBALL

tury, however, the game was appealing to a broader audience. The 1893 Princeton-Yale game drew fifty thousand spectators, and informal games were played in yards and playgrounds throughout the country.

But college football's violence and use of "tramp athletes," nonstudents hired to help teams win, sparked a national scandal. Critics accused football of mirroring undesirable features of American society. An editor of *The Nation* charged in 1890 that "the lack of moral scruple which pervades the struggles of the business world meets with temptations equally irresistible in the miniature contests of the football field."

The scandals climaxed in 1905, when 18 players died from game-related injuries and over 150 were seriously injured. President Theodore Roosevelt, a strong advocate of athletics, convened a White House conference to discuss ways to eliminate brutality and foul play. The gathering founded the Intercollegiate

Japanese Baseball

Baseball, the "American pastime," was one of the new leisure-time pursuits that Americans took with them to different parts of the world. The Shanghai Base Ball Club was founded by Americans in China in 1863, but was denounced by the Imperial Court as spiritually corrupting. However, when Horace Wilson, an American teacher, taught the rules of baseball to his Japanese students around 1870, the game received enthusiastic welcome as a reinforcement of traditional virtues and quickly became an entrenched aspect of Japanese culture.

During the 1870s, Japanese high schools and colleges organized baseball games, and in 1883 Hiroshi Hiraoka, a railroad engineer who had studied in Boston, founded the first official local team, the Shimbashi Athletic Club Athletics.

Prior to baseball, the Japanese had no team sports or recreational athletics. When they learned about baseball, they found that the idea of a team sport fit into their culture very well. But to the Japanese, baseball was serious business, often involving brutal training. Practices at Ichiko, one of Japan's two great high-school teams in the late nineteenth century, were dubbed "Bloody Urine" because many players passed blood after a day of drilling. There was a spiritual quality as well, linked to Buddhist values. According to one Japanese coach, "Student baseball must be the baseball of self-discipline, or trying to attain the truth, just as in Zen Buddhism." This attitude prompted Japanese to consider baseball as a new method to pursue the spirit of Bushido, the way of the samurai.

When Americans played baseball in Japan, the Japanese appreciated their talent, but found them lacking in discipline and respect. Americans insulted the Japanese by refusing to remove their hats and bow when they stepped up to bat. An international dispute occurred in 1891 when William Imbrie, an American professor at Meijo University in Tokyo, arrived late for a local game and climbed over the fence. The fence, however, was sacred, and Japanese fans attacked him for his sacrilege, causing him facial injuries. Americans assumed that their game would encourage Japanese to become like westerners, but the Japanese transformed the American pastime into a uniquely Japanese expression of discipline and nationalism.

Replete with bats, gloves, and uniforms, this Japanese baseball team of 1890 very much resembles its American counterpart of that era. The Japanese adopted baseball soon after Americans became involved in their country, but added their cultural qualities to the game.
(Japanese Baseball Hall of Fame)

Athletic Association (renamed the National College Athletic Association in 1910) to police college sports. In 1906 the association altered the game to make it less violent and more open.

As more women enrolled in college, they participated in sports such as rowing, track, and swimming. Eventually women made basketball their most popular intercollegiate sport. Invented in 1891 as a winter sport for men, basketball received women's rules (which limited dribbling and running and encouraged passing) from Senda Berenson of Smith College.

American show business also became a mode of leisure created by and for common people. After the

CIRCUSES, POPULAR DRAMA, AND MUSICAL COMEDY
Civil War, railroads enabled circuses to reach towns across the country. Circuses offered two main attractions: oddities of nature, both human and animal, and the temptation and conquest of death.

Three branches of American show business—popular drama, musical comedy, and vaudeville—matured with the growth of cities. Theatrical performances offered audiences escape into melodrama, adventure, and comedy. For urban people unfamiliar with the frontier, popular plays made the mythical Wild West and Old South come alive through stories of Davy Crockett, Buffalo Bill, and the Civil War. Virtue and honor always triumphed in melodramas such as *Uncle Tom's Cabin* and *The Old Homestead,* reinforcing faith that goodness would prevail.

The American musical derived from Europe's lavishly costumed operettas. George M. Cohan, a spirited singer, dancer, and songwriter born into an Irish family of entertainers, became master of American musical comedy after the turn of the century. Drawing on patriotism and traditional values in songs like "Yankee Doodle Boy" and "You're a Grand Old Flag," Cohan bolstered morale during World War I. American comic operas initially imitated European musicals, but by the early 1900s, composers like Victor Herbert were writing themes appealing directly to American audiences.

Because of its variety, vaudeville was probably the most popular mass entertainment in early-twentieth-century America. Shows included,

VAUDEVILLE
in rapid succession, acts of jugglers, pantomimists, magicians, puppeteers, acrobats, comedians, singers, and

dancers. Shrewd entrepreneurs made vaudeville a big business. The famous producer Florenz Ziegfeld brilliantly packaged shows in a stylish format—the Ziegfeld Follies—and gave the nation a new model of femininity, the Ziegfeld Girl, whose graceful dancing and alluring costumes suggested a haunting sensuality.

Show business provided new opportunities for female, African American, and immigrant performers, but it also encouraged stereotyping and exploitation. Comic opera diva Lillian Russell, vaudeville singer-comedienne Fanny Brice, and burlesque queen Eva Tanguay attracted intensely loyal fans and commanded handsome fees. In contrast to the demure Victorian female, they conveyed an image of pluck and creativity. There was something both shocking and confident about Eva Tanguay singing "It's All Been Done Before But Not the Way I Do It." But lesser female performers and showgirls (called "soubrettes") were often exploited by male promoters and theater owners, who wanted to profit by titillating the public with scantily clad women.

Before the 1890s, the chief form of commercial entertainment employing African Americans was the minstrel show, but vaudeville opened new opportunities to them. Pandering to prejudices of white audiences, composers and performers of both races ridiculed blacks. As songs like "He's Just a Little Nigger, But He's Mine All Mine" confirm, blacks were demeaned on stage much as they were in society. Burt Williams, a highly paid black performer, achieved success by playing stereotypical roles but was tormented by the humiliation he had to suffer.

Immigrants occupied the core of American show business. Vaudeville in particular used ethnic humor, exaggerated dialects, and other national traits. Skits and songs reinforced stereotypes, but such distortions were more sympathetic than those directed at blacks. A typical scene involving Italians, for example, highlighted a character's uncertain grasp of English, which caused him to confuse *mayor* with *mare, diploma* with the *plumber,* and *pallbearer* with *polar bear.* The conditions of African Americans, however, were subject to more vicious jokes.

Shortly after 1900, live entertainment began to yield to motion pictures. Perfected by Thomas Edison

MOVIES
in the 1880s, movies began as slot-machine peepshows in penny arcades and billiard parlors. Eventually

images were projected onto a screen for large audiences. At first, subjects of films hardly mattered; scenes of speeding trains, acrobats, and writhing belly dancers were thrilling enough.

Producers soon discovered that a film could tell a story in exciting ways, and motion pictures became a distinct art form. D. W. Griffith's *Birth of a Nation* (1915), an epic film about the Civil War and Reconstruction, fanned racial prejudice by depicting African Americans as threats to white moral values. The National Association for the Advancement of Colored People (NAACP), formed in 1909, led organized protests against it. But the film's innovative techniques—close-ups, fade-outs, and battle scenes—heightened the drama. By 1920, movies appealed to all classes, and audiences idolized film stars such as Mary Pickford, Lillian Gish, and Charlie Chaplin.

By mass-producing sound and images, technology made entertainment a desirable consumer good. The still camera, modernized by inventor George Eastman, enabled ordinary people to record visual images and preserve family memories. The phonograph, another Edison invention, brought musical performances into the home. News also became a consumer product. Using high-speed printing presses, cheap paper, and profits from growing advertisement revenues, shrewd publishers created a much-desired medium. Increased leisure time seemed to nurture a fascination with the sensational, and from the 1880s onward, popular urban newspapers increasingly whetted that appetite.

Joseph Pulitzer, a Hungarian immigrant who bought the *New York World* in 1883, pioneered journalism as a branch of mass culture. Pulitzer filled the *World* with stories of disasters, crimes, and scandals and printed screaming headlines, set in large bold type like that used for advertisements. *World* reporter Nellie Bly (real name, Elizabeth Cochrane) faked her way into an insane asylum and wrote a brazen exposé of the sordid conditions she found. Pulitzer also popularized comics, and the yellow ink they were printed in gave rise to the term *yellow journalism* as a synonym for sensationalism.

In one year the *World*'s circulation increased from 20,000 to 100,000, and by the late 1890s it reached 1 million. Soon other publishers, such as William Randolph Hearst, who bought the *New York Journal*

YELLOW JOURNALISM

in 1895 and started a newspaper empire, adopted Pulitzer's techniques. Pulitzer, Hearst, and their rivals boosted circulation further by emphasizing sports and women's news. Newspapers had previously reported sporting events, but yellow-journalism papers gave such stories greater prominence with separate, expanded sports pages. Newspapers also added special sections devoted to household tips, fashion, decorum, and club news to capture female readers.

By the early twentieth century, mass-circulation magazines overshadowed expensive elitist journals of earlier eras. Publications such as *McClure's*, *Saturday Evening Post*, and *Ladies' Home Journal* offered human-interest stories, exposés, fiction, photographs, colorful covers, and eye-catching ads. Meanwhile, the total number of published books more than quadrupled between 1880 and 1917. This reflected growing literacy. Between 1870 and 1920, the proportion of Americans over age ten who could not read or write fell from 20 percent to 6 percent.

OTHER MASS-MARKET PUBLICATIONS

Other forms of communication also expanded. In 1891 there was less than 1 telephone for every 100 people in the United States; by 1901 the number reached 2.1, and by 1921 it swelled to 12.6. In 1900 Americans used 4 billion postage stamps; in 1922 they bought 14.3 billion. More than ever before, people in different parts of the country knew about and discussed the same news event. America was becoming a mass society where the same products, technology, and information dominated everyday life, regardless of region.

To some extent, the cities' new amusements allowed ethnic and social groups to share common experiences. Yet different consumer groups used parks, ball fields, movies, and newspapers to reinforce their own cultural habits. To the dismay of reformers who hoped that public recreation and holidays would assimilate newcomers and teach them habits of restraint, immigrants used picnics for special ethnic gatherings and Fourth of July celebrations for boisterous drinking and sometimes violent behavior. Young working-class men and women resisted parents' and moralists' warnings and frequented urban dance halls, where they explored their own forms of courtship and sexual behavior. Thus, leisure—like work and politics—was shaped by the pluralistic forces that thrived in urban life.

Summary *Online Study Center* ACE the Test

*a*merican cities experienced an "unheralded triumph" by the early 1900s. Amid corruption and political conflict, urban engineers modernized local infrastructures with sewer, water, and lighting services, and urban governments made the environment safer by expanding professional police and fire departments. When native inventiveness met the traditions of European, African, and Asian cultures, a new kind of society emerged. The jumble of social classes, ethnic and racial groups, political organizations, and professional experts sometimes lived in harmony, sometimes not.

Amid bewildering diversity, native-born whites tried to Americanize and uplift immigrants, but newcomers stubbornly protected their cultures. Optimists had envisioned the American nation as a melting pot, where various nationalities would fuse into a unified people. Instead, many ethnic groups proved unmeltable, and racial minorities got burned on the bottom of the pot. Instead, the United States became a pluralistic society—more like a salad bowl, where ingredients retained their original flavor and occasionally blended.

Pluralism and interest-group loyalties enhanced the importance of politics, with different groups competing for power, wealth, and status. By 1920, immigrants outnumbered the native-born in many cities, and the national economy depended on these new workers and consumers. Migrants and immigrants transformed the United States into an urban nation. They gave American culture its varied texture, and they laid the foundations for the liberalism that characterized American politics in the twentieth century.

LEGACY FOR A PEOPLE AND A NATION
Ethnic Food

The American taste for ethnic food has a complicated history. Since the nineteenth century, the food business has offered immigrant entrepreneurs lucrative opportunities, many of which involved products unrelated to their own ethnic background. The industry is replete with success stories such as Hector Boiardi (Chef Boyardee), William Gebhardt (Eagle Brand chili and tamales), Jeno Paulucci (Chun-King), and Alphonse Biardot (Franco-American), all of whom immigrated to the United States in the late nineteenth or early twentieth century. But Americans have also supported unheralded local immigrant merchants and restaurateurs who have offered special and regional fare—German, Chinese, Italian, Tex-Mex, "soul food," or Thai—in every era.

The evolution of American eating habits was one of the true melting pots. Occasionally criticisms developed, such as when dietitians and reformers in the early twentieth century charged that the rich foods of eastern European Jews made them overly emotional and less capable of assimilating. But as historian Donna Gabaccia has observed, relatively conflict-free sharing and borrowing have characterized American food ways far more than intolerance. And mass marketers have been quick to capitalize.

As each wave of immigrants has entered the nation—and especially as these newcomers have occupied the cities, where cross-cultural contact has been inevitable—food has given them certain ways of becoming American, of finding some group acceptance, while also confirming their identity.

GILDED AGE POLITICS 1877–1900

*K*nown to friends as the "People's Joan of Arc" and to enemies as the "Kansas Pythoness," Mary Elizabeth Lease was an electrifying orator who, one observer said, could "set a crowd hooting and harrahing at her will." Born in 1853 in Pennsylvania, she lived most of her adult life in Kansas. Married at age twenty, Lease bore five children, took in washing, and studied law by pinning her notes above her washtub.

In 1885, Lease became the first woman admitted to the Kansas bar and an ardent activist. Joining the Women's Christian Temperance Union and the Farmers' Alliance, she became a spokesperson for the Populist party, making over 160 speeches in 1890 on behalf of downtrodden farmers and laboring people. She later ran for the U.S. Senate, but damaged her party's fortune by refusing to unite with Democrats in opposition to big business and political corruption. "This is a nation of inconsistencies," proclaimed Lease, who backed prohibition, women's suffrage, and birth control. "We fought England for our liberty and put chains on four million blacks. We wiped out slavery and [then] by our tariff laws and national banks began a system of white wage slavery worse than the first."

Lease's turbulent career paralleled an eventful era, characterized by three themes: special-interest ascendancy, legislative accomplishment, and political exclusion. When she attacked the railroads and big business for exploiting farmers, she expressed the growing dissatisfaction with the greed and abuses of power exerted by large corporations and wealthy individuals. The era's venality seemed so widespread that when, in 1874, Mark Twain and Charles Dudley Warner satirized America as a land of shallow money grubbers in their novel *The Gilded Age*, the name stuck.

At the same time, Lease's rhetoric obscured economic and political accomplishments at the state and national levels. Between 1877 and 1900, Congress achieved legislative landmarks in railroad regulation, tariff and currency reform, and civil service despite partisan and regional rivalries. Meanwhile, the judiciary actively supported big business by defending property

The Nature of Party Politics

Issues of Legislation

LINKS TO THE WORLD
Missionaries

The Presidency Restrengthened

Discrimination, Disfranchisement, and Response

Agrarian Unrest and Populism

The Depression and Protests of the 1890s

The Silver Crusade and the Election of 1896

LEGACY FOR A PEOPLE AND A NATION
Interpreting a Fairy Tale

Online Study Center
This icon will direct you to interactive map and primary source activities on the website http://college.hmco.com/pic/nortonbrief7e

CHRONOLOGY

1873 • Congress ends coinage of silver dollars

1873–78 • Economic hard times hit

1876 • Hayes elected president

1878 • Bland-Allison Act requires Treasury to buy between $2 and $4 million in silver each month

1880 • Garfield elected president

1881 • Garfield assassinated; Arthur assumes the presidency

1883 • Pendleton Civil Service Act introduces merit system
• Supreme Court strikes down 1875 Civil Rights Act

1884 • Cleveland elected president

1886 • *Wabash* case declares that only Congress can limit interstate commerce rates

1887 • Farmers' Alliances form
• Interstate Commerce Commission begins regulating rates and practices of interstate shipping

1888 • B. Harrison elected president

1890 • McKinley Tariff raises tariff rates
• Sherman Silver Purchase Act commits Treasury to buying 4.5 million ounces of silver each month

• "Mississippi Plan" uses poll taxes and literacy tests to prevent African Americans from voting
• National American Woman Suffrage Association formed

1892 • Populist convention in Omaha draws up reform platform
• Cleveland elected president

1893 • Sherman Silver Purchase Act repealed

1893–97 • Major economic depression hits United States

1894 • Wilson-Gorman Tariff passes
• Coxey's army marches on Washington, D.C.

1895 • Cleveland deal with bankers saves gold reserves

1896 • McKinley elected president
• *Plessy v. Ferguson* establishes separate-but-equal doctrine

1899 • *Cummins v. County Board of Education* applies separate-but-equal doctrine to schools

1900 • Gold Standard Act requires all paper money to be backed by gold
• McKinley reelected president

rights against state and federal regulation. The presidency was occupied by respectable men who prepared the office for its more activist character after the turn of the century. Even so, exclusion—the third phenomenon—prevented the majority of Americans—including women, southern blacks, Indians, uneducated whites, and unnaturalized immigrants—from access to the tools of democracy.

Until the 1890s, special interests, accomplishment, and exclusion existed within a delicate political equilibrium characterized by a stable party system and balance of power among geographical sections. Then in the 1890s, rural discontent rumbled through the West and South, and a deep economic depression bared flaws in the industrial system. The 1896 presidential campaign stirred Americans with near-religious fervor. A new party arose, old parties split, sectional unity dissolved, and fundamental disputes about the nation's future climaxed. ◼

The Nature of Party Politics

*P*ublic interest in elections reached an all-time high between 1870 and 1896, with around 80 percent of eligible voters (white and black males in the North, somewhat lower rates among mostly white males in the South) consistently voting. (Under 50 percent typically do so today.) Politics served as a form of recreation, more popular than baseball, and included parades, picnics, and speeches.

As different groups competed for power and wealth, they formed coalitions. With some excep-

CULTURAL-
POLITICAL
ALIGNMENTS

tions, groups who opposed government interference in personal liberty identified with the Democratic Party; those who believed government could be an agent of moral reform identified with the Republican Party. Democrats included immigrant Catholics and Jews; Republicans consisted mostly of native-born Protestants. Democrats would restrict government power. Republicans believed in direct government action.

Adherents battled over how much government should control people's lives. The most contentious issues were use of leisure time and celebration of Sunday, the Lord's day. Protestant Republicans wanted to keep the Sabbath holy through legislation that would close bars, stores, and commercial amusements on Sundays. Immigrant Democrats, accustomed to feasting after church, fought saloon closings and other restrictions.

Allegiances to national parties and candidates were so evenly divided that no faction gained control for very long. Between 1877 and 1897, Republicans held the presidency for three terms, Democrats for two. Rarely did one party control the presidency and Congress simultaneously. From 1876 through 1892, presidential elections were extremely close. The outcome often hinged on the popular vote in a few populous northern states—Connecticut, New York, New Jersey, Ohio, Indiana, and Illinois.

Internal quarrels split both the Republican and Democratic parties. Among Republicans, New York's

PARTY FACTIONS

pompous senator Roscoe Conkling led one faction, known as "Stalwarts," and worked the spoils system to win government jobs for his supporters. The Stalwarts' rivals were the "Half

Breeds," led by James G. Blaine, who pursued influence as blatantly as Conkling did. On the sidelines stood more idealistic Republicans, or "Mugwumps" (supposedly an Indian term meaning "mug on one side of the fence, wump on the other"). Mugwumps such as Senator Carl Schurz of Missouri believed that only righteous men should govern. Meanwhile, Democrats subdivided into white-supremacy southerners, immigrant-stock and working-class urban political machines, and business-oriented advocates of low tariffs.

In each state, one party usually dominated, and often the state "boss" was a senator who parlayed his state power into national influence. Until the Seventeenth Amendment to the Constitution was ratified in 1913, state legislatures elected U.S. senators, and a senator could wield enormous influence with his command of federal jobs, and many brazenly did so.

Issues of Legislation

*W*ell into the 1880s, bitter hostilities from the Civil War and Reconstruction continued to divide Americans. Republicans capitalized on war memories by "waving the bloody shirt." As one Republican orator harangued in 1876, "Every man that tried to destroy this nation was a Democrat. . . . Soldiers, every scar you have on your heroic bodies was given you by a Democrat." In the South, Democratic candidates also waved the bloody shirt, calling Republicans traitors to white supremacy and states' rights.

The Grand Army of the Republic, an organization of 400,000 Union Army veterans, allied with the Republican Party and cajoled Congress into generous pensions for former Union soldiers and their widows. The Union Army spent $2 billion to fight the Civil War; veterans' pensions ultimately cost $8 billion, one of the largest welfare commitments the federal government has ever made. By 1900 soldiers' pensions accounted for roughly 40 percent of the federal budget. Confederate veterans received none of this money, though some southern states funded small pensions and built old-age homes for ex-soldiers.

The practice of awarding government jobs to party workers regardless of their qualifications, known

CIVIL SERVICE
REFORM

as the spoils system, predated the Civil War and flourished afterward. As the postal service and other

During the Gilded Age, American Christians contributed more money toward missionary work than toward other popular political and social causes. First intended to teach native peoples about the Bible, missionary projects focused increased attention overseas as the nineteenth century progressed, sending funds and volunteers to every part of the globe, including the Middle East, Africa, and China. Expanding beyond pure preaching, mission organizations sponsored construction of schools and hospitals and taught secular subjects as well as biblical learning.

American missionaries altered the educational climate in several countries. In Syria, they opened the American University of Beirut (first called the Syrian Protestant College), and the school soon developed departments of medicine, pharmacy, and commerce. Its nursing program was one of the few places where Middle Eastern women could receive technical training. Missionaries' efforts in the Middle East also increased interest in Arabic literature. Their use of Arabic printing presses to translate the Bible advanced the mass production of books for Middle Easterners.

In Africa, almost all leaders of the earliest independent African states had been educated in schools founded and taught by European and American missionaries, many of whom were African American. Protestant denominations believed that African American missionaries would be more effective than white missionaries in Africa.

By 1890, there were one hundred missionary physicians in China, who brought American medical techniques to 350,000 patients per year. Many other missionaries to China were unmarried American women whose feminist impulses fueled their opposition to practices such as foot binding, which they considered debasing to women.

American foreign missionaries in the late nineteenth century did not come close to realizing their goal of converting the world to Christ. When they tried to impose western customs, they were often rejected and sometimes persecuted. Yet they established churches that lasted for decades and schools that influenced native educational efforts. In the United States, divisions between liberals and fundamentalists in the 1920s destroyed the evangelical unity that previously made large missionary societies possible, and by the 1930s the heyday of American foreign missions was over.

Missionary work enabled American women to undertake humanitarian projects in foreign lands. Using both her gentility and her strength of character, Dr. Kate Woodall, shown in this photo from 1895, carried out her missionary work in China by training female medical students. (ABCFM Picture Collection: Individuals, Woodhull, Kate C., Houghton Library, Harvard College Library)

government agencies expanded, the number of federal jobs tripled, from 53,000 in 1865 to 166,000 in 1891. Elected officials scrambled to control these jobs to benefit themselves and their party. In return for comparatively short hours and high pay, appointees to federal positions pledged votes and a portion of their earnings to their patrons.

Shocked by such corruption, especially after the revelation of scandals in the Grant administration, some reformers began advocating appointments based on merit. Civil service reform accelerated in 1881 with the formation of the National Civil Service Reform League. That year, the assassination of President James Garfield by a distraught job seeker hastened the drive for change. The Pendleton Civil Service Act, which Congress passed in 1882 and President Chester Arthur signed in 1883, created the Civil Service Commission to oversee competitive examinations for government positions. The act gave the commission jurisdiction over only 10 percent of federal jobs, though the president could expand the list. Because the Constitution barred Congress from interfering in state affairs, civil service at the state and local levels developed more haphazardly.

But economic policy furnished the main issue of the Gilded Age. Railroads particularly provoked controversy. In their quest for customers, railroads engaged in rate wars, which hurt profits and angered shippers with inconsistent freight charges. On noncompetitive routes, railroads often boosted charges to compensate for unprofitably low rates on competitive routes. Railroads also played favorites, reducing rates to large shippers and offering free passenger passes to preferred customers and politicians.

Such favoritism stirred farmers, small merchants, and reform politicians to demand rate regulation. By **RAILROAD REGULATION** 1880 fourteen states had established commissions to limit freight and storage charges of state-chartered lines. Railroads fought back, arguing that the Constitution guaranteed them freedom to acquire and use property without government restraint. But in 1877, in *Munn v. Illinois,* the Supreme Court upheld state regulation, declaring that grain warehouses owned by railroads acted in the public interest and therefore must submit to regulation for "the common good."

But only the federal government could limit rates involving interstate commerce, as affirmed by the Supreme Court in the *Wabash* case of 1886. In 1887 Congress passed the Interstate Commerce Act. The law prohibited pools, rebates, and long-haul/short-haul rate discrimination, and created the Interstate Commerce Commission (ICC), the nation's first regulatory agency, to investigate railroad rate-making methods and issue cease-and-desist orders against illegal practices. The legislation's weak provisions for enforcement, however, left railroads room for evasion, and federal judges chipped away at ICC powers. In the *Maximum Freight Rate* case (1897), the Supreme Court ruled that the ICC lacked power to set rates, and in the *Alabama Midlands* case (1897), it overturned prohibitions against long-haul/short-haul discrimination. Even if weakened, regulation remained in force.

In 1816 Congress initially created a tariff, which levied duties (taxes) on imported goods, to protect **TARIFF POLICY** American products from European competition. But tariffs quickly became a tool by which special interests could enhance their profits. By the 1880s, these interests had succeeded in obtaining tariffs on more than four thousand items. A few economists and farmers argued for free trade, but most politicians still insisted that tariffs were necessary to support industry and preserve jobs.

The Republican Party put protective tariffs at the core of its agenda. Democrats complained that tariffs made prices artificially high by keeping out less expensive foreign goods, thereby benefiting domestic manufacturers while hurting farmers whose crops were not protected and consumers.

During the Gilded Age, revenues from tariffs and other levies created a surplus in the federal budget. Most Republicans, being businessmen, liked the idea that the government was earning more than it spent and hoped to keep the extra money as a Treasury reserve or for projects that would aid commerce. Democrats acknowledged a need for protection of some manufactured goods and raw materials, but they favored lower tariff duties to encourage foreign trade and reduce the Treasury surplus.

Manufacturers and their congressional allies firmly controlled tariff policy. The McKinley Tariff of 1890 boosted already-high rates by another 4 percent. When House Democrats passed a bill to trim tariffs in 1894, Senate Republicans added six hundred amendments restoring most cuts (Wilson-Gorman

Tariff). In 1897 the Dingley Tariff raised rates further. Attacks on duties made tariffs a symbol of privileged business in the public mind.

Monetary policy inflamed stronger emotions than tariffs. When increased industrial and agricul-

MONETARY
POLICY

tural production caused prices to fall after the Civil War, debtors and creditors had opposing reactions. Farmers suffered because their incomes dropped. And because high demand for a relatively limited amount of available money raised interest rates on loans, it was costly for them to borrow to pay off mortgages and other debts. They

■ Taking advantage of the new fad of bicycling (see Chapter 19), a cartoonist in an 1886 issue of the humor magazine *Puck* illustrates the controversy over silver coinage. Depicting two uncoordinated wheels, one a silver coin and the other a gold coin, the illustration conveys the message of how hard it was to proceed with conflicting kinds of currency. (Private Collection)

favored the coinage of silver to increase the amount of currency in circulation, which would reduce interest rates. Small businessmen agreed. Large businesses and bankers favored a stable, limited money supply backed only by gold, fearing that anything else would fluctuate and threaten investors' confidence in the U.S. economy.

Creditor-debtor tension translated into class divisions between haves and have-nots. The debate also reflected sectional cleavages: western silver-mining areas and agricultural regions of the South and West against the industrial Northeast.

By the 1870s, the currency controversy boiled down to gold versus silver. Previously, the government had bought gold and silver to back the national currency at a ratio that made a gold dollar worth sixteen times more than a silver dollar. The gold rush of 1848, however, increased the gold supply and lowered its market price relative to that of silver. Consequently, silver dollars disappeared as owners hoarded them. In 1873 Congress officially stopped coining them. The United States and many of its trading partners unofficially adopted the gold standard, meaning that their currency was backed chiefly by gold.

But within a few years, new mines in the American West began to flood the market with silver, and its price dropped. Because gold now was relatively less plentiful, it became worth more than sixteen times silver (the ratio reached twenty to one by 1890). Silver producers now wanted the government to resume buying silver at the old sixteen-to-one ratio.

Congress tried to compromise. The Bland-Allison Act (1878) authorized the Treasury to buy between $2 million and $4 million worth of silver monthly, and the Sherman Silver Purchase Act (1890) increased the government's silver purchase by specifying weight (4.5 million ounces) rather than dollars. Neither group was satisfied, however. Creditors wanted the government to stop buying silver, while debtors felt the legislation failed to expand the money supply satisfactorily. The issue would intensify during the 1896 presidential election.

In the Gilded Age, senators and representatives earned small salaries yet had to maintain residences

LEGISLATIVE
ACCOMPLISHMENTS

in their home district and in Washington. They had no private offices, worked long hours, wrote their own speeches, and paid for staff out of their own pockets.

The Presidency Restrengthened

*O*perating under the cloud of Andrew Johnson's impeachment, Grant's scandals, and doubts about the legitimacy of the 1876 election (see Chapter 16), American presidents between 1877 and 1900 moved to restore authority to their office. Proper and honest, Presidents Rutherford Hayes (1877–1881), James Garfield (1881), Chester Arthur (1881–1885), Grover Cleveland (1885–1889 and 1893–1897), Benjamin Harrison (1889–1893), and William McKinley (1897–1901) tried to act as legislative as well as administrative leaders. Each president initiated legislation and used the veto to guide national policy.

Rutherford B. Hayes had been a Union general and an Ohio congressman and governor before his

HAYES, GARFIELD, AND ARTHUR

disputed election to the presidency, which prompted opponents to label him "Rutherfraud." Hayes saw himself as reformer and conciliator, emphasizing national harmony over sectional rivalry. He tried to overhaul the spoils system by appointing civil service reformer Carl Schurz and battling New York's patronage king, Senator Conkling.

When Hayes declined to run for reelection in 1880, Republicans nominated another Ohio congressman and Civil War hero, James A. Garfield, who won by just 40,000 votes out of 9 million cast. By winning the pivotal states of New York and Indiana, however, Garfield carried the electoral college by 214 to 155. Garfield hoped to reduce the tariff, develop economic relations with Latin America, and fight patronage. But his chance to make lasting contributions ended in July 1881 when Charles Guiteau shot him in a Washington railroad station. Garfield lingered for seventy-nine days before dying.

Garfield's successor was Vice President Chester A. Arthur, a New York spoilsman whom Hayes had fired in 1878. Arthur became a temperate executive. He signed the Pendleton Civil Service Act, urged Congress to modify outdated tariff rates, and supported federal regulation of railroads. But congressional partisans frustrated his plans for reducing the tariff and strengthening the navy. Arthur lost the 1884 presidential nomination to James G. Blaine at the Republican National Convention.

Democrats nominated New York governor Grover Cleveland, a bachelor who had tainted his reputation when he admitted to fathering an illegitimate son. On election day Cleveland won by only 29,000 popular votes; his tiny margin of 1,149 votes in New York secured that state's 36 electoral votes, enough for a 219-to-182 victory in the electoral college. Cleveland may have won New York due to remarks by a Protestant minister, who equated Democrats with "rum, Romanism, and rebellion." Democrats eagerly publicized the slur among New York's large Irish Catholic population, urging voters to protest by supporting Cleveland.

Cleveland, the first Democratic president since James Buchanan (1857–1861), expanded civil service,

CLEVELAND AND HARRISON

vetoed hundreds of private pension bills, and urged Congress to cut tariff duties. When advisers worried about his chances for reelection, the president retorted, "What is the use of being elected or reelected, unless you stand for something?" But when Democrats renominated Cleveland for the presidency in 1888, businessmen in the party convinced him to moderate his attacks on tariffs.

Republicans in 1888 nominated Benjamin Harrison, former senator from Indiana and grandson of President William Henry Harrison (1841). Bribery and multiple voting helped Harrison win Indiana by 2,300 votes and New York by 14,000, ensuring his victory. (Democrats also indulged in such cheating, but Republicans proved more successful at it.) Although Cleveland outpolled Harrison by 90,000 popular votes, Harrison secured 233 electoral votes to Cleveland's 168.

The first president since 1875 whose party had majorities in both houses of Congress, Harrison influenced legislation with threats of vetoes, informal dinners, and consultations with politicians. The Congress of 1889–1891 passed 517 bills, 200 more than the average passed by Congresses between 1875 and 1889. Harrison appointed reformer Theodore Roosevelt as civil service commissioner. But under pressure from special interests, he signed the Dependents' Pension Act, which doubled the number of welfare recipients from 490,000 to 966,000 by providing pensions for disabled Union veterans and aid to their widows and minor children.

The Pension Act and other appropriations in 1890 pushed the federal budget past $1 billion for the first time. Voters reacted by unseating seventy-eight Republicans in the 1890 congressional elections. Seeking to capitalize on voter unrest, Democrats nominated Grover Cleveland to run against Harrison again in 1892. With large contributions from business, Cleveland beat Harrison by 370,000 popular votes (3 percent of the total) and won the electoral vote.

In office again, Cleveland's actions reflected political weakness and the power of business interests. Cleveland campaigned on sweeping tariff reform, but he failed to line up support in the Senate, where protectionists undercut his efforts. And when 120,000 boycotting railroad workers paralyzed commerce in the Pullman strike of 1894, Cleveland bowed to requests from railroad managers to send in troops (see Chapter 18).

Discrimination, Disfranchisement, and Response

Issues of race gave a peculiar quality to politics in the South. There, poor whites feared that newly enfranchised African American men would challenge their political and social superiority (real and imagined). Wealthy white landowners and merchants fanned these fears, using racism to divide whites and blacks from protesting their similar economic subjugation.

Most African Americans lived in the South and worked in agriculture. In 1880, 90 percent of all

VIOLENCE
AGAINST
AFRICAN
AMERICANS

southern blacks worked in farming or personal and domestic service—just as they had as slaves. Weapons, including a gun commonly known as a "nigger killer," were plentiful, and whites used them. Between 1889 and 1909, over seventeen hundred African Americans were lynched in the South, typically in sparsely populated districts where whites felt threatened by an influx of migrant blacks. Most lynching victims were accused of assault—rarely proved—on a white woman.

Protests arose on several fronts. In Memphis, for example, Ida B. Wells, a teacher in an African American school, reacted by establishing an antilynching newspaper in 1892, *The Free Speech and Headlight*. She urged local blacks to migrate to the West and fled to England to escape death threats. But she soon returned and wrote *A Red Record* (1895), which tabulated statistics on racial lynchings and served as a foundation for further protest campaigns.

Despite threats and intimidation, blacks formed the backbone of the southern Republican Party and

DISFRANCHISEMENT

won numerous elective offices, even after Reconstruction. In North Carolina, for example, eleven African Americans served in the state Senate and forty-three in the House between 1877 and 1890. White politicians sought restrictions that would disfranchise blacks, or deprive them of their right to vote. Beginning with Tennessee in 1889 and Arkansas in 1892, southern states levied poll taxes of $1 to $2, prohibitive to most blacks, who were poor and deep in debt. Other schemes disfranchised blacks who could not read.

The Supreme Court determined in *U.S. v. Reese* (1876) that Congress had no control over local and state elections other than upholding the Fifteenth Amendment, which prohibits states from denying the vote "on account of race, color, or previous condition of servitude." State legislatures found other ways to exclude black voters. For instance, an 1890 state constitutional convention established the "Mississippi Plan," requiring voters to pay a poll tax eight months before each election, to present the tax receipt at election time, and to prove that they could read and interpret the state constitution. Registration officials applied stiffer standards to blacks, even declaring black college graduates ineligible on grounds of illiteracy.

Such restrictions proved highly effective. In South Carolina, for example, 70 percent of eligible blacks voted in the 1880 presidential election; by 1896 the rate had dropped to 11 percent. By the 1900s, African Americans had effectively lost political rights in the South. Disfranchisement also affected poor whites, few of whom could meet poll tax, property, and literacy requirements. Thus, the total number of eligible voters in Mississippi shrank from 257,000 in 1876 to 77,000 in 1892.

Racial discrimination and legal segregation expanded. In a series of cases during the 1870s, the

LEGAL
SEGREGATION

Supreme Court opened the door to discrimination by ruling that the Fourteenth Amendment protected citizens' rights only against infringement by state governments but not from individuals or organizations. If blacks wanted legal protection from individual prejudice, the Court said, they must seek it from state laws because under the Tenth Amendment, states retained all powers not specifically assigned to Congress. These rulings climaxed in 1883 when the Court struck down the 1875 Civil Rights Act, which prohibited segregation in public facilities such as streetcars, theaters, and parks.

States, however, still could segregate on a "separate-but-equal" basis, as upheld by the Supreme Court in the famous case of *Plessy v. Ferguson* (1896). This case began in 1892 when the Citizens Committee, an organization of prominent New Orleans African Americans, chose Homer Plessy, a dark-skinned Creole, to stage a sit-in in a whites-only railroad car. The Citizens Committee hoped to challenge the law through Plessy's arrest. But in upholding Plessy's conviction, the Court stated that a state law providing for separate facilities for the two races was not unconstitutional because "a distinction which is founded in the color of the two races, and which must always exist so long as white men are distinguished from the other race by color—has no tendency to destroy the legal equality of the two races." In 1899 the Court legitimated school segregation in *Cummins v. County Board of Education,* until it was overturned by *Brown v. Board of Education* in 1954.

Segregation laws—known as Jim Crow laws—multiplied throughout the South, reminding African Americans of their inferior status. State and local statutes restricted them to the rear of streetcars, separate public drinking fountains and toilets, and separate sections of hospitals and cemeteries. Mobile, Alabama, passed a curfew requiring blacks to be off the streets by 10:00 P.M., and Atlanta mandated separate Bibles for swearing in black witnesses in court.

African American women and men challenged discrimination. Some boycotted racist businesses; others

AFRICAN
AMERICAN
ACTIVISM

considered moving to Africa. Still others promoted "Negro business enterprise." In 1898 Atlanta University professor John Hope urged blacks to become their own employers and supported Negro Business Men's Leagues. In the optimistic days following Reconstruction, many blacks saw higher education as a means of elevating their status. In all-black teachers' colleges, men and women sought opportunities for themselves and their race.

While disfranchisement pushed African American men out of public life, African American women used traditional roles as mothers, educators, and moral guardians to seek services and reforms. They successfully lobbied southern local and state governments for cleaner city streets, better public health, expanded charity services, and vocational education. Ida B. Wells moved to Chicago and continued her equal rights crusade by founding the Women's Era Club, the first civic organization for African American women. While black and white women sometimes united to improve the general community, white women often joined men in white supremacy campaigns.

In the North, white women sought equality through the vote; their successes, however, were lim-

WOMAN
SUFFRAGE

ited. Prior to 1869, each state determined who was qualified to vote. That year, the Fifteenth Amendment forbade states from denying the vote "on account of race, color or previous condition" but omitted any reference to sex. For the next twenty years, two organizations—the National Woman Suffrage Association (NWSA) and the American Woman Suffrage Association (AWSA)—crusaded for female suffrage. The NWSA, led by Elizabeth Cady Stanton and Susan B. Anthony, advocated women's rights in courts and workplaces as well as at the ballot box. The AWSA, led by former abolitionists Lucy Stone and Thomas Wentworth Higginson, focused narrowly on suffrage.

In 1878 Anthony persuaded Senator A. A. Sargent of California to introduce a constitutional amendment stating that the right to vote "shall not be denied or abridged by the United States or by any state on account of sex." A Senate committee killed the bill, but the NWSA had it reintroduced repeatedly over the next eighteen years. On the few occasions it did reach the Senate floor, it was rejected with the claim that suffrage would interfere with women's family obligations.

Meanwhile, the AWSA worked to amend state constitutions. (The groups merged in 1890 to form the National American Woman Suffrage Association.)

■ Livingstone College in North Carolina was one of several institutions of higher learning established by and for African Americans in the late nineteenth century. With a curriculum that emphasized training for educational and religious work in the South and in Africa, these colleges were coeducational, operating on the belief that both men and women could have public roles.   (Courtesy of Heritage Hall, Livingstone College, Salisbury, North Carolina)

Between 1870 and 1910, eleven states (mostly in the West) legalized limited woman suffrage. By 1890 nineteen states allowed women to vote on school issues, and three granted suffrage on tax and bond issues. Just as important, these campaigns helped train a corps of female leaders in political organizing and public speaking.

Agrarian Unrest and Populism

conomic inequities sparked a mass movement that would shake American society. The agrarian revolt began in Grange organizations in the early 1870s and accelerated within a decade as Farmers' Alliances formed in Texas and across the Cotton Belt and Great Plains. The movement flourished where tenancy, debt, weather, and insects endangered struggling farmers and inspired visions of a truly cooperative and democratic society.

Southern agriculture did not benefit much from mechanization (see Chapter 17). Tobacco and cotton, the principal southern crops, required constant hoeing and weeding by hand. Tobacco could not be harvested all at once because the leaves matured at different rates and stems were too fragile for machines. Thus, after the Civil War, southern landlords employed sharecroppers and tenant farmers to replace slaves.

SHARECROPPING AND TENANT FARMING IN THE SOUTH

Sharecropping and tenant farming entangled millions of black and white southerners in a web of debt and humiliation, at whose center stood the crop lien. Most farmers, too poor to have ready cash, borrowed to buy necessities, offering their future crop as collateral. After the crop was harvested and brought to market, the lender claimed the portion of the crop that would satisfy the loan. But often the debt exceeded the crop's value. So the farmer would pay off part of the debt, but borrow more for food and supplies for the coming year, sinking even deeper into debt.

Merchants frequently took advantage by inflating prices and charging interest ranging from 33 to 200 percent. Farmers, having pledged more than their crop's worth against such debts, often fell behind in payments and never recovered.

In the southern backcountry, farmers now devoted all of their land to cotton and had to purchase supplies such as flour, potatoes, and corn that they had grown prior to the Civil War. This shift toward commercial farming came about for two reasons: debts incurred during the war and Reconstruction forced farmers to grow crops that would bring in cash, and railroads enabled them to transport cotton to markets more easily than before. As they grew fewer subsistence crops, backcountry yeomen found themselves frequently at the mercy of merchants.

Online Study Center Improve Your Grade
Interactive Map:
The Expansion of Agriculture, 1860–1900

In the Midwest, as growers cultivated more land, as mechanization boosted productivity, and as foreign competition increased, supplies of agricultural products exceeded worldwide demand, leading to steady price drops for staple crops. A bushel of wheat that sold for $1.45 in 1866 brought only 80 cents in the mid-1880s and 49 cents by the mid-1890s. Meanwhile, transportation and storage fees remained high. In order to buy necessities and pay bills, farmers had to produce more, but the more they produced, the lower crop prices dropped.

HARDSHIP IN THE MIDWEST AND WEST

The West suffered special hardships. In Colorado absentee capitalists seized control of technology as well as access to transportation and water. Charges of monopolistic control by railroads echoed among farmers, miners, and stockmen in Wyoming and Montana. In California, Washington, and Oregon, wheat and fruit growers found their opportunities blocked by railroads' control of transportation and storage rates.

With aid from Oliver H. Kelley, a clerk in the Department of Agriculture, farmers in almost every state during the 1860s and 1870s founded local organizations called Granges. By 1875 the Grange had twenty thousand branches and a mil-

GRANGE MOVEMENT

lion members. Strongest in the Midwest and South, Granges first served a social function, sponsoring meetings and educational events to relieve the loneliness of farm life. Family-oriented, local Granges welcomed women's participation.

As membership flourished, Granges turned to economic and political action. Local branches formed cooperative associations to buy supplies and market crops and livestock. Some Grangers operated farm-implement factories and insurance companies. Most enterprises failed, however, because farmers lacked capital for large-scale buying and because large manufacturers undercut them.

Granges declined in the late 1870s, after convincing states to establish agricultural colleges, electing sympathetic legislators, and securing state laws regulating transportation and storage rates. But corporations won court support to overturn Granger laws in the *Wabash* case of 1886. Disavowing party politics, Granges did not challenge business interests within the two major parties. As a result, Granges again became farmers' social clubs.

In the Southwest, migrations of English-speaking ranchers into Mexican pastureland sparked another agrarian protest. In the late 1880s, a group calling itself Las Gorras Blancas, or White Hats, struggled to control ancestral lands, harassing Anglo ranchers and destroying fences on public land. Their cause, however, could not halt Anglos from legally buying and using public land, and by 1900 many Hispanics had given up farming to work as agricultural laborers or migrate into the cities.

THE WHITE HATS

By 1890, two networks of Farmers' Alliances—one in the Great Plains, one in the South—became the center of rural activism. The first Farmers' Alliances arose in Texas, where hard-pressed small farmers rallied against crop liens, merchants, and railroads. Using traveling lecturers to build membership, the southern Alliance extended into other states and boasted 2 million members by 1889. A separate Colored Farmers' National Alliance claimed 1 million black members. The Plains movement in the late 1880s organized 2 million members in Kansas, Nebraska, and the Dakotas.

FARMERS' ALLIANCES

Farmers' Alliances fostered loyalty through rallies, educational meetings, and cooperative buying and selling agreements, and encouraged women's participation.

They also proposed a subtreasury plan to relieve the most serious rural problems: shortages of cash and credit. The plan first called for the federal government to construct warehouses where farmers could store nonperishable crops while awaiting higher prices; the government would then loan farmers Treasury notes valued at 80 percent of the market price of stored crops. Farmers could use these notes for debts and purchases. Once the crops were sold, farmers would repay the loans plus small interest and storage fees, thereby avoiding the exploitative crop-lien system.

The subtreasury plan's second part would provide low-interest government loans to farmers to buy land.

PROBLEMS IN ACHIEVING ALLIANCE UNITY These loans, along with the Treasury notes for stored crops, would inject cash into the economy and encourage the kind of inflation that advocates hoped would raise crop prices without raising other prices.

If Farmers' Alliances had been able to unite, they could have made a formidable force, but racial and sectional differences and personality clashes thwarted such attempts. Racist voting restrictions weakened potential Alliance voter strength. Also, racism impeded acceptance of blacks by white Alliances. Many poor white farmers came from families that had supported the Ku Klux Klan during Reconstruction. Some had owned slaves, considered African Americans inferior, and took comfort in the belief that there always would be people worse off than they were.

Northern and southern Alliances favored government regulation of transportation and communications, equitable taxation, currency reform, and prohibition of landownership by foreign investors, but regional differences further prevented unity. Northern farmers, mostly Republicans, wanted protective tariffs to keep out foreign grain. White southerners, mostly Democrats, wanted low tariffs to hold down costs of foreign manufactured goods.

Online Study Center Improve Your Grade
Primary Source:
Tom Watson Indicts Corporate Plunder

Growing membership drew Alliances into politics. By 1890 farmers had elected several officeholders sympathetic to their cause, especially in the South, where Alliances controlled four governorships, eight state legislatures, and forty-seven seats in

RISE OF POPULISM

Congress (forty-four in the House, three in the Senate). In the Midwest, Alliance candidates often ran on third-party tickets, with some success in Kansas, Nebraska, and the Dakotas. Leaders crisscrossed the country to solidify support for a new party. In summer 1890, the Kansas Alliance held a "convention of the people" and nominated candidates who swept the state's fall elections. Formation of this People's, or Populist, Party gave a title to Alliance political activism. (Populism is the political doctrine that asserts the rights and powers of the common people in their struggle with the privileged elite.) By 1892 southern Alliance members joined northern counterparts in St. Louis in summoning a People's Party convention in Omaha, Nebraska, on July 4 to draft a platform and nominate a presidential candidate.

As its presidential candidate, the party nominated James B. Weaver of Iowa, a former Union general and supporter of an expanded money supply. Charging that inequality (between white classes) threatened to splinter American society, the new party's platform declared, "The fruits of the toil of millions are boldly stolen to build up colossal fortunes for a few." Claiming that "wealth belongs to him that creates it," the document addressed three central sources of rural unrest: transportation, land, and money. Frustrated with weak regulation, Populists demanded government ownership of railroad and telegraph lines. The monetary plank called for the government to make more money available for farm loans and to base money on free and unlimited coinage of silver. Other planks advocated a graduated income tax, postal savings banks, direct election of U.S. senators, and a shorter workday.

The Populist campaign featured dynamic personalities such as Mary Elizabeth Lease and "Sockless Jerry" Simpson, an unschooled but canny rural reformer who got his nickname after he ridiculed wealthy people for their silk stockings, causing a reporter to carp that Simpson probably wore no stockings at all. The South produced leaders such as Texas's Charles W. Macune, Georgia's Tom Watson, and North Carolina's Leonidas Polk. Minnesota's Ignatius Donnelly, pseudoscientist and writer of apocalyptic novels, became chief ideologue of the northern plains and penned the platform's thunderous language.

POPULIST SPOKESPEOPLE

Not since 1856 had a third party done so well in its first national effort. Weaver garnered 8 percent of the popular vote in 1892, majorities in four states, and twenty-two electoral votes. Nevertheless, the party faced a dilemma of whether to stand by its principles or compromise to gain power. Populist candidates were mainly successful in the West. The vote-rich Northeast ignored Weaver, and Alabama was the only southern state that gave Populists as much as one-third of its votes.

Still, Populism gave rural southerners and westerners faith in the future, especially the 1896 presidential election. Amid hardship, millions of people came to believe that a cooperative democracy in which government would ensure equal opportunity could overcome corporate power.

The Depression and Protests of the 1890s

I n 1893, shortly before Grover Cleveland's second presidency, the Philadelphia and Reading Railroad, once profitable, went bankrupt. Like other railroads, it had borrowed heavily to lay track and build stations and bridges. Overexpansion cut into profits, and ultimately the company was unable to pay its debts.

Similar problems beset manufacturers. For example, output at McCormick farm machinery factories was nine times greater in 1893 than in 1879, but revenues had only tripled. The company bought more equipment and squeezed more work out of fewer laborers, but it only enlarged debt and unemployment. Jobless workers also could not pay their bills, and banks suffered when customers defaulted. The failure of the National Cordage Company in May 1893 sparked a chain reaction of business and bank closings: five hundred banks and sixteen hundred businesses failed by year's end. Between 1893 and 1897, the nation suffered a devastating economic depression.

Nearly 20 percent of the labor force was jobless during the depression. Falling demand caused prices to drop between 1892 and 1895, but layoffs and wage cuts more than offset declining living costs. Many people could not afford basic necessities. The New York police estimated that twenty thousand homeless and jobless people roamed city streets.

As the depression deepened, the currency dilemma reached a crisis. The Sherman Silver Purchase Act of 1890 had committed the government to use Treasury notes (silver certificates) to buy 4.5 million ounces of silver each month. Recipients could redeem these certificates for gold, at the ratio of one ounce of gold for every sixteen ounces of silver. But a western mining boom increased silver supplies, causing its market value to fall and prompting holders of Sherman silver notes and Civil War greenbacks to exchange their notes for more valuable gold. As a result, the nation's gold reserve dwindled, falling below $100 million in early 1893.

CONTINUING CURRENCY PROBLEMS

If investors believed that the country's gold reserve was disappearing, they would lose confidence in America's economic stability and refrain from investing. British capitalists, for example, owned some $4 billion in American stocks and bonds and were likely to stop investing if dollars were to depreciate. The lower the gold reserve dropped, the more people rushed to redeem their money. Panic spread, causing more bankruptcies and unemployment.

To protect the gold reserves, President Cleveland called a special session of Congress to repeal the Sherman Silver Purchase Act. Repeal passed in late 1893, but the run on gold continued through 1894. In early 1895 reserves fell to $41 million, and Cleveland accepted an offer of 3.5 million ounces of gold for $65 million in federal bonds from a banking syndicate led by financier J. P. Morgan. When the bankers resold the bonds, they made a $2 million profit. Cleveland claimed that he had saved the reserves, but discontented farmers, workers, silver miners, and some of Cleveland's Democratic allies saw only his humiliation at the hands of businessmen.

The deal between Cleveland and Morgan did not end the depression. After improving slightly in 1895, the economy plunged again. Farm income, declining since 1887, continued to slide; factories closed; banks restricted withdrawals. The tight money supply depressed housing construction and dried up jobs. Cities such as Detroit allowed citizens to cultivate "potato patches" on vacant land to alleviate food shortages. Urban police stations filled up nightly with vagrants who had no other place to stay.

In the final years of the century, gold discoveries in Alaska, good harvests, and industrial growth

CONSEQUENCES OF THE DEPRESSION

brought relief. But the downturn hastened the crumbling of the old economic system and the emergence of a new one. The American economy had become national rather than sectional. When farmers in the West fell into debt, they affected the economic health of railroads, farm-implement manufacturers, and banks in other regions. Moreover, the corporate consolidation that characterized the new business system was beginning to solidify as the depression hit. When contraction occurred, companies that had expanded too rapidly were dragged down by their reckless debts, and they pulled other industries with them.

A new global marketplace was emerging, forcing American farmers to contend not only with discriminatory transportation rates and falling crop prices at home, but also with Canadian and Russian wheat growers, Argentine cattle ranchers, Indian and Egyptian cotton manufacturers, and Australian wool producers. And the glutted domestic market persuaded American businessmen to seek new markets abroad (discussed in Chapter 22).

The depression exposed fundamental tensions in the industrial system. Technological and organiza-

DEPRESSION-ERA PROTESTS

tional changes had been widening the gap between employees and employers for half a century (see Chapter 18). Protests began with the railroad strikes of 1877. The vehemence of those strikes, and their support by working-class people, raised fears that the United States would experience a popular uprising like the one in Paris six years earlier, which had briefly overturned the government and introduced communist principles. The Haymarket riot of 1886, a general strike in New Orleans in 1891, and the prolonged strike at the Carnegie Homestead Steel plant in 1892 heightened anxieties. In 1892 violence erupted at a silver mine in Coeur d'Alene, Idaho, where striking miners, angered by wage cuts and a lockout, seized the mine and battled federal troops.

In 1894 there were over thirteen hundred strikes and countless riots. Contrary to accusations of business leaders, few protesters were anarchists or communists. Instead, they were men and women who believed that in a democracy their voices should be heard.

Small numbers of socialists did participate in these and other confrontations. Furthermore, personal ex-

SOCIALISTS

perience convinced many workers who never became socialists to agree with Karl Marx (1818–1883), the German philosopher and father of communism, that whoever controls the means of production determines how well people live. Marx wrote that industrial capitalism generates profits by paying workers less than the value of their labor and that mechanization and mass production alienate workers from their labor. According to Marx, only by abolishing the return on capital—profits—could labor receive its true value, possible only if workers owned the means of production. Marx predicted that workers worldwide would revolt and seize factories, farms, banks, and transportation lines. This revolution would establish a socialist order of justice and equality.

In America, socialism suffered from lack of strong leadership and disagreement over how to achieve Marx's vision. Much of the movement consisted of ideas brought by immigrants—first Germans, later Russian Jews, Italians, Hungarians, and Poles. It splintered into small groups, such as the Socialist Labor Party, which failed to attract the mass of unskilled laborers because it often focused on doctrine while ignoring workers' everyday needs. Social mobility and the philosophy of individualism also undermined socialist aims. Workers hoped to benefit through education, through property acquisition, or by becoming their own boss; thus, most American workers sought individual advancement rather than the betterment of all.

In 1894 an inspiring Socialist leader arose in response to the government's quashing of the Pullman

EUGENE V. DEBS

strike and of the newly formed American Railway Union. Eugene V. Debs converted to socialism while serving a six-month prison term for defying an injunction against the strike. Once released, he became the leading spokesman for American socialism, combining visionary Marxism with Jeffersonian and Populist antimonopolism. Debs captivated audiences with indignant attacks on the free-enterprise system. "Many of you think you are competing," he would lecture. "Against whom? Against Rockefeller?

About as I would if I had a wheelbarrow and competed with the Santa Fe [railroad] from here to Kansas City." By 1900 the group soon to be called the Socialist Party of America was uniting around Debs.

In 1894 Debs shared public attention with Jacob S. Coxey, a quiet businessman from Massillon, Ohio.

COXEY'S ARMY — Coxey believed that the government should aid debtors by issuing $500 million of "legal tender" paper money, making low-interest loans to local governments, and using the loaned money to pay the unemployed to build roads and other public works. He planned to publicize his scheme by leading a march from Massillon to Washington, D.C., gathering a "petition in boots" of unemployed workers along the way.

Coxey's army, about 200 strong, left in March 1894. Moving across Ohio into Pennsylvania, the marchers received food and housing in depressed industrial towns and rural villages and added new recruits. A dozen similar marches from places such as Seattle, San Francisco, and Los Angeles also began the trek eastward. Sore feet prompted some to commandeer trains, but most processions were law-abiding.

Coxey's band of 500, including women and children, entered Washington on April 30. The next day (May Day, a date traditionally associated with socialist demonstrations), the group, armed with "war clubs of peace," marched to the Capitol. When Coxey and a few others vaulted the wall surrounding the Capitol grounds, mounted police routed the crowd. Police dragged Coxey away as he tried to speak from the Capitol steps. As arrests and clubbings continued, Coxey's dream demonstration of 400,000 jobless workers dissolved.

Unlike socialists, who wished to replace the capitalist system, Coxey's troops merely wanted more jobs and better living standards. The brutal reactions of officials, however, reveal how threatening dissenters such as Coxey and Debs were to the existing social order.

The Silver Crusade and the Election of 1896

ocial protest and economic depression made the presidential election of 1896 seem pivotal. Debates over money and power were climax-

ing, Democrats and Republicans battled to control Congress and the presidency, and the Populist party stood at the center of the political whirlwind.

As late as 1894, Populist candidates made good showings in western and southern elections, but the

POPULIST PARTY — party was underfinanced and underorganized. It had strong candidates, but not enough of them to effectively challenge the major parties and convince voters to abandon the Republicans or Democrats.

The Populist crusade against "money power" settled on the issue of silver, which many believed would solve the nation's complex ills.

FREE SILVER — To them, free coinage of silver symbolized an end to special privileges for the rich and the return of government to the people by lifting common people out of debt, increasing the cash in circulation, and reducing interest rates.

As the election of 1896 approached, Populists had to decide whether to join with sympathetic factions of the major parties, thus risking a loss of identity, or remain an independent third party. Except in mining areas of the Rocky Mountain states, where free coinage of silver had strong support, Republicans were unlikely allies because their support for the gold standard and big business represented what Populists opposed.

Alliance with northern and western Democrats was more plausible, since there the Democratic Party retained vestiges of antimonopoly ideology and sympathy for a looser currency system despite the influence of "gold Democrats" such as President Cleveland and Senator David Hill of New York. Fusion with southern Democrats seemed less likely, since there the party constituted the very power structure against which farmers had revolted in the late 1880s. Whatever they chose to do, Populists ensured that the election of 1896 would be the most issue oriented since 1860.

Each party was divided. For a year, Ohio industrialist Marcus A. Hanna had been maneuvering to

REPUBLICAN NOMINATION OF MCKINLEY — win the Republican nomination for Ohio's governor, William McKinley, and had corralled enough delegates to succeed. The Republicans' only distress occurred when they adopted a moderate platform supporting gold, rejecting a prosilver stance proposed by Colorado senator Henry M. Teller. Teller, who had been among the party's founders forty years earlier, walked out in tears, taking a small group of silver Republicans with him.

At the Democratic convention, prosilver delegates wearing silver badges and waving silver banners paraded through the Chicago Amphitheatre. A *New York World* reporter remarked that "all the silverites need is a Moses." They found one in William Jennings Bryan.

WILLIAM JENNINGS BRYAN

Bryan, age thirty-six, arrived at the Democratic convention as a member of a contested Nebraska delegation. A former congressman whose support for coinage of silver had annoyed President Cleveland, Bryan found the depression's impact on midwestern farmers distressing. Shortly after the convention seated Bryan, he joined the resolutions committee and helped write a platform calling for free coinage of silver. Bryan addressed the full convention, and his now-famous words ignited the delegates:

> Having behind us the producing masses of this nation and the world, supported by the commercial interests, the laboring interests, and the toilers everywhere, we will answer [the wealthy classes'] demand for a gold standard by saying to them: You shall not press down upon the brow of labor this crown of thorns, you shall not crucify mankind upon a cross of gold.

After that speech, delegates had no trouble supporting Bryan as presidential nominee. In accepting the silverite goals of southerners and westerners and repudiating Cleveland's policies, the Democratic Party became more attractive to discontented farmers. But it too alienated a dissenting minority wing of gold Democrats, who withdrew and nominated their own candidate.

Bryan's nomination presented the Populist party convention with a dilemma. Should Populists join Democrats in support of Bryan, or should they nominate their own candidate? Some reasoned that supporting a different candidate would split the anti-McKinley vote and guarantee a Republican victory. The convention compromised, first naming Tom Watson as its vice-presidential nominee to preserve party identity (Democrats had nominated Maine

shipping magnate Arthur Sewall for vice president) and then nominating Bryan for president.

The campaign, as Kansas journalist William Allen White observed, "took the form of religious frenzy." Bryan preached that "every great economic question is in reality a great moral question." Republicans countered Bryan's attacks on privilege by predicting chaos if he won. Hanna invited thousands of people to McKinley's home in Canton, Ohio, where the candidate plied them with homilies on moderation and prosperity, promising something for everyone. In an appeal to working-class voters, Republicans stressed the new jobs that a protective tariff would create.

The election revealed that the political standoff had finally ended. McKinley, symbol of urban and corporate ascendancy, beat Bryan by over 600,000 popular votes and won in the electoral college by 271 to 176.

ELECTION RESULTS

Bryan worked hard to rally the nation, but obsession with silver undermined his effort and prevented Populists from building the urban-rural coalition that would have expanded their political appeal. Urban workers, who might have benefited from Populist goals, shied away from the silver issue out of fear that free coinage would shrink the value of their wages. Labor leaders such as the AFL's Samuel Gompers, though partly sympathetic, would not commit themselves fully because they viewed farmers as businessmen, not workers. And socialists such as Daniel DeLeon denounced Populists as "retrograde" because they believed in free enterprise. Although Populists and fusion candidates won a few state and congressional elections, the Bryan-Watson ticket of the Populist party polled only 222,600 votes nationwide. Thus, the Populist crusade collapsed.

As president, McKinley signed the Gold Standard Act (1900), requiring that all paper money be backed by gold. A seasoned politician, McKinley had guided passage of record-high tariff rates in 1890 when he was a congressman from Ohio. He accordingly supported the Dingley Tariff of 1897, which raised duties even higher. An upward swing of the business cycle and a money supply enlarged by gold discoveries in Alaska, Australia, and South Africa helped restore prosperity. To sustain prosperity at home, McKinley encouraged

THE MCKINLEY PRESIDENCY

imperialistic ventures in Latin America and the Pacific (covered in Chapter 22). Good times and victory in the Spanish-American War enabled him to beat Bryan again in 1900.

Summary *Online Study Center* ACE the Test

politicians during the Gilded Age prepared the nation for the twentieth century. Laws encouraging economic growth with some principles of regulation, measures expanding government agencies while reducing crass patronage, federal intervention in trade and currency issues, and a more active presidency all evolved during the 1870s and 1880s.

True to Mary Lease's characterization, the United States remained a "nation of inconsistencies." Those who supported disfranchisement of African Americans and continued discrimination against blacks and women still polluted politics. Nor could the system tolerate radical views such as those expressed by socialists, Coxey, or Populists.

The 1896 election realigned national politics. The Republican Party, founded in the 1850s amid a crusade against slavery, became the majority party by emphasizing government aid to business, attracting urban workers, and playing down its moralism. The Democratic Party miscalculated on the silver issue and held its traditional support only in the South. After 1896, suspicion of party politics increased, and voter participation rates declined.

Populism failed because the political system lacked the ability to accept third parties. The structure of Congress gave the two-party system enormous power, making it difficult for the few Populist representatives to speak, let alone serve on committees and promote reform legislation.

Nevertheless, by 1920, many Populist goals were achieved, including regulation of railroads, banks, and utilities; shorter workdays; a variant of the subtreasury plan; a graduated income tax; direct election of senators; and the secret ballot. These reforms succeeded because immigration, urbanization, and industrialization had transformed the United States into a pluralistic society in which compromise had become a political fact of life. As the Gilded Age ended, business was still in the ascendancy, and large segments of the population were still excluded from political and economic opportunity. But the winds of reform had begun to blow more strongly.

LEGACY FOR A PEOPLE AND A NATION
Interpreting a Fairy Tale

The Wizard of Oz, one of the most popular movies of all time, began as a work of juvenile literature by journalist L. Frank Baum in 1900. Originally titled *The Wonderful Wizard of Oz,* the story used memorable characters to create an adventurous quest.

Adults, however, were tempted to search for hidden meanings. In 1964 one scholar, Henry M. Littlefield, asserted that Baum really intended to write a Populist parable about the conditions of overburdened farmers and laborers. Dorothy symbolized the well-intentioned common person; the Scarecrow, the struggling farmer; the Tin Man, the industrial worker. Hoping for a better life, these friends, along with the Cowardly Lion (William Jennings Bryan), followed a yellow brick road (the gold standard) that led nowhere. The Emerald City they find is presided over by a wizard. A typical politician, the wizard tries to be all things to all people, but Dorothy reveals him as a fraud. Dorothy is able to leave this muddled society and return to her simple Kansas farm family of Aunt Em and Uncle Henry by using her magical silver slippers (representing coinage of silver, though the movie made them red).

Subsequent theorists found additional supportive symbols, such as Oz being the abbreviation for ounces (oz.), the chief measurement of gold; the Wicked Witch of the East—who, Baum wrote, made the little people (Munchkins) "slaves for her night and day"—could represent industrial capitalism.

But in 1983, historian William R. Leach asserted that Baum's masterpiece actually was a celebration of urban consumer culture. Its language exalted the opulence of Emerald City, which to Leach resembled the "White City" of the Chicago World's Fair of 1893. Baum's career supported this new interpretation. Before he was a writer, he designed display windows and was involved in theater— activities that gave him an appreciation of modern urban life.

The real legacy of *The Wonderful Wizard of Oz* has been its ability to provoke differing interpretations. Baum's fairy tale, the first real American work of this sort, has bequeathed many fascinating images about the diversity and contradictions of American culture.

THE PROGRESSIVE ERA 1895–1920

a coworker once described Florence Kelley as a "guer-rilla warrior" in the "wilderness of industrial wrongs." A com-manding woman, Kelley was a leader in guiding the United States out of the tangled swamp of unregulated industrial capitalism into the twentieth-century welfare state.

The daughter of a Republican congressman from Philadelphia, Kelley graduated from Cornell University in 1883. She prepared to study law but was denied admission to the University of Pennsylvania because she was fe-male. Instead, she traveled to Europe and joined a group of socialists in Zurich, who alerted her to the plight of the underprivileged. She married a so-cialist Russian medical student and returned to New York City in 1886. When the marriage collapsed from debts and physical abuse, Kelley took her three children to Chicago in 1891. She moved into Hull House, a settlement-house residence in the slums where middle-class reformers lived, while assist-ing and learning from working-class immigrants.

Until the 1890s, Kelley's life had been male oriented, influenced first by her father, then by her husband. At Hull House, Kelley entered a female-dominated environment, where women applied helping skills to better society.

Over the next decade, Kelley became the nation's most ardent advocate of improved conditions for working-class women and children. She investi-gated and publicized the exploitative sweatshop system in Chicago's garment industry, lobbied for laws prohibiting child labor and regulating women's working hours, and served as Illinois's first factory inspector. Her work helped create new professions for women in social service, and her strategy of investigating and crusading for action became a model for reform.

During the 1890s, economic depression, labor violence, political up-heaval, and foreign entanglements shook the nation. By 1900, however, the political tumult had calmed, and economic depression seemed to be over. The nation emerged victorious from a war against Spain (covered in Chapter 22), and a new era of dynamic political leaders such as Theodore Roosevelt and Woodrow Wilson was dawning. A sense of renewal both intensified anxiety

The Varied Progressive Impulse

Governmental and Legislative Reform

LINKS TO THE WORLD
Russian Temperance

New Ideas in Social Institutions

Challenges to Racial and Sexual Discrimination

Theodore Roosevelt and the Revival of the Presidency

Woodrow Wilson and the Extension of Reform

LEGACY FOR A PEOPLE AND A NATION
Margaret Sanger, Planned Parenthood, and the Birth-Control Controversy

Online Study Center
This icon will direct you to interactive map and primary source activities on the website
http://college.hmco.com/pic/nortonbrief7e

CHRONOLOGY

1895 • Booker T. Washington gives Atlanta Compromise speech
• National Association of Colored Women founded

1898 • *Holden v. Hardy* upholds limits on miners' working hours

1900 • McKinley reelected

1901 • McKinley assassinated; T. Roosevelt assumes the presidency

1904 • T. Roosevelt elected president
• *Northern Securities* case dissolves railroad trust

1905 • *Lochner v. New York* removes limits on bakers' working hours

1906 • Hepburn Act tightens ICC control over railroads
• Meat Inspection Act passed
• Pure Food and Drug Act passed

1908 • Taft elected president
• *Muller v. Oregon* upholds limits on women's working hours

1909 • NAACP founded

1910 • Mann-Elkins Act reinforces ICC powers
• White Slave Traffic Act (Mann Act) prohibits transportation of women for "immoral purposes"

1911 • Society of American Indians founded

1912 • Woodrow Wilson elected president

1913 • Sixteenth Amendment ratified, legalizing federal income tax
• Seventeenth Amendment ratified, providing for direct election of U.S. senators
• Underwood Tariff institutes income tax
• Federal Reserve Act establishes central banking system

1914 • Federal Trade Commission created to investigate unfair trade practices
• Clayton Anti-Trust Act outlaws monopolistic business practices

1916 • Wilson reelected
• Adamson Act mandates eight-hour workday for railroad workers

1919 • Eighteenth Amendment ratified, establishing prohibition of alcoholic beverages

1920 • Nineteenth Amendment ratified, giving women the vote in federal elections

over continuing social and political problems and raised hopes that democracy could be reconciled with capitalism.

Between 1895 and 1920, a series of complex reform movements emerged, seeking to restore American society, values, and institutions. By the 1910s reformers were calling themselves "Progressives," and two years later they formed a political party. Historians have used the term *Progressivism* to refer to the

era's spirit while disagreeing over its meaning and over which groups and individuals actually were Progressive.

The reform impulse indeed had many sources. Industrial capitalism had created awesome technology, unprecedented productivity, and vast consumer goods. But it also brought harmful overproduction, domineering monopolies, labor strife, and the spoiling of natural resources. Burgeoning cities facilitated cultural amenities but also bred poverty, disease, and crime. Rising immigration and a new professional class reconfigured the social order. And the depression of the 1890s led many leaders to conclude that the central promise of American life was not being kept; equality of opportunity was a myth.

Progressives organized around three goals. First, they sought to end abuses of power. Progressives made trustbusting, consumers' rights, and good government compelling political issues.

Second, Progressives aimed to supplant corrupt power with humane institutions such as schools and medical clinics. They abandoned notions that hard work and good character guaranteed success and that the poor were responsible for their plight. Instead, Progressives acknowledged that society bore responsibility for improving individual lives, and they believed that government must protect the common good and elevate public interest above self-interest. Their attitude challenged entrenched views on women's roles, race relations, education, legal and scientific thought, and morality.

Third, Progressives wanted to establish bureaus of experts that would end wasteful competition and promote social and economic order. Just as corporations applied scientific method—planning, control, and predictability—to ensure economic efficiency, Progressives advocated expertise and planning to achieve social and political efficiency.

Progressives had faith in the ability of humankind to create a better world. Rising incomes, new educational opportunities, and increased availability of goods and services inspired confidence that social improvement would follow. Judge Ben Lindsey of Denver, who spearheaded juvenile delinquency reform, expressed the Progressive creed when he wrote, "In the end the people are bound to do the right thing, no matter how much they fail at times." ■

The Varied Progressive Impulse

*a*s the twentieth century dawned, party loyalty eroded and voter turnout declined. In northern states, voter participation in presidential elections dropped from Gilded Age levels of 80 percent to less than 60 percent. In southern states, where poll taxes and literacy tests excluded most African Americans and many poor whites from voting, it fell below 30 percent. At the same time, the political system was opening to new interest groups, each championing its own cause.

Many local voluntary organizations became national after 1890 and tried to shape public policy.

NATIONAL ASSOCIATIONS AND FOREIGN INFLUENCES

These organizations included professional associations such as the American Bar Association; women's organizations such as the National American Woman Suffrage Association, issue-oriented groups such as the National Consumers League, civic clubs such as the National Municipal League, and minority associations such as the National Negro Business League. Because they were usually independent from political parties, these groups made politics more fragmented and issue driven than in earlier eras.

American reformers transferred foreign ideas for reorganizing society to America. Some were introduced by Americans such as Florence Kelley who had observed reforms in England, France, and Germany, and others by foreigners traveling in the United States. The settlement-house model was directly copied from England; other reforms, such as old-age insurance, subsidized workers' housing, city planning, and rural reconstruction, were modified to suit America. Although Populist, rural-based goals of moral regeneration, political democracy, and antimonopolism lingered, the Progressive quest for social justice and educational and legal reform had a largely urban bent.

The new middle class—men and women in law, medicine, engineering, settlement house and social

THE NEW MIDDLE CLASS AND MUCKRAKERS

work, religion, teaching, and business—formed the vanguard of Progressive reform. Offended by inefficiency and immorality in business and government, these people sought to apply the rationalism of their professions to social problems.

Progressive views were conveyed by journalists whom Theodore Roosevelt dubbed muckrakers (after a character in the Puritan allegory *Pilgrim's Progress* who, rather than looking heavenward at beauty, looked downward and raked the muck to find what was wrong with life). Muckrakers fed public taste for scandal by exposing social, economic, and political wrongs. Investigative articles in popular magazines attacked adulterated foods, fraudulent insurance, prostitution, and political corruption. Lincoln Steffens hoped his exposés of bosses' misrule in *McClure's* (later published as *The Shame of the Cities* in 1904) would inspire mass outrage and reform. Other well-known muckraking works included Upton Sinclair's novel *The Jungle* (1906), highlighting the perils of the meatpacking industry; and Ida M. Tarbell's critical history of Standard Oil (first published in *McClure's*, 1902–1904).

Progressives advocated nominating candidates through direct primaries instead of party caucuses. To make officeholders more responsible, they urged adoption of the initiative permitting voters to propose new laws; the referendum, which enabled voters to accept or reject a law; and the recall, which allowed voters to remove offending officials from office.

The Progressive spirit also attracted some businessmen and wealthy women. Executives like Alexander Cassatt of the Pennsylvania Railroad

UPPER-CLASS REFORMERS

supported some government regulation to protect their interests from more radical reformers. Others, like E. A. Filene, founder of a Boston department store, were humanitarians who worked unselfishly for social justice. Business-dominated organizations like the Municipal Voters League and U.S. Chamber of Commerce thought that running schools, hospitals, and local government like efficient businesses would stabilize society. Elite women led organizations like the Young Women's Christian Association (YWCA), which aided unmarried working women, and they joined middle- and working-class women in many causes of the Woman's Christian Temperance Union (WCTU), the largest women's organization of its time.

Vital elements of what became modern American liberalism derived from working-class urban experiences. By 1900 many urban workers were pressing for "bread-and-butter reforms" such as safe factories,

WORKING-CLASS REFORMERS

shorter workdays, workers' compensation, and better housing. Often these were the same people who supported political bosses, but bossism was not necessarily at odds with humanitarianism. "Big Tim" Sullivan, an influential boss in New York City's Tammany Hall political machine, said he supported shorter workdays for women because "I had seen me sister go out to work when she was only fourteen and . . . we ought to help these gals by giving 'em a law which will prevent 'em from being broken down while they're still young."

After 1900, urban working-class voters elected Progressive legislators trained in machine politics. New York's Alfred E. Smith and Robert F. Wagner, Massachusetts's David I. Walsh, and Illinois's Edward F. Dunne—all from immigrant backgrounds—wanted government to alleviate the hardships of urban-industrial growth. But as protectors of individual liberty, they opposed reforms such as prohibition, Sunday closing laws, civil service, and nonpartisan elections.

Disillusioned immigrant intellectuals, industrial workers, miners, and women's rights activists wanted

SOCIALISTS

a different society altogether and turned to socialism. They wanted the United States to follow the example of Germany, England, and France, where the government sponsored low-cost housing, social insurance and old-age pensions, public ownership of municipal services, and labor reform. Rarely did these reforms gain wide acceptance. Labor unions, for example, opposed social insurance because it would increase taxes.

Most socialists united behind Eugene V. Debs, the American Railway Union organizer who drew nearly 100,000 votes as the Socialist Party's presidential candidate in 1900. A spellbinding spokesman for causes such as peace and antimaterialism, Debs polled over 900,000 votes in 1912 at the pinnacle of his party's career. With rebukes of unfair privilege, socialists won over some Progressives, such as Florence Kelley. But most Progressives had too large a stake in capitalism. Municipal ownership of public utilities represented their limit of drastic change.

Progressive reform in the South similarly focused on railroad and utility regulation, factory safety, and

SOUTHERN PROGRESSIVISM

pure food and drug legislation. The South pioneered some reforms: the direct primary originated in North

■ Though their objectives sometimes differed from those of middle-class Progressive reformers, socialists also became a more active force in the early twentieth century. Socialist parades on May Day, such as this one in 1910, were meant to express the solidarity of all working people.   (Library of Congress)

Carolina; the city commission plan arose in Galveston, Texas; and the city manager plan began in Staunton, Virginia. Progressive governors introduced business regulation that rivaled that of their northern counterparts.

Yet racial discrimination tainted southern Progressivism. The disenfranchisement of black men through poll taxes, literacy requirements, and other means meant that electoral reforms affected only white men with enough cash and education to satisfy voting prerequisites.

Southern women's reform efforts also remained racially distinct. White women crusaded against child labor, founded social service organizations, and challenged unfair wages. African American women, using a guise as homemakers and religious leaders, which was more acceptable to whites than political activism, advocated street cleaning, better education, and health reforms.

It would be a mistake to assume that a Progressive spirit captured all of American society between 1895 and 1920. Defenders of free enterprise opposed regulatory measures, believing government programs undermined the individual initiative and competition central to a free-market system. "Old guard" Republicans like Senator Nelson W. Aldrich of Rhode Island and House Speaker Joseph Cannon of Illinois championed the notion that government intervention contradicted the natural law of survival of the fittest.

OPPONENTS OF PROGRESSIVISM

Moreover, prominent Progressives were not always progressive. Governor Hiram Johnson of California promoted discrimination against Japanese Americans, New Jersey's Woodrow Wilson had no sympathy for African Americans, and northern settlement houses segregated blacks and whites.

Nevertheless, Progressive reformers generally occupied the center of the ideological spectrum, believing on one hand that laissez faire was obsolete and on the other that a radical departure from free enterprise was dangerous. Like Thomas Jefferson, they expressed faith in the conscience and will of the people; like Alexander Hamilton, they desired a strong central government to act in the interest of conscience.

Governmental and Legislative Reform

*T*raditionally, mistrust of tyranny had prompted most Americans to believe that government should interfere in private affairs only in extreme circumstances. In the late 1800s, this viewpoint weakened when economic problems led corporations to pursue government aid for their enterprises. Discontented farmers sought government regulation of railroads and monopolistic businesses. And city dwellers, accustomed to the favors of political machines, expected government to act on their behalf.

Progressive reformers endorsed the principle that government should ensure justice and counteract

RESTRUCTURING GOVERNMENT

exploitation. But to use such power effectively, activists would have to reclaim government from politicians whose greed they believed had soiled the democratic system. Between 1870 and 1900, opponents of urban bosses tried to restructure government through such reforms as civil service, nonpartisan elections, and tight scrutiny of public expenditures. After 1900, reform campaigns installed city-manager and commission forms of government (in which urban officials were chosen for professional expertise rather than political connections) and public ownership of utilities (to prevent gas, electric, and transit companies from profiting at public expense).

Reformers found the city too small an arena, however, and saw greater legislative opportunities in state and federal governments. In the Plains and West, reformers sought railroad regulation and government control of natural resources. In the South, they continued the Populist crusade against big business and autocratic politicians. In the Northeast and Midwest, they attacked corrupt politics and unsafe labor conditions.

Faith in a fair-minded executive prompted Progressives to support a number of skillful governors,

ROBERT M. LA FOLLETTE

particularly Wisconsin's Robert M. La Follette. A small-town lawyer, La Follette rose through the state Republican Party to become governor in 1900. There, he initiated direct primaries, more equitable taxes, and regulation of railroad rates. After three terms, La Follette was elected to the U.S. Senate. "Battling Bob" asserted that his "goal was not to 'smash' corporations, but to drive them out of politics."

Political reformers achieved a major goal in 1913 with the Seventeenth Amendment, which provided for direct election of U.S. senators (they previously had been elected by state legislatures, which Progressives suspected were corrupt). By 1916 all but three states had direct primaries, and many had adopted the initiative, referendum, and recall. But party bosses were still able to control elections. Efforts to use the initiative, referendum, and recall often failed because special-interest groups spent large sums to influence the voting.

Middle- and working-class reformers sometimes united around labor laws. A coalition of the middle

LABOR REFORM

and working classes pushed many states to use their constitutional police power to protect public health and enact factory inspection laws. By 1916 nearly two-thirds of the states required victims' compensation for industrial accidents. Some legislatures even granted aid to mothers with dependent children. Under pressure from the National Child Labor Committee, nearly every state set minimum employment ages (varying from twelve to sixteen) and prohibited employers from making children work more than eight or ten hours a day. Such laws had a limited effect, though, because they seldom provided for the close inspection of factories that enforcement required. And families needing extra income encouraged children to lie about their ages.

Several groups united to achieve restricted working hours for women. After the Supreme Court, in *Muller v. Oregon*, upheld Oregon's ten-hour limit in 1908 (see Chapter 18), more states passed laws protecting female workers. In 1914 the American Association for Old Age Security secured old-age pensions in Arizona. Judges struck down the law, but demand for pensions continued, and in the 1920s many states enacted such laws.

Russian Temperance

When American temperance advocates secured nationwide prohibition with the 1919 constitutional amendment, they were five years behind Russia. Vodka and other spirits had been outlawed there since 1914, when Czar Nicholas II decreed nationwide prohibition, following a twenty-seven-year effort launched when author Leo Tolstoy started a temperance society.

While American reformers feared the moral and economic consequences of drunkenness, some Russians linked alcohol to deficiencies in strength and valor, believing Russia had lost the war with Japan in 1905 because excessive drinking made their soldiers unfit. Both Russians and Americans agreed that alcohol had negative effects on health. Adopting American treatments, Russian doctors opened clinics to help alcoholics overcome their addiction.

In contrast to the United States, where the Woman's Christian Temperance Union spearheaded alcohol reform, Russian women never formed a temperance society. Upper-class Russian women were more interested in obtaining the vote, and working-class women opted for personal persuasion. One group of peasant women installed a lock on the village liquor store door to prevent their husbands from buying vodka. Moreover, all women worried about how a ban on alcohol might undermine Russian hospitality, which required a hostess to serve vodka and wine.

When Bolsheviks seized power in 1917, they extended prohibition. But as in the United States, Russians who wanted to drink found substitutes, some of them dangerous, such as wood alcohol or varnish. Eventually the Bolshevik regime abandoned prohibition just as Americans would, because they needed the tax revenues from alcoholic beverage sales.

In 1925 Russia restored the state vodka monopoly, which guaranteed the government a steady flow of income. Alcohol abuse increased, as did alcohol-related diseases such as liver cancer and fetal alcohol syndrome, problems that remain today. On a lesser scale, similar difficulties resulted after Americans ended prohibition with the Twenty-first Amendment in 1933. The dilemma of excessive drinking and alcoholism linked the United States to Russia, but both discovered that prohibition would not fight alcohol's resulting problems.

Like Americans, other people—in this instance, Ukrainians—used posters as propaganda for a cause. Here, the temperance movement in the Ukraine in the early twentieth century depicted a dissolute alcoholic with bottle in hand, and the text links his drinking with the work of the Devil. (© Rykoff Collection/CORBIS)

Reformers did not always agree about whether states should regulate drinking and sexual behavior.

TEMPERANCE AND PROHIBITION

The Anti-Saloon League, formed in 1893, allied with the Woman's Christian Temperance Union (founded in 1874) to publicize alcoholism's role in health problems like liver disease. Reformers successfully shifted temperance from individual responsibility to the alleged link between drinking and accidents, poverty, and reduced productivity.

The war on saloons prompted many areas to restrict liquor consumption. By 1900 almost one-fourth of the nation's population lived in "dry" communities, prohibiting liquor sales. But alcohol consumption, especially beer, increased after 1900, convincing prohibitionists that a nationwide ban was the best solution. In 1918 Congress passed the Eighteenth Amendment (ratified in 1919 and implemented in 1920), outlawing the manufacture, sale, and transportation of intoxicating liquors. Although not all prohibitionists were Progressives and vice versa, the Eighteenth Amendment embodied the Progressive strategy of using legislation to protect the family and workplace.

Moral outrage erupted when muckraking journalists charged that international gangs were kidnapping

PROSTITUTION AND WHITE SLAVERY

young women and forcing them into prostitution, a practice called "white slavery." More imagined than real, these charges alarmed moralists, who falsely perceived a link between immigration and prostitution. Reformers prodded governments to investigate and pass corrective legislation. The Chicago Vice Commission, for example, undertook a "scientific" survey and published its findings as *The Social Evil in Chicago* in 1911. The report concluded that poverty, gullibility, and desperation drove women into prostitution.

Investigations found rising numbers of prostitutes but failed to prove that criminal organizations deliberately lured women into "the trade." Reformers nonetheless believed they could attack prostitution by punishing its promoters. In 1910 Congress passed the White Slave Traffic Act (Mann Act), prohibiting interstate and international transportation of a woman for immoral purposes. By 1915 nearly every state had outlawed brothels and solicitation of sex. Such laws failed to address the more serious problem of sexual

violence that women suffered from family, presumed friends, and employers.

New Ideas in Social Institutions

*P*reoccupation with efficiency and scientific management infiltrated education, law, religion, and the social sciences. Darwin's theory of evolution had challenged traditional beliefs in a God-created world, immigration had created complex social diversity, and technology had made old habits of production obsolete. Professionals grappled with how to embrace progress yet preserve the best of the past.

As late as 1870, when families needed children to work on farms, Americans attended school only a

JOHN DEWEY AND PROGRESSIVE EDUCATION

few months a year for four years on average. By 1900, however, laws required children to attend school to age fourteen. The number of public high schools grew from five hundred in 1870 to ten thousand in 1910. In the late nineteenth century, psychologist G. Stanley Hall and philosopher John Dewey asserted that in modern education, personal development should be the focus of the curriculum.

Progressive education, based on Dewey's *The School and Society* (1899) and *Democracy and Education* (1916), stressed that learning should involve real-life problems and that children should be taught to use ingenuity to control their environments. Dewey and his wife, Alice, practiced these ideas in their Laboratory School at the University of Chicago.

Making curriculum practical similarly drove higher-education reform. Previously American col-

GROWTH OF COLLEGES AND UNIVERSITIES

leges had resembled their European counterparts in training a select few for careers in law, medicine, and religion. But in the late 1800s, institutions of higher learning multiplied, aided by land grants. Between 1870 and 1910, the number of colleges and universities in the United States grew from 563 to nearly 1,000. Educators sought to make learning more appealing and to keep up with technological and social changes. Harvard University, under President Charles W. Eliot, pioneered new teaching methods and substituted electives for required courses. Many schools, private and public, considered athletics vital to a student's growth, and intercollegiate sports became a permanent fixture.

Southern states set up segregated land-grant colleges for blacks and whites. Although African Americans continued to suffer from inferior educational opportunities, they found intellectual stimulation in all-black colleges and used their education to help uplift their race.

Between 1890 and 1910, the number of women in colleges swelled from 56,000 to 140,000. Of these, 106,000 attended coeducational institutions (mostly state universities); the rest enrolled in women's colleges. By 1920, 283,000 women attended college, accounting for 47 percent of total enrollment. But discrimination lingered. Women were encouraged (and usually sought) to take home economics and education courses, and most medical schools and many private institutions refused to admit them. Instead they attended separate schools, most of which were founded in the late nineteenth century—such as Women's Medical College of Philadelphia and Smith College.

By 1920, 78 percent of children ages five to seventeen were enrolled in public schools; another 8 percent attended private and parochial schools. There were 600,000 college and graduate students in 1920 versus 52,000 in 1870. Yet critical analysis seldom tested the faith that schools could promote equality and justice as well as personal growth and responsible citizenship.

Oliver Wendell Holmes Jr., associate justice of the Supreme Court between 1902 and 1932, led the

PROGRESSIVE LEGAL THOUGHT attack on the traditional view of law as universal and unchanging, arguing instead that law should reflect society's needs. Louis D. Brandeis, a lawyer who later joined Holmes on the Supreme Court, insisted that judges' opinions be based on scientifically gathered information about social realities. Using this Progressive approach, Brandeis collected extensive data on the harmful effects of long working hours to convince the Supreme Court, in *Muller v. Oregon* (1908), to uphold Oregon's ten-hour limit on women's workday.

Judges raised on laissez-faire economics and strict interpretation of the Constitution overturned laws Progressives thought necessary for reform. In 1905 the Supreme Court, in *Lochner v. New York*,

revoked a New York law limiting bakers' working hours. The Court's majority argued that the Fourteenth Amendment protected an individual's right to make contracts without government interference.

Several decisions beginning with *Holden v. Hardy* (1898), in which the Supreme Court sustained a Utah law regulating miners' hours, confirmed the use of state police power to protect health, safety, and morals. Judges also affirmed federal police power and Congress's authority over interstate commerce by upholding federal legislation such as the 1906 Pure Food and Drug Act, the Meat Inspection Law, and the Mann Act.

But even if one agreed that laws should address society's needs, whose needs should prevail in a diverse nation? In many localities, a native-born Protestant majority imposed Bible reading in public schools (offending Catholics and Jews), required businesses to close on Sundays, limited women's rights, restricted religious practices of Mormons and other groups, prohibited interracial marriage, and enforced racial segregation. Justice Holmes asserted that laws should be made for "people of fundamentally differing views," but were such laws possible?

Social science—the study of society and its institutions—underwent changes of its own. Young

SOCIAL SCIENCE economics scholars used statistics to argue that laws governing economic relationships were not timeless but should reflect prevailing social conditions. A new breed of sociologists led by Lester Ward, Albion Small, and Edward A. Ross agreed, adding that citizens should work to cure social ills rather than wait for problems to solve themselves.

Meanwhile, Progressive historians Frederick Jackson Turner, Charles A. Beard, and Vernon L. Parrington examined the past to explain present American society. Beard, like other Progressives, believed that the Constitution was a flexible document. His influential *Economic Interpretation of the Constitution* (1913) argued that merchants and lawyers created the Constitution to defend private property. If the Constitution had served special interests in one age, it could be changed to serve broader interests in another age.

In public health, organizations such as the National Consumers League (NCL) joined physicians and social scientists to secure far-reaching Progressive reforms. Founded by Florence Kelley in 1899, NCL activities included woman suffrage, protection of female and child laborers, and elimination of health hazards. Local branches united with women's clubs to advance consumer protection measures such as the licensing of food vendors and inspection of dairies and urged city governments to provide medical care to the poor.

Much of Progressive reform rested on religious underpinnings. A movement known as the Social Gospel, led by Protestant ministers

THE SOCIAL GOSPEL

Walter Rauschenbusch, Washington Gladden, and Charles Sheldon, would counter the brutality of competitive capitalism by interjecting Christian churches into worldly matters such as arbitrating industrial harmony and improving the environment of the poor. Believing that service provided individual salvation and God's kingdom on earth, Social Gospelers actively participated in social reform.

The Social Gospel served as a response to Social Darwinism, the application of biological natural selection and survival of the fittest to human interactions. But another movement, eugenics, sought to apply Darwinian principles to society scientifically. The brainchild of Francis Galton, an English statistician and cousin of Charles Darwin, eugenics rested on the belief that human character could be inherited, including bad traits such as criminality, insanity, and what some people called feeblemindedness. Eugenicists believed society had an obligation to prevent the reproduction of the mentally defective, the criminally inclined, and the generally inferior. Inevitably such ideas targeted immigrants and people of color.

EUGENICS

Eugenicists advocated two basic means to prevent the proliferation of people who might threaten American progress: sterilization and immigration restrictions. In 1907 Indiana enacted the country's first statute permitting involuntary sterilization of "confirmed criminals, idiots, imbeciles, and rapists." By 1915 thirteen states had such laws, and by 1930 the number reached thirty. Meanwhile, Madison Grant's *The Passing of the Great Race* (1916) strongly bolstered theories that immigrants from southern and eastern Europe threatened to weaken American society because they were inferior mentally and morally to earlier Nordic immigrants. Thus, many people, including some Progressives, wanted new laws to curtail the influx of Poles, Italians, Jews, and other eastern and southern Europeans, as well as Asians. In the 1920s restrictive legislation did just that.

Challenges to Racial and Sexual Discrimination

The white male reformers of the Progressive era dealt primarily with politics and institutions, and ignored issues directly affecting former slaves, nonwhite immigrants, American Indians, and women. Yet activists within these groups made strides toward their own advancement. Their efforts, however, posed a dilemma. Should women and nonwhites seek to be on a par with white men, or was there something unique about racial and sexual cultures that they should preserve at the risk of broader gains?

In 1900 nine-tenths of African Americans lived in the South, where repressive Jim Crow laws had multiplied in the 1880s and 1890s. In 1910 only 8,000 out of 970,000 high-school-age blacks in the South were enrolled in high schools. Denied voting rights and officially segregated, blacks met with relentless intimidation and violence, including lynching.

CONTINUED DISCRIMINATION FOR AFRICAN AMERICANS

Many African Americans moved north in the 1880s, accelerating their migration after 1900. Although conditions were better, job discrimination, inferior schools, and segregated housing prevailed in the North too. White authorities confined blacks to separate and inferior schools, hospitals, and other institutions. And most whites still believed that blacks were inferior and incapable of citizenship.

African American leaders differed sharply over how—and whether—to pursue assimilation. In the wake of emancipation, ex-slave Frederick Douglass urged "ultimate assimilation through self-assertion." Others supported emigration to Africa or the establishment of all-black communities in Oklahoma Territory and Kansas. Others, as bitter as white racists, advocated militancy, believing, as one writer stated, "Our people must die to be saved."

■ Booker T. Washington's Tuskegee Institute helped train young African Americans in useful crafts such as shoemaking and shoe repair, as illustrated here. At the same time, Washington's intentions and the Tuskegee curriculum reinforced what many whites wanted to believe: that blacks were unfit for anything except manual labor.   (Tuskegee University Library)

Most blacks could neither escape nor conquer white society. Self-help, a strategy articulated by educator Booker T. Washington, offered one popular alternative. Born into slavery in backcountry Virginia in 1856, Washington obtained an education and in 1881 founded Tuskegee Institute in Alabama, an all-black vocational school. There he developed a philosophy that blacks' best hopes lay in at least temporarily accommodating to whites. Washington counseled African Americans to work hard, acquire property, and prove they were worthy of respect. "Dignify and glorify common labor," he urged in a speech at the Atlanta

BOOKER T. WASHINGTON AND SELF-HELP

Exposition in 1895, which became known as the Atlanta Compromise. Washington observed that "in all things that are purely social we can be as separate as the fingers, yet one as the hand in all matters essential to mutual progress."

Because he said what they wanted to hear, white businesspeople, reformers, and politicians welcomed Washington as representative of all African Americans. Washington never argued that blacks were inferior to whites; he asserted that they could enhance their dignity through self-improvement.

Some blacks concluded that Washington favored a degrading second-class citizenship. In 1905 a group of "anti-Bookerites" convened near Niagara Falls and pledged militant pursuit of unrestricted voting, economic opportunity, integration, and equality before the law. Representing the Niagara movement was W. E. B. Du Bois, an outspoken critic of the Atlanta Compromise.

Online Study Center **Improve Your Grade**
Primary Source: Atlanta Exposition Address

A New Englander and the first black to receive a Ph.D. degree from Harvard, Du Bois was both a

W. E. B. DU BOIS AND THE "TALENTED TENTH"

Progressive and a member of the black elite. While a faculty member at Atlanta University, Du Bois compiled sociological studies of black urban life and wrote in support of civil rights. He treated Booker T. Washington politely but could not accept white domination.

Du Bois believed that an intellectual vanguard of highly trained blacks, the "Talented Tenth," could use their skill to pursue racial equality. In 1909 he joined with white liberals similarly discontent with Washington's accommodationism to form the National Association for the Advancement of Colored People (NAACP). Du Bois and his allies wanted the organization to end racial discrimination and obtain voting rights through legal redress in the courts. By 1914 the NAACP had fifty branch offices and six thousand members.

African Americans who managed to acquire property and education encountered continued oppression. Woodrow Wilson, a southerner, condoned segregation. During his presidency, southern cabinet members preserved racial separation in restrooms, restaurants, and government office buildings and balked at hiring black workers.

African Americans struggled with questions about their place in white society. Du Bois voiced this dilemma, observing that "one ever feels his twoness— an American, a Negro, two souls, two thoughts, two unreconciled strivings, two warring ideals in one dark body." As he wrote in 1903, a black "would not bleach his Negro soul in a flood of white Americanism, for he knows that Negro blood has a message for the world. He simply wishes to make it possible for a man to be both a Negro and an American."

In 1911 educated middle-class Indians formed their own association, the Society of American Indi-

SOCIETY OF AMERICAN INDIANS

ans (SAI), to work for better education, civil rights, and healthcare. It also sponsored "American Indian Days" to cultivate pride and offset images of savage peoples promulgated in Wild West shows.

The SAI's emphasis on racial pride, however, was squeezed between pressures for assimilation from one side and tribal allegiance on the other. Its small membership did not fully represent the diverse and unconnected Indian nations. Individual hard work was not enough to overcome white prejudice and condescension, and attempts to redress grievances through legal action faltered for lack of funds. Ultimately the SAI had to rely on rhetoric and moral exhortation, which had little effect on poverty-stricken Indians. Torn by internal disputes, the association folded in the early 1920s.

Women's groups shared similar questions about the tactics they should use to achieve equality. Could

"THE WOMAN MOVEMENT"

women achieve equality with men and at the same time change male-dominated society?

The answers that women found involved a subtle but important shift in women's politics. Before 1910, women's rights advocates called themselves "the woman movement." Often middle class, these women sought to move beyond the household into higher education and paid professions in social welfare, and argued that legal and voting rights were indispensable to such moves. They claimed that women's special, even superior, traits as guardians of family and morality would humanize all of society. Settlement-house founder Jane Addams, for example, endorsed woman suffrage by asking, "If women have in any sense been responsible for the gentler side of life which softens and blurs some of its harsher conditions, may not they have a duty to perform in our American cities?"

Originating as middle-class literary and educational organizations, women's clubs began taking

WOMEN'S CLUBS

stands on public affairs in the late nineteenth century. They asserted traditional female responsibilities for home and family as the rationale for reforming society through an enterprise called social housekeeping. These women worked for factory inspection, regulation of children's and women's labor, improved housing and education, and consumer protection.

African American women had their own club movement, including the Colored Women's Federation, which sought to establish a training school for "colored girls." Founded in 1895, the National Association of Colored Women was the nation's first African American social service organization; it concentrated on establishing nurseries, kindergartens, and retirement homes. Black women also developed reform organizations within black Baptist and African Methodist Episcopal churches.

Around 1910 some of those concerned with women's place in society began using the term *feminism* to represent their ideas.

FEMINISM Whereas the woman movement spoke of duty and moral purity, feminists emphasized rights and self-development. On one hand, feminists argued that all women should unite in the struggle for rights because of their shared disadvantages as women. On the other hand, feminists insisted that sex typing—treating women differently from men—must end because it resulted in discrimination.

Feminism focused primarily on economic and sexual independence. Charlotte Perkins Gilman, a major figure in the movement, declared in her book *Women and Economics* (1898) that domesticity was obsolete and attacked men's monopoly on economic opportunity. Arguing that paid employees should handle domestic chores, Gilman asserted that modern women must take jobs in industry and the professions to secure independence.

Feminists also supported a single standard of behavior for men and women, and several feminists joined the birth-control movement

MARGARET SANGER'S CRUSADE led by Margaret Sanger. A former visiting nurse, Sanger helped reverse state and federal "Comstock laws"—named after a nineteenth-century New York moral reformer—that had banned distribution of information about sex and contraception. Despite opposition from those who saw birth control as a threat to family, Sanger formed the American Birth Control League in 1921, successfully enlisting physicians and social workers to convince judges to allow distribution of birth-control information. Most states still prohibited the sale of contraceptives, but Sanger succeeded in initiating public debate.

Online Study Center **Improve Your Grade**
Interactive Map: Woman Suffrage Before 1920

During the Progressive era, a generation of feminists, represented by Harriot Stanton Blatch, daughter of nineteenth-century suffragist Elizabeth Cady Stanton, carried on

WOMAN SUFFRAGE women's battle for the vote. Blatch, whose chief goal was improvement of women's working conditions, saw the vote as the means to achieve such improvement. Thus, women would exercise the vote to promote and protect their economic roles.

Nine states, all in the West, allowed women to vote in state and local elections by 1912 (see Map 21.1). Suffragists' tactics ranged from moderate but persistent letter-writing and publications of the National American Woman Suffrage Association, led by Carrie Chapman Catt, to spirited meetings and militant marches of the National Woman's Party, led by Alice Paul. More decisive was women's service during the First World War as factory laborers, medical volunteers, and municipal workers. Legislators, who could no longer deny that women could shoulder public responsibilities, passed the national suffrage amendment (the Nineteenth) in 1920.

The Progressive era helped women clarify issues that concerned them, but major reforms were not achieved until later. Women's clubs, feminists, and suffragists failed to create an interest group united enough to overcome men's political, economic, and social control. As feminist Crystal Eastman observed in the aftermath of suffrage, "Men are saying perhaps, 'Thank God, this everlasting women's fight is over!' But women, if I know them, are saying, 'Now at last we can begin.' . . . Now they can say what they are really after, in common with all the rest of the struggling world, is freedom."

Theodore Roosevelt and the Revival of the Presidency

*T*he Progressive era's reform efforts focused on the federal government as the foremost agent of change. Though the federal government had notable accomplishments during the Gilded Age (see Chapter 20), its role was mainly to support rather than

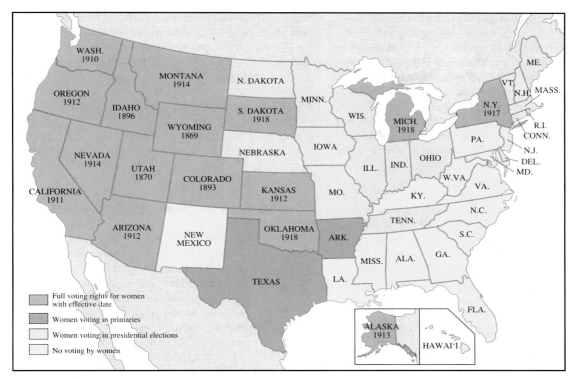

Map 21.1   Woman Suffrage Before 1920

Before Congress passed and the states ratified the Nineteenth Amendment, woman suffrage already existed, but mainly in the West. Several midwestern states allowed women to vote only in presidential elections, but legislatures in the South and Northeast generally refused such rights until forced to do so by constitutional amendment.

control economic expansion. Then, in September 1901, the assassination of President William McKinley by anarchist Leon Czolgosz vaulted Theodore Roosevelt, the vigorous young vice president, into the White House. As governor of New York, Roosevelt had angered Republican bosses by showing sympathy for regulatory legislation. He would become the nation's most forceful president since Lincoln and would bestow the office with much of its twentieth-century character.

Driven throughout his life by an obsession to overcome the physical limitations of asthma and near-sightedness that plagued his youth, Roosevelt exerted a zest for action and display of courage that contemporaries called "manliness." In his

THEODORE
ROOSEVELT

teens, he became an expert marksman and horseman and later competed on Harvard's boxing and wrestling teams. In the 1880s he lived on a Dakota ranch, roping cattle and brawling with cowboys. Roosevelt had wealth, but he also inherited a sense of civic responsibility that guided him into public service. He served three terms in the New York State Assembly, ran for mayor of New York City in 1886 (finishing third), sat on the federal Civil Service Commission, served as New York City's police commissioner, was assistant secretary of the navy, and earned a reputation as a combative, crafty leader. In 1898 Roosevelt thrust himself into the Spanish-American War by organizing a volunteer cavalry brigade, called the Rough Riders, to fight in Cuba. Although his dramatic act had little impact on the war's outcome, it made him a media hero.

Only forty-two years old when he assumed the presidency in 1901, Roosevelt carried his youthful exuberance into the White House. A Progressive, he concurred with allies that a small, uninvolved government would not suffice in the industrial era. Instead, he believed that economic development necessitated a government powerful enough to guide national affairs broadly. Especially in economic matters, he wanted the government to decide when big business was good and when it was bad.

The federal economic regulation that characterized twentieth-century America began with Roosevelt's presidency. Although labeled a "trustbuster," Roosevelt actually considered business consolidation an efficient means toward material progress. He believed in distinguishing between good and bad trusts and preventing bad ones from manipulating markets. Thus, he instructed the Justice Department to use antitrust laws to prosecute railroad, meatpacking, and oil trusts, which he believed unscrupulously exploited the public. Roosevelt triumphed in 1904 when the Supreme Court ordered the breakup of Northern Securities Company, the huge railroad combination created by J. P. Morgan and his business allies (the *Northern Securities* case). Roosevelt did not attack other trusts, such as U.S. Steel, another of Morgan's creations.

REGULATION OF TRUSTS

When prosecution of Northern Securities began, Morgan reportedly asked Roosevelt, "If we have done anything wrong, send your man to my man and they can fix it up." The president refused but was more sympathetic to cooperation between business and government than it might seem. He urged the Bureau of Corporations (part of the newly created Department of Labor and Commerce) to assist companies to merge and expand. Through investigation and cooperation, the administration cajoled businesses to regulate themselves.

Roosevelt also supported regulatory legislation. After a year of wrangling, Roosevelt persuaded Congress to pass the Hepburn Act (1906), which gave the Interstate Commerce Commission (ICC) greater authority to set railroad freight and storage rates, though it did allow courts to overturn rate decisions. Progressive senator Robert La Follette complained that Roosevelt had compromised to ensure the bill's passage. But Roosevelt focused on achievable regulation rather than idealistic objectives.

Roosevelt was also willing to compromise to secure pure food and drug legislation. For decades reformers had sought government regulation of processed meat and patent medicines. Public outrage flared in 1906 when Upton Sinclair published *The Jungle,* a fictionalized exposé of Chicago meatpacking plants. Sinclair, a socialist who sought to improve working conditions, shocked the public with vivid descriptions:

PURE FOOD AND DRUG LAWS

> There would be meat stored in great piles in rooms; and the water from the leaky roofs would drip over it, and thousands of rats would race about on it. It was too dark in these storage places to see well, but a man could run his hand over these piles of meat and sweep off handfuls of dried dung of rats. These rats were a nuisance, and the packers would put poisoned bread out for them; they would die, and then rats, bread, and meat would go into the hoppers together.

Roosevelt ordered an investigation, and finding Sinclair's descriptions accurate, he supported the Meat Inspection Act (1906). This law required government agents to monitor the quality of processed meat. But as part of a compromise to pass the bill, the government had to finance inspections, and meatpackers could appeal adverse decisions. Nor were companies required to provide date-of-processing information on canned meats. Most large meatpackers benefited because the legislation helped them force out smaller competitors and restored foreign confidence in American meat products.

The Pure Food and Drug Act (1906) also addressed abuses in the patent medicine industry. Makers of tonics and pills had long been making exaggerated claims about their products' effects and liberally using alcohol and narcotics as ingredients. The law required that labels list the ingredients, a goal consistent with Progressive confidence that with the truth, people would make wiser purchases.

In Roosevelt's mind, there were good and bad labor organizations (socialists, for example, were bad), just as there were good and bad business combinations. When the United Mine Workers struck against Pennsylvania coal mine owners in 1902 over an eight-hour workday and higher pay, the president employed investigation and arbitration. Owners refused to recognize the union or arbitrate grievances. As winter approached and fuel shortages loomed, Roosevelt threatened to use federal troops to reopen the mines, thus forcing management to accept arbitration. The arbitration commission supported higher wages and reduced hours and required management to deal with grievance committees, but it did not mandate recognition of the union. The settlement embodied Roosevelt's belief that the president or his representatives should determine which labor demands were legitimate and which were not.

Roosevelt's Progressive impulse for efficiency and love for the outdoors inspired lasting contributions to

CONSERVATION

resource conservation. Government establishment of national parks had begun in the late nineteenth century (see Chapter 17). Roosevelt advanced the movement by favoring conservation over preservation. Thus, he not only exercised presidential power to declare national monuments of natural wonders such as the Grand Canyon in Arizona but also backed a policy of "wise use" of forests, waterways, and other resources. Previously, the government had transferred ownership of natural resources on federal land to the states and private interests, but Roosevelt believed the federal government should retain management over lands in the public domain.

Roosevelt exerted federal authority over resources by protecting waterpower sites from sale to private interests and charging permit fees for those who wanted to produce hydroelectricity. He also supported the Newlands Reclamation Act of 1902, which controlled sale of irrigated federal land in the West. He tripled the number of national forests and supported conservationist Gifford Pinchot in creating the U.S. Forest Service.

As principal advocate of the "wise use" policy, Pinchot promoted scientific management of the nation's

GIFFORD PINCHOT

woodlands. He obtained Roosevelt's support for transferring management of the national forests from the Interior Department to his bureau in the Agriculture Department. The Forest Service charged fees for grazing livestock within the national forests, supervised bidding for the cutting of timber, and hired university-trained foresters as federal employees.

Pinchot and Roosevelt did not seek to lock up—preserve—resources permanently; rather they wanted to guarantee—conserve—their efficient use and prevent big corporations from demanding more federal land. Many of those involved in natural-resource exploitation welcomed such a policy because it enabled them to minimize overproduction and restrict competition. As a result of new federal policies, the West and its resources fell under the Progressive spell of management.

In 1907 a financial panic caused by reckless speculation forced some New York banks to close to prevent frightened depositors from

PANIC OF 1907

withdrawing money. J. P. Morgan helped stem the panic by persuading financiers to stop dumping their stocks. In return for Morgan's aid, Roosevelt approved a deal allowing U.S. Steel to absorb the Tennessee Iron and Coal Company—a deal at odds with Roosevelt's trustbusting aims.

During his last year in office, Roosevelt retreated from the Republican Party's friendliness to big business. He supported stronger business regulation and heavier taxation of the rich. Promising he would not seek reelection, Roosevelt backed Secretary of War William Howard Taft in 1908. Taft handily defeated third-time Democratic nominee William Jennings Bryan by 1.25 million popular votes and a 2-to-1 margin in the electoral college.

Taft faced political problems that Roosevelt had postponed: foremost, excessively high tariffs. Honor-

TAFT ADMINISTRATION

ing Taft's pledge to cut rates, the House passed a bill providing numerous reductions. Protectionists in the Senate prepared to amend the House bill and revise rates upward. But Senate Progressives organized a stinging attack on the tariff, trapping Taft between reformers who claimed to be preserving Roosevelt's antitrust campaign and protectionists who still dominated the Republican Party. In the end, Senator Aldrich and other protectionists restored many of the cuts, and Taft signed what became known as the Payne-Aldrich Tariff (1909). In the eyes of Progressives, Taft had failed to fill Roosevelt's shoes.

In reality, Taft was as sympathetic to reform as Roosevelt. He prosecuted more trusts than Roosevelt; expanded national forest reserves; signed the Mann-Elkins Act (1910), which bolstered regulatory powers of the ICC; and supported labor reforms such as the eight-hour workday and mine safety legislation. The Sixteenth Amendment, which legalized the federal income tax as a permanent part of federal power, and the Seventeenth Amendment, which provided for direct election of U.S. senators, were initiated during Taft's presidency (and ratified in 1913). Like Roosevelt, Taft compromised with big business, but unlike Roosevelt, he lacked the ability to manipulate the public with spirited rhetoric. Roosevelt had expanded presidential power. Taft, by contrast, believed in the strict restraint of law. He had been a successful lawyer and judge and returned to the bench as chief justice of the United States between 1921 and 1930.

In 1910, when Roosevelt returned from a hunting trip in Africa boasting three thousand animal trophies, he found his party frag-

SPLIT OF THE REPUBLICAN PARTY

mented. While one wing remained loyal to Taft, reformers formed the National Progressive Republican League and rallied behind Robert La Follette for president in 1912, though many hoped Roosevelt would run. Disappointed by Taft, Roosevelt spoke out in favor of "the welfare of the people" and stronger regulation of business. When La Follette became ill early in 1912, Roosevelt, proclaiming himself fit as a "bull moose," sought the Republican presidential nomination.

Taft's supporters controlled the Republican convention and nominated him for a second term. In protest, Roosevelt's supporters formed a third party—the Progressive, or Bull Moose, Party—and nominated the fifty-three-year-old former president. Democrats took forty-six ballots to select New Jersey's Progressive governor Woodrow Wilson. Socialists, by now a growing party, again nominated Eugene V. Debs.

Central to Roosevelt's campaign was a scheme called the "New Nationalism." Roosevelt foresaw an

NEW NATIONALISM VERSUS NEW FREEDOM

era of national unity in which government would coordinate and regulate economic activity. He would not destroy big business, but instead would establish regulatory commissions of experts to protect citizens' interests and ensure wise use of economic power.

Dubbing his program the "New Freedom," Wilson argued that concentrated economic power threatened individual liberty and that monopolies should be bro-

ken up to ensure a free marketplace. But he would not restore laissez faire. Like Roosevelt, Wilson would enhance government authority to protect and regulate. "Without the watchful . . . resolute interference of the government, there can be no fair play between individuals and such powerful institutions as the trust," he declared. Wilson stopped short, however, of advocating the cooperation between business and government that characterized Roosevelt's New Nationalism.

Roosevelt and Wilson stood closer than their rhetoric implied. Both believed in individual freedom. Both supported equality of opportunity (chiefly for white males), conservation of natural resources, fair wages, and social betterment for all. And both would expand government through strong leadership and bureaucratic reform.

The popular vote was inconclusive. The victorious Wilson won just 42 percent, though he did capture 435 out of 531 electoral votes. Roosevelt received 27 percent of the popular vote and 88 electoral votes; Taft polled 23 percent of the popular vote and 8 electoral votes. Debs won 901,000 votes, 6 percent of the total, but no electoral votes. Three-quarters of the electorate supported alternatives to Taft's view of restrained government.

Woodrow Wilson and the Extension of Reform

D espite receiving a minority of the total vote in 1912, Wilson interpreted the election as a mandate to subdue trusts and broaden the government's role in social reform. On inauguration day in 1913, he proclaimed, "The feelings with which we face this new age of right and opportunity sweep across our heartstrings like some air out of God's own presence, where justice and mercy are reconciled and the judge and the brother are one."

Born in Virginia in 1856 and raised in the South, Wilson was the son of a Presbyterian minister. He

WOODROW WILSON

earned a B.A. degree at Princeton University, studied law at the University of Virginia, received a Ph.D. degree from Johns Hopkins University, and became a professor of history, jurisprudence, and political economy. Between 1885 and 1908, he published several respected books on American history and government.

A superb orator, Wilson could inspire loyalty with religious imagery and eloquent expressions of American ideals. In 1902 he became president of Princeton and upset tradition with curricular reforms and battles against aristocratic elements. In 1910 New Jersey's Democrats, eager for respectability, nominated Wilson for governor. Once elected, Wilson repudiated the party bosses and promoted Progressive legislation. A poor administrator, he often lost his temper, but his accomplishments nevertheless won him the Democratic nomination for president in 1912.

As president, Wilson blended New Freedom competition with New Nationalism regulation. His

WILSON'S POLICY ON BUSINESS REGULATION

administration sought to prevent corporate abuses with passage in 1914 of the Clayton Anti-Trust Act and a bill creating the Federal Trade Commission (FTC). The Clayton Act corrected deficiencies of the Sherman Anti-Trust Act of 1890 (see Chapter 18) by outlawing such practices as price discrimination (efforts to destroy competition by lowering prices in some regions but not in others) and interlocking directorates (management of two or more competing companies by the same executives). The FTC could investigate and issue cease-and-desist orders against unfair trade practices.

Wilson expanded banking regulation with the Federal Reserve Act (1913), which established the nation's first central banking system since 1836. The act intended to break the power that banking syndicates held over money supply and credit. It created twelve district banks supervised by the Federal Reserve Board to lend money to member banks at low interest rates called the "discount rate." By adjusting this rate (and thus the amount a bank could afford to borrow), district banks could increase or decrease the amount of money in circulation, enabling the Federal Reserve Board to loosen or tighten credit as needed. Monetary affairs no longer would depend on the gold supply, and interest rates would be fairer.

Wilson attempted to restore competition with the Underwood Tariff, passed in 1913. By the 1910s,

TARIFF AND TAX REFORM

prices for some consumer goods had become unnaturally high because tariffs discouraged the importation of cheaper foreign goods. By reducing or eliminating certain tariff rates, the Underwood Tariff encouraged imports. To replace revenues lost because of tariff reductions, the act levied a graduated income tax on U.S. residents. Incomes under $4,000 were exempt; thus, almost all factory workers and farmers escaped taxation. Individuals and corporations earning between $4,000 and $20,000 had to pay a 1 percent tax; thereafter, rates rose to a maximum of 6 percent on earnings over $500,000.

By 1916, the First World War, raging in Europe since 1914, and that year's upcoming presidential election prompted Wilson to support stronger reforms. He backed the Federal Farm Loan Act, which created twelve federally supported banks (not to be confused with the Federal Reserve banks) that could lend money at moderate interest to farmers who belonged to credit institutions—a watered-down version of the Populists' subtreasury plan proposed a generation earlier.

To forestall railroad strikes, Wilson in 1916 pushed passage of the Adamson Act, which mandated eight-hour workdays and time-and-a-half overtime pay. He pleased Progressives by appointing Louis Brandeis, the "people's advocate," to the Supreme Court, though anti-Semitism almost blocked Senate approval of the Court's first Jewish justice. Wilson also backed laws regulating child labor and providing workers' compensation for federal employees who suffered work-related injuries or illness.

Republicans snubbed Theodore Roosevelt as their candidate in 1916, choosing Charles Evans Hughes,

ELECTION OF 1916

Supreme Court justice and former reform governor of New York. Aware of the First World War's impact on national affairs, Wilson ran on a platform of peace, Progressivism, and preparedness; his slogan was "He Kept Us Out of War." Republicans could not muzzle Roosevelt, whose bellicose speeches suggested that Republicans would drag Americans into war. Wilson received 9.1 million votes to Hughes's 8.5 million and barely won in the electoral college, 277 to 254. The Socialist candidate drew only 600,000 votes, down from 901,000 in 1912, largely because Wilson's reforms had won over some socialists and because the ailing Debs was no longer the party's standard-bearer.

During Wilson's second term, U.S. involvement in the First World War increased government regulation of the economy. Mobilization for war, he came to believe, required coordination of production and cooperation between the public and private sectors. The War Industries Board exemplified this cooperation: private businesses submitted to the board's control on condition that their profit motives would be satisfied. After the war, Wilson's administration dropped these measures, including farm price supports, guarantees of collective bargaining, and high taxes. This retreat from regulation stimulated an era of business ascendancy in the 1920s.

Summary ☼ *Online Study Center* ACE the Test

By 1920 a quarter-century of reform had wrought momentous changes. In their efforts to end abuses of power, Progressives established the principle of public intervention to ensure fairness, health, and safety. For every American who suffered some form of poverty or deprivation, three or four enjoyed unprecedented material comforts. Although Progressive values lingered after the First World War, growing affluence and a mass-consumer society refocused people's attention away from reform to materialism.

Multiple and sometimes contradictory goals characterized the Progressive era because there was no single Progressive movement. Programs on the national level ranged from Roosevelt's faith in big government as a coordinator of big business to Wilson's promise to dissolve economic concentrations and legislate open competition. At state and local levels, reformers pursued causes as varied as neighborhood improvement, government reorganization, public ownership of utilities, and better working conditions. New consciousness about identity confronted women and African Americans, and although women made some inroads into public life, both groups still found themselves in confined social positions.

Their remarkable successes aside, the failure of many Progressive initiatives indicates the strength of the opposition, as well as weaknesses within the reform movements. Courts asserted constitutional and liberty-of-contract doctrines in striking down key Progressive legislation, notably the federal law prohibiting child labor. On the federal level, regulatory agencies rarely had enough resources for thorough

investigations and had to depend on information from the very companies they policed. In 1920, as in 1900, government remained under the influence of business.

Yet Progressive era reforms reshaped the national outlook. Trustbusting, however faulty, forced industrialists to become more sensitive to public opinion. Progressive legislation equipped government with tools to protect consumers against price fixing and dangerous products. The income tax, created to redistribute wealth, also became a source of government revenue. Although the questions they raised about American life remained unresolved, Progressives made the nation acutely aware of its principles and promises.

LEGACY FOR A PEOPLE AND A NATION

Margaret Sanger, Planned Parenthood, and the Birth-Control Controversy

Some reforms of the Progressive era illustrate how earnest intentions can become tangled in divisive issues of morality. Such is the legacy of birth-control advocate Margaret Sanger. In 1912 Sanger wrote an advice column on sex education in the *New York Call* titled "What Every Girl Should Know." Censors accused her of writing obscene literature because she discussed venereal disease publicly. She counseled poor women on New York's Lower East Side about how to avoid the pain of frequent childbirth, miscarriage, and bungled abortion. In 1914 Sanger launched *The Woman Rebel*, a radical monthly advocating a woman's right to birth control. Indicted for distributing obscenity through the mails, Sanger fled to England, where she gave speeches promoting birth control.

Back in the United States, Sanger opened the first birth-control clinic in Brooklyn in 1916. She was arrested and jailed, but when a court exempted physicians from a law prohibiting distribution of contraceptive information, she set up a doctor-run clinic in 1923. Staffed by female doctors and social workers, the Birth Control Clinical Research Bureau became a model for other clinics. Sanger organized the American Birth Control League (1921) and tried to win support from medical and social reformers, including the eugenics movement, for legalized birth control. After a falling-out with some of her allies, she resigned from the American Birth Control League in 1928.

The movement continued, however, and in 1938, the American Birth Control League and the Birth Control Clinical Research Bureau merged to form the Birth Control Federation of America, renamed the Planned Parenthood Federation of America (PPFA) in 1942. The organization's name defined its mission to strengthen the family and stabilize society rather than to protect a woman's right to voluntary motherhood. Throughout the 1940s, PPFA emphasized family planning through increased availability of contraceptives. In 1970 it began receiving federal funds.

In the 1960s, feminist agitation for women's rights and rising concerns about overpopulation expanded issues of birth control to include abortion. The intense debate between a woman's "choice" and an unborn child's "right to life" drew PPFA into the fray, especially after 1973, when the Supreme Court validated women's right to abortion in *Roe v. Wade*. PPFA fought legislative and court attempts to make abortions illegal and helped organize a women's march on Washington in 1989. But some Latino and African American groups attacked PPFA's stance, charging that abortion was a kind of eugenics program meant to reduce births among nonwhite races.

Because of PPFA's involvement in abortion politics, several of its clinics have been targets of picketing and even violence by those who believe abortion is immoral. PPFA now operates nearly nine hundred health centers providing medical services and education. But birth control's legacy includes disagreement over whose rights and whose morality should prevail.

THE QUEST FOR EMPIRE 1865–1914

"Foreign devil!" they shouted at Lottie Moon. The Southern Baptist missionary, half a world from home in the 1880s, braced herself against the Chinese "rabble" she came to convert to Christianity. She walked "steadily and persistently" through the hecklers, vowing silently to win their acceptance and their souls.

Born in 1840 in Virginia and educated at what is now Hollins College, Charlotte Diggs Moon volunteered in 1873 for "woman's work" in northern China. There she taught and proselytized, largely among women and children until her death in 1912.

Lottie Moon (Mu Ladi, or 幕拉第) made sometimes dangerous evangelizing trips in the 1870s and 1880s to isolated Chinese hamlets. Curious peasant women pinched her, purring, "How white her hand is!" They questioned: "How old are you?" and "Where do you get money to live on?" Speaking in Chinese, she held high a picture book on Jesus Christ, drawing attention to the "foreign doctrine" that she hoped would displace Confucianism, Buddhism, and Taoism.

In the 1890s a "storm of persecution" against foreigners swept China, and missionaries became targets. One missionary conceded that by "believing Jesus," girls and women alarmed men, who worried that "disobedient wives and daughters" would no longer "worship the idols when told." In the village of Shaling in early 1890, Lottie Moon's Christian converts were beaten. For months in 1900, during the violent Boxer Rebellion, she had to leave China altogether.

Lottie Moon and thousands of other missionaries managed to convert to Christianity only a small minority of the Chinese people. Although she, like other missionaries, probably never shed the Western view that she represented a superior religion and culture, she felt great affection for the Chinese. In letters and articles directed to a U.S. audience, she lobbied to recruit "a band of ardent, enthusiastic, and experienced Christian women," to stir up "a mighty wave of enthusiasm for Woman's Work for Woman."

Imperial Dreams

Ambitions and Strategies

Crises in the 1890s: Hawai'i, Venezuela, and Cuba

The Spanish-American War and the Debate over Empire

Asian Encounters: War in the Philippines, Diplomacy in China

LINKS TO THE WORLD
The U.S. System of Education in the Philippines

TR's World

LEGACY FOR A PEOPLE AND A NATION
The Status of Puerto Rico

Online Study Center
This icon will direct you to interactive map and primary source acivities on the website
http://college.hmco.com/pic/nortonbrief7e

CHRONOLOGY

1861–69 • Seward sets expansionist course

1867 • United States acquires Alaska and Midway

1876 • Pro-U.S. Díaz begins thirty-four-year rule in Mexico

1878 • U.S. gains naval rights in Samoa

1885 • Strong's *Our Country* celebrates Anglo-Saxon destiny of dominance

1887 • U.S. gains naval rights to Pearl Harbor, Hawai'i

1890 • Alfred Thayer Mahan publishes *The Influence of Sea Power upon History*
• McKinley Tariff hurts Hawaiian sugar exports

1893 • Economic crisis leads to business failures and mass unemployment
• Pro-U.S. interests stage successful coup against Queen Lili'uokalani of Hawai'i

1895 • Cuban revolution against Spain begins
• Japan defeats China in war, annexes Korea and Formosa (Taiwan)

1898 • United States formally annexes Hawai'i
• U.S. battleship *Maine* blows up in Havana harbor
• United States defeats Spain in Spanish-American War

1899 • Treaty of Paris enlarges U.S. empire
• United Fruit Company forms and becomes influential in Central America
• Philippine insurrection breaks out, led by Emilio Aguinaldo

1901 • McKinley assassinated; Theodore Roosevelt becomes president

1903 • Panama grants canal rights to United States
• Platt Amendment subjugates Cuba

1904 • Roosevelt Corollary declares U.S. a hemispheric "police power"

1905 • Portsmouth Conference ends Russo-Japanese War

1906 • San Francisco School Board segregates Asian schoolchildren
• U.S. invades Cuba to quell revolt

1907 • "Great White Fleet" makes world tour

1910 • Mexican revolution threatens U.S. interests

1914 • U.S. troops invade Mexico
• First World War begins
• Panama Canal opens

Like many other Americans who went overseas in the late nineteenth and early twentieth centuries, Lottie Moon helped spread American culture abroad. Some adopted and others rejected American ways. American participants likewise became transformed. Lottie Moon, for example, strove to understand the Chinese and learn their language. She abandoned derogatory phrases like "heathen Chinese" and assumed Chinese dress. She reminded less sensitive missionaries that the Chinese rightfully took pride in their own ancient history.

Lottie Moon also changed—in her own words—from "a timid self-distrustful girl into a brave self-reliant woman." As she questioned the Chinese confinement of women, most conspicuous in arranged marriages, foot binding, and sexual segregation, she advanced women's rights. She also challenged the male domination of America's religious missions. When the Southern Baptist Foreign Mission Board denied women missionaries the right to vote in meetings, she resigned in protest. The board soon reversed itself.

In later decades, critics labeled missionaries' activities as "cultural imperialism," accusing them of subverting indigenous traditions and sparking cultural clashes. Defenders of missionary work have celebrated their efforts to break down cultural barriers. Either way, Lottie Moon's story illustrates how Americans in the late nineteenth century interacted with the rest of the world, how the categories "domestic" and "foreign" intersected, and how they expanded abroad not only to seek land, trade, investments, and strategic bases but also to promote American culture.

Between the Civil War and the First World War, an expansionist United States joined the great world powers. Before the Civil War, Americans had extended the frontier: they pushed Indians out of the path of white migration, seized California and other areas from Mexico, and acquired southern parts of present-day Arizona and New Mexico from Mexico in the Gadsden Purchase. Americans had also developed international trade and promoted American culture everywhere.

By the 1870s, Europe's powers were carving up Africa and large parts of Asia and Oceania. By 1900 they had conquered over 10 million square miles (one-fifth of the earth's land) and 150 million people. As the century turned, France, Russia, and Germany were spending heavily on modern steel navies, challenging an overextended Great Britain. In Asia, a rapidly modernizing Japan expanded at the expense of both China and Russia.

Engineering advances altered the world's political geography through the Suez Canal (1869), the British Trans-Indian railroad (1870), and the Russian Trans-Siberian Railway (1904), while steamships, machine guns, telegraphs, and malaria drugs facilitated the imperialists' task. Simultaneously, Europe's optimism of the 1850s and 1860s gave way to a pessimistic sense of impending warfare informed by notions of racial conflict and survival of the fittest.

Observant Americans argued that the United States risked being "left behind" if it failed to join the scramble for territory and markets. Republican senator Henry Cabot Lodge of Massachusetts advised that "the United States must not fall out of the line of march," because "civilization and the advancement of the [Anglo-Saxon] race" were at stake. Such thinking enticed Americans to reach beyond the continental United States for more land, markets, cultural influence, and power.

By 1900 the United States had emerged as a great power with particular clout in Latin America, especially as Spain declined and Britain disengaged from the Western Hemisphere. In the Pacific, the new U.S. empire included Hawai'i, American Samoa, and the Philippines. In the decade that followed, President Theodore Roosevelt would seek to consolidate this power.

Most Americans applauded expansionism—the outward movement of goods, ships, dollars, people, and ideas. But many became uneasy when it gave way to imperialism—the imposition of control over other peoples and the undermining of their sovereignty. Abroad, native nationalists, commercial competitors, and other imperial nations tried to block the spread of U.S. influence. ■

Imperial Dreams

*a*t the end of the nineteenth century, Americans shifted from internal emphases on industrialization, railroad construction, and western settlement to foreign policy. Political and business leaders began to advocate a more activist approach to world affairs. The motives of these expansionists were complex, but all emphasized the supposed benefits to the country's domestic health.

The leaders who guided America's expansionism also guided the economic development of the machine age, forged the transcontinental railroad, built America's bustling cities and giant corporations, and shaped a mass culture. They unabashedly believed that the United States was an exceptional nation, different from and superior to others because of its Anglo-

Saxon heritage and its God-favored and prosperous history.

Along with exceptionalism, the American march toward empire embraced nationalism, capitalism, Social Darwinism, and a paternalistic attitude toward foreigners. "They are children and we are men in these deep matters of government," the future president Woodrow Wilson announced in 1898. His words reveal the gender and age bias of American attitudes. Where these attitudes intersected with foreign cultures, the result was often tension and rejection.

Foreign policy is usually dominated by what scholars have labeled the "foreign policy elite"—opinion leaders in politics, journalism, business, agriculture, religion, education, and the military. Better read and better traveled than most other Americans and more politically active in the post–Civil War era, this small group, whom Secretary of State Walter Q. Gresham called "the thoughtful men of the country," believed that U.S. prosperity and security depended on exerting U.S. influence abroad. Increasingly in the late nineteenth century, the expansionist-minded elite urged both formal and informal imperialism. They often met in Washington, D.C., at the homes of the historian Henry Adams and the writer and diplomat John Hay (who became secretary of state in 1898) or at the Metropolitan Club. They talked about building a bigger navy and digging a canal across Panama, Central America, or Mexico; establishing colonies; and selling surpluses abroad. Theodore Roosevelt, appointed assistant secretary of the navy in 1897, was among them; so were Senator Henry Cabot Lodge, who joined the Foreign Relations Committee in 1896, and the corporate lawyer Elihu Root, who later would serve as both secretary of war and secretary of state.

FOREIGN POLICY ELITE

These American leaders believed that selling, buying, and investing in foreign marketplaces were important to the United States. One reason was profits from foreign sales. Another was that foreign markets could offset American economic imbalances, particularly since the nation's farms and factories produced more than Americans could consume, especially during the 1890s depression. By exporting surpluses, foreign commerce might relieve overproduction, unemployment, economic depression, and the social tension that arose from them. Economic ties also enabled Americans to exert political influence abroad and helped spread the American way of life, especially capitalism.

Foreign trade contributed to the United States's tremendous economic growth after the Civil War. Foreign commerce stimulated the building of a larger navy, the professionalization of the foreign service, calls for more colonies, and a more interventionist foreign policy. In 1865 U.S. exports totaled $234 million; by 1900 they topped $1.5 billion (see Figure 22.1). By 1914, exports had reached $2.5 billion. In 1874 the United States reversed its historically unfavorable balance of trade (importing more than it exported) and began to enjoy a long-term favorable balance. Most of America's products went to Britain, continental Europe, and Canada, but increasing amounts flowed to new markets in Latin America and Asia. And direct American investments abroad reached $3.5 billion by 1914, placing the United States among the top four investor countries.

FOREIGN TRADE EXPANSION

Agricultural goods accounted for about three-fourths of total exports in 1870 and about two-thirds in 1900, with grain, cotton, meat, and dairy products topping the list. Farmers' livelihoods thus became tied to world-market conditions and foreign wars. Wisconsin cheesemakers shipped to Britain; the Swift and Armour meat companies exported refrigerated beef to Europe.

In 1913 manufactured goods led U.S. exports for the first time (see Figure 22.1). America's steel, copper, and petroleum were sold abroad, making many workers in those industries dependent on American exports.

In expanding U.S. influence overseas, officials championed sometimes racist notions of American supremacy. For decades, the Western scientific establishment had classified humankind by race, and students of physical anthropology drew on phrenology and physiognomy—the measurement of skull size and the comparison of facial features—to produce a hierarchy of superior and inferior races. One prominent French researcher claimed that blacks represented a "female race" and "like the woman, the black is deprived of political and scientific intelligence. . . . But on the other hand he has great virtues of sentiment. Like women he also likes jewelry, dancing, and singing."

RACE THINKING AND THE MALE ETHOS

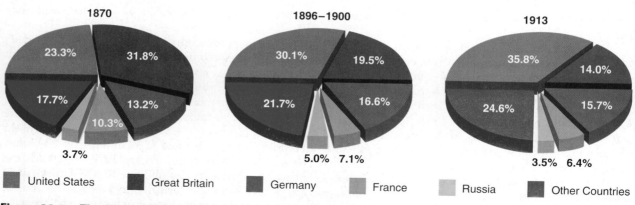

Figure 22.1   The Rise of U.S. Economic Power in the World

These pie charts showing percentage shares of world manufacturing production for the major nations of the world demonstrate that the United States came to surpass Great Britain in this significant economic measurement of power.   (Source: League of Nations data presented in Aaron L. Friedberg, *The Weary Titan: Britain and the Experience of Relative Decline, 1895–1905* [Princeton, N.J.: Princeton University Press, 1988], p. 26.)

The language of U.S. leaders was also weighted with words such as *manliness* and *weakling*. The warrior and president Theodore Roosevelt viewed people of color (or "darkeys," as he called them) as effeminate weaklings who lacked the ability to govern themselves and could not cope with world politics. Americans regularly debased Latin Americans as half-breeds needing supervision or distressed damsels begging for manly rescue. The gendered imagery prevalent in U.S. foreign relations joined race thinking to place women, people of color, and nations weaker than the United States low in the hierarchy of power and, hence, in a necessarily dependent status justifying U.S. dominance.

"As America goes, so goes the world," declared Reverend Josiah Strong, author of the influential *Our Country* (1885), which celebrated an Anglo-Saxon race destined to lead others. Social Darwinists saw Americans as a superior people certain to overcome all competition. Secretary of State Thomas F. Bayard (1885–1889) applauded the "overflow of our population and capital" into Mexico to "saturate those regions with Americanism."

Race thinking—popularized in world's fairs, magazine cartoons, postcards, school textbooks, museums, and political orations—reinforced notions of American greatness, influenced the way U.S. leaders dealt with other peoples, and obviated the need to think about the subtle textures of other societies. *National Geographic*, which published its first issue in 1888, featured pictures of exotic, premodern people who had not yet become "Western" and regularly pictured women with naked breasts. Fairs also put so-called uncivilized people of color on display in the "freaks" or "midway" section. Dog-eating Filipinos aroused comment at the 1904 St. Louis World's Fair. Such racism downgraded diplomacy and justified domination and war, because self-proclaimed superiors do not negotiate with people ranked as inferiors.

Similar thinking permeated attitudes toward immigrants, whose entry into the United States was first restricted in these years. Although the Burlingame Treaty (1868) had provided for free immigration between the United States and China, riots against Chinese immigrants continuously erupted in the American West. A new treaty in 1880 permitted Congress to suspend Chinese immigration. But hostility continued: in 1885 white coal miners and railway workers in Rock Springs, Wyoming, massacred at least twenty-five Chinese.

In 1906 the San Francisco School Board ordered the segregation of all Chinese, Koreans, and Japanese in special schools. Tokyo protested this discrimination, and President Roosevelt quieted the crisis by striking a "gentleman's agreement" with Tokyo restricting the inflow of Japanese immigrants. San Francisco then rescinded its segregation order. Relations with Tokyo were jolted again in 1913 when the California legislature denied Japanese residents the right to own property.

Expansionists believed that empire benefited both Americans and those who came under their control.

THE "CIVILIZING" IMPULSE

When the United States intervened in weaker states, Americans claimed they were extending liberty and prosperity to less fortunate people. William Howard Taft, as civil gover-

nor of the Philippines (1901–1904), described the U.S. mission in its new colony as lifting up Filipinos "to a point of civilization" that will make them "call the name of the United States blessed." Later, Taft said about the Chinese that "the more civilized they become . . . the wealthier they become, and the better market they become for us."

Missionaries dispatched to Asia and Africa helped spur the transfer of American culture and power abroad—"the peaceful conquest of the world," as Reverend Frederick Gates put it. In 1915 10,000 American missionaries worked overseas. In China, by 1915 over 2,500 American Protestant missionaries, most of them female, labored to preach the gospel, teach, and administer medical care.

■ As part of "Anthropology Days" during the 1904 St. Louis World's Fair, organizers put on a series of athletic events showing "primitive" people participating in games such as running, high-jumping, archery, and spear throwing. In this photo by Jessie Tarbox Beals, Igorots from the Philippines compete in a spear-throwing contest. The winners were given American flags. Meanwhile, the 1904 Olympic Games took place on an irregular basis during the fair featuring white "civilized" athletes (the vast majority from the United States) who received gold medals for their victories. (Special Collections, St. Louis Public Library)

Ambitions and Strategies

The U.S. empire grew gradually, sometimes haltingly, as American leaders defined guiding principles and built institutions to support overseas ambitions. William H. Seward, one of its chief architects, argued relentlessly for extension of the American frontier as senator from New York (1849–1861) and secretary of state (1861–1869). Seward envisioned a large U.S. empire encompassing Canada, the Caribbean, Cuba, Central America, Mexico, Hawai'i, Iceland, Greenland, and the Pacific islands. This empire would be the result of a natural process of gravitation toward the United States. Commerce would hasten the process, as would a canal across Central America, a transcontinental American railroad, and a telegraph system to speed communications.

Most of Seward's grandiose plans did not reach fruition in his lifetime. In 1867 a treaty with Denmark

SEWARD'S QUEST FOR EMPIRE to buy the Danish West Indies (Virgin Islands) was scuttled by his political foes in the Senate and a hurricane in St. Thomas. The Virgin Islanders, who had voted for annexation, would gain official U.S. status in 1917. Seward's scheme with unscrupulous Dominican Republic leaders to gain a Caribbean naval base at Samaná Bay similarly failed. The corruption surrounding this deal foiled President Ulysses S. Grant's initiative in 1870 to buy the island nation.

Anti-imperialism blocked Seward. Senator Carl Schurz and E. L. Godkin, editor of *The Nation*, argued that creating a showcase of democracy and prosperity on unsettled land at home would best persuade other peoples to adopt American ways. Some anti-imperialists, sharing the racism of the times, opposed the annexation of territory populated by dark-skinned people.

Seward did enjoy some successes. In 1866, citing the Monroe Doctrine (see Chapter 10), he sent troops to the Mexican border and demanded that France abandon its puppet regime there. Also facing angry Mexican nationalists, Napoleon III abandoned the Maximilian monarchy that he forcibly installed three years earlier. In 1867 Seward paid Russia $7.2 million for the 591,000 square miles of Alaska—resource rich and twice the size of Texas. That same year,

Seward claimed the Midway Islands (two small islands and a coral atoll northwest of Hawai'i).

In 1866, through the efforts of financier Cyrus Field, an underwater transatlantic cable linked Euro-

INTERNATIONAL COMMUNICATIONS pean and American telegraph networks. Backed by J. P. Morgan, communications pioneer James A. Scrymser strung telegraph lines to Latin America, entering Chile in 1890. In 1903 a submarine cable spanned the Pacific to the Philippines; three years later it reached Japan and China. Wire telegraphy—like radio (wireless telegraphy) later—shrank the globe. Nellie Bly, a reporter for the *New York World*, accented the impact of new technology in 1890 when she completed a well-publicized trip around the world in seventy-two days. Drawn closer through improved communications and transportation, nations found that faraway events had greater impact on their prosperity and security.

Increasingly, American diplomats negotiated with their European counterparts as equals, signaling that the United States had arrived on the international stage. Seward's successor, Hamilton Fish (1869–1887), for example, achieved a diplomatic victory in resolving tensions with Great Britain, which had built the *Alabama* and other vessels for the Confederacy during the Civil War to prey on Union shipping. Senator Charles Sumner demanded that Britain pay $2 billion in damages or cede Canada to the United States. But in 1871, Fish's negotiations led to the Washington Treaty, whereby Britain apologized and agreed to the creation of a tribunal, which later awarded the United States $15.5 million.

Washington officials also squared off with European powers over Samoa, South Pacific islands 4,000 miles from San Francisco on the trade route to Australia. In 1878 the United States gained exclusive right to a coaling station at Samoa's coveted port of Pago Pago. Eyeing the same prize, Britain and Germany began to cultivate ties with Samoan leaders. Tensions grew, and war seemed possible. Britain, Germany, and the United States met in Berlin in 1889 and, without consulting the Samoans, devised a three-part protectorate that limited Samoa's independence. Ten years later, the three powers partitioned Samoa: the United States received Pago Pago through annexation of part of the islands (now called American Samoa), Germany took what is today independent Western Samoa, and

Britain obtained the Gilbert Islands and Solomon Islands.

Calling attention to the naval buildup by the European powers, notably Germany, U.S. expansionists argued for a bigger, modernized navy that would add the "blue water" command of the seas to its traditional role of coastline defense. Captain Alfred Thayer Mahan, a major popularizer for this "New Navy," whose ideas were published in *The Influence of Sea Power upon History* (1890), argued that because foreign trade was essential, the nation required an efficient navy to protect its shipping; in turn, a navy required colonies for bases. Theodore Roosevelt and Henry Cabot Lodge consulted Mahan, sharing his belief in the links between trade, navy, and colonies and his alarm over "the aggressive military spirit" of Germany.

ALFRED T. MAHAN AND NAVALISM

Moving toward modernization, Congress in 1883 authorized construction of the first steel-hulled warships. American factories produced steam engines, high-velocity shells, powerful guns, and precision instruments. The navy shifted from sail power to steam and from wood construction to steel. New ships such as the *Maine, Oregon,* and *Boston* earned the United States naval prominence.

Crises in the 1890s: Hawai'i, Venezuela, and Cuba

In the depression-plagued 1890s, crises in Hawai'i and Cuba and the belief that the frontier had closed at home buoyed the expansionist argument. In 1893 historian Frederick Jackson Turner postulated that the expanding continental frontier, which had shaped the American character, was gone. He did not say that a new frontier had to be found overseas, but he did claim that "American energy will continually demand a wider field for its exercise."

Hawai'i, the Pacific Ocean archipelago of eight major islands located 2,000 miles from the U.S. West Coast, emerged as America's new frontier. The Hawaiian Islands had long commanded American

ANNEXATION OF HAWAI'I

attention—commercial, religious missionary, naval, and diplomatic. By 1881 Secretary of State James Blaine had declared the Hawaiian Islands "essentially a part of the American system." By 1890 Americans owned about three-quarters of Hawai'i's wealth and subordinated its economy to that of the United States through sugar exports that entered the U.S. marketplace duty free.

In Hawai'i's multiracial society, Chinese and Japanese nationals far outnumbered Americans, who represented just 2.1 percent of the population. Prominent Americans on the islands organized secret clubs and military units to contest the royal government. In 1887 they forced the king to accept a constitution that allowed foreigners to vote and shifted decision making from the monarchy to the legislature. The same year, Hawai'i granted the United States naval rights to Pearl Harbor. Many native Hawaiians believed that the *haole* (foreigners), especially Americans, were taking their country from them.

The native government was further undermined when the McKinley Tariff of 1890 eliminated the duty-free status of Hawaiian sugar exports in the United States. Suffering declining sugar prices, the American island elite pressed for annexation by the United States, thereby classifying their sugar as domestic. When Princess Lili'uokalani assumed the throne in 1891, she sought to roll back the political power of the *haole*. The next year, the white oligarchy—questioning her moral rectitude and fearing Hawaiian nationalism—formed the subversive Annexation Club.

The annexationists struck in January 1893 in collusion with John L. Stevens, the chief American diplomat in Hawai'i, who dispatched troops from the U.S.S. *Boston* to occupy Honolulu. The queen, arrested and confined, surrendered. Rather than yield to the new provisional regime, headed by Sanford B. Dole, son of missionaries and a prominent attorney, she relinquished authority to the U.S. government. President Benjamin Harrison hurried an annexation treaty to the Senate.

Sensing foul play, incoming President Grover Cleveland ordered an investigation, which confirmed a conspiracy and revealed that most Hawaiians opposed annexation. But when Hawai'i proved a strategic and commercial way station to Asia and the Philippines during the Spanish-American War, President William McKinley maneuvered annexation through Congress on July 7, 1898. Under the Organic Act of June 1900, the people of Hawai'i became U.S. citizens with the right to vote in local elections and to send a nonvoting delegate to Congress. Statehood came in 1959.

The Venezuelan crisis of 1895 also saw the United States in an expansive mood. For decades Venezuela and Great Britain had quarreled over the border between Venezuela and British Guiana, a territory containing gold deposits and a commercial gateway to South America via the Orinoco River. Venezuela sought U.S. help, and Secretary of State Richard Olney brashly lectured the British that the Monroe Doctrine prohibited European powers from denying self-government to nations in the Western Hemisphere. The British, seeking international friends to counter intensifying competition from Germany, quietly retreated. With almost no Venezuelan input, in 1896 an Anglo-American arbitration board divided the disputed territory between Britain and Venezuela. Thus, the United States displayed a typical imperialist trait: disregard for the rights of small nations.

VENEZUELAN BOUNDARY DISPUTE

In 1895 Cuba was the site of another crisis. From 1868 to 1878 the Cubans had battled Spain for their independence, winning the end of slavery only. While the Cuban economy suffered, repressive Spanish rule continued. Insurgents committed to *Cuba libre* waited for another chance, and José Martí, one of the heroes of Cuban history, collected money, arms, and men in the United States.

REVOLUTION IN CUBA

Cubans of all classes settled in Baltimore, New York, Boston, and Philadelphia, and prominent Cubans on the island sent their children to school in the United States. When Cuban expatriates returned home, many spoke English, had American names, played baseball, and jettisoned Catholicism for Protestant denominations.

The Cuban and U.S. economies were also intertwined. American investments of $50 million dominated the island. Over 90 percent of Cuba's sugar was exported to the United States, and most island imports came from the United States. Havana's famed cigar factories relocated to Key West and Tampa to evade protectionist U.S. tariff laws. Martí, however,

feared that "economic union means political union," for "the nation that buys, commands" and "the nation that sells, serves."

Martí's fears were prophetic. In 1894 the Wilson-Gorman Tariff imposed a duty on Cuban sugar. The Cuban economy, highly dependent on exports, plunged into crisis, hastening the island's revolution against Spain and its further incorporation into "the American system."

From American soil, Martí launched the revolution against Spain. Rebels burned sugar-cane fields and razed mills. U.S. investments went up in smoke, and Cuban-American trade dwindled. To separate the insurgents from their supporters, Spanish general Valeriano Weyler instituted a policy of "reconcentration." Some 300,000 Cubans were herded into fortified towns and camps, where starvation and disease led to tens of thousands of deaths. As reports of atrocity made headlines in the United States, Americans sympathized with the insurrectionists. In late 1897, a new government in Madrid modified reconcentration and promised some autonomy for Cuba, but the insurgents continued to gain ground.

President William McKinley assumed office as an imperialist who advocated foreign bases for the New Navy, the export of surplus production, and U.S. supremacy in the Western Hemisphere. Vexed by the turmoil in Cuba, he explored purchasing it for $300 million. In January 1898, when antireform pro-Spanish loyalists and army personnel rioted in Havana, Washington ordered the battleship *Maine* to Havana harbor to demonstrate U.S. concern and protect American citizens.

SINKING OF THE MAINE

On February 15 an explosion ripped the *Maine*, killing 266 of 354 American officers and crew. A week earlier, William Randolph Hearst's inflammatory *New York Journal* had published a stolen private letter written by the Spanish minister in Washington, Enrique Dupuy de Lôme, belittling McKinley and suggesting that Spain would fight on. Congress complied unanimously with McKinley's request for $50 million in defense funds. Vengeful Americans blamed Spain. (Later, official and unofficial studies attributed the sinking to an accidental internal explosion.)

Though reluctant to go to war, McKinley sent Spain an ultimatum: accept an armistice, end recon-

■ On July 1, 1898, U.S. troops stormed Spanish positions on San Juan Hill near Santiago, Cuba. Both sides suffered heavy casualties. A *Harper's* magazine correspondent reported a "ghastly" scene of hundreds killed and thousands wounded. The American painter William Glackens (1870–1938) put to canvas what he saw. Because Santiago surrendered on July 17, propelling the United States to victory in the war, and because Rough Rider Theodore Roosevelt fought at San Juan Hill and later gave a self-congratulatory account of the experience, the human toll has often gone unnoticed. (Wadsworth Atheneum Museum of Art, Hartford, CT, Gift of Henry Schnakenberg)

MCKINLEY'S ULTIMATUM AND WAR DECISION centration, and designate McKinley as arbiter. Madrid made concessions. It abolished reconcentration and rejected, then accepted, an armistice. The president would no longer tolerate chronic disorder 90 miles off the U.S. coast. On April 11 McKinley asked Congress for authorization to use force "to secure a full and final termination of hostilities between . . . Spain and . . . Cuba, and to secure in the island the establishment of a stable government, capable of maintaining order."

McKinley listed the reasons for war: the "cause of humanity"; the protection of American life and property; the "very serious injury to the commerce, trade, and business of our people"; and, referring to the destruction of the *Maine,* the "constant menace to our peace." On April 19 Congress declared Cuba

free and independent and directed the president to use force to remove Spanish authority. The legislators also passed the Teller Amendment, which disclaimed any U.S. intention to annex Cuba or control the island except to ensure its "pacification." Believing that the Cubans were not ready for self-government, McKinley successfully argued against recognizing the rebel government in favor of a period of American tutoring.

The Spanish-American War and the Debate over Empire

B y the time the Spanish concessions were on the table, prospects for compromise appeared dim. Advancing Cuban insurgents wanted nothing less than independence, and no Spanish government could have granted that and remained in office. Nor did the United States welcome a truly independent Cuban government that might reduce U.S. interests.

McKinley's April message expressed a humanitarian impulse to stop the bloodletting and a concern for

MOTIVES FOR WAR

commerce and property as justification for war. Republican politicians wanted the Cuban question solved to secure the party's victory in the upcoming congressional elections. Many businesspeople and farmers believed that ejecting Spain would open new markets for surplus production.

Imperialists saw the war as an opportunity to fulfill expansionist dreams, while conservatives, alarmed by Populism and labor strikes, welcomed it as a national unifier. One senator commented that "internal discord" was disappearing in the "fervent heat of patriotism." Assistant Secretary of the Navy Theodore Roosevelt and others too young to remember the Civil War looked on war as adventure.

More than 263,000 regulars and volunteers served in the army and 25,000 in the navy during the war. Most, however, never left the United States. The typical volunteer was young (early twenties), white, unmarried, native-born, and working class. Deaths numbered 5,462, mostly from a typhoid epidemic in Tennessee, Virginia, and Florida. Only 379 died in combat. About 10,000 African Americans, assigned to segregated regiments, found no relief from racism, even though black troops were central to the victorious battle for Santiago de Cuba. For all, food, sanitary conditions, and medical care were bad. Although Roosevelt's Rough Riders, a motley unit of Ivy Leaguers and cowboys, proved undisciplined and ineffective, Roosevelt's self-serving publicity ensured that they received good press.

The first war news came not from Cuba but the Spanish colony of the Philippine Islands, where

DEWEY IN THE PHILIPPINES

Filipinos were also seeking independence. On May 1, 1898, Commodore George Dewey's ship *Olympia* led an American squadron into Manila Bay and wrecked the Spanish fleet. Dewey received orders from Washington in February to attack the islands if war broke out. Manila was a choice harbor, and the Philippines sat on the way to China's potentially huge market.

Facing Americans and rebels in Cuba and the Philippines, Spanish resistance collapsed rapidly. U.S.

ships blockaded Cuban ports, and insurgents cut off supplies from the countryside, causing starvation and illness for Spanish soldiers. American troops landed near Santiago de Cuba on June 22 and laid siege to the city. On July 3, U.S. warships sank the Spanish Caribbean squadron in Santiago harbor. American forces then assaulted the Spanish colony of Puerto Rico, winning another Caribbean naval base and pushing Madrid to defeat.

On August 12, 1898, Spain and the United States signed an armistice, and in December, they agreed on

TREATY OF PARIS

the peace terms: independence for Cuba and cession of the Philippines, Puerto Rico, and the Pacific island of Guam to the United States in exchange for $20 million. The U.S. empire now stretched deep into Asia, and the annexation of Wake Island (1898), Hawai'i (1898), and Samoa (1899) gave American traders, missionaries, and naval promoters other steppingstones to China.

During the war, the *Washington Post* detected that "the taste of empire is in the mouth of the people." But anti-imperialists such as author Mark Twain, Nebraska politician William Jennings Bryan, reformer Jane Addams, and industrialist Andrew Carnegie argued against annexation of the Philippines. Their concern that a war to free Cuba had led to empire stimulated a debate over American foreign policy.

Imperial control could be imposed either formally (by military occupation, annexation, or colonialism)

ANTI-IMPERIALIST ARGUMENTS

or informally (by economic domination, political manipulation, or the threat of intervention). Anti-imperialist ire focused mostly on formal imperial control. Some critics cited the Declaration of Independence and the Constitution, arguing that the conquest of people against their wills violated the right of self-determination.

Online Study Center **Improve Your Grade**
Primary Source:
American Anti-Imperialist League Program

Other anti-imperialists feared that the American character was being corrupted by imperialist zeal. Seeing children play war games on Chicago streets, Jane Addams noted that they were not freeing Cubans but slaying Spaniards. Hoping to build a foreign policy constituency from women's organizations, Addams and others championed peace and an end to imperial conquest.

Some anti-imperialists protested that the United States was practicing a double standard—"offering liberty to the Cubans with one hand, cramming liberty down the throats of the Filipinos with the other, but with both feet planted upon the neck of the negro," as an African American politician from Massachusetts put it. Still other anti-imperialists warned that annexing people of color would undermine Anglo-Saxon purity and supremacy at home.

For Samuel Gompers and other anti-imperialist labor leaders, the issue was jobs. Might not the new colonials be imported as cheap labor to drive down American wages? Would not exploitation of the weak abroad lead to further exploitation at home?

The anti-imperialists never launched an effective campaign. Although they organized the Anti-Imperialist League in November 1898, they differed so profoundly on domestic issues that it was difficult to speak with one voice on a foreign question.

The imperialists appealed to patriotism, destiny, and commerce. They envisioned American greatness:

IMPERIALIST ARGUMENTS merchant ships plying the waters to boundless Asian markets, naval vessels cruising the Pacific to protect American interests, missionaries uplifting inferior peoples. It was America's duty, they insisted, quoting a then-popular Rudyard Kipling poem, to "take up the white man's burden." Furthermore, Filipino insurgents were beginning to resist U.S. rule, and it seemed cowardly to pull out under fire, especially with Germany and Japan ready to seize them. National honor dictated that Americans keep what they had shed blood to take.

In February 1899, by a 57-to-27 vote (just 1 more than the minimum two-thirds majority), the Senate passed the Treaty of Paris, ending the war with Spain. Most Republicans voted yes and most Democrats no. An amendment promising independence once the Filipinos formed a stable government lost only by the tie-breaking ballot of the vice president.

Asian Encounters: War in the Philippines, Diplomacy in China

 he Philippine crisis was far from over. Emilio Aguinaldo, the Philippine nationalist leader who had been battling the Spanish for years, believed that American officials had promised independence for his country. But after the victory, U.S. officers ordered Aguinaldo out of Manila. In early 1899, he proclaimed an independent Philippine Republic and took up arms.

Both sides fought viciously: American soldiers burned villages and tortured captives, while Filipinos staged brutal hit-and-run guerrilla ambushes. U.S. troops introduced a variant of the Spanish reconcentration policy. In the province of Batangas, for instance, U.S. troops forced residents to live in designated zones to separate insurgents from local supporters. Poor sanitation, starvation, and malaria and cholera killed thousands. Outside secure areas, Americans destroyed food supplies to starve out the rebels. At least one-quarter of the population of Batangas died or fled.

PHILIPPINE INSURRECTION AND PACIFICATION

Before the Philippine insurrection was suppressed in 1902, over 200,000 Filipinos and 5,000 Americans lay dead. Resistance to U.S. rule, however, continued. When the fiercely independent, often violent Muslim Filipinos of Moro Province refused to knuckle under, the U.S. military threatened extermination. In 1906, 600 of them, including women and children, were slaughtered at the Battle of Bud Dajo.

U.S. officials soon tried to Americanize the Philippines, including a new education system with English as the primary language. Architect Daniel Burnham, leader of the City Beautiful movement (see Chapter 19), planned modern Manila. The Philippine economy grew as an American satellite, and a sedition act sent U.S. critics to prison. In 1916 the Jones Act vaguely promised independence once the Philippines established a "stable government," but the United States did not end its rule until 1946.

McKinley had greater success with negotiations in China. Outsiders had been pecking away at China since the 1840s. The major powers took advantage of the Qing (Manchu) dynasty's weakness and carved out spheres of influence (regions over which they claimed political control and exclusive commercial privileges): Germany in Shandong; Russia in Manchuria; France in Yunnan and Hainan; Britain in Kowloon and Hong Kong. Then, in 1895, Japan claimed victory over China in a short war and assumed control of Formosa, Korea,

CHINA AND THE OPEN DOOR POLICY

The U.S. System of Education in the Philippines

In the Philippines, U.S. officials moved swiftly after 1898 to create a school system based on the American notion of universal education. Under the Spanish, education had been limited and run largely by the Catholic Church. U.S. leaders hoped improved schools would be a show of goodwill. By 1901, a national education system had been established. Most instruction would be in English rather than native Philippine languages (only a small minority spoke Spanish), which rankled many Filipinos.

To overcome a teacher shortage, the United States recruited thousands of young American educators. Over a thousand arrived in 1901–1902 alone. One ship, the U.S.S. *Thomas,* carried 540 teachers, both male and female, who opened local schoolhouses across the country.

American officials also helped promising Filipinos attend universities in the United States. After returning, these students provided a cadre of well-trained medical doctors, engineers, and other professionals in the public and private sectors. Other Filipinos earned degrees at home, many at the University of the Philippines, founded in 1908.

Public schools for boys and girls, and higher education for women—at home and in the United States—allowed women to qualify as professionals for the first time. Many seized the chance, earning degrees, entering the public sphere, and founding their own colleges. Although male students outnumbered females initially, women outnumbered men at the university level by the end of the twentieth century.

But the U.S. goal of universal education never became a complete reality. Schools varied widely in quality, and Filipino elites proved better able than the less privileged to take advantage of the system. The result was a widening gap between the entitled few and the masses in the decades of U.S. colonial rule (which ended in 1946) and postcolonial independence.

Still, for millions in the Philippines, the arrival of the Americans linked the two countries through education. The irony was not lost on educated Filipinos, who knew they owed their schooling partly to the colonial power.

Boys in Normal High School, Manila, Philippines, 1900.   (Library of Congress)

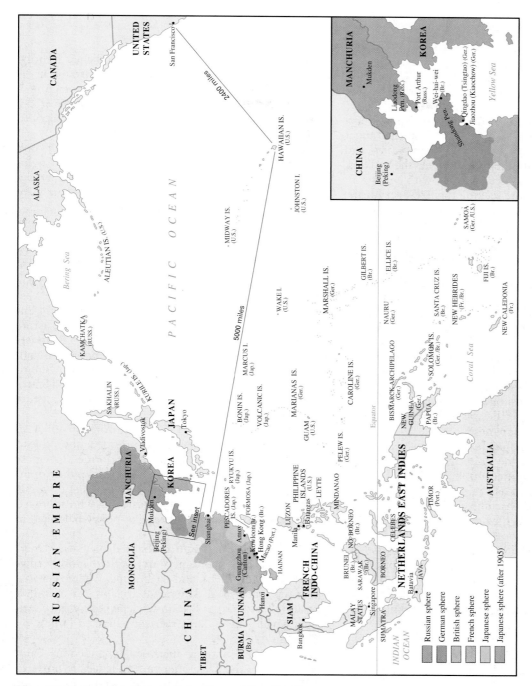

Map 22.1   Imperialism in Asia: Turn of the Century

China and the Pacific region had become imperialist hunting grounds by the turn of the century. The European powers and Japan controlled more areas than the United States, which nonetheless participated in the imperial race by annexing the Philippines, Wake, Guam, Hawai'i, and Samoa; announcing the Open Door policy; and expanding trade. As the spheres of influence in China demonstrate, that besieged nation succumbed to outsiders despite the Open Door policy.

and parts of China proper (see Map 22.1). American religious and business leaders petitioned Washington to halt the dismemberment of China before they were closed out.

Secretary of State John Hay knew that missionaries had become targets of Chinese nationalist anger and that American oil and textile companies had been disappointed with their investments there. Thus, in September 1899 Hay sent nations with spheres of influence in China a note seeking their respect for the principle of equal trade opportunity—an Open Door. The recipients sent evasive replies, privately complaining that the United States was seeking for free in China the trade rights that they had gained at considerable cost.

The next year, the Boxers, a Chinese secret society (so named in the Western press because some members were martial artists), sought to expel foreigners. They rioted, killing many outsiders and laying siege to the foreign legations in Beijing. The United States joined other imperialist powers in sending troops. Hay also sent a second Open Door note instructing other nations to preserve China's territorial integrity and honor "equal and impartial trade." China continued for years to be fertile soil for foreign exploitation, especially by the Japanese.

The Open Door policy became a cornerstone of U.S. diplomacy. While the United States had long opposed barriers to its international commerce, after 1900, when it emerged as the premier world trader, the Open Door policy became an instrument first to pry open markets and then to dominate them. The Open Door also developed several tenets: first, that America's domestic well-being required exports; second, that foreign trade would suffer interruption unless the United States intervened abroad; and third, that the closing of any area to American products, citizens, or ideas threatened the survival of the United States.

TR's World

*T*heodore Roosevelt played an important role in shaping U.S. foreign policy in the McKinley administration. As assistant secretary of the navy (1897–1898), as a Spanish-American War hero, and then as vice president in McKinley's second term, Roosevelt worked to build U.S. global prominence.

Long fascinated by power, he also relished hunting and killing. After an argument with a girlfriend in his youth, he vented his anger by shooting a neighbor's dog. Roosevelt justified the slaughtering of American Indians, if necessary, and took his Rough Riders to Cuba, desperate to get in on the fighting.

Like many Americans of his day, Roosevelt took for granted the superiority of Protestant Anglo-American culture and believed in using American power to shape world affairs. In TR's view, there were "civilized" and "uncivilized" nations; the former, primarily white and Anglo-Saxon or Teutonic, had a duty to intervene in the affairs of the latter (generally non-white, Latin, or Slavic, and therefore "backward") to preserve order, even if that included violence.

Roosevelt's love of the good fight made many rue his ascension to the presidency after McKinley's assassination in September 1901. But this "cowboy" was also an astute analyst of foreign policy. TR understood that American power, though growing year by year, remained limited, and in many parts of the world the United States would have to rely on diplomacy to achieve satisfactory outcomes.

PRESIDENTIAL AUTHORITY

Roosevelt sought to centralize foreign policy in the White House, believing the president should lead foreign relations as he did domestic priorities. Congress was too large and unwieldy, and he saw public opinion as "the voice of the devil, or what is still worse, the voice of the fool." Most presidents who followed TR shared the notion that foreign policy belonged in the executive branch.

Roosevelt's first efforts focused on Latin America, where U.S. economic interests and power towered (see Map 22.2), and on Europe, where repeated tensions persuaded Americans to develop friendlier relations with Great Britain while avoiding the continent's troubles, which Americans blamed largely on Germany.

As U.S. economic interests expanded in Latin America, so did U.S. political influence. Exports to Latin America rose from over $50 million in the 1870s to more than $120 million in 1901, and they reached $300 million in 1914. Investments by U.S. citizens in Latin America climbed to $1.26 billion in 1914. In 1899 two large banana importers had merged to form the United Fruit Company, owning much of the land in Central America (more than 1

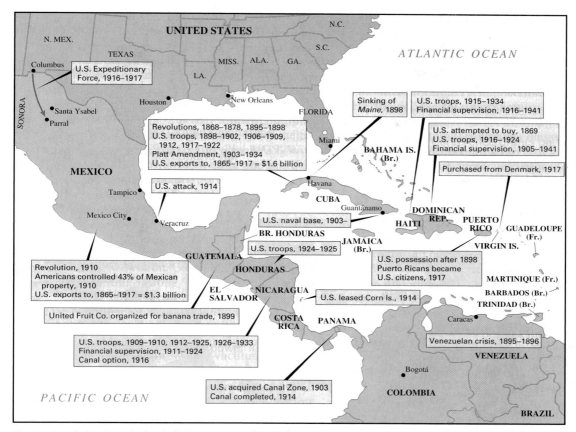

Map 22.2   U.S. Hegemony in the Caribbean and Latin America

Through many interventions, territorial acquisitions, and robust economic expansion, the United States became the predominant power in Latin America in the early twentieth century. The United States often backed up the Roosevelt Corollary's declaration of a "police power" in 1904 by dispatching troops to Caribbean nations, where they met nationalist opposition.

million acres in 1913) and the railroad and steamship lines.

After the war in Cuba, U.S. business interests dominated the island's economy, controlling the sugar,

CUBA AND THE PLATT AMENDMENT

mining, tobacco, and utilities industries and most of the rural lands. Private U.S. investments grew from $50 million before the revolution to $220 million by 1913, and U.S. exports rose from $26 million in 1900 to $196 million in 1917. The Teller Amendment outlawed the annexation of Cuba, but Washington offi-

cials used its call for "pacification" to justify U.S. control and keeping troops there until 1902.

U.S. authorities restricted voting rights largely to propertied Cuban males, excluding two-thirds of adult men and all women. American officials also forced Cubans to add the Platt Amendment to their constitution in 1903. This statement prohibited Cuba from making treaties that might impair its independence; in practice, it meant that all treaties required U.S. approval. Most important, the Platt Amendment granted the United States "the right to intervene" to preserve the island's independence and maintain order. Finally, it required Cuba to lease a naval base to the United States (at Guantánamo Bay, still under U.S. jurisdiction today). Formalized in a 1903 treaty, the amendment governed Cuban-American relations until 1934.

Cubans widely protested the Platt Amendment, and a rebellion in 1906 prompted another U.S. invasion. The marines stayed until 1909; they returned briefly in 1912 and again from 1917 to 1922. U.S. officials helped develop a transportation system, expand the public schools, establish a national army, and increase sugar production. When Dr. Walter Reed's experiments, based on the theory of Cuban physician Carlos Juan Finlay, proved that mosquitoes transmitted yellow fever, sanitary engineers eradicated the disease.

Puerto Rico, the Caribbean island taken as a spoil of war in the Treaty of Paris, at first welcomed the United States as an improvement over Spain. But the U.S. military governor, General Guy V. Henry, disdained Puerto Ricans as children who needed "kindergarten instruction in controlling themselves without allowing them too much liberty." Some residents warned against the "Yankee peril"; others applauded the "Yankee model" and futilely anticipated statehood (see the end of this chapter).

Panama meanwhile became the site of a bold U.S. expansionist venture. In 1869 the world had marveled when the newly completed Suez Canal facilitated travel between the Indian Ocean and Mediterranean Sea and enhanced the power of the British Empire. Surely that feat could be duplicated in the Western Hemisphere, possibly in Panama, a province of Colombia. Business interests joined politicians, diplomats, and navy officers in insisting that the United States control such an interoceanic canal.

PANAMA CANAL

The trouble was that the Clayton-Bulwer Treaty with Britain (1850) had provided joint control of a canal. The British, recognizing their diminishing influence and cultivating friendship with the United States as a counterweight to Germany, permitted a solely U.S.-run canal in the Hay-Pauncefote Treaty (1901). When Colombia resisted Washington's terms, Roosevelt encouraged Panamanian rebels to declare independence and ordered American warships to back them.

In 1903 the new Panama awarded the United States a canal zone and long-term rights to its con-

trol, and Panama received its independence. (In 1922 the United States paid Colombia $25 million in "conscience money" but did not apologize.) A technological achievement, the Panama Canal was completed in 1914.

Online Study Center **Improve Your Grade**
Interactive Map:
The Panama Canal

Worried that Latin American nations' defaults on debts owed to European banks were provoking European intervention, Theodore Roosevelt in 1904 issued the Roosevelt Corollary to the Monroe Doctrine. The corollary warned Latin Americans to stabilize their politics and finances, or risk "intervention by some civilized nation." Roosevelt's declaration provided the rationale for frequent U.S. interventions in Latin America.

ROOSEVELT COROLLARY

From 1900 to 1917, U.S. presidents ordered American troops to Cuba, Panama, Nicaragua, the Dominican Republic, Mexico, and Haiti to quell civil wars, thwart challenges to U.S. influence, gain ports and bases, and forestall European meddling (see Map 22.2). U.S. authorities ran elections, trained national guards, and shifted foreign debts to U.S. banks. They also controlled tariff revenues and government budgets (as in the Dominican Republic, from 1905 to 1941).

U.S. officials focused particular attention on Mexico, where long-time dictator Porfirio Díaz (1876–1910) aggressively recruited foreign investors through tax incentives and land grants. In the 1890s, the United States dominated Mexico's foreign trade. By 1910 Americans controlled 43 percent of Mexican property and produced over half the country's oil; in the state of Sonora, 186 of 208 mining companies were American owned. The Mexican revolutionaries who ousted Díaz in 1910 wanted to end their economic dependence on the United States.

U.S.-MEXICO RELATIONS

The revolution descended into a bloody civil war with strong anti-Yankee overtones, and the Mexican government intended to nationalize American-owned properties. President Woodrow Wilson twice ordered troops to Mexican soil: once in 1914, at Veracruz, to overthrow President Victoriano Huerta, and again in 1916, in northern Mexico, where General John J. "Black Jack" Pershing spent months pursuing Mexican rebel Pancho Villa for raiding an American border town. Failing to capture Villa and facing another nationalistic government, U.S. forces departed in January 1917.

As the United States demonstrated the power to enforce the Monroe Doctrine, European nations reluctantly honored U.S. hegemony in Latin America. In turn, the United States continued to stand outside European embroilments. Theodore Roosevelt did help settle a Franco-German clash over Morocco by mediating a settlement at Algeciras, Spain (1906), but he drew American criticism for this involvement. Americans endorsed the Hague peace conferences (1899 and 1907) and negotiated arbitration treaties but generally stayed outside the European arena, except for trade.

In East Asia, Roosevelt and his successor, William Howard Taft, sought to preserve the Open Door and

PEACEMAKING IN EAST ASIA

contain Japan's rising power. The United States gradually made concessions to Japan to protect the Philippines and sustain the Open Door policy. Japan continued to plant interests in China and then smashed the Russians in the Russo-Japanese War (1904–1905). President Roosevelt mediated the negotiations at the Portsmouth Conference in New Hampshire in 1905 and won the Nobel Peace Prize for helping to preserve a balance of power in Asia.

In 1905, in the Taft-Katsura Agreement, the United States conceded Japanese hegemony over Korea in return for Japan's respect for the U.S. position in the Philippines. Three years later, in the Root-Takahira Agreement, Washington recognized Japan's interests in Manchuria, and Japan again pledged the security of the U.S. Pacific possessions and endorsed the Open Door in China. Roosevelt also deterred the Japanese with reinforced naval power; in late 1907 he sent the navy's "Great White Fleet" on a world tour. Impressed, the Japanese expanded their navy.

President Taft hoped to counter Japanese advances in Asia through dollar diplomacy—the use of

DOLLAR DIPLOMACY

private funds to serve American diplomatic goals while simultaneously garnering profits for American financiers. Taft induced American bankers to join an international consortium building a railway in China. But it seemed only to embolden Japan to extend its holdings in China.

In 1914, when the First World War broke out in Europe, Japan seized Shandong and some Pacific islands from the Germans. In 1915 Japan issued its Twenty-One Demands, insisting on hegemony over China. The United States lacked power in Asia to block Japan's imperialism. A new president, Woodrow Wilson, worried about how the "white race" could blunt the rise of the "yellow race."

British officials shared this concern, though their attention focused on rising tensions in Europe. Anglo-

ANGLO-AMERICAN RAPPROCHEMENT

American cooperation blossomed in the TR-Taft years. The intense German-British rivalry and the rise of the United States to world power furthered London's quest for friendship with Washington. Americans not only shared their language and respect for private property rights, but also appreciated British support in the 1898 war and the Hay-Pauncefote Treaty, London's endorsement of the Roosevelt Corollary, and withdrawal of British warships from the Caribbean.

British-American trade and U.S. investment in Britain also secured ties. By 1914 over 140 American companies operated in Britain, including H. J. Heinz's processed foods and F. W. Woolworth's "penny markets." Many decried an Americanization of British culture. But such exaggerated fears gave way to cooperation, especially in 1917 when the United States entered the First World War supporting Britain against Germany.

Summary *Online Study Center*   ACE the Test

By 1914 Americans held extensive economic, strategic, and political interests across the globe. The outward reach of U.S. foreign policy from Seward to Wilson sparked opposition from domestic critics, other imperial nations, and foreign nationalists, but expansionists prevailed, and the trend toward empire endured.

Economic and strategic needs motivated and justified expansion. The belief that the U.S. economy needed foreign markets to absorb surplus production joined missionary zeal to reform other societies through American influence. Notions of racial and male supremacy and appeals to national greatness also fed the appetite for foreign adventure. The greatly augmented navy became a primary means for satisfying America's expansionist impulses.

Revealing the diversity of America's intersection with the rest of the world, missionaries, generals, companies, and politicians carried American ideas, guns, and goods abroad to a mixed reception. When world war broke out in August 1914, the United States's self-proclaimed greatness and political isolation from Europe were put to the test.

LEGACY FOR A PEOPLE AND A NATION
The Status of Puerto Rico

Since the U.S. invasion of their island in July 1898 and subsequent transfer from Spain to the United States, Puerto Ricans have debated their status. Colony? Territory? Nation? State? Or the "Commonwealth of Puerto Rico" that the U.S. Congress designated in 1952? A small island with 3.8 million people, Puerto Rico has held nonbinding plebiscites in 1967, 1993, and 1998, each time rejecting statehood and independence in favor of commonwealth. The U.S. Congress, which holds constitutional authority over Puerto Rico, is similarly uneasy with the ambivalence of commonwealth status.

Puerto Ricans remain troubled by their incomplete political status. The island governs itself, and Puerto Ricans are U.S. citizens (made so by the Jones Act of 1916). They pay no federal income taxes, but contribute to Social Security, and they cannot elect representatives to Congress or vote in U.S. elections. In 1999 many Puerto Ricans marched against the U.S. Navy's decades-long use of its Vieques islands as a bombing range. Two years later, President George W. Bush announced plans to vacate that installation by May 2003.

Puerto Ricans have rejected statehood because they fear it would mean forfeiting their Latin American culture and Spanish language. Most Puerto Ricans today, although bilingual, prefer Spanish over English and oppose mandatory English courses. Puerto Rico's concerns are a legacy of the era of empire building. Then as now, the issue centered on self-determination—in this case, the right of a people to sustain their own culture.

AMERICANS IN THE GREAT WAR 1914–1920

On May 7, 1915, Secretary of State William Jennings Bryan was having lunch with cabinet members in Washington when he received a bulletin: the British luxury ocean liner *Lusitania* had been sunk, apparently by a German submarine. He rushed to his office and at 3:06 P.M. received confirmation from London: "THE LUSITANIA WAS TORPEDOED OFF THE IRISH COAST AND SANK IN HALF AN HOUR." In truth, the giant vessel sank in just eighteen minutes: 1,198 people died, including 128 Americans. With Europe at war, Bryan had feared such a calamity. Britain had imposed a naval blockade against Germany, and the Germans responded with submarine warfare against Allied shipping, proclaiming the North Atlantic a danger zone and then sinking numerous British and Allied ships. As a passenger liner, the *Lusitania* was supposed to be spared, but German officials had warned Americans in newspaper ads that they traveled on British or Allied ships at their own risk: passenger liners suspected of carrying munitions or other contraband were subject to attack. For weeks Bryan had urged President Woodrow Wilson to stop Americans from booking passage on British ships; Wilson had refused.

The *Lusitania*, it soon emerged, was carrying munitions. Desperate to keep the United States out of the war, Bryan urged Wilson to condemn Germany and Britain equally and to ban Americans from traveling on belligerent ships. Others, including former president Theodore Roosevelt, called the sinking "an act of piracy" and pressed for war. Wilson did not want war, but disagreed with Bryan. He sent a strong note to Berlin, insisting Germany end its submarine warfare.

As Bryan pressed his case, he became increasingly isolated within the administration. When in early June Wilson refused to ban Americans from belligerent ships and sent a second protest note to Germany, Bryan resigned.

Americans were similarly divided over Europe's war. Eastern newspapers charged Bryan with stabbing the country in the back. In the Midwest and

Precarious Neutrality

The Decision for War

Winning the War

Mobilizing the Home Front

LINKS TO THE WORLD
The Influenza Pandemic of 1918

Civil Liberties Under Challenge

Red Scare, Red Summer

The Defeat of Peace

LEGACY FOR A PEOPLE AND A NATION
Freedom of Speech and the ACLU

Online Study Center
This icon will direct you to interactive map and primary source activities on the website http://college.hmco.com/pic/nortonbrief7e

C H R O N O L O G Y

1914 • First World War begins in Europe

1915 • Germans sink *Lusitania* off the coast of Ireland

1916 • After torpedoing the *Sussex*, Germany pledges not to attack merchant ships without warning
• National Defense Act expands military

1917 • Germany declares unrestricted submarine warfare
• Russian Revolution ousts the czar; Bolsheviks later take power
• United States enters the First World War
• Selective Service Act creates the draft
• Espionage Act limits First Amendment rights
• Race riot breaks out in East St. Louis, Illinois

1918 • Wilson announces Fourteen Points for new world order
• Sedition Act further limits free speech

• U.S. troops at Château-Thierry help blunt German offensive
• U.S. troops intervene in Russia against Bolsheviks
• Spanish flu pandemic kills 20 million worldwide
• Armistice ends the First World War

1919 • Paris Peace Conference punishes Germany and launches League of Nations
• May Day bombings help instigate Red Scare
• American Legion organizes for veterans' benefits and antiradicalism
• Wilson suffers stroke after speaking tour
• Senate rejects Treaty of Versailles and U.S. membership in League of Nations
• *Schenck v. U.S.* upholds Espionage Act

1920 • Palmer Raids round up suspected radicals

South, however, Bryan won praise from pacifists and German American groups. A few weeks later, speaking to fifteen thousand people at Madison Square Garden in New York City, Bryan was loudly applauded when he warned against "war with any of the belligerent nations." Although many Americans agreed with Wilson that honor was more important than peace, others shared Bryan's position that some sacrifice of neutral rights was reasonable to keep the country out of the fighting.

To many, war seemed unthinkable. The new machine guns, howitzers, submarines, and dreadnoughts were awesome death engines; one social reformer lamented that using them would mean "civilization is all gone, and barbarism come."

For almost three years, Wilson kept America out of the war while protecting U.S. trade interests and improving the nation's military posture. But American property, lives, and neutrality fell victim to British and German naval warfare. When the president fi-

nally asked Congress for a declaration of war, two years after the *Lusitania* went down, he insisted America would not just win the war but "make the world safe for democracy."

A year and a half later, the Great War was over. Some 10 million soldiers perished. Europeans suffered the destruction of ideals and goodwill, not to mention immense economic damage. The Great War toppled four empires of the Old World—German, Austro-Hungarian, Russian, and Ottoman Turkish—and left two others, British and French, drastically weakened.

Losses for the United States were comparatively small, yet American involvement tipped the scales in favor of the Allies with the infusion of troops, supplies, and loans. The war years also witnessed a massive international transfer of wealth from Europe across the Atlantic, as the United States went from being the world's largest debtor nation to the largest creditor. The conflict marked the United States as a world power.

At home, though, World War I intensified social divisions. Racial tensions accompanied the northward migration of southern blacks, and pacifists and German Americans were harassed. The federal government trampled on civil liberties to promote patriotism and silence critics. And after Russia's communist revolution, a Red Scare in America repressed radicals and tarnished its democratic image. Although reformers continued to devote themselves to issues such as prohibition and woman suffrage, the war splintered the Progressive movement.

Abroad, Americans who had marched to battle grew disillusioned with the peace process. They recoiled from the victors' squabbling over the spoils and chided Wilson for failing to deliver his promised "peace without victory." Americans again debated foreign policy. After negotiating the Treaty of Versailles at Paris following World War I, the president urged U.S. membership in the new League of Nations, which he believed would reform world politics. The Senate rejected his appeal (the League nonetheless organized without U.S. membership) because many Americans feared that the organization might threaten the U.S. empire and entangle America in Europe's problems. ■

Precarious Neutrality

*W*orld War I grew from years of European competition over trade, colonies, allies, and armaments. Two powerful alliance systems had formed: the Triple Alliance of Germany, Austria-Hungary, and Italy and the Triple Entente of Britain, France, and Russia. All had imperial holdings and wanted more, but as Germany challenged Britain for world leadership, many Americans saw Germany as an excessively militaristic nation that threatened U.S. interests in the Western Hemisphere.

Crises in the Balkans triggered a chain of events that shattered Europe's delicate balance of power.

OUTBREAK OF THE FIRST WORLD WAR

Slavic nationalists sought to enlarge independent Serbia by annexing regions such as Bosnia, then a province of the Austro-Hungarian Empire. On June 28, 1914, Archduke Franz Ferdinand, heir to the Austro-Hungarian throne, was assassinated by a Serbian nationalist while in Sarajevo, the capital of Bosnia. Austria-Hungary consulted its Triple Alliance partner Germany, which urged toughness. When Serbia called on its Slavic friend Russia for help, Russia looked for backing from its ally France. In late July, Austria-Hungary declared war against Serbia. Russia began to mobilize its armies.

Germany struck first, declaring war against Russia on August 1 and against France two days later. When German forces slashed into neutral Belgium to get France, London declared war against Germany on August 4. Eventually Turkey (the Ottoman Empire) joined Germany and Austria-Hungary as the Central Powers, and Italy (switching sides) and Japan teamed up with Britain, France, and Russia as the Allies. Japan seized Shandong, Germany's sphere of influence in China.

President Wilson at first distanced America by proclaiming neutrality, the traditional U.S. policy toward European wars. Privately, the president worried that without neutrality, "our mixed populations would wage war on each other."

Despite Wilson's appeal for unity at home, ethnic groups did take sides. Many German Americans and

TAKING SIDES

anti-British Irish Americans (Ireland was trying to break free from British rule) cheered for the Central Powers. Americans with roots in Allied nations championed the Allied cause. Germany's attack on Belgium confirmed for many that it was the archetype of unbridled militarism.

The pro-Allied sympathies of Wilson's administration also weakened the U.S. neutrality proclamation. Wilson shared the conviction with British leaders that a German victory would destroy free enterprise and government by law. If Germany won the war, he prophesied, "it would change the course of our civilization and make the United States a military nation."

U.S. economic ties with the Allies also rendered neutrality difficult, if not impossible. England, a longtime customer, flooded America with new orders, especially for arms. Sales to the Allies helped end an American recession. Between 1914 and 1916, American exports to England and France grew 365 percent, from $753 million to $2.75 billion. Largely because of Britain's naval blockade, exports to Germany dropped by more than 90 percent, from $345 million to only $29 million. Loans to Britain and France from private American banks—totaling $2.3 billion during neutrality—financed much of U.S. trade with the Allies. Germany received only $27 million in the same period.

To Germans, the huge U.S. trade with the Allies was an act of unneutrality that had to be stopped. Americans, however, worried that cutting their economic ties with Britain would constitute an unneutral act in favor of Germany. Under international law, Britain—which controlled the seas—could buy both contraband (war-related goods) and noncontraband from neutrals. It was Germany's responsibility, not America's, to stop such trade as international law prescribed by blockading the enemy's territory, seizing contraband from neutral (American) ships, or confiscating goods from belligerent (British) ships.

WILSONIANISM   "Wilsonianism," the cluster of ideas Wilson espoused, consisted of traditional American principles (such as democracy and the Open Door) and a vision of the United States as a beacon of freedom. Only the United States could lead the convulsed world into a peaceful era of unobstructed commerce, free-market capitalism, democratic politics, and open diplomacy.

"America had the infinite privilege of fulfilling her destiny and saving the world," Wilson claimed. Critics, however, charged that Wilson often violated his own credos while forcing them on others—as his military interventions in Mexico in 1914, Haiti in 1915, and the Dominican Republic in 1916 testified. Nonetheless, his ideals served American commercial purposes.

To say that American neutrality was never a possibility given ethnic loyalties, economic ties, and Wilsonian preferences is not to say that Wilson sought to enter the war. In early 1917, the president remarked, "We are the only one of the great white nations that is free from war today, and it would be a crime against civilization for us to go in." What, then, finally brought the United States into the war?

The short answer is that Americans got caught in the Allied–Central Power crossfire. The British sought to cripple the German economy by severing neutral trade. They seized cargo and defined a broad list of contraband (including foodstuffs) that they prohibited neutrals from ship-

VIOLATIONS OF NEUTRAL RIGHTS

ping to Germany. Furthermore, to counter German submarines, the British flouted international law by arming their merchant ships and flying neutral (sometimes American) flags. Wilson frequently protested Britain's actions, but London deflected Washington's criticism by paying for confiscated cargoes, while German provocations made British behavior appear less offensive by comparison.

Germany looked for victory at sea by using its submarines. In February 1915 Berlin declared a war zone around the British Isles, warned neutral vessels to stay away so as not to be mistakenly attacked, and advised passengers to stay off Allied ships. Wilson informed Germany that it would be accountable for any losses of American life and property.

Wilson held a strict interpretation of international law and expected Germans to warn passenger or merchant ships before attacking, so that passengers and crew could disembark safely into lifeboats. The Germans thought that surfacing its slender and sluggish *Unterseebooten* (U-boats) would risk their advantage and leave them vulnerable to attack. Berlin protested that Wilson was denying it the one weapon that could break the British economic stranglehold, disrupt the Allies' substantial connection with U.S. producers and bankers, and win the war. To British, Germans, and Americans, naval warfare became a matter of life and death.

Online Study Center **Improve Your Grade**
Interactive Map:
The War in Europe, 1914–1918

The Decision for War

In early 1915 German U-boats sank ship after ship, notably the *Lusitania* on May 7. Germany's subsequent brief promise to refrain from attacking passenger liners ended in mid-August when another British vessel, the *Arabic,* was sunk off Ireland, claiming three Americans' lives. The Germans quickly pledged that an unarmed passenger ship would never again be attacked without warning. But the *Arabic* incident led critics to ask why Americans could not be required to sail on American craft. After all, from August 1914 to March 1917, 190 Americans were killed on belligerent ships in contrast to 3 deaths on an American ship (the tanker *Gulflight,* sunk by a German U-boat in May 1915).

■ Initially underestimated as a weapon, the German U-boat proved to be frighteningly effective against Allied ships. At the beginning of the war, Germany had about twenty operational submarines in its High Seas Fleet, and officials moved swiftly to speed up production. This photograph shows a German U-boat under construction in 1914. (Bibliothek für Zeitgeschichte, Stuttgart)

In March 1916, a U-boat attack on the *Sussex*, a French vessel crossing the English Channel, injured four more Americans. Wilson threatened Berlin that the United States would sever diplomatic relations if the attacks continued. Again the Germans retreated. At the same time, U.S.-British relations soured after Britain's crushing response to the Easter Rebellion in Ireland and further British restriction of U.S. trade with the Central Powers.

PEACE ADVOCATES

As the United States became more entangled in the war, many Americans urged Wilson to keep the peace. In early 1915, Jane Addams, Carrie Chapman Catt, and other suffragists helped found the Woman's Peace Party, the U.S. section of the Women's International League for Peace and Freedom. "The mother half of humanity," claimed women peace advocates, had a special role as "the guardians of life." Later that year, pacifist Progressives organized the antiwar American Union Against Militarism. Businessmen Andrew Carnegie and Henry Ford financed peace efforts, as did socialists such as Eugene Debs.

Antiwar advocates emphasized that war drained a nation of its youth, resources, and reform impulse; that it fostered repression at home; that it violated Christian morality; and that wartime business barons reaped huge profits at the expense of the people. Militarism and conscription, Addams pointed out, were what millions of immigrants had left behind in Europe. Although the peace movement was splintered, it articulated several ideas that Wilson, who campaigned on a peace platform in 1916, shared. Wilson futilely labored to bring the belligerents to the conference table, urging them in early 1917 to temper their acquisitive war aims and embrace "peace without victory."

In Germany, Wilson's overture went unheeded. Since August 1916, leaders in Berlin had debated whether to resume the unrestricted U-boat campaign. Opponents feared a break with the United States, but proponents claimed that only through an all-out attack on Britain's supply shipping could Germany win the war. True, the United States might enter the war, but victory might be achieved before U.S. troops crossed the Atlantic. Consequently, in early February 1917, Germany launched unrestricted submarine warfare, attacking all warships and merchant

UNRESTRICTED SUBMARINE WARFARE

vessels—belligerent or neutral—in the declared war zone. Wilson then broke diplomatic relations with Berlin.

In late February, British intelligence intercepted and passed to U.S. officials a telegram addressed to the German minister in Mexico from German foreign secretary Arthur Zimmermann. Its message was that if Mexico joined an alliance against the United States, Germany would help Mexico recover the territories it had lost in 1848. Zimmermann hoped to "set new enemies on America's neck—enemies which give them plenty to take care of over there."

Although Mexico City rejected Germany's offer, Wilson judged Zimmermann's telegram "a conspiracy against this country." The prospect of a German-Mexican collaboration helped turn the tide of opinion in the American Southwest, where antiwar sentiment had been strong.

Soon afterward, Wilson asked Congress for "armed neutrality" to defend American lives and commerce, seeking authority, for example, to arm American merchant ships. Antiwar senators Robert M. La Follette and George Norris, among others, saw the armed-ship bill as a blank check for the president to move the country to war, and they filibustered it to death. Wilson armed America's commercial vessels anyway, but acted too late to prevent the sinking of several American ships. War cries heightened. In late March, Wilson called Congress into special session.

On April 2, 1917, the president stepped before a hushed Congress and enumerated U.S. grievances:

WAR MESSAGE AND WAR DECLARATION Germany's violation of freedom of the seas, disruption of commerce, interference with Mexico, and breach of human rights by killing innocent Americans. Congress declared war against Germany on April 6 by a vote of 373 to 50 in the House and 82 to 6 in the Senate. (This vote was for war against Germany only; a declaration of war against Austria-Hungary came several months later, on December 7.) Montana's Jeannette Rankin, the first woman in Congress, cast a ringing "no" vote.

For principle, for morality, for honor, for commerce, for security, for reform—for all of these reasons, Wilson took the United States into the Great War. The submarine was certainly the culprit that drew a reluctant president and nation into the maelstrom. Critics blamed Wilson's rigid definition of in-

ternational law and his contention that Americans should be entitled to travel anywhere, even on a belligerent ship loaded with contraband. Most Americans came to accept Wilson's view that the Germans had to be checked to ensure an open, orderly world in which U.S. principles and interests would be safe.

America went to war to reform world politics, not to destroy Germany. By early 1917 the president concluded that America would be unable to claim a seat at the postwar peace conference unless it became a combatant. At the peace conference, Wilson intended to promote the principles he thought essential to a stable world order, to advance democracy and the Open Door, and to outlaw revolution and aggression. In designating the United States an "Associate" rather than an Allied nation, Wilson tried to preserve part of his country's neutral status, but to no avail.

Winning the War

Even before the U.S. declaration of war, the Wilson administration strengthened the military under the banner of "preparedness." The National Defense Act of 1916 provided for increases in the army and National Guard and for summer training camps modeled on the one in Plattsburgh, New York, where some of America's social and economic elite had trained in 1915 as "citizen soldiers." The Navy Act of 1916 started the largest naval expansion in American history.

To raise an army, Congress in May 1917 passed the Selective Service Act, requiring all males between the ages of twenty-one and thirty (later changed to eighteen and forty-five) to register. National service, proponents believed, would prepare the nation for battle and instill patriotism and respect for democracy and personal sacrifice. Critics, however, feared it would lead to the militarization of American life.

THE DRAFT AND THE SOLDIER

On June 5, 1917, more than 9.5 million men signed up for the "great national lottery." By war's end, 24 million had been registered by local draft boards. The typical soldier was in his early to mid-twenties, white, single, American born, and poorly educated (most had not attended high school, and perhaps 30 percent could not read or write). Tens of thousands of women enlisted in the army Nurse Corps, served as "hello girls" (volunteer bilingual telephone operators) in the army Signal Corps, and became clerks in the navy and Marine Corps.

Some 400,000 African Americans also served in the military. Many southern politicians feared arming African Americans, but the army drafted them into segregated units and assigned them to menial labor; they endured miserable conditions. Ultimately over 42,000 blacks would see combat in Europe, and several black units served with distinction in the French army. The all-black 369th Infantry Regiment, for example, spent more time in the trenches—191 days—and received more medals than any other American outfit.

Although French officers had their share of racial prejudice and often treated the soldiers from their own African colonies poorly, black Americans serving with the French reported a degree of respect lacking in the American army. The irony was not lost on African American leaders such as W. E. B. Du Bois, who had endorsed the National Association for the Advancement of Colored People's (NAACP) support for the war and urged blacks to volunteer to help make the world safe for democracy.

Approximately 3 million men evaded draft registration. Some were arrested, others fled to Mexico or Canada, but most stayed at home and were never discovered. Another 338,000 men who had registered—mostly lower-income agricultural and industrial laborers—never showed up for induction. Nearly 65,000 draftees applied for conscientious-objector (CO) status (refusing to bear arms for religious or pacifistic reasons), but some changed their minds or failed preinduction examinations. Quakers and Mennonites were numerous among the 4,000 inductees classified as COs. COs who refused noncombat service, such as in the medical corps, faced imprisonment.

U.S. General John J. Pershing, head of the American Expeditionary Forces (AEF), insisted that his

TRENCH WARFARE

"sturdy rookies" remain a separate army. He refused to turn over his "doughboys" (so termed, apparently, because the large buttons on American uniforms in the 1860s resembled a deep-fried bread of that name) to Allied commanders, who favored deadly trench warfare. Since the fall of 1914, zigzag trenches fronted by barbed wire and mines stretched across France. Between the muddy, stinking trenches lay "no man's

land," denuded by artillery fire. Soldiers would charge enemy trenches, only to face machine-gun fire and poison gas.

First used by the Germans in April 1915, chlorine gas stimulated overproduction of fluid in the lungs, leading to death by drowning. Gas in various forms (mustard and phosgene, in addition to chlorine) would continue in use throughout the war, sometimes blistering, sometimes incapacitating, often killing.

The death toll in trench warfare was immense. At the Battle of the Somme in 1916, the British and French suffered 600,000 dead or wounded to earn only 125 square miles; the Germans lost 400,000 men. At Verdun that same year, 336,000 Germans perished, while at Passchendaele in 1917, over 370,000 British men died to gain about 40 miles of mud and barbed wire.

Not long after arriving on the French front, American soldiers faced the horrors caused by advanced

SHELL SHOCK

weaponry. Some suffered shell shock, a form of mental illness also known as war psychosis. Symptoms included a fixed, empty stare; violent tremors; paralyzed limbs; listlessness; jabbering; screaming; and haunting dreams. The illness could strike anyone; even soldiers appearing courageous cracked after days of incessant shelling and inescapable human carnage. Providing some relief were Red Cross canteens, staffed by women volunteers, which offered haircuts, food, and recreation.

In Paris, where forty large houses of prostitution thrived, venereal disease became such a problem

AMERICAN UNITS IN FRANCE

that French prime minister Georges Clemenceau offered licensed, inspected prostitutes in "special houses" to the American army. Still, by war's end, about 15 percent of America's soldiers had contracted venereal disease, costing the army $50 million and 7 million days of active duty. Periodic inspections, chemical prophylactic treatments, and the threat of court-martial kept the problem from being greater.

Overseas soldiers filled their diaries and letters with descriptions of "ancient" architecture and noted how the war-torn French countryside bore little resemblance to the groomed landscapes they had seen in paintings. "Life in France for the American soldier meant marching in the dirt and mud, living in cellars in filth, being wet and cold and fighting," the chief of staff of the Fourth Division remarked, ". . . but these French people did not seem to appreciate him at all."

With both sides virtually exhausted, the Americans tipped the balance toward the Allies. But not at first. Initially, the U.S. Navy battled submarines and escorted troop carriers; pilots in the U.S. Air Service, flying mostly British and French aircraft, saw limited action. American "aces" such as Eddie Rickenbacker defeated their German counterparts in aerial "dog-fights" and became heroes, as much in France as at home. But only ground troops could make a decisive difference, and American units did not engage in much combat until after the harsh winter of 1917–1918.

The military and diplomatic situation changed dramatically as a result of the Bolshevik Revolution

THE BOLSHEVIK REVOLUTION

in Russia. In November 1917, the liberal-democratic government of Aleksander Kerensky, which had led the country since the czar's abdication early in the year, was overthrown by V. I. Lenin's radical socialists. Lenin vowed to change world politics and end imperial rivalries on terms that challenged Wilson's. To Lenin, the war signaled the impending end of capitalism and the rise of a global revolution of workers. For Western leaders, the prospect of Bolshevik-style revolutions worldwide was too frightening to contemplate.

In the weeks following their takeover, the Bolsheviks attempted to embarrass the capitalist governments and incite world revolution by publishing several Allied secret agreements for dividing up the colonies and other territories in the event of an Allied victory. Wilson confided to Colonel House that he wanted to tell the Bolsheviks to "go to hell," but he accepted the colonel's argument that he would have to address Lenin's claims that there was little to distinguish the two warring sides and that socialism represented the future.

In the Fourteen Points, unveiled in January 1918, Wilson reaffirmed America's commitment to an inter-

FOURTEEN POINTS

national system governed by laws and renounced territorial gains as a legitimate war aim. The first five points called for diplomacy "in the public view," freedom of the seas, lower tariffs, reductions in armaments, and the decolonization of empires. The next eight points specified the evacuation of foreign troops from Russia, Belgium, and France and appealed for self-determination for

nationalities in Europe, such as the Poles. For Wilson, the fourteenth point was the mechanism for achieving the others: "a general association of nations," or League of Nations.

Lenin was unimpressed and called for an immediate end to the fighting, the eradication of colonialism, and self-determination for all peoples. He also made a separate peace with Germany—the Treaty of Brest-Litovsk, signed on March 3, 1918. The deal erased centuries of Russian expansion, as Poland, Finland, and the Baltic states were taken from Russia and Ukraine was granted independence. One of Lenin's motives was to allow Russian troops loyal to the Bolsheviks to return home to fight anti-Bolshevik forces attempting to oust his government.

In March 1918, the Germans launched a major offensive, transferring troops from the Russian front

AMERICANS IN BATTLE

to France, and by May they were within 50 miles of Paris. U.S. First Division troops helped blunt the German advance at Cantigny (see Map 23.1). In June the Third Division and French forces held positions along the Marne River at Château-Thierry, and the Second Division attacked the Germans in the Belleau Wood. American soldiers won the battle after three weeks of fighting, but thousands died or were wounded in sacrificial frontal assaults against German machine guns.

Allied victory in the Second Battle of the Marne in July 1918 stemmed German advances. In September, French and American forces took St. Mihiel in a ferocious battle. Then, in the Meuse-Argonne offensive, over 1 million Americans joined British and French troops in weeks of combat in which some 26,000 Americans were killed before the Allies claimed the Argonne Forest on October 10. For Germany—its ground and submarine war stymied, its troops and cities mutinous, its allies Turkey and Austria dropping out, its kaiser having abdicated—peace became imperative. The Germans accepted a punishing armistice effective November 11, 1918.

The cost of the war is impossible to compute: the belligerents counted 10 million soldiers and 6.6 mil-

CASUALTIES

lion civilians dead and 21.3 million people wounded. Fifty-three thousand American soldiers died in battle and another 62,000 from disease, mainly a virulent strain of influenza in late 1918. Economic damage was colossal and output dwindled,

Map 23.1   American Troops at the Western Front, 1918

America's 2 million troops in France met German forces head-on, ensuring the defeat of the Central Powers in 1918.

contributing to widespread starvation in Europe during the winter of 1918–1919.

The German, Austro-Hungarian, Ottoman, and Russian empires were no more. For a time it appeared that the Bolshevik Revolution might spread westward, as communist uprisings shook Germany and parts of central Europe. Even before the armistice, revolutionaries temporarily took power in the German cities of Bremen, Hamburg, and Lübeck. In Moscow, the new Soviet state sought to consolidate its power.

Mobilizing the Home Front

*T*he war had a tremendous impact on America. The federal government expanded its power to meet war needs and intervened in American life. The enlarged Washington bureaucracy managed the economy, labor force, military, public opinion, and more. Federal expenditures increased as the government spent more than $760 million a month from April 1917 to August 1919. As tax revenues lagged, the administration resorted to deficit spending. To

The Influenza Pandemic of 1918

In the summer and fall of 1918, as World War I neared its end, an outbreak of influenza swept the earth. It claimed more than twice as many as the Great War itself—somewhere between 25 and 40 million lives. In the United States, 675,000 people died.

The first cases were identified in midwestern military camps in early March. At Fort Riley, Kansas, 48 men died. Soldiers shipped out to Europe in large numbers (84,000 in March), some unknowingly carrying the virus. The illness appeared on the western front in April, and by June, an estimated 8 million Spaniards were infected.

In August, after a midsummer lull, a deadlier form of the influenza erupted simultaneously in three cities on three continents: Freetown, Sierra Leone, in Africa; Brest, France, the port of entry for many American soldiers; and Boston, Massachusetts. In September, the disease swept down the East Coast, killing 12,000 Americans.

People could be healthy at the start of the weekend and dead by the end of it. Some experienced a rapid accumulation of fluid in the lungs and literally drowned. Others died slowly. Mortality rates were highest for twenty- to twenty-nine-year-olds—the same group dying in the trenches.

In October, the epidemic hit full force, spreading to Japan, India, Africa, and Latin America and claiming 200,000 American lives. There was a nationwide shortage of caskets and gravediggers, and funerals were limited to fifteen minutes. Bodies were left in gutters or on front porches, to be picked up by trucks that drove the streets.

Suddenly, for reasons still unclear, the epidemic eased in November, though the dying continued into 1919. In England and Wales, the final toll was 200,000. Samoa lost a quarter of its population, and in India, the epidemic may have claimed a staggering 20 million. It was, in historian Roy Porter's words, "the greatest single demographic shock mankind has ever experienced." Americans, accustomed to thinking that two great oceans could isolate them, were reminded that they were immutably linked to the rest of humankind.

A nurse at a special camp for influenza victims on the grounds of Corey Hill Hospital in Brookline, Massachusetts, September 1918. The gauze mask she and countless others wore that autumn proved to be useless: the microbe could pass right through it. (© Underwood & Underwood/CORBIS)

Progressives of the New Nationalist persuasion (see Chapter 21), the wartime expansion and centralization of government power were welcome, but others worried about the dangers of concentrated federal power.

The federal government and private business became partners during the war. Early on, the government relied on industrial committees for advice on purchases and prices. But evidence of self-interested businesspeople cashing in on the national interest aroused public protest. The head of the aluminum advisory committee, for example, was also president of the largest aluminum company. Consequently, the committees were replaced in July 1917 with a single manager, the War Industries Board. The government also suspended antitrust laws and signed cost-plus contracts, guaranteeing companies healthy profits and a means to head off labor strikes with higher wages. Competitive bidding was virtually abandoned, and big business grew bigger.

BUSINESS-GOVERNMENT COOPERATION

Hundreds of new government agencies, staffed primarily by businesspeople, used economic controls to shift the nation's resources to the Allies, the AEF, and war-related production. The Food Administration, led by engineer and investor Herbert Hoover, urged Americans to grow "victory gardens" and eat meatless and wheatless meals, but it also regulated prices and distribution. The Railroad Administration took over the railway industry; the Fuel Administration controlled coal supplies and rationed gasoline. When strikes threatened the telephone and telegraph companies, the federal government seized and ran them.

The largest of the superagencies was the War Industries Board (WIB), headed by the financier Bernard Baruch. This Wall Streeter threatened Henry Ford that he would dispatch the military to seize his plants unless the automaker accepted WIB limits on car production. Designed as a clearing-house to coordinate the national economy, the WIB made purchases, allocated supplies, and fixed prices at levels that business requested. The WIB also ordered the standardization of goods to streamline production. The varieties of automobile tires, for example, were reduced from 287 to 3.

About a quarter of all American production was diverted to war needs. As farmers enjoyed boom years, they put more acreage into production and mechanized. Gross farm income from 1914 to 1919 increased

ECONOMIC PERFORMANCE

over 230 percent. Although manufacturing output leveled off in 1918, wartime demand fueled substantial growth for some industries such as steel, which enjoyed a peak production of 45 million tons in 1917, twice the prewar figure. Overall, the gross national product in 1920 stood 237 percent higher than in 1914.

There were mistakes in the rush to production. Weapons deliveries fell short, and the bloated bureaucracy of the War Shipping Board failed to build enough ships. In the severe winter of 1917–1918, coal companies withheld production to raise prices; railroads did not have enough coal cars; and harbors froze, closing out coal barges. People died from pneumonia and freezing. A Brooklyn man went to forage for coal in the morning and returned to find his two-month-old daughter frozen to death in her crib.

To pay its wartime bills, the government dramatically increased taxes. The Revenue Act in 1916 started by raising the surtax on high incomes and corporate profits, imposing a federal tax on large estates, and significantly increasing the tax on munitions manufacturers. Still, the government financed only one-third of the war through taxes. The other two-thirds came from loans, including Liberty bonds sold to the American people. The War Revenue Act of 1917 provided for a more steeply graduated personal income tax, a corporate income tax, an excess-profits tax, and increased excise taxes on alcoholic beverages, tobacco, and luxury items.

Although these taxes did curb excessive corporate profiteering, there were loopholes. Sometimes companies inflated costs to conceal profits. Corporate net earnings for 1913 totaled $4 billion; in 1917 they reached $7 billion; and in 1918, after the tax bite and the war's end, they still stood at $4.5 billion. The abrupt cancellation of billions of dollars' worth of contracts at war's end, however, caused a brief economic downturn, a short boom, and then an intense decline (discussed in Chapter 24).

For American workers, the full-employment wartime economy increased earnings. With the higher cost of living, however, workers saw minimal improvement in their economic standing. Turnover rates escalated as workers switched jobs, seeking better pay and conditions. Some employers sought to overcome labor shortages by expanding welfare and social programs and establishing personnel departments.

LABOR SHORTAGE

To meet the labor crisis, the Department of Labor's U.S. Employment Service matched laborers with job vacancies, attracting workers from the South and Midwest to war industries in the East. The department also temporarily relaxed the literacy-test and head-tax provisions of immigration law to attract farm labor, miners, and railroad workers from Mexico. As workers crammed into cities, the U.S. Housing Corporation and Emergency Fleet Corporation built row houses in Newport News, Virginia, and Eddystone, Pennsylvania.

The tight wartime labor market meant new work opportunities for women. In Connecticut, a special motion picture, *Mr. and Mrs. Hines of Stamford Do Their Bit*, appealed to housewives' patriotism, urging them to take factory jobs. Although the total number of working women increased slightly, the real story was that many moved into formerly male domains. Some white women left domestic service for factories, shifted from clerking in department stores to stenography and typing, or departed textile mills for firearms plants. For the first time, department stores employed black women as elevator operators and cafeteria waitresses. But most working women were single and remained concentrated in the sex-segregated occupations of typists, nurses, teachers, and domestic servants.

Women also participated in the war effort as volunteers, making clothing for refugees and soldiers, serving at Red Cross facilities, and teaching French to nurses assigned to the war zone. Many worked for the Women's Committee of the Council of National Defense, a network of state and local organizations publicizing government mobilization programs, encouraging home gardens, sponsoring drives to sell Liberty bonds, and promoting social welfare reforms. This patriotic work improved prospects of passing the Nineteenth Amendment granting woman suffrage (see Chapter 21). "We have made partners of women in this war," Wilson said in 1918. "Shall we admit them only to a partnership of suffering and sacrifice . . . and not to a partnership of privilege and right?"

War mobilization encouraged a great migration of southern blacks to northern cities to work in railroad yards, packinghouses, steel mills, shipyards, and coal mines. Between 1910 and 1920, Cleveland's black population swelled by more than 300 percent, Detroit's by more than 600 percent, and Chicago's by 150 percent, with most of it occurring between 1916 and 1919. All told, about a half-million African Americans moved to the North, with families pooling savings or selling household goods to pay for the journey. Most of the migrants were unmarried and skilled or semiskilled males in their early twenties. Northern wartime jobs provided an escape from low wages, sharecropping, tenancy, crop liens, debt peonage, lynchings, and political disfranchisement. One African American wrote to a friend in Mississippi: "I just begin to feel like a man. . . . I don't have to humble to no one. I have registered. Will vote the next election."

To keep factories running smoothly, Wilson instituted the National War Labor Board (NWLB) in early 1918. The NWLB discouraged strikes and lockouts and urged management to negotiate with existing unions. In July, after the Western Union Company fired eight hundred union members for trying to organize the firm's workers, the president nationalized the telegraph lines and put the laborers back to work. But in September the NWLB ordered striking Bridgeport, Connecticut, machinists back to munitions factories, threatening to revoke the draft exemptions they received for working in an "essential" industry.

NATIONAL WAR LABOR BOARD

Many labor leaders hoped the war would lead to recognition and better pay through partnership with government. Samuel Gompers threw the AFL's loyalty to Wilson, promising to deter strikes. He and other moderate labor leaders accepted appointments to federal agencies. The antiwar Socialist Party blasted the AFL for becoming a "fifth wheel on [the] capitalist war chariot," but union membership climbed from roughly 2.5 million in 1916 to more than 4 million in 1919.

The AFL, however, could not curb strikes by the radical Industrial Workers of the World (IWW, also known as "Wobblies") or rebellious AFL locals, especially those controlled by socialists. In the nineteen war months, more than six thousand strikes expressed workers' demands for a "living wage" and improved working conditions. Unions sought to create "industrial democracy," a more representative workplace with a role for labor in determining job categories and content. Defying the AFL, labor parties had sprung up in twenty-three states by 1920.

Civil Liberties Under Challenge

*W*ilson and his advisers enjoyed the support of newspapers, religious leaders, and public officials, but they were less certain about ordinary Americans. An official and unofficial campaign soon began to silence dissenters who were questioning Wilson's decision for war or protesting the draft. The Wilson administration had one of the worst civil liberties records in American history.

The targets of governmental and quasi-vigilante repression included hundreds of thousands of antiwar Americans and aliens: pacifists, conscientious objectors, socialists, radical labor groups, the debt-ridden Oklahoma tenant farmers who staged the Green Corn Rebellion against the draft, the Non-Partisan League, reformers such as Robert La Follette and Jane Addams, and countless others. In the wartime debate over democratic free speech, the concept of "civil liberties" emerged for the first time as a major public policy issue (see the end of this chapter).

Spearheading the administration's war campaign was the Committee on Public Information (CPI),

COMMITTEE ON PUBLIC INFORMATION

formed in April 1917 and headed by Progressive journalist George Creel. Employing talented writers and scholars, the CPI used propaganda to shape public opinion. Pamphlets and films demonized the Germans, and CPI "Four-Minute Men" spoke at movie theaters, schools, and churches to pump up patriotism. Encouraged by the CPI, film companies and the National Association of the Motion Picture Industry produced documentaries, newsreels, and anti-German movies such as *The Kaiser, the Beast of Berlin* (1918).

The committee also urged the press to practice "self-censorship" and encouraged people to spy on their neighbors. Ultrapatriotic groups such as the Sedition Slammers and the American Defense Society used vigilantism. In Hilger, Montana, citizens burned history texts mentioning Germany. To avoid trouble, the Kaiser-Kuhn grocery in St. Louis changed its name to Pioneer Grocery. Germantown, Nebraska, became Garland, and the townspeople in Berlin, Iowa, henceforth hailed from Lincoln. The German shepherd became the Alsatian shepherd.

Towns had Liberty Loan quotas and sometimes bullied "slackers" into purchasing bonds. Nativist advocates of "100% Americanism" exploited the atmosphere to exhort immigrants to throw off their Old World cultures. Companies offered English-language and naturalization classes and refused jobs and promotions to those who did not learn English fast enough.

Even institutions that had long practiced tolerance were contaminated. Wellesley College economics professor Emily Greene Balch was fired for her pacifist views (she won the Nobel Peace Prize in 1946). Three Columbia University students were apprehended in mid-1917 for circulating an antiwar petition. Columbia fired Professor J. M. Cattell, a distinguished psychologist, for his antiwar stand. His colleague Charles Beard, a prowar historian, resigned in protest. Local school boards also dismissed teachers who questioned the war.

The Wilson administration guided through an obliging Congress the Espionage Act (1917) and the

ESPIONAGE AND SEDITION ACTS

Sedition Act (1918), giving the government wide latitude to crack down on critics. The first statute forbade "false statements" designed to impede the draft or promote military insubordination, and it banned from the mails materials considered treasonous. The Sedition Act made it unlawful to obstruct the sale of war bonds and to use "disloyal, profane, scurrilous, or abusive" language to describe the government, the Constitution, the flag, or the military uniform. More than two thousand people were prosecuted under the acts, with many others intimidated into silence.

Progressives and conservatives used the war emergency to throttle the Industrial Workers of the World and the Socialist Party. Government agents raided IWW meetings, and the army put down IWW strikes. By war's end, most of the union's leaders were in jail. In summer 1918, Socialist Party leader Eugene V. Debs was arrested by federal agents for an oration extolling socialism and freedom of speech—including the freedom to criticize Wilson on the war. Debs told the court what many thought of the Espionage Act: it was "a despotic enactment in flagrant conflict with democratic principles and with the spirit of free institutions." Handed a ten-year sentence, Debs remained in prison until he was pardoned in late 1921.

The Supreme Court endorsed such convictions. In *Schenck v. U.S.* (1919), the Court unanimously upheld the conviction of a Socialist Party member who had mailed pamphlets urging draft resistance. In war, Justice Oliver Wendell Holmes wrote, the First Amendment could be restricted: when words "are of such a nature as to create a clear and present danger that they will bring about the substantial evils that Congress has a right to prevent," free speech could be limited.

Red Scare, Red Summer

The line between wartime suppression of dissent and the postwar Red Scare is not easily drawn. Together they stabbed at the Bill of Rights and wounded radicalism in America. But where wartime fears focused on subversion, after the armistice it was revolution; and where the prewar target was often German Americans, in 1919 it was frequently organized labor. Already alarmed by the Russian Revolution and communist uprisings in Europe, American fears grew in 1919 when the Soviet leadership formed the Communist International (or Comintern) to export revolution throughout the world. Terrified conservatives sought out pro-Bolshevik sympathizers (or "Reds," from the red flag used by communists) in the United States, especially in immigrant groups and labor unions.

Labor union leaders emerged from the war determined to secure higher wages for workers and retain wartime bargaining rights, while employers rescinded benefits they had been forced to grant during the war, including recognition of unions. The result was more than thirty-three hundred strikes involving 4 million laborers nationwide. On May 1, a day of celebration for workers around the world, bombs were sent to prominent Americans, though they were intercepted and dismantled. Police never captured the conspirators, but many blamed anarchists and others bent on destroying the American way of life. When the Boston police went on strike in September, some claimed a Bolshevik conspiracy, but others thought it ridiculous to label Boston's Irish American Catholic cops "radicals."

LABOR STRIKES

Unrest in the steel industry in September stirred more fears of Bolshevism. Many steelworkers worked twelve hours a day, seven days a week, and lived in squalid housing, counting on the National Committee for Organizing Iron and Steel Workers to improve their lives. When postwar industry unemployment climbed and the U.S. Steel Corporation refused to meet with committee representatives, some 350,000 workers walked off the job demanding the right to collective bargaining, a shorter workday, and a living wage. The steel barons hired strikebreakers and sent agents to club strikers. The strike collapsed in early 1920.

Business and political leaders dismissed the steel strike as a foreign threat orchestrated by American radicals. There was no conspiracy, and the American left was badly splintered. Two defectors from the Socialist Party, John Reed and Benjamin Gitlow, founded the Communist Labor Party in 1919. The rival Communist Party of the United States of America, composed largely of aliens, was launched the same year. But their combined membership did not exceed seventy thousand, and in 1919 the harassed Socialist Party could muster barely thirty thousand members.

Although divisiveness signified weakness, both Progressives and conservatives interpreted the rise of new communist parties as strengthening the radical menace. Organized in May 1919 to lobby for veterans' benefits, the American Legion soon preached an antiradicalism that fueled the Red Scare. By 1920, 843,000 Legion members, mostly middle and upper class, embraced an Americanism demanding conformity.

AMERICAN LEGION

Wilson's attorney general, A. Mitchell Palmer, also insisted that Americans think alike. A Progressive reformer, Quaker, and ambitious politician, Palmer appointed J. Edgar Hoover to head the Radical Division of the Department of Justice. Hoover compiled index cards naming allegedly radical individuals and organizations. During 1919 agents jailed IWW members; Palmer also made sure that 249 alien radicals, including anarchist Emma Goldman, were deported to Russia.

States passed peacetime sedition acts and arrested hundreds of people. Vigilante groups flourished, their numbers swelled by returning veterans. In November 1919 in Centralia, Washington, American Legionnaires broke from a parade to storm the IWW hall. Several were wounded, others were arrested, and one Wobbly, an ex-soldier, was taken from jail by a mob, then beaten, castrated, and shot. The New York State legislature expelled five duly elected Socialist Party members in early 1920.

Online Study Center Improve Your Grade
Primary Source:
    Case Against the "Reds"

The Red Scare reached a climax in January 1920 in the Palmer Raids. Planned and directed by Hoover,

PALMER RAIDS

government agents in thirty-three cities broke into meeting halls and homes without search warrants, jailing over four thousand people and denying them counsel. In Boston some four hundred people were detained on bitterly cold Deer Island: two died of pneumonia, one leaped to his death, and another went insane. Because of court rulings and the courageous efforts of Assistant Secretary of Labor Louis Post, most of the arrestees were released, although nearly six hundred were deported in 1920–1921.

Palmer's disregard for elementary civil liberties drew criticism, with many charging that his tactics violated the Constitution. When Palmer called for a peacetime sedition act, he alarmed both liberal and conservative leaders. His dire prediction that pro-Soviet radicals would incite violence on May Day 1920 proved mistaken, as the day remained peaceful. Palmer, who had called himself the "Fighting Quaker," was jeered as the "Quaking Fighter."

Palmer also blamed communists for the racial violence that gripped the nation in these years,

RACIAL UNREST

though the charge was equally baseless. African Americans realized well before the war ended that their participation did little to change discriminatory white attitudes. Segregation remained social custom. The Ku Klux Klan was reviving, and racist films such as D. W. Griffith's *The Birth of a Nation* (1915) fed prejudice with its celebration of the Klan and its demeaning depiction of blacks. Despite wartime declarations of humanity, 382 blacks were lynched in America between 1914 and 1920, some of them in military uniform.

Northern whites who resented "the Negro invasion" rioted, as in East St. Louis, Illinois, in July 1917 (see Chapter 19) and a month later in Houston. During the bloody "Red Summer" of 1919 (so named by black author James Weldon Johnson for the blood that was spilled), race riots rocked two dozen cities and

towns. The worst violence occurred in Chicago, a favorite destination for migrating blacks. In the hot days of July 1919, a black youth swimming at a segregated white beach was hit by a rock and drowned. Soon blacks and whites were battling one another. Stabbings, burnings, and shootings continued for days until state police restored calm. Thirty-eight people died, twenty-three African Americans and fifteen whites. A disillusioned W. E. B. Du Bois vowed a struggle: "We return. We return from fighting. We return fighting." And poet Claude McKay put it this way in his poem, "If We Must Die":

Like men we'll face the murderous cowardly pack.
Pressed to the wall, dying, but fighting back.

Du Bois and McKay reflected a newfound militancy among black veterans and northern black

BLACK MILITANCY

communities. Editorials in African American newspapers subjected white politicians to increasingly harsh criticism and implored readers to embrace their own prowess and beauty. The NAACP stepped up its campaign for civil rights and equality, vowing in 1919 to publicize the terrors of lynching and seek legislation against it. Other blacks, doubting the potential for equality, turned instead to charismatic Jamaican immigrant Marcus Garvey, who called on African Americans to seek a separate black nation (as detailed in Chapter 24).

The crackdown on laborers and radicals and the resurgence of racism in 1919 dashed wartime hopes. Although the passage of the Nineteenth Amendment in 1920, guaranteeing women the right to vote, showed that reform could happen, it was the exception. Unemployment, inflation, racial conflict, labor upheaval, a campaign against free speech—all inspired disillusionment in the immediate postwar years.

The Defeat of Peace

resident Wilson seemed more focused on confronting the threat of radicalism abroad than at home. In mid-1918, he revealed his ardent anti-Bolshevism when he ordered five thousand American troops to northern Russia and ten thousand more to Siberia, where they joined other Allied contingents in fighting what was now a Russian civil war. Wilson did not consult Congress. He said the military expeditions would guard Allied supplies and Russian railroads from German seizure and would also rescue a group of Czechs who wished to fight the Germans.

Seeking to smash the infant Bolshevik government, Wilson backed an economic blockade of Russia, sent arms to anti-Bolshevik forces, and refused to recognize Lenin's government. The United States also secretly passed military information to anti-Bolshevik forces and used food relief to shore up Soviet opponents in the Baltic region. Later, at the Paris Peace Conference, Russia was denied a seat. U.S. troops did not leave Siberia until spring 1920, after the Bolsheviks had demonstrated their staying power.

Wilson faced a monumental task in securing a postwar settlement, though some observers suggested he underestimated his task. During the 1918 congressional elections, Wilson misstepped in suggesting that patriotism required the election of a Democratic Congress; Republicans blasted the president for questioning their love of country and gained control of both houses. This was trouble because a peace treaty would require approval from a potentially hostile Senate and because the election results diminished Wilson's stature in the eyes of foreign leaders. Wilson aggravated his political problems by not naming a senator to his advisory American Peace Commission and refusing to bring any prominent Republicans with him or to consult with the Senate Foreign Relations Committee before the Paris Peace Conference.

Wilson was greeted by adoring crowds in Paris, London, and Rome, but their leaders—Georges Clemenceau of France, David Lloyd George of Britain, and Vittorio Orlando of Italy (with Wilson, the Big Four)—became formidable adversaries. After four years of horrible war, the Allies were not about to be cheated out of the fruits of victory. The late-arriving Americans had not suffered as France and Great Britain had. Germany would have to pay big for the calamity it had caused.

The Big Four tried to work out an agreement at the conference. The victors demanded that Germany

PARIS PEACE CONFERENCE

(which had been excluded from the proceedings) pay a huge reparations bill. Wilson instead called for a small indemnity, fearing that an economically hobbled Germany might turn

to Bolshevism. Unable to moderate the Allied position, the president reluctantly agreed to a clause blaming the war on the Germans and to the creation of a commission to determine reparations (later set at $33 billion). Wilson acknowledged that the peace terms were "hard," but he also came to believe that "the German people must be made to hate war."

As for dismantling empires and the principle of self-determination, Wilson could achieve only some of his goals. Creating a League-administered "mandate" system, the conferees gave Japan authority over Germany's colonies in the Pacific, while France obtained what became Lebanon and Syria and Britain received the three former Ottoman provinces that became Iraq. Britain also secured Palestine, on the condition that it promote "the establishment in Palestine of a national home for the Jewish people" without prejudice to "the civil and religious rights of existing non-Jewish communities"—the so-called Balfour Declaration of 1917.

Elsewhere in Europe, Wilson's prescriptions fared better. Out of Austria-Hungary and Russia came the newly independent states of Austria, Hungary, Yugoslavia, Czechoslovakia, and Poland. Wilson and his colleagues also built a *cordon sanitaire* (buffer zone) of new westward-looking nations (Finland, Estonia, Latvia, and Lithuania) around Russia to quarantine the Bolshevik contagion.

Wilson worked hardest on the charter for the League of Nations, the centerpiece of his plans for

LEAGUE OF NATIONS AND ARTICLE 10

the postwar world. He envisioned the League as having power over all disputes among states; as such, it could transform international relations. Even so, the great powers would have preponderant say: the organization would have an influential council of five permanent members and elected delegates from smaller states, an assembly of all members, and a World Court.

Wilson identified Article 10 as the "kingpin" of the League covenant: "The Members of the League undertake to respect and preserve as against external aggression the territorial integrity and existing political independence of all Members of the League." Wilson insisted the League charter become part of the peace treaty, arguing that there could be no future peace without a league to oversee it.

German representatives at first refused to sign the punitive treaty but submitted in June 1919. They gave up 13 percent of Germany's territory, 10 percent of its population, all of its colonies, and a huge portion of its national wealth. Many people wondered how the League could function in the poisoned postwar atmosphere of humiliation and revenge.

In March 1919, thirty-nine senators (enough to deny the treaty the necessary two-thirds vote) signed a petition stating that the League's

CRITICS OF THE TREATY

structure did not adequately protect U.S. interests. Wilson denounced his critics as "pygmy" minds, but persuaded the peace conference to exempt the Monroe Doctrine and domestic matters from League jurisdiction. But Wilson would budge no more. Could his critics not see that League membership would give the United States "leadership in the world"?

By summer, criticism intensified: Wilson had bastardized his own principles. He had conceded Shandong to Japan and killed a provision affirming the racial equality of all peoples. The treaty ignored freedom of the seas, and tariffs were not reduced. Reparations on Germany promised to be punishing. Critics on the left protested that the League would perpetuate empire. Conservative critics feared it would limit American freedom of action in world affairs, stymie U.S. expansion, and intrude on domestic questions. And Article 10 raised serious questions: Would the United States be *obligated* to use armed force to ensure collective security? And would the League feel compelled to crush colonial rebellions, such as in Ireland or India?

Henry Cabot Lodge of Massachusetts led the Senate opposition. A Harvard-educated Ph.D. and partisan Republican who intensely disliked Wilson, Lodge packed the Foreign Relations Committee with critics and introduced several reservations to the treaty, most importantly that Congress had to approve any obligation under Article 10.

In September 1919 Wilson embarked on a speaking tour of the United States. Growing more exhausted, he dismissed his antagonists as "contemptible quitters." While doubts about Article 10 multiplied, Wilson highlighted neglected features of the League charter—such as the arbitration of disputes and an international conference to abolish child labor. In Colorado, the president awoke to nausea and uncontrollable facial twitching. A few days later, he suffered a massive stroke that paralyzed his left side. He

became peevish and even more stubborn, increasingly unable to conduct presidential business. Advised to placate Lodge and other senatorial critics so the Versailles treaty might receive congressional approval, Wilson rejected "dishonorable compromise."

Twice in November the Senate rejected the Treaty of Versailles and thus U.S. membership in the

SENATE REJECTION OF THE TREATY AND LEAGUE

League. In March 1920 the Senate again voted; this time, a majority (49 for and 35 against) favored the treaty with reservations, but the tally fell short of the two-thirds needed. Had Wilson permitted Democrats to compromise—to accept reservations—he could have achieved his fervent goal of membership in the League, which came into being without the United States.

At the core of the debate lay a basic issue in American foreign policy: whether the United States would endorse collective security or continue the more solitary path articulated in George Washington's Farewell Address and the Monroe Doctrine. In a world dominated by imperialist states unwilling to subordinate their strategic ambitions to an international organization, Americans preferred their traditional nonalignment and freedom of choice over binding commitments to collective action. Wilson countered that the League promised something better than the status quo for the United States and the rest of the world: collective security in place of the frail protection of alliances and the instability of a balance of power.

World War I did not make the world safe for democracy, but it did make the United States an even

AN UNSAFE WORLD

greater world power. By 1920 the United States was the leading global economic power, producing 40 percent of the world's coal, 70 percent of its petroleum, and half of its pig iron. It also ranked first in world trade. American companies used the war to nudge the Germans and British out of foreign markets, especially in Latin America. Meanwhile, the United States shifted from a debtor to a creditor nation, becoming the world's leading banker.

After the disappointment of Versailles, the peace movement revitalized, and the military became more professional. The Reserve Officers Training Corps (ROTC) became permanent; military "colleges" provided upper-echelon training; and the Army Industrial College, founded in 1924, pursued business-military cooperation in logistics and planning. The National Research Council, created in 1916 with government money and Carnegie and Rockefeller funds, continued as a defense research alliance. Tanks, quick-firing guns, armor-piercing explosives, and oxygen masks for pilots were among the technological advances emerging from the First World War.

The international system born in these years was unstable. Nationalist leaders active during the First World War, such as Ho Chi Minh of Indochina and Mohandas K. Gandhi of India, vowed independence for their peoples. Communism became a disruptive force in world politics, and the Soviets bore a grudge against those who had tried to thwart their revolution. The new states in central and eastern Europe proved weak. Germans bitterly resented the harsh peace settlement, and German war debts and reparations dogged international order for years.

Summary *Online Study Center* ACE the Test

*T*he war years marked the emergence of the United States as a world power, and Americans could take justifiable pride in their contribution to the Allied victory. But the war exposed deep divisions among Americans: white versus black, nativist versus immigrant, capital versus labor, men versus women, radical versus Progressive and conservative, pacifist versus interventionist, nationalist versus internationalist.

During the war, the federal government intervened in the economy and influenced people's everyday lives as never before. Although the Wilson administration shunned reconversion plans (war housing projects, for example, were sold to private investors) and quickly dismantled the many governmental agencies, the World War I experience of the activist state served as guidance for reformers battling the Great Depression in the 1930s (the topic of Chapter 25). The partnership of government and business in managing the wartime economy advanced the development of a mass society through the standardization of products and the promotion of efficiency. Wilsonian wartime policies also nourished the concentration of corporate ownership by suspending antitrust laws. Business

power dominated the next decade, while labor entered lean years.

Although the disillusionment of Versailles did not cause the United States to adopt isolationism (as discussed in Chapter 26), skepticism about America's ability to right wrongs abroad marked the nation's postwar mood. People recoiled from photographs of shell-shocked faces and bodies dangling from barbed wire. American soldiers, tired of idealism, craved regular jobs. Many Progressives lost their enthusiasm for crusades, disgusted by the bickering of the victors.

By 1920 idealism had faded at home and abroad. Americans were unsure what their country's new-found status as a world power meant for the future. With uneasiness and a mixed legacy from the Great War, the country entered the 1920s.

LEGACY FOR A PEOPLE AND A NATION
Freedom of Speech and the ACLU

Before World War I, those with radical views often received harsh treatment for exercising their freedom of speech. During the war, however, the Wilson administration's suppression of dissidents led some Americans to reformulate the traditional definition of allowable speech. Roger Baldwin, a conscientious objector, and women's suffrage activist Crystal Eastman were among the first to advance the idea that the content of political speech could be separated from the identity of the speaker and that patriotic Americans could—indeed, should—defend the right of others to express political beliefs abhorrent to their own. After defending conscientious objectors, Baldwin and Eastman—joined by activists such as Jane Addams, Helen Keller, and Norman Thomas—formed the American Civil Liberties Union (ACLU).

Since 1920 the ACLU, which today has some 300,000 members, has aimed to protect the civil liberties of all Americans. It has been involved in almost every major civil liberties case in U.S. courts, among them the John Scopes "monkey trial" (1925) concerning the teaching of evolution at a Tennessee school and the landmark *Brown v. Board of Education* case (1954) that ended federal tolerance of racial segregation.

Conservatives have long criticized the ACLU for its opposition to official prayers in public schools and its support of abortion, as well as its decisions on whose freedom of speech to defend. ACLU proponents counter that it has also defended those on the right, such as Oliver North, a key figure in the Iran-contra scandal of the 1980s.

Either way, the principle of free speech is today broadly accepted by Americans, so that even ACLU bashers take it for granted. Ironically, the Wilson administration's crackdown on dissent produced an expanded commitment to freedom of speech for a people and a nation.

The New Era 1920–1929

Eager to win $25,000 offered by a hotel owner to the first person to fly nonstop between New York and Paris, three different airplane crews at Roosevelt Airfield accepted the challenge in the spring of 1927. One man, Charles A. Lindbergh, young, handsome, and the only one piloting solo, risked drizzly weather to start the trip on May 20. For thirty-three hours, his craft, *The Spirit of St. Louis,* bounced across the Atlantic skies. The flight captivated Americans as newspaper and telegraph reports followed Lindbergh's progress. When he landed at Le Bourget Airfield, the nation rejoiced. President Calvin Coolidge dispatched a warship to bring "Lucky Lindy" home. Celebrants sent Lindbergh 55,000 telegrams and feted him during a triumphant homecoming parade.

Although his was not the first transatlantic flight (in 1919, two men had piloted a plane from Newfoundland to Ireland), Lindbergh's venture turned him into one of the most celebrated heroes in American history. One newspaper exclaimed that he had accomplished "the greatest feat of a solitary man in the history of the human race." Lindbergh received the Distinguished Flying Cross and the Congressional Medal of Honor. Promoters offered him millions of dollars for a world air tour and $700,000 for a movie contract. Texas named a town after him.

The celebration and publicity surrounding Lindbergh's flight reveal the impact of commercialism, technology, and mass entertainment on American culture. Lindbergh epitomized achievement, self-reliance, and courage—old-fashioned values that vied for public allegiance in a new era.

During the 1920s, consumerism flourished. Although poverty beset small farmers, workers in declining industries, and nonwhites in inner cities, most others enjoyed a high standard of living relative to previous generations. Spurred by advertising and installment buying, Americans acquired radios, automobiles, real estate, and stocks. As in the Gilded Age, government maintained a favorable climate for business. And in contrast to the Progressive era, few people worried about abuses of power. Still, state and local governments undertook important reforms.

Big Business Triumphant

Politics and Government

Materialism Unbound

Cities, Migrants, and Suburbs

New Rhythms of Everyday Life

LINKS TO THE WORLD
Pan American Airways

Lines of Defense

The Age of Play

Cultural Currents

The Election of 1928 and the End of the New Era

LEGACY FOR A PEOPLE AND A NATION
Intercollegiate Athletics

Online Study Center
This icon will direct you to interactive map and primary source activities on the website http://college.hmco.com/pic/nortonbrief7e

C H R O N O L O G Y

1920 • Nineteenth Amendment ratified, legalizing the vote for women in federal elections
• Harding elected president
• KDKA transmits first commercial radio broadcast

1920–21 • Postwar deflation and depression occurs

1921 • Federal Highway Act funds national highway system
• Emergency Quota Act establishes immigration quotas
• Sacco and Vanzetti convicted
• Sheppard-Towner Act allots funds to states to set up maternity and pediatric clinics

1922 • Economic recovery raises standard of living
• *Coronado Coal Company v. United Mine Workers* rules that strikes may be illegal actions in restraint of trade
• *Bailey v. Drexel Furniture Company* voids restrictions on child labor
• Federal government ends strikes by railroad shop workers and miners
• Fordney-McCumber Tariff raises rates on imports

1923 • Harding dies; Coolidge assumes the presidency
• *Adkins v. Children's Hospital* overturns a minimum-wage law affecting women

1923–24 • Government scandals (Teapot Dome) exposed

1924 • National Origins Act revises immigration quotas
• Coolidge elected president

1925 • Scopes trial highlights battle between religious fundamentalists and modernists

1927 • Sacco and Vanzetti executed
• Lindbergh pilots solo transatlantic flight
• Ruth hits sixty home runs
• *The Jazz Singer,* the first movie with sound, is released

1928 • Stock market soars
• Hoover elected president

1929 • Stock market crashes; Great Depression begins

As Lindbergh's adventure reveals, it was an era of contrast and complexity. Fads and frivolities coincided with creativity in the arts and advances in science and technology. Changes in work habits, family responsibilities, and healthcare fostered new uses of time and new attitudes about behavior. Material bounty and leisure enticed Americans into new amusements. The era's modernism and materialism were appealing to many but unsettling to those who embraced tradition and scorned liberal ideas.

The glitter of consumer culture blinded Americans to rising debts and uneven prosperity. They were thoroughly unprepared when a devastating depression brought the era to a close. ■

Big Business Triumphant

*T*he 1920s began with economic decline. After the First World War ended, industrial output dropped and unemployment rose as wartime orders dried up, consumer spending dwindled, and demobilized soldiers flooded the work force. Unemployment, around 2 percent in 1919, passed 12 percent in 1921. Railroads and mining industries suffered, and New England textile companies abandoned outdated factories for the convenient raw materials and cheap labor of the South.

Electric energy prompted a recovery in 1922 that continued unevenly until 1929. *NEW ECONOMIC EXPANSION* By decade's end, factories using electric motors dominated industry, increasing productivity. Most urban households now had electric lighting and could use new appliances such as refrigerators and vacuum cleaners.

As Americans acquired spending money and leisure time, service industries such as restaurants, beauty salons, and movie theaters boomed. Installment, or time-payment, plans drove the new consumerism. Of 3.5 million automobiles sold in 1923, 80 percent were bought on credit.

Although Progressive era trustbusting reined in big business, it had not eliminated oligopoly, the con-

OLIGOPOLIES AND "NEW LOBBYING" trol of an industry by a few large firms. By the 1920s oligopolies dominated production, marketing, distribution, and finance. In industries such as steel and electrical equipment, a few companies, such as U.S. Steel and General Electric, predominated.

Business and professional organizations also expanded in the 1920s. Retailers and manufacturers formed trade associations to swap information. Farm bureaus promoted scientific agriculture and tried to stabilize markets. These special-interest groups participated in the "new lobbying." With government playing an increasingly influential role, hundreds of organizations sought to convince legislators to support their interests.

Government policies helped business thrive, and legislators came to depend on lobbyists' expertise. Congress cut taxes on corporations and wealthy individuals in 1921, and the next year raised tariff rates in the Fordney-McCumber Tariff Act. Presidents Warren G. Harding, Calvin Coolidge, and Herbert Hoover appointed cabinet officers who were favorable toward business. Regulatory agencies such as the Federal Trade Commission and Interstate Commerce Commission cooperated with, rather than regulated, corporations.

Key Supreme Court decisions sheltered business from government regulation and hindered organized labor. In *Coronado Coal Company v. United Mine Workers* (1922), Chief Justice William Howard Taft, the former president, ruled that a striking union, like a trust, could be prosecuted for illegal restraint of trade. Yet in *Maple Floor Association v. U.S.* (1929), the Court decided that trade associations that distributed anti-union information were not acting in restraint of trade. The Court also voided restrictions on child labor (*Bailey v. Drexel Furniture Company*, 1922)

and overturned a minimum-wage law affecting women because it infringed on liberty of contract (*Adkins v. Children's Hospital*, 1923).

Public opinion turned against organized labor in the 1920s, linking it with communism brought to

SETBACKS FOR ORGANIZED LABOR America by radical immigrants. Using Red Scare tactics, the Harding administration in 1922 obtained a sweeping court injunction to quash a strike by 400,000 railroad shop workers. State and federal courts issued injunctions to prevent strikes and permitted businesses to sue unions for damages suffered from labor actions.

Some corporations countered the appeal of unions by offering pensions, profit sharing (which amounted to withholding wages for later distribution), and company-sponsored picnics and sporting events—a policy known as welfare capitalism. State legislators aided employers by prohibiting closed shops (workplaces where union membership was mandatory) and permitting open shops (which could discriminate against unionized workers). As a result of these efforts, union membership fell from 5.1 million in 1920 to 3.6 million in 1929.

Agriculture suffered during the 1920s, as farmers faced international competition and tried to increase

LANGUISHING AGRICULTURE productivity by investing in new machines such as harvesters and tractors. Debt increased, while overproduction and foreign competition depressed crop and livestock prices, in turn reducing incomes. Early in the decade, for example, the price of cotton dropped by two-thirds, and that of hogs and cattle fell by half. Farm income never recovered. Many farmers became tenants because they lost their land; more quit farming altogether.

Politics and Government

a series of Republican presidents extended Theodore Roosevelt's government-business cooperation, but they made government a compliant coordinator rather than the active manager Roosevelt had advocated. President Warren G. Harding, elected in 1920, was a symbol of government's goodwill toward business. He captured 16 million popular votes to 9 million for the Democratic nominee, Ohio governor James M. Cox. (The total vote in the 1920 presidential election increased 36 percent over 1916, reflecting the participation of women voters for the first time.)

A small-town newspaperman and senator from Ohio, Harding appointed assistants who promoted business growth, notably Secretary of State Charles Evans Hughes, Secretary of Commerce Herbert Hoover, Secretary of the Treasury Andrew Mellon, and Secretary of Agriculture Henry C. Wallace. Harding also backed reforms such as the Budget and Accounting Act of 1921 to streamline federal spending, and he supported antilynching legislation and efforts to assist farm cooperatives and liberalize farm credit.

Harding was plagued by problems, among them his extramarital affairs. For example, in 1917, he

SCANDALS OF HARDING ADMINISTRATION

began a relationship with Nan Britton, thirty-one years his junior, that resulted in a daughter in 1919. Britton reputedly visited Harding in the White House, although Harding never acknowledged his illegitimate offspring.

Of greater consequence, Harding often appointed cronies who used government positions for personal gain. Charles Forbes of the Veterans Bureau went to federal prison, convicted of fraud and bribery in connection with government contracts. Most notorious, a congressional inquiry in 1923 and 1924 revealed that Secretary of the Interior Albert Fall had accepted bribes to lease oil-rich government property to private oil companies. He was fined $100,000 and spent a year in jail for his role in the so-called Teapot Dome scandal, named for the oil reserve he turned over to the Mammoth Oil Company.

By mid-1923, Harding had become disillusioned. On a speaking tour, he became ill and died in San Francisco on August 2. Although his death preceded revelation of the Teapot Dome scandal, some speculated that Harding committed suicide to avoid impeachment or was poisoned by his wife. Most evidence, however, points to death from natural causes, probably a heart attack. Vice President Calvin Coolidge, who now became president, was more aloof than Harding. As governor of Massachusetts, Coolidge had attracted national attention in 1919 with his stand against striking Boston policemen, winning him business support and the vice-presidential nomination in 1920.

Respectful of private enterprise and aided by Andrew Mellon, who was retained as secretary of

COOLIDGE PROSPERITY

the treasury, Coolidge's administration reduced federal debt, lowered income-tax rates (especially for the wealthy), and began a national highway system. Meanwhile, with farm prices falling, Congress twice passed bills to establish government-backed price supports for staple crops (the McNary-Haugen bills of 1927 and 1928). Resembling the Farmers' Alliances' subtreasury scheme of the 1890s (see Chapter 20), these bills would have established a system whereby the government would buy surplus farm products and either hold them until prices rose or sell them abroad. Coolidge, however, vetoed the measures as improper government interference in the market economy.

"Coolidge prosperity" was the decisive issue in the presidential election of 1924. Both major parties ran candidates who favored private initiative over government intervention. At their national convention, Democrats voted 542 to 541 against condemning the revived Ku Klux Klan, and deadlocked for 103 ballots between southern prohibitionists, who supported former secretary of the treasury William G. McAdoo, and antiprohibition easterners, backing New York's governor Alfred E. Smith. They compromised on John W. Davis, a New York corporation lawyer.

Remnants of the Progressive movement, along with various farm, labor, and socialist groups, formed a new Progressive Party and nominated Robert M. La Follette, the aging Wisconsin reformer. The new party stressed public ownership of utilities, aid to farmers, rights for organized labor, and regulation of business. Coolidge beat Davis by 15.7 million to 8.4 million popular votes and 382 to 136 electoral votes. La Follette received 4.8 million popular votes and only 13 electoral votes.

The urgency for political and economic reform that inspired the previous generation faded in the

EXTENSIONS OF PROGRESSIVE REFORM

1920s, with important reforms continuing primarily at state and local levels. Following pre–World War I initiatives, thirty-four states instituted or expanded workers' compensation laws in the 1920s. Many states established employee-funded old-age pensions and welfare programs for the indigent. By 1926 every major city and many smaller ones had planning and zoning commissions to harness physical growth to the common good. Statehouses, city halls, and universities trained a new generation of reformers who later influenced national affairs.

Organizations such as the Indian Rights Association, the Indian Defense Association, and the General Federation of Women's Clubs worked to obtain justice and social services for Native Americans, including better education and return of tribal lands. But like other minorities, Indians generally met discrimination and pressure to assimilate. Severalty, the policy created by the Dawes Act of 1887 of allotting land to individuals rather than to tribes, failed to make Indians self-supporting. Deeply attached to their land, even struggling Indian farmers were unlikely to move to cities. Whites still hoped to convert native peoples into "productive" citizens, typically ignoring indigenous cultures. Reformers were especially critical of Indian women, who refused to adopt middle-class homemaking habits and balked at sending their children to boarding schools.

INDIAN AFFAIRS

Citizenship remained unclear. The Dawes Act had conferred citizenship on Indians who accepted land allotments but not those who remained on reservations. After several court challenges, Congress passed a law in 1924 granting citizenship to all Indians. President Herbert Hoover's administration reorganized the Bureau of Indian Affairs and increased expenditures for health, education, and welfare. Much of the money, however, went to enlarge the bureaucracy rather than to Indians.

Ratification of the Nineteenth Amendment in 1920 gave women the vote, but they nonetheless remained outside local and national power structures. Instead, they worked through voluntary associations to lobby legislators on issues such as birth control, peace, education, Indian affairs, or opposition to lynching.

WOMEN AND POLITICS

Women's groups persuaded Congress to pass the Sheppard-Towner Act (1921), granting funds to states to create maternity and pediatric clinics. (The measure ended in 1929, when Congress, under pressure from private physicians, canceled funding.) The Cable Act of 1922 reversed the law under which an American woman who married a foreigner assumed her husband's citizenship, allowing her to retain U.S. citizenship. At state levels, women achieved rights, such as the ability to serve on juries.

As new voters, however, most women pursued diverging interests. Women in the National Association of Colored Women, for example, fought for the rights of minorities. Other groups, such as the National Woman's Party, pressed for an equal rights amendment (ERA) to ensure women's equality under the law. But the ERA alienated organizations such as the National Consumers League, the Women's Trade Union League, and the League of Women Voters, which supported special protective legislation to limit the hours and improve conditions for employed women.

Materialism Unbound

Between 1919 and 1929, the gross national product—the total value of all goods and services produced in the United States—swelled by 40 percent. Wages and salaries also grew, while the cost of living remained relatively stable. People enjoyed greater purchasing power (see Table 24.1). By 1929 two-thirds of all Americans had electricity at home, compared with one-sixth in 1912. In 1929 one-fourth of all families owned vacuum cleaners. Many could afford such goods as radios, washing machines, and movie tickets only because several family members worked or because the breadwinner took a second job. Nevertheless, new products and services were available to more than just the rich.

During the 1920s automobile registrations soared from 8 million to 23 million, and by 1929 there was one car for every five Americans. Mass production and competition made cars affordable. A Ford Model T cost less than $300, and a Chevrolet sold for $700 by 1926—when factory workers earned about $1,300 a year and clerical workers about $2,300. At those prices, people could consider the car a necessity rather than a luxury.

EFFECTS OF THE AUTOMOBILE

Cars altered American life. City streets became cleaner as autos replaced the horses that had dumped tons of manure every day. Women who learned to drive achieved newfound independence, traveling by themselves or with female friends. By 1927 most au-

TABLE 24.1	
Consumerism in the 1920s	
1900	
2 bicycles	$ 70.00
wringer and washboard	5.00
brushes and brooms	5.00
sewing machine (mechanical)	25.00
TOTAL	$ 105.00
1928	
automobile	$ 700.00
radio	75.00
phonograph	50.00
washing machine	150.00
vacuum cleaner	50.00
sewing machine (electric)	60.00
other electrical equipment	25.00
telephone (per year)	35.00
TOTAL	$1,145.00

From *Another Part of the Twenties,* by Paul Carter. Copyright 1977 by Columbia University Press. Reprinted by permission of the author.

Note: These figures, taken from an article in *Survey Magazine* in 1928, contrast one family's expenditures on consumer goods in 1900 with those of 1928.

tos were enclosed (they previously had open tops), creating new private space for courtship and sex. Most important, the car was the ultimate symbol of social equality. As one writer observed in 1924, "It is hard to convince Steve Popovich, or Antonio Branca, or plain John Smith that he is being ground into the dust by Capital when at will he may drive the same highways, view the same scenery, and get as much enjoyment from his trip as the modern Midas."

After the First World War, motorists joined farmers and bicyclists in their decades-old campaign for improved roads. In 1921 Congress passed the Federal Highway Act, providing funds for state roads, and in 1923 the Bureau of Public Roads planned a national highway system. Road building inspired technological developments such as mechanized road graders and concrete mixers, and mass-produced tires and plate

glass. The oil refining industry, aided by chemistry, became vast and powerful, with the United States producing about 65 percent of the world's oil in 1920. Public officials paid more attention to traffic control, with General Electric Company producing the first timed stop-and-go traffic light in 1924.

By 1929 more money was spent on advertising than on formal education. Blending psychological theory with practical cynicism, advertising theorists asserted that people's tastes could be manipulated. For example, cosmetics manufacturers such as Max Factor and the African American entrepreneur Madame C. J. Walker used movie stars and beauty advice in magazines to entice female customers. Baseball star Babe Ruth was hired to endorse food and sporting goods.

ADVERTISING

Radio became an influential advertising medium. By 1929 over 10 million Americans owned radios, spending $850 million annually on radio equipment. In the early 1920s, Congress decided that radio should be a private enterprise, not a tax-supported public service as in Great Britain. American programming focused on entertainment—such as Lindbergh's flight—rather than on educational content because of the larger audiences—and therefore advertising profits. Station KDKA in Pittsburgh, at first noncommercial, pioneered broadcasting in 1920. In 1922 an AT&T-run station in New York ran advertisements—"commercials." Other stations followed, and by 1922 there were 508 commercial stations.

RADIO

Radio transformed political culture when both parties broadcast their presidential nominating conventions for the first time in 1924. And radio's mass marketing and standardized programming blurred ethnic boundaries and created—at least in one way—a homogeneous "American" culture, which television and other mass media extended throughout the twentieth century.

Some new trends benefited the working classes, especially in cities. Indoor plumbing and electricity became more common, and canned foods and ready-made clothes were more affordable. A little cash and a lot of credit enabled many wage earners to purchase an automobile. Spending became a national pastime.

■ During the 1920s, the desire to own an automobile spread to members of all classes, races, and ethnic groups. Low prices and available credit enabled this family from Beaumont, Texas, to own a "touring car." (Tyrrell Historical Library, Beaumont, Texas)

Cities, Migrants, and Suburbs

*T*he 1920 federal census revealed that for the first time, a majority of Americans lived in urban areas (defined as places with 2,500 or more people). Growth in manufacturing and services helped propel urbanization. Industries such as steel, oil, and auto production energized Birmingham, Houston, and Detroit; services and retail trades boosted expansion in Seattle, Atlanta, and Minneapolis.

During the 1920s, 6 million Americans left their farms for the city. Irrigation and mechanization made large-scale farming so efficient that fewer farmers could produce more crops. As a result, crop prices plummeted, and small landholders could not make a living. Midwesterners, particularly young single people, moved to regional centers like Kansas City and Indianapolis or to the West. Between 1920 and 1930, California's population increased 67 percent, and California became one of the most urbanized states while retaining its status as a leading agricultural state.

African Americans, in what is called the Great Migration, made up a sizable portion of people on the move. Pushed from cotton farming by a boll weevil plague and lured by industrial jobs, 1.5 million blacks moved cityward during the 1920s, doubling the African American populations of New York, Chicago, Detroit, and Houston. Forced by low wages and discrimination to seek cheap housing, black newcomers squeezed into low-rent ghettos. The only way to expand their housing opportunities was to spill into nearby white neighborhoods, which sparked resistance and violence. Fears of such "invasion" prompted white neighborhood associations to adopt restrictive covenants, whereby homeowners pledged not to sell or rent property to blacks.

AFRICAN AMERICAN MIGRATION

In response to discrimination and violence, thousands of urban blacks joined movements that glorified racial independence. The most influential was the Universal Negro Improvement Association (UNIA), headed by Marcus Garvey, a Jamaican immigrant who believed blacks should separate from corrupt white society. *Negro World*, Garvey's newspaper, refused to publish ads for products foreign to black culture, such as hair straightening and skin-lightening cosmetics, and he founded the Black Star shipping line to help blacks emigrate to Africa.

MARCUS GARVEY

The UNIA declined in the mid-1920s after ten UNIA leaders were arrested on charges of anarchism, and Garvey was deported for mail fraud involving the bankrupt Black Star line; the company's main problem was that unscrupulous dealers had sold it dilapidated ships. Black leaders like W. E. B. Du Bois opposed the UNIA, fearing its extremism would undermine their efforts. Nevertheless, in big cities, the organization attracted a large following (contemporaries estimated 500,000; Garvey claimed 6 million), and Garvey's speeches instilled many African Americans with a heightened sense of racial pride.

The newest immigrants to American cities came from Mexico and Puerto Rico, where declining fortunes pushed people off the land. During the 1910s, Anglo farmers' associations encouraged Mexican immigration to provide cheap agricultural labor, and by the 1920s, Mexican migrants made up three-fourths of farm labor in the American West. Growers treated Mexican laborers as slaves, providing them low wages and poor healthcare. Though some achieved middle-class status, most crowded into low-rent districts plagued by poor sanitation, poor police protection, and poor schools. Mexicans moved back and forth across the border, creating a way of life that Mexicans called *sin fronteras*—without borders.

NEWCOMERS FROM MEXICO AND PUERTO RICO

The 1920s also witnessed an influx of Puerto Ricans to the mainland as a shift in the island's economy from sugar to coffee production created a labor surplus. Attracted by contracts from employers seeking cheap labor, most Puerto Rican migrants moved to New York City, where they created *barrios* (communities) in Brooklyn and Manhattan and found jobs in manufacturing, hotels, restaurants, and domestic service.

Puerto Ricans and Mexicans practiced traditional customs and developed businesses—*bodegas* (grocery stores), cafés, boarding houses—and social organizations to help them adapt to American society. Educated elites—doctors, lawyers, business owners—often became community leaders.

Prosperity and automobile transportation in the 1920s made suburbs more accessible to those wishing to flee congested urban neighborhoods. Between 1920 and 1930, suburbs of Chicago (such as Oak Park and Evanston), Cleveland (Shaker Heights), and Los Angeles (Burbank and Inglewood) grew five to ten times faster than nearby central cities. Los Angeles builders alone opened 3,200 subdivisions and erected 250,000 homes. Most suburbs were middle- and upper-class bedroom communities; some, like Highland Park (near Detroit), were industrial satellites.

GROWTH OF SUBURBS

Suburbanites wanted to escape big-city crime, grime, and taxes, and they fought urban annexation efforts, preserving control over their own police, schools, and water and gas services. Particularly in the Northeast and Midwest, the suburbs' independence prevented central cities from accessing the resources and tax bases of wealthier suburban communities. Moreover, population dispersal spread the environmental problems of city life—trash, pollution, noise—across the entire metropolitan area.

Most of the consumers who jammed movie houses and sporting arenas and who embraced fads like crossword puzzles, miniature golf, and marathon dancing lived in or around cities. People there defied law and tradition by patronizing speakeasies (illegal saloons during prohibition), wearing outlandish clothes, and listening to jazz, while moralists strained to resist modernism, and many reminisced about the simplicity of a world gone by.

New Rhythms of Everyday Life

*a*mid changes, people increasingly split daily life into distinct compartments: work, family, and leisure. Increased mechanization and higher productivity enabled many employers to shorten the workweek for industrial laborers from six days to

Pan American Airways

Air transportation and air mail service between the United States and Latin America began in the 1920s, but anti-American hostility in the region made it difficult. In 1926 the U.S. government, fearful that German aircraft might drop bombs on the Panama Canal in future conflicts, signed a treaty with Panama giving American airplanes exclusive rights to Panamanian airports. Charles Lindbergh and a formerly obscure pilot, Juan Trippe, played key roles in expanding American air service to Latin America.

With help from his father-in-law, Trippe established Pan American Airways (informally known as Pan Am) in 1927 and won a contract to carry mail between Florida and Cuba. In December of that year, Lindbergh charmed the Mexicans into accepting airline links to the United States. The next year, Lindbergh joined Pan Am and helped Trippe initiate mail and passenger service to Panama, Mexico, and other Latin American countries in 1929. Trippe advertised to wealthy Americans the opportunity to escape prohibition and enjoy Caribbean beaches.

Pan Am built airports that became essential connections between Latin America and the rest of the world. Pan Am air service also helped unite parts of Latin America that previously were divided by impenetrable mountain ranges. But to build an airport, Pan Am cooperated with dictators, engaged in bribery, and violated human rights, in one case helping Bolivian police corral Indians behind barbed wire for days to clear a new airport.

Still, Pan Am facilitated global travel. In 1942 its aircraft became the first to fly around the world. In the 1940s, the company began offering flights to Europe and Africa. Until its demise in 1991, Pan Am provided a leading link between the United States and the rest of the world.

Providing air transport connections to the Caribbean, Central America, and South America, Pan American Airways established the first major passenger and cargo links between the United States and other nations. By the early 1930s, flights were so numerous that the timetable announced in this illustration consisted of twelve pages. (The Pan American Heritage Web Site)

five and a half. White-collar employees often worked a forty-hour week, enjoyed a full weekend off, and received annual vacations.

Family size decreased between 1920 and 1930 as birth control became more widely practiced. Over half the women married in the 1870s and 1880s had five or more children; only 20 percent of their counterparts marrying in the 1920s had similar childbirth patterns. The divorce rate jumped from 1 divorce for every 7.5 marriages in 1920 to 1 in 6 by 1929. With longer life expectancy, lower birth rates, and more divorce, adults devoted a smaller portion of their lives to child rearing.

Although housework was still arduous, machines lightened some household chores. Especially in middle-

HOUSEHOLD MANAGEMENT

class households, electric irons and washing machines simplified housewives' toil. Gas- and oil-powered central heating and hot-water heaters eliminated hauling wood, coal, and water; keeping up a kitchen fire; and removing ashes.

But technology and economic change also created new demands on women's time. The availability of washing machines, hot water, vacuum cleaners, and commercial soap put greater pressure on wives to keep everything clean. No longer a producer of food and clothing as her ancestors were, a housewife now also became the chief shopper. And the automobile also made her the family's chauffeur. One survey found that urban housewives spent 13 percent of their work time, seven and a half hours per week, driving to shop and to transport children.

Nutrition added a scientific dimension to housewives' responsibilities. With the discovery of vitamins

HEALTH AND LIFE EXPECTANCY

between 1915 and 1930, nutritionists began advocating certain foods to prevent illness, and giant food companies advertised their products as filled with vitamins and minerals. Other companies made lofty claims that were hard to dispute because little was known about these invisible, tasteless ingredients. Welch's Grape Juice, for example, avoided mentioning its excess of sugars when it advertised that it was "Rich in Health Values," containing vitamins, minerals, and "the laxative properties you cannot do without."

Better diets and improved hygiene made Americans healthier. Life expectancy at birth increased from fifty-four to sixty years between 1920 and 1930, and infant mortality decreased by two-thirds. Public sanitation and research in bacteriology and immunology reduced life-threatening diseases such as tuberculosis and diphtheria. But infant mortality rates were 50 to 100 percent higher among nonwhites, and tuberculosis in inner-city slums remained alarmingly common. Nevertheless, the total population over age sixty-five grew 35 percent between 1920 and 1930.

Industrialism put premiums on youth and agility, pushing older people into poverty from forced retirement and reduced income. Most

OLDER AMERICANS AND RETIREMENT

European countries established state-supported pension systems in the early 1900s. Many Americans, however, believed pensions smacked of socialism and that individuals should prepare for old age by saving in their youth.

Most inmates in state poorhouses were older people, and almost one-third of Americans age sixty-five and older depended financially on someone else. Few employers, including the federal government, provided for retired employees. Resistance to pension plans finally broke at the state level in the 1920s. Led by Isaac Max Rubinow and Abraham Epstein, reformers persuaded voluntary associations, labor unions, and legislators to endorse old-age assistance. By 1933 almost every state provided at least minimal support to needy elderly people, opening the door to a national program of old-age insurance.

New cultural influences altered habits and values. Women and men wore more casual and gaily colored

SOCIAL VALUES

clothes than their parents' generation. The line between acceptable and inappropriate behavior blurred as smoking, drinking, swearing, and frankness about sex became fashionable. Birth-control advocate Margaret Sanger, who a decade earlier had been accused of promoting race suicide, gained a large following. Newspapers, motion pictures, and popular songs (such as "Hot Lips" and "Burning Kisses") made certain that Americans did not suffer from "sex starvation."

Because child-labor laws and compulsory-attendance rules kept children in school longer than in the past, peer groups played a more influential role in socializing youngsters. Graded school classes, sports, and clubs constantly brought together children of the same age, separating them from the company and influence of adults. Meanwhile, parents relied less on traditions of childcare and more on experts who wrote manuals on successful child rearing.

Online Study Center **Improve Your Grade**
Primary Source: Wild Young People

After the First World War, women continued to stream into the labor force. By 1930, 10.8 million

WOMEN IN THE
WORK FORCE

women held paying jobs, an increase of 2 million since war's end. Most notably, the proportion of women working in agriculture shrank, while it grew or held steady in urban job categories (see Figure 24.1). Sex segregation persisted; most women took jobs that men seldom sought. Over 1 million women worked as professionals, primarily teachers and nurses. Some 2.2 million women were typists, bookkeepers, and filing clerks, a tenfold increase since 1920. Although almost 2 million women worked in manufacturing, their numbers hardly grew over the decade. Women's wages seldom exceeded half of those paid to men.

Family economic needs were paramount among women's reasons for working. Consumerism pro-

vided an additional push. Although the majority of married women did not work outside the home (only 12 percent were employed in 1930), married women as a proportion of the work force rose by 30 percent, and the number of employed married women swelled from 1.9 million to 3.1 million.

Minority women were twice as likely to be employed as white women. Often they entered the labor

EMPLOYMENT
OF MINORITY
WOMEN

force because their husbands were unemployed or underemployed. The majority of employed African American women held domestic jobs doing cooking, cleaning, and laundry. The few working in factories performed the least desirable, lowest-paying tasks. Some opportunities opened for educated black women in social work, teaching, and nursing, but even these women faced discrimination and low incomes.

Next to black women, Japanese American women were the most likely to have paying jobs, similarly working as field hands and domestics facing racial bias and low pay. Economic necessity also drew thousands of Mexican women into wage labor, although

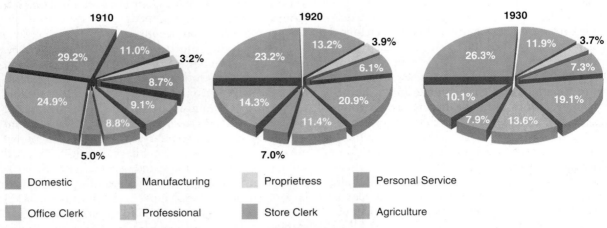

Figure 24.1   Changing Dimensions of Paid Female Labor, 1910–1930

These charts reveal the extraordinary growth in clerical and professional occupations among employed women and the accompanying decline in agricultural labor in the early twentieth century. Notice that manufacturing employment peaked in 1920 and that domestic service fluctuated as white immigrant women began to move out of these jobs and were replaced by women of color.

their tradition resisted female employment. Most worked as field laborers, operatives in garment factories, and domestic servants.

Many women cast aside previous images of femininity that included heavy, floor-length dresses and

ALTERNATIVE
IMAGES OF
FEMININITY

long hair, opting instead for the independence and sexual freedom of the 1920s "flapper" with her short skirts and bobbed hair. Although few women lived the flapper life, office workers, store clerks, and college coeds adopted the look. New models of female behavior included movie temptresses like Clara Bow, known as the "It Girl," and Gloria Swanson, notorious for love affairs on and off the screen. Women increasingly asserted a new social equality with men. One observer described "the new woman" as intriguingly independent:

> She takes a man's point of view as her mother never could. . . . She will never make you a hatband or knit you a necktie, but she'll drive you from the station . . . in her own little sports car. . . . [S]he'll dive as well as you, perhaps better, she'll dance as long as you care to, and she'll take everything you say the way you mean it.

The era's sexual openness enabled the underground homosexual culture to surface. In nontradi-

HOMOSEXUAL
CULTURE

tional city neighborhoods, such as New York's Greenwich Village and Harlem, cheap rents and an apparent tolerance attracted gays and lesbians who patronized dance halls, speakeasies, and cafés. Still, gay establishments remained targets for police raids, demonstrating that there was little acceptance by the rest of society.

These trends represented a break with the more restrained culture of the nineteenth century. But social change rarely proceeds smoothly. As the decade proceeded, groups mobilized to defend older values.

Lines of Defense

*E*arly in 1920 the leader of a newly formed organization hired two public relations experts to recruit members. The experts, Edward Clarke and Elizabeth Tyler, canvassed the South, Southwest, and Midwest, where they found thousands of men eager to pay a $10 membership fee and $6 for a white uniform. Clarke and Tyler pocketed $2.50 from each membership and secured 5 million members by 1923.

This was the Ku Klux Klan, a revived version of the hooded order that had terrorized southern com-

KU KLUX KLAN

munities after the Civil War. It appealed to fear, vowing to protect female, racial, and ethnic purity. As one pamphlet declared, "Every criminal, every gambler, every thug, every libertine, every girl ruiner, every home wrecker, every wife beater, every dope peddler, every moonshiner, every white slaver, every Rome-controlled newspaper, every black spider—is fighting the Klan. . . . Which side are you on?"

Reconstituted in 1915 by William J. Simmons, an Atlanta evangelist and insurance salesman, the Klan revived the hoods, intimidating tactics, and mystical terminology of its forerunner (its leader was the Imperial Wizard, its book of rituals the Kloran). But the new Klan fanned outward from the Deep South, wielding power in places as diverse as Oregon, Oklahoma, and Indiana. Members included many from the middle class who were fearful of losing social and economic gains and nervous about a new youth culture that eluded family control. An estimated half-million women joined.

One phrase summed up Klan goals: "Native, white, Protestant supremacy." Native meant no immigration, no "mongrelization" of American culture. According to Imperial Wizard Hiram Wesley Evans, "The world has been so made so that each race must fight for its life, must conquer, accept slavery, or die." Evans accused the Catholic Church of discouraging assimilation and enslaving people to a foreign pope.

Using threatening assemblies, violence, and political and economic pressure, Klansmen meted out vigilante justice to suspected bootleggers, wife beaters, and adulterers; forced schools to adopt Bible reading and stop teaching the theory of evolution; campaigned against Catholic and Jewish political candidates; and fueled racial tensions against Mexicans in Texas border cities. Klan women both promoted native white Protestantism and worked for women's rights. By 1925, scandal undermined its moral base. Indiana Grand Dragon David Stephenson was convicted of second-degree murder after he kidnapped and raped a woman who later died. More generally, the Klan's negative, exclusive brand of patriotism could not compete in a pluralistic society.

The KKK was not alone. Intolerance pervaded American society in the 1920s. Nativists charged that Catholic and Jewish immigrants clogged city slums, flouted community norms, and stubbornly held to alien religious and political beliefs. Naturalist Madison Grant, whose study of zoology fueled his belief that certain human races, mainly Nordics, were superior, wrote in *The Passing of the Great Race* (1916): "These immigrants adopt the language of the native American, they wear his clothes, they steal his name and they are beginning to take his women, but they seldom adopt his religion or understand his ideals."

Efforts to restrict immigration gathered support. Labor leaders warned that aliens would depress wages and raise unemployment. Business executives, who formerly desired cheap immigrant laborers, now realized that they could keep wages low by mechanizing and by hiring blacks. In response to these pressures, Congress set yearly immigration quotas for each nationality. By restricting annual immigration of a given nationality to 3 percent of the number of immigrants from that nation residing in the United States in 1910, the Emergency Quota Act of 1921 favored northern and western Europeans and discriminated against immigrants from southern and eastern Europe, whose numbers were comparatively small in 1910.

IMMIGRATION QUOTAS

In 1924 Congress replaced the Quota Act with the National Origins Act. This law limited the influx to 150,000 people by setting quotas at 2 percent of each nationality residing in the United States in 1890, except for Asians, who were banned completely. The act further restricted southern and eastern Europeans, since fewer of those groups lived in the United States in 1890 than in 1910, though it allowed wives and children of U.S. citizens to enter as nonquota immigrants. As a result, the 1921 quotas for southern and eastern Europeans fell by 84 percent, while those for northern and western Europeans dropped by only 29 percent. Revisions beginning in 1929 redefined quotas to be distributed among European countries in proportion to the "national origins" (country of birth or descent) of American inhabitants in 1920. People from Canada, Mexico, and Puerto Rico did not fall under the quotas (except for those whom the Labor Department defined as potential paupers) and became the largest immigrant groups (see Figure 24.2).

Fear of immigrant radicalism was evident in 1921 when a court convicted Nicola Sacco and Bartolomeo Vanzetti, two immigrant anarchists, of murdering a guard and paymaster during a robbery in South Braintree, Massachusetts. Though evidence failed to prove their guilt, Judge Webster Thayer openly sided with the prosecution and privately called the defendants "anarchist bastards." Appeals failed to win a new trial, and the prisoners were executed in 1927, touching off protests in Europe, Asia, and South America and leaving doubts that the United States truly nurtured freedom of belief.

SACCO AND VANZETTI CASE

The pursuit of spiritual purity stirred religious fundamentalists as millions sought salvation from what they perceived as the irreverence of a materialistic, hedonistic society. Resolutely believing that God's miracles created earth and its life, they rejected Darwin's theory of evolution as speculation. Where fundamentalists constituted a majority, as they did throughout the South, they sought to determine what schools taught. Their enemies were "modernists," who interpreted "truths" critically, believing that biblical accuracy was less important than the historical relevance of God in culture and the role of science in advancing knowledge.

FUNDAMENTALISM

In 1925 Christian fundamentalism clashed with modernism when the Tennessee state legislature outlawed public schools from teaching the theory that humans had evolved from lower forms of life rather than descended from Adam and Eve. High-school teacher John Thomas Scopes volunteered to serve in a test case and was arrested for violating the law. William Jennings Bryan, former secretary of state and three-time presidential candidate, argued for the prosecution, and civil liberties lawyers headed by Clarence Darrow represented the defense. News correspondents crowded into town, and radio stations broadcast the trial.

SCOPES TRIAL

Scopes was convicted—clearly he had broken the law—but modernists claimed victory in showing the illogic of fundamentalism. The trial's climax occurred when Bryan took the witness stand as an expert on

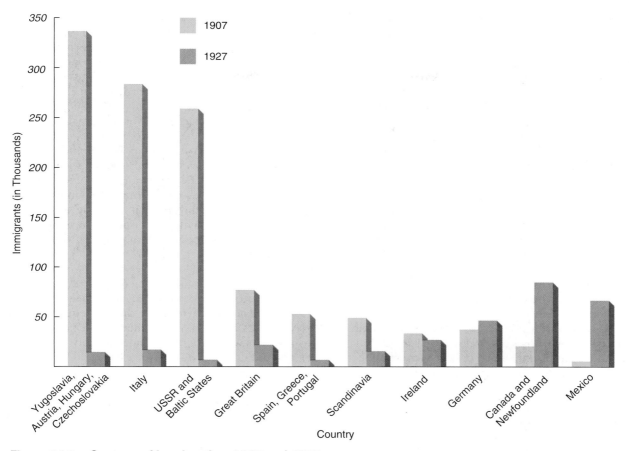

Figure 24.2   Sources of Immigration, 1907 and 1927

Immigration peaked in 1907 and 1908, when newcomers from southern and eastern Europe poured into the United States. After immigration restriction laws were passed in the 1920s, the greatest number of immigrants came from the Western Hemisphere (Canada and Mexico), which was exempted from the quotas, and the number coming from eastern and southern Europe shrank.

religion and science. He asserted that Eve really had been created from Adam's rib, that the Tower of Babel was responsible for the diversity of languages, and that a biblical "day" could have lasted thousands of years. Spectators in Dayton cheered Bryan, but the liberal press mocked him. Nevertheless, fundamentalists convinced school boards to ban the teaching of evolution and influenced the content of high-school biology books. They also created an independent subculture of schools, camps, radio ministries, and missionary societies.

Klan rallies, immigration restriction, and fundamentalist literalism might appear as last gasps of a rural society struggling against modern urban-industrial values. Yet half the Klan's members lived in cities, especially in working-class neighborhoods. Even urban reformers backed immigration restriction as a means of controlling poverty and assimilating immigrants.

Urban Pentecostal churches attracted blacks and whites struggling with economic insecurity, nervous

about modernism's attack on old-time religion, and swayed by the notion of a personal God. Using modern advertising and elaborately staged services broadcast on radio, magnetic preachers such as Aimee Semple McPherson of Los Angeles, former baseball player Billy Sunday, and Father Divine (George Baker, an African American who amassed an interracial following especially in eastern cities) stirred revivalist fervor. Clergy of all faiths condemned drinking, dancing, new dress styles, and sex in movies and in parked cars. Many urban dwellers supported prohibition, believing that it would win the battle against poverty, vice, and corruption. Yet most people sincerely wanted balance as they tried to adjust to the modern order in one way or another. Americans sought fellowship in civic organizations. Membership swelled in Rotary, Elks, and women's clubs, and the number of Community Chests—associations that coordinated local welfare projects—grew from 12 in 1919 to 361 in 1930. Perhaps most important, more people were finding release in recreation and leisure time.

The Age of Play

*a*mericans embraced commercial entertainment, spending $2.5 billion on leisure in 1919; by 1929, it topped $4.3 billion. Spectator amusements—movies, music, and sports—accounted for 21 percent of the 1929 total; the rest involved participatory recreation, such as games, hobbies, and travel.

Entrepreneurs fed this appetite for fads, fun, and "ballyhoo." Games and fancies particularly attracted newly affluent middle-class families; early in the 1920s, mahjong, a Chinese tile game, was the craze. In the mid-1920s, crossword puzzles, printed in mass-circulation newspapers and magazines, were the rage, and by 1930 the nation boasted thirty thousand miniature golf courses. Dance crazes like the Charleston and recorded music on radio boosted the growing popularity of jazz.

Americans also enjoyed watching movies and sports. In total capital investment, motion pictures

became one of the nation's leading industries. In 1922 movies attracted 40 million viewers weekly; by

decade's end, nearly 100 million—at a time when the nation's population was 120 million and total weekly church attendance was 60 million. Between 1922 and 1927, the Technicolor Corporation developed a means to produce movies in color. That, along with the introduction of sound in *The Jazz Singer* in 1927, made movies more exciting.

The most popular films were spectacles such as Cecil B. DeMille's *The Ten Commandments* (1923); lurid dramas such as *A Woman Who Sinned* (1924); and slapstick comedies starring Fatty Arbuckle, Harold Lloyd, and Charlie Chaplin. Ironically, comedies, with their poignant satires of the human condition, carried the most thought-provoking messages. In 1927 movie producers, bowing to political pressure, instituted self-censorship, forbidding nudity, rough language, and plots that did not end with justice and morality triumphant.

Spectator sports also boomed. Gate receipts from college football surpassed $21 million by the late 1920s, as sports provided the drama people craved. Newspapers and radio magnified this tension, glorifying events with such unrestrained narrative that promoters did not need advertising.

Baseball's drawn-out suspense, variety of plays, and potential for keeping statistics attracted a huge following. After the "Black Sox scandal" of 1919, when eight members of the Chicago White Sox were banned for allegedly throwing the World Series to the Cincinnati Reds (even though a jury acquitted them), baseball transformed itself. Discovering that home runs excited fans, the leagues redesigned the ball. A record 300,000 people attended the six-game 1921 World Series between the New York Giants and New York Yankees. Millions enjoyed professional games on the radio.

As technology and mass society made the individual less significant, people clung to sports, movie, and

news heroes as a means of identifying with the unique. Bill Tilden in tennis, Gertrude Ederle in swimming (the first woman to swim across the English Channel), and Bobby Jones in golf were famous. But boxing, football, and baseball produced the most popular sports heroes. Heavyweight champion Jack Dempsey, the "Manassa (Colorado) Brawler," attracted the first of several million-dollar gates in his fight with French boxer Georges Carpentier in 1921.

Baseball's foremost hero was George Herman "Babe" Ruth, who began his career as a pitcher but broke records hitting home runs. He hit twenty-nine in 1919, fifty-four in 1920 (the year the Boston Red Sox traded him to the New York Yankees), fifty-nine in 1921, and sixty in 1927. Known for overindulgence in food, drink, and sex, he nonetheless charmed fans with public appearances and visits to hospitalized children.

Americans fulfilled a yearning for romance and adventure through movie idols. One of the decade's

MOVIE STARS AND PUBLIC HEROES

most ballyhooed personalities was Rudolph Valentino, whose image exploited the era's sexual liberalism. In his most famous film, Valentino played a passionate sheik who carried away beautiful women to his tent. When he died at age thirty-one of complications from ulcers and appendicitis, the press turned his funeral into a public extravaganza.

The Eighteenth Amendment (1919) and ensuing federal law (1920) prohibited the manufacture, sale,

PROHIBITION

and transportation of alcoholic beverages (see Chapter 21), and prohibition worked well at first. Per capita consumption of liquor dropped, as did arrests for drunkenness. But it was hardly enforced: in 1922 Congress gave the Prohibition Bureau just three thousand employees and less than $7 million for nationwide enforcement.

After 1925, prohibition broke down as thousands made their own wine and bathtub gin, and bootleg importers easily evaded the few patrols that existed. Moreover, drinking was a business with willing customers, and criminal organizations capitalized on public demand. The most notorious of such mobs belonged to Al Capone, who seized control of illegal liquor and vice in Chicago, maintaining his grip on politicians and the business through intimidation, bribery, and violence. Americans wanted liquor, and until 1931 when a federal court convicted and imprisoned him for income-tax evasion (the only charge for which authorities could obtain hard evidence), Capone supplied them.

Cultural Currents

 ntellectuals exposed the era's hypocrisy. Writers and artists felt at odds with society, and their rejection of conformity was biting and bitter.

Several writers from the so-called Lost Generation, including novelist Ernest Hemingway and poets

LITERATURE OF ALIENATION

Ezra Pound and T. S. Eliot, abandoned the United States for Europe. Others, such as novelists William Faulkner and Sinclair Lewis, remained in America but expressed disillusionment with the materialism they witnessed. F. Scott Fitzgerald's *This Side of Paradise* (1920) and *The Great Gatsby* (1925) and Eugene O'Neill's plays derided Americans' preoccupation with money. Edith Wharton explored the clash of old and new moralities in novels such as *The Age of Innocence* (1920).

Inspired by spiritual discontent, middle-class, educated black writers rejected white culture and exalted

HARLEM RENAISSANCE

the militantly assertive "New Negro." In the "Negro Mecca" of New York's Harlem, black intellectuals and artists, aided by a few white patrons, celebrated black culture and created the Harlem Renaissance.

The popular 1921 musical comedy *Shuffle Along* is often credited with launching the Harlem Renaissance and showcased African American artists such as composer Eubie Blake and singer Josephine Baker. Harlem also fostered gifted writers, including Langston Hughes, Countee Cullen, Zora Neale Hurston, Jessie Fauset, and Alain Locke.

Though cherishing their African heritage, these artists and intellectuals realized that blacks had to make peace with themselves as Americans. Langston Hughes wrote, "We younger Negro artists who create now intend to express our individual dark-skinned selves without fear or shame. If white people are pleased, we are glad. If they are not, it doesn't matter. We know we are beautiful."

The Jazz Age, as the 1920s is sometimes called, owes its name to the music of black culture. Evolving

JAZZ

from African and black American folk music, early jazz communicated exuberance, humor, and authority that African Americans seldom experienced in their public and political lives. Jazz's emotional rhythms and improvisation blurred the distinction between composer and performer. Music recorded by black artists—among them trumpeter Louis Armstrong and blues singer Bessie Smith—and aimed at black consumers (sometimes called "race records") gave African Americans a place in consumer culture. More important, jazz endowed America with its most distinctive and popular art form.

In many ways, the 1920s were the nation's most creative years. Artists such as Georgia O'Keeffe, Aaron Douglas, and John Marin forged a uniquely American style of painting. Composers such as Henry Cowell pioneered electronic music, and Aaron Copland built orchestral works around native folk motifs. George Gershwin blended jazz rhythms, classical forms, and folk melodies in serious compositions (*Rhapsody in Blue*, 1924, and the Piano Concerto in F, 1925) and hit tunes such as "Someone to Watch Over Me." In architecture the skyscraper boom drew worldwide attention to American forms. The "emotional and aesthetic starvation" that essayist Harold Stearn lamented at the beginning of the decade were long gone by the end.

The Election of 1928 and the End of the New Era

Intellectuals' uneasiness about materialism seldom affected the confident rhetoric of politics. Herbert Hoover voiced that confidence when he accepted the Republican nomination for president in 1928. "We in America today," Hoover boasted, "are nearer to the final triumph over poverty than ever before in the history of any land."

As the Republican candidate in 1928 (Coolidge did not seek reelection), Hoover fused individual hard

HERBERT HOOVER

work with modern emphasis on collective action. A Quaker from Iowa, orphaned at age ten, Hoover put himself through Stanford University and became a wealthy mining engineer. During and after the First World War, he distinguished himself as U.S. food administrator.

As secretary of commerce under Harding and Coolidge, Hoover practiced "associationalism." Recognizing that nationwide associations dominated commerce and industry, Hoover sought business and government cooperation by making the Commerce Department a center for the promotion of business, encouraging the formation of trade associations, holding conferences, and issuing reports, all aimed at improving productivity, marketing, and profits.

In sharp contrast, Democrats chose New York's governor Alfred E. Smith as their candidate. Hoover

AL SMITH

had rural, native-born, Protestant, business roots and had never before run for public office. Smith was an urbane politician of immigrant stock with a career embedded in New York City's Tammany Hall political machine, who relished the give-and-take of city streets.

Smith was the first Roman Catholic to run for president on a major party ticket. His religion enhanced his appeal among urban ethnics, who voted in increasing numbers, but intense anti-Catholic sentiments lost him southern and rural votes. Smith had a strong record on Progressive reform and civil rights, but his campaign stressed issues like opposition to prohibition that alienated many farmers and city dwellers.

Hoover won the popular vote by 21 million to 15 million, the electoral vote by 444 to 87. Smith carried the nation's twelve largest cities, formerly Republican strongholds, and he lured millions of foreign-stock voters to the polls for the first time. For the next forty years or so, the Democratic Party solidified this urban base, which in conjunction with its traditional strength in the South, made the party a formidable force in national elections.

At his inaugural, Hoover proclaimed a New Day, "bright with hope." His cabinet featured mostly

HOOVER'S ADMINISTRATION

businessmen, including six millionaires. In low-ranking posts, Hoover appointed young professionals who similarly believed that scientific methods could solve national problems. Americans widely agreed that individuals were responsible for their own success and that poverty suggested personal weakness. Prevailing opinion also held that ups and downs of the business cycle were natural and not to be tampered with by government.

This trust dissolved in the fall of 1929 when stock market prices suddenly plunged after soaring in

STOCK MARKET CRASH

1928, and on October 24, "Black Thursday," panic set in. Prices of many stocks hit record lows; some sellers could find no buyers. At noon, leading bankers put up $20 million and ceremoniously began buying stocks. The mood brightened, and some stocks rallied, lifting hopes. But as news spread, panicked investors sold off stock to avoid further losses. On "Black Tuesday," October 29, prices plummeted again. Hoover assured Americans that "the crisis will be over in sixty days." He shared the popular assumptions that the economy was strong enough to endure until the market righted itself. Instead, the crash fueled a devastating depression.

The economic weakness that underlay the Great Depression had several interrelated causes. Since mid-

DECLINING DEMAND

1928, demand for new housing had faltered, reducing sales of building materials and increasing unemployment. Growth industries such as automobiles and electric appliances also saw demand level off, but initially frenzied expansion continued. Consequently, unsold inventories stacked up in warehouses, and laborers were laid off. Retailers also had amassed large inventories and in turn started ordering less. Farm prices continued to sag, leaving farmers with less income for new machinery and goods. As wages and purchasing power stagnated, workers could not afford to buy consumer products. Thus, by 1929, a sizable population of underconsumers was causing serious repercussions.

The widening divisions in income distribution meant the rich grew richer, while middle- and lower-income Americans barely made modest gains. Although average per capita disposable income (income after taxes) rose about 9 percent between 1920 and 1929, the income of the wealthiest 1 percent rose 75 percent. Much of this increase was put into stock market investments, not consumer goods.

Furthermore, many businesses overloaded themselves with debt. To obtain loans, they misrepresented

CORPORATE DEBT

their assets in ways that weakened their ability to repay. Overlooked by lending agencies, this practice put the nation's banking system on precarious footing.

The depression also resulted from risky stock market speculation. Individuals bought heavily on mar-

STOCK MARKET SPECULATION

gin, meaning that they purchased stock with a down payment of only a fraction of the stock's price and then used these stocks as collateral for more stock purchases. When stock prices stopped rising, people tried to unload what they bought on margin, but as numerous investors sold simultaneously, prices dropped. Brokers then demanded full payment for stocks bought on margin. Bankers in turn needed cash and pressured businesses to pay back their loans. The more obligations went unmet, the more banks and investment companies collapsed.

International economic woes also contributed. During and after the First World War, Americans

INTERNATIONAL ECONOMIC TROUBLES

loaned billions to European nations. By the late 1920s, however, American investors instead opted for the more lucrative U.S. stock market. Europeans, unable to borrow more or sell goods in America because of high tariffs, bought less from the United States. Moreover, the Allied nations depended on German war reparations to pay their debts to the United States, and the German government depended on American bank loans to pay those war reparations. When the crash cut off American loans, the world economy ground to a halt.

The government refrained from regulating wild speculation. In supporting business expansion, the

FAILURE OF FEDERAL POLICIES

Federal Reserve Board pursued easy credit policies, charging low discount rates (interest on loans to member banks) even though easy money was financing the speculative mania.

Neither the experts nor people on the street realized what really had happened in 1929. Conventional wisdom, based on previous depressions, held that downturns simply had to run their course. Farmers in the country's midsection, where drought parched some of the lands that would become the Dust Bowl of the 1930s, had already begun to feel the pinch of hard times. But in 1929 most people waited, never realizing that the era of expansion and frivolity had come to an end.

Online Study Center Improve Your Grade
Interactive Map: The Dust Bowl

Summary *Online Study Center* ACE the Test

*T*wo disturbing events, the end of the First World War and the beginning of the Great Depression, marked the boundaries of the 1920s. After the war, traditional customs weakened as many women and men replaced old-fashioned values with new liberation. Modern science and technology touched rich and poor alike through the mass media, movies, automobiles, and electric appliances. Moreover, the decade's prosperity and freewheeling attitudes enabled ordinary Americans to emulate wealthier people by consuming more and speculating in the stock market.

Beneath the "era of excess," prejudice and intergroup tensions resurfaced, tainting the American Dream. Prohibitionists, Klansmen, and immigration restrictionists encouraged discrimination against racial minorities and ethnic groups. Meanwhile, the distinguishing forces of twentieth-century life—technological change, bureaucratization, mass culture, and growth of the middle class—accelerated, making the decade truly a "new era."

LEGACY FOR A PEOPLE AND A NATION
Intercollegiate Athletics

In 1924 brutality, academic fraud, and illegal payments to recruits prompted the Carnegie Foundation for the Advancement of Higher Education to undertake a five-year investigation of college sports. Its 1929 report condemned coaches and alumni supporters, but had minimal impact. Football was big, and other sports followed as universities built stadiums to attract spectators, bolster alumni allegiance, and enhance revenues.

For most of the twentieth century, intercollegiate athletics ranked as a major national commercial entertainment. Still, American colleges struggled to reconcile conflicts between the commercialism of athletic competition and the restraints of educational missions. The economic potential of college sports coupled with burgeoning athletic departments—including administrators, staffs, and tutors as well as coaches and trainers—has created programs that compete with and sometimes overshadow an institution's academic operations.

Since the 1920s, recruiting scandals, cheating incidents, and academic fraud in college sports have sparked continual controversy. In 1952, after revelations of point-shaving (fixing the outcome) of basketball games at several colleges, the American Council on Education undertook its own study. Its recommendations, including the abolition of football bowl games, went largely unheeded. In 1991 further abuses prompted the Knight Foundation Commission on Intercollegiate Athletics to urge college presidents to reform intercollegiate athletics. After a follow-up study in 2001, few significant changes resulted, though by 2005 the NCAA had attempted to bolster the importance of academics.

The most sweeping reforms followed court rulings in the 1990s mandating that women's sports be treated equally under Title IX of the Educational Amendments Act of 1972. Enforcement, however, provoked a backlash that resulted in changes to prevent men's teams from being cut. With millions of dollars involved, the system established in the 1920s has withstood most pressures for change.

THE GREAT DEPRESSION AND THE NEW DEAL 1929–1941

*I*n 1931 the rain stopped in the Great Plains. As temperatures reached 115 degrees in Iowa, the soil baked. Farmers watched rich black dirt turn to gray dust.

Then the winds began to blow. Farmers had stripped the Plains of native grasses in the 1920s, using tractors to put millions of acres into production. Now, with nothing to hold the earth, it began to blow away. The dust storms began in 1934 and worsened in 1935. Cattle, blinded by blowing grit, ran in circles until they died. Boiling clouds of dust filled and darkened the skies over Kansas, Colorado, Oklahoma, Texas, and New Mexico—the Dust Bowl.

In late 1937 on a farm near Stigler, Oklahoma, Marvin Montgomery counted up his assets: $53 and a car—a 1929 Hudson he had just bought. On December 29, 1937, Montgomery and his wife and four children—along with their furniture, bedding, pots, and pans—squeezed into the Hudson. Traveling on Route 66, the Montgomerys headed for California.

At least a third of farms in the Dust Bowl were abandoned in the 1930s, and many families headed west, lured by advertisements promising work in California fields. The plight of families like the Montgomerys, captured in the federal government–sponsored Farm Security Administration (FSA) photographs, came to represent the suffering of the Great Depression.

The Montgomerys ran out of money in Arizona and worked the cotton fields there for five weeks, before traveling on to California. There, the wages were low, and migrant families found little welcome. Because they took over agricultural labor formerly done by Mexicans and Mexican Americans, rural Californians regarded these migrants as forfeiting their "whiteness." "Negroes and 'Okies' upstairs," read a sign in a San Joaquin valley movie theater.

While most migrants lived in squalid makeshift camps, the Montgomerys secured housing provided by the federal Farm Security Administration (FSA).

Hoover and Hard Times: 1929–1933

Franklin D. Roosevelt and the Launching of the New Deal

Political Pressure and the Second New Deal

Labor

Federal Power and the Nationalization of Culture

LINKS TO THE WORLD
The 1936 Olympic Games

The Limits of the New Deal

LEGACY FOR A PEOPLE AND A NATION
Social Security

Online Study Center
This icon will direct you to interactive map and primary source activities on the website http://college.hmco.com/pic/nortonbrief7e

C H R O N O L O G Y

1929 • Stock market crash (Oct.); Great Depression begins

1930 • Hawley-Smoot Tariff raises rates on imports

1931 • "Scottsboro Boys" arrested in Alabama

1932 • Banks fail throughout nation
- Bonus Army marches on Washington
- Hoover's Reconstruction Finance Corporation tries to stabilize banks, insurance companies, and railroads
- Roosevelt elected president

1933 • 13 million Americans unemployed
- "First Hundred Days" of Roosevelt administration offers major legislation for economic recovery and poor relief
- National bank holiday halts run on banks
- Agricultural Adjustment Act (AAA) encourages decreased farm production
- National Industrial Recovery Act (NIRA) attempts to spur industrial growth
- Tennessee Valley Authority established

1934 • Long starts Share Our Wealth Society
- Townsend proposes old-age pension plan
- Indian Reorganization (Wheeler-Howard) Act restores lands to tribal ownership

1935 • National Labor Relations (Wagner) Act guarantees workers' right to unionize
- Social Security Act establishes insurance for the aged, the unemployed, and needy children
- Works Progress Administration creates jobs in public works projects
- Revenue (Wealth Tax) Act raises taxes on business and the wealthy

1936 • 9 million Americans unemployed
- United Auto Workers win sit-down strike against General Motors

1937 • Roosevelt's court-packing plan fails
- Memorial Day massacre of striking steelworkers
- "Roosevelt recession" begins

1938 • 10.4 million Americans unemployed
- 80 million movie tickets sold each week

1939 • Marian Anderson performs at Lincoln Memorial
- Social Security amendments add benefits for spouses and widows

The FSA camp had 240 tents and 40 small houses. The Montgomerys' experience shows the human costs of the Great Depression, but statistics are necessary to give a sense of its magnitude. Between 1929 and 1933, the U.S. gross national product was cut in half. Corporate profits fell from $10 billion to $1 billion; 100,000 businesses shut their doors. Four million workers were unemployed in January 1930; by November the number had jumped to 6 million. When President Herbert Hoover left office in 1933, 13 million workers—about one-fourth of the labor force—were idle, and millions more had only part-time work. There was no national safety net: no welfare system, no unemployment compensation, no Social Security. And as thousands of banks failed, with no federally guaranteed deposit insurance, families' savings disappeared.

Herbert Hoover, who had been elected president in the prosperous late 1920s, looked first to private enterprise for solutions. By the end of his term, he had extended the federal government's role in managing an economic crisis further than his predecessors had. Yet the depression continued to deepen. The economic catastrophe exacerbated existing racial and class tensions. In Germany, the international economic crisis propelled Adolf Hitler to power. By late 1932 many feared the depression was a crisis of capitalism, and even of democracy itself.

In 1932 voters replaced Hoover with a man who promised a New Deal. Franklin Delano Roosevelt seemed willing to experiment, and although he did not end the depression (only the massive mobilization for World War II did that), New Deal programs did alleviate suffering. For the first time, the federal government assumed responsibility for the nation's economy and the welfare of its citizens, thus strengthening its power in relation to the states.

As it transformed the role and power of the federal government, the New Deal nevertheless maintained America's existing economic and social systems. Although some Americans saw the economic crisis as an opportunity for major economic change—even revolution—Roosevelt's goal was to save capitalism. New Deal programs increased federal regulation of the economy without altering the capitalist system or the distribution of wealth. And despite pressure (even within his administration) to attack racist discrimination, Roosevelt never directly challenged legal segregation in the South—in part because he relied on southern white Democrats to pass New Deal legislation.

Despite its limits, the New Deal preserved America's democratic experiment through a time of uncertainty and crisis. By the end of the decade, the widening force of world war shifted America's focus from domestic to foreign policy. But the changes set in motion by the New Deal continued to transform the United States for decades to come. ■

Hoover and Hard Times: 1929–1933

*a*s the depression deepened in the early 1930s, tens of millions of Americans were desperately poor. In cities, the hungry lined up at soup kitchens. In West Virginia and Kentucky, wide-spread hunger and limited resources meant that the American Friends Service Committee distributed food only to those who were 10 percent below the normal weight for their height. In November 1932, *The Nation* told readers that one-sixth of the American population risked starvation over the coming winter. In Albany, New York, a ten-year-old girl died of starvation in her elementary school classroom.

Families, unable to pay rent, were evicted. The new homeless poured into shantytowns, called "Hoovervilles" in ironic tribute to the formerly popular president. Over a million men took to the road or the rails in search of work. The average marriage age rose by over two years during the 1930s. Married people delayed having children, and in 1933 the birth rate sank below replacement rates. (Contraceptive sales, with condoms costing at least $1 per dozen, did not fall during the depression.) More than 25 percent of women who were between the ages of twenty and thirty during the Great Depression never had children.

The agricultural sector, which employed almost a quarter of American workers and did not share in 1920s prosperity, was hit hard by the depression. As urbanites spent less and foreign competitors dumped agricultural surpluses into the global market, farm prices hit bottom. Farmers tried to compensate for lower prices by producing more, thus adding to the surplus and further depressing prices. By 1932, a bushel of wheat that cost North Dakota farmers 77 cents to produce brought only 33 cents. Cash-strapped farmers could not pay their property taxes or mortgages. Banks, facing their own ruin, foreclosed. In Mississippi, on a single day in April 1932, approximately one-fourth of all farmland was being auctioned off to meet debts. By the middle of the decade, the ecological crisis of the Dust Bowl would drive thousands of farmers from their land.

FARMERS AND INDUSTRIAL WORKERS

America's industrial workers had seen their standard of living improve during the 1920s, and their consumer spending had bolstered the nation's economic growth. But as Americans had less money to spend, sales of manufactured goods plummeted and factories closed: more than seventy thousand had gone out of business by 1933. As car sales dropped from 4.5 million in 1929 to 1 million in 1933, Ford laid off more than two-thirds of its Detroit workers. Almost a quarter of industrial workers were unemployed,

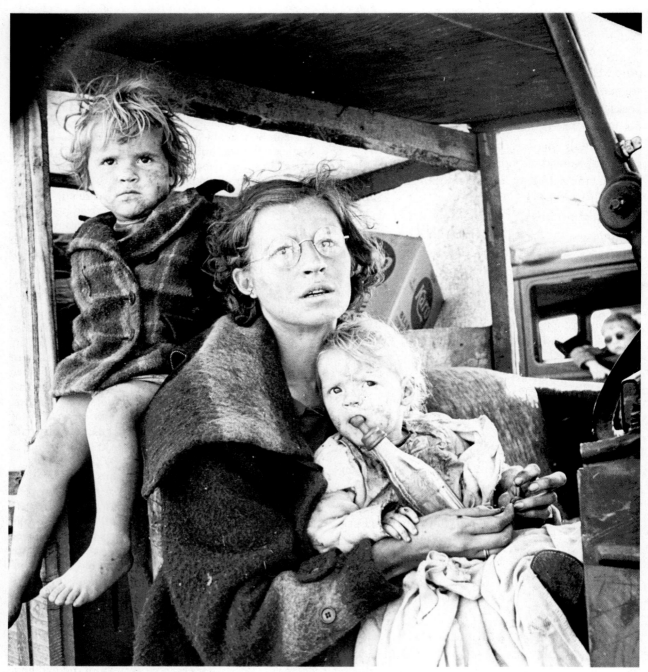

■ This 1939 photograph, titled "Mother and Children on the Road," was taken in Tule Lake, California, by Farm Security Administration photographer Dorothea Lange. The FSA used photos like this one to build public support for New Deal programs to assist migrant workers and the rural poor.   (Library of Congress)

and those with jobs saw the average wage fall by almost one-third.

For workers on the lowest rungs of the employment ladder, the depression was a crushing blow. In

MARGINAL WORKERS

the South, positions most white men had considered undignified before the depression—street cleaners, bellhops, garbage collectors—became desirable as other jobs disappeared, thereby increasing pressure for "Negro removal." In 1930 a short-lived fascist-style organization, the Black Shirts, recruited forty thousand members with the slogan, "No Jobs for Niggers Until Every White Man Has a Job!" Northern blacks did not fare much better. An Urban League survey of 106 cities found black unemployment rates averaged 30 to 60 percent higher than whites'. By 1932, African American unemployment reached almost 50 percent.

Mexican Americans and Mexican nationals in the American Southwest also felt the twin impacts of depression and racism. Their wages on California farms fell from a miserable 35 cents an hour in 1929 to a cruel 14 cents an hour by 1932. Throughout the Southwest, campaigns against "foreigners" hurt not only Mexican immigrants but also American citizens of Hispanic background whose families had lived in the Southwest for centuries, long before the land belonged to the United States. In 1931 the Labor Department announced plans to deport illegal immigrants to free jobs for Americans. The policy hit people of Mexican origin hardest, since even those who immigrated legally often lacked full documentation, and officials ignored that children born in the United States were U.S. citizens. The U.S. government deported eighty-two thousand Mexicans between 1929 and 1935, but almost half a million people repatriated to Mexico during the 1930s. Some left voluntarily, but many were coerced into believing they had no choice.

Even before the economic crisis, women were barred from many jobs and were paid significantly less than men. As the economy worsened, discrimination heightened. With widespread male unemployment, it was easy to believe that women who worked took jobs from men. In fact, men laid off from U.S. Steel would not have been hired as teachers, secretaries, "sales girls," or maids. Nonetheless, when a 1936 Gallup poll asked whether wives should work if their husbands had jobs, 82 percent (including 75

percent of the women) answered no. Such beliefs translated into policy. In 1930 and 1931, 77 percent of urban school systems refused to hire married women as teachers, and 63 percent fired female teachers who married.

At first, women lost jobs more quickly than men did. Women in low-wage manufacturing jobs were laid off before male employees, who were presumed to be supporting families. Middle-class families economized by firing household help. Almost a quarter of women in domestic service—a high percentage of them African American—were unemployed by January 1931. And as jobs disappeared, women of color lost even poorly paid positions to white women. But as the depression progressed, "women's jobs," such as teaching, clerical work, and switchboard operators, were not hit as hard as "men's jobs" in heavy industry, and women—including married women who previously did not work for wages—increasingly sought employment. Still, by 1940 only 15.2 percent of married women worked outside the home.

Although unemployment climbed to 25 percent, most Americans did not lose their homes or jobs dur-

MIDDLE-CLASS WORKERS AND FAMILIES

ing the depression. Professional and white-collar workers did not fare as badly as industrial workers and farmers. Many middle-class families, however, made do with less. "Use it up, wear it out, make it do, or do without," the saying went, and middle-class women cut back on household expenses by canning food or making their own clothes. Although most families' incomes fell, the impact was cushioned by declining prices of consumer goods, especially food. But even for the relatively affluent, the human toll of the depression was visible everywhere, and no one took economic security for granted any more.

Although Herbert Hoover, "the Great Engineer," had a reputation as a problem solver, no one knew

HOOVER'S LIMITED SOLUTIONS

what to do about the crisis. Experts disagreed about the causes of the depression and about the proper course of action. Many prominent business leaders believed that financial panics and depressions, no matter how painful, were part of a natural and ultimately beneficial "business cycle." Economic depressions, according to this theory, brought down inflated prices and cleared the way for real economic growth.

Herbert Hoover disagreed. "The economic fatalist," he said, "believes that these crises are inevitable. . . . I would remind these pessimists that exactly the same thing was once said of typhoid, cholera, and smallpox." Hoover had faith in "associationalism": business and professional organizations coordinated by the federal government and working together to solve the nation's problems. The federal government's role was limited to serving as a clearinghouse for ideas and plans that state and local governments, along with private industry, could voluntarily choose to implement.

While many Americans thought Hoover was doing nothing to fight the downturn, in truth he stretched his beliefs about the role of government to their limit. He tried voluntarism, exhortation, and limited government intervention. First, he sought voluntary pledges from business groups to keep wages stable and renew investment. But when they looked at their bottom lines, few could keep those promises.

As unemployment climbed, Hoover continued his focus on volunteerism, creating the President's Organization on Unemployment Relief (POUR) to generate private contributions to aid the destitute. Although 1932 saw record charitable contributions, they were inadequate. By mid-1932, one-quarter of New York's private charities, funds exhausted, had closed their doors. State and city officials found their treasuries drying up too.

Hoover held firm, fearing that government "relief" would destroy self-reliance in the poor. Thus, he authorized federal funds to feed drought-stricken livestock but rejected a smaller grant providing food for impoverished farm families. Many Americans were angry at Hoover's seeming insensitivity. When Hoover, trying to restore confidence, said, "What this country needs is a good big laugh," the resulting jokes were not what he expected. "Business is improving," one man tells another. "Is Hoover dead?" asks his companion. Two years after his election, Hoover was the most hated man in America.

Hoover eventually endorsed limited federal action to combat the crisis, but it was too little. Federal public works projects, such as the Grand Coulee Dam in Washington, created some jobs. The Federal Farm Board, created in 1929, supported crop prices by lending money to cooperatives to buy crops and keep them off the market. But the board soon ran short of money, and unsold surpluses jammed warehouses.

Hoover also signed into law the Hawley-Smoot Tariff (1930) to support American farmers and manufacturers by raising import duties to a staggering 40 percent. Instead it hampered international trade as other nations created their own protective tariffs. And as other nations sold less to the United States, they had less money to repay their U.S. debts or buy American products. Fearing the collapse of the international monetary system, Hoover in 1931 announced a moratorium on the payment of First World War debts and reparations.

In January 1932, the administration took its most forceful action with the Reconstruction Finance Corporation (RFC). It provided federal loans to banks, insurance companies, and railroads, which Hoover hoped would shore up those industries and halt disinvestment in the American economy. Hoover compromised his principles: this was direct government intervention, not "voluntarism." If he would support assistance to private industries, why not direct relief to the millions of unemployed?

More and more Americans had begun to ask that question. As the depression deepened, social unrest and violence began to surface. Increasing

PROTEST AND SOCIAL UNREST

violence raised the specter of popular revolt, and Chicago mayor Anton Cermak told Congress that if the federal government did not send his citizens aid, it would have to send troops instead.

Throughout the nation, tens of thousands of farmers took the law into their own hands. Angry crowds forced auctioneers to accept just a few dollars for foreclosed property and then returned it to the original owners. In August 1932 a new group, the Farmers' Holiday Association, encouraged farmers to hold back agricultural products to limit supply and drive prices up. In the Midwest, farmers barricaded roads to stop other farmers' trucks and then dumped the contents in roadside ditches.

In cities, the most militant actions came from Unemployed Councils, local groups similar to unions for unemployed workers that were created and led by Communist Party members. Communist leaders believed that the depression demonstrated capitalism's failure and offered an opportunity for revolution. Few of the quarter-million Americans joining local

Unemployed Councils sought revolution, but they did demand action. "Fight, Don't Starve," read banners in a Chicago demonstration.

As social unrest spread, so did racial violence. Vigilante committees offered bounties to force African Americans off the Illinois Central Railroad's payroll: $25 for maiming and $100 for killing black workers. Ten men were murdered and at least seven wounded. The Ku Klux Klan reemerged, and at least 140 attempted lynchings were recorded between January 1930 and February 1933. In most cases, local authorities were able to prevent the lynchings, but white mobs tortured, hung, and mutilated thirty-eight black men during the early years of the Great Depression. Racial violence was not restricted to the South; lynchings took place in Pennsylvania, Minnesota, Colorado, and Ohio as well.

The worst confrontation occurred in summer 1932. More than fifteen thousand unemployed World War I veterans and their families

BONUS ARMY

converged on the nation's capital as Congress debated a bill authorizing immediate payment of cash "bonuses" that veterans had been scheduled to receive in 1945. Calling themselves the Bonus Army, they set up a "Hooverville" shantytown across the river from the Capitol. Concerned about the federal budget, President Hoover opposed the bill, and the Senate voted it down.

Most of the Bonus Marchers left Washington, but several thousand stayed. Calling them "insurrectionists," the president set a deadline for their departure. On July 28, Hoover sent in General Douglas MacArthur and four infantry companies, four troops of cavalry, a machine-gun squadron, and six tanks. What followed shocked the nation: men and women chased by horsemen; children teargassed; shacks set afire. The next day, newspapers carried photographs of U.S. troops attacking their own citizens.

Many worried about an even greater danger in the growing disillusionment with democracy. As the depression worsened, the appeal of a strong leader—someone who would take action, unencumbered by constitutionally mandated checks and balances—grew. In February 1933 the U.S. Senate passed a resolution calling for newly elected president Franklin D. Roosevelt to assume "unlimited power." The rise to power of Hitler and his National Socialist Party in depression-ravaged Germany was an obvious parallel.

Franklin D. Roosevelt and the Launching of the New Deal

In the presidential campaign of 1932, Democratic challenger Franklin Delano Roosevelt insisted that the federal government had to play a much greater role than the limited federal intervention Hoover espoused. Roosevelt supported direct relief payments for the unemployed, declaring that such government aid was "a matter of social duty." During the campaign, he was never explicit about the outlines of his "New Deal." His most concrete proposals, in fact, were sometimes contradictory. But all understood that he had committed to use the power of the federal government to combat the paralyzing economic crisis. Roosevelt's 22.8 million popular votes far outdistanced Hoover's 15.8 million. Third-party Socialist candidate Norman Thomas drew nearly 1 million votes.

Franklin Roosevelt, the twentieth-century president most beloved by America's "common people,"

FRANKLIN D. ROOSEVELT

was born into upper-class privilege. After graduating from Harvard College and Columbia Law School, he married Eleanor Roosevelt, Theodore Roosevelt's niece and his own fifth cousin, once removed. He served in the New York State legislature, was appointed assistant secretary of the navy by Woodrow Wilson, and at age thirty-eight ran for vice president in 1920 on the Democratic Party's losing ticket.

In 1921 Roosevelt was stricken with polio and was bedridden for two years. He lost the use of his legs but gained, according to his wife, Eleanor, a new strength of character. By 1928 Roosevelt was sufficiently recovered to run for—and win—the governorship of New York, and then the Democratic Party's presidential nomination in 1932.

Elected in November 1932, Roosevelt did not take office until March 4, 1933. (The Twentieth Amendment to the Constitution shifted all future inaugurations to January 20.) In this long interregnum, the American banking system reached the verge of collapse.

The origins of the banking crisis lay in the flush years of World War I and the 1920s, when American banks made risky loans. After real-estate and stock market bubbles burst in 1929 and agricultural prices collapsed, many of these loans soured. As a result, banks lacked sufficient funds to cover their customers' deposits. Fearful of losing their savings, depositors pulled money out of banks and put it into gold or under mattresses. "Bank runs," in which crowds of angry customers demanded their money, became common.

BANKING CRISIS

By the 1932 election, the bank crisis was escalating rapidly. Hoover, the lame-duck president, refused to take action without Roosevelt's support, while Roosevelt refused to endorse actions he could not control. By Roosevelt's March 4 inauguration, every state had either suspended banking operations or restricted depositors' access to their money. The new president understood that the collapse of the U.S. banking system would threaten the nation's survival.

Standing in a cold rain on the Capitol steps, Roosevelt vowed in his inaugural address to face the crisis "frankly and boldly." The lines we remember from his speech are words of comfort: "The only thing we have to fear is fear itself—nameless, unreasoning, unjustified terror." But the only loud cheers came when Roosevelt asserted that, if need be, "I shall ask the Congress for the one remaining instrument to meet the crisis—broad Executive power to wage a war against the emergency, as great as the power that would be given to me if we were in fact invaded by a foreign foe."

The next day Roosevelt, using powers legally granted by the World War I "Trading with the Enemy" Act, closed the nation's banks for a four-day "holiday" and summoned Congress to an emergency session. He immediately introduced the Emergency Banking Relief Bill, which was passed sight unseen by unanimous House vote, approved 73 to 7 in the Senate, and signed into law the same day. It provided federal authority to reopen solvent banks and reorganize the rest, and authorized federal money to shore up private banks. Roosevelt had attacked "unscrupulous money changers," and many critics of the failed banking system had hoped he planned to remove the banks from private hands. Instead, Roosevelt's banking policy was much like Hoover's—a fundamentally conservative approach that upheld the status quo.

The banking bill could save the U.S. banking system only if Americans were confident enough to deposit money in the reopened banks. In the first of his radio "Fireside Chats," the president reached out to the people. "We have provided the machinery to restore our financial system," he said. "It is up to you to support and make it work." The next morning when the banks opened, people lined up—this time, most of them to deposit money. In his first action as president, Roosevelt demonstrated that he was not as radical as some wished or as others feared.

During the ninety-nine-day-long special session of Congress, which journalists dubbed "The First Hundred Days," the federal government took on dramatically new roles. Roosevelt set out to revive the economy, aided by advisers—lawyers, university professors, and social workers, collectively nicknamed "the Brain Trust"—and by the enormously capable First Lady. These "New Dealers" had no coherent plan, and Roosevelt alternated between attempts to balance the budget and massive deficit spending (spending more than is taken in in taxes and borrowing the difference). But with a strong mandate for action and the support of a Democrat-controlled Congress, the administration produced a flood of legislation. Two basic strategies emerged: New Dealers experimented with national economic planning, and they created a range of "relief" programs to help the needy.

FIRST HUNDRED DAYS

At the heart of the New Deal experiment in planning were the National Industrial Recovery Act (NIRA) and the Agricultural Adjustment Act (AAA). The NIRA was based on the belief that "destructive competition" had worsened industry's economic woes. Skirting antitrust regulation, the NIRA authorized competing businesses to cooperate in crafting industrywide "codes." Thus, automobile manufacturers, for example, would cooperate to limit production and establish industrywide prices and wages. With wages and prices stabilized, the theory went, consumer spending would increase, thereby allowing industries to rehire workers.

NATIONAL INDUSTRIAL RECOVERY ACT

Administered by the National Recovery Administration (NRA), participation was voluntary—with one catch. Businesses that adhered to the industrywide "codes" could display the NRA "Blue Eagle" symbol; the government urged consumers to boycott businesses without the Blue Eagle. Still, this voluntary program, while larger than previous efforts, was not very different from Hoover-era "associationalism."

As small-business owners had feared, big business easily dominated the NRA-mandated cartels. NRA staff lacked the training to stand up to the representatives of corporate America. The twenty-six-year-old NRA staffer who oversaw the creation of the petroleum industry code was "helped" by twenty highly paid oil industry lawyers. The majority of the 541 codes approved by the NRA reflected the interests of major corporations, not small-business owners, labor, or consumers. Most fundamental, the NRA did not deliver economic recovery. In 1935 the Supreme Court put an end to the fragile, floundering system when it found that the NRA extended federal power past its constitutional bounds.

The Agricultural Adjustment Act (AAA) had a more enduring effect. Establishing a national system

AGRICULTURAL ADJUSTMENT ACT of crop controls, it offered subsidies to farmers who agreed to limit production of specific crops. (Overproduction drove crop prices down.) The subsidies would ideally provide farmers the same purchasing power they had had during the prosperous period before World War I. In 1933 the nation's farmers destroyed 8.5 million piglets and plowed under crops in the fields. Millions of hungry Americans found it difficult to understand this waste of food.

AAA crop control policies hurt tenant farmers and sharecroppers, who were turned off the land as landlords cut production. In the South the number of sharecropper farms dropped by almost a third between 1930 and 1940. The result was a homeless population of dispossessed Americans—many of them African American—heading to cities and towns. But the subsidies did help many. In the Dakotas, government payments accounted for almost three-quarters of the total farm income for 1934.

In 1936 the Supreme Court found that the AAA, like the NRA, was unconstitutional. But the AAA (unlike the NRA) was too popular with its constituency, American farmers, to disappear. The legislation was rewritten to meet the Supreme Court's objections, and farm subsidies continued into the twenty-first century.

Roosevelt also moved quickly to implement poor relief, with $3 billion in federal funds allocated in

RELIEF PROGRAMS 1935. New Dealers, like many other Americans, disapproved of direct relief payments. Thus, New Deal programs emphasized "work relief." By January 1934, the Civil Works Administration gave jobs to 4 million people, most earning $15 a week. And the Civilian Conservation Corps (CCC) paid unmarried young men $1 a day to do hard outdoor labor: building dams and reservoirs, creating trails in national parks. The program was segregated by race but brought together young men from very different backgrounds. By 1942 the CCC had employed 2.5 million men, including 80,000 Native Americans working on western Indian reservations.

The Public Works Administration (PWA), created by Title II of the National Industrial Recovery Act, appropriated $3.3 billion for public works in 1933. PWA workers built the Grand Coulee Dam (begun during Hoover's administration) and the Triborough Bridge in New York City, as well as hundreds of public buildings. But the PWA's main purpose was to pump federal money into the economy. This huge appropriation shows the Roosevelt administration's willingness to use the controversial deficit spending to stimulate the economy.

In the three months until Congress adjourned on June 16, 1933, Roosevelt delivered fifteen messages to Congress proposing major legislation, and Congress had passed fifteen significant laws (see Table 25.1). The United States had rebounded from near collapse. As these and other New Deal programs were implemented, unemployment fell from 13 million in 1933 to 9 million in 1936. Farm prices rose, along with wages and salaries, and business failures abated (see Figure 25.1).

Political Pressure and the Second New Deal

he unprecedented popular and congressional support for Roosevelt's New Deal did not last. The dramatic actions of the First Hundred Days were possible as responses to a national emergency, but once the immediate crisis was averted, the struggle over solutions began in earnest. Some sought to stop the expansion of government power; others

TABLE 25.1

New Deal Achievements

Year	Labor	Agriculture and Environment	Business and Industrial Recovery	Relief	Reform
1933	Section 7(a) of NIRA	Agricultural Adjustment Act	Emergency Banking Relief Act	Civilian Conservation Corps	Tennessee Valley Authority
		Farm Credit Act	Economy Act	Federal Emergency Relief Act	Federal Securities Act
			Beer-Wine Revenue Act	Home Owners Refinancing Act	
			Banking Act of 1933 (guaranteed deposits)	Public Works Administration	
			National Industrial Recovery Act	Civil Works Administration	
1934	National Labor Relations Board	Taylor Grazing Act			Securities Exchange Act
1935	National Labor Relations (Wagner) Act	Resettlement Administration		Works Progress Administration	Social Security Act
		Rural Electrification Administration		National Youth Administration	Public Utility Holding Company Act
					Revenue Act (wealth tax)
1937		Farm Security Administration			
1938	Fair Labor Standards Act	Agricultural Adjustment Act of 1938		National Housing Act	

Source: Adapted from Charles Sellers, Henry May, and Neil R. McMillen, *A Synopsis of American History,* 6th ed. Copyright © 1985 by Houghton Mifflin Company. Reprinted by permission.

pushed for increased governmental action to combat continuing poverty and inequality.

Many wealthy business leaders criticized the New Deal. Some charged that there was too much taxation and government regula-

BUSINESS OPPOSITION tion. Others condemned the deficit financing of relief and public works. In 1934 several corporate leaders joined former presidential candidate Al Smith and disaffected conservative Democrats to establish the American Liberty League and campaigned against New Deal "radicalism." In an attempt to turn southern whites against the New Deal and splinter the Democratic Party, the Liberty League secretly channeled funds to a racist group in the South, which circulated incendiary pictures of the First Lady with African Americans.

Meanwhile, other Americans (sometimes called populists) thought the government favored business over the common people. Unemploy-

DEMAGOGUES AND POPULISTS ment had decreased, but 9 million people were still jobless. In 1934 a wave of strikes hit the nation, affecting 1.5 million workers. In 1935 dust storms enveloped the southern plains states, killing livestock and driving families from their land. As

Figure 25.1   The Economy Before and After the New Deal, 1929–1941

The New Deal reduced bank closings, business failures, and unemployment, and it increased farm prices, wages, and salaries. Some of the nation's most persistent economic problems, however, did not disappear until the advent of the Second World War.

dissatisfaction mounted, so did the appeal of demagogues, who sought power by playing to people's prejudices.

Father Charles Coughlin, a Roman Catholic priest whose weekly radio sermons reached 30 million listeners, appealed to people who felt they'd lost control of their lives to distant elites. Increasingly anti–New Deal, he was also anti-Semitic, telling listeners that an international conspiracy of Jewish bankers caused their problems.

Another challenge came from Dr. Francis E. Townsend, a public health officer in Long Beach, California, who lost his job at age sixty-seven with only $100 in savings. His situation was common. With social welfare left to the states, only about 400,000 of the 6.6 million elderly Americans received a state-supplied pension. As employment and savings disappeared, many older people fell into poverty. Townsend proposed that Americans over the age of sixty receive a government pension of $200 a month, financed by a new "transaction" (sales) tax. Townsend's plan was fiscally impossible (almost three-quarters of working Americans earned just $200 a month or less). Nonetheless, 20 million Americans, or one in five adults, signed petitions supporting this plan.

Then there was Huey Long, perhaps the most successful populist demagogue in American history. As a U.S. senator, Long initially supported the New Deal, but later believed Roosevelt had fallen captive to big business. Long countered in 1934 with the Share Our Wealth Society, advocating the seizure (by taxation) of all income exceeding $1 million a year and of wealth in excess of $5 million per family. From these funds, the government would provide each American family an annual income of $2,000 and a one-time homestead allowance of $5,000. (Long's plan was fiscally impossible too.) By mid-1935, Long's movement claimed 7 million members. An assassin's bullet extinguished his ambition in September 1935.

The political left also gained ground. In Wisconsin the left-wing Progressive Party reelected Robert La

LEFT-WING CRITICS Follette Jr. to the Senate in 1934, provided seven of the state's ten representatives to Congress, and placed La Follette's brother Philip in the governorship. Muckraker and socialist Upton Sinclair won the Democratic gubernatorial nomination in California in 1934. Disclaiming any intention to overthrow the U.S. government, the U.S. Communist Party proclaimed that "Communism Is Twentieth Century Americanism," and cooperated with left-wing labor unions, student groups, and writers' organizations in a "Popular Front" against fascism abroad and racism at home. In 1938, at its high point, the party had fifty-five thousand members.

Owing to Eleanor Roosevelt's influence, the administration included activists committed to progressive causes. Frances Perkins,

SHAPING THE SECOND NEW DEAL America's first woman cabinet member, came from a social work background, as did Roosevelt's close adviser, Harold Ickes. Women activists in government and the Democratic Party, attached to Eleanor Roosevelt, were strong advocates for social reform. In 1936 at least fifty African Americans held relatively important positions in New Deal agencies and cabinet-level departments. Journalists called these officials—who met on Friday evenings at the home of Mary McLeod Bethune, Director of Negro Affairs for the National Youth Administration—the "black cabinet."

Roosevelt also drew political lessons from populist demagogues and leftist politicians. Many Americans hit hard by the depression looked to the New Deal for help. Other Americans with a tenuous hold on the middle class were afraid of continued disorder and wanted stability. Still others, frightened by the populist promises of Long and Coughlin, wanted the New Deal to preserve American capitalism. In the 1936 presidential election, Roosevelt took initiative once more.

During the period historians call "the Second New Deal," Roosevelt introduced progressive programs aimed at providing "greater security for the average man than he has ever known before." The first triumph of the Second New Deal was a law Roosevelt called "the Big Bill." The Emergency Relief Appropriation Act provided $4 billion in new deficit spending, primarily for massive public works programs for the jobless. Programs included the Resettlement Administration, which resettled destitute families and organized rural homestead communities and suburban greenbelt towns for low-income workers; the Rural Electrification Administration, which brought electricity to isolated areas; and the National Youth Administration, which sponsored work-relief programs for young adults.

The largest and best-known program was the Works Progress Administration (WPA), later renamed

WORKS PROGRESS ADMINISTRATION the Work Projects Administration. The WPA employed over 8.5 million people who built 650,000 miles of highways and roads and 125,000 public buildings, as well as bridges, reservoirs, irrigation systems, sewage treatment plants, parks, playgrounds, and swimming pools nationwide. WPA workers built or renovated schools and hospitals, operated nurseries for preschool children, and taught 1.5 million adults to read and write.

The WPA also sponsored cultural programs, which provided employment for artists, musicians, writers, and actors and offered art to the people. The WPA's Federal Theater Project brought vaudeville, circuses, and theater, including African American and Yiddish plays, to cities and towns; its Arts Project hired painters and sculptors to teach their crafts in rural schools and commissioned artists to decorate post office walls with murals depicting ordinary life in America. Perhaps the most ambitious was the WPA's Federal Writers Project (FWP), which hired authors such as John Steinbeck and Richard Wright to create guidebooks for every state and write about the people of the United States. More than two thousand elderly former slaves told their stories to FWP writers as "slave narratives." Life stories of sharecroppers and textile workers were published as *These Are Our Lives* (1939). WPA projects were controversial, for many of the artists, performers, and writers sympathized with the struggles of workers and farmers, and some of the artists were communists. However, the goal of this "Popular Front" culture was not to overthrow the government, but to remember and celebrate artistically the lives and labor of America's plain folk.

Big Bill programs offered a short-term "emergency" strategy, but Roosevelt's long-term strategy centered around the Social Security **SOCIAL SECURITY ACT** Act, which created for the first time a federal system to provide for the social welfare of American citizens. Its key provision was a federal pension system in which eligible workers paid mandatory Social Security taxes on their wages and their employers contributed an equivalent amount; these workers then received federal retirement benefits. The Social Security Act also created several welfare programs, including a cooperative federal-state system of unemployment compensation and Aid to Dependent Children (later renamed Aid to Families with Dependent Children, AFDC) for needy children in families without fathers present.

Compared with systems of social security already available in most western European nations, U.S. Social Security was fairly conservative. First, the government did not pay for old-age benefits; workers and their employers did. Second, the tax was regressive in that the more workers earned, the less they were taxed proportionally. Finally, the law did not cover agricultural labor, domestic service, and "casual labor not in the course of the employer's trade or business" (for example, janitorial work at a hospital). Thus, a disproportionally high number of people of color, who worked as farm laborers, domestic servants, and service workers, received no benefits. The act also excluded public sector employees, so many teachers, nurses, librarians, and social workers, the majority of whom were women, went uncovered. (Although the original Social Security Act provided no retirement benefits for spouses or widows of covered workers, Congress added these benefits in 1939.) Despite these limitations, with its passage, the federal government took responsibility for the economic security of the aged, the temporarily jobless, dependent children, and people with disabilities.

As the 1936 election approached, Roosevelt adopted the populist language of his critics. Denouncing the "unjust concentration of **ROOSEVELT'S POPULIST STRATEGIES** wealth and power," he proposed that government should "cut the giants down to size" through antitrust suits and heavy corporate taxes. He also supported the Wealth Tax Act, which helped slightly redistribute income by raising income taxes of the wealthy. It imposed a new tax on business profits and increased taxes on inheritances, large gifts, and profits from the sale of property.

Roosevelt won by a landslide, defeating the Republican nominee, Governor Alf Landon of Kansas, by a margin of 27.8 million votes to 16.7 million. The Democrats also won majorities in the House and Senate. Roosevelt had forged a powerful "New Deal coalition" consisting of the urban masses—especially immigrants from southern and eastern Europe—organized labor, the eleven states of the Confederacy (the "Solid South"), and northern blacks. African Americans in northern cities now constituted voting blocks, and the New Deal drew them away from the

Republican Party, which they had long supported as the party of Lincoln. With the New Deal coalition, the Democratic Party would occupy the White House for most of the next thirty years.

Labor

*D*uring the worst years of the depression, American workers continued to struggle for the rights of labor. Management, however, resisted unionization vigorously, with some refusing to negotiate with union representatives and others hiring armed thugs to intimidate workers. When workers walked off the job, employers replaced them with strikebreakers. Workers tried to keep the strikebreakers from crossing picket lines, and the situation often turned violent. Local police or National Guard troops frequently intervened for management. As strikes spread, violence erupted in the steel, automobile, and textile industries, among lumber workers in the Pacific Northwest, and among teamsters in the Midwest.

The Roosevelt administration responded with the 1935 National Labor Relations (Wagner) Act, guaranteeing workers the right to organize unions and bargain collectively. It outlawed "unfair labor practices" such as firing workers who joined unions, prohibited management from sponsoring company unions, and required employers to bargain with labor's elected union representatives to set wages, hours, and working conditions. Critically important, it also created a mechanism for enforcement: the National Labor Relations Board (NLRB). By decade's end, the NLRB played a key role in mediating disputes. Union membership grew: in 1929, it stood at 3.6 million; in mid-1938, it surpassed 7 million.

The Wagner Act further alienated business leaders. The business-sponsored Liberty League insisted that the Supreme Court would soon find the Wagner Act unconstitutional.

The rapid growth and increasing militancy of the labor movement exacerbated an internal division between "craft" and "industrial" unions. Craft unions represented labor's elite—the skilled workers in a particular trade, such as carpentry. Industrial unions represented all the workers, skilled and unskilled, in a given industry, such as automobile

RIVALRY BETWEEN CRAFT AND INDUSTRIAL UNIONS

manufacture. In the 1930s, industrial unions grew dramatically.

Craft unions dominated the American Federation of Labor, the powerful union umbrella organization. Most AFL leaders offered little support for industrial organizing, and many looked down on industrial workers, disproportionately immigrants from southern and eastern Europe—"the rubbish at labor's door," in the words of the Teamsters' president. Conservative craft unionists were alarmed at what they saw as the radicalism of industrial unions.

In 1935 John L. Lewis, head of the United Mine Workers and the nation's most prominent labor leader, resigned as vice president of the AFL. He and other industrial unionists created the Committee for Industrial Organization (CIO); the AFL suspended CIO unions. In 1938 the slightly renamed Congress of Industrial Organizations had 3.7 million members, slightly more than the AFL's 3.4 million. Unlike the AFL, the CIO included women and people of color, giving these "marginal" workers greater employment security and the benefits of collective bargaining.

The most decisive labor conflict came when the United Auto Workers (UAW) demanded recognition from General Motors (GM), Chrysler, and Ford. When GM refused, on December 30, 1936, workers at the Fisher Body plant in Flint, Michigan, responded with a sit-down strike *inside* the Fisher One factory, thus immobilizing a key part of the GM production system. GM tried to force the workers out by turning off the heat. When the police tried tear gas, strikers turned the plant's water hoses on the police.

SIT-DOWN STRIKES

As the sit-down strike spread, production plummeted. General Motors obtained a court order to evacuate the plant, but the strikers stood firm, risking imprisonment and fines. Michigan's governor refused to send in the National Guard. After forty-four days, GM agreed to recognize the union, and Chrysler followed. Ford held out until 1940.

On Memorial Day 1937, picnicking workers and their families marched toward the Republic Steel plant in Chicago, intending to support strikers there. Police ordered them to disperse. A marcher threw something, and the police attacked. Ten men were killed, seven of them shot in the back. Thirty marchers were wounded, includ-

MEMORIAL DAY MASSACRE

ing a woman and three children. Many Americans, fed up with labor strife, showed little sympathy for the workers.

Gradually the violence receded as the National Labor Relations Board proved effective in mediating disputes. Unionized workers—about 23 percent of the nonagricultural work force—saw their standards of living rise.

Federal Power and the Nationalization of Culture

In the 1930s, the expansion of federal power meant government policies played an increasingly important role in the lives of Americans from different regions, classes, and ethnic backgrounds. During the depression, political power moved from the state and local levels to the White House and Congress. By the end of the 1930s, almost 35 percent of the population had received some federal benefit, whether crop subsidies through the AAA or a WPA job. As political analyst Michael Barone argues, "The New Deal changed American life by changing the relationship between Americans and their government." Americans now expected the federal government to play an active role in the life of the nation.

The New Deal changed the American West more than any other region, as federally sponsored construction of dams and other public works projects reshaped the region's economy and environment. During the 1930s, the federal Bureau of Reclamation, an obscure agency created in 1902, expanded its mandate dramatically to build large multipurpose dams that controlled entire river systems. The Boulder Dam (later renamed for Herbert Hoover) harnessed the Colorado River, providing water to southern California municipalities and using hydroelectric power to produce electricity for Los Angeles and southern Arizona.

New Deal in the West

The water from these dams opened new areas to agriculture and allowed western cities to expand; the cheap electricity they produced attracted industry. After the completion of Washington State's Grand Coulee Dam in 1941, the federal government controlled a great deal of water and hydroelectric power

in the region—which meant control over the region's future.

The federal government also brought millions of acres of western land under its control in the 1930s, limiting agricultural production to keep prices from falling further and to combat the environmental disaster of the Dust Bowl. In 1934 the Taylor Grazing Act imposed new restrictions on ranchers' use of public lands for grazing stock. Federal livestock reduction programs probably saved the western cattle industry, but they destroyed the traditional economy of the Navajos by forcing them to reduce the size of their sheep herds on federal reservation lands. The large farms and ranches of the West benefited from federal subsidies and crop supports through the AAA, but such programs also increased federal government control in the region.

New federal activism included Native Americans. Previous federal policy toward Native Americans, especially those on western Indian reservations, had been disastrous. The Bureau of Indian Affairs (BIA) was riddled with corruption; in its attempts to "assimilate" Native Americans, it had separated children from their parents, suppressed native languages, and outlawed tribal religious practices. Division of tribal lands failed to promote individual landownership. In the early 1930s, Native Americans were the poorest group in the nation, with an infant mortality rate twice that of white Americans.

New Deal for Native Americans

In 1933 Roosevelt named one of the BIA's most vocal critics to head the agency. John Collier, founder of the American Indian Defense Agency, sought to reverse the failed course of Indian policy. The Indian Reorganization Act (IRA, 1934) worked toward ending forced assimilation and restoring Indian lands to tribal ownership. Indian tribes had regained their status as semisovereign nations, guaranteed "internal sovereignty" in matters not limited by acts of Congress.

Some Indians rejected the IRA as a "back-to-the-blanket" measure based on romantic notions of "authentic" Indian culture. The tribal government structure specified by the IRA was perplexing to tribes such as the Papagos, whose language had no word for "representative." The Navajo nation also refused to ratify the IRA, especially since the vote occurred during the federally mandated destruction of Navajo sheep herds. Eventually, however, 181 tribes organized under the IRA, which laid the groundwork for future economic development and limited political autonomy among native peoples.

Online Study Center **Improve Your Grade**
Primary Source: Economic Conditions of the South

NEW DEAL IN THE SOUTH

Well before the Great Depression, the South was mired in debilitating poverty. In 1929 the South's per capita income of $365 per year was less than half of the West's $921. More than half of southern farm families were tenants or sharecroppers with no land of their own. Almost 15 percent of South Carolina's people could not read or write.

The largest federal intervention in the South was the Tennessee Valley Authority (TVA), authorized by Congress during Roosevelt's First Hundred Days in 1933. The TVA was created to develop a water and hydroelectric power project similar to the multipurpose dams of the West. However, confronted with the poverty of the Tennessee River Valley region (which included parts of Virginia, North Carolina, Tennessee, Georgia, Alabama, Mississippi, and Kentucky), the TVA broadened to promote economic development, bring electricity to rural areas, restore fields worn out from overuse, and fight malaria.

Though an economic miracle, the TVA proved a monumental environmental disaster over time. TVA strip mining caused soil erosion. Its coal-burning generators released sulfur oxides, which combined with water vapor to produce acid rain. Above all, the TVA degraded the water by dumping untreated sewage, toxic chemicals, and metal pollutants from strip mining into streams and rivers.

Online Study Center **Improve Your Grade**
Interactive Map: The Tennessee Valley Authority

Southern senators benefited from the flow of federal dollars to their states but were suspicious of federal intervention. When federal action threatened the South's racial hierarchy, they resisted passionately. As the nation's poorest and least educated region, the South would not easily be integrated into the national culture and economy. But New Deal programs began that process and improved the lives of at least some of the region's people.

America's national popular culture played a critical role in the life of Americans throughout the 1930s.

MASS MEDIA AND POPULAR CULTURE

The national mass medium of radio broke down regional boundaries, fostered national connections, and helped millions survive hard times. Manufacturers rushed to produce cheaper models, and by 1937 Americans were buying radios at the rate of twenty-eight a minute. By the end of the decade 27.5 million households owned radios, and families listened on average five hours a day.

In a time of uncertainty, radio gave citizens immediate access to political news and the actual voices of their elected leaders. It also offered escape: for children, the adventures of *Flash Gordon*, and for housewives, the new soap operas such as *The Romance of Helen Trent*. Families gathered to listen to the comedy of ex-vaudevillians George Burns and Gracie Allen, and Jack Benny.

Listeners were carried to New York City for performances of the Metropolitan Opera on Saturday afternoons; to the Moana Hotel on the beach at Waikiki through the live broadcast of *Hawaii Calls;* to major league baseball games (begun by the St. Louis Cardinals in 1935) in distant cities. Millions shared the horror of the kidnapping of aviator Charles Lindbergh's son in 1932; black Americans in the urban North and the rural South shared the triumphal moment when African American boxer Joe Louis knocked out white heavyweight champion James Braddock in 1937. Radio lessened the isolation of individuals and helped to create a more homogeneous mass culture.

The shared popular culture of 1930s America also centered around Hollywood movies. Although the film industry suffered in the initial years of the depression—almost one-third of all movie theaters closed, and ticket prices fell from 30 cents to 20 cents—it rebounded after 1933. In a nation of fewer than 130 million people, 80 to 90 million movie tickets were sold weekly by the mid-1930s. Comedies were especially popular, from the slapstick of the Marx Brothers to the sophisticated banter of *My Man Godfrey*.

Finally, federal policies intended to channel jobs to male heads of households strengthened the power of national popular culture. During Roosevelt's first two years in office, 1.5 million youths lost jobs and

The 1936 Olympic Games

GERMANY
XIth OLYMPIC GAMES
1936
1st — 16th AUGUST
BERLIN

The 1936 Olympic Games scheduled to take place in Berlin, under the Nazi regime, created a dilemma for the United States and other nations. Would participation in the Nazi-orchestrated spectacle lend credence to Hitler? Or would victories by other nations undermine Hitler's claims about the superiority of Germany's "Aryan race"?

From the first Olympic Games in 1896, international politics were always near the surface. Germany was excluded in 1920 and 1924 following its defeat in World War I. The International Olympic Committee's choice (in 1931) of Berlin for the XI Olympiad was intended to welcome Germany back into the world community. However, with Hitler's rise to power in 1933, Germany determined to use the games as propaganda for the Nazi state. Soon after, campaigns to boycott the Berlin Olympics emerged in several nations, including the United States.

Americans were divided over the boycott. Some U.S. Jewish groups led campaigns against U.S. participation in Berlin, while many African Americans hoped to demonstrate on the fields of Berlin just how wrong Hitler's notions of Aryan superiority were.

The debate over the Berlin Olympics also revealed pockets of American anti-Semitism. Faced with the prospect of a boycott, the president of the American Olympic Committee (AOC), Avery Brundage, attributed the boycott movement to a "conspiracy" of Jews and communists.

In the end, the United States sent 312 athletes to Berlin, including eighteen African Americans, who won fourteen medals, or almost one-quarter of the U.S. total of fifty-six. Track and field star Jesse Owens earned four gold medals.

Despite the initial controversy, the XI Olympiad was a public relations triumph for Germany in the United States. As participants and spectators flocked to swastika-bedecked Berlin, Hitler's vow that the Olympic Games would thereafter take place in Germany "for all time to come" seemed suddenly possible. The vision of nations linked in peaceful athletic competition hit a low point at the 1936 Olympics. The 1940 Olympic Games, scheduled for Tokyo, were cancelled because of the escalating world war.

The eleventh summer Olympic Games in Berlin were carefully crafted as propaganda for the Nazi state. And the spectacle of the 1936 games, as represented in this poster, was impressive. But on the athletic fields, Nazi claims of Aryan superiority were challenged by athletes such as African American Jesse Owens, who is shown breaking the Olympic record in the 200-meter race. (Above: © Leonard de Selva/ CORBIS; left: © Bettmann/CORBIS)

469

■ Radio provided the backdrop for family life and household chores during the 1930s, with programs ranging from operas to soap operas. The largest audience for any single program during the decade listened to the Joe Louis–Max Schmeling boxing match in June 1938.

(AP/Wide World Photo)

many young people who would have gone to work at the age of fourteen in better times decided to stay in school. By the end of the decade, three-quarters of American youth went to high school—up from one-half in 1920—and graduation rates doubled. As more young people went to high school, more participated in national youth culture, increasingly listening to the same music and adopting the same styles of clothing, dance, and speech. Paradoxically, the hard times of the depression caused youth culture to spread more widely among America's young.

The Limits of the New Deal

Roosevelt began his second term with a strong mandate for reform. Almost immediately, however, the president's actions undermined his New Deal agenda. Labor strife and racial issues divided America. As fascism spread in Europe, domestic initiatives lost ground to foreign affairs and defense. By late 1938, New Deal reform had ground to a halt.

In safeguarding his progressive agenda in 1936, Roosevelt perceived the Supreme Court as the great-

COURT-PACKING PLAN

est danger to his programs. In ruling unconstitutional both the National Industrial Recovery Act (in 1935) and the Agricultural Adjustment Act (in 1936), the Court rejected not only specific provisions of New Deal legislation but the expansion of presidential and federal power. Only three of the nine justices were consistently sympathetic to New Deal "emergency" measures, and Roosevelt was convinced the Court would invalidate most of the Second New Deal legislation. Citing the advanced age and heavy workload of the nine justices, he asked Congress for authority to appoint up to six new justices. But in an era that had seen the rise to power of Hitler, Mussolini, and Stalin, many Americans saw Roosevelt's plan as an attack on constitutional government. Congress rebelled, and Roosevelt experienced his first major congressional defeat.

During the long public debate over court packing, key swing-vote justices began to favor liberal, pro–New Deal rulings. The Court upheld both the Wagner Act (*NLRB v. Jones & Laughlin Steel Corp.*), ruling that Congress's power to regulate interstate commerce also involved regulating the production of goods for interstate commerce, and the Social Security Act. Moreover, a new judicial pension program encouraged older judges to retire, and the president appointed seven new associate justices, including notables such as Hugo Black, Felix Frankfurter, and William O. Douglas. In the end, Roosevelt got what he wanted, but the court-packing plan damaged his political credibility.

Another New Deal setback was the recession of 1937–1939, sometimes called the "Roosevelt recession." In 1937, confident that the depression had largely been cured, Roosevelt cut back government spending. At the same time, the Federal Reserve Board, concerned about a 3.6 percent inflation rate, tightened credit. The actions sent the economy into a tailspin: unemployment climbed from 7.7 million in 1937 to 10.4 million in 1938.

ROOSEVELT RECESSION

New Dealers struggled over the direction of liberal reform. Some urged trustbusting; others advocated the resurrection of national economic planning as it had existed under the National Recovery Administration. But Roosevelt chose deficit financing to stimulate consumer demand and create jobs. And in 1939, with conflict over the world war in Europe commanding more of the nation's attention, the New Deal came to an end.

No president had ever served more than two terms, and many Americans speculated whether Franklin Roosevelt would run for a third term in 1940. Roosevelt seemed undecided until spring, when Adolf Hitler's military advances convinced him to stay on. Roosevelt expanded military contracts, thereby reducing unemployment. Roosevelt also promised Americans, "Your boys are not going to be sent into any foreign wars."

ELECTION OF 1940

On election day, the New Deal did not deliver the landslide victory it had in the 1936 election. Roosevelt again won in the cities, primarily among blue-collar workers, ethnic Americans, and African Americans, and carried every state in the South.

While many Americans benefited, the New Deal fell short of equality for people of color. Over and over, national New Deal programs lost to local custom in the South and the West. In the South, African Americans received lower relief payments than whites and were paid

RACE AND THE LIMITS OF THE NEW DEAL

less for WPA jobs. In Tucson, Arizona, Federal Emergency Relief Agency officials divided applicants into four groups—Anglos, Mexican Americans, Mexican immigrants, and Indians—and allocated relief payments in descending order.

The case of the Scottsboro Boys illustrates the power of racism in the conflict between local and national power in 1930s America. One night in March 1931, young black and white "hobos" fought on a Southern Railroad freight train as it passed through Alabama. The black youths tossed the whites off the train. A posse stopped the train and threw the black youths in the Scottsboro, Alabama, jail. Two white women "riding the rails" claimed these young men had raped them. The youths were barely saved from a lynch mob. Medical evidence later showed that the women were lying. But within two weeks, eight of the so-called Scottsboro Boys were convicted of rape by all-white juries and sentenced to death. The ninth, a boy of thirteen, was saved from the death penalty by one vote. The case, clearly a product of southern racism, became a cause célèbre, both nationally and, through the Communist Party, around the world.

The Supreme Court intervened, ruling that Alabama deprived black defendants of equal protection under the law by systematically excluding African Americans from juries and that the defendants had been denied counsel. Alabama staged new trials, however, convicting five of the young men, who spent almost two decades in prison. On issues of race, the South would not yield easily to federal power.

Roosevelt could not secure passage of his New Deal without southern Democrats, and they were willing to hold him hostage over race. For example, in 1938, southern Democrats blocked an antilynching bill with a six-week-long filibuster in the Senate. Roosevelt refused to use his political capital to break the filibuster and pass the bill. He knew that blacks would not desert the Democratic Party, but without southern senators, his legislative agenda was dead. Roosevelt wanted all Americans to enjoy the benefits of democracy, but he had no strong commitment to civil rights.

African Americans supported Roosevelt and the New Deal, despite discriminatory policies, because it helped them. By the end of the 1930s, almost one-third of African American households survived on income from a WPA job. African Americans held significant positions in the Roosevelt administration.

When the acclaimed black contralto Marian Anderson was barred from performing in Washington's Constitution Hall by the Daughters of the American Revolution, First Lady Eleanor Roosevelt arranged for Anderson to sing at the Lincoln Memorial on Easter Sunday, 1939. Such public commitment to equality was enormously important to African Americans.

With the New Deal's limits, some blacks concluded that self-help and direct-action movements were the only road to equality. In 1934 black tenant farmers and sharecroppers joined with poor whites to form the Southern Tenant Farmers' Union. In the North, African American consumers began to boycott white merchants who refused to hire blacks. Their slogan was "Don't Buy Where You Can't Work." And the Brotherhood of Sleeping Car Porters, under the leadership of A. Philip Randolph, fought for black workers. Such actions helped to improve the lives of black Americans during the 1930s.

Assessments of Roosevelt varied widely during his presidency: he was passionately hated and just as passionately loved. When he spoke

AN ASSESSMENT OF THE NEW DEAL

to Americans in his Fireside Chats, thousands wrote to him, asking for his help and offering their advice.

Eleanor Roosevelt, the nation's First Lady, played an unprecedented role in the Roosevelt administration. She worked tirelessly for social justice, bringing reformers, trade unionists, and advocates for the rights of women and African Americans to the White House. Sometimes described as the conscience of the New Deal, she took public positions—especially on African American civil rights—far more progressive than those of her husband's administration. In some ways, she deflected criticism from her husband to herself; in others, she cemented allegiances of groups such as African Americans to the New Deal.

Most scholars consider Franklin Roosevelt a truly great president, citing his courage and self-confidence, his willingness to experiment, and his capacity to inspire the nation. Some who see the New Deal as a squandered opportunity for true change charge that Roosevelt lacked vision. They judge Roosevelt by goals that were not his own: Roosevelt was a pragmatist whose goal was to preserve the system. But even critics agree that he transformed the presidency.

During his more than twelve years in office, Roo-sevelt strengthened the presidency and the federal government. Through New Deal programs, the government greatly added to its regulatory responsibilities, including overseeing the nation's financial systems. For the first time, the federal government offered relief to the jobless and the needy and used deficit spending to stimulate the economy. Millions of Americans benefited from programs that are still operating today, among them, Social Security.

As late as 1939, more than 10 million men and women were still jobless, and the nation's unemployment rate stood at 19 percent. In 1941, as a result of mobilization for war, unemployment declined to 10 percent, and in 1944, at the height of the war, only 1 percent of the labor force was jobless. World War II, not the New Deal, would reinvigorate the American economy.

Summary *Online Study Center* ACE the Test

In the 1930s, a major economic crisis threatened the nation. By 1933, almost a quarter of America's workers were unemployed, and millions were homeless and hungry. Herbert Hoover, elected president in 1928, believed that government should play only a limited role in managing the economy. He tried to solve the nation's economic problems through a voluntary partnership of businesses and the federal government known as associationalism. In the 1932 presidential election, voters turned to the candidate who promised them a "New Deal."

The New Deal was a liberal reform program that developed within the parameters of America's capitalist and democratic system, expanding the power of the federal government. New Deal reforms forced banks, utilities, stock markets, farms, and most businesses to operate within federal guidelines. The government guaranteed workers' right to join unions, and federal law required employers to negotiate with unions to set wages, hours, and working conditions. Many unemployed workers, elderly and disabled Americans, and dependent children were protected by a national welfare system, administered through the federal government.

The New Deal had its detractors. Business leaders attacked New Deal regulations and support of organized labor. As the federal government expanded its role, tensions between national and local authority sometimes flared, and differences in regional ways of life and social and economic structures presented challenges to national policymakers. Both the West and the South were transformed by federal government action, but citizens of both regions were suspicious of federal intervention, and white southerners resisted challenges to the racial system of Jim Crow. The political realities of a fragile New Deal coalition and strong opposition shaped—and limited—New Deal programs of the 1930s and the social welfare systems Americans still live with today.

LEGACY FOR A PEOPLE AND A NATION
Social Security

The New Deal's Social Security system resulted in a secure old age for millions of Americans. Although Social Security initially excluded some of America's neediest citizens, such as farm and domestic workers, amendments expanded eligibility. Today, almost 99 percent of American workers are covered by Social Security.

The Social Security system faces an uncertain future, and its troubles are due in part to decisions made during the 1930s. President Franklin Roosevelt did not want Social Security to be confused with poor relief and instead created a system financed by payments from workers and their em-

ployers. But if benefits came from their own contributions, workers who began receiving payments in 1940 would have received less than a dollar a month. Therefore, Social Security payments from current workers covered the benefits of those already retired.

Over time, this financing system has become increasingly unstable. In 1935 average life expectancy was under sixty-five years, the age one could collect benefits. Today, on average, American men live to over eighty, and women live nearly twenty years past retirement age. In 1935 there were 16 workers paying into the system for each person receiving benefits. In 2000 there were fewer than 3.5 workers per retiree. Unless the system is reformed, many argue, the retirement of 77 million baby boomers born from the 1940s to the 1960s could bankrupt the system.

While the stock market soared in the 1990s, some proposed that since Social Security paid only a fraction of what individuals might have earned by investing their Social Security tax payments in the stock market, Americans be allowed to do just that. Opponents declared this proposal too risky; others argued that if current workers kept their money to invest, where would benefits for current retirees come from? Debates over Social Security would play a crucial role in the second term of President George W. Bush.

PEACESEEKERS AND WARMAKERS: AMERICANS IN THE WORLD 1920–1941

*I*n 1921 the Rockefeller Foundation dedicated several million dollars for projects to control yellow fever in Latin America, beginning with Mexico. Transmitted by mosquitoes, the virus causes severe headaches, vomiting, jaundice (yellow skin), and often death. Learning from the pioneering work of Carlos Juan Finlay of Cuba, Oswaldo Cruz of Brazil, and U.S. Army surgeon Walter Reed, scientists sought to destroy the mosquito in its larval stage, before it became an egg-laying adult.

U.S. diplomats, military officers, and business executives agreed that the disease threatened public health, which in turn disturbed political and economic order. When outbreaks occurred, ports were closed and quarantined, disrupting trade and immigration. The infection struck American officials, merchants, investors, and soldiers abroad and incapacitated workers. Insufficient official attention to epidemics stirred public discontent against regimes the United States supported. When the Panama Canal opened in 1914, leaders feared that the disease would spread, even reinfecting the United States, which suffered its last epidemic in 1905.

Gradually overcoming local anti-U.S. feelings, Rockefeller personnel inspected breeding places and deposited larvae-eating fish in public waterworks. In 1924 La Fundación Rockefeller declared yellow fever eradicated in Mexico. Elsewhere in Latin America, the foundation's antimosquito campaign proved successful in maritime and urban areas but less so in rural and jungle regions. Politically, Rockefeller Foundation efforts in the 1920s and 1930s strengthened central governments by providing a public health infrastructure and diminishing anti-U.S. sentiment.

The Rockefeller Foundation's program offers insights into Americans' fervent but futile efforts to build a stable international order after the First

Searching for Peace and Order in the 1920s

The World Economy, Cultural Expansion, and Great Depression

U.S. Dominance in Latin America

The Course to War in Europe

Japan, China, and a New Order in Asia

U.S. Entry into World War II

LINKS TO THE WORLD
Radio News

LEGACY FOR A PEOPLE AND A NATION
Presidential Deception of the Public

Online Study Center
This icon will direct you to interactive map and primary source activities on the website http://college.hmco.com/pic/nortonbrief7e

CHRONOLOGY

1921–22 • Washington Conference limits naval arms
• Rockefeller Foundation begins battle against yellow fever in Latin America

1922 • Mussolini comes to power in Italy

1924 • Dawes Plan eases German reparations

1928 • Kellogg-Briand Pact outlaws war

1929 • Great Depression begins
• Young Plan reduces German reparations

1930 • Hawley-Smoot Tariff raises duties

1931 • Japan seizes Manchuria

1933 • Adolf Hitler becomes chancellor of Germany
• United States extends diplomatic recognition to Soviet Union
• U.S. announces Good Neighbor policy for Latin America

1934 • Fulgencio Batista comes to power in Cuba

1935 • Italy invades Ethiopia
• Congress passes first Neutrality Act

1936 • Germany reoccupies the Rhineland
• Spanish Civil War breaks out

1937 • Sino-Japanese War breaks out
• Roosevelt makes "quarantine speech" against aggressors

1938 • Mexico nationalizes American-owned oil companies
• Munich Conference grants part of Czechoslovakia to Germany

1939 • Germany and Soviet Union sign nonaggression pact
• Germany invades Poland, and Second World War begins

1940 • Germany invades Denmark, Norway, Belgium, the Netherlands, and France
• Selective Training and Service Act starts first U.S. peacetime draft

1941 • Lend-Lease Act gives aid to Allies
• Germany attacks Soviet Union
• U.S. freezes Japanese assets
• Roosevelt and Churchill sign Atlantic Charter
• Japanese flotilla attacks Pearl Harbor, Hawai'i, and U.S. enters Second World War

---

World War. Despite the "isolationist" label sometimes applied to U.S. foreign relations during the interwar decades, Americans remained active in world affairs in the 1920s and 1930s—from gunboats on Chinese rivers, to negotiations in European financial centers, to marine occupations in Haiti and Nicaragua, to oil wells in the Middle East, to campaigns against diseases in Africa and Latin America. President Wilson said after the First World War that the United States had "become a determining factor in the history of mankind."

Notwithstanding the nation's overseas projects—colonies, spheres of influence, naval bases, investments, trade, missionary activity, humanitarian efforts—many Americans did think of themselves as isolationists, meaning that they wanted no part of Europe's political squabbles, military alliances and interventions, or the League of Nations, which might drag them into war. Internationalist-minded Americans, including most senior officials, also wanted to steer clear of future European war but were more willing than isolationists to attempt to reshape the world.

A stable world would better facilitate American prosperity and security. In the interwar years, American diplomats increasingly exercised U.S. power through conferences, humanitarian programs, cultural penetration ("Americanization"), calls for peace, nonrecognition of disapproved regimes, arms control, and economic and financial ties under the Open Door principle.

But a stable world order proved elusive. Public health projects saved lives but could not address staggering poverty across the globe. World War I debts and reparations bills bedeviled the 1920s. The Great Depression shattered world trade and threatened America's prominence in international markets. It also spawned political extremism, militarism, and war in Europe and Asia. As Nazi Germany marched to war, the United States adopted a policy of neutrality. The United States also defended its interests in Asia against Japanese aggression by invoking the Open Door policy.

After the outbreak of European war in September 1939, many Americans agreed with President Franklin D. Roosevelt that Germany and Japan imperiled U.S. interests because they were building self-sufficient spheres of influence based on military and economic domination. Roosevelt first pushed for American military preparedness and then favored aiding Britain and France. A German victory, he reasoned, would destroy traditional economic ties, threaten U.S. influence in the Western Hemisphere, and place at the pinnacle of European power Adolf Hitler, whose ambitions and barbarities seemed limitless.

At the same time, Japan seemed determined to dismember America's friend China, destroy the Open Door principle, and endanger a U.S. colony: the Philippines. To deter the Japanese, the United States cut off supplies of vital American products such as oil. Japan's surprise attack on Pearl Harbor, Hawai'i, in December 1941 finally brought the United States into the Second World War. ■

Searching for Peace and Order in the 1920s

he First World War left Europe in shambles. Between 1914 and 1921, Europe suffered tens of millions of casualties from world war, civil wars, massacres, epidemics, and famine. Germany and France lost 10 percent of their workers. The American Relief Administration and private charities delivered food to needy Europeans, including Russians wracked by famine in 1921 and 1922. Through their generosity, Americans also hoped to dampen any appeal political radicalism might have. Secretary of State Charles Evans Hughes and other leaders expected American economic expansion to promote international stability—a prosperity that would render unnecessary ideological extremes, revolution, arms races, aggression, and war.

Collective security, as envisioned by Woodrow Wilson (see Chapter 23), elicited little enthusiasm among Republican leaders. Senator Henry Cabot Lodge gloated in 1920 that "we have destroyed Mr. Wilson's League of Nations." The Geneva-headquartered League of Nations, envisioned as a peacemaker, proved feeble, not just because the United States did not join but because members failed to use it to settle disputes. Still, starting in the mid-1920s, American officials participated discreetly in League meetings on public health, prostitution, drug and arms trafficking, counterfeiting of currency, and other issues. American jurists served on the Permanent Court of International Justice (World Court). The Rockefeller Foundation donated $100,000 a year to the League's public health efforts.

During the interwar years, peace groups drew widespread support. Women gravitated to their own organizations because they lacked influence in the male-dominated groups and because of the popular assumption that women—as nurturing mothers—had a unique aversion to war. Carrie Chapman Catt's moderate National Conference on the Cure and Cause of War, formed in 1924, and the U.S. Section of the Women's International League for Peace and Freedom (WILPF), organized in 1915 by Jane Addams and Emily Greene Balch, became the largest women's peace groups. When Addams won the Nobel Peace Prize in 1931, she gave her award money to the League of Nations.

PEACE GROUPS

Peace groups differed over strategies to ensure world order. Some urged cooperation with the League of Nations and the World Court. Others championed arbitration, disarmament and arms reduction, the outlawing of war, and strict neutrality during wars. The WILPF called for an end to U.S. economic imperialism, which, it claimed, compelled the United States to intervene militarily in Latin America to protect U.S. business interests. The Women's Peace Union (organized in 1921) lobbied for a constitutional amendment requiring a national referendum on a declaration of war. Quakers, YMCA officials, and Social Gospel clergy in 1917 created the American Friends Service Committee to identify pacifist alternatives to warmaking.

Peace advocates influenced Warren G. Harding's administration to convene the Washington Naval Conference of November 1921–

WASHINGTON NAVAL CONFERENCE

February 1922. Delegates from Britain, Japan, France, Italy, China, Portugal, Belgium, and the Netherlands joined a U.S. team to discuss limiting naval armaments. American leaders worried that huge military spending endangered economic rehabilitation and that an expansionist Japan, with the world's third largest navy, would overtake the United States, ranked second behind Britain.

Secretary of State Charles Evans Hughes opened the conference with the stunning proposal to scrap thirty major U.S. ships, totaling 846,000 tons. He urged the British and Japanese delegations to do away with smaller amounts. The final limit was 500,000 tons each for the Americans and the British, 300,000 tons for the Japanese, and 175,000 tons each for the French and Italians, as agreed to in the Five-Power Treaty. The treaty set a ten-year moratorium on building capital ships (battleships and aircraft carriers). The governments also pledged not to build new fortifications in their Pacific possessions (such as the Philippines).

Next, the Nine-Power Treaty reaffirmed the Open Door in China, recognizing Chinese sovereignty. Finally, in the Four-Power Treaty, the United States, Britain, Japan, and France agreed to respect one another's Pacific possessions. These treaties did not limit submarines, destroyers, or cruisers, and did not provide enforcement powers for the Open Door. Still, Hughes achieved arms limitation and improved America's strategic position in the Pacific regarding Japan.

Peace advocates also welcomed the Locarno Pact of 1925, a set of agreements among European nations that sought to reduce tensions

KELLOGG-BRIAND PACT

between Germany and France, and the Kellogg-Briand Pact of 1928. In the latter document, sixty-two nations agreed to "condemn recourse to war for the solution of international controversies, and renounce it as an instrument of national policy." The accord passed the Senate 85 to 1, but it lacked enforcement provisions. The Kellogg-Briand Pact reflected popular opinion that war was barbaric and stimulated public discussion on the topic. But arms limitations, peace pacts, and efforts by peace groups failed to eradicate war, which fed on the economic troubles that upended world order.

The World Economy, Cultural Expansion, and Great Depression

While Europe struggled after the First World War, the international economy wobbled. Then, in the 1930s, the Great Depression set off a political chain reaction that carried the world to war. Cordell Hull, secretary of state from 1933 to 1944, argued that political extremism and militarism sprang from maimed economies. Hull proved right.

Because of World War I, the United States became a creditor nation and the financial capital of the world

ECONOMIC AND CULTURAL EXPANSION

(see Figure 26.1). From 1914 to 1930, private investments abroad grew fivefold to more than $17 billion. By the late 1920s, the United States produced nearly half of the world's industrial goods and ranked first among exporters ($5.2 billion worth of shipments in 1929). Britain and Germany lost ground to American businesses in Latin America, where Standard Oil operated in eight nations and the United Fruit Company became a huge landowner.

With America's economic prominence, cultural exportation easily followed. Hollywood movies saturated the global market and stimulated interest in American ways and products. Although some foreigners warned against "Americanization," others aped American mass-production methods and modernization. Coca-Cola opened a bottling plant in Essen, Germany, and Ford built an automobile plant in Cologne.

Germans marveled at Henry Ford's industrial techniques ("Fordismus"). In the 1930s, Nazi leader Adolf Hitler sent German car designers to Detroit

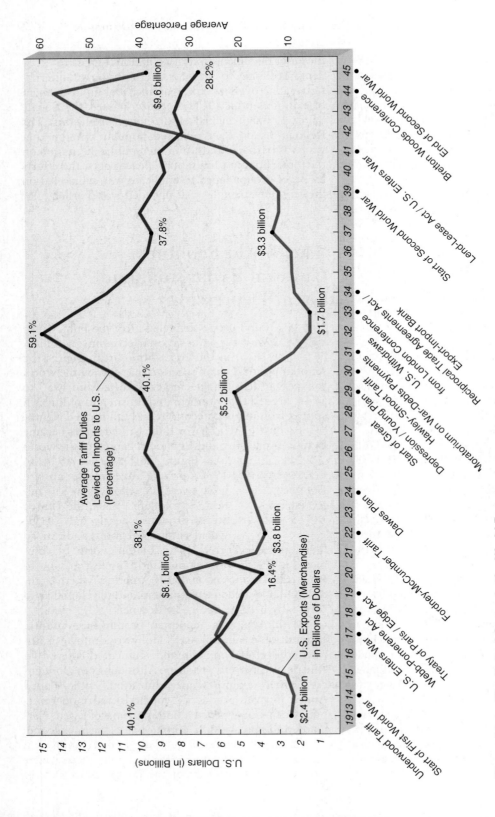

Figure 26.1 The United States in the World Economy

In the 1920s and 1930s, global depression and war scuttled the United States's hope for a stable economic order. This graph suggests, moreover, that high American tariffs meant lower exports, further impeding world trade. The Reciprocal Trade Agreements program initiated in the early 1930s was designed to ease tariff wars with other nations. (Source: U.S. Bureau of the Census, *Historical Statistics of the United States, Colonial Times to 1970* [Washington, D.C., 1975].)

before launching the Volkswagen. The Phelps-Stokes Fund further adverted the American capitalist model, exporting to black Africa Booker T. Washington's Tuskegee philosophy of education, while the Rockefeller Foundation supported colleges training doctors in Lebanon and China and funded medical research and nurses' training in Europe.

The U.S. government assisted this expansion. The Webb-Pomerene Act (1918) excluded from antitrust prosecution those combinations set up for export trade; the Edge Act (1919) permitted American banks to open foreign-branch banks; and the overseas offices of the Department of Commerce distributed valuable market information. The federal government also stimulated foreign loans by American investors. U.S. government support for the expansion of the telecommunications industry helped International Telegraph and Telephone (IT&T), Radio Corporation of America (RCA), and the Associated Press (AP) become international giants by 1930.

Europeans branded the United States stingy for its handling of World War I debts and reparations.

WAR DEBTS AND GERMAN REPARATIONS
Twenty-eight nations were involved in inter-Allied government debts, totaling $26.5 billion ($9.6 billion of it owed to the U.S. government). Europeans owed private American creditors another $3 billion and urged Americans to erase the government debts as a magnanimous contribution to the war effort. During the war, they angrily charged, Europe had bled while America profited. American leaders insisted on repayment, some pointing out that the victorious European nations had gained vast territory and resources as war spoils.

The debts question became linked to Germany's $33 billion reparations bill—which some believed Germany had the capacity but not the willingness to pay. When Germany defaulted on its payment, American bankers loaned millions to keep the nation afloat and forestall the radicalism that might thrive on economic troubles. A triangular relationship developed: American investors' money flowed to Germany, Germany paid reparations to the Allies, and the Allies then paid some of their debts to the United States. The American-crafted Dawes Plan of 1924 reduced Germany's annual payments, extended the repayment period, and provided more loans. The United States also gradually scaled down Allied obligations, cutting the debt by half during the 1920s.

But everything hinged on continued German borrowing in the United States, and in 1928 and 1929, American lending abroad dropped sharply as funds shifted to more lucrative opportunities in the stock market (see Chapters 24 and 25). The U.S.-negotiated Young Plan of 1929, which reduced Germany's reparations, salvaged little as the world economy sputtered and collapsed. By 1931, the Allies had paid back only $2.6 billion. Staggered by the Great Depression—an international catastrophe—they defaulted on the rest. Annoyed, Congress in 1934 passed the Johnson Act, which forbade U.S. government loans to foreign governments in default to the United States.

As the depression deepened, tariff wars reinvigorated economic nationalism. By 1932 twenty-five

DECLINE IN TRADE
nations retaliated against rising American tariffs (created in the Fordney-McCumber Act of 1922 and the Hawley-Smoot Act of 1930) by imposing higher tariffs on foreign imports. From 1929 to 1933, world trade declined by 40 percent. Exports of American merchandise slumped from $5.2 billion to $1.7 billion.

For Secretary of State Hull, finding a way out of the crisis depended on reviving world trade, which he believed would also boost the chances for global peace. He successfully pressed Congress to pass the Reciprocal Trade Agreements Act in 1934, which empowered the president to reduce U.S. tariffs by up to 50 percent through special agreements with foreign countries. The act's central feature was the most-favored-nation principle, whereby the United States was entitled to the lowest tariff rate set by any nation with which it had an agreement.

In 1934 Hull also helped create the Export-Import Bank, a government agency providing loans to foreigners purchasing American goods. The bank stimulated trade and became a diplomatic weapon, allowing the United States to exact concessions by approving or denying loans. In the short term, Hull's ambitious programs brought mixed results.

The Roosevelt administration's move to extend diplomatic recognition to the Soviet Union was also

U.S. RECOGNITION OF THE SOVIET UNION
economically driven. Throughout the 1920s, the Republicans refused diplomatic relations with the Soviet government, which had failed to pay $600 million for confiscated American-owned property and repudiated

preexisting Russian debts. Nonetheless, in the late 1920s, American businesses such as General Electric and International Harvester entered the Soviet marketplace, and Henry Ford signed a contract to build an automobile plant there. By 1930 the Soviet Union had become the largest buyer of American farm and industrial equipment.

Roosevelt speculated that closer Soviet-American relations might help the economy while deterring Japanese expansion. In 1933 Roosevelt granted U.S. diplomatic recognition to the Soviet Union in return for Soviet agreement to discuss its debts, forgo subversive activities in the United States, and grant Americans in the Soviet Union religious freedom and legal rights.

U.S. Dominance in Latin America

Through the Platt Amendment, the Roosevelt Corollary, the Panama Canal, military intervention, and economic preeminence, the United States had thrown an imperial net over Latin America in the early twentieth century (see Chapter 22). U.S. dominance in the hemisphere grew after the First World War. A prominent State Department officer patronizingly remarked that Latin Americans were of "low racial quality" and therefore "very easy people to deal with if properly managed."

American-made schools, roads, telephones, and irrigation systems dotted Central America and the Caribbean. American "money doctors" in Colombia and Peru helped reform tariff and tax laws and invited U.S. companies to build public works. Washington forced private high-interest loans on the Dominican Republic and Haiti. Republican administrations curtailed U.S. military intervention in the hemisphere, temporarily withdrawing troops from the Dominican Republic (1924) and Nicaragua (1925). But the marines returned to Nicaragua in 1926 to end fighting between conservative and liberal Nicaraguans and protect American property. In Haiti, the U.S. troop commitment made under Woodrow Wilson in 1915 lasted until 1934, the soldiers there to keep pro-Washington governments in power.

By 1929 direct American investments in Latin America (excluding bonds and securities) totaled $3.5 billion, while U.S. exports dominated the region's trade. Country after country experienced the repercussions of U.S. economic and political decisions. For example, the price that Americans set for Chilean copper determined the health of Chile's economy.

Latin American nationalists protested that their resources were being drained away by U.S. companies, leaving many nations in a dependent state. Unapologetic Americans believed that they were bringing material improvements and the blessings of liberty to Latin American neighbors.

DEPENDENCY STATUS

Criticism of U.S. imperialism in the region mounted in the interwar years. In 1928, at the Havana Inter-American conference, U.S. officials unsuccessfully tried to kill a resolution stating that "no state has a right to intervene in the internal affairs of another." Two years later, a Chilean newspaper warned that the American "Colossus" had "financial might" and that its aim was "Americas for the Americans— of the North." In the United States, Senator William Borah of Idaho urged that Latin Americans be granted the right of self-determination, to decide their own futures. Business leaders feared that Latin American nationalists would direct their anti-Yankee feelings against American-owned property.

Renouncing unpopular military intervention, the United States switched strategies to maintain its influence in Latin America: Pan-Americanism (a fifty-year-old concept strengthening ties between North and South America), support for strong local leaders, the training of national guards, economic and cultural penetration, Export-Import Bank loans, financial supervision, and political subversion. Dubbed the Good Neighbor policy by Franklin Roosevelt in 1933, it meant that the United States would be less blatant in its domination—avoiding exploitative business practices and military expeditions and consulting with Latin Americans.

GOOD NEIGHBOR POLICY

Most notably, Roosevelt ordered home the U.S. military forces stationed in Haiti (since 1915) and Nicaragua (since 1912, with a hiatus in 1925–1926), and he restored some sovereignty to Panama and increased that nation's income from the canal. Roosevelt's popularity in Latin America grew when, in a series of pan-American conferences, he joined in pledging that no nation in the hemisphere would intervene in the "internal or external affairs" of any other.

But Roosevelt promised more than he could deliver. His administration continued to bolster dictators in the region, believing that they would preserve U.S. economic interests. And when a revolution brought a radical government to power in Cuba in 1933, FDR instructed the American ambassador in Havana to work with conservative Cubans to replace the new government with one friendlier to U.S. interests. With Washington's support, army sergeant Fulgencio Batista took power in 1934.

During the Batista era (which ended when he was dethroned by Fidel Castro in 1959), Cuba protected U.S. investments and aligned itself with U.S. foreign policy. In return, the United States provided military aid and Export-Import Bank loans, abrogated the unpopular Platt Amendment, and gave Cuban sugar a favored position in the United States. American tourists flocked to Havana's night life of rum, rumba, prostitution, and gambling. Nationalistic Cubans protested that their nation had become a mere extension of the United States.

In Mexico, Roosevelt again showed a level of restraint that his predecessors had lacked. Since

CLASH WITH MEXICAN NATIONALISM

Woodrow Wilson sent troops to Mexico in 1914 and again in 1916, U.S.-Mexican relations had faltered as the two governments wrangled over economic interests. Still, by 1934, the United States accounted for 61 percent of Mexico's imports and received 52 percent of its exports. That year, however, a new government under Lázaro Cárdenas pledged "Mexico for the Mexicans" and strengthened trade unions to strike against foreign corporations.

In 1937 workers struck foreign oil companies for higher wages and recognition, but the companies, including Standard Oil, rejected union appeals, hoping to send a message across the hemisphere that economic nationalism could never succeed. The following year, the Cárdenas government boldly expropriated the property of all foreign-owned petroleum companies, calculating that the approaching war in Europe would restrain the United States from attacking Mexico. The United States countered by reducing purchases of Mexican silver and promoting a multinational business boycott. But Roosevelt rejected appeals to intervene militarily, fearing that Mexicans would increase oil sales to Germany and Japan. Tense negotiations led to a compromise in 1942 whereby the United States conceded that Mexico owned and could control its raw materials, and Mexico compensated the companies for their lost property.

While the United States remained the dominant power in the hemisphere, the Good Neighbor policy under Roosevelt filled Latin Americans with hope that a new era had dawned. The more sober-minded nationalists in the region knew that deepening tensions in Europe and Asia might have influenced Washington's restraint. But these threats also created a sense that nations in the Western Hemisphere should stand together.

The Course to War in Europe

*O*n March 5, 1933, one day after Roosevelt's inauguration, Germany's parliament granted dictatorial powers to the new chancellor, Adolf Hitler, leader of the Nazi Party. It was a stunning rise to power for Hitler, whose Nazis would probably have remained a fringe party had the Great Depression not hit Germany so hard. Production plummeted 40 percent, and unemployment ballooned to 6 million, meaning that two of every five workers were jobless. The disintegrating banking system, which robbed millions of their savings, and widespread resentment over the post–World War I Versailles settlement further fueled mass discontentment. While the communists preached a workers' revolution, German businessmen and property owners supported Hitler, believing they could manipulate him once he thwarted the communists. They were wrong.

Like Benito Mussolini, who gained control of Italy in 1922, Hitler was a fascist. Fascism (called Nazism, or National Socialism, in Germany) celebrated supremacy of the state over the individual; dictatorship over democracy; authoritarianism over freedom of speech; a state-regulated economy over the free market; and militarism over peace. The Nazis vowed to revive Germany, cripple communism, and "purify" the German "race" by destroying Jews and others, such as homosexuals and Gypsies, whom Hitler deemed inferior. The Nuremberg Laws of 1935 stripped Jews of citizenship and outlawed intermarriage with Germans. Half of all German Jews were without work.

Determined to get out from under the Versailles treaty, Hitler withdrew Germany from the League

GERMAN AGGRESSION UNDER HITLER

of Nations, ended reparations payments, and began to rearm. While secretly laying plans to conquer neighboring states, he watched admiringly as Mussolini's troops invaded Ethiopia in 1935. The next year Hitler ordered his own troops into the Rhineland, an area demilitarized by the Versailles treaty.

In 1936 Italy and Germany formed an alliance called the Rome-Berlin Axis. Shortly after, Germany and Japan united against the Soviet Union in the Anti-Comintern Pact. Britain and France responded with a policy of appeasement, hoping to curb Hitler's expansionism by permitting him a few territorial gains. Instead, the German leader continually raised his demands.

Online Study Center **Improve Your Grade**
Interactive Map:
German and Italian Expansion, 1933–1942

The Spanish Civil War in 1936 made matters worse. Beginning in July, about three thousand American volunteers, known as the Abraham Lincoln Battalion of the "International Brigades," joined Spanish Loyalists in defending Spain's elected republican government against Francisco Franco's fascist movement. The Soviet Union also backed the Loyalists. Hitler and Mussolini sent military aid to Franco, who won in 1939, tightening fascism's grip on the European continent.

Early in 1938 Hitler again tested European tolerance when he sent soldiers to annex his birth nation,

THE MUNICH CONFERENCE

Austria. In September he seized the Sudeten region of Czechoslovakia. France and Britain, without consulting the Czechs, agreed to allow Hitler this territorial bite, in exchange for a pledge that he would not take more. British prime minister Neville Chamberlain returned home to proclaim "peace in our time." In March 1939 Hitler swallowed the rest of Czechoslovakia.

Many Americans sought to maintain distance from Europe's tumult by embracing isolationism,

ISOLATIONIST VIEWS IN THE UNITED STATES

either because they abhorred war or because they opposed U.S. alliances with other nations. Americans learned powerful lessons from the First World War: that war damages reform movements, undermines civil liberties, dangerously expands federal power, disrupts the economy, and accentuates racial and class tensions (see Chapter 23). In a 1937 Gallup poll, nearly two-thirds said U.S. participation in World War I was a mistake.

Conservative isolationists feared higher taxes and increased executive power if the nation went to war again. Liberal isolationists worried that domestic problems might go unresolved with increased military spending. Many isolationists predicted that in attempting to spread democracy abroad, Americans would lose their freedoms at home. The vast majority of isolationists opposed fascism, but they did not think the United States should do what Europeans refused to do: block Hitler.

A congressional committee headed by Senator Gerald P. Nye held hearings from 1934 to 1936 on the

NYE COMMITTEE HEARINGS

role of business in the U.S. decision to enter the First World War. The Nye committee did not prove that American munitions makers dragged the nation into war, but it uncovered evidence that corporations had bribed foreign politicians to bolster arms sales in the 1920s and 1930s.

Isolationists grew suspicious of American business ties with Nazi Germany and fascist Italy. Twenty-six of the top American corporations, including DuPont, Standard Oil, and General Motors, had contracts in 1937 with German firms. And after Italy attacked Ethiopia in 1935, American petroleum, copper, scrap iron, and steel exports to Italy increased substantially, despite Roosevelt's call for a moral embargo. Other businesses, such as the Wall Street law firm of Sullivan and Cromwell, severed ties with Germany to protest the Nazi persecution of Jews.

Roosevelt signed a series of neutrality acts. Congress meanwhile outlawed the kinds of contacts that

NEUTRALITY ACTS

had compromised U.S. neutrality during World War I. The Neutrality Act of 1935 prohibited arms shipments to either side in a war once the president had declared the existence of belligerency. The Neutrality Act of 1936 forbade loans to belligerents. The Neutrality Act of 1937 introduced the cash-and-carry principle: warring nations would have to pay cash for nonmilitary purchases and carry the goods from U.S. ports in their own ships. The act also forbade Americans from traveling on the ships of belligerent nations.

President Roosevelt shared isolationist views in the early 1930s. Although prior to World War I

**ROOSEVELT'S
EVOLVING VIEWS**

he was an expansionist and interventionist like his cousin Theodore, during the interwar period FDR talked more about the horrors of war. In a passionate speech in August 1936 at Chautauqua, New York, Roosevelt appealed to pacifist voters in the upcoming election. The United States, he promised, would remain unentangled in the European conflict. During the crisis over Czechoslovakia in 1938, Roosevelt endorsed appeasement.

All the while, Roosevelt grew troubled by the arrogance of Germany, Italy, and Japan—aggressors he tagged the "three bandit nations." He condemned Nazi persecution of the Jews and the Japanese slaughter of Chinese civilians. In November 1938, Hitler launched *Kristallnacht* (or "Crystal Night," named for the shattered glass that littered streets after the attack on Jewish synagogues, businesses, and homes) and sent tens of thousands of Jews to concentration camps. Shocked, Roosevelt recalled the U.S. ambassador and allowed fifteen thousand refugees on visitor permits to remain longer in the United States. But he would not break trade relations with Hitler or push Congress to loosen immigration laws. Congress rejected all measures, including a bill to admit twenty thousand children under age fourteen. Motivated by economic concerns and widespread anti-Semitism, over 80 percent of Americans supported Congress's decision to uphold immigration restrictions.

Even the tragic voyage of the *St. Louis* did not change government policy. The vessel left Hamburg in mid-1939 carrying 930 desperate Jewish refugees. Denied entry to Havana, the *St. Louis* headed for Miami, where Coast Guard cutters prevented it from docking and forced its return to Europe. Some refugees took shelter in countries that later were overrun by Hitler's legions.

Quietly, though, Roosevelt began readying for war. In early 1938 he successfully pressured the House of Representatives to defeat a constitutional amendment that would require a majority vote in a national referendum before a congressional declaration of war could take effect (unless the United States were attacked). Later, in the wake of the Munich crisis, Roosevelt asked Congress for funds to fortify the air force, which he believed essential to deter aggression. In January 1939 the president secretly decided to sell bombers to France. Although these five hundred combat planes did not deter war, French orders spurred growth of the U.S. aircraft industry.

Hitler's swallowing of Czechoslovakia in March 1939 proved a turning point for Western leaders. Until then, they could explain away Hitler's actions by saying he was only trying to reunite German-speaking peoples. Now they knew it would require force to stop him. When Hitler began eyeing Poland, London and Paris stood by the Poles. Undaunted, Berlin signed a nonaggression pact with Moscow in August 1939, including a top-secret protocol that carved eastern Europe into German and Soviet zones, and let the Soviets grab the eastern half of Poland and the Baltic states of Lithuania, Estonia, and Latvia, formerly part of the Russian Empire.

Early on September 1, 1939, German tanks rolled into Poland while fighting planes covered them, thereby

**POLAND
AND THE
OUTBREAK OF
WORLD WAR II**

launching a new type of warfare, the *blitzkrieg* (lightning war)—highly mobile land forces and armor combined with tactical aircraft. Within forty-eight hours, Britain and France declared war on Germany.

**REPEAL OF THE
ARMS EMBARGO**

With Europe at war, Roosevelt declared neutrality and pressed for repeal of the arms embargo. After much debate, Congress in November lifted the embargo on contraband and approved cash-and-carry exports of arms. Using "methods short of war," Roosevelt thus began to aid the Allies. Hitler sneered that a "half Judaized, half negrified" United States was "incapable of conducting war."

Japan, China, and a New Order in Asia

n Asia, Japan flexed its muscle. The United States had interests at stake in Asia: the Philippines and Pacific islands, religious missions, trade and investments, and the Open Door in China. In missionary fashion, Americans believed that they were China's friend and protector. Pearl Buck's best-selling novel and later film *The Good Earth* (1931) countered prevailing images of the "heathen Chinee" by representing the Chinese as noble, persevering peasants. By contrast, the aggressive Japan loomed as a threat to American interests. The Tokyo government seemed bent on subjugating China and unhinging the Open Door doctrine of equal trade and investment.

The Chinese were uneasy about the U.S. presence in Asia and shared Japan's interest in reducing Western influence. The Chinese Revolution of 1911 still rumbled in the 1920s as antiforeign riots damaged American property and imperiled American missionaries. Chinese nationalists criticized Americans for extraterritoriality (the exemption of foreigners from Chinese legal jurisdiction) and demanded an end to this affront to Chinese sovereignty.

In the late 1920s, civil war broke out in China when Jiang Jieshi (Chiang Kai-shek) ousted Mao

JIANG JIESHI

Zedong and his communist followers from the ruling Guomindang Party. Americans applauded this anti-Bolshevism and Jiang's conversion to Christianity in 1930. Jiang's new wife, American-educated Soong Meiling, won their hearts with her flawless English and Western fashion. Warming to Jiang, U.S. officials signed a treaty in 1928 restoring control of tariffs to the Chinese. U.S. gunboats and marines still remained in China to protect American citizens and property.

The Japanese grew suspicious of U.S. ties with China. In the early twentieth century, Japanese-American relations deteriorated as Japan gained influence in Manchuria, Shandong, and Korea. The Japanese sought to dominate Asian territories that produced the raw materials that their import-dependent island nation required. The Japanese also resented the discriminatory immigration law of 1924, which excluded them from emigrating to the United States. Secretary Hughes called the law "a lasting injury" to Japanese-American relations. Although Japanese-American trade was twice that of Chinese-American trade, commercial rivalry strained relations between Japan and the United States.

Relations further soured in 1931 after the Japanese military seized Manchuria from China (see Map

MANCHURIAN CRISIS

26.1). Larger than Texas, Manchuria served Japan as a buffer against the Soviets and was a vital source of coal, iron, timber, and food. More than half of Japan's foreign investments rested in Manchuria. Although the seizure of Manchuria violated the Nine-Power Treaty and the

Kellogg-Briand Pact, the United States could not compel Japanese withdrawal, and the League of Nations merely condemned the Tokyo government. The American response came as a moral lecture known as the Stimson Doctrine: the United States would not recognize any impairment of China's sovereignty or of the Open Door policy, Secretary Stimson declared in 1932.

Japan continued to pressure China, leading to the Sino-Japanese War in 1937. Japanese forces seized Beijing and cities along the coast. The gruesome bombing of Shanghai intensified anti-Japanese sentiment in the United States. In an effort to help China by permitting it to buy American arms, Roosevelt refused to declare the existence of war, thus avoiding activation of the Neutrality Acts.

In a speech on October 5, 1937, the president called for a "quarantine" to curb the "epidemic of

ROOSEVELT'S QUARANTINE SPEECH

world lawlessness." People who thought Washington had been too gentle with Japan cheered. Isolationists feared that Roosevelt was edging toward war. On December 12 Japanese aircraft sank the American gunboat *Panay,* an escort for Standard Oil Company tankers on the Yangtze River. Two American sailors died. Roosevelt was relieved when Tokyo apologized and offered to pay for damages.

Japan's declaration of a "New Order" in Asia, in the words of one American official, "banged, barred, and bolted" the Open Door. Alarmed, the Roosevelt administration during the late 1930s gave loans and sold military equipment to Jiang's Chinese government, while embargoing airplane shipments to Japan. In mid-1939, the United States abrogated its trade treaty with Tokyo, yet Americans continued to ship oil, cotton, and machinery to Japan. The administration hesitated to initiate sanctions because it might spark a Japanese-American war when Germany posed a more serious threat and the United States was unprepared for war. That left Japanese-American relations stalemated when Europe's war erupted in 1939.

U.S. Entry into World War II

a stalemate was fine with many Americans if it kept the United States out of war. Roosevelt remarked in 1939 that the United States could not "draw a line of defense around this country and

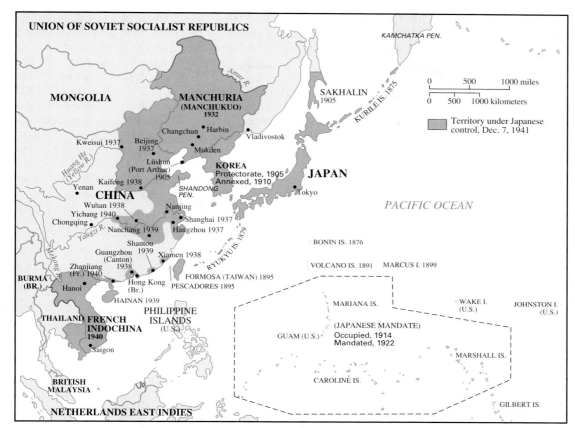

Map 26.1   Japanese Expansion Before Pearl Harbor

The Japanese quest for predominance began at the turn of the century and intensified in the 1930s. China suffered the most at the hands of Tokyo's military. Vulnerable U.S. possessions in Asia and the Pacific proved no obstacle to Japan's ambitions for a Greater East Asia Co-Prosperity Sphere.

live completely and solely to ourselves" or remain insulated from world war. Polls showed that Americans favored the Allies and supported aid to Britain and France, but the great majority emphatically wanted the United States to remain at peace. Troubled by this conflicting advice—oppose Hitler, aid the Allies, but stay out of the war—the president gradually moved the nation from neutrality to undeclared war against Germany and then, after the Japanese attack on Pearl Harbor, to full-scale war.

Unprecedented numbers of Americans spoke out on foreign affairs and joined organizations addressing foreign policy from 1939 through 1941. The widespread use of radio, the nation's chief source of news,

helped stimulate public interest, as did ethnic affiliations with the various belligerents and victims. The American Legion, the League of Women Voters, labor unions, and local chapters of the Committee to Defend America by Aiding the Allies and the isolationist America First Committee amassed citizen participation in the national debate. African American churches organized anti-Italian boycotts to protest Mussolini's pummeling of Ethiopia.

In March 1940 the Soviet Union invaded Finland. In April Germany conquered Denmark and Norway (see Map 26.2). On May 10, 1940,

FALL OF FRANCE Germany attacked Belgium, the Netherlands, and France, ultimately pushing French and British forces back to the English Channel. At Dunkirk, France, between May 26 and June 6, more than 300,000 Allied soldiers frantically escaped to Britain on a flotilla of small boats. The Germans occupied Paris a week later. A new French government in the town of Vichy collaborated with the Nazis and, on June 22, surrendered France to Berlin. The German Luftwaffe (air force) launched massive bombing raids against Great Britain.

Online Study Center **Improve Your Grade**
Primary Source:
   Propaganda in Films

Alarmed by the swift defeat of one European nation after another, Americans shed their isolationism. Insisting that New Deal reforms would not be sacrificed for military preparedness, the president began to aid the beleaguered Allies to prevent the fall of Britain. In May 1940 he ordered the sale of old surplus military equipment to Britain and France. In July he cultivated bipartisan support by naming Republicans Henry L. Stimson and Frank Knox, backers of aid to the Allies, secretaries of war and the navy, respectively. In September, the president traded fifty over-age American destroyers for leases to eight British military bases, including Newfoundland, Bermuda, and Jamaica.

Map 26.2   The German Advance, 1939–1942

Hitler's drive to dominate Europe pushed German troops deep into France and the Soviet Union. Great Britain took a beating but held on with the help of American economic and military aid before the United States itself entered the Second World War in late 1941.

Radio News

In radio's early years, network executives believed their job was to entertain Americans and left current affairs to newspapers. Yet radio had the revolutionary potential of reporting events as they happened.

Franklin Roosevelt was among the first to grasp radio's promise. As governor of New York he occasionally went on the air, and after becoming president he commenced his Fireside Chats, reassuring Americans during the depression that the government was working hard to help them. The broadcasts were so successful that one journalist remarked, "The President has only to look toward a radio to bring Congress to terms."

Across the Atlantic, Adolf Hitler also used radio to carry speeches directly to the German people. His message: Germany had been wronged by enemies abroad and by Marxists and Jews at home. But under Hitler, the Nazis promised to restore the country's former greatness. As "Sieg Heil!" thundered over the airwaves, millions of Germans saw Hitler as their salvation.

In 1938, as events abroad escalated, American radio networks increased news coverage. When Hitler annexed Austria in March, NBC and CBS broke into scheduled programs to deliver bulletins. Then, on March 13, CBS broadcast the first international news roundup, a half-hour show featuring live reports. A new era in American radio was born. In the words of author Joseph Persico, what made the broadcast revolutionary "was the listener's sensation of being on the scene" in far-off Europe.

When leaders from France and Britain met with Hitler in Munich later that year, millions of Americans eagerly listened to live radio updates. Correspondents became well known, in particular, Edward R. Murrow of CBS. During the Nazi air blitz of London in 1940–1941, Murrow's understated, nicotine-scorched voice kept Americans spellbound as he tried to "report suffering to people [Americans] who have not suffered."

Without a doubt Murrow's reports strengthened interventionist voices in Washington by emphasizing Winston Churchill's greatness and England's bravery. Furthermore, radio reports from Europe made Americans feel closely linked to people living an ocean away.

Edward R. Murrow at his typewriter in wartime London.
(Library of Congress)

Two weeks later Roosevelt signed the hotly debated and narrowly passed Selective Training and Service Act, the first peacetime military draft in American history. The law called for the registration of all men between the ages of twenty-one and thirty-five, with over 16 million men signing up. Meanwhile, Roosevelt won reelection in November 1940 with promises of peace: "Your boys are not going to be sent into any foreign wars."

FIRST PEACETIME
MILITARY DRAFT

Roosevelt claimed that the United States could avoid war by enabling the British to win. In January 1941 Congress debated the president's Lend-Lease bill. Because Britain was broke, the president explained, the United States should lend rather than sell weapons. In March 1941, with pro-British sentiment running high, the House passed the Lend-Lease Act by 317 votes to 71; the Senate followed with a 60-to-31 tally. The initial appropriation was $7 billion, but by war's end, it reached $50 billion, more than $31 billion of it for Britain.

To ensure delivery of Lend-Lease goods, Roosevelt ordered the U.S. Navy to patrol halfway across the Atlantic and sent American troops to Greenland. In July, the president dispatched marines to Iceland, arguing that it was essential for safeguarding the Western Hemisphere. He also sent Lend-Lease aid to the Soviet Union, which Hitler had attacked in June (thereby shattering the 1939 Nazi-Soviet nonaggression pact). If the Soviets could hold off two hundred German divisions in the east, Roosevelt calculated, Britain would gain some breathing space.

In August 1941 Roosevelt and British prime minister Winston Churchill met for four days on a British battleship off the coast of Newfoundland. The two leaders issued the Atlantic Charter, a set of war aims reminiscent of Wilsonianism (see Chapter 23): collective security, disarmament, self-determination, economic cooperation, and freedom of the seas. Churchill later recalled that the president told him that he could not ask Congress to declare war against Germany but "he would wage war" and "become more and more provocative."

ATLANTIC
CHARTER

On September 4, a German submarine launched torpedoes at (but did not hit) the American destroyer *Greer*. Henceforth, Roosevelt said, the U.S. Navy would shoot on sight. He also made good on a prom-ise to Churchill: American warships would convoy British merchant ships across the ocean. Thus, the United States entered into an undeclared naval war with Germany. When in October the destroyer *Reuben James* went down with the loss of more than one hundred American lives, Congress scrapped the cash-and-carry policy and revised the Neutrality Acts to permit transport of munitions to Britain on armed American merchant ships. The United States was very close to being a belligerent.

It seems ironic that the Second World War came to the United States by way of Asia. Roosevelt had wanted to avoid war with Japan to concentrate on defeating Germany. In September 1940, after Germany, Italy, and Japan had signed the Tripartite Pact (to form the Axis powers), Roosevelt slapped an embargo on shipments of aviation fuel and scrap metal to Japan. After Japanese troops occupied French Indochina in July 1941, Washington froze Japanese assets in the United States, virtually ending trade (including oil) with Japan. "The oil gauge and the clock stood side by side" for Japan, wrote one observer.

U.S. DEMANDS
ON JAPAN

Tokyo recommended a summit between President Roosevelt and Prime Minister Prince Konoye, but American officials insisted that the Japanese first agree to respect China's sovereignty and honor the Open Door policy. Roosevelt supported Secretary Hull's hard line against Japan's pursuit of the Greater East Asia Co-Prosperity Sphere—the name Tokyo gave to the Asian region it intended to dominate.

Roosevelt told his advisers to string out ongoing Japanese-American talks to gain time to fortify the Philippines and check the fascists in Europe. By deciphering intercepted messages, American officials learned that Tokyo's patience was dissipating. In late November the Japanese rejected American demands to withdraw from Indochina. An intercepted message on December 3 instructed the Japanese embassy in Washington to burn codes and destroy cipher machines—a step suggesting that war was coming.

In a daring raid on Pearl Harbor in Hawai'i, an armada of sixty Japanese ships, including six carriers bearing 360 airplanes, crossed 3,000 miles of the Pacific Ocean, maintaining radio silence to avoid detection. Early on December 7, some 230 miles northwest of Hon-

SURPRISE
ATTACK ON
PEARL HARBOR

olulu, the carriers unleashed their planes, dropping torpedoes and bombs on the unsuspecting American naval base and nearby airfields.

The battleship U.S.S. *Arizona* fell to a Japanese bomb that ignited explosives below deck, killing over one thousand sailors. The U.S.S. *Nevada* tried to escape by heading out to sea but was hit. Altogether the invaders sank or damaged eight battleships, many smaller vessels, and more than 160 aircraft on the ground. A total of 2,403 died; 1,178 were wounded. Even so, from the perspective of the war's outcome the Pearl Harbor tragedy amounted to a military inconvenience more than a disaster.

American cryptanalysts may have broken Japanese code, but the intercepted messages offered few details: there were no specifics on Japan's military plans and no mention of Pearl Harbor. Roosevelt did not, as some critics charged, conspire to leave the fleet vulnerable so that the United States could enter the Second World War through the "back door" of Asia. The base at Pearl Harbor was not on red alert because a message from Washington warning of the imminence of war was transmitted by a slow method and had arrived too late. Base commanders believed Hawai'i was

EXPLAINING PEARL HARBOR

■ The stricken U.S.S. *West Virginia* was one of eight battleships caught in the surprise Japanese attack at Pearl Harbor, Hawai'i, on December 7, 1941. In this photograph, sailors on a launch attempt to rescue a crew member from the water as oil burns around the sinking ship. (U.S. Army)

too far from Japan to be a target. Like Roosevelt's advisers, they expected an assault against British Malaya, Thailand, or the Philippines (see Map 26.1). The Pearl Harbor calamity stemmed from mistakes and insufficient information, not from conspiracy.

Roosevelt described the December 7 attack as "a date which will live in infamy," and the next day asked Congress for a declaration of war against Japan. He noted that the Japanese had also attacked Malaya, Hong Kong, Guam, the Philippines, Wake, and Midway. A unanimous vote in the Senate and a 388-to-1 vote in the House thrust America into war. Representative Jeannette Rankin of Montana voted no, as she had for World War I. Britain declared war on Japan, but the Soviet Union did not. Three days later, Germany and Italy, honoring the Tripartite Pact they had signed with Japan in September 1940, declared war against the United States.

At the core, the war resulted from a fundamental clash of systems. Germany and Japan preferred a world divided into closed spheres of influence. The United States sought a liberal capitalist world order. American principles manifested respect for human rights; fascists in Europe and militarists in Asia did not. The United States prided itself on democracy; Germany and Japan embraced authoritarian regimes. When the United States protested against German and Japanese expansion, Berlin and Tokyo charged that Washington conveniently ignored its sphere of influence in Latin America and its history of military and economic aggrandizement. These incompatible objectives obstructed diplomacy and made war likely.

Summary ⚙ *Online Study Center* **ACE the Test**

In the 1920s and 1930s, America could not create a peaceful and prosperous world order. The Washington Conference treaties failed to curb a naval arms race or protect China, and both the Dawes Plan and the Kellogg-Briand Pact were ineffective. U.S. trade policies, shifting from protectionist tariffs to reciprocal trade agreements, only minimally improved U.S. or international commerce during the Great Depression. Recognition of the Soviet Union had little effect. Most ominous, the aggressors Germany and Japan ignored repeated U.S. protests. Even where American policies seemed to satisfy Good Neighbor goals—in Latin America—nationalist resentments simmered and Mexico challenged U.S. dominance.

During the late 1930s and early 1940s, President Roosevelt hesitantly but steadily moved the United States from neutrality to aiding the Allies, to belligerency, and finally to war after the attack on Pearl Harbor. Congress gradually revised and retired the Neutrality Acts in the face of growing danger.

The Second World War offered another opportunity for Americans to set things right. As the publisher Henry Luce wrote in *American Century* (1941), the United States must "exert upon the world the full impact of our influence." Isolationists joined the president's call for victory when he said, "We are going to win the war, and we are going to win the peace that follows."

LEGACY FOR A PEOPLE AND A NATION
Presidential Deception of the Public

Before U-652 launched two torpedoes at the *Greer,* heading for Iceland on September 4, 1941, the U.S. destroyer stalked the German submarine for hours. After the attack, which missed its mark, the *Greer* also released depth charges. But when President Roosevelt described the encounter in a radio Fireside Chat on September 11, he declared that the German submarine had fired the first shot and accused Germany of violating freedom of the seas.

Roosevelt misled the American people about the events of September 4. The incident had little to do with freedom of the seas—which related to neutral merchant ships, not to U.S. warships in a war zone. Roosevelt's words were a call to arms, yet he never asked Congress for a declaration of war against Germany. The president believed that deceiving the public would move hesitant Americans toward war as noble and necessary. The practice worked: public opinion polls soon demonstrated that most Americans approved Roosevelt's shoot-on-sight policy after the *Greer* incident.

While some defended Roosevelt and accused the public of being shortsighted, his critics—even those agreeing that Nazi Germany had to be stopped—have seen in his methods a danger to the democratic process, which cannot work with dishonesty and a usurping of congressional powers. In the 1960s, during America's descent into the Vietnam War, Senator J. William Fulbright of Arkansas recalled the *Greer* incident: "FDR's deviousness in a good cause made it easier for LBJ to practice the same kind of deviousness in a bad cause." Indeed, during the Tonkin Gulf crisis of 1964, President Lyndon B. Johnson shaded the truth to gain from Congress wide latitude in waging war.

Since Roosevelt, presidents have found it easier to distort, withhold, or lie about foreign relations to garner public support. The result: the growth of the "imperial presidency"—grabbing power from Congress and using questionable means to reach presidential objectives. The practice of deception—even for a noble end—was one of Roosevelt's legacies for a people and a nation.

THE SECOND WORLD WAR AT HOME AND ABROAD 1941–1945

*W*illiam Dean Wilson was sixteen in 1942 when U.S. Marine Corps recruiters came to Shiprock, New Mexico, where he attended the Navajo boarding school. Five years too young to be drafted and a year too young to volunteer for the marines, he lied about his age. He also removed the note reading "Parents will not consent" from his recruiting file and was inducted into the Marine Corps.

Wilson and fellow Navajo recruits trained for a crucial project. Battles were won or lost because nations broke the codes enemies used to transmit messages, and the marines wanted a code based on the highly complex Navajo language, Diné. In 1942 there was no written form, and fewer than thirty non-Navajos worldwide—none of them Japanese—understood it. Unlike written ciphers, this code promised to be unbreakable. Navajo words represented the first letter of their English translations; thus *wol-la-chee* ("ant") stood for the letter *A*. The Navajo "code-talkers" memorized words representing 413 basic military terms and concepts. *Dah-he-tih-hi* ("humming-bird") meant fighter plane; *ne-he-mah,* "our mother," was the United States; *beh-na-ali-tsosie,* "slant-eye," stood for Japan.

Beginning with the Battle of Guadalcanal, Wilson and the other 420 code talkers participated in every marine assault in the Pacific from 1942 to 1945. Usually two code talkers were assigned to a battalion, one going ashore with assault forces and the other receiving messages on ship. Often under hostile fire, code talkers set up their equipment and began transmitting enemy sightings and directing shelling by American detachments. "Were it not for the Navajos," declared Major Howard Conner, Fifth Marine Division signal officer, "the Marines would never have taken Iwo Jima. . . . Six Navajo radio sets operating around the clock . . . sent and received over eight hundred messages without error."

The United States at War

The Production Front and American Workers

Life on the Home Front

The Limits of American Ideals

LINKS TO THE WORLD
War Brides

Life in the Military

Winning the War

LEGACY FOR A PEOPLE AND A NATION
Atomic Waste

Online Study Center
This icon will direct you to interactive map and primary source activities on the website
http://college.hmco.com/pic/nortonbrief7e

C H R O N O L O G Y

1941 • Government war-preparedness study concludes U.S. not ready for war before June 1943
- Roosevelt issues Executive Order No. 8802, forbidding racial discrimination by defense industry
- Japan attacks Pearl Harbor
- United States enters World War II

1942 • War Production Board created to oversee conversion to military production
- Millions of Americans move to take jobs in war industries
- Allies losing war in Pacific to Japan; U.S. victory at Battle of Midway in June is turning point
- Office of Price Administration creates rationing system for food and consumer goods
- U.S. pursues "Europe First" war policy; Allies reject Stalin's demands for a second front and invade North Africa
- West Coast Japanese Americans relocated to internment camps
- Manhattan Project set up to create atomic bomb
- Congress of Racial Equality established

1943 • Soviet army defeats German troops at Stalingrad
- Congress passes War Labor Disputes (Smith-Connally) Act following coal miners' strike
- Zoot suit riots in Los Angeles; race riots break out in Detroit, Harlem, and forty-five other cities
- Allies invade Italy
- Roosevelt, Churchill, and Stalin meet at Teheran Conference

1944 • Allied troops land at Normandy on D-Day, June 6
- Roosevelt elected to fourth term as president
- U.S. retakes Philippines

1945 • Roosevelt, Stalin, and Churchill meet at Yalta Conference
- British and U.S. forces firebomb Dresden, Germany
- Battles of Iwo Jima and Okinawa result in heavy Japanese and American losses
- Roosevelt dies; Truman becomes president
- Germany surrenders; Allied forces liberate Nazi death camps
- Potsdam Conference calls for Japan's "unconditional surrender"
- U.S. uses atomic bombs on Hiroshima and Nagasaki
- Japan surrenders
- More than 55 million people worldwide have perished in WWII

Wartime service changed the Navajo code talkers' lives, broadening their horizons and often deepening their ambitions. William Dean Wilson, for example, later became a tribal judge. Most Navajo veterans were happy to return to their traditional culture in 1945, participating in purification ceremonies to dispel battlefield ghosts and invoke blessings for the future.

The Second World War marked a turning point for millions of Americans and also in the history of the United States. For forty-five months, Americans fought abroad. Although the war began badly for the United States, the Allies halted the Axis powers' advance by mid-1942. In June 1944, American troops, together with Canadian, British, and Free French units, launched a massive invasion across the English Channel, landing at Normandy and pushing into Germany the following spring. Battered by bombing raids, leaderless after Adolf Hitler's suicide, and pressed by a Soviet advance, the Nazis capitulated in May 1945. In the Pacific, Americans drove Japanese forces back, island by island. America's devastating conventional bombing of Japanese cities, followed by the atomic bombs that demolished Hiroshima and Nagasaki in August 1945, led to the surrender of Japan. Throughout the war, the "Grand Alliance"—Britain, the Soviet Union, and the United States—united in defeating Germany but disagreed about how best to fight and how to shape the postwar world. Prospects for postwar international cooperation seemed bleak.

Although the war was fought far from the United States, it had a major impact on American society. America's leaders committed the United States to become the "arsenal of democracy," producing vast quantities of arms. All sectors of the economy were mobilized for victory. America's big businesses got even bigger, as did its central government, labor unions, and farms. The federal government had the monumental task of coordinating these spheres and two new ones: higher education and science.

During the war, nearly one of every ten Americans moved permanently to another state, most heading for war-production centers in the North and West Coast cities. Japanese Americans were rounded up by the army and placed in internment camps. And while the war encouraged African Americans to demand citizenship rights, competition for jobs and housing sparked race riots. For women, the war offered new job opportunities in the armed forces and war industries.

On the home front, Americans supported the war by collecting scrap iron, rubber, and newspapers for recycling and planting "victory gardens." At war's end, although many Americans grieved for lost loved ones and worried about the postwar order, the United States enjoyed unprecedented power and prosperity. ■

The United States at War

merican antiwar sentiment evaporated as Japanese bombs fell in the U.S. territory of Hawai'i and Franklin Roosevelt responded by declaring war with Japan on December 8. When Germany formally declared war on the United States three days later, America joined British and Soviet Allied nations in the ongoing war against the Axis powers of Japan, Germany, and Italy. The American public's shift from caution—even isolationism—to fervent support for war seemed dramatic. But in truth, the U.S. entry into World War II had been coming. America's embargo of shipments to Japan and refusal to accept Japan's expansionist policies brought the two nations to the brink of war, and the United States was deeply involved in an undeclared naval war with Germany well before Japan's attack on Pearl Harbor. By December 1941, Roosevelt had long since instituted a peacetime draft, created war mobilization agencies, and commissioned war plans for simultaneous struggle in Europe and the Pacific.

Nonetheless, the nation was not militarily ready for war. Throughout the 1930s, military funding had

A NATION UNPREPARED

been a low priority. In September 1939 (when Hitler invaded Poland and began the Second World War), the U.S. army ranked forty-fifth in size among the world's armies and could fully equip only one-third of its 227,000 men. A peacetime draft instituted in 1940 expanded the U.S. military to 2 million men, but Roosevelt's 1941 survey of war preparedness estimated that the United States could not be ready to fight before June 1943.

In December 1941, the Allies were losing (see Map 26.2). Hitler claimed Austria, Czechoslovakia, Poland, the Netherlands, Denmark, and Norway. Romania was lost, then Greece and Bulgaria. France had fallen in 1940. Britain fought on, but German planes rained bombs on London. More than 3 million German soldiers penetrated deep into the Soviet Union and Africa. German U-boats controlled the Atlantic from the Arctic to the Caribbean and in 1942 sank 216 vessels, some so close to American shores that residents could see the glow of burning ships.

In the Pacific, the war was largely America's. The Soviets had not declared war on Japan, and there

WAR IN THE PACIFIC

were too few British troops protecting England's Asian colonies to make much difference. By late spring 1942, Japan had captured most of the European colonial possessions in Southeast Asia. The Japanese attacked the Philippines hours after Pearl Harbor and destroyed U.S. air capability in the region. American and Filipino troops retreated to the Bataan Peninsula, hoping to hold the main island, Luzon, but Japanese forces were superior. In March 1942, General Douglas MacArthur, the commander of U.S. forces in the Far East, departed the Philippines for Australia, proclaiming, "I shall return."

Left behind were almost eighty thousand American and Filipino troops. Starving and decimated by disease, they held on for nearly a month before surrendering. The Japanese troops, lacking supplies themselves, were unprepared to deal with such a large number of prisoners, and most believed the prisoners had forfeited honorable treatment by surrendering. In what came to be known as the Bataan Death March, the Japanese force-marched their captives to prison camps 80 miles away, denying them food and water and bayoneting or beating to death those who fell behind. As many as ten thousand Filipinos and six hundred Americans died. Tens of thousands of Filipino refugees and prisoners died under Japanese occupation.

The United States struck back. On April 18, sixteen American B-25s released bombs above Tokyo and other cities. The Doolittle raid (named after the mission's leader) did little harm to Japan, but the image of American bombers so close pushed Japanese commander Yamamoto to bold action: attempting to

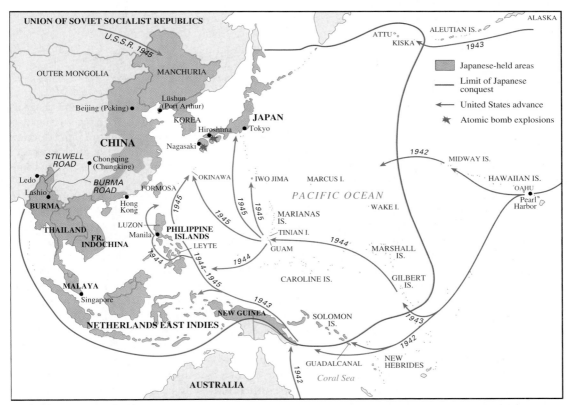

Map 27.1   The Pacific War

The strategy of the United States was to "island-hop"—from Hawai'i in 1942 to Iwo Jima and Okinawa in 1945. Naval battles were also decisive, notably the Battles of the Coral Sea and Midway in 1942. The war in the Pacific ended with Japan's surrender on August 15, 1945 (V-J Day).   (Source: Thomas G. Paterson, J. Garry Clifford, Kenneth J. Hagan, *American Foreign Policy: A History*, vol. 2, 3d ed. Copyright © 1991 by D. C. Heath Company. Used by permission of Houghton Mifflin Company.)

lure the weakened United States into a "decisive battle." The target was Midway—two tiny islands about 1,000 miles northwest of Honolulu, where the U.S. Navy had a base. If Japan could take Midway—not implausible, given Japan's string of victories—it would have a secure defensive perimeter far from the home islands (see Map 27.1). By using Guam, the Philippines, and perhaps even Australia as hostages, Japan could dictate a negotiated peace with the United States.

What General Yamamoto did not know was that America's codebreaking machines were deciphering Japanese messages. When the Japanese fleet arrived, it found the U.S. Navy lying in wait. The Battle of Midway in June 1942 was a turning point in the Pacific war. Japan's hope of forcing the United States to withdraw, leaving Japan to control the Pacific, vanished. Now Japan was on the defensive.

Despite the importance of these early Pacific battles, America's war strategy was "Europe First." U.S. military leaders believed that if Germany conquered the Soviet Union, it might directly threaten the United States. Roosevelt also feared that the Soviet Union, suffering almost unimaginable losses, might pursue a separate peace with Germany and so destroy the coalition of Allies. Thus, America would work with Britain and the USSR to defeat Germany, then deal with an isolated Japan.

"EUROPE FIRST" STRATEGY

British prime minister Winston Churchill and Soviet premier Joseph Stalin disagreed over strategy. By late 1941, German troops had nearly reached Moscow and Leningrad (present-day St. Petersburg) and slashed deeply into Ukraine, claiming the lives of over a million Soviet soldiers. Stalin pressed for British and American troops to attack Germany from the west to draw Germans away from the Soviet front. Roosevelt agreed and promised to open a second front before the end of 1942. Churchill, however, blocked this plan. He argued that it was essential to win control of the North Atlantic shipping lanes first, and promoted air attacks on Germany and a smaller, safer attack on Axis positions in North Africa. Churchill meant to halt the Germans in North Africa to protect British possessions in the Mediterranean and the oil-rich Middle East.

Against his advisers' advice, Roosevelt accepted Churchill's plan. The U.S. military was not yet ready for a major campaign, and Roosevelt needed to demonstrate wartime success to the American public before the end of 1942. Thus, instead of helping the USSR, the British and Americans made a joint landing in North Africa in November 1942, winning quick victories in Algeria and Morocco. In Egypt, the British confronted General Erwin Rommel and his Afrika Korps in a struggle over the Suez Canal and Middle East oil fields, with Rommel's army surrendering after six months. Meanwhile, the Soviet army, fighting block by block for control of Stalingrad in the deadly cold, defeated the German Sixth Army. By the spring of 1943, Germany, like Japan, was on the defensive. Relations among the Allies remained precarious as the United States and Britain continued to resist Stalin's demand for a second front.

The Production Front and American Workers

*a*lthough the war would be fought on the battlefields of Europe and the Pacific, the nation's strategic advantage lay on the "production front" at home. America would serve as the world's "great arsenal of democracy," making the machines that would win the war for the Allies.

Goals for military production were staggering. In 1940 American factories built only 3,807 airplanes. Following Pearl Harbor, Roosevelt asked for 60,000 aircraft in 1942 and double that in 1943. Plans called for the manufacture of 16 million tons of shipping and 120,000 tanks. During the war, military production took precedence over civilian goods. Automobile plants built tanks and airplanes instead of cars; dress factories sewed military uniforms. The War Production Board, established by Roosevelt in early 1942, had allocated resources and coordinated production among thousands of independent factories.

During the war, American businesses overwhelmingly cooperated with government war-production plans. Patriotism was one reason, but generous incentives were another. In 1940, as the United States produced armaments for the Allies, the American economy began to recover from the depression. Auto

BUSINESSES, UNIVERSITIES, AND THE WAR EFFORT

manufacturers, for example, expected to sell 4 million cars in 1941, a 25 percent increase over 1939. The massive retooling necessary to produce planes or tanks instead of cars would be expensive and leave manufacturers dependent on a single client—the federal government.

The federal government, however, paid for retooling and factory expansions; it guaranteed profits by allowing corporations to charge it production costs plus a fixed profit; it created tax write-offs and exemptions from antitrust laws. Consequently, corporations doubled their net profits between 1939 and 1943.

Most military contracts went to America's largest corporations, which had the facilities to guarantee rapid, efficient production. From mid-1940 through September 1944, the government awarded contracts totaling $175 billion, with two-thirds going to the top one hundred corporations. General Motors alone received 8 percent of the total. This approach made sense for a nation that wanted enormous quantities of war goods manufactured in the shortest possible time; most small businesses lacked the necessary capacity. However, wartime government contracts further consolidated American manufacturing in the hands of a few giant corporations.

Wartime needs also created a new relationship between science and the U.S. military. Federally sponsored research programs developed new technologies of warfare, such as radar, and millions of dollars went to fund research at America's largest universities. The most important government-sponsored scientific research was the Manhattan Project, a $2 billion secret effort to build an atomic bomb. Roosevelt was convinced by scientists fleeing the Nazis in 1939 that Germany was creating an atomic weapon, and he resolved to beat them to it. The Manhattan Project achieved the world's first sustained nuclear chain reaction at the University of Chicago in 1942, and in 1943 the government established a secret community for atomic scientists and their families at Los Alamos, New Mexico. Although the expression "military-industrial complex" had not yet been coined (president and former five-star general Dwight Eisenhower would do so in 1961), the web of military-business-university interdependence had begun.

MANHATTAN PROJECT

America's new defense factories required millions of workers. At first they were plentiful: 9 million Americans were unemployed in 1940 when war mobilization began. But the armed forces took 16 million men, forcing industry to look elsewhere for workers. Women, African Americans, Mexican Americans, and poor whites from Appalachia and the Deep South streamed into defense plant jobs.

NEW OPPORTUNITIES FOR WORKERS

But many industries refused to hire African Americans. A. Philip Randolph, head of the Brotherhood of Sleeping Car Porters, proposed a march on Washington, D.C., to demand equal access to defense jobs. Roosevelt, fearing race riots, offered the March on Washington movement a deal: in exchange for canceling the march, he issued Executive Order No. 8802, which prohibited discrimination in war industries and government jobs. With this federal protection, more than 1.5 million black Americans migrated from the South to the industrial cities of the North and West during the war.

Mexican workers also filled wartime jobs in the United States. About 200,000 Mexican farm workers, or *braceros,* were offered short-term agricultural contracts as Americans shifted to more lucrative war work. Mexican and Mexican American workers faced discrimination and segregation, but they seized these new economic opportunities. In 1941 not a single Mexican American worked in the Los Angeles shipyards; by 1944, seventeen thousand were employed there.

At first, employers insisted that women were not suited for industrial jobs. But as labor shortages loomed, employers did an about-face: posters and billboards urged women to "Do the Job HE Left Behind." The government's War Manpower Commission glorified the invented worker "Rosie the Riveter," who was featured on posters, in magazines, and in recruitment jingles.

WOMEN AT WORK

Rosie the Riveter was an inspiring, albeit inaccurate, image of working women. Only 16 percent of women workers held jobs in defense plants, and only 4.4 percent of the so-called skilled jobs (such as riveting). Nonetheless, during the war, over 6 million women entered the labor force, and the number of working women increased by 57 percent. More than 400,000 African American women abandoned domestic service for higher-paying industrial jobs with union benefits. Seven million women moved to war-production areas, such as Willow Run, Michigan, and southern California. Women workers in all fields kept the American economy going.

Workers in defense plants were often expected to work ten days for every day off or accept difficult night shifts. Businesses and the federal government provided new support to keep workers on the job. The West Coast Kaiser shipyards offered high pay, childcare, subsidized housing, and healthcare. The federal government also funded childcare centers and before- and after-school programs, with 130,000 preschoolers and 320,000 school-age children enrolled during the programs' peak.

The federal government attempted to ensure that labor strikes, so common in the 1930s, would not interrupt wartime production. *ORGANIZED LABOR DURING WARTIME* Days after Pearl Harbor, a White House labor-management conference agreed to a no-strike/no-lockout pledge. In 1942 Roosevelt created the National War Labor Board (NWLB) to settle disputes. The NWLB forged a temporary compromise between union demands for a "closed shop," in which only union members could work, and management's desire for "open" shops. Workers could not be required to join a union, but unions could enroll as many members as possible. Between 1940 and 1945, union membership ballooned from 8.5 million to 14.75 million.

The government did restrict union power if it threatened war production. When coal miners in the United Mine Workers union went on strike in 1943, following an NWLB attempt to limit wage increases to a cost-of-living adjustment, lack of coal halted railroads and shut down steel mills essential to war production. Congress responded with the War Labor Disputes (Smith-Connally) Act, granting the president authority to seize and operate any strike-bound plant deemed necessary to national security.

For nearly four years, American factories operated twenty-four hours a day, seven days a week, *SUCCESS ON THE PRODUCTION FRONT* turning out roughly 300,000 airplanes, 102,000 armored vehicles, 77,000 ships, 20 million small arms, 40 billion bullets, and 6 million tons of bombs. By war's end, the United States was producing 40 percent of the world's weaponry. This feat depended on transforming formerly skilled work into assembly-line mass production. Henry Ford, now seventy-eight years old, created a massive bomber plant not far from Detroit, with assembly lines almost a mile long turning out one B-24 Liberator bomber every hour. On the West Coast, William Kaiser cut construction time for Liberty ships—the huge, 440-foot-long cargo ships transporting tanks, guns, and bullets overseas—from 355 to 56 days. The ships were not well made; welded hulls sometimes split in rough seas. However, as the United States struggled to produce cargo ships faster than Germans could sink them, production speed surpassed quality in importance.

Life on the Home Front

*a*mericans worried about family and friends fighting in distant places and grieved the loss of loved ones. And although their lives were disrupted, the United States was protected by two oceans, and thereby spared the war that other nations experienced. Bombs did not fall on American cities; invading armies did not burn and rape and kill. Instead, war mobilization ended the Great Depression and brought prosperity. American civilians experienced the paradox of good times amid global conflagration.

Still, the war was a constant presence for Americans on the home front. Families planted 20 million *SUPPORTING THE WAR EFFORT* "victory gardens" to free up food supplies for the military. Housewives saved cooking fat and returned it to butchers, because it yielded glycerin to make black powder used in bullets. Children collected scrap metal: the iron in one old shovel blade was enough for four hand grenades, and tin cans helped make a tank or ship.

Many consumer goods were rationed or unavailable during the war. To save wool for military use, the War Production Board (WPB) redesigned men's suits, narrowing lapels, shortening jackets, and eliminating vests and pant cuffs. Bathing suits, the WPB specified, must shrink by 10 percent. When silk and nylon were diverted from stockings to parachutes, women used makeup on their legs. The Office of Price Administration (OPA), created by Congress in 1942, established a nationwide rationing system. Every citizen—regardless of age—received two ration books each month with 48 blue stamps for canned fruits and vegetables and 54 red points for meat, fish, and dairy. Sugar was tightly rationed, and people saved for months to make a birthday cake. Feeding a family required complex calculations. A black market existed, but most Americans understood that sugar produced alcohol for weapons manufacture and meat went to feed "our boys" overseas.

Despite widespread support, government leaders worried that in a long war, public willingness to sacrifice might lag. To boost public support, in 1942 Roosevelt created the Office of War Information (OWI), which hired Hollywood filmmakers and New York copywriters to sell the war at home. OWI posters exhorted Americans to save and sacrifice and reminded them to watch what they said, for "loose lips sink ships."

PROPAGANDA AND POPULAR CULTURE

Popular culture reinforced wartime messages. A vacuum cleaner advertisement in the *Saturday Evening Post* urged women war workers to fight "for freedom and all that means to women everywhere. You're fighting for a little house of your own, and a husband to meet every night at the door." Songs urged Americans to "Remember December 7th" or to "Accentuate the Positive." Others made fun of America's enemies ("You're a sap, Mr. Jap / You make a Yankee cranky").

Movies drew 90 million viewers a week in 1944—out of a total population of 132 million. Hollywood sought to meet Eleanor Roosevelt's challenge to "Keep 'em laughing." *A WAVE, a WAC, and a Marine* promised "no battle scenes, no message, just barrels of fun and jive to make you happy you're alive." Others, such as *Bataan* or *Wake Island*, portrayed actual—if sanitized—events in the war. Even in comedies, however, the war was always present. Theaters held "plasma premieres," offering free admission to those who donated a half-pint of blood to the Red Cross. Audiences sang "The Star Spangled Banner," then watched newsreels with censored combat footage. In movie theaters, Americans saw the horror of Nazi death camps in May 1945.

Although Americans made sacrifices, American per capita income rose from $691 to $1,515 between 1939 and 1945. Price controls kept inflation down so wage increases didn't disappear to higher costs. With little to buy, savings rose.

WARTIME PROSPERITY

World War II cost approximately $304 billion (more than $3 trillion in today's dollars), which the United States financed through deficit spending, borrowing money by selling war bonds. The national debt grew from $49 billion in 1941 to $259 billion in 1945 (the debt was not paid off until 1970). However, wartime revenue acts increased the number of Americans paying personal income tax from 4 million to 42.6 million—at rates ranging from 6 to 94 percent—and introduced a new system where employers "withheld" taxes from employee paychecks. For the first time, individuals paid more taxes than corporations did.

Online Study Center　**Improve Your Grade**

Interactive Map: The Home Front

Despite hardships and fears, the war also offered home-front Americans new opportunities. More than 15 million civilians moved during the war. People who had never traveled before found themselves on the other side of the country—or the world, moving for defense jobs or to be near loved ones at stateside military posts.

A NATION IN MOTION

The rapid influx of war workers to cities and small towns strained resources. Migrants crowded into substandard housing, such as woodsheds, tents, or cellars or into trailer parks without adequate sanitary facilities. Disease spread: scabies and ringworm, polio, tuberculosis. Many native citizens found the war workers—especially the unmarried men—a rough bunch.

In and around Detroit, where car factories were producing tanks and planes, established residents called war workers from southern Appalachia "hillbillies" and "white trash." Many migrants knew little about urban life. One young man from rural Tennessee, unfamiliar with traffic lights and street signs, navigated by counting the number of trees between his home and the war plant where he worked. Some Appalachian "trailer-ites" appalled neighbors by building outdoor privies or burying garbage in their yards.

As people from different backgrounds confronted one another, tensions rose and racism flared. In 1943 almost 250 racial conflicts exploded in forty-seven cities. In June in Detroit, white mobs, undeterred by police, roamed the city attacking

RACIAL CONFLICTS

blacks. Blacks hurled rocks at police and dragged whites off streetcars. After thirty hours of rioting, twenty-five blacks and nine whites lay dead.

In Los Angeles in 1943, young Mexican American gang members, or *pachucos,* wore zoot suits: long jackets with wide shoulders, loose pants "pegged" below the knee, and wide-brimmed hats. With cloth rationed, wearing pants requiring five yards of fabric was a purposeful rejection of wartime sacrifice. Although a high percentage of Mexican Americans served in the military, many white servicemen believed otherwise. Racial tensions fueled rumors that *pachucos* had attacked white sailors, and violence resulted. For four days, mobs of white men—mainly soldiers and sailors—attacked and stripped zoot-suiters. Los Angeles outlawed zoot suits, but the riots ended only when naval personnel were removed from the city.

The war changed family life. Despite policies initially exempting married men and fathers from the draft, almost 3 million families were broken up. The divorce rate of 16 per 1,000 marriages in 1940 almost doubled to 27 per 1,000 in 1944. At the same time, the marriage rate climbed. Some couples scrambled to marry before the man went overseas; others married and had children for military deferments. Total births rose from about 2.4 million in 1939 to 3.1 million in 1943. Many were "goodbye babies," conceived to guarantee the continuation of the family if the father died in battle.

FAMILIES IN WARTIME

On college campuses, women complained along with song lyrics, "There is no available male." But other young women enjoyed male company, sparking concern about wartime threats to sexual morality. *Youth in Crisis,* a newsreel shown nationwide in 1943, featured a girl with "experience far beyond her age" necking with a soldier. These "victory girls" or "cuddle bunnies" allegedly supported the war by giving their all to men in uniform. Many young men and women behaved as they never would in peacetime, which often meant hasty marriages to virtual strangers, especially if a baby was on the way. Wartime mobility created opportunities for young men and women to explore same-sex attraction, and gay communities grew in such cities as San Francisco.

In many ways, the war reinforced traditional gender roles weakened by the depression, restoring a pseudo-breadwinner role with men defending the nation while women "kept the home fires burning."

Some women took "men's jobs," but those who were motivated by patriotism rather than need understood it to be "for the duration." Either way, women who worked were blamed for creating an "epidemic" of juvenile delinquency. Nonetheless, millions of women took on new responsibilities and enjoyed greater independence, and many husbands returned to find that the lives of their wives and children seemed complete without them.

The Limits of American Ideals

The U.S. government worked hard to explain the reasons for citizens' wartime sacrifices. In 1941 Roosevelt pledged America to defend "four essential human freedoms"—freedom of speech, freedom of religion, freedom from want, and freedom from fear—and government-sponsored films contrasted democracy and totalitarianism, freedom and fascism, equality and oppression.

As America fought the totalitarian regimes of the Axis powers, the nation confronted difficult questions. What limits on civil liberties were justified in the interest of national security? How freely could information flow without revealing military secrets and costing American lives? How could the United States protect itself against spies or saboteurs, especially from German, Italian, or Japanese citizens living in the United States? And what about America's ongoing problem of race? The answers revealed tensions between the nation's democratic ideals and its wartime practices.

In civil liberties, American leaders mostly embraced a "strategy of truth," declaring that citizens required a truthful accounting of the war's progress. However, the government closely controlled military information, as seemingly unimportant details might tip off enemies about troop movements. While government-created propaganda sometimes dehumanized the enemy, such hate mongering was used much less frequently than during the First World War.

More complex was how to handle dissent and guard against the possibility that enemy agents were operating within the nation's borders. The Alien Registration (Smith) Act, passed in 1940, made it unlawful to advocate the overthrow of the U.S. government by force or violence. After Pearl Harbor, the government arrested thousands of Germans, Italians, and

War Brides

During and immediately after World War II, more than 60,000 American servicemen married women from other nations. The U.S. government promised servicemen that it would deliver their wives and babies home, free of charge.

Beginning in Britain in 1946, the U.S. Army's "Operation War Bride" eventually transported more than 70,000 women and children. The first group—455 British women and their 132 children—arrived in the United States on February 4, 1946. As the former WWII transport *Argentina* sailed into New York harbor in the predawn darkness, the Statue of Liberty was specially illuminated. Women who had sung "There'll Always Be an England" as they set sail from Southampton, England, gathered on the deck to attempt "The Star Spangled Banner." These women, many of them teenagers, had left their homes and families behind to join their new husbands in a strange land.

Women from war-destroyed cities were impressed by America's material abundance and the warm welcome they received. But America's racial prejudice shocked Shanghai native Helen Chia Wong, wife of Staff Sgt. Albert Wong, when she and her husband were refused rental of a house with the explanation, "The neighbors wouldn't like it." It wasn't always easy, but most war brides settled into their new communities, becoming part of their new nation and helping to forge an intimate link between America and other nations of the world.

The army's "Operation War Bride" (sometimes called "Operation Mother-in-Law" or "the Diaper Run") began in Britain in early 1946. Employing eleven former World War II troopships, including the *Queen Mary,* the U.S. government relocated the wives and babies of U.S. servicemen from dozens of nations to the United States. These English war brides, with babies their fathers have not yet seen, are waiting to be reunited with their husbands in Massachusetts, Missouri, and Iowa.   (Bettmann/CORBIS)

other Europeans suspected as spies and potential traitors. The government interned 14,426 Europeans in Enemy Alien Camps and prohibited ten thousand Italian Americans from living or working in restricted zones along the California coast.

In March 1942, Roosevelt ordered that all 112,000 foreign-born Japanese and Japanese Americans living in California, Oregon, and the state of Washington (the vast majority of the mainland population) be removed from the West Coast to "relocation centers." There were no individual charges as was the case with Germans and Italians; Japanese and Japanese Americans were imprisoned solely because they were of Japanese descent.

INTERNMENT OF JAPANESE AMERICANS

Anger at Japan's "sneak attack" on Pearl Harbor fueled calls for internment, as did fears that West Coast cities might come under enemy attack. Long-standing racism also played a critical role, and people in economic competition with Japanese Americans were among the strongest supporters of internment. Although Japanese nationals were forbidden to gain U.S. citizenship, American-born Nissei (second generation) and Sansei (third generation) were increasingly successful in business and agriculture. The relocation order forced Japanese Americans to sell property valued at $500 million for a fraction of its worth.

The internees were sent to flood-damaged lands at Relocation, Arkansas; to the intermountain terrain of Wyoming and the desert of western Arizona; and to other arid and desolate spots in the West. The camps were bleak: behind barbed wire, entire families lived in a single room in tar-papered wooden barracks with cots, blankets, and a bare light bulb. Toilets, bathing, and dining facilities were communal; privacy was almost nonexistent. People nonetheless attempted to sustain community life, setting up schools and clubs to battle monotony.

Feeling betrayed, almost 6,000 internees renounced U.S. citizenship and demanded to be sent to Japan. Some Japanese Americans sought legal remedy, but the Supreme Court upheld the government's action in *Korematsu v. U.S.* (1944). Others sought to

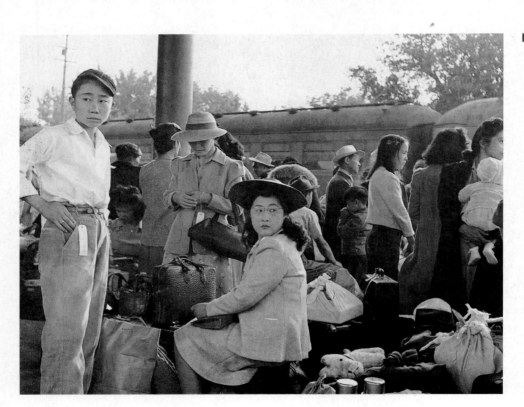

■ In February 1942 President Franklin D. Roosevelt ordered that all Japanese Americans living on the West Coast be rounded up and placed in prison camps. These families were awaiting a train to take them to an assembly center in Merced, California; from there, they would be sent to relocation camps in remote inland areas. (National Archives)

demonstrate their loyalty. The all–Japanese American 442nd Regimental Combat Team, drawn heavily from internees, was the most decorated unit of its size, receiving a Congressional Medal of Honor, 47 Distinguished Service Crosses, 350 Silver Stars, and more than 3,600 Purple Hearts. In 1988 Congress issued a public apology and symbolic payment of $20,000 each to the 60,000 surviving Japanese American internees.

Meanwhile, African American leaders wanted the nation to confront the parallels between the Nazi racist doctrines and the persistence of Jim Crow segregation in the United States. Proclaiming a "Double V" campaign (victory at home and abroad), groups such as the National Association for the Advancement of Colored People (NAACP) hoped "to persuade, embarrass, compel and shame our government and our nation . . . into a more enlightened attitude toward a tenth of its people." The NAACP, 50,000 strong in 1940, had 450,000 members by 1946. In 1942 civil rights activists founded the Congress of Racial Equality (CORE), which stressed "nonviolent direct action" and staged sit-ins to desegregate restaurants and movie theaters in northern cities and Washington, D.C.

AFRICAN AMERICANS AND "DOUBLE V"

Military service was a key issue for African Americans, who understood the link between duty and citizenship. But the U.S. military remained segregated by race and resisted using black units as combat troops. As late as 1943, less than 6 percent of the armed forces were African American: the marines initially refused to accept African Americans at all, and the navy approximated segregation by assigning black men to service positions in which they would rarely interact with nonblacks as equals or superiors.

The U.S. federal government and War Department decided that the world war was not the time to integrate the armed forces. The majority of Americans (approximately 89 percent of Americans were white) opposed integration. Racism was so entrenched that the Red Cross segregated blood plasma during the war. In southern states, racial segregation was the law. Integration of military installations, the majority of which were in the South, would have provoked a crisis as federal power contradicted state law. Pointing to outbreaks

A SEGREGATED MILITARY

of racial violence in southern training camps, government and military officials argued that wartime integration would provoke more racial violence and hinder America's war effort. General Marshall proclaimed that it was not the army's job to "solve a social problem that has perplexed the American people throughout the history of this nation." Hopes for racial justice were another casualty of the war.

Despite discrimination, African Americans stood up for their rights. Lt. Jackie Robinson refused to move to the back of the bus at the army's Camp Hood, Texas, in 1944—and faced court-martial, even though military regulations forbade racial discrimination on military vehicles. Black sailors disobeyed orders to return to work after an explosion that destroyed two ships and killed 320 men—an explosion caused by navy practice of assigning untrained black stevedores to load bombs onto Liberty ships. When they were court-martialed for mutiny, future Supreme Court justice and chief counsel for the NAACP Thurgood Marshall asked why only black sailors did this work. He proclaimed: "This is the Navy on trial for its whole vicious policy toward Negroes."

African American servicemen did eventually fight on the front lines. The Marine Corps commandant in the Pacific proclaimed that "Negro Marines are . . . Marines, period." The "Tuskegee Airmen," trained at the Tuskegee Institute in Alabama, saw heroic service in all-black units such as the Ninety-ninth Pursuit Squadron, which won eighty Distinguished Flying Crosses. After the war, African Americans called on their wartime service to claim the full rights of citizenship and shared fully in veterans' benefits under the GI Bill (discussed in Chapter 29). The war was a turning point for equal rights.

America failed to live up to its democratic ideas in refusing to assist European Jews and others attempting to flee Hitler's Germany. In 1942 American papers reported the "mass slaughter" of Jews and other "undesirables" (Gypsies, homosexuals, the physically and mentally disabled) under Hitler. Roosevelt knew about Nazi death camps capable of killing two thousand people an hour using the gas Zyklon-B. Still, American leaders did not divert airpower from principal German targets to destroy the camps.

AMERICA AND THE HOLOCAUST

British and American representatives met in Bermuda in 1943 but took no action. Appalled,

Secretary of the Treasury Henry Morgenthau Jr. charged that the State Department made the United States an accessory to murder. Early in 1944, stirred by Morgenthau, Roosevelt created the War Refugee Board, establishing refugee camps in Europe and helping to save 200,000 Jews. But, it came too late. By war's end, the Nazis had systematically murdered almost 11 million people.

Life in the Military

More than 16 million men and approximately 350,000 women served in the U.S. armed forces during World War II. Eighteen percent of American families had a father, son, or brother in the armed forces. Some men (and all of the women) volunteered. But over 10 million were draftees. The World War II draft extended fairly equitably across the population. Almost 10,000 Princeton students or alumni served—as did all four of the Roosevelts' sons.

The Selective Service Act provided for deferments, but the small number of college deferments was offset

SELECTIVE SERVICE

by deferments for many "critical occupations," including war workers and almost 2 million agricultural workers. Most deferments were for those deemed physically or mentally unqualified for military service. Army physicians discovered the impact of the depression as draftees arrived with rotted teeth and deteriorated eyesight—signs of malnutrition. Army dentists pulled 15 million teeth; optometrists prescribed 2.5 million pairs of glasses. Up to one-third of African American draftees were functionally illiterate. Forty-six percent of African Americans and almost a third of European American draftees were classified "4-F"—unfit for service.

Nonetheless, almost 12 percent of America's total population served in the military. Regional differences were profound, and northerners and southerners often could not understand one another. Ethnic differences complicated things further. Although African Americans and Japanese Americans served in separate units, Hispanics, Native Americans—including the Navajo code talkers—and Chinese Americans served in "white" units. Furthermore, the differences among "whites"—the "Italian" kid from Brooklyn and the one from rural Mississippi (or rural

Montana)—were profound. The result was often tension, but many became less prejudiced as they served with men unlike themselves.

Military service was widespread, but the burdens of combat were not equally shared. Women's roles in

FIGHTING THE WAR

the U.S. military were much more restricted than in the British or Soviet militaries. In the United States, the recruiting slogan for the WACs (Women's Army Corps) was "Release a Man for Combat," with women typically serving as nurses, in communications offices, and as typists or cooks. However, most men never saw combat either; one-quarter never left the United States. One-third of U.S. military personnel served in clerical positions, with educated men most likely slotted into noncombat positions. African Americans, though assigned dirty and dangerous tasks, were largely kept from combat. Lower-class, less-educated white men bore the brunt of the fighting.

Combat in World War II was horrible. Hollywood war films depicted men dying bravely, shot cleanly and comforted by buddies in their last moments. In reality, fewer than 10 percent of casualties were from bullets; most were killed or wounded by mortars, bombs, or grenades. Seventy-five thousand American men remained missing at the end of the war, blown into fragments too small to identify. Combat meant using flamethrowers that burned at 2,000 degrees Fahrenheit on other human beings. It meant being violently ill on a landing craft steering through floating body parts of those who had gone ahead, knowing that if you tripped, you would likely drown under the sixty-eight-pound weight of your pack, and that if you made it ashore, you would likely be blown apart by artillery. Service was "for the duration" of the war. Only death, serious injury, or victory offered release.

In forty-five months of war, close to 300,000 American servicemen died in combat, and nearly 1 million were wounded, half of them seriously. Medical advances, such as penicillin and the use of blood plasma to prevent shock, helped wounded men survive—but many never fully recovered. Between 20 and 30 percent of combat casualties were psychoneurotic. The federal government strictly censored images of American combat deaths for most of the war, consigning them to a secret file called "the chamber of horrors." Americans at home rarely understood what combat was like, and many men never talked about their experiences in the war.

Winning the War

*a*xis hopes for victory depended on a short war. Leaders in Germany and Japan recognized that if the United States had time to fully mobilize, the war was lost. Hitler, blinded by racial arrogance, stated shortly after declaring war on the United States, "I don't see much future for the Americans. . . . It's a decayed country. . . . American society [is] half Judaized, and the other half Negrified. How can one expect a State like that to hold together." By mid-1942 Axis powers realized that they had underestimated American resolve and the willingness of other Allies to sacrifice their citizens to stop the Axis advance (see Map 27.2). The chance of an Axis victory grew slim as months passed, and although the outcome was virtually certain after spring 1943, two more years of bloody fighting lay ahead.

The Allies' suspicions of one another undermined cooperation. The Soviets continued to press Britain

TENSIONS AMONG THE ALLIES

and the United States to open a second front to draw German troops away from the USSR. The English-speaking Allies, however, continued to delay. When Italy surrendered in September 1943 to American and British officers, Stalin grumbled that the arrangement smacked of a separate peace.

With the alliance badly strained, the three Allied leaders met in Teheran, Iran, in December 1943. Stalin dismissed Churchill's justifications for delaying the second front. Roosevelt also rejected Churchill's proposal for another peripheral attack, this time through the Balkans to Vienna. The three agreed to launch Operation Overlord—the cross-Channel invasion of France—in early 1944. And the Soviet Union promised to aid the Allies against Japan once Germany was defeated.

The second front opened in the dark morning hours of June 6, 1944—D-Day. In the largest am-

WAR IN EUROPE

phibious landing in history, 200,000 Allied troops commanded by American general Dwight D. Eisenhower scrambled ashore at Normandy, France. Landing craft and soldiers immediately en-

countered the enemy; they triggered mines and were pinned down by fire from cliffside pillboxes. Although heavy aerial and naval bombardment and the clandestine work of saboteurs had softened the German defenses, the fighting was ferocious.

Allied troops spread across the countryside, liberating France and Belgium and entering Germany in September. In December, German armored divisions counterattacked in Belgium's Ardennes Forest, hoping to get to Antwerp and halt Allied supplies through that Belgian port. After weeks of heavy fighting in what has come to be called the Battle of the Bulge, the Allies gained control in late January 1945. Meanwhile, Soviet troops marched through Poland and cut a path to Berlin. American forces crossed the Rhine River in March 1945 and captured the industrial Ruhr valley. Several units peeled off to enter Austria and Czechoslovakia, where they met up with Soviet soldiers.

Allied leaders began planning the peace in early 1945. Franklin Roosevelt, by this time very ill, called

YALTA CONFERENCE

for a summit meeting. The three Allied leaders convened at Yalta, in the Russian Crimea, in February 1945, each with definite goals for the postwar world. Britain, its formerly powerful empire now vulnerable and shrinking, sought to protect its colonial possessions and limit Soviet power, in part by insisting that France be included in plans for postwar control of Germany, thus reducing the Soviet sphere of influence from one-third to one-quarter. The Soviet Union, with 21 million dead, wanted reparations from Germany for its massive rebuilding effort. The Soviets hoped to expand their sphere of influence throughout eastern Europe and guarantee their national security; Germany, Stalin insisted, must be permanently weakened so it could never again attack the Soviet Union.

The United States also wanted to expand its influence and control the peace. Roosevelt lobbied for the United Nations Organization, approved in principle the previous year at Dumbarton Oaks in Washington, D.C., and through which the United States hoped to exercise influence. The United States sought to avoid the debts-reparations fiasco that had plagued Europe after the First World War. U.S. goals included self-determination for liberated peoples; gradual and orderly decolonization; and management of world affairs by the Soviet Union, Great Britain, the United

Map 27.2 **The Allies on the Offensive in Europe, 1942–1945**

The United States pursued a "Europe First" policy: first defeat Germany, then focus on Japan. American military efforts began in North Africa in late 1942 and ended in Germany in 1945 on May 8 (V-E Day).

Legend:
- Nov. 1942 boundaries
- Hitler's Greater Germany
- Other Axis nations
- Axis-occupied areas
- Allied nations
- Neutral nations
- Limit of Axis advance, Nov. 1942
- Allied advance
- Limit of Allied advance, May 1945
- ☆ Major battles

ATLANTIC OCEAN

IRELAND · Dublin

GREAT BRITAIN · London

PORTUGAL · Lisbon

SPAIN · Madrid
Gibraltar (Great Britain)

MOROCCO (Vichy France) · Casablanca
Allied landings Nov. 1942

ALGERIA (Vichy France) · Oran · Algiers

North Sea

NORWAY · Oslo

SWEDEN · Stockholm

DENMARK · Copenhagen

NETH.
BELG.
Battle of the Bulge Dec. 1944–Jan. 1945
Paris Liberated, Aug. 1944
Normandy June 1944

FRANCE · Vichy

VICHY FRANCE · Marseilles

Corsica
Sardinia

Hamburg
Cologne ☆
Apr. 1945
Rhine R.
Aug. 1944

SWITZ.

GERMANY
Munich
Berlin Apr.–May 1945 ☆
Elbe R.
Prague

Baltic Sea

FINLAND · Helsinki
Leningrad

U. S. S. R.
Moscow
Riga
Minsk
Warsaw Aug. 1944–Jan. 1945 ☆
Kiev
Dnieper R.
Kursk July 1943 ☆
Kharkov
Rostov
Don R.
Volga R.
Stalingrad Aug. 1942–Feb. 1943 ☆

CZECHOSLOVAKIA
Vienna
HUNGARY · Budapest

ITALY · Rome · Anzio Jan. 1945 ☆
Po R.
Sept. 1943
Salerno ☆

YUGOSLAVIA · Belgrade

ROMANIA · Bucharest
Danube R.
BULGARIA · Sofia

ALBANIA

GREECE · Athens

Odessa
CRIMEA
Yalta
Black Sea

TURKEY · Ankara

Kasserine Pass Feb. 1943 ☆
TUNISIA (Vichy France) · Tunis
July 1943
Sicily
Malta (Great Britain)
Tripoli
LIBYA

Mediterranean Sea

Crete
Cyprus (Great Britain)

SYRIA (France)
LEBANON
PALESTINE (Great Britain)
TRANSJORDAN (Great Britain)

IRAQ

SAUDI ARABIA

El Alamein Oct.–Nov. 1942 ☆
Alexandria
Cairo ·
EGYPT

Scale: 0   300   600 miles
0   300   600 kilometers

States, and China. (Roosevelt hoped China might help stabilize Asia after the war; the United States abolished the Chinese Exclusion Act in 1943 to consolidate ties between the two nations.) The United States was also determined to limit Soviet influence in the postwar world.

Military positions during the Yalta Conference helped shape negotiations. Soviet troops occupied eastern European countries, including Poland, where Moscow installed a pro-Soviet regime despite a British-supported Polish government-in-exile in London.

With Soviet troops in place, Britain and the United States were limited in negotiating the future of eastern Europe. The Big Three agreed that some eastern German territory would be transferred to Poland and the remainder divided into four zones (the fourth to be administered by France). Berlin, within the Soviet zone, would also be divided among the four victors. In exchange for U.S. promises to support Soviet claims on territory lost to Japan in the Russo-Japanese War of 1904–1905, Stalin agreed to a treaty of friendship with Jiang Jieshi (Chiang Kai-shek), America's ally,

■ The three Allied leaders—Winston Churchill, Franklin D. Roosevelt, and Joseph Stalin—met at Yalta in February 1945. Having been president for twelve years, Roosevelt showed signs of age and fatigue. Two months later, he died of a massive cerebral hemorrhage.   (Franklin D. Roosevelt Library)

rather than with the communist Mao Zedong (Mao Tse-tung), and to declare war on Japan within three months of Hitler's defeat.

Franklin D. Roosevelt, reelected to an unprecedented fourth term in November 1944, did not live to see the war's end. He died on April 12, making Vice President Harry S Truman president. Truman, who had replaced former vice president Henry Wallace as Roosevelt's running mate in 1944, was inexperienced in foreign policy and was not informed about the top-secret atomic weapons project until after he became president. Eighteen days into Truman's presidency, Adolf Hitler killed himself in a bunker in bomb-ravaged Berlin. On May 8 Germany surrendered.

HARRY TRUMAN

As the great powers jockeyed for influence after Germany's surrender, the Grand Alliance began to crumble. At the Potsdam Conference in mid-July, Truman—a novice at international diplomacy—was less patient with the Soviets than Roosevelt had been. Truman also was emboldened by learning during the conference that a test of the new atomic weapon had been successful; the United States no longer needed or wanted the Soviet Union in the Pacific war. The Allies did agree that Japan must surrender unconditionally. But with the end of the European war, the wartime bonds between the Allies were strained.

With Hitler defeated, the Pacific war continued. Since the Battle of Midway in June 1942, American strategy had been to "island-hop" toward Japan, skipping the most fortified islands and taking the weaker ones, aiming to strand the Japanese armies on their island outposts. To cut off supplies, Americans also attempted to sink the Japanese merchant marine. By 1944 Allied troops—from the United States, Britain, Australia, and New Zealand—had secured the Solomon, Gilbert, Marshall, and Mariana Islands. General Douglas MacArthur landed at Leyte to retake the Philippines for the United States in October 1944.

WAR IN THE PACIFIC

In February 1945, U.S. and Japanese troops battled for Iwo Jima, an island less than 5 miles long, about 700 miles south of Tokyo. Twenty-one thousand Japanese defenders occupied the island's high ground. Hidden in caves, trenches, and underground tunnels, they were protected from the aerial bombardment U.S. forces used to make way for an amphibious landing. The island offered no cover, and marines were slaughtered as they came ashore. For twenty days, U.S. forces fought their way up Mount Suribachi, the highest and most heavily fortified point on Iwo Jima. Iwo Jima claimed 6,821 Americans and more than 20,000 Japanese—some of whom committed suicide rather than surrender. Only 200 Japanese survived.

A month later, American troops landed on Okinawa, an island at the southern tip of Japan, from which Allied forces planned to invade the main Japanese islands. Fighting raged for two months. The monsoon rains began in May, turning battlefields into seas of mud with decaying corpses. The supporting fleet endured waves of mass *kamikaze* (suicide) attacks, in which Japanese pilots intentionally crashed bomb-laden planes into American ships. On Okinawa, 7,374 American soldiers died, and nearly the entire Japanese garrison of 100,000 was killed. Approximately 80,000 civilians—about one-quarter of the population—perished.

With American forces just 350 miles from Japan's main islands, a powerful military faction was nonetheless determined to avoid the humiliation of an unconditional surrender and to preserve the emperor's sovereignty. On March 9, 1945, 333 American B-29 Superfortresses dropped a mixture of explosives and incendiary devices on a 4-by-3-mile area of Tokyo. They created a firestorm, a fierce blaze that sucked all the oxygen from the air, creating hurricane-force winds and growing hot enough to melt concrete and steel. Almost 100,000 people were incinerated, suffocated, or boiled to death hiding in canals. Over the following five months, American bombers attacked sixty-six Japanese cities, leaving 8 million people homeless and killing almost 900,000.

BOMBING OF JAPAN

Meanwhile, Japan was attempting to bomb the U.S. mainland. Thousands of bomb-bearing high-altitude balloons, constructed by schoolgirls of rice paper and flour-potato paste, were launched into the jetstream. As General Yamamoto had realized at the war's beginning, American resources would far outlast Japan's.

Early in the summer of 1945, Japan sent out peace feelers through the Soviets. Japan was not, however, willing to accept the "unconditional surrender" terms that Allied leaders had agreed to at Potsdam, and Truman chose not to pursue a negotiated peace. U.S. troops were mobilizing to invade the Japanese home islands, highly aware of the death tolls on Iwo Jima and Okinawa. The Manhattan Project offered another option, and Truman took it. Using atomic bombs on Japan, Truman believed, would end the war quickly and save American lives.

Historians still debate Truman's decision to use the atomic bomb rather than negotiate surrender terms. Was Japan on the verge of an unconditional surrender, as some argue? Or was the antisurrender faction of Japanese military leaders strong enough to prevail? Truman knew the bomb could give the United States real and psychological power in negotiating the peace. How much did his desire to demonstrate the bomb's power to the Soviet Union influence him? Did racism or retaliation play any role? No matter the answers to these ongoing debates, bombing (whether conventional or atomic) fit the established U.S. strategy of using machines rather than men whenever possible.

The decision to use the bomb did not seem as momentous to Truman as it does in retrospect. The moral line had already been crossed with the bombing of civilian populations: the Japanese bombed Shanghai, China, in 1937; Germans "terror-bombed" Warsaw, Rotterdam, and London. British and American bombers created firestorms in German cities, killing 225,000 people in Dresden. The American bombing of Japanese cities with conventional weapons had killed nearly 1 million people and destroyed 56 square miles of Tokyo alone. What distinguished the atomic bombs from conventional bombs was their power and their efficiency—not that they killed huge numbers of innocent civilians in unspeakably awful ways.

Online Study Center
Primary Source: Effects of the Atomic Bomb

On July 26, 1945, the Allies delivered an ultimatum to Japan: promising that the Japanese people would not be "enslaved," the Potsdam Declaration called for unconditional surrender or "prompt and utter destruction." Tokyo radio announced that the government would respond with *mokusatsu* (literally, "kill with silence," or ignore the ultimatum). On August 6, 1945, the B-29 bomber *Enola Gay* dropped an atomic bomb above the city of Hiroshima, killing 130,000 people. Tens of thousands more would suffer radiation poisoning.

On August 8, the Soviet Union declared war on Japan. On August 9, Americans dropped a second atomic bomb on Nagasaki, killing 60,000 people. Five days later, Japan surrendered. The Allies promised that the Japanese emperor could remain as the nation's titular head. The Second World War was over.

Summary *Online Study Center* ACE the Test

*H*itler once prophesied, "We may be destroyed, but if we are, we shall drag a world with us." World War II devastated much of the globe. In Asia and Europe, people wandered through rubble, searching for food. One out of nine people in the Soviet Union had perished: at least 21 million civilians and military were dead. The Chinese lost 10 million; the Germans and Austrians 6 million; the Japanese 2.5 million. Almost 11 million people had been murdered in Nazi death camps. Across the globe, the Second World War killed at least 55 million people.

War required Allied nations with very different goals to cooperate. Tensions remained high as Stalin unsuccessfully pushed the United States and Britain to open a second front to draw German soldiers away from the Soviet Union. The United States, meanwhile, was fighting the Japanese in the Pacific. When Japan surrendered in August 1945, the strains between the Soviet Union and its English-speaking Allies made postwar stability unlikely.

American servicemen covered the globe, while on the home front, Americans worked around the clock to make weapons. Despite wartime sacrifices, including almost 300,000 lives, many Americans found that the war improved their lives. Mobilization ended the Great Depression. Americans moved in huge numbers to job-rich war-production centers. The influx strained the resources of existing communities and sometimes led to social friction and violence. But many Americans—African Americans, Mexican Americans, women, poor whites from the South—found new opportunities in well-paid war jobs.

The federal government became a stronger presence—regulating business and employment, overseeing the military, and even controlling what people could buy to eat or wear. The Second World War was a powerful engine of social change.

At war's end, only the United States had the economic resources to spur international recovery; only the United States was more prosperous than when war began. In the struggle to fashion a new world, soon to be called the Cold War, the United States held a commanding position. For better or worse, the Second World War was a turning point in the nation's history.

LEGACY FOR A PEOPLE AND A NATION
Atomic Waste

Victory in the Second World War may have been sweet to Americans, but the war's environmental legacy proved noxious, not to mention toxic and deadly. War industries fouled the water and the soil with both solid and petrochemical wastes. The production of synthetic rubber spewed forth sulfur dioxide, carbon monoxide, and other dangerous gases. Air pollution—smog—was first detected in Los Angeles in 1943, the result of rapid wartime industrialization and widespread automobile dependence.

No wartime or postwar weapons program became more threatening to the environment than the atomic bomb. Many of its ingredients—notably, plutonium, beryllium, and mercury—are highly toxic contaminants. Radioactive waste was initially stored at Oak Ridge, Tennessee, and Hanford, Washington, where plutonium was produced. During the postwar arms race, the United States opened other production facilities—for example, at Rocky Flats in Colorado and on the Savannah River in South Carolina. There, radioactive waste seeped from leaky barrels into the soil and water, threatening human life and killing wildlife. Nuclear testing between 1945 and 1963 killed an estimated 800,000 Americans from cancers attributable to radioactive fallout.

The biggest problem of the new millennium remains how to dispose of radioactive materials. Scientists are skeptical that current technology is up to the task of cleaning soil and water at the nuclear weapons sites. "The technology . . . used to remediate contaminated sites," said the chairman of a National Resource Council task force that studied the problem, "is simply ineffective and unable to accomplish the massive job that needs to be done."

THE COLD WAR AND AMERICAN GLOBALISM 1945–1961

*O*n July 16, 1945, the "Deer" Team leader parachuted into northern Vietnam. Colonel Allison Thomas and the five members of his Office of Strategic Services (OSS) unit followed their mission: to work with the Vietminh, a nationalist Vietnamese organization, to sabotage Japanese forces that in March had seized Vietnam from France. A banner proclaimed, "Welcome to Our American Friends." Ho Chi Minh, head of the Vietminh, greeted the OSS team. The next day Ho denounced the French but added, "We welcome 10 million Americans." "Forget the Communist Bogy," Thomas radioed OSS headquarters in China.

A communist dedicated to winning his nation's independence from France, Ho joined the French Communist Party after World War I. For the next two decades, living in China, the Soviet Union, and elsewhere, Ho planned and fought to free his nation from French colonialism. During World War II, Ho's Vietminh warriors harassed French and Japanese forces and rescued downed American pilots. In March 1945 Ho met with U.S. officials in China. Receiving no aid from ideological allies in the Soviet Union, Ho hoped the United States would favor his nation's quest for liberation.

Other OSS personnel soon parachuted into Kimlung, including a male nurse who diagnosed Ho's ailments as malaria and dysentery; quinine and sulfa drugs restored his health, but Ho remained frail. Everywhere the Americans went, impoverished villagers thanked them with gifts of food and clothing, interpreting the foreigners' presence as a sign of U.S. anticolonial and anti-Japanese sentiments. In early August, the Deer Team gave Vietminh soldiers weapons training. Ho said he hoped young Vietnamese could study in the United States and that American technicians could help build an independent Vietnam. Ho remarked that "your statesmen make eloquent speeches about . . . self-determination. We are self-determined. Why not help us?"

A second OSS unit, the "Mercy" Team, headed by Captain Archimedes Patti, arrived in Hanoi on August 22. But unbeknown to these OSS members,

From Allies to Adversaries

Containment in Action

The Cold War in Asia

The Korean War

Unrelenting Cold War

LINKS TO THE WORLD
The People-to-People Campaign

The Struggle for the Third World

LEGACY FOR A PEOPLE AND A NATION
The National Security State

Online Study Center

This icon will direct you to interactive map and primary source activities on the website
http://college.hmco.com/pic/nortonbrief7e

CHRONOLOGY

1945 • Roosevelt dies; Truman becomes president
• Atomic bombings of Japan

1946 • Kennan's "long telegram" criticizes USSR
• Vietnamese war against France erupts

1947 • Truman Doctrine seeks aid for Greece and Turkey
• Marshall offers Europe economic assistance
• National Security Act reorganizes government

1948 • Communists take power in Czechoslovakia
• Truman recognizes Israel
• U.S. organizes Berlin airlift

1949 • NATO founded as anti-Soviet alliance
• Soviet Union explodes atomic bomb
• Mao's communists win power in China

1950 • NSC-68 recommends major military buildup
• Korean War starts in June; China enters in fall

1951 • U.S. signs Mutual Security Treaty with Japan

1953 • Eisenhower becomes president
• Stalin dies
• U.S. helps restore shah to power in Iran
• Korean War ends

1954 • Geneva accords partition Vietnam
• CIA-led coup overthrows Arbenz in Guatemala

1955 • Soviets create Warsaw Pact

1956 • Soviets crush uprising in Hungary
• Suez crisis sparks war in Middle East

1957 • Soviets fire first ICBM and launch *Sputnik*

1958 • U.S. troops land in Lebanon
• Berlin crisis

1959 • Castro ousts Batista in Cuba

1960 • Eighteen African colonies become independent
• Vietcong organized in South Vietnam

who believed that President Franklin D. Roosevelt's sympathy for eventual Vietnamese independence remained U.S. policy, the new Truman administration wanted France to decide Vietnam's fate. That policy shift explains why Ho never received answers to the several letters and telegrams he sent to Washington beginning August 30, 1945.

On September 2, 1945, with OSS personnel present, an emotional Ho Chi Minh read his declaration of independence for the Democratic Republic of Vietnam: "All men are created equal; they are endowed by their Creator with certain unalienable Rights; among these are Life, Liberty, and the pursuit of Happiness." Having borrowed from the internationally renowned 1776 American document, Ho then itemized Vietnamese grievances against France.

In a last meeting with Captain Patti, Ho expressed his sadness that the United States had armed the French to reestablish their colonial rule in Vietnam. Sure, Ho said, U.S. officials in Washington judged him a "Moscow puppet" because he was a communist. But Ho claimed that he drew inspiration from the American struggle for independence. If necessary, Ho insisted, the Vietnamese would go it alone. And they did—first against the French and eventually against more than half a million U.S. troops in what became America's longest war.

Because Ho Chi Minh and his nationalist followers declared themselves communists, U.S. leaders rejected their appeal. Endorsing the containment doctrine against communism, American presidents from Truman to George H. W. Bush believed that a ruthless Soviet Union directed a worldwide communist conspiracy against peace, free-market capitalism, and democracy. Soviet leaders from Joseph Stalin to Mikhail Gorbachev protested that a militarized, economically aggressive United States sought world domination. This protracted contest between the United States and the Soviet Union acquired the name "Cold War."

The primary feature of world affairs for over four decades, the Cold War was fundamentally a contest between the United States and the Soviet Union over spheres of influence. The face-off between the capitalist "West" and the communist "East" dominated international relations and eventually took the lives of millions, cost trillions of dollars, spawned fears of doomsday, and destabilized several nations. On occasion the two superpowers negotiated and signed agreements to temper their dangerous arms race; at other times they went to the brink of war and armed allies to fight vicious Third World conflicts. Sometimes these allies had their own ambitions and resisted pressure from one or both superpowers.

Vietnam was part of the Third World, a general term for nations that during the Cold War era wore neither the "West" (the "First World") nor the "East" (the "Second World") label. Sometimes called "developing countries," Third World nations on the whole were nonwhite, nonindustrialized, and located in the southern half of the globe—in Asia, Africa, the Middle East, and Latin America. Many had been colonies of European nations or Japan and were vulnerable to the Cold War rivalry. U.S. leaders often interpreted their anticolonialism as Soviet inspired rather than as expressions of indigenous nationalism. Vietnam became one among many sites where Cold War fears and Third World aspirations intersected, prompting American intervention and a globalist foreign policy that regarded the entire world as the appropriate sphere for America's influence.

Critics in the United States challenged Cold War exaggerations of threats from abroad, meddlesome interventions in the Third World, and the militarization of foreign policy. But when leaders such as Truman described the Cold War as a life-and-death struggle against a monstrous enemy, critics' questions were drowned out by charges that dissenters were "soft on communism," if not un-American. U.S. leaders successfully cultivated a Cold War consensus that stifled debate and shaped the mindset of generations of Americans. ■

From Allies to Adversaries

The Second World War unsettled the international system. At its end, Germany was in ruins; Great Britain was overstrained and exhausted; after five years of Nazi occupation, France was rent by internal division; and Italy was drastically weakened. Japan was decimated and under occupation, and China was headed toward a renewed civil war. Throughout Europe and Asia, factories, transportation, and communications links were reduced to rubble, and agricultural production plummeted. The United States and the Soviet Union, though they had been allies in the war, proposed very different solutions. The collapse of Germany and Japan, moreover, created power vacuums that drew the two major powers into collision over former Axis-influenced countries. For example, in Greece and China, where civil wars raged between leftists and conservative regimes, the two powers supported different sides.

With empires disintegrating, a new Third World was created, especially as financial constraints and nationalist rebellions forced the imperial states to set their colonies free. Britain exited India (and Pakistan) in 1947 and Burma and Sri Lanka (Ceylon) in 1948. The Philippines gained independence from the United States in 1946. After four years of battling nationalists in Indonesia, the Dutch left in 1949. In the Middle East, Lebanon (1943), Syria (1946), and Jordan (1946) gained independence, while in Palestine, British officials faced pressure from Zionists intent on creating a Jewish homeland and from Arab leaders opposed to it. In Iraq, nationalist agitation increased against the British-installed government. Washington and Moscow regarded these new or emerging Third World states as potential allies that might provide military bases, resources, and markets.

DECOLONIZATION

However, some new nations stayed out of the Cold War.

The United States and the Soviet Union assessed their most pressing tasks in very different terms. The

STALIN'S AIMS

Soviets, though committed to victory over the capitalist countries, were most concerned about preventing another invasion of their homeland. The USSR land mass was three times larger than the United States, but it had only 10,000 miles of seacoast, which was under ice much of the year. Russian leaders before and after the revolution had made increased maritime access a chief foreign policy aim.

Worse, the USSR's geographical frontiers were hard to defend. Siberia, vital for its mineral resources, lay 6,000 miles east of Moscow and was vulnerable to encroachment by Japan and China. In the west, the border with Poland had generated violent clashes since World War I. With World War II claiming at least 20 million lives and causing massive physical destruction, Soviet leaders wanted no dangers along their western borders.

Overall, however, Soviet territorial objectives were limited. Although many Americans compared Stalin to Hitler, Stalin's aims resembled those of czars before him: he wanted the USSR's borders to include the Baltic states of Estonia, Latvia, and Lithuania, as well as the eastern part of prewar Poland. To the south, Stalin wanted a presence in northern Iran, and he pressed the Turks for naval bases and free access out of the Black Sea. Economically suspicious of their European neighbors, the Soviets did not promote rapid rebuilding of the war-ravaged economies of the region or expanded world trade.

The United States, by contrast, came out of the war secure of its borders. Separated from other world

U.S. ECONOMIC AND STRATEGIC NEEDS

powers by two oceans, the American home base had been virtually immune from attack during the fighting. American casualties were fewer than any of the other major combatants. With its fixed capital intact, its resources more plentiful than ever, and in lone possession of the atomic bomb, the United States was the strongest world power at war's end.

But Washington officials guarded against complacency. Some other power—almost certainly the USSR—could take advantage of instability in war-torn Europe and Asia and seize control of these areas, with dire implications for America's security. Therefore Washington officials sought bases overseas to keep an airborne enemy at bay. To enhance U.S. security, American planners sought the quick reconstruction of nations—including former enemies Germany and Japan—and a world economy based on free trade.

The Soviets refused to join the new World Bank and International Monetary Fund (IMF), created at the July 1944 Bretton Woods Conference by forty-four nations to stabilize trade. They held that the United States dominated both institutions and used them to promote private investment and open international commerce, which Moscow saw as capitalist tools of exploitation. With the United States as its largest donor, the World Bank opened in 1945 and made loans to finance members' reconstruction projects; the IMF, also heavily U.S. backed, helped members meet balance-of-payments through currency loans.

Joseph Stalin, though hostile to the Western powers and capable of ruthlessness against his own people

STALIN AND TRUMAN

(his periodic purges since the 1930s had taken the lives of millions), did not want war. He was aware of his country's weakness in relation to the United States and believed he could achieve his aspirations through cooperation with the Americans and British. But Stalin believed that Germany and Japan would eventually threaten the USSR again, and his suspicion of capitalist powers was boundless. Many suspected Stalin was clinically paranoid. As historian David Reynolds has noted, this paranoia, coupled with Stalin's xenophobia (fear of anything foreign) and his Marxist-Leninist ideology, created in him a mental map of "them" versus "us" that decisively influenced his approach to world affairs.

To a lesser degree, Harry Truman too was prone to a "them" versus "us" worldview. He often glossed over ambiguities and counterevidence, preferring the simple, decisive answer. Truman exaggerated, as when he declared in his undelivered farewell address that he had "knocked the socks off the communists" in Korea. When Truman protested in 1945 that the Soviets were not fulfilling the Yalta agreement on Poland, the Soviet commissar of foreign affairs, V. M. Molotov, stormed out of their meeting. Truman self-consciously developed what he called his "tough method," and his toughness became a trademark of American Cold War diplomacy.

There are no precise dates for the beginning of the Cold War. It resulted more from an ongoing process that arguably began in 1917 with the Bolshevik Revolution and Western powers' hostile response, but which in a more meaningful sense began in mid-1945 as World War II ended. By spring 1947, certainly, the struggle was underway.

THE BEGINNING OF THE COLD WAR

One of the first Soviet-American clashes came in Poland in 1945, when the Soviets blocked the Polish government-in-exile in London from participating in the communist government that Moscow sponsored. The Soviets also extinguished civil liberties in Romania, arguing that the United States similarly manipulated Italy. Moscow initially allowed free elections in Hungary and Czechoslovakia, but as the Cold War accelerated and U.S. influence in Europe expanded, the Soviets encouraged communist coups in Hungary (1947) and Czechoslovakia (1948). Yugoslavia was unique: its independent communist government, led by Josip Broz Tito, successfully broke with Stalin in 1948.

To defend their actions, Moscow officials noted that the United States was reviving their traditional enemy, Germany, and was meddling in eastern Europe. The Soviets cited clandestine American meetings with anti-Soviet groups, repeated calls for elections likely to produce anti-Soviet regimes, and the use of loans to gain political influence (financial diplomacy). Moscow charged that the United States was pursuing a double standard—intervening in eastern Europe but demanding that the Soviet Union stay out of Latin America and Asia. Americans called for free elections in the Soviet sphere, Moscow noted, but not in the U.S. sphere in Latin America.

The Soviets believed that the United States was practicing "atomic diplomacy"—maintaining a nuclear monopoly to scare the Soviets into diplomatic concessions. Secretary of State James F. Byrnes thought the atomic bomb could deter Soviet expansion, but Secretary of War Henry L. Stimson disagreed in 1945. If Americans continued to have "this weapon rather ostentatiously on our hip," he warned Truman, the Soviets' "suspicions and their distrust of our purposes and motives will increase."

ATOMIC DIPLOMACY

In this tense atmosphere, Truman refused to turn over the weapon to an international authority. In 1946 he backed the Baruch Plan, named after its author, financier Bernard Baruch, which provided for U.S. abandonment of its atomic monopoly only after the world's fissionable materials were controlled by an international agency. The Soviets retorted that it would require them to shut down their atomic-bomb development project while the United States continued its own. Washington and Moscow soon became locked in a frightening nuclear arms race.

By mid-1946, the Soviets and Americans clashed on numerous fronts. When the United States declined a Soviet reconstruction loan but gave Britain a loan, Moscow upbraided Washington for using its dollars to manipulate foreign governments. The two Cold War powers also backed different groups in Iran, where the United States helped bring the pro-West shah to the throne. Unable to agree on the unification of Germany, the former allies built up their zones independently.

After Stalin gave a speech in February 1946 depicting the world as threatened by capitalist acquisitiveness, the American chargé d'affaires in Moscow, George F. Kennan, sent a pessimistic "long telegram" to Washington. His widely circulated report fed a growing belief among American officials that only toughness would work with the Soviets. The following month, in Fulton, Missouri, former British prime minister Winston Churchill warned that a Soviet-erected "iron curtain" had cut off eastern European countries from the West. With an approving Truman nearby, Churchill called for Anglo-American partnership to resist the new menace.

WARNINGS FROM KENNAN AND CHURCHILL

The growing Soviet-American tensions had major implications for the United Nations. The delegates who gathered in San Francisco in April 1945 to sign the U.N. charter agreed on an organization that included a General Assembly of all member states and a smaller Security Council spearheading peace and security issues. Five great powers were given permanent seats on the council—the United States, the Soviet Union, Great Britain, China, and France—and could exercise a veto against any proposed action. To be effective, therefore, the U.N. needed great-power cooperation. Of the fifty-one founding states, twenty-two came from the Americas and another fifteen from Europe, which effectively gave the United States a majority in the assembly. In retaliation, Moscow exercised its veto in the Security Council.

Some high-level U.S. officials were dismayed by the administration's harsh anti-Soviet posture. Secretary of Commerce Henry A. Wallace charged that Truman's get-tough policy substituted atomic and economic coercion for diplomacy. Wallace told a Madison Square Garden audience in September 1946 that "'getting tough' never brought anything real and lasting—whether for schoolyard bullies or businessmen or world powers." Truman fired Wallace, blasting him privately as "a real Commy."

East-West tensions escalated further in early 1947, when the British requested American help

TRUMAN DOCTRINE

defending their conservative client-government (a government that is dependent on the economic or military support of a more powerful country) in Greece in a civil war against leftists. Truman requested $400 million in aid from Congress. The Republican Eightieth Congress wanted less spending, and many had little respect for the Democratic president after voters in the 1946 elections gave the GOP ("Grand Old Party," the Republican Party) majorities in both houses of Congress. Republican senator Arthur Vandenberg of Michigan, a bipartisan leader, told the president he would have to "scare hell out of the American people" to gain congressional approval.

With that in mind, the president delivered a speech laced with alarmist language outlining America's role in the postwar world. Truman claimed that communism imperiled the world. "If Greece should fall under the control of an armed minority," he concluded in an early version of the domino theory (discussed later in this chapter), "the effect upon its neighbor, Turkey, would be immediate and serious. Confusion and disorder might well spread throughout the entire Middle East." Truman articulated what became known as the Truman Doctrine: "I believe that it must be the policy of the United States to support free peoples who are resisting attempted subjugation by armed minorities or by outside pressures."

Critics correctly pointed out that the Soviet Union was little involved in the Greek civil war, that the communists in Greece were more pro-Tito than pro-Stalin, and that the resistance movement had non-communist as well as communist members. Truman countered that should communists gain control of Greece, they might open the door to Soviet power in the Mediterranean. The Senate approved Truman's

request by 67 to 23 votes. Using U.S. dollars and military advisers, the Greek government defeated the insurgents in 1949, and Turkey became a staunch U.S. ally on the Soviets' border.

Months after Truman's speech, the term *Cold War* slipped into the lexicon as a description of the Soviet-American relationship.

INEVITABLE COLD WAR?

Within two years of the victory over the Axis powers, the two Grand Alliance members were locked in a struggle for world dominance that would last almost half a century. Even before World

■ On March 5, 1946, former British prime minister Winston S. Churchill (1874–1965) delivered a speech, which he intended for a worldwide audience, at Westminster College in Fulton, Missouri. President Harry S Truman (*right*) had encouraged Churchill (*seated*) to speak on two themes: the need to block Soviet expansion and the need to form an Anglo-American partnership. Always eloquent and provocative, Churchill denounced the Soviets for drawing an "iron curtain" across eastern Europe. This speech became one of the landmark statements of the Cold War. (Terry Savage/Harry S Truman Presidential Library)

War II ended, perceptive observers anticipated that the United States and the USSR would seek to fill the power vacuum. The two countries had a history of tension and were militarily powerful. Most of all, they were divided by sharply differing political economies with divergent needs and a deep ideological chasm.

Far less clear is that the conflict had to result in a cold war. The "cold peace" that had prevailed through World War II could conceivably have been maintained into the postwar years. Neither side's leadership wanted war. Both hoped, at least initially, that a spirit of cooperation could be maintained. The Cold War resulted from decisions by individual human beings who might have done more, for example, to maintain diplomatic dialogue and negotiated solutions to complex international problems. For decades, Americans would wonder if the high price they were paying for victory in the superpower confrontation was necessary.

Containment in Action

*T*o counter Soviet and communist expansion, the Truman team relied on a policy of containment. George Kennan, now at the State Department in Washington, published an influential statement of the containment doctrine, under the pseudonym "Mr. X," in the July 1947 issue of *Foreign Affairs* magazine. Kennan advocated a "policy of firm containment, designed to confront the Russians with unalterable counterforce at every point where they show signs of encroaching upon the interests of a peaceful and stable world." Such counterforce, Kennan argued, would foster a "mellowing" of Soviet behavior. Kennan's "X" article joined the Truman Doctrine as another key manifesto of Cold War policy.

The veteran journalist Walter Lippmann took issue with the containment doctrine in his slim but pow-

LIPPMANN'S CRITIQUE
erful book *The Cold War* (1947), calling it a "strategic monstrosity" that failed to distinguish between areas vital and peripheral to U.S. security. Nor did Lippmann share Truman's conviction that the Soviet Union wanted to take over the world. Ironically, Kennan agreed with much of Lippmann's critique and soon distanced himself from the doctrine he had helped to create.

Invoking the containment doctrine, the United States in 1947 and 1948 began to build an international economic and defensive network to protect American prosperity and advance U.S. hegemony. In western Europe, the region of primary concern, American diplomats pursued economic reconstruction; the ouster of communists from governments, as occurred in 1947 in France and Italy; and blockage of "third force," or neutralist, tendencies. U.S. officials kept the decolonization of European empires orderly. Meanwhile, American culture—consumer goods, music, consumption ethic, and production techniques—permeated European societies, and while some resisted, transatlantic ties were strengthened.

Online Study Center   Improve Your Grade
Interactive Map: Divided Europe

Americans, who already had spent billions of dollars on European relief and recovery by 1947, remembered all too well the troubles of the

MARSHALL PLAN
1930s: global depression, political extremism, and war born of economic discontent. Such cataclysms could not be allowed to happen again; communism must not replace fascism. Hence, in June 1947, Secretary of State George C. Marshall announced that the United States would finance a massive European recovery program. Launched in 1948, the Marshall Plan sent $12.4 billion to western Europe until 1951 (see Map 28.1). To stimulate business at home, the legislation required that Europeans spend this aid on American-made products. The Marshall Plan proved a mixed success: it caused inflation, failed to solve a balance-of-payments problem, took only tentative steps toward economic integration, and further divided Europe between "East" and "West." But the program spurred impressive western European industrial production and investment, started the region toward self-sustaining economic growth, and contained communism.

Truman streamlined U.S. defense by working with Congress on the National Security Act of July

NATIONAL SECURITY ACT
1947. The act created the Office of Secretary of Defense (which became the Department of Defense two years later) to oversee the armed services, the National Security Council (NSC) of high-level officials to advise the president, and the Central Intelligence Agency (CIA) to conduct spy and

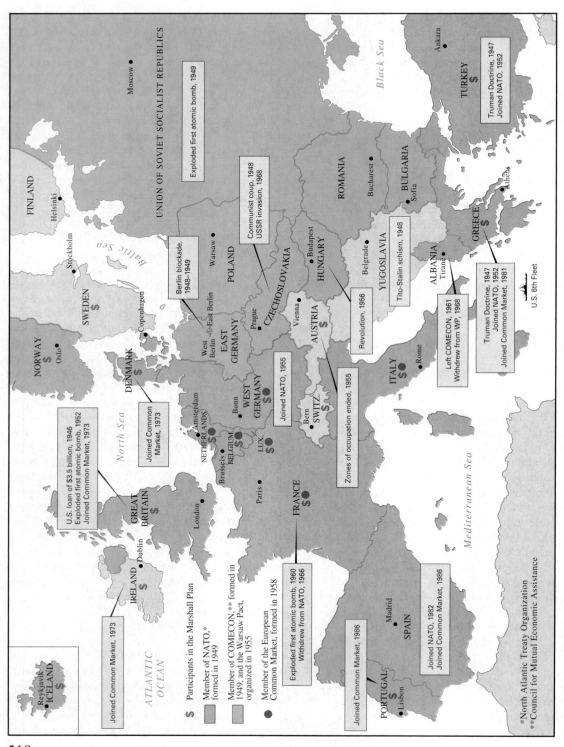

Map 28.1 Divided Europe

After the Second World War, Europe broke into two competing camps. When the United States launched the Marshall Plan in 1948, the Soviet Union countered with its own economic plan the following year. When the United States created the North Atlantic Treaty Organization (NATO) in 1949, the Soviet Union answered with the Warsaw Pact in 1955. On the whole, these two camps held firm until the late 1980s.

Map labels:

ATLANTIC OCEAN

ICELAND $ — Reykjavík — Joined Common Market, 1973

IRELAND $ — Dublin

GREAT BRITAIN $ — London — U.S. loan of $3.5 billion, 1946; Exploded first atomic bomb, 1952; Joined Common Market, 1973

North Sea

NORWAY $ — Oslo

SWEDEN $ — Stockholm

FINLAND — Helsinki

Baltic Sea

DENMARK $ — Copenhagen — Joined Common Market, 1973

NETHERLANDS $ — Amsterdam

BELGIUM $ — Brussels

LUX. $

FRANCE $ — Paris — Exploded first atomic bomb, 1960; Withdrew from NATO, 1966

WEST GERMANY $ — Bonn — Joined NATO, 1955

EAST GERMANY — West Berlin / East Berlin

POLAND — Warsaw — Berlin blockade, 1948–1949

UNION OF SOVIET SOCIALIST REPUBLICS — Moscow — Exploded first atomic bomb, 1949

CZECHOSLOVAKIA — Prague — Communist coup, 1948; USSR invasion, 1968

SWITZ. $ — Bern

AUSTRIA $ — Vienna — Zones of occupation ended, 1955

HUNGARY — Budapest — Revolution, 1956

ROMANIA — Bucharest

YUGOSLAVIA — Belgrade — Tito-Stalin schism, 1948

BULGARIA — Sofia

ALBANIA — Tiranë — Left COMECON, 1961; Withdrew from WP, 1968

ITALY $ — Rome

GREECE $ — Athens — Truman Doctrine, 1947; Joined NATO, 1952; Joined Common Market, 1981

TURKEY — Ankara — Truman Doctrine, 1947; Joined NATO, 1952

Black Sea

Mediterranean Sea

U.S. 6th Fleet

SPAIN — Madrid — Joined NATO, 1982; Joined Common Market, 1986

PORTUGAL $ — Lisbon — Joined Common Market, 1986

Legend:

$ Participants in the Marshall Plan

   Member of NATO,* formed in 1949

   Member of COMECON,** formed in 1949, and the Warsaw Pact, organized in 1955

● Member of the European Common Market, formed in 1958

*North Atlantic Treaty Organization
**Council for Mutual Economic Assistance

518

information gathering overseas. By the early 1950s the CIA had expanded to include covert (secret) operations aimed at overthrowing unfriendly foreign leaders. The National Security Act gave the president increased powers regarding foreign policy.

In response, Stalin forbade communist satellite governments in eastern Europe to accept Marshall Plan aid and ordered communist parties in western Europe to work to thwart it. He also created the Cominform, an organization designed to coordinate communist activities around the world. Whereas American planners saw the Marshall Plan as protecting their European friends against a potential Soviet threat, to Stalin it raised anew the specter of capitalist penetration. He tightened his grip on eastern Europe—most notably, engineering a coup in Czechoslovakia in February 1948 that ensured Soviet control—which heightened anxiety in the United States.

In June 1948, the Americans, French, and British agreed to fuse their German zones and integrate

BERLIN
BLOCKADE
AND AIRLIFT

West Germany (the Federal Republic of Germany) into the western European economy. Fearing a resurgent Germany tied to the American Cold War camp, the Soviets cut off access to the jointly occupied city of Berlin inside the Soviet zone. President Truman then ordered a massive airlift of food, fuel, and other supplies to Berlin. The Soviets finally lifted the blockade in May 1949 and founded the German Democratic Republic, or East Germany.

The successful airlift may have saved Truman's political career: he narrowly defeated Republican Thomas E. Dewey in the November 1948 presidential election. Truman next formalized the military alliance among the United States, Canada, and western Europe. In April 1949, twelve nations signed a mutual defense treaty, agreeing that an attack on one of them would be considered an attack on all, and establishing the North Atlantic Treaty Organization (NATO) (see Map 28.1).

Not since 1778 had the United States entered a formal European military alliance, and some critics, such as Senator Robert A. Taft, Republican of Ohio, claimed that NATO would provoke rather than deter war. Administration officials responded that should the Soviets ever probe westward, NATO would bring the full force of the United States to bear on the Soviet Union. Truman officials also hoped that NATO

would keep western Europeans from embracing communism or even neutralism in the Cold War. The Senate ratified the treaty by 82 votes to 13, and the United States began spending billions of dollars under the Mutual Defense Assistance Act.

By the summer of 1949, Truman and his advisers were basking in the successes of their foreign policy. Containment was working, West Germany was on the road to recovery, the Berlin blockade had been defeated, and NATO had been formed. True, there was trouble in China, where the communists under Mao Zedong were winning a civil war. But that struggle would likely wax and wane for years to come. Just possibly, some dared to think, Harry Truman was on his way to winning the Cold War.

Then, suddenly, in late September, came the "twin shocks," two momentous developments that made

TWIN SHOCKS

Americans feel in greater danger than ever before. First, an American reconnaissance aircraft detected unusually high radioactivity in the atmosphere: the Soviets had exploded an atomic bomb. With the American nuclear monopoly erased, western Europe seemed more vulnerable. The communists in China completed their conquest sooner than many expected. Now the world's largest and most populous countries were ruled by communists, and one of them had the atomic weapon. Rejecting appeals for high-level negotiations, Truman in early 1950 gave the go-ahead for production of a hydrogen bomb, the "Super." Kennan bemoaned the militarization of the Cold War and was replaced at the State Department by Paul Nitze. The National Security Council delivered to the president in April 1950 a significant top-secret document tagged NSC-68. Predicting continued tension with expansionistic communists, the report, authored primarily by Nitze, urged a much enlarged military budget and the mobilization of public support. The Cold War was about to become vastly more expensive and far-reaching.

The Cold War in Asia

*a*sia gradually became ensnared in the Cold War. Indeed, the consequences of an expansive containment doctrine would exact its heaviest price on the United States in large-scale wars in Korea and Vietnam. Though less important to both superpowers than Europe, Asia was where the Cold War turned hot.

From the start, Japan was crucial to U.S. strategy. The United States monopolized Japan's reconstruction through a military occupation directed by General Douglas MacArthur. Truman disliked "Mr. Prima Donna, Brass Hat" MacArthur, but MacArthur wrote a democratic constitution, gave women voting rights, revitalized the economy, and destroyed the nation's weapons. U.S. authorities Americanized Japan by censoring films critical of the United States (for the destruction of Hiroshima, for example) or depicting Japanese customs such as suicide, arranged marriages, and swordplay. In 1951, against Soviet protests, the United States and Japan signed a separate peace that restored Japan's sovereignty and ended the occupation. The Mutual Security Treaty that year provided for U.S. forces in Japan, including a base on Okinawa.

The administration had less success in China. The United States had long backed the Nationalists

CHINESE CIVIL WAR

of Jiang Jieshi (Chiang Kai-shek) against Mao Zedong's communists. But after the Second World War, Generalissimo Jiang's government had become corrupt, inefficient, and out of touch with discontented peasants, whom the communists enlisted with promises of land reform. Jiang also subverted American efforts to negotiate a cease-fire and a coalition government. American officials divided on the question of whether Mao was an Asian Tito—communist but independent—or, as most believed, part of an international communist movement that might give the Soviets a springboard into Asia. Thus, when the Chinese communists made secret overtures to the United States for diplomatic talks in 1945 and 1949, American officials declined. Mao leaned to the Soviet side in the Cold War. Because of China's fierce independence, however, a Sino-Soviet schism opened.

With his victory in September 1949, Mao proclaimed the People's Republic of China (PRC). Truman hesitated to extend diplomatic recognition to the new government. U.S. officials became alarmed by the 1950 Sino-Soviet Treaty and the harassment of Americans in China. Truman also chose nonrecognition because vocal Republican critics, the so-called China lobby, pinned Jiang's defeat on Truman. The president argued that despite billions of dollars in American aid, Jiang proved a poor instrument of containment. Not until 1979 did official Sino-American relations resume.

Mao's victory in China drew urgent American attention to Indochina, the southeast Asian peninsula

VIETNAM'S QUEST FOR INDEPENDENCE

held by France for nearly a century. The Japanese wrested control over Indochina during World War II, but still the Vietnamese nationalist movement grew. Their leader, Ho Chi Minh, hoped to use Japan's defeat to assert Vietnamese independence and sought U.S. support. American officials rejected Ho's appeals over restoring French rule. Paris warned that American support of Vietnamese independence would strengthen the French Communist Party, perhaps even drive France into the arms of the USSR. In addition, the Truman administration feared that Ho Chi Minh was an "agent of international communism," who would assist Soviet and, after 1949, Chinese expansionism. Overlooking the native roots of the nationalist rebellion against French colonialism, Washington interpreted events in Indochina through a Cold War lens.

When war between the Vietminh and France broke out in 1946, the United States initially took a hands-off approach. But after Jiang's regime collapsed in China three years later, the Truman administration in February 1950 recognized the French puppet government of Bao Dai, a playboy and former emperor. To many Vietnamese, the United States thus became an ally of the hated French. Second, in May, the administration agreed to send weapons and military advisers to sustain the French. From 1945 to 1954, the United States gave $2 billion of the $5 billion that France spent to keep Vietnam within its empire—to no avail. How Vietnam ultimately became the site of America's longest war, covered in Chapters 30 and 31, is one of the most tragic stories of modern history.

The Korean War

Early on June 25, 1950, a large military force of the Democratic People's Republic of Korea (North Korea) moved into the Republic of Korea (South Korea). Colonized by Japan since 1910, Korea was split in two after Japan's defeat in 1945.

Although the Soviets armed the North and Americans armed the South (U.S. aid reached $100 million a year), the Korean War began as a civil war. Since its division, the two parts had been skirmishing while antigovernment (and anti-U.S.) guerrilla fighting flared in the South.

Both the North's communist leader, Kim Il Sung, and the South's president, Syngman Rhee, sought to reunify their nation. Kim's military especially gained strength when tens of thousands returned home in 1949 after serving in Mao's army. President Truman claimed that the Soviets had masterminded the North Korean attack.

Actually, Stalin reluctantly approved the attack only after Kim predicted an easy, early victory and after Mao backed Kim. When the U.N. Security Council voted to defend South Korea, the Soviet representative was not present because the Soviets were boycotting the United Nations for its refusal to admit the People's Republic of China. During the war, Moscow gave limited aid to North Korea and China, reneging on promised Soviet airpower. Aware of his strategic inferiority in relation to the United States, Stalin did not want war.

STALIN'S DOUBTS

The president first ordered General Douglas MacArthur to send arms and troops to South Korea. He did not seek congressional approval—fearing lawmakers would initiate a lengthy debate—and thereby set the precedent of waging war on executive authority alone. After the Security Council voted to assist South Korea, MacArthur became commander of U.N. forces in Korea. Sixteen nations contributed troops, but 40 percent were South Korean and 50 percent American. In the early weeks, North Korean tanks and superior firepower sent the South Korean army into retreat. The first American soldiers, taking heavy casualties, could not stop the North Koreans from pushing them and the South Koreans and Americans into the tiny Pusan perimeter at the tip of South Korea.

U.S. FORCES INTERVENE

General MacArthur planned a daring amphibious landing at heavily fortified Inchon, several hundred miles behind North Korean lines. After U.S. bombs pounded Inchon, marines sprinted ashore on September 15, 1950, liberating the South Korean capital of Seoul and pushing the North Koreans back.

Truman meanwhile redefined the U.S. war goal from the containment of North Korea to the reunification of Korea by force.

In September U.S. troops drove deep into North Korea, and American aircraft began strikes against bridges on the Yalu River, the border between North Korea and China. Mao publicly warned that China could not permit the bombing of its transportation links with Korea and would not accept the annihilation of North Korea. MacArthur shrugged off the warnings, and Washington officials agreed, confident that the Soviets were not preparing for war.

CHINESE ENTRY INTO THE WAR

MacArthur was right about the Soviets, but wrong about the Chinese. On October 25 Mao sent Chinese soldiers into the war near the Yalu. Perhaps to lure American forces into a trap or signal willingness to negotiate, they pulled back after a successful offensive against South Korean troops. Then, on November 26, tens of thousands of Chinese troops surprised American forces and drove them southward. One U.S. officer described "the men of a whole United States Army fleeing from a battlefield, abandoning their wounded, running for their lives."

Online Study Center Improve Your Grade
Primary Source:
MacArthur Outlines His Objectives in Korea

By 1951 the front stabilized around the 38th parallel. Both Washington and Moscow welcomed negotiations, but MacArthur called for an attack on China and Jiang's return. Denouncing limited war (war without nuclear weapons, confined to one place), MacArthur hinted that the president was practicing appeasement. In April, backed by the Joint Chiefs of Staff, Truman fired MacArthur, who nonetheless returned home a hero. Truman's popularity sagged as he weathered scattered demands for his impeachment.

TRUMAN'S FIRING OF MACARTHUR

Armistice talks began in July 1951, but the fighting continued for two years. Defying the Geneva Prisoners of War Convention (1949), U.S. officials announced that only North Korean and Chinese prisoners of war (POWs) who wished to go home would be returned. While Americans resisted forced repatriation, the

North Koreans denounced forced retention. Both sides undertook "reeducation" or "brainwashing" on POWs.

As the POW issue stalled negotiations, U.S. officials made deliberately vague public statements about

PEACE AGREEMENT

using atomic weapons in Korea. Casualties on all sides mounted. Not until July 1953 was an armistice signed. Stalin's death in March and a more conciliatory Soviet government helped enable a settlement that the Chinese especially welcomed. The combatants agreed to hand the POW question to a special panel of neutral nations, which gave prisoners the choice to stay or leave. The North Korean–South Korean borderline was set near the 38th parallel, the prewar boundary, and a demilitarized zone was created between them.

American casualties totaled 54,246 dead and 103,284 wounded. Nearly 5 million Asians died: 2 million North Korean civilians and 500,000 soldiers; 1 million South Korean civilians and 100,000 soldiers; and at least 1 million Chinese soldiers—ranking Korea as one of the costliest wars of the twentieth century.

The Korean War carried major domestic political consequences. The failure to achieve victory and

CONSEQUENCES OF THE WAR

the public's impatience undoubtedly helped elect Republican Dwight Eisenhower to the presidency in 1952, as this former general promised to end the war. The powers of the presidency grew as Congress repeatedly deferred to Truman. The president never asked Congress for a declaration of war, believing that as commander-in-chief, he had the authority to send troops wherever he wished. He saw no need to consult Congress— except to get the $69.5 billion Korean War bill paid. In addition, Republican lawmakers, including Wisconsin senator Joseph McCarthy, accused Truman and Secretary of State Dean Acheson of being "soft on communism," which pushed the administration into an uncompromising position in the negotiations.

The Sino-American hostility generated by the war made U.S. reconciliation with the Beijing government impossible and made South Korea and Formosa major recipients of American foreign aid. The alliance with Japan strengthened as its economy boomed after filling large U.S. procurement orders. Australia and New Zealand joined the United States in a mutual defense agreement, the ANZUS Treaty (1951). The United States sent four army divisions to Europe and initiated plans to rearm West Germany. The military budget jumped from $14 billion in 1949 to $44 billion in 1953; it remained between $35 billion and $44 billion a year throughout the 1950s. The Soviet Union matched this military buildup, resulting in an arms race. Truman's legacy was a highly militarized U.S. foreign policy on a global scale.

Unrelenting Cold War

President Eisenhower and Secretary of State John Foster Dulles largely sustained Truman's Cold War foreign policies. As a World War II general, Eisenhower had traveled in Europe, Asia, and Latin America and had negotiated with world leaders. After the war, he had served as army chief of staff and NATO supreme commander. Dulles had been closely involved with U.S. diplomacy since the first decade of the century.

Eisenhower and Dulles accepted the Cold War consensus about the threat of communism and the

EISENHOWER AND DULLES

need for global vigilance. Although Democrats promoted an image of Eisenhower as a bumbling, aging hero, the president in fact commanded the policymaking process and occasionally tamed the more hawkish proposals of Dulles and Vice President Richard Nixon. Even so, the secretary of state was influential. Few Cold Warriors rivaled Dulles's anticommunism, often expressed in biblical terms. A graduate of Princeton and George Washington Universities, Dulles had assisted Woodrow Wilson at Versailles and later became a senior partner in a prestigious Wall Street law firm and an officer of the Federal Council of Churches. He struck people as arrogant and averse to an essential ingredient in successful diplomacy: compromise. But his assertion that neutrality was an "immoral and short-sighted conception" did not sit well with Third World leaders, who resented being told they had to choose between East and West.

Dulles conceded much to the anticommunist McCarthyites, who claimed that the State Department was infested with communists (discussed in the next chapter). The State Department's chief security officer targeted homosexuals and other "incompatibles," making few distinctions between New Dealers and communists. Dulles thus forced many talented officers out of the Foreign Service, among them, Asia specialists. "The wrong done," the journalist Theodore A. White wrote, "was to poke out the eyes and ears of the State Department on Asian affairs, to blind American foreign policy."

Considering containment too defensive, Dulles called instead for "liberation," freeing eastern Europe from Soviet control. "Massive retal-

"MASSIVE RETALIATION" iation" was the administration's plan for the nuclear obliteration of the Soviet state or its assumed client, the People's Republic of China, if either one took aggressive action.

In the military, Eisenhower and Dulles emphasized airpower and nuclear weaponry. The president's preference for heavy weapons stemmed in part from his desire to trim the federal budget ("more bang for the buck," as the saying went). Galvanized by the successful test of the world's first hydrogen bomb in November 1952, Eisenhower oversaw a massive stockpiling of nuclear weapons—from 1,200 at the start of his presidency to 22,229 at the end. With this huge arsenal, the United States could practice "brinkmanship": not backing down, even if it took the nation to the brink of war. Eisenhower also popularized the "domino theory": that small, weak nations would fall to communism like a row of dominoes unless they were backed by the United States.

Eisenhower increasingly used the Central Intelligence Agency as an instrument of foreign policy. The

CIA AS FOREIGN POLICY INSTRUMENT CIA put foreign leaders (such as King Hussein of Jordan) on its payroll; subsidized foreign labor unions, newspapers, and political parties; planted false stories in newspapers through "disinformation" projects; and trained foreign military officers. It hired American journalists and professors, used business executives as "fronts," and conducted experiments on unsuspecting Americans to determine the effects of "mind control" drugs (the MKULTRA program). The CIA also launched covert operations (including assassination schemes) to subvert governments in the Third World, helping to overthrow the governments of Iran (1953) and Guatemala (1954).

The American intelligence community embraced the principle of plausible deniability: covert operations should be conducted in such a way, and the decisions that launched them concealed so well, that the president could deny any knowledge of them. Thus, Eisenhower disavowed any U.S. role in Guatemala, even though he had ordered the operation. He and his successor, John F. Kennedy, also denied instructing the CIA to assassinate Cuba's Fidel Castro, whose regime after 1959 became stridently anti-American.

Leaders in Moscow quickly became aware of Eisenhower's covert actions, as well as his stockpiling of nuclear weapons. The Soviets in-

NUCLEAR BUILDUP creased their intelligence and tested their first H-bomb in 1953. Four years later, they fired the world's first intercontinental ballistic missile (ICBM) and propelled the satellite *Sputnik* into outer space. Americans felt more vulnerable to air attack, even though in 1957 the United States had 2,460 strategic weapons and a nuclear stockpile of 5,543, compared with the Soviet Union's 102 and 650, respectively. The administration deployed intermediate-range missiles in Europe, targeted against the Soviet Union. At the end of 1960, the United States added Polaris missile–bearing submarines to its navy. To foster future technological advancement, the National Aeronautics and Space Administration (NASA) was created in 1958.

Overall, though, Eisenhower sought to avoid military confrontation with the Soviet Union and China, content to follow Truman's containment of communism. Eisenhower declined to use nuclear weapons and proved more reluctant than other Cold War presidents to send soldiers into battle. Convinced that the struggle against Moscow would be largely decided by international public opinion, he wanted to win the "hearts and minds" of people overseas. The "People-to-People" campaign, launched in 1956, used ordinary Americans and nongovernmental organizations to enhance the international image of the United States and its people.

Sometimes the propaganda war was waged on the Soviets' turf. In 1959 Vice President Richard Nixon traveled to Moscow for an American products fair. In the display of a modern American kitchen, Nixon extolled capitalist consumerism, while Soviet premier Nikita Khrushchev, Stalin's successor, touted

The People-to-People Campaign

Just after the start of the Cold War, U.S. officials determined that the Soviet-American confrontation was as much psychological and ideological as military and economic. One result was the People-to-People campaign, a state-private venture initiated by the U.S. Information Agency (USIA) in 1956 that aimed to win the "hearts and minds" of people around the world. American propaganda experts used ordinary Americans, businesses, civic organizations, labor groups, and women's clubs to promote confidence abroad in American goodness. The People-to-People campaign, one USIA pamphlet said, made "every man an ambassador."

Campaign activities resembled the home-front mobilization efforts of World War II. Americans were told that thirty dollars could send a ninety-nine-volume portable library of American books to schools and libraries overseas. Publishers donated magazines and books for free distribution to foreign countries. People-to-People committees organized sister-city affiliations and pen-pal letter exchanges, hosted exchange students, and organized traveling "People-to-People delegations." The travelers were urged to behave like goodwill ambassadors and "help overcome any feeling that America is a land that thinks money can buy everything."

Camp Fire Girls in over three thousand communities took photographs on the theme "This is our home. This is how we live. These are my People." The photographs were sent to girls in Latin America, Africa, Asia, and the Middle East. The Hobbies Committee connected people with interests in radio, photography, coins, stamps, and horticulture.

The persistence to this day of the widespread impression that Americans are a provincial, materialistic people promotes skepticism about the People-to-People campaign's success. But alongside this negative image is a positive one that sees Americans as open, friendly, optimistic, and pragmatic. Whatever role the People-to-People campaign played in the larger Cold War struggle, it certainly linked ordinary Americans more closely to other parts of the world.

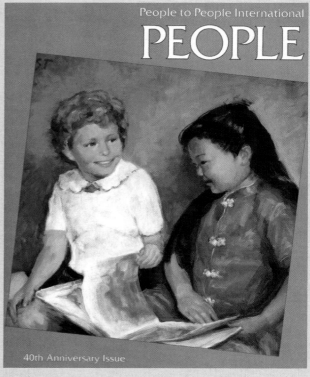

This Alice Nast painting of two girls—one from the United States and one from Taiwan—was commissioned by the Kansas City chapter of People to People and the Kansas City, Tainan Sister City Commission. The painting was presented by Zelma Millman, Chairman of the Kansas City / Tainan Sister City Commission to the mayor of Tainan in September 1994, prior to the 11th Worldwide Conference of People-to-People International. (The Cover of 40th Anniversary issue is reprinted with permission of Alice Nast, Artist / Courtesy of *People to People International* Magazine)

communism. The encounter became famous as the "kitchen debate."

In February 1956, Khrushchev called for "peaceful coexistence" between capitalists and communists,

REBELLION IN HUNGARY

denounced Stalin, and suggested that Moscow would tolerate different brands of communism. Testing Khrushchev, revolts erupted in Poland and Hungary. After a new Hungarian government in 1956 withdrew from the Warsaw Pact (the Soviet military alliance formed in 1955 with communist countries of eastern Europe), Soviet troops and tanks crushed the rebellion.

Although the Eisenhower administration's propaganda encouraged liberation efforts, U.S. officials could not aid the rebels without igniting a world war. Instead, they promised only to welcome more Hungarian immigrants than American quota laws allowed. The West could have reaped some propaganda advantage had not British, French, and Israeli troops—U.S. allies—invaded Egypt during the Suez crisis just before the Soviets smashed the Hungarian uprising (detailed in the next section).

The turmoil had barely subsided when the divided city of Berlin again became a Cold War flash point. The Soviets railed against American bombers capable of carrying nuclear warheads in West Germany and complained that West Berlin had become an escape route for East Germans. In 1958 Khrushchev announced that the Soviet Union would recognize East German control of all of Berlin unless the United States and its allies began talks on German reunification and rearmament. The United States refused; Khrushchev backed down but promised to press the issue again.

Two weeks before a summit in Paris on May 1, 1960, a U-2 spy plane carrying high-powered cameras

U-2 INCIDENT

crashed 1,200 miles inside the Soviet Union. Moscow admitted shooting down the plane and promptly displayed captured CIA pilot Francis Gary Powers and the pictures he had been snapping of Soviet military sites. Khrushchev demanded an apology for violation of Soviet airspace. When Washington refused, the Soviets walked out of the Paris summit.

Meanwhile, both sides kept an eye on the People's Republic of China. Despite evidence of a widening Sino-Soviet split, most American officials treated communism as a monolithic world movement. In 1954,

in a dispute over Jinmen (Quemoy) and Mazu (Matsu), two tiny islands off the Chinese coast, the United States and China lurched toward the brink. Taiwan's Jiang Jieshi used these islands to raid the mainland. Communist China bombarded the islands in 1954. Thinking U.S. credibility was at stake, Eisenhower defended the outposts, even hinting he might use nuclear weapons. "Let's keep the Reds guessing," advised Dulles.

In early 1955, Congress passed the Formosa Resolution, authorizing the president to deploy troops to

FORMOSA RESOLUTION

defend Formosa and adjoining islands. In so doing, Congress formally surrendered to the president what it had informally given up in the 1950 Korea decision: the constitutional power to declare war. The crisis passed, but war loomed again in 1958 over Jinmen and Mazu. This time, as Jiang withdrew some troops, China relaxed its bombardments. But Eisenhower's nuclear threats persuaded the Chinese that they too needed nuclear arms. In 1964 China exploded its first nuclear bomb.

The Struggle for the Third World

In much of the Third World, the process of decolonization that began during the First World War accelerated after the Second World War, when the economically wracked imperial countries proved incapable of resisting their colonies' demands for freedom. A cavalcade of new nations cast off their colonial bonds (see Map 28.2). From 1943 to 1994, 125 countries, including 18 in Africa in 1960 alone, became independent (the figure includes the former Soviet republics that departed the USSR in 1991). The emergence of so many new states in the 1940s shook the foundations of the international system. In the traditional U.S. sphere of influence, Latin America, nationalists once again challenged Washington's dominance.

By the late 1940s, Soviet-American rivalry shifted increasingly to the Third World. The new nations

INTERESTS IN THE THIRD WORLD

could buy American goods, supply raw materials, and invite investments (more than one-third of America's private foreign investments were in

Map 28.2   The Rise of the Third World: Newly Independent Nations Since 1943

Accelerated by the Second World War, decolonization liberated many peoples from imperial rule. New nations emerged in the postwar international system dominated by
the Cold War rivalry of the United States and the Soviet Union. Many newly independent states became targets of great-power intrigue but chose nonalignment in the
Cold War.

Third World countries in 1959). Both great powers looked to these new states for votes in the United Nations and military and intelligence bases. But many new nations wanted to end the economic, military, and cultural hegemony of the West and set the two superpowers against each other to garner more aid and arms. U.S. interventions in the Third World, American leaders believed, became necessary to impress Moscow with Washington's might against threats to American interests.

To thwart nationalist, radical, and communist challenges, over 90 percent of U.S. foreign aid went to developing nations by 1961. Washington also allied with undemocratic but anticommunist regimes, meddled in civil wars, and unleashed CIA covert operations. When some of the larger Third World states—notably India, Ghana, Egypt, and Indonesia—refused to take sides in the Cold War, Secretary of State Dulles declared that neutralism was a step on the road to communism, insisting with Eisenhower that every nation take sides.

American leaders argued that technologically "backward" Third World countries needed Western-induced capitalist development to enjoy economic growth and political moderation. Often U.S. officials ascribed stereotyped race- and gender-based characteristics to Third World peoples, seeing them as dependent, emotional, and irrational, and therefore dependent on the fatherly tutelage of the United States. American officials also suggested that Third World countries were "weak women"—passive and servile, unable to resist the menacing communists. Eisenhower condescendingly described neutralist India as a place where "emotion rather than reason seems to dictate policy."

Racism influenced U.S. relations with Third World countries. In 1955 G. L. Mehta, the Indian ambassa-

RACISM AND SEGREGATION AS U.S. HANDICAPS dor to the United States, was refused service in the whites-only section of a restaurant at Houston International Airport. The insult stung deeply, as did many similar indignities experienced by other Third World diplomats. Dulles apologized to Mehta and thought U.S. racial segregation was a "major international hazard."

Thus, developments in race relations (covered in the next chapter) came into play. When the Supreme Court announced its decision in *Brown v. Board of Education* in 1954, the government quickly broadcast

news of the desegregation order around the world in thirty-five languages on its Voice of America overseas radio network. But the problem did not go away. For example, after the 1957 Little Rock crisis, Dulles remarked that racial bigotry was "ruining our foreign policy." Still, when a State Department office countered Soviet anti-American race propaganda with a 1958 World's Fair exhibit in Brussels titled "The Unfinished Work"—on U.S. strides toward desegregation—southern conservatives kicked up such a furor that the Eisenhower administration closed the display.

U.S. hostility toward revolution also obstructed its quest for influence in the Third World. In the twentieth century, the United States opposed revolutions in Mexico, China, Russia, Cuba, Vietnam, Nicaragua, and Iran, largely because many Third World revolutions rose against America's Cold War allies and threatened American investments, markets, and military bases. Preferring to maintain the status quo, the United States usually supported its European allies or the conservative, propertied classes in the Third World during revolutionary crises.

Yet idealism also drove U.S. policy. Believing that Third World peoples craved modernization and the

DEVELOPMENT AND MODERNIZATION American economic model of private enterprise, American policymakers launched various "development" projects. Such projects held out the promise of sustained economic growth, prosperity, and stability, which the benefactors hoped would undermine radicalism. In the 1950s the Carnegie, Ford, and Rockefeller Foundations worked with the U.S. Agency for International Development (AID) to sponsor the Green Revolution promoting agricultural production. The Rockefeller Foundation supported foreign universities' efforts to train national leaders committed to nonradical development.

To persuade Third World peoples against radical doctrines, American leaders created propaganda campaigns. The U.S. Information Agency (USIA), founded in 1953, used films, radio broadcasts, the magazine *Free World*, exhibitions, and libraries (in 162 cities worldwide by 1961) to trumpet the "People's Capitalism." Citing America's economic success—contrasted with "slave-labor" conditions in the Soviet Union—it showcased well-paid American workers, political democracy, and religious freedom. To counter ugly pictures of segregation, the USIA applauded success stories of individual African Americans, such as the boxers Floyd Patterson and Sugar Ray Robinson. In 1960 some 13.8 million people visited U.S. pavilions abroad.

Undoubtedly, the American way of life had appeal for some Third World peoples. Hollywood movies offered enticing glimpses of middle-class materialism, as American films dominated many overseas markets. Blue jeans, advertising billboards, and soft drinks flooded foreign societies. Foreigners both envied and resented Americans for wasting so much while poorer peoples went without. The people of many countries, moreover, resented the profits that U.S. corporations extracted from them. Americans were often blamed for the persistent poverty in the developing world, even though leaders of those nations made decisions hindering their own progress, such as pouring millions of dollars into their militaries while their people needed food. Anti-American resentments materialized in the late 1950s attacks on USIA libraries in Calcutta, India; Beirut, Lebanon; and Bogotá, Colombia.

When the more benign techniques of containment—aid, trade, cultural relations—proved insufficient to prompt Third World nations to the American side, the Eisenhower administration pressed harder. Guatemala was an early test case. In 1951 the leftist Jacobo Arbenz Guzmán was elected president of Guatemala, a poor country whose largest landowner was the powerful American-owned United Fruit (UF) Company, which held 3 million acres across Latin America and operated railroads, ports, ships, and telecommunications facilities. Arbenz expropriated UF's uncultivated land and offered compensation. The company declined and charged that Arbenz posed a communist threat. The CIA began a secret plot to overthrow Arbenz, who turned to Moscow for military aid, thus reinforcing American suspicions. The CIA airlifted arms into Guatemala, and in mid-1954, CIA-supported Guatemalans struck from Honduras. U.S. planes bombed the capital city, driving Arbenz from power. The new pro-American regime returned United Fruit's land, but an ensuing civil war staggered the nation for decades.

Eisenhower was apprehensive as turmoil gripped Cuba in the late 1950s. In early 1959 Fidel Castro's rebels, or *barbudos* ("bearded ones"), driven by anti-American nationalism, ousted Fulgencio Batista, a

INTERVENTION IN GUATEMALA

THE CUBAN REVOLUTION AND FIDEL CASTRO

long-time U.S. ally whose corrupt regime had turned Havana into a haven for gambling, prostitution, and organized crime. Cubans had resented U.S. domination since the early twentieth century, when the Platt Amendment compromised their independence. Castro sought to break the U.S. grasp on Cuban trade and roll back American business, which invested some $1 billion on the island.

In early 1960, after Cuba signed a trade treaty with the Soviet Union, Eisenhower ordered the CIA to organize Cuban exiles to overthrow the Castro government. The agency also began to plot an assassination of the Cuban leader. When the president drastically cut U.S. sugar purchases, Castro seized all North American–owned companies that had not yet been nationalized. Castro appealed to the Soviet Union, which offered loans and expanded trade. Before leaving office in early 1961, Eisenhower broke diplomatic relations with Cuba and advised president-elect John F. Kennedy to advance plans for the invasion.

In the Middle East, meanwhile, ongoing tensions between Arabs and Jews posed additional challenges (see Map 33.1). Before the end of World War II, only France and Britain had been much concerned with this region. But the dissolution of empires and the rise of Cold War tensions drew Washington in, as did trouble in British-held Palestine. From 1945 to 1947, Britain tried to enlist U.S. officials to help resolve how to split Palestine between the Arabs and Jews. The Truman administration declined, and the British in 1947 turned the issue over to the United Nations, which voted to partition Palestine into separate Arab and Jewish states. Arab leaders opposed the decision, but in May 1948, Jewish leaders announced the creation of Israel.

ARAB-ISRAELI CONFLICT

The United States, which lobbied to secure the U.N. vote, extended recognition to the new state minutes after the act of foundation. A moral conviction that Jews deserved a homeland and that Zionism would create a democratic Israel influenced Truman, as did the belief that Jewish votes might swing some states to the Democrats in the 1948 election. These beliefs trumped concerns on the part of some senior officials that Arab oil producers might turn against the United States. The Soviet Union recognized the new nation, but Israel kept Moscow at arm's length. Palestinian Arabs, displaced from land they considered theirs, joined with Israel's Arab neighbors to make immediate war on the new state. The Israelis fought for six months until a U.N.-backed truce was called.

Thereafter, American Middle East policy centered on ensuring Israel's survival and cementing ties with Arab oil producers. American companies produced about half of the region's petroleum in the 1950s. Oil-rich Iran became a special friend, as its shah granted American oil companies a 40 percent interest in a new petroleum consortium in return for CIA help in the successful overthrow, in 1953, of his rival, Mohammed Mossadegh.

American officials faced a formidable foe in Egypt's Gamal Abdul Nasser, a towering figure in a pan-Arabic movement who vowed to expel the British from the Suez Canal and the Israelis from Palestine. The United States wished neither to anger the Arabs, for fear of losing valuable oil supplies, nor to alienate its ally Israel, supported at home by politically active American Jews. When Nasser declared neutrality in the Cold War, Dulles lost patience.

In 1956 the United States abruptly reneged on its offer to Egypt to help finance the Aswan Dam, a

SUEZ CRISIS

project to provide inexpensive electricity and water for Nile valley farmland. Nasser responded by nationalizing the British-owned Suez Canal, intending to use its profits to build the dam. Fully 75 percent of western Europe's oil came from the Middle East, most of it through the Suez. Fearing an interruption in trade, the British and French conspired with Israel to bring down Nasser. On October 29, 1956, the Israelis invaded Suez, joined two days later by British and French forces.

Eisenhower fumed. America's allies had not consulted him, and the president feared the invasion would cause Nasser to seek help from the Soviets, inviting them into the Middle East. Eisenhower sternly demanded that London, Paris, and Tel Aviv pull their troops out, and they did. Egypt took possession of the canal, the Soviets built the Aswan Dam, and Nasser became a hero. The United States countered Nasser by supporting the notoriously corrupt King Ibn Saud of Saudi Arabia, who renewed America's lease of an air base.

Washington officials worried that a vacuum existed in the Middle East and that the Soviets might fill

EISENHOWER DOCTRINE

it. To protect American interests there, the president proclaimed in the 1957 Eisenhower Doctrine that the United States would intervene in the Middle East if any government threatened by a communist takeover asked for help. In 1958 fourteen thousand American troops scrambled to quell a political dispute in Lebanon that Washington feared might be exploited by pro-Nasser groups or communists.

Cold War concerns also drove Eisenhower's policy in Vietnam. Despite substantial U.S. aid, the French

NATIONALIST VICTORY IN VIETNAM

lost steadily to the Vietminh. Finally, in early 1954, Ho's forces surrounded the French fortress at Dienbienphu in northwest Vietnam (see Map 30.1). The United States had advised and bankrolled the French, but had not committed troops to the war.

Eisenhower pressed the British to help form a coalition to address the Indochinese crisis, but they refused. At home, influential members of Congress—including Lyndon Baines Johnson of Texas, who as president would wage large-scale war in Vietnam—told Eisenhower they wanted "no more Koreas" and warned him against any U.S. military commitment. The issue became moot on May 7, when French defenders at Dienbienphu surrendered.

Peace talks, already under way in Geneva, brought Cold War and nationalist contenders together—the

GENEVA ACCORDS

United States, the Soviet Union, Britain, the People's Republic of China, Laos, Cambodia, and the competing Vietnamese regimes of Bao Dai and Ho Chi Minh. The 1954 Geneva accords, signed by France and Ho's Democratic Republic of Vietnam, temporarily divided Vietnam at the 17th parallel; Ho's government was confined to the North, Bao Dai's to the South. The 17th parallel was meant to serve as a military truce line; the country was scheduled to be reunified after national elections in 1956. In the meantime, neither North nor South was to join a military alliance or permit foreign bases on its soil.

Sure that the Geneva agreements would spell communist victory, the United States tried to undermine them. Soon after the conference, a CIA team undertook secret operations against the North, including commando raids across the 17th parallel. In the South, the United States helped Ngo Dinh Diem push Bao Dai aside and inaugurate the Republic of Vietnam. Diem was a dedicated nationalist and anticommunist, but he had little mass support. When Ho and some in the world community pressed for national elections, Diem and Eisenhower refused, fearing that the popular Vietminh leader would win. From 1955 to 1961, the Diem government received more than $1 billion in American aid, most of it military. American advisers organized and trained Diem's army, and American agriculturalists improved crops. Diem's Saigon regime became dependent on the United States for its very existence.

Diem proved a difficult ally. He abolished elections and appointed people beholden to him. He threw

NATIONAL
LIBERATION
FRONT

dissenters in jail and shut down newspapers criticizing him. Noncommunists and communists alike began to strike back at Diem's repressive government. In Hanoi, Ho's government in the late 1950s sent aid to southern insurgents, who assassinated hundreds of Diem's village officials. In late 1960, southern communists, at Hanoi's direction, organized the National Liberation Front (NLF), known as the Vietcong. The Vietcong in turn attracted other anti-Diem groups in the South. The Eisenhower administration, aware of Diem's shortcomings, affirmed its commitment to an independent, noncommunist South Vietnam.

Summary   *Online Study Center*   **ACE the Test**

The United States emerged from the Second World War as the preeminent world power. But Washington officials worried that the unstable international system, an unfriendly Soviet Union, and the decolonizing Third World could upset American plans for the postwar peace. Locked with the Soviet Union in a "Cold War," U.S. leaders marshaled their nation's superior resources to influence other countries. Foreign economic aid, atomic diplomacy, military alliances, client states, covert operations, propaganda, and cultural infiltration became the instruments of the Cold War, which began as a

conflict over Europe's future but soon encompassed the globe.

America's international leadership was welcomed by those who feared Soviet intentions. The reconstruction of former enemies Japan and (West) Germany helped those nations recover swiftly and become staunch members of the Western alliance. But U.S. policy also sparked resistance. Communist countries condemned financial and atomic diplomacy, while Third World nations sought to undermine America's European allies and sometimes identified the United States as an imperial co-conspirator. On occasion, even America's allies bristled at a United States that boldly proclaimed itself economic master and global policeman and haughtily touted its hegemonic status.

At home, critics protested that Presidents Truman and Eisenhower exaggerated the communist threat, wasting U.S. assets on immoral foreign ventures. Still, these presidents and their successors held firm to the mission of creating a nonradical, capitalist, free-trade international order. Determined to contain Soviet expansion, fearful of domestic charges of being "soft on communism," they enlarged the U.S. sphere of influence and held the line against the Soviet Union and the People's Republic of China, and revolution everywhere. One consequence was a dramatic increase in presidential power over foreign affairs—what historian Arthur M. Schlesinger Jr. called "the Imperial Presidency"—as Congress ceded constitutional power.

The globalist perspective of the United States prompted Americans to interpret troubles in the developing world as Cold War conflicts, inspired, if not directed, by Soviet-backed communists. The intensity of the Cold War obscured for Americans the indigenous roots of most Third World troubles, as the wars in Korea and Vietnam attested. Nor could the United States abide developing nations' drive for economic independence—for gaining control of their own raw materials and economies. Intertwined in the global economy as importer, exporter, and investor, the United States read challenges from this "periphery" as threats to the American standard of living.

LEGACY FOR A PEOPLE AND A NATION
The National Security State

For decades, America's Cold War religion has been national security; its texts the Truman Doctrine, the "X" article, and NSC-68; and its cathedral the national security state. During the Cold War, embracing preparedness for total war, the U.S. government transformed itself into a huge military headquarters that interlocked with corporations and universities.

Overseen by the president and his National Security Council, the national security state's core, once called the National Military Establishment, in 1949 became the Department of Defense. This department ranks as a leading employer; its payroll by 2000 included 1.3 million people on active duty and almost 600,000 civilian personnel, giving it more employees than ExxonMobil, Ford, General Motors, and GE combined. Almost a quarter of a million of these troops and civilians served overseas, in 130 countries. Although national defense spending declined after the Cold War, it never fell below $290 billion. In the aftermath of the terrorist attacks of September 11, 2001, the military budget rose again, reaching $400 billion in 2003.

Joining the Department of Defense as instruments of national security policy were the Joint Chiefs of Staff, Central Intelligence Agency, and dozens more government bodies. The focus of all of these entities was finding the best means to combat real and potential threats from foreign governments. But what about threats from within? The terrorist attacks of September 2001 made starkly clear that enemies existed who, while perhaps beholden to a foreign entity, launched their attacks from inside the nation's borders. In 2002 President George W. Bush created the Department of Homeland Security, which would have 170,000 employees and would encompass all or part of twenty-two agencies, including the Coast Guard, the Customs Service, the Federal Emergency Management Administration, and the Internal Revenue Service. It would involve the biggest overhaul of the federal bureaucracy since the Department of Defense was created, and it signified a more expansive notion of national security.

In 1961 President Eisenhower had warned against a "military-industrial complex," while others feared a "warfare state." Despite the warnings, the national security state remained vigorous in the early twenty-first century, a lasting legacy of the early Cold War period for a people and a nation.

AMERICA AT MIDCENTURY 1945–1960

*E*venings after supper, when the sticky heat of the Georgia summer days ebbed, families on Nancy Circle enjoyed a walk. Parents stood chatting as children played.

In 1959 the twenty houses on Nancy Circle were a couple of years old. They stood on land once belonging to the Cherokees, in a development carved from the old Campbell plantation, along the route General William Tecumseh Sherman had taken in his march to the sea during the Civil War. Slaves picked cotton there a century before, but no African Americans lived in those homes.

Nancy Circle was part of a new suburban development in Smyrna, Georgia, northwest of Atlanta, but few residents worked in the city. Most traveled to the massive Lockheed Georgia airplane plant created, in large part, by Cold War defense spending. With three bedrooms for about $17,000, the houses were affordable to young families.

Children ran in and out of each other's houses and women gathered to drink coffee in the mornings after the men left for work. There were aerospace engineers, three career military men, an auto mechanic, and a musician. Only two women held paid jobs: one had almost-grown children and taught second grade, and the other was divorced and worked as a secretary. People were suspicious of her but liked her sister, born with dwarfism, who had left her job in a North Carolina textile mill to help care for her nephew. Two war brides—one Japanese and one German—lived in the neighborhood. The Japanese woman spoke little English; the German woman taught the girls in the neighborhood to crochet.

The people who lived on Nancy Circle read magazines criticizing the homogeneity and conformity of suburban life, but that wasn't their experience. On this single street, people from deep Appalachia lived next to people who had grown up in city tenement apartments, and women who'd done graduate work baked Christmas cookies with women who had not finished high school. These new suburbanites were creating for themselves a new world and a new

Shaping Postwar America

Domestic Politics in the Cold War Era

Cold War Fears and Anticommunism

The Struggle for Civil Rights

Creating a Middle-Class Nation

Men, Women, and Youth at Midcentury

LINKS TO THE WORLD
Barbie

The Limits of the Middle-Class Nation

LEGACY FOR A PEOPLE AND A NATION
The Pledge of Allegiance

Online Study Center
This icon will direct you to interactive map and primary source activities on the website
http://college.hmco.com/pic/nortonbrief7e

CHRONOLOGY

1945 • World War II ends

1946 • Marriage and birth rates skyrocket, creating baby boom
• More than 1 million veterans enroll in colleges under GI Bill
• More than 5 million U.S. workers go on strike

1947 • Taft-Hartley Act limits power of unions
• Truman orders loyalty investigation of 3 million government employees
• Mass-production techniques used to build Levittown houses

1948 • Truman issues executive order desegregating armed forces and federal government
• Truman elected president

1949 • Soviet Union explodes atomic bomb
• National Housing Act promises decent housing for all Americans

1950 • Korean War begins
• McCarthy alleges communists in government
• "Treaty of Detroit" creates model for new labor-management relations

1952 • Eisenhower elected president

1953 • Korean War ends
• Congress adopts termination policy for Native American tribes
• Rosenbergs executed as atomic spies

1954 • *Brown v. Board of Education* decision reverses "separate-but-equal" doctrine
• Senate condemns McCarthy

1955 • Montgomery bus boycott begins

1956 • Highway Act launches interstate highway system
• Eisenhower reelected
• Elvis Presley appears on *Ed Sullivan Show*

1957 • King elected first president of Southern Christian Leadership Conference
• School desegregation crisis in Little Rock, Arkansas
• Congress passes Civil Rights Act
• Soviet Union launches *Sputnik*

1958 • Congress passes National Defense Education Act

middle-class culture. Having grown up with the Great Depression and world war, these new suburbanites believed they had found good lives.

The United States had emerged from World War II stronger and more prosperous. Europe and Asia had been devastated, but America's farms, cities, and factories were intact. U.S. production capacity increased during the war, and the fight against fascism gave Americans a unity of purpose. Victory seemed to confirm their struggles. But memories of sixteen years of depression and war would continue to shape the choices Americans made in their private lives, domestic policies, and relations with the rest of the world.

In the postwar era, the actions of the federal government and the choices individual Americans made began a profound reconfiguration of American society. Postwar social policies that sent millions of veterans to college on the GI Bill, linked the nation with interstate highways, fostered the growth of suburbs and the Sunbelt, and disrupted regional isolation helped to create a national middle-class culture encompassing an unprecedented majority of the nation's citizens. Countless individual decisions—to go to college, marry young, have a large family, move to the suburbs, start a business—were made possible by federal initiatives. Americans in the postwar era defined a new American Dream: one that centered on the family, a new level of material comfort and consumption, and a shared sense of belonging to a common culture.

Nevertheless, almost a quarter of Americans did not share in the postwar prosperity—but they were invisible to the middle-class majority. Rural poverty continued, and inner cities became increasingly impoverished as more affluent Americans moved to the suburbs and new migrants—poor black and white southerners, new immigrants from Mexico and Puerto Rico, Native Americans resettled by the federal government from tribal lands—arrived.

As class and ethnicity became less important in suburbia, race continued to divide Americans. The 1950s saw important federal actions to protect the civil rights of African Americans, including the Supreme Court's school desegregation decision in *Brown v. Board of Education*. African Americans increasingly took direct action, and in 1955, the year-long Montgomery bus boycott launched the modern civil rights movement.

The economic boom that began with the end of the war lasted twenty-five years. Although fears—of nuclear war, of returning hard times—lingered, new prosperity bred complacency by the late 1950s. The most significant domestic political ferment, in fact, was a byproduct of the Cold War: a ferocious anticommunism that narrowed the boundaries of acceptable dissent. Instead, by decade's end, people sought satisfaction in their families and in the consumer pleasures newly available to so many. ■

Shaping Postwar America

*a*t the end of World War II, many Americans feared that the economy would plunge back into depression—and in the immediate aftermath of the war, unemployment rose and a wave of strikes rocked the nation. But dire predictions were wrong: the economy flourished, and Americans' standard of living improved. The GI Bill and other federal programs created new opportunities that fundamentally changed the nation.

As the end of the war approached and the American war machine slowed, factories began to lay off workers. Ten days after the victory over Japan, 1.8 million people nationwide received pink slips, and 640,000 filed for unemployment compensation. More than 15 million GIs awaited demobilization.

POSTWAR ECONOMIC UNCERTAINTY

In the spring of 1944—a year before V-E Day—Congress, anticipating a postwar crisis, unanimously passed the Servicemen's Readjustment Act, known as the GI Bill of Rights. It showed the nation's gratitude but also attempted to keep demobilized veterans from swamping the U.S. economy: year-long unemployment benefits meant they could be gradually absorbed into civilian employment, and higher-education benefits would keep men out of the job market. In winter 1945, congressional Democrats introduced the Full Employment Act guaranteeing work through public sector employment if necessary. By the time Truman signed it into law in early 1946, key provisions guaranteeing work had virtually disappeared. But the act reaffirmed the federal government's responsibility for managing the economy and created the Council of Economic Advisors to help prevent economic downturns.

Conversion to a peacetime economy hit workers hard, especially as the inflation rate skyrocketed. More than 5 million workers walked off the job the first year. Unions shut down the coal, automobile, steel, and electric industries and halted railroad and maritime transportation. So disruptive were the strikes that Americans began hoarding food and gasoline.

POSTWAR STRIKES AND THE TAFT-HARTLEY ACT

By spring 1946, Americans grew impatient with the strikes. When unions threatened a national railway strike, President Truman announced that if strikers in an industry vital to national security refused a presidential order to return to work, he would ask Congress to draft them into the armed forces. The Democratic Party would not offer unlimited support to organized labor.

Then, in 1947, the Taft-Hartley Act permitted states to enact right-to-work laws that outlawed "closed shops," in which all workers were required to join the union if a majority of their number favored a union shop. The law also mandated an eighty-day cooling-off period before unions initiated strikes imperiling national security. These restrictions limited unions' ability to expand their membership. Truman did not want to see union power so limited, but Congress passed the Taft-Hartley Act over Truman's veto.

Despite initial difficulties, the economy recovered quickly, fueled by consumer spending. Although Amer-

ECONOMIC GROWTH

icans had brought home steady paychecks during the war, they had had little on which to spend them. No new cars, for example, had been built since 1942. When new cars and appliances appeared at war's end, Americans were ready to buy. Because most factories around the world were in ruins, U.S. corporations expanded their global dominance and grew dramatically in size. America's ten largest corporations were in automobiles (GM, Ford, Chrysler), oil (Standard Oil of New Jersey, Mobil, Texaco), and electronics and communications (GE, IBM, IT&T, AT&T).

In the agricultural sector, new machines, such as mechanical cotton-, tobacco-, and grape-pickers and crop-dusting planes, revolutionized farming, and the increased use of fertilizers and pesticides raised the total value of farm output from $24.6 billion in 1945 to $38.4 billion in 1961. Large investors were drawn to agriculture by its increased profitability, and the average size of farms increased from 195 to 306 acres.

Economic growth was also fueled by government programs. By 1949, veterans received close to $4 billion in unemployment compensation, low-interest loans for homes or businesses, and—perhaps most significant—money for higher education.

Before the war, only about 7.5 percent of young Americans had gone to college. With GI benefits, almost half of America's returning veterans sought higher education. The resulting increase in the number of well-educated or technically trained workers benefited the American economy. And the flood of students and federal dollars into the nation's colleges and universities created a golden age for higher education.

Education created social mobility: children of barely literate menial laborers became white-collar professionals. The GI Bill fostered the emergence of a national middle-class culture, for as colleges exposed people to new ideas and experiences, students became less rooted in ethnic or regional cultures.

The end of the war brought a boom in marriage and birth rates. In 1946 the U.S. marriage rate was

BABY BOOM

higher than that of any other record-keeping nation (except Hungary). The birth rate soared, reversing the downward trend of the past 150 years. "Take the 3,548,000 babies born in 1950," wrote Sylvia F. Porter in her syndicated newspaper column. "Bundle them into a batch. . . . What do you get? Boom. The biggest, boomiest boom ever known in history. Just imagine how much these extra people, these new markets, will absorb—in food, clothing, in gadgets, in housing, in services." Although the baby boom peaked in 1957, more than 4 million babies were born every year until 1965 (see Figure 29.1). As this vast cohort

Figure 29.1   Birth Rate, 1945–1964

The birth rate began to rise in 1942 and 1943, but it skyrocketed during the postwar years beginning in 1946, reaching its peak in 1957. From 1954 to 1964, the United States recorded more than 4 million births every year. (Source: Adapted from U.S. Bureau of the Census, *Historical Statistics of the United States, Colonial Times to 1970,* Bicentennial Edition [Washington, D.C.: U.S. Government Printing Office, 1975], p. 49.)

grew older, it had successive impacts on housing, schools, fads, popular music, the job market, and retirement funds, including Social Security.

Scarcely any new housing had been built since the 1920s. Almost 2 million families were doubled up with relatives in 1948; 50,000 people were living in Quonset huts, and housing was so tight in Chicago that 250 used trolley cars were sold as homes.

In the postwar years, white Americans moved to the suburbs. Some escaped crowded cities. People from rural areas moved closer to city jobs. Some white families left urban neighborhoods because African American families were moving in. Most, however, simply wanted to own their own homes, and suburban developments offered affordable housing. Although suburban development predated World War II, the massive migration of 18 million Americans to the suburbs between 1950 and 1960 was on a wholly different scale (see Table 29.1).

SUBURBANIZATION

In 1947 builder William Levitt adapted Henry Ford's assembly-line methods to revolutionize home building. By 1949, instead of 4 or 5 custom homes per year, Levitt's company built 180 houses a week. They were very basic: four and a half rooms on a 60-by-100-foot lot, all with identical floor plans disguised by four different exteriors. By rotating seven paint colors, Levitt guaranteed that only one in every twenty-eight houses would be identical. The basic house sold for $7,990. Other homebuilders quickly adopted Levitt's techniques.

Suburban development happened on such a large scale because federal policies encouraged it. The Federal Housing Administration (FHA) offered low-interest mortgages. New highways also promoted suburban development. Congress authorized construction of a 37,000-mile chain of highways in 1947 and in 1956 passed the Highway Act to create a 42,500-mile interstate highway system. Intended to facilitate commerce and rapid mobilization of the military, highways allowed workers to live farther from their jobs in central cities.

Postwar federal programs did not benefit all Americans equally. First, federal policies often assisted men at the expense of women. As industry laid off civilian workers to make room for veterans, women lost their jobs at a rate 75 percent higher than men. Many stayed in the work force but were pushed into lower-paying jobs. Universities made room for veterans on the GI Bill by excluding qualified women students.

INEQUALITY IN BENEFITS

Inequities were also based on race. African American, Native American, Mexican American, and Asian American veterans, like European American veterans, received educational benefits and hiring preference in civil service jobs. But war workers from these groups were among the first laid off. Federal loan officers and bankers often labeled African American or racially mixed neighborhoods "high risk," denying mortgages to racial minorities regardless of individual creditworthiness. This practice, called "redlining" because such neighborhoods were outlined in red on lenders' maps, kept African Americans and many Hispanics from enjoying the economic explosion of the postwar era, as white families who bought homes with federally guaranteed mortgages saw their small investments grow dramatically over the years.

TABLE 29.1

Geographic Distribution of the U.S. Population, 1930–1970 (in Percentages)

Year	Central Cities	Suburbs	Rural Areas and Small Towns
1930	31.8%	18.0%	50.2%
1940	31.6	19.5	48.9
1950	32.3	23.8	43.9
1960	32.6	30.7	36.7
1970	31.4	37.6	31.0

Source: Adapted from U.S. Bureau of the Census, *Decennial Censuses, 1930–1970* (Washington, D.C.: U.S. Government Printing Office).

Domestic Politics in the Cold War Era

lthough the major social and economic transformations in postwar America were largely due to federal policies and programs, foreign affairs were politically paramount, given the challenges of the expanding Cold War. Domestically, Truman attempted to build on the New Deal's liberal agenda, while Eisenhower called for balanced budgets and business-friendly policies. But neither administration approached the legislative activism of the New Deal.

Harry Truman, a former haberdasher from Missouri, never expected to be president. In 1944,

HARRY S TRUMAN AND POSTWAR LIBERALISM

when Franklin Roosevelt asked him to be his vice-presidential candidate, he almost refused. But with the war in its fourth year, the busy president had little time for his new vice president and left Truman in the dark about everything from the Manhattan Project to plans for postwar domestic policy. When Roosevelt died suddenly in April 1945, Truman was unprepared to take his place.

Truman nevertheless stepped forward, placing a sign on his desk: "The Buck Stops Here." Most of Truman's presidency focused on foreign relations, as he led the nation through the end of World War II into the Cold War with the Soviet Union. Domestically, he oversaw reconversion from war to peace and attempted to keep a liberal agenda—the legacy of Roosevelt's New Deal—alive.

In his 1944 State of the Union address, Roosevelt offered Americans a "Second Bill of Rights": the right to employment, healthcare, education, food, and housing. This notion of government responsibility was the cornerstone of postwar liberalism. Truman proposed an increase in the minimum wage and national housing legislation offering loans for mortgages, and he supported the Full Employment Act. To pay for his proposed social welfare programs, he gambled that full employment would generate sufficient tax revenue and that consumer spending would fuel economic growth.

The gamble paid off, but the conservative coalition of Republicans and southern Democrats that stalled Roosevelt's New Deal legislation in the late 1930s was less inclined to support Truman. Congress gutted the Full Employment Act, refused to raise the minimum wage, and passed the anti-union Taft-Hartley Act. With powerful congressional opposition, Truman had little chance of major legislative accomplishments. As Truman presided over the rocky transition from a wartime to a peacetime economy, he faced massive inflation (briefly hitting 35 percent), shortages of consumer goods, and a wave of strikes that slowed production and drove prices up. His ap-

proval rating plunged from 87 percent in late 1945 to 32 percent in 1946.

By 1948 it seemed that Republicans would win the White House in November, and the party nominated

1948 ELECTION

Thomas Dewey, the man Roosevelt defeated in 1944, as its candidate. Republicans hoped schisms in the Democratic Party would ensure victory. Former New Dealer Henry Wallace ran for president on the Progressive Party ticket, advocating friendly relations with the Soviet Union, racial desegregation, and nationalization of basic industries. A fourth party, the Dixiecrats (States' Rights Democratic Party), was organized by white southerners who left the 1948 Democratic convention when it adopted a pro–civil rights plank. They nominated the fiercely segregationist governor of South Carolina, Strom Thurmond.

Truman refused to give up. He resorted to red-baiting, denouncing "Henry Wallace and his communists." Most important, he appealed to the burgeoning population of African American voters in northern cities, becoming the first presidential candidate to campaign in Harlem. In the end, Truman prevailed. Roosevelt's New Deal coalition—African Americans, union members, northern urban voters, and most southern whites—had endured.

In his 1949 State of the Union message, Truman stated, "I expect to give every segment of our popula-

TRUMAN'S FAIR DEAL

tion a fair deal." Unlike Roosevelt, Truman pushed legislation supporting the civil rights of African Americans, including antilynching laws. He proposed national health insurance and federal aid for education. However, southern conservatives in Congress destroyed his civil rights legislation. The American Medical Association denounced his health insurance plan as "socialized medicine," and the Roman Catholic Church opposed educational assistance because it would not include parochial schools.

When Truman ordered troops to Korea in June 1950 (see Chapter 28), Americans grumbled as the nation again mobilized for war. People remembered the shortages of the previous war and stocked up on sugar, coffee, and canned goods. Fueled by panic buying, inflation rose again. An unpopular war and charges of influence peddling by Truman's cronies pushed the president's public approval rating to an all-time low of 23 percent in 1951, where it stayed for a year.

"It's Time for a Change" was the Republican campaign slogan in 1952, and voters agreed. Americans hoped that candidate General

EISENHOWER'S DYNAMIC CONSERVATISM

Dwight D. Eisenhower, the immensely popular World War II hero, could end the Korean War. Eisenhower appealed to moderates in both parties (the Democrats tried to recruit him as their presidential candidate).

Smiling Ike, with his folksy style, garbled syntax, and frequent escapes to the golf course, was no stranger to hard work. His low-key style played down his role as politician and highlighted his role as chief of state. Relying heavily on his staff, Eisenhower delegated authority to cabinet members and sometimes appeared out of touch with his own government, but he was not, and he remained a popular president.

With a Republican in the White House for the first time in twenty years, conservatives hoped to roll back New Deal programs such as Social Security. Instead, Eisenhower adopted what he called "dynamic conservatism": being "conservative when it comes to money and liberal when it comes to human beings." In 1954 Eisenhower signed into law amendments to the Social Security Act that raised benefits and added 7.5 million workers, mostly self-employed farmers, to its rolls. His administration, motivated by Cold War fears, also increased government funding for education. When the Soviet Union launched *Sputnik,* the first earth-orbiting satellite, in 1957 (and America's first launch exploded seconds after liftoff), education became an issue of national security. Congress responded in 1958 with the National Defense Education Act (NDEA), which funded enrichment of school programs in mathematics, foreign languages, and the sciences and offered fellowships and loans to college students.

Overall, Eisenhower's administration was an ally of business and industry. The Eisenhower tax reform

GROWTH OF THE MILITARY-INDUSTRIAL COMPLEX

bill raised business depreciation allowances, and the Atomic Energy Act of 1954 allowed private companies to own reactors and nuclear materials to produce electricity. Eisenhower balanced only three of his eight budgets, turning to deficit spending to cushion the impact of three recessions (in

1953–1954, 1957–1958, and 1960–1961) and fund America's global activities. In 1959 federal expenditures climbed to $92 billion, about half of which went to the military, mostly for developing new weapons.

Before leaving office in 1961 at the end of his second term, Eisenhower delivered his farewell address. Because of the Cold War, he observed, the United States had a large standing army—3.5 million men—and spent ever greater percentages of its budget developing weapons. Condemning the new "conjunction of an immense military establishment and a large arms industry," Eisenhower warned, "The total influence—economic, political, even spiritual—is felt in every city, every statehouse, every office of the federal government" and threatened the nation's democratic process. Eisenhower, former five-star general and war hero, urged Americans to "guard against . . . the military-industrial complex."

Cold War Fears and Anticommunism

International relations had a profound influence on America's domestic politics in the years following World War II. Americans were frightened by Cold War tensions between the United States and the Soviet Union, and their reasonable fears spilled over into anticommunist demagoguery and witch hunts, allowing the trampling of civil liberties, the suppression of dissent, and the persecution of innocent Americans.

Anticommunism was not new: a "red scare" had swept the nation following the Russian Revolution of 1917, and opponents of America's labor movement had used charges of communism to block unionization through the 1930s. Many saw the Soviet Union's virtual takeover of eastern Europe after World War II as an alarming parallel to Nazi Germany's takeover of neighboring states. People remembered the failure of "appeasement" at Munich and worried about being "too soft" toward the Soviet Union.

In addition, American intelligence officers in a top-secret project code-named "Venona" decrypted

ESPIONAGE AND NUCLEAR FEARS

almost three thousand Soviet telegraphic cables that proved spies had infiltrated U.S. government agencies and nuclear programs. (The United

States also had spies within the Soviet Union.) To prevent the Soviets from realizing their codes were compromised, intelligence officials withheld this evidence from the American public.

Fear of nuclear war contributed to American anticommunism. When the Soviet Union joined the United States in possessing atomic weapons in 1949, President Truman initiated a national atomic civil defense program, advising: "I cannot tell you when or where the attack will come or that it will come at all. I can only remind you that we must be ready when it does come." Children practiced "duck-and-cover" positions in school classrooms, learning how to shield their faces from the atomic flash. *Life* magazine featured backyard fallout shelters. Americans worried that the United States was vulnerable to attack.

THE POLITICS OF ANTICOMMUNISM

American leaders did not always draw a sufficient line between prudent attempts to prevent Soviet spies from infiltrating government agencies and anticommunist scare-mongering. Republican politicians effectively used red-baiting against Democratic opponents, eventually targeting the Truman administration. In 1947 President Truman ordered investigations into the loyalty of more than 3 million government employees. As anticommunist hysteria grew, the government discharged people deemed "security risks," among them alcoholics, homosexuals, and debtors thought susceptible to blackmail. In most cases, there was no evidence of disloyalty.

Leading the anticommunist crusade was the House Un-American Activities Committee (popularly known as HUAC). Created in 1938 to investigate "subversive and un-American propaganda," the committee lost credibility by charging that film stars, including eight-year-old Shirley Temple, were Communist Party dupes. By 1947, HUAC attacked Hollywood again, using Federal Bureau of Investigation (FBI) files and testimony of people such as Screen Actors Guild president Ronald Reagan (a secret informant for the FBI). Screenwriters and directors known as the "Hollywood Ten" were sent to prison when they refused to "name names" of suspected communists. At least a dozen others committed suicide. Studios blacklisted screenwriters, directors, and even makeup artists suspected of communist affiliations. With no evidence of wrongdoing, careers were ruined.

MCCARTHYISM AND THE GROWING "WITCH HUNT"

University professors were targeted in 1949, when HUAC demanded lists of the textbooks used at eighty-one universities. When the board of regents at the University of California, Berkeley, instituted a loyalty oath and fired twenty-six faculty members resisting on principle, protests nationwide forced the regents to back down. But many professors began to downplay controversial material in their courses. In the labor movement, the CIO expelled eleven unions, over 900,000 members, for alleged communist domination. The red panic reached its nadir in February 1950, when Joseph R. McCarthy of Wisconsin, a relatively obscure U.S. senator, charged that the U.S. State Department was "thoroughly infested with Communists." McCarthy first claimed there were 205 communists in the State Department, then 57, then 81. He had a severe drinking problem and a record of dishonesty as a lawyer and judge. But McCarthy crystallized Americans' anxieties, and anticommunist excesses came to be known as "McCarthyism."

The anticommunist crusade was embraced by labor union officials, religious leaders, and the media, as well as by politicians. Women in New York who lobbied for the continuation of wartime daycare programs were denounced as communists by the *New York World Telegram*.

ANTICOMMUNISM IN CONGRESS

In such a climate, most public figures found it too risky to stand up against McCarthyist tactics. In 1950, with bipartisan support, Congress passed the Internal Security (McCarran) Act, which required members of "Communist-front" organizations to register with the government and prohibited them from holding government jobs or traveling abroad. In 1954 the Senate passed the Communist Control Act sponsored by Senator Hubert H. Humphrey of Minnesota, which effectively made membership in the Communist Party illegal.

In 1948 Congressman Richard Nixon of California, a member of HUAC, was propelled onto the national stage when he accused former State Department official Alger Hiss of espionage. In 1950 Hiss was convicted of lying about his contacts with Soviet agents. That same year, Ethel and Julius Rosenberg were arrested for passing atomic secrets to the Soviets;

they were found guilty of treason and executed in 1953. For decades, many historians believed that the Rosenbergs were victims of a witch hunt, but there was evidence of Julius Rosenberg's guilt in cables decrypted by the Venona Project. They were not presented at trial for national security reasons and remained top secret until 1995.

The excesses of Cold War anticommunism waned when Senator McCarthy was discredited on national

THE WANING OF THE RED SCARE

television in 1954. McCarthy was a master at using the press and making sensational accusations— front-page material—just before reporters' deadlines. When Mc-

Carthy's charges proved untrue, retractions appeared in the back pages of the newspapers.

But McCarthy's crucial mistake was charging on television that the army was shielding communists, citing the case of one army dentist. The so-called Army-McCarthy hearings, held by a Senate subcommittee in 1954, became a showcase for the senator's abusive treatment of witnesses. McCarthy, apparently drunk, alternately ranted and slurred his words. When army counsel Joseph Welch protested, "Have you no sense of decency, sir?" the gallery erupted in applause. In December 1954, the Senate voted to "condemn" McCarthy for sullying the dignity of Congress. He remained a senator, but exhaustion and alcohol took their toll, and he died in 1957 at the age of forty-eight. With McCarthy discredited, the most virulent anticommunism had run its course.

Online Study Center   **Improve Your Grade**

Primary Source: Army-McCarthy Hearings

The Struggle for Civil Rights

*T*he Cold War also shaped African American struggles for social justice and the nation's responses to them. As the Soviet Union pointed out, the United States could hardly pose as the leader of the free world or condemn the denial of human rights in eastern Europe while practicing segregation. Nor could the United States convince new African and Asian nations of its dedication to human rights if African Americans were subjected to segregation, discrimination, disfranchisement, and racial violence. Many Americans, however, viewed such criticism as a Soviet-inspired attempt to weaken the United States. The FBI and local law enforcement commonly used anticommunist fears to justify attacking civil rights activists. In this heated environment, African Americans struggled to seize the political initiative.

African Americans who had helped win the Second World War were determined to enjoy better lives in

GROWING BLACK POLITICAL POWER

postwar America. Politicians such as Harry Truman were paying attention to black aspirations, especially as black voters in some urban-industrial states began to influence the balance of power.

President Truman had compelling political reasons for supporting African American civil rights and genuinely believed that every American, regardless of race, should enjoy full citizenship. Truman was disturbed by a resurgence of racial terrorism, as a revived Ku Klux Klan burned crosses and murdered blacks seeking civil rights after World War II. But what really horrified Truman was the report that police in Aiken, South Carolina, had gouged out the eyes of a black sergeant just three hours after his army discharge. In December 1946, Truman signed an executive order establishing the President's Committee on Civil Rights. Its report, *To Secure These Rights*, would become the civil rights movement agenda for the next twenty years. It called for antilynching and antisegregation legislation and for laws guaranteeing voting rights and equal employment opportunity. For the first time since Reconstruction, a president had acknowledged the federal government's responsibility to protect blacks and strive for racial equality.

In 1948 Truman issued two executive orders ending racial discrimination in the federal government. One proclaimed a policy of "fair employment throughout the federal establishment" and created the Employment Board of the Civil Service Commission to hear discrimination charges. The other ordered the racial desegregation of the armed forces. Segregated units were phased out by the Korean War.

At the same time, African Americans challenged racial discrimination in the courts. In 1939 the

SCHOOL DESEGREGATION AND SUPREME COURT VICTORIES

NAACP established its Legal Defense and Education Fund under Charles Hamilton Houston and Thurgood Marshall. By the 1940s, Marshall (who in 1967 would become the first African American

Supreme Court justice) and his colleagues worked to destroy the separate-but-equal doctrine established in *Plessy v. Ferguson* (1896). Because of NAACP lawsuits, African Americans gained admission to professional and graduate schools at many formerly segregated state universities. The NAACP also won victories through the Supreme Court in *Smith v. Allwright* (1944), which outlawed the whites-only primaries held by the Democratic Party in some southern states; *Morgan v. Virginia* (1946), which struck down segregation in interstate bus transportation; and *Shelley v. Kraemer* (1948), which held that racially restrictive covenants (private agreements among white homeowners not to sell to blacks) could not legally be enforced.

Changing social attitudes accompanied these gains. Gunnar Myrdal's social science study *An American Dilemma* (1944) and Richard Wright's novel *Native Son* (1940) and his autobiography, *Black Boy* (1945), increased white awareness of racial injustice. A new and visible black middle class emerged, composed of college-educated activists, veterans, and union workers. Blacks and whites worked together in CIO unions and service organizations such as the National Council of Churches. In 1947 a black baseball player, Jackie Robinson, broke the major league color barrier and electrified Brooklyn Dodgers fans.

Even so, blacks continued to suffer disfranchisement, job discrimination, and violence, including the bombing murder in 1951 of the Florida state director of the NAACP and his wife. But in 1954 the NAACP won a historic victory. *Brown v. Board of Education of Topeka*, which Thurgood Marshall argued, incorporated school desegregation cases from several states. Written by Chief Justice Earl Warren, the Court's unanimous decision concluded that "in the field of public education the doctrine of 'separate but equal' has no place. Separate educational facilities are inherently unequal." But the ruling that overturned *Plessy v. Ferguson* did not demand immediate compliance. A year later the Court ordered school desegregation, but without a timetable, southern states resisted.

The forces of white resistance urged southern communities to defy the Court. The Klan experienced

WHITE RESISTANCE

another resurgence, and white violence against blacks increased. In 1955 Emmett Till, a fourteen-year-old from Chicago, was murdered by white men in Mississippi who took offense at the way he spoke to a white woman. Business and professional people created White Citizens' Councils, known familiarly as "uptown Ku Klux Klans," and used economic power against black civil rights activists. When FBI director J. Edgar Hoover briefed President Eisenhower on southern racial tensions in 1956, he warned of communist influences among civil rights activists, and even suggested that Citizens' Councils might "control the rising tension."

White resistance also mounted in northern cities, such as Chicago, where the African American population increased due to migration from 275,000 to 800,000 between 1940 and 1960. The newcomers found good jobs and enjoyed political power, but faced housing segregation. So racially divided was Chicago that the U.S. Commission on Civil Rights in 1959 described it as "the most residentially segregated city in the nation." Other northern cities were not far behind.

Although President Eisenhower disapproved of racial segregation, he objected to "compulsory federal

FEDERAL AUTHORITY AND STATES' RIGHTS

law," believing instead that race relations would improve "only if [desegregation] starts locally." He also feared that the ugly public confrontations over desegregation would jeopardize Republican inroads in the South. Thus, Eisenhower did not state forthrightly that the federal government would enforce the *Brown* decision as law.

Events in Little Rock, Arkansas, forced the president to get involved. In September 1957 Arkansas governor Orval E. Faubus defied court-ordered desegregation for Little Rock's Central High School, saying on television that "blood would run in the streets" if black students tried to enter the high school. Eight black teenagers tried to enter Central High but were turned away by the Arkansas National Guard. The ninth was surrounded by jeering whites and narrowly escaped the mob with the help of a sympathetic white woman.

The "Little Rock Nine" entered Central High more than two weeks later, after a federal judge intervened. Television broadcast the scene to the world. Eisenhower, fearing violence, nationalized the Arkansas National Guard (placing it under federal, not state, control) and dispatched one thousand army paratroopers to guard the students for the rest of the year. Eisenhower's use of federal power was a critical step toward racial equality, directly confronting the conflict between federal authority and states' rights. However, the state triumphed the following year when Faubus closed all public high schools in Little Rock rather than desegregate them.

By the mid-1950s, African Americans were increasingly engaged in a grassroots struggle for civil rights. In 1955 Rosa Parks, a department store seamstress and long-time NAACP activist, was arrested when she refused to give up her seat to a white man on a public bus in Montgomery, Alabama. Her arrest enabled local black women's organizations and civil rights groups to organize a boycott of the city's bus system. They selected Martin Luther King Jr., a recently ordained minister, as their leader. King launched the boycott declaring, "If we are wrong, the Constitution is wrong. If we are wrong, God Almighty is wrong. . . . If we are wrong, justice is a lie."

MONTGOMERY BUS BOYCOTT

Martin Luther King Jr. was a twenty-six-year-old Baptist minister with a recent Ph.D. from Boston University. Schooled in the teachings of India's leader Mohandas K. Gandhi, King believed in nonviolent civil disobedience as a vehicle to focus the nation's attention on the immorality of Jim Crow.

During the year-long Montgomery bus boycott, blacks rallied in their churches. They maintained their boycott through heavy rains and steamy summer heat, often walking miles a day. With the bus company near bankruptcy and downtown merchants hurt by declining sales, city officials adopted harassment tactics to end the boycott. But the black people of Montgomery persevered: thirteen months later, the Supreme Court declared Alabama's bus segregation laws unconstitutional.

The boycott propelled King to the forefront of a new grassroots civil rights activism, with black churches playing a major role. In 1957 he became the first president of the Southern Christian Leadership Conference (SCLC), organized to coordinate civil rights activities. That same year, Congress passed the first Civil Rights Act since Reconstruction, creating the Commission on Civil Rights to investigate sys-

■ In 1957 white teenagers in Little Rock, Arkansas, angrily confront African American students who, under federal court order, are attempting to enter, and thus desegregate, Central High School. The Supreme Court's *Brown* decision of 1954 was resisted by whites throughout the South. (AP/Wide World Photos, Inc.)

tematic discrimination, such as in voting. This measure proved ineffective; however, with success in Montgomery and gains in the Supreme Court, African Americans were poised for a major civil rights movement in the decade to come.

Creating a Middle-Class Nation

*D*espite resistance to civil rights in the 1950s, the United States was becoming increasingly inclusive. National prosperity offered more Americans material comfort and economic security—entrance into an economic middle class. Old European ethnic identities faded as an ever smaller percentage of America's people were first- or second-generation immigrants. In the new suburbs, people from different backgrounds worked together to create communities. Middle-class Americans increasingly looked to national media for advice on matters ranging from how to celebrate Thanksgiving to how to raise children. New opportunities for consumption—whether teenage fads or suburban ranch-style homes—also tied disparate Americans together. In the postwar years, a new middle-class way of life was transforming the United States.

During the 1950s, sustained economic growth created unprecedented levels of prosperity and economic

PROSPERITY FOR MORE AMERICANS

security. In great part, the boom was driven by consumer spending, as Americans eagerly bought goods unavailable during the war, and industries expanded production. As the Cold War deepened, government spending for defense created jobs and further stimulated the economy.

A new era of peaceful labor relations helped bring prosperity to more Americans. By 1950, the United Auto Workers (UAW) and General Motors led the way for other corporations in providing workers with health insurance, pension plans, and guaranteed cost-of-living adjustments, or COLAs. The 1950 agreement gave GM's workers a five-year contract with regular wage increases tied to corporate productivity. With wage increases linked to productivity, labor cast its lot with management: workplace stability and efficiency, not strikes, would boost wages. During the 1950s, wages and benefits propelled union families into the ranks of the middle class.

During World War II, new defense plants and military training camps channeled federal money

THE SUNBELT AND ECONOMIC GROWTH

to the South, stimulating economic growth. In the postwar era, massive defense spending continued to shift economic development to the South and Southwest—the Sunbelt (see Map 29.1). Government actions—including generous tax breaks for oil companies, siting of military bases, and defense and aerospace contracts—were crucial to the region's new prosperity.

The Sunbelt's spectacular growth was due to agribusiness, the oil industry, real-estate development, and recreation. Sunbelt states aggressively—and successfully—sought foreign investment and drew industry with lower taxes and heating bills as well as right-to-work laws outlawing closed shops. The development of air-conditioning was also crucial, making bearable even the hottest summer days. Houston, Phoenix, Los Angeles, San Diego, Dallas, and Miami all boomed, and by 1963 California was the most populous state in America.

Cold War military and aerospace spending created a need for highly educated scientists, engineers, and other white-collar professionals. By the early 1960s, universities and academic researchers received several billion dollars in space program research funding alone. Their research transformed American industry and society with inventions like the transistor in the 1950s, which sparked the computer revolution, and everyday consumer goods like the transistor radio.

By the 1950s, America was becoming a middle-class nation. Unionized blue-collar workers gained

A NEW MIDDLE-CLASS CULTURE

middle-class incomes, and veterans with GI Bill college educations swelled the growing managerial and professional class. In 1956, for the first time, the United States had more white-collar workers than blue-collar workers, and most families—60 percent—had incomes in the middle-class range (approximately $3,000 to $9,000 a year in the mid-1950s).

Paradoxically, the strength of unions in the postwar era contributed to a decline in working-class identity: as large numbers of blue-collar workers participated in suburban middle-class culture, the lines separating working class and middle class seemed less important. Increasingly, a family's standard of living mattered more than what sort of work made the

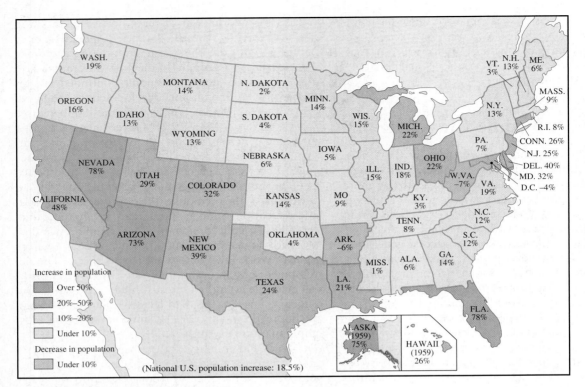

Map 29.1   Rise of the Sunbelt, 1950–1960

The years after the Second World War saw a continuation of the migration of Americans to the Sunbelt states of the Southwest and the West Coast.

standard of living possible. Although people of color did not share equally in America's postwar prosperity, many middle-income African Americans, Latinos, and Asian Americans did participate in middle-class culture.

The emergence of a national middle-class culture was possible, in part, because America's population

WHITENESS AND NATIONAL CULTURE

was more homogeneous in the 1950s than before or since. In the nineteenth and early twentieth centuries, the United States had restricted or prohibited immigration from Asia, Africa, and Latin America while accepting millions of Europeans to America's shores. This large-scale European immigration was shut off in the 1920s, so that by 1960, only 5.7 percent of Americans were foreign born (compared with approximately 15 percent in 1910 and 10 percent in 2000). In 1950, 88 percent of Americans were of Eu-

ropean ancestry (compared with 69 percent in 2000), 10 percent of the population was African American, 2 percent was Hispanic, and Native Americans and Asian Americans each accounted for about one-fifth of 1 percent.

Although the new suburbs were peopled mostly by white families, these suburbs were more diverse than the communities from which their residents had come. America's small towns and urban ethnic enclaves were homogeneous and intolerant of challenges to traditional ways. In the suburbs, paradoxically, many people encountered different customs and beliefs, but new suburbanites frequently adopted the norms of the developing national middle class.

Because many white Americans were new to the middle class, they were uncertain about what was ex-

TELEVISION

pected of them and turned to the national mass media for answers.

Women's magazines helped housewives replace the ethnic and regional dishes with "American" recipes created from national brand-name products—such as casseroles made with Campbell's cream of mushroom soup. Television also fostered America's shared national culture. Although televisions cost about $300—the equivalent of $2,000 today—almost half of American homes had them by 1953, and ownership rose to 90 percent by 1960.

On television, suburban families such as the Andersons (*Father Knows Best*) and the Cleavers (*Leave It to Beaver*) ate at a properly set dining room table. June Cleaver did housework in carefully ironed dresses. Every crisis was resolved through paternal wisdom. These popular family situation comedies reinforced the suburban middle-class ideal many American families sought.

The "middle-classness" of television programming was due in part to advertising. Corporations buying airtime did not want to offend potential consumers. Thus, while African American musician Nat King Cole drew millions of viewers to his NBC show, it could not find a sponsor because companies feared that being linked to a black performer would hurt sales among whites, especially in the South. Since African Americans made up only about 10 percent of the population and often had little disposable income, they did not influence advertising decisions. The *Nat King Cole Show* was canceled within a year; it was a decade before the networks again anchored a show around a black performer.

With only three TV networks available—ABC, CBS, and NBC—at any one time 70 percent or more of all viewers might be watching the same popular program. (In the early twenty-first century, the most popular shows might attract 12 percent of the viewing audience.) Television gave Americans a shared set of experiences and helped create a homogeneous, white-focused, middle-class culture.

Americans also found common ground in a new abundance of consumer goods. After decades of

CONSUMER CULTURE

scarcity, Americans had a dazzling array of consumer goods from which to choose, and even utilitarian objects got two-tone paint jobs or rocket-ship details. People used consumer choices to express personal identities and claim status. Cars, more than anything else, embodied consumer fantasies. Expensive Cadillacs were the

first to develop tailfins, soon added to midrange Chevys, Fords, and Plymouths. Americans spent $65 billion on automobiles in 1955—equivalent to almost 20 percent of the gross national product. To pay for cars, suburban houses, and modern appliances, consumer debt rose from $5.7 billion in 1945 to $58 billion in 1961.

The uncertainties of the nuclear age likely contributed to the resurgence of religion, as church

RELIGION

membership doubled (primarily in mainline Christian churches) between the end of World War II and the early 1960s. The media played a role, as preachers such as Billy Graham created national congregations from television audiences, preaching a message that combined salvation with Cold War patriotism. Local churches and synagogues offered new suburbanites a sense of community, celebrating life's rituals and supporting the sick and bereaved, who were often far from their extended families and old communities.

Men, Women, and Youth at Midcentury

*H*aving survived the Great Depression and a world war, many Americans pursued "the good life" and sought refuge from the Cold War through homes and families. They saw their familial commitment as an expression of faith in the future. Yet despite the satisfactions many Americans found in family life, both men and women felt limited by social pressures to conform to narrowly defined gender roles.

During the 1950s, few Americans remained single, and most people married very young. By 1959,

MARRIAGE AND FAMILIES

almost half of American brides were younger than nineteen; their husbands were usually only a year or so older. Early marriage was endorsed by experts and approved by most parents, in part to prevent premarital sex. As Americans accepted psychotherapeutic insights, they worried not only that premarital sex might leave the young woman pregnant but that the experience could damage her psychologically so she would never adjust to "normal" marital relations. One popular women's magazine argued, "When two people are ready for sexual intercourse at the fully human level they are ready for marriage. . . . And society has no right to stand in their way."

Many young couples found freedom from parental authority by marrying. Most newlyweds quickly had babies—an average of three—completing their families in their twenties. Birth control (condoms and diaphragms) was widely available and used, as couples planned the size of their families. Two children were the American ideal in 1940; by 1960, most couples wanted four. About 88 percent of children under age eighteen lived with two parents (in 2000, the figure was 69 percent), and fewer were born outside marriage; only 3.9 percent of births were to unmarried women in 1950 (compared with more than one-third of births in 2000). As late as 1960, there were only 9 divorces per 1,000 married couples.

In fifties families, men and women usually adopted distinct roles, with male breadwinners and female homemakers. Contemporary commentators insisted this was based on essential differences between the sexes. In fact, the economic structure and cultural values of postwar America determined the choices available to men and women.

GENDER ROLES IN FIFTIES FAMILIES

During the 1950s, it was possible for many families to live in modest middle-class comfort on one (male) salary. Good childcare was rarely available, and fewer families lived close to relatives. Childcare experts, including Dr. Spock, whose 1946 *Baby and Child Care* sold millions of copies, insisted that a mother's full-time attention was necessary to her child's well-being. Because of hiring discrimination, women who could afford to stay home often didn't find the jobs available to them attractive enough to justify juggling cooking and housework too. Instead, America's schools and religious institutions benefited immensely from women's volunteer labor.

Suburban domesticity left many women feeling isolated from the larger world their husbands inhabited. The popular belief that one should find complete emotional satisfaction in private life put unrealistic pressures on marriages. And despite near-universal celebration of women's domestic roles, many women were manag-

WOMEN AND WORK

ing both job and family responsibilities (see Figure 29.2). Twice as many women were employed in 1960 as in 1940, including 39 percent of women with children between the ages of six and seventeen. Most worked part time for a specific family goal, like a new car or college tuition. These jobs were in service to the family, not a means to independence from it.

Figure 29.2   Marital Distribution of the Female Labor Force, 1944–1970

The composition of the female labor force changed dramatically from 1944 to 1970. In 1944, 41 percent of women in the labor force were single; in 1970, only 22 percent were single. During the same years, the percentage of the female labor force who had a husband in the home jumped from 34 to 59. The percentage who were widowed or divorced remained about the same from 1944 to 1970.   (Source: Adapted from U.S. Bureau of the Census, *Historical Statistics of the United States, Colonial Times to 1970,* Bicentennial Edition [Washington, D.C.: U.S. Government Printing Office, 1975], p. 133.)

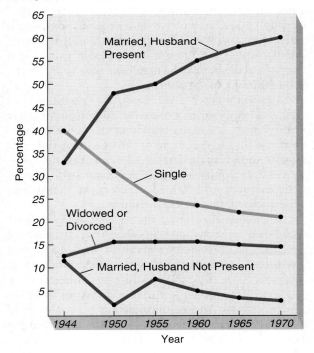

Women nonetheless faced discrimination in the work force. Want ads were divided into "Help Wanted—Male" and "Help Wanted—Female" categories. Female full-time workers earned, on average, 60 percent of what men were paid and were restricted to lower-paid "female" fields: maids, secretaries, teachers, and nurses. A popular book, *Modern Woman: The Lost Sex,* claimed that ambitious women and "feminists" suffered from "penis envy." College psychology textbooks warned women not to "compete" with men, and magazine articles described "career women" as a "third sex." Medical schools limited female admissions to 5 percent of each class. In 1960 less than 4 percent of lawyers and judges were female. When future Supreme Court Justice Ruth Bader Ginsburg graduated at the top of her Columbia Law School class in 1959, she could not find a job.

Academics and mass media critics devoted equal attention to the plight of the American male. American men faced a "crisis of masculinity," proclaimed the nation's mass-circulation magazines. In a best-selling book, sociologist William H. Whyte explained that postwar corporate employees had become "organization men," succeeding through cooperation and conformity, not through initiative and risk. And experts insisted women's "natural" desire for security and comfort was stifling men's natural instincts for adventure. Men who did not conform to standards of male responsibility—husband, father, breadwinner—were also condemned. Some linked concerns about masculinity to the Cold War, arguing that unless men recovered masculinity diminished by white-collar work or a family-centered existence, the nation's future was at risk.

"THE CRISIS OF MASCULINITY"

Sexuality was complicated terrain in postwar America. Only heterosexual intercourse within marriage was socially acceptable. Women who became pregnant outside marriage were often ostracized by friends and family and expelled from school. Homosexuality was grounds for job dismissal, expulsion from college, even jail. In his works on human sexuality, *Sexual Behavior in the Human Male* (1948) and *Sexual Behavior in the Human Female* (1953), Dr. Alfred Kinsey, director of the Institute for Sex Research at Indiana University, noted that while 80 percent of his female sample disapproved of premarital

SEXUALITY

sex, half of them had had premarital sex. He also reported that 37 percent of American men had had "some homosexual experience." The *Chicago Tribune* called him a "menace to society." While Kinsey's samples did not provide a complete picture of American sexual behavior, they told many Americans they were not alone in breaking certain rules.

Another challenge to sexual norms came when Hugh Hefner launched *Playboy* magazine in 1953. Within three years, it had a circulation of 1 million. Hefner saw *Playboy* as an attack on America's "ferocious anti-sexuality" and his nude "playmates" as a means for men to combat the increasingly "blurred distinctions between the sexes" in suburban culture.

The sheer numbers of "baby boom" youth made them a force in American society. As this group moved from childhood to youth, a distinct youth culture developed. Its customs and rituals were created within peer groups and were shaped by national media—teen magazines, movies, radio, advertising, music—targeted toward this huge potential audience. America's corporations quickly learned the power of youth, as children's fads launched multimillion-dollar industries. Mr. Potato Head, probably the first toy advertised on television, had $4 million in sales in 1952. In the mid-1950s, when Walt Disney's television show *Disneyland* featured Davy Crockett, "King of the Wild Frontier," every child in America *had* to have a coonskin cap. As these baby boom children grew up, their buying power shaped American popular culture.

YOUTH CULTURE

By 1960, America's 18 million teenagers were spending $10 billion a year. Seventy-two percent of movie tickets in the 1950s were sold to teenagers, and Hollywood created a flood of teen films, ranging from forgettable B-movies to controversial films such as James Dean's *Rebel Without a Cause*. Adults worried about teens' copying the delinquency romanticized by the film, and teenage boys did emulate Dean's rebellious look. The film, however, blamed parents for teenage confusion, drawing heavily on popular psychological theories about sexuality and the "crisis of masculinity."

Nothing defined youth culture as much as its music. Young Americans were electrified by the driving energy of Bill Haley and the Comets, Chuck Berry, Little Richard, and Buddy Holly. Elvis Presley's 1956 appearance on TV's *Ed Sullivan Show* touched off a

Barbie

Barbie, the "All-American Doll," is—like many Americans—an immigrant. Though introduced in 1959 by the American toy company Mattel, Barbie's origins lie in Germany, where she was called Lilli.

The German Lilli doll was based on a character that cartoonist Reinhard Beuthien drew to fill space in the June 24, 1952, edition of the German tabloid *Das Bild.* Lilli was so popular that she became a regular feature. Soon Lilli appeared in three-dimensional form as *Bild* Lilli, an eleven-and-a-half-inch-tall blonde doll—with the figure Barbie would make famous (equivalent to 39-21-31 in human proportions). Dressed in a variety of sexy outfits, Lilli was sold in tobacco shops and bars as a "novelty gift" for men, not girls.

Lilli came to America with Ruth Handler, one of the founders of the Mattel toy corporation. When she glimpsed Lilli while vacationing in Europe, Handler bought three—one for her daughter Barbara, after whom Lilli would be renamed. Mattel bought the rights to Lilli (the doll and the cartoon, which Mattel quietly retired) and unveiled "Barbie" in March 1959. Despite mothers' hesitations about a doll that looked like Barbie, within the year Mattel had sold 351,000 Barbies at $3 each (or about $17 in 2000 dollars). The billionth Barbie was sold in 1997.

In 2002 labor-rights groups called for a boycott of Barbie. They cited studies showing that half of all Barbies are made by exploited young women in mainland China: of the $10 retail cost of an average Barbie, Chinese factories receive only 35 cents to cover their costs, including labor. But the eleven-and-a-half-inch doll remains popular, selling in over 150 countries. Today the average American girl has ten Barbies—and the typical German girl owns five.

Before Barbie became an American child's toy, she was "Lilli," a German sex symbol. Mattel transformed the doll into a wholesome American teenager with a new wardrobe to match. (Spielzeug Museum, Munich)

frenzy of teen adulation—and a flood of letters from parents scandalized by his "gyrations." Though few white musicians acknowledged it, the roots of rock 'n' roll lay in African American rhythm and blues. The raw energy and sometimes sexually suggestive lyrics of early rock music faded as the music industry sought white performers, such as Pat Boone, to do blander, more acceptable "cover" versions of music by black artists.

The distinct youth culture of the 1950s made many adults uneasy. Parents worried that "going steady" might encourage teens to "go too far" sexually. Juvenile delinquency was a major concern. Crime rates for young people had risen dramatically after World War II, but much juvenile delinquency was "status" crimes (activities that were criminal only because of the person's age): curfew violations, sexual experimentation, and underage drinking. Congress held extensive hearings on juvenile delinquency, with experts testifying to the corrupting power of youth-oriented popular culture, comic books in particular. Most youthful behavior, however, fit squarely into the consumer culture that youth shared with their parents.

The Limits of the Middle-Class Nation

*D*uring the 1950s, America's popular culture and mass media celebrated new opportunities. But influential critics condemned middle-class culture as a wasteland of conformity, homogeneity, and ugly consumerism.

Some of the most popular fiction of the postwar era, such as J. D. Salinger's *The Catcher in the Rye* (1951) and Norman Mailer's *The Naked and the Dead* (1948), was profoundly critical of American society, and Americans devoured them. They even made bestsellers of difficult academic works such as David Riesman's *The Lonely Crowd* (1950) and William H. Whyte's *The Organization Man* (1955), both of which criticized conformity in American life. Versions of these critiques also appeared in mass-circulation magazines like *The Ladies' Home Journal* and *Reader's Digest*. Steeped in such cultural criticism, many Americans under-

CRITICS OF CONFORMITY

stood *Invasion of the Body Snatchers*—a 1956 film in which zombie-like aliens grown in pods gradually replace a town's human inhabitants—as criticism of the bland homogeneity of postwar culture.

Americans did lose some autonomy at work as large corporations replaced smaller businesses; they experienced the homogenizing force of mass production and a national consumer culture; they saw distinctions among ethnic groups and socioeconomic classes decline in importance. Critics were often elitist and antidemocratic, seeing only bland conformity and sterility in the emerging middle-class suburban culture. However, identical houses did not produce identical souls; instead, inexpensive suburban housing provided healthier, and perhaps happier, lives to millions who had grown up in dank, dark tenements or ramshackle farmhouses without indoor plumbing.

The new consumer culture encouraged wastefulness and harmed the environment. *Business Week* noted that corporations need not rely on "planned obsolescence," purposely designing a product to wear out. Americans replaced products because they were "out of date," not because they didn't work; hence, automakers revamped designs annually. By the 1960s the United States, with only 5 percent of the world's population, consumed more than one-third of the world's goods and services.

ENVIRONMENTAL DEGRADATION

The rapid economic growth that made the middle-class consumer culture possible exacted environmental costs. Steel mills, coal-powered generators, and car engines burning lead-based gasoline polluted the atmosphere and imperiled people's health. As suburbs spread farther from jobs and neighborhoods were built without public transportation, Americans relied on private automobiles, consuming the nonrenewable resources of oil and gasoline and filling cities and suburbs with smog. Water was diverted from lakes and rivers to service burgeoning Sunbelt cities, including the swimming pools and golf courses that dotted parched Arizona and southern California.

Defense contractors and farmers were among the country's worst polluters. Refuse from nuclear weapons facilities at Hanford, Washington, and at Colorado's Rocky Flats arsenal poisoned soil and water resources. Agriculture used pesticides and other chemicals. DDT, a chemical used during the war to kill mosquitoes and lice on Pacific islands, was used widely in the United States until 1962, when wildlife biologist Rachel Carson specifically indicted DDT for the deaths of mammals, birds, and fish in her best-selling book *Silent Spring*.

The nation was moving toward a postindustrial economy in which providing goods and services to consumers was more important than manufacturing goods. Therefore, although union members prospered during the 1950s, union membership grew slowly—as most new jobs were created in the union-resistant white-collar service trades. Technological advances increased productivity and also pushed people from relatively well-paid blue-collar jobs into the growing and less-well-paid service sector.

Even as fewer Americans were excluded because of ethnic identities, racial discrimination remained

CONTINUING RACISM

largely unchallenged in most of 1950s America. Suburbs, both North and South, were almost always racially segregated. Many white Americans had little or no contact in their daily lives with people of different races, partly because the relatively small populations of nonwhite Americans were not equally dispersed nationwide. In 1960 there were 68 people of Chinese descent and 519 African Americans in Vermont; 181 Native Americans lived in West Virginia; Mississippi had just 178 Japanese American residents. Most white Americans in the 1950s, especially those outside the South, gave little thought to race. Instead, they regarded the emerging middle-class culture not as "white," but as "American," marginalizing people of color in image as in reality.

In an age of abundance, more than one in five Americans still lived in poverty. One-fifth of the poor were people of color, including almost half of the nation's African American population and more than half of all Native Americans. Two-thirds lived in households headed by a person with an eighth-grade education or less, one-fourth in households headed by a single woman. More than one-third were under age eighteen. One-fourth were over age sixty-five; Social Security payments helped, but many retirees were not yet covered, and in the years before Medicare, medical costs drove many older Americans into poverty.

As millions of Americans (most of them white) settled in the suburbs, the poor concentrated in inner

POVERTY IN AN AGE OF ABUNDANCE

cities. African American migrants were joined by poor whites from the southern Appalachians, moving to Chicago, Cincinnati, Baltimore, and Detroit. Latin Americans arrived in growing numbers from Mexico, the Dominican Republic, Colombia, Ecuador, and Cuba. According to the 1960 census, over a half-million Mexican Americans had migrated to the Los Angeles–Long Beach area since 1940. And New York City's Puerto Rican population exploded from 70,000 in 1940 to 613,000 in 1960.

Because of the strong economy, many newcomers gained the higher standard of living they sought. But discrimination limited their advances, and they endured crowded and decrepit housing and poor schools. In addition, the federal programs that helped middle-class Americans sometimes made the lives of the poor worse. For example, the National Housing Act of 1949, passed to make available "a decent home . . . for every American family," provided for "urban redevelopment." Redevelopment meant slum clearance, replacing the only housing many poor people had with high-rise buildings, parking lots, or highways.

The growth of large "agribusinesses" pushed more tenant farmers and small farmers off the land. From 1945 to 1961 the nation's farm population declined from 24.4 million to 14.8 million. When the harvesting of cotton in the South was mechanized in the 1940s and 1950s, more than 4 million people were displaced. Southern tobacco growers dismissed tenant farmers, bought tractors to plow the land, and hired migratory workers. In the West and Southwest, Mexican citizens served as cheap migrant labor under the *bracero* program. Almost 1 million Mexican workers came legally to the United States in 1959. Entire families labored, enduring conditions little better than in the Great Depression of the 1930s.

Native Americans were America's poorest people, with an average annual income barely half that of the poverty level. Conditions were worsened by "termination," a federal policy implemented during the Eisenhower administration. "Termination" reversed the Indian Reorganization Act of 1934, allowing Indians to terminate their tribal status and so remove reservation lands from federal protection prohibiting their sale. Sixty-one tribes were terminated between 1954 and 1960. Termination could take place only with a tribe's agreement, but pressure was sometimes intense, especially when reservation land was rich in natural resources. Enticed by cash payments, almost four-fifths of the Klamaths of Oregon voted to sell their shares of the forest land. Many Indians left reservation land for the city. By the time termination ceased in the 1960s, observers compared the situation of Native Americans to the devastation of their forebears in the nineteenth century.

Online Study Center **Improve Your Grade**

Interactive Map: American Indian Reservations

Overall, Americans enjoyed relative prosperity in the postwar era. But those who made it to the comfortable middle class often ignored the plight of those left behind. It would be their children—the generation of the baby boom—who would see racism, poverty, and the self-satisfaction of postwar suburban culture as a failure of American ideals.

Summary *Online Study Center* **ACE the Test**

*a*s the economic depression and world war receded, people married and had children in record numbers. Millions of veterans used the GI Bill to attend college, buy homes, and start businesses. Although American leaders feared the nation would lapse into economic depression after wartime government spending ended, consumer spending fueled growth. Sustained economic growth lifted a majority of Americans into an expanding middle class.

The Cold War presidencies of Truman and Eisenhower focused more on international relations than on domestic politics. Within the United States, Cold War fears provoked an extreme anticommunism that stifled political dissent and diminished Americans' civil liberties and freedoms.

The continuing African American struggle for civil rights drew national attention during the Montgomery bus boycott. African Americans won victories in the Supreme Court, including the landmark *Brown v. Board of Education*. Truman and Eisenhower used federal power to guarantee the rights of black Americans as a national civil rights movement began to coalesce.

Despite continued racial divisions, the United States became a more inclusive nation in the 1950s as a majority of Americans participated in a national, consumer-oriented, middle-class culture. This culture largely ignored the poverty in the nation's cities and rural areas. For the growing number in the middle class, the American Dream seemed a reality.

LEGACY FOR A PEOPLE AND A NATION
The Pledge of Allegiance

The Pledge of Allegiance Americans recite today was shaped by the Cold War. Congress added the phrase "under God" to the pledge in 1954 to emphasize the difference between the God-fearing United States and the "godless communists" of the Soviet Union.

The Pledge of Allegiance was not always an important part of American public life. The original version was written in 1892 by Francis Bellamy, editor of *The Youth's Companion*, to commemorate the four hundredth anniversary of Columbus's arrival in North America. In 1942 Congress officially adopted a revised version as an act of wartime patriotism. The Supreme Court ruled in 1943, however, that schoolchildren could not be forced to say the "Pledge to the Flag."

During the Cold War years, the pledge became an increasingly important symbol of U.S. loyalty. Cold War fears fueled a campaign by the Knights of Columbus, a Catholic men's service organization, to include "under God" in the pledge. Supporting the bill, President Eisenhower proclaimed that

> in this way we shall constantly strengthen those spiritual weapons which forever will be our country's most powerful resource in peace and war. From this day forward, the millions of our schoolchildren will daily proclaim in every city and town, every village

and every rural schoolhouse, the dedication of our nation and our people to the Almighty.

Some Americans, citing the doctrine of separation of church and state, have protested including "under God." In June 2002, the Ninth District Court (covering California and eight other western states) sparked a controversy by ruling that the 1954 version of the pledge was unconstitutional because it conveyed "state endorsement" of a religious belief. Questions about the proper role of religion in American life remain controversial, a legacy for a people and a nation becoming more diverse in the twenty-first century.

THE TUMULTUOUS SIXTIES 1960–1968

*I*t was late, and Ezell Blair had an exam the next day. But he and friends in the dormitory sat talking—as they often did—about injustice, about living in a nation that proclaimed equality for all but denied full citizenship to some because of the color of their skin. They were complaining about all the do-nothing adults, condemning the black community of Greensboro, when Franklin McCain said, "It's time to fish or cut bait." Joe McNeil and McCain's roommate, David Richmond, agreed they should do something. Blair hesitated. "I was thinking about my grades," he said later, just "trying to deal with that architecture and engineering course I was taking."

But the next day, February 1, 1960, after their classes at North Carolina Agricultural and Technical College, the four freshmen walked into town. At the F. W. Woolworth's on South Elm Street, one of the most profitable stores in the national chain, each bought a few small things. Then, nervously, they sat down at the lunch counter and tried to order coffee. These seventeen- and eighteen-year-olds were prepared to be arrested, even physically attacked. The counter help just ignored them, until one worker said, "We don't serve colored here." An elderly white woman told the boys how proud she was of them. Still nothing happened. The store closed; the manager turned out the lights. After forty-five minutes, the four men who had begun the sit-in movement left.

The next day they returned with twenty fellow students. By February 3, sixty-three of the sixty-five seats were taken. On February 4, the sit-in spread to the S. H. Kress store across the street. By February 7, there were sit-ins in Winston-Salem; by February 8, in Charlotte; by February 9, in Raleigh. By the third week in February, students were picketing Woolworth's stores in the North. On July 26, 1960, F. W. Woolworth's ended segregation in all its stores.

The sit-in at the Greensboro Woolworth's signaled the beginning of a decade of public activism as millions of Americans—many of them young—marched for civil rights or against the war in Vietnam. Passion over contemporary issues

Kennedy and the Cold War

Marching for Freedom

Liberalism and the Great Society

Johnson and Vietnam

A Nation Divided

1968

LINKS TO THE WORLD
The British Invasion

LEGACY FOR A PEOPLE AND A NATION
The Immigration Act of 1965

Online Study Center

This icon will direct you to interactive map and primary source activities on the website
http://college.hmco.com/pic/nortonbrief7e

CHRONOLOGY

1960 • Sit-ins begin in Greensboro
 • Birth-control pill approved for contraceptive use
 • John F. Kennedy elected president
 • Young Americans for Freedom write Sharon Statement
 • Freedom Rides protest segregation in transportation

1962 • Students for a Democratic Society issues Port Huron Statement
 • Cuban missile crisis courts nuclear war

1963 • Civil rights March on Washington for Jobs and Freedom draws more than 250,000
 • John F. Kennedy assassinated; Lyndon B. Johnson becomes president

1964 • Civil Rights Act outlaws discrimination in hiring and public accommodation
 • Race riots break out in first of the "long, hot summers"
 • Free Speech Movement begins at UC Berkeley
 • Lyndon B. Johnson elected president

1965 • Lyndon Johnson launches Great Society programs
 • Voting Rights Act outlaws practices that prevent most African Americans from voting in southern states
 • Immigration and Nationality Act lowers barriers to immigration from Asia and Latin America
 • Malcolm X assassinated
 • Watts riot leaves thirty-four dead

1967 • Summer of Love in San Francisco's Haight-Ashbury district
 • Race riots erupt in Newark, Detroit, and other cities

1968 • Tet Offensive causes fear of losing war in Vietnam
 • Martin Luther King Jr. assassinated
 • Robert Kennedy assassinated
 • Antiwar protests escalate
 • Violence erupts at Democratic National Convention
 • Richard Nixon elected president

revitalized democracy—and threatened to tear the nation apart.

John F. Kennedy, the nation's youngest president, told Americans as he took office in 1961: "The torch has been passed to a new generation." But Kennedy had only modest success implementing his domestic agenda. In his third year as president, however, Kennedy offered greater support for civil rights and proposed more ambitious domestic policies. When he was assassinated in November 1963, his death seemed to many the end of an era of hope.

Lyndon Johnson, Kennedy's successor, summoned the memory of the martyred president to launch an ambitious program of civil rights and other liberal legislation. Calling his vision the Great Society, John-

son intended to use federal power to eliminate poverty and guarantee equal rights to all Americans.

Despite liberal triumphs, social tensions escalated during the mid-1960s. A revitalized conservative movement emerged, and Franklin Roosevelt's old New Deal coalition fractured as white southerners abandoned the Democratic Party. Angry that discrimination and poverty persisted even with landmark civil rights laws, many African Americans, especially in the North, rioted. White youth culture increasingly rejected the values and lifestyle of its elders, creating "the generation gap."

Meanwhile, after the 1962 Cuban missile crisis brought the Soviet Union and the United States close to nuclear disaster, Kennedy and Khrushchev deescalated tensions in 1963 and lessened Cold War pressures in Europe. Everywhere else, however, the superpowers competed frantically. Throughout the 1960s, the United States tried a variety of approaches—including foreign aid, CIA covert actions, military assaults, cultural penetration, economic sanctions, and diplomacy—to win the Cold War. In Vietnam, Kennedy expanded U.S. involvement significantly. Johnson increased U.S. troops to more than half a million in 1968.

By 1968, the Vietnam War divided Americans and undermined Johnson's Great Society. With the assassinations that spring of Martin Luther King Jr. and Robert Kennedy, two of America's brightest leaders, cities in flames, and tanks on Chicago streets in August, the fate of the nation hung in the balance. ■

Kennedy and the Cold War

*Y*oung, handsome, and intellectually inquisitive, John F. Kennedy brought wit and sophistication to the White House. His Irish American grandfather had been mayor of Boston, and his millionaire father, Joseph P. Kennedy, served as ambassador to Great Britain. In 1946 the young Kennedy returned from the Second World War a naval hero (the boat he commanded was sunk by a Japanese destroyer in 1943, and Kennedy saved his crew) and campaigned to represent Boston in the U.S. House of Representatives. He served three terms in the House and in 1952 was elected to the Senate.

As a Democrat, Kennedy inherited the New Deal commitment to America's social welfare system. He

JOHN
FITZGERALD
KENNEDY

generally voted with the pro-labor sentiments of his low-income, blue-collar constituents, but avoided controversial issues such as civil rights. Kennedy won a Pulitzer Prize for his *Profiles in Courage* (1956), a study of principled politicians, but he shaded the truth in claiming sole authorship, when it was written largely by aide Theodore Sorensen (from over a hundred pages of notes dictated by Kennedy). In foreign pol-

icy, Senator Kennedy endorsed the Cold War policy of containment. Despite an unimpressive legislative record, he enjoyed an enthusiastic following, especially after his landslide Senate reelection in 1958.

Kennedy cultivated an image as a happy and healthy family man. But he was a chronic womanizer, even after his 1953 marriage to Jacqueline Bouvier. As a child he had almost died of scarlet fever and developed severe back problems, which worsened during World War II. After the war, Kennedy was diagnosed with Addison's disease, an adrenalin deficiency causing chronic pain that required daily cortisone injections. As president he would require plenty of bed rest and frequent therapeutic swims in the White House pool.

Kennedy beat Republican Richard Nixon in 1960 by a narrow 118,000 votes out of nearly 69 million.

ELECTION
OF 1960

Kennedy achieved mixed success in the South, but ran well in the Northeast and Midwest. His Roman Catholic faith hurt him in states where voters feared he would take direction from the pope, but helped in states with large Catholic populations. As the sitting vice president, Nixon had to answer for sagging economic figures and the Soviet downing of a U-2 spy plane (see Chapter 28). Perhaps worse, when asked to list Nixon's significant decisions as vice president, Eisenhower replied, "If you give me a week, I might think of one."

The new president surrounded himself with mostly young advisers; the writer David Halberstam called them "the best and the brightest." Secretary of Defense Robert McNamara (age forty-four) had been an assistant professor at Harvard at twenty-four and later the whiz-kid president of the Ford Motor Company. Kennedy's special assistant for national security affairs, McGeorge Bundy (age forty-one), had become a Harvard dean at thirty-four with only a bachelor's degree. Secretary of State Dean Rusk, at fifty-two the oldest, had been a Rhodes scholar in his youth. Kennedy was only forty-three, and his brother Robert, the attorney general, was thirty-five.

Kennedy gave top priority to the Cold War. In the campaign he accused Eisenhower of an unimaginative foreign policy that failed to reduce the threat of nuclear war with the Soviet Union and of weakening America's standing in the Third World.

Once in office, Kennedy understood sooner than his advisers the limits of American power abroad.

NATION
BUILDING AND
COUNTER-
INSURGENCY

More than his predecessor, he proved willing to initiate dialogue with the Soviets, sometimes using his brother Robert as a secret channel to Moscow. Yet Kennedy also sought victory in the Cold War. After Soviet leader Nikita Khrushchev endorsed "wars of national liberation" such as the one in Vietnam, Kennedy called for "peaceful revolution" based on nation building. The administration helped developing nations with aid to improve agriculture, transportation, and communications. Kennedy oversaw the creation of the multibillion-dollar Alliance for Progress in 1961 to spur economic development in Latin America. That year, too, he created the Peace Corps, dispatching American teachers, agricultural specialists, and health workers, many of them recent graduates, to assist in developing nations.

Cynics then and later dismissed the Alliance and Peace Corps as Kennedy's Cold War tools for countering anti-Americanism and defeating communism in the developing world. True enough, but they were also humanitarian. As historian Elizabeth Cobbs Hoffman has written, "the Peace Corps broached an age-old dilemma of U.S. foreign policy: how to reconcile the imperatives and temptations of power politics with the ideals of freedom and self-determination for all nations."

Although Kennedy and his aides were supportive of social revolution in the Third World, they could not accept communist involvement in these uprisings. Therefore, the administration also relied on counter-insurgency to defeat revolutionaries who challenged pro-American Third World governments. American military and technical advisers trained native troops and police to quell unrest.

The Alliance for Progress was only partly successful; infant mortality rates improved, but Latin American economies registered unimpressive growth, and class divisions widened, exacerbating political unrest. Although many foreign peoples welcomed U.S. economic assistance and American material culture, they resented meddling by outsiders. And because aid was usually funneled through a self-interested elite, it often never reached the poor. To people who preferred the quick fix of a managed economy, moreover, the American emphasis on private enterprise seemed inappropriate.

The administration's first year witnessed little movement on controlling the nuclear arms race or

SOVIET-
AMERICAN
TENSIONS

even getting a superpower ban on testing nuclear weapons in the atmosphere or underground. Kennedy and Soviet leader Nikita Khrushchev could not agree on these issues or other preconditions for peace at a summit in Vienna in June 1961. Instead, both superpowers continued testing and accelerated their arms production. In 1961 the U.S. military budget shot up 15 percent; by mid-1964, U.S. nuclear weapons had increased by 150 percent. Government advice to citizens to build fallout shelters in their backyards intensified public fear of devastating war.

If war occurred, many expected Berlin would be the proximate cause. In mid-1961 Khrushchev demanded an end to Western occupation of West Berlin and a reunification of East and West Germany. Kennedy replied that the United States would honor its commitment to West Germany. In August the Soviets, at the urging of the East German regime, erected a concrete and barbed-wire barricade to halt the exodus of East Germans into the more prosperous and politically free West Berlin. The Berlin Wall inspired protests throughout the noncommunist world, but Kennedy privately sighed that "a wall is a hell of a lot better than a war."

Kennedy knew that Khrushchev would continue to press elsewhere, and he was particularly rankled

BAY OF PIGS
INVASION

by growing Soviet assistance to Fidel Castro's Cuban government. The Eisenhower administration had contested the Cuban revolution and bequeathed to Kennedy a partially developed CIA plan to overthrow Castro (see Chapter 28): CIA-trained Cuban exiles would land and secure a beachhead; the Cuban people would rise up against Castro and welcome a new U.S.-backed government.

The attack took place on April 17, 1961, as twelve hundred exiles landed at the swampy Bay of Pigs in Cuba. Instead of discontented Cubans, they were greeted by Castro's loyal troops and were quickly captured. Kennedy tried to keep U.S. participation in the operation hidden, but the CIA's role swiftly became public. Anti-American sentiments swept the region. Castro, concluding that the United States might launch another invasion, looked increasingly toward the Soviet Union for military and economic assistance.

Embarrassed, Kennedy vowed to bring Castro down. The CIA soon hatched a project called Operation Mongoose to disrupt the island's trade, support raids on Cuba from Miami, and plot to kill Castro. The agency's assassination schemes included providing Castro with cigars laced with explosives and deadly poison. The United States also tightened its economic blockade and undertook military maneuvers in the Caribbean. The Joint Chiefs of Staff sketched plans to spark a rebellion in Cuba that would be followed by an invasion of U.S. troops.

Both Castro and Khrushchev believed an invasion was coming, which partly explains the Soviet leader's risky decision in 1962 to secretly deploy nuclear missiles in Cuba as a deterrent. But Khrushchev also hoped the move would improve the Soviet position in the nuclear balance of power and force Kennedy to finally resolve the German problem. Khrushchev worried that Washington might provide West Germany with nuclear weapons, and believed he could prevent it by putting Soviet missiles just 90 miles off the coast of Florida. The world soon faced a frightening example of brinkmanship.

CUBAN MISSILE CRISIS

In mid-October 1962 a U-2 plane flying over Cuba photographed the missile sites. The president immediately organized a special executive committee of advisers to find a way to force the missiles and their nuclear warheads out of Cuba. Options considered ranged from full-scale invasion to limited bombing to quiet diplomacy. Defense Secretary McNamara proposed a solution acceptable to the president: a naval quarantine of Cuba.

Kennedy addressed the nation on October 22, demanding that the Soviets retreat. U.S. warships began crisscrossing the Caribbean, while B-52s with nuclear bombs took to the skies. Khrushchev agreed to withdraw the missiles if the United States pledged never to attack Cuba and promised to remove American Jupiter missiles aimed at the Soviet Union from Turkey. For several days, the world teetered on the brink of disaster. Then, on October 28, came a compromise: the United States agreed to Soviet demands in exchange for the withdrawal of Soviet offensive forces from Cuba. Fearing Castro might make matters worse, Khrushchev settled without consulting the Cubans.

Many observers then and later called it Kennedy's finest hour, although critics claimed Kennedy may have triggered the crisis with his anti-Cuban projects. Either way, the Cuban missile crisis was a watershed in the Soviet-American relationship. Both Kennedy and Khrushchev acted with greater prudence in its aftermath, taking steps toward improved relations. In August 1963 the adversaries signed a treaty banning nuclear tests in the atmosphere, the oceans, and outer space. They also installed a coded wire-telegraph "hot line" staffed around the clock to allow near-instant communication between the capitals. Both sides refrained from further confrontation in Berlin.

Together, these small steps began to build mutual trust. By the autumn of 1963, the Cold War in Europe was drawing to a close, as both sides accepted the status quo of a divided continent and a fortified border. But the arms race continued and accelerated, and the superpower competition in the Third World continued.

Marching for Freedom

*W*hile President Kennedy saw the Cold War as the most important issue Americans faced, many African Americans believed civil rights should become a national priority. In the early 1960s, young civil rights activists seized the national stage and demanded that the federal government mobilize behind them.

In 1960, six years after the *Brown* decision declared "separate but equal" unconstitutional, little had changed for African Americans in the South. Fewer than 7 percent of black students attended integrated schools. Water fountains were still labeled "White Only" and "Colored Only." One year after the young men had sat down at the all-white lunch counter in Greensboro, more than seventy thousand Americans—most of them college students—participated in sit-ins.

STUDENTS AND THE MOVEMENT

The young people who created the Student Nonviolent Coordinating Committee (SNCC) in the spring of 1960 to coordinate the growing movement were committed to nonviolence. In years to come, SNCC stalwarts—including activist Diane Nash; future NAACP chair Julian Bond; future Washington, D.C., mayor Marion Barry; and future member of the U.S. House of Representatives John Lewis—would risk their lives in the struggle for social justice.

On May 4, 1961, thirteen members of the Congress of Racial Equality (CORE), a nonviolent civil rights organization (see Chapter 27), *FREEDOM RIDES* purchased bus tickets in Washington, D.C., for a 1,500-mile trip through the South to New Orleans. Calling themselves Freedom Riders, this racially mixed group sought to demonstrate that despite Supreme Court rulings ordering the desegregation of interstate buses, Jim Crow still ruled the South. They knew they were risking their lives, and some suffered serious injuries. One bus was firebombed outside Anniston, Alabama. Riders were badly beaten in Birmingham, and in Montgomery, a thousand whites attacked riders with baseball bats and steel bars. Police stayed away.

News of the violent attacks made headlines worldwide. Soviet commentators decried the "savage nature of American freedom and democracy." One southern business leader, in Tokyo to promote Birmingham as a site for international business development, saw Japanese interest evaporate once photos of the Birmingham attacks appeared in Tokyo newspapers.

In America, the violence forced many to confront racial discrimination and hatred in their nation. Middle- and upper-class white southerners had resisted integration following the *Brown* decision. The Freedom Rides made some think differently. Even the *Atlanta Journal* editorialized: "It is time for the decent people . . . to muzzle the jackals." The national and international outcry pushed a reluctant President Kennedy to send federal marshals to safeguard Freedom Riders in Alabama. But bowing to white southern pressure, he allowed Freedom Riders to be arrested in Mississippi.

Beginning in 1961, thousands of SNCC volunteers, many of them high-school and college students, risked their lives encouraging African Americans in rural Mississippi and Georgia to resist segregation and register to vote. They formed Freedom Schools, teaching literacy and constitutional rights. Some SNCC volunteers were white and some were from the North, but many were black southerners who understood first-hand the impact of racism, powerlessness, and poverty.

These efforts achieved national attention during the Freedom Summer of 1964. Because Mississippi laws made it almost impossible for *FREEDOM SUMMER* blacks to vote, the Freedom Summer volunteers created a racially integrated grassroots political party, the Mississippi Freedom Democratic Party. Project workers were arrested over a thousand times and were shot at, bombed, and beaten. Local black activist James Cheney and two white volunteers, Michael Schwerner and Andrew Goodman, were murdered by a Klan mob. That summer, black and white activists risked their lives together.

The Freedom Riders had captured the attention of the nation and the larger Cold War world, and had forced the hand of the president. *BIRMINGHAM AND THE CHILDREN'S CRUSADE* Martin Luther King Jr., having risen through the Montgomery bus boycott to leadership in the movement, concluded that only by provoking a crisis would the civil rights struggle advance. King and the SCLC planned a 1963 campaign in the most violently racist city in America: Birmingham, Alabama. Anticipating a violent response to their nonviolent protests, they called their plan "Project C"—for "confrontation." King wanted all Americans to see the racist hate and violence that marred their nation.

In a controversial action, King and the parents of Birmingham put children on the front lines. As about a thousand black children, some as young as six, marched, police commissioner Eugene "Bull" Connor ordered his police to train "monitor" water guns—powerful enough to strip bark from a tree at 100 feet—on them. The water guns mowed down the children, and then police loosed attack dogs as the nation watched in horror on television. President Kennedy demanded that Birmingham's white business and political elite negotiate a settlement. The Birmingham movement won and, more important, pushed civil rights to the fore of Kennedy's political agenda.

Kennedy was sympathetic—though not terribly committed—to the civil rights movement, and he knew that racial oppression hurt the United *KENNEDY AND CIVIL RIGHTS* States in the Cold War struggle for international opinion. Domestically, however, he knew that if he alienated conservative southern Democrats in Congress, his legislative programs would founder. Thus, he appointed five die-hard segregationists to the federal bench in the Deep South and delayed issuing an executive order forbidding segregation in federally subsidized housing (a pledge made in the 1960 campaign) until late 1962. He allowed FBI director J. Edgar Hoover to harass Martin Luther King and other activists, using wiretaps and surveillance to gather personal information and circulating rumors of communist connections and personal improprieties to discredit them.

But grassroots civil rights activism—and the violence of white mobs—forced Kennedy's hand. In September 1962, the president ordered 500 U.S. marshals to protect James Meredith, the first African American to attend the University of Mississippi. Thousands of whites attacked the marshals with guns, gasoline bombs, bricks, and pipes, killing two and seriously wounding 160. Neither the marshals nor James Meredith backed down.

The following spring, Kennedy confronted the defiant Alabama governor, George C. Wallace, who promised to "bar the schoolhouse door" to prevent the desegregation of the University of Alabama. With Wallace vowing, "Segregation now, segregation tomorrow, segregation forever!" Kennedy committed

the federal government to guarantee racial justice—even over the opposition of individual states. In a televised address Kennedy said: "Now the time has come for this nation to fulfill its promise." That night, civil rights leader Medgar Evers was murdered in his driveway in Jackson, Mississippi. A week later, the president asked Congress to pass a comprehensive civil rights bill ending racial discrimination in the entire United States.

On August 28, 1963, a quarter of a million Americans gathered on the Washington Mall to show support for Kennedy's civil rights bill. Behind the scenes, organizers from the major civil rights groups—SCLC, CORE, SNCC, the NAACP, the Urban League, and A. Philip Randolph's Brotherhood of Sleeping Car Porters—grappled with growing tensions. SNCC activists saw Kennedy's legislation as too little, too late, and wanted radical action. King and other older leaders counseled moderation. The movement was splintering.

MARCH ON WASHINGTON

What Americans saw, however, was a celebration of unity. Black and white celebrities joined hands; folk singers sang freedom songs. Television aired Martin Luther King Jr.'s prophesy of a day when "all

A historic moment for the civil rights movement was the March on Washington on August 28, 1963. The Reverend Martin Luther King Jr. (*center*) joined a quarter of a million black people and white people in their march for racial equality. Addressing civil rights supporters, and the nation, from the steps of the Lincoln Memorial, King delivered his "I Have a Dream" speech. (R. W. Kelley/Getty Images)

God's children, black men and white men, Jews and Gentiles, Protestants and Catholics, will be able to join hands and sing in the words of the old Negro spiritual, 'Free at last! Free at last! Thank God Almighty, we are free at last!'" The 1963 March on Washington for Jobs and Freedom was a triumph, powerfully demonstrating African Americans' commitment to equality and justice. Days later, white supremacists bombed the Sixteenth Street Baptist Church in Birmingham, killing four black girls.

Liberalism and the Great Society

By 1963, Kennedy seemed to be taking a new path. Campaigning in 1960, he promised to lead America into a "New Frontier," with the federal government working to eradicate poverty, guarantee healthcare to the elderly, and ensure decent schools for all children. But few of Kennedy's initiatives were passed into law. Lacking a popular mandate in the election and fearful of alienating southern Democrats in Congress, Kennedy let his social policy agenda languish.

Instead, Kennedy focused on the economy, believing that continued prosperity would solve America's social problems. Kennedy's vision was perhaps best realized in America's space program. As the Russians moved ahead in the space race, Kennedy vowed in 1961 to put a man on the moon before the decade's end. With billions in new funding, the National Aeronautics and Space Administration (NASA) began the Apollo program. And in February 1962, astronaut John Glenn orbited the earth in the space capsule *Friendship Seven*.

On November 22, 1963, Kennedy visited the home state of Vice President Lyndon Johnson. Riding with

THE KENNEDY ASSASSINATION

his wife, Jackie, in an open-top limousine, Kennedy was cheered by thousands along the motorcade's route. Suddenly gunshots rang out. The president crumpled, shot in the head. Tears ran down the cheeks of CBS anchorman Walter Cronkite as he announced to the nation later that day that the president was dead.

That same day, police captured a suspect: Lee Harvey Oswald, a former U.S. Marine (dishonorably discharged) who had once attempted to gain Soviet citizenship. Two days later, television cameras rolled as Oswald was shot dead by nightclub owner Jack Ruby. Was Ruby silencing Oswald to prevent him from implicating others? Americans wondered. The seven-member Warren Commission, headed by U.S. Supreme Court Chief Justice Earl Warren, concluded that Oswald acted alone. But debates still rage over whether Kennedy's death was a conspiracy.

Millions of Americans watched their president's funeral on television: the brave young widow; a riderless horse; three-year-old "John-John" saluting his father's casket. People would remember Kennedy less for any specific accomplishment than for his inspirational rhetoric and the romance he brought to American political life. In the post-assassination grief, Lyndon Johnson invoked Kennedy's memory to push through the most ambitious legislative program since the New Deal.

Whereas Kennedy had been raised with wealth and was educated at Harvard, Johnson had grown

JOHNSON AND THE GREAT SOCIETY

up in modest circumstances in the Texas hill country and graduated from Southwest Texas State Teachers' College. He was as earthy as Kennedy was elegant, prone to colorful curses, and willing to use his physical size to his advantage. Johnson had a long political career, beginning when he filled an empty congressional seat from Texas in 1937. As Senate majority leader from 1954 to 1960, he learned how to manipulate people and wield power, and in the presidency, he used these skills to unite the nation.

Johnson, a liberal in the style of Franklin D. Roosevelt, believed the federal government should actively improve the lives of Americans. In a 1964 commencement address at the University of Michigan, he described his vision of "abundance and liberty for all . . . demand[ing] an end to poverty and racial injustice . . . where every child can find knowledge to enrich his mind and to enlarge his talents." Johnson called this vision "The Great Society."

Johnson signed into law the Civil Rights Act of 1964, ending legal discrimination on the basis of

CIVIL RIGHTS ACT

race, color, religion, national origin, and sex in federal programs, voting, employment, and public accommodation. The original bill did not include discrimination on the basis of sex; that was added by a southern congressman who hoped it would torpedo the bill. But a bipartisan group of women members of the House of Representatives ensured it was passed. The Civil Rights Act of 1964 gave the government enforcement power, including the authority to withhold federal funds from public agencies or federal contractors that discriminated and establishing the Equal Employment Opportunity Commission (EEOC) to investigate and judge claims of job discrimination.

Many Americans did not believe it was the federal government's job to end racial discrimination or poverty. White southerners resented federal intervention, and millions of conservative Americans believed that since the New Deal, the federal government had been overstepping its constitutional boundaries and wanted a return to local control and states' rights. In the 1964 election, this vision was championed by the Republican candidate, Arizona senator Barry Goldwater.

Goldwater not only voted against the 1964 Civil Rights Act; he opposed the national Social Security system. Like many conservatives, he believed that individual liberty, not equality, mattered most. Goldwater also believed that the United States needed a more powerful national military to fight communism; in campaign speeches, he suggested that the United States should use tactical nuclear weapons against its enemies.

THE ELECTION OF 1964

Goldwater's campaign slogan, "In your heart you know he's right," was turned against him by Johnson supporters: "In your heart you know he's right . . . far right," one punned. Johnson campaigned on a record unemployment rate below 4 percent and economic growth above 6 percent. But his civil rights support severed the New Deal coalition and, he told an aide, "delivered the south to the Republican Party for my lifetime and yours."

Tensions mounted at the 1964 Democratic National Convention. Two delegations arrived from Mississippi, each demanding to be seated. The Democratic Party's official delegation was exclusively white; the Mississippi Freedom Democratic Party (MFDP) was racially mixed. White southern delegates threatened to leave if the MFDP delegates were seated. MFDP delegate Fannie Lou Hamer told the convention's credentials committee about the threats and violence she'd faced when she tried to register to vote. Johnson sought a compromise, but the MFDP declined. "We didn't come all this way

for no two seats," Hamer said, and the delegation walked out.

Though Johnson won the election by a landslide, he lost the Deep South—the first Democrat since the Civil War to do so. But voters also elected the most liberal Congress in history. With a record 61.1 percent of the popular vote, Johnson launched his Great Society. Congress responded in 1965 and 1966 with the most sweeping reform legislation since 1935.

Johnson signed the 1965 Voting Rights Act, which outlawed practices that prevented most blacks in the Deep South from voting and provided for federal oversight of elections. Within two years, the percentage of African Americans registered to vote in Mississippi jumped from 7 percent to more than 60 percent. Black elected officials became increasingly common in southern states over the following decade.

IMPROVING AMERICAN LIFE

Seeking to improve the quality of American life, the Johnson administration established new student loan and grant programs to help low- and moderate-income Americans attend college and created the National Endowment for the Arts and the National Endowment for the Humanities. The Immigration Act of 1965 ended racially based quotas. And Johnson supported consumer protection legislation, including the 1966 National Traffic and Motor Vehicle Safety Act, inspired by Ralph Nader's exposé of the automobile industry, *Unsafe at Any Speed* (1965). Johnson signed "preservation" legislation protecting America's wilderness and addressing environmental pollution.

WAR ON POVERTY

At the heart of Johnson's Great Society was the War on Poverty, which included major legislation beginning in 1964 (see Table 30.1). Johnson and other liberals believed that in a time of affluence, the nation should use its resources to end "poverty, ignorance and hunger as intractable, permanent features of American society."

Johnson's goal was "to offer the forgotten fifth of our people opportunity, not doles." Billions of federal dollars were channeled to municipalities and school districts to improve opportunities for the poverty stricken, from preschoolers (Head Start) to high schoolers (Upward Bound) to young adults (Job Corps). The Model Cities program offered federal funds to upgrade employment, housing, education, and health in targeted urban neighborhoods, and

TABLE 30.1

Great Society Achievements, 1964–1966

	1964	1965	1966
Civil Rights	Civil Rights Act Equal Employment Opportunity Commission Twenty-fourth Amendment	Voting Rights Act	
War on Poverty	Economic Opportunity Act Office of Economic Opportunity Job Corps Legal Services for the Poor VISTA		Model Cities
Education		Elementary and Secondary Education Act Head Start Upward Bound	
Environment		Water Quality Act Air Quality Act	Clean Water Restoration Act

**New
Government
Agencies**
		Department of
		    Housing and Urban
		    Development
		National Endowments for
		    the Arts and Humanities
			Department of
			    Transportation

Miscellaneous		Medicare and Medicaid Immigration and Nationality Act	

The Great Society of the mid-1960s saw the biggest burst of reform legislation since the New Deal of the 1930s.

Community Action Programs involved the poor in creating local grassroots antipoverty programs.

The Johnson administration also expanded the Food Stamp program and earmarked billions for constructing public housing and subsidizing rents. Two massive federal programs provided healthcare: Medicare for those sixty-five and older and Medicaid for the poor. Finally, Aid to Families with Dependent Children (AFDC), the welfare program created during the New Deal, increased benefits and eligibility.

The War on Poverty was controversial. Leftists believed the government was doing too little to change structural inequality. Conservatives argued that Great Society programs created dependency among America's poor. Policy analysts noted that specific programs were ill conceived and badly implemented.

Decades later, most historians judge the War on Poverty a mixed success. It did alleviate poverty, directly addressing debilitating housing, health, and nutritional deficiencies that hurt America's poor. Between 1965 and 1970, federal spending for Social Security, healthcare, welfare, and education more than doubled. By 1975, the number of Americans receiving food stamps had increased from 600,000 (in 1965) to 17 million. Poverty among the elderly fell from about 40 percent in 1960 to 16 percent in 1974, due largely to increased Social Security benefits and Medicare (see Figure 30.1).

But War on Poverty programs less successfully addressed the root causes of poverty. Neither the Job Corps nor Community Action Programs showed significant results. Economic growth largely sparked the

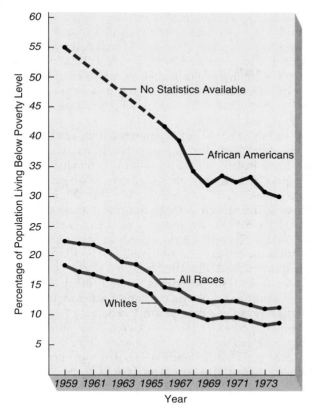

Figure 30.1   Poverty in America for Whites, African Americans, and All Races, 1959–1974

Because of rising levels of economic prosperity, combined with the impact of Great Society programs, the percentage of Americans living in poverty in 1974 was half as high as in 1959. African Americans still were far more likely than white Americans to be poor. In 1959 more than half of all blacks (55.1 percent) were poor; in 1974 the figure remained high (30.3 percent). The government did not record data on African American poverty for the years 1960 through 1965.

dramatic decrease in poverty rates during the 1960s—from 22.4 percent of the population in 1959 to 11 percent in 1973. Unchanged was the fact that 11 million Americans in female-headed households remained poor—the same number in 1969 as in 1963.

Political compromises created long-term problems. For example, Congress accommodated doctors and hospitals in Medicare legislation by allowing federal reimbursements of hospitals' "reasonable costs" and doctors' "reasonable charges" in treating elderly patients. With no incentives to hold prices down, national healthcare expenditures as a percentage of the gross national product rose by almost 44 percent from 1960 to 1971. Nevertheless, problems aside, Johnson's Great Society marked the moment in which many Americans believed they could and should eliminate poverty, disease, and discrimination.

Johnson and Vietnam

*I*n foreign policy, Johnson held firmly to ideas about U.S. superiority and the menace of communism. But international affairs held little interest for him, and he had little appreciation for foreign cultures. At the Taj Mahal in India, Johnson tested the monument's echo with a Texas cowboy yell. And on a trip to Senegal, he ordered that an American bed, a special showerhead, and cases of Cutty Sark be sent along with him. "Foreigners," Johnson quipped early in his administration, only half-jokingly, "are not like the folks I am used to."

Online Study Center   **Improve Your Grade**
Interactive Map: The Vietnam War, 1954–1975

Yet Johnson knew that foreign policy, especially regarding Vietnam, would demand his attention. Since the late 1950s, hostilities in Vietnam had increased, as Ho Chi Minh's North assisted Vietcong guerrillas in the South in reunifying the country under a communist government. President Kennedy had increased aid to the Diem regime in Saigon, airdropped more raiding teams in North Vietnam, and launched herbicide crop destruction to starve the Vietcong. Kennedy also strengthened the U.S. military presence in South Vietnam: by 1963 over sixteen thousand military advisers were there, some authorized to join the U.S.-equipped Army of the Republic of Vietnam (ARVN) in combat.

KENNEDY'S LEGACY IN VIETNAM

Meanwhile, opposition to Diem's repressive regime increased. Peasants objected to being removed from their villages, and Buddhist monks, protesting the Roman Catholic Diem's religious persecution, poured gasoline and ignited themselves in the streets of Saigon. Although Diem was honest, he countenanced corruption in his government and jailed critics. Eventually U.S. officials encouraged ambitious South Vietnamese generals to remove Diem; they murdered him on November 1, 1963.

The timing of Kennedy's assassination a few weeks later ensured that Vietnam would be the most controversial aspect of his legacy. He had expanded U.S. involvement and approved a coup against Diem, but despite the urgings of top advisers, he had refused to commit American ground forces. Over time he became skeptical about South Vietnam's prospects and hinted he would end the American commitment after winning reelection in 1964. Kennedy arrived in Dallas that fateful day uncertain about how to proceed in solving the Vietnam problem.

With the 1964 election looming, Lyndon Johnson did not want to do anything in Vietnam that could keep him from winning the presidency, and so he kept Vietnam on the back burner. Yet Johnson also sought victory there, and throughout 1964, the administration secretly considered expanding the war to North Vietnam.

TONKIN GULF INCIDENT AND RESOLUTION

In early August 1964, U.S. destroyers reported coming under attack from North Vietnamese patrol boats in the Gulf of Tonkin twice in three days (see Map 30.1). Despite conflicting evidence as to whether the second attack occurred, Johnson ordered retaliatory air strikes against North Vietnamese patrol boat bases and an oil depot. By a vote of 416 to 0 in the House and 88 to 2 in the Senate, Congress quickly passed the Gulf of Tonkin Resolution, giving the president the authority to "take all necessary measures to repel any armed attack against the forces of the United States and to prevent further aggression." In so doing, Congress essentially surrendered its war-making powers to the executive branch.

President Johnson also appreciated how the Gulf of Tonkin affair boosted his public approval ratings and effectively removed Vietnam as a campaign issue for GOP presidential nominee Barry Goldwater. On the ground in South Vietnam, however, the outlook remained grim, as the Vietcong made gains. U.S. officials secretly planned to escalate American involvement.

DECISION FOR ESCALATION

In February 1965, in response to Vietcong attacks on American installations in South Vietnam that killed thirty-two Americans, Johnson ordered Operation Rolling Thunder, a bombing program that continued until October 1968. On March 8, the first U.S. combat battalions came ashore near Danang. The North Vietnamese hid in shelters and increased infiltration into the South. In Saigon, meanwhile, coups and countercoups by self-serving military leaders undermined U.S. efforts.

In July 1965, Johnson convened high-level discussions about U.S. war policy, partially to manipulate the historical record to show him agonizing over a decision he had in truth already made about America's open-ended involvement. On July 28, Johnson publicly announced a significant troop increase, with others to follow. By the end of 1965, more than 180,000 U.S. ground troops were in South Vietnam; in 1966 there were 385,000; and in 1968 U.S. troop strength reached 536,100. In 1967 alone, U.S. warplanes flew 108,000 sorties and dropped 226,000 tons of bombs on North Vietnam. Each American escalation brought a new North Vietnamese escalation, and increased material assistance to the Hanoi government from the Soviet Union and China.

Rolling Thunder and the U.S. troop commitment "Americanized" the war, transforming it from a civil war between North and South into an American war against the communist Hanoi government. Not everyone embraced the decision.

OPPOSITION TO AMERICANIZATION

Democratic leaders in the Senate, major newspapers such as the *New York Times* and the *Wall Street Journal*, and prominent columnists like Walter Lippmann warned against deepening involvement, as did Vice President Hubert H. Humphrey and Undersecretary of State George W. Ball. Abroad, virtually all of America's allies—including France, Britain, Canada, and Japan—cautioned against escalation and urged a political settlement. Remarkably, many top U.S. officials knew that the odds of success were small, but hoped the new measures would cause Hanoi to end the insurgency in the South.

Leaders feared that if the United States failed in Vietnam, other countries would find American power less credible. The Soviets and Chinese would challenge U.S. interests elsewhere, and allied governments might conclude they could not depend on Washington. Johnson worried that failure in Vietnam would harm his domestic agenda and feared the personal humiliation. As for helping a South Vietnamese ally

Map 30.1   Southeast Asia and the Vietnam War

To prevent communists from coming to power in Vietnam, Cambodia, and Laos in the 1960s, the United States intervened massively in Southeast Asia. The interventions failed, and the remaining American troops made a hasty exit from Vietnam in 1975, when the victorious Vietcong and North Vietnamese took Saigon and renamed it Ho Chi Minh City.

repulse external aggression, that did not figure into the equation as much as it would have if the Saigon government—wracked with infighting and possessing little popular support—had done more in its own defense.

To minimize publicity about the war, Johnson refused to call up reserve units. This forced the military to rely heavily on the draft, which made Vietnam a young man's war—the average age of soldiers was twenty-two, compared with twenty-six in World War II. It also became a war of the poor and the working class. Through the years of heavy escalation (1965–1968), college students could get deferments, as could teachers and engineers. (In 1969 the draft was changed so that some students were called up through a lottery system.) The armed services recruited hard in poor communities, many of them heavily African American and Latino, advertising the mili-

AMERICAN SOLDIERS IN VIETNAM

tary as an avenue of training and advancement. Once in uniform, those with fewer skills were far more likely to see combat, and hence to die.

Infantrymen maneuvered into thick jungles, where booby traps and land mines were a constant threat. The enemy was hard to find, often burrowed into elaborate underground tunnels or melded into the population, where any Vietnamese might be a Vietcong.

The entry of American forces into the conflict in 1965 helped stave off a South Vietnamese defeat, thereby achieving Americanization's most immediate and basic objective. But as the North Vietnamese matched each American escalation with one of their own, the war became a stalemate. The U.S. commander, General William Westmoreland, mistakenly believed that a strategy of attrition represented the key to victory. Thus, the measure of success became the "body count"—the number of North Vietnamese and Vietcong corpses found after battle. But the counts were manipulated by officers eager to demonstrate an

■ Wounded American soldiers after a battle in Vietnam.   (Larry Burrows/Getty Images)

operation's success. Worse, the American reliance on massive military technology—including carpet bombing, napalm (jellied gasoline), and crop defoliants that destroyed forests—alienated many South Vietnamese and brought new recruits to the Vietcong.

As television coverage brought the war—its body bags, burned villages, and weeping refugees—into homes nightly, opposition grew. College professors and students organized debates and lectures on American policy, which became a form of protest, called "teach-ins" after the sit-ins of the civil rights movement. Pacifist groups such as the American Friends Service Committee and the Women's International League for Peace and Freedom also organized early protests.

DIVISIONS AT HOME

In early 1966 Senator William Fulbright held televised hearings on whether the national interest was being served by pursuing the war. To the surprise of some, George F. Kennan testified that his containment doctrine was meant for Europe, not volatile Southeast Asia. America's "preoccupation" with Vietnam, Kennan asserted, was undermining its global obligations. Fulbright provoked Americans to think about the conflict and the nation's role in it and illustrated deep divisions among public officials.

Defense Secretary Robert McNamara, who championed the Americanization of the war in 1965, became increasingly troubled by the killing and destructiveness of the bombing. As early as November 1965, he expressed skepticism that victory could ever be achieved. American credibility was suffering, McNamara feared. But Johnson was determined to prevail in Vietnam. Although on occasion he halted the bombing to encourage Ho Chi Minh to negotiate, such pauses often were accompanied by increases in American troop strength. The North demanded a complete suspension of bombing raids before negotiating. And Ho rejected American terms, which amounted to abandonment of his dream of an independent, unified Vietnam.

A Nation Divided

 s Johnson struggled with Vietnam, his Great Society faced challenges at home. America was fracturing not only over the Vietnam war, but also along many different lines: black and white, youth and age, radical and conservative.

URBAN UNREST

Shortly after President Johnson signed into law the 1964 landmark Civil Rights Act, racial violence erupted in northern cities. Angry residents of Harlem took to the streets after a white police officer shot a black teenager in July 1964. The following summer, in the predominantly black Watts section of Los Angeles, crowds burned, looted, and battled police for five days and nights. The riot, which began when a white police officer attempted to arrest a black resident on suspicion of drunken driving, left thirty-four dead and more than one thousand injured. In July 1967 twenty-six people were killed in street battles between African Americans and police and army troops in Newark, New Jersey. A week later, in Detroit, forty-three died as 3 square miles went up in flames. In 1967 there were 167 violent outbreaks in 128 cities.

The "long, hot summers" of urban unrest in the 1960s differed from almost all previous race riots. Where past riots were typically started by whites, now black residents exploded in anger over the lack of opportunity in their lives. They looted and burned stores, most of them white owned, while also devastating their own neighborhoods.

In 1968 the National Advisory Commission on Civil Disorders, chaired by Governor Otto Kerner of Illinois, warned that America was "moving towards two societies, one white, one black—separate and unequal," and blamed white racism for the riots. "What white Americans have never fully understood—but what the Negro can never forget—is that white society is deeply implicated in the ghetto. White institutions created it, white institutions maintain it, and white society condones it," concluded the Kerner Commission. Some white Americans disagreed, while others wondered why African Americans were venting their frustration just when they were making real progress.

Online Study Center **Improve Your Grade**
Primary Source:
The Negro Family: The Case for National Action

The answer stemmed, in part, from regional differences. The civil rights movement focused mostly on fighting legal discrimination in the South and ignored problems in the North. Increasingly concentrated in deteriorating inner-city ghettos, most northern

African Americans faced discrimination in housing, credit, and employment. The median income of northern blacks was roughly half that of whites, and their unemployment rate was twice as high. Many northern blacks had given up on both the civil rights movement and the Great Society.

In this climate, the voice of Malcolm X, one-time pimp and street hustler who converted in prison to the Nation of Islam faith, carried a powerful message, urging blacks to seize their freedom "by any means necessary." Members of the Nation of Islam, commonly known as Black Muslims, espoused black pride and separatism from white society. Their faith combined traditional Islam with a belief that whites were subhuman "devils" whose race would soon be destroyed. By the early 1960s, Malcolm X had become the Black Muslims' chief spokesperson. But his murder in 1965 by members of the Nation of Islam who felt betrayed when he started his own more racially tolerant organization, transformed Malcolm X into a powerful symbol of black defiance and self-respect.

BLACK POWER

A year after Malcolm X's death, Stokely Carmichael, SNCC chairman, denounced "the betrayal of black dreams by white America." To end white oppression, Carmichael proclaimed, blacks had to "stand up and take over" by electing black candidates and organizing their own schools and institutions. "Black Power," his listeners chanted. That year, SNCC expelled its white members and repudiated both nonviolence and integration. CORE followed in 1967.

The best-known black radicals were the Black Panthers, formed in Oakland, California, in 1966. Blending black separatism and revolutionary communism, the Panthers focused on destroying capitalism and its "military arm," the police. Male Panthers dressed in commando gear, carried weapons, and talked about killing "pigs"—and did kill eleven officers by 1970. Police responded in kind; most infamously, Chicago police murdered Panther leader Fred Hampton in his bed. However, the group—led by female members—also worked to improve their neighborhoods by instituting free breakfast and healthcare for ghetto children, offering courses in African American history, and demanding jobs and housing. Before the end of the decade, a vocal minority of America's young of varying races and ethnicities would also call for revolution.

By the mid-1960s, 41 percent of the American population was under age twenty. These young people spent more time with peers than any previous generation, as three-quarters of them graduated from high school (up from one-fifth in the 1920s) and almost half attended college (up from 16 percent in 1940). As this large baby boom generation came of age, many believed they must provide democratic leadership for their nation. Inspired by the sit-in movement started at black colleges, white students committed themselves to changing the system.

YOUTH AND POLITICS

In the fall of 1960, a group of conservative college students met at William F. Buckley's estate in Sharon, Connecticut, to create Young Americans for Freedom (YAF). Their manifesto, the "Sharon Statement," endorsed Cold War anticommunism and a vision of limited government directly opposed to New Deal liberalism. The YAF planned to capture the Republican Party and move it to the political right; Goldwater's selection as the Republican candidate for president in 1964 demonstrated their early success.

At the other end of the political spectrum, an emerging New Left also rejected liberalism. While conservatives believed liberalism's activist government encroached on individual liberty, the New Left believed liberalism was not enough to bring equality to all Americans. Meeting in Port Huron, Michigan, in 1962, founding members of Students for a Democratic Society (SDS) drafted their "Port Huron Statement," condemning racism, poverty in the midst of plenty, and the Cold War. Calling for "participatory democracy," SDS sought to wrest power from the corporations, the military, and the politicians and return it to "the people."

The rise of white youth activism crystallized at the University of California, Berkeley in fall 1964, when the university banned political activity—including recruiting volunteers for civil rights work in Mississippi—from its traditional place along a university-owned sidewalk. When police tried to arrest a CORE worker who defied the order, some four thousand students surrounded the police car. Berkeley graduate student

FREE SPEECH MOVEMENT

and Mississippi Freedom Summer veteran Mario Savio encouraged the students: "You've got to put your bodies upon the levers . . . [and] you've got to indicate to the people who run it . . . that unless you're free, the machine will be prevented from working at all."

Student political groups, left and right, united to create the Free Speech Movement (FSM). The FSM won back the right to political speech, but not before state police arrested almost eight hundred student protesters. Many saw the administration's actions as a failure of America's democratic promises, but the FSM's victory also demonstrated to students their potential power. By decade's end, the activism born at Berkeley would spread to hundreds of colleges and universities.

Student protesters sought greater control over their education, demanding more relevant classes, more

STUDENT ACTIVISM

freedom in course selection, and a greater voice in the running of universities. A major target was the doctrine of in loco parentis, which until the late 1960s put universities legally "in the place of parents," allowing control over student behavior that went beyond the law. In loco parentis fell heaviest on women, who had strict curfew regulations called *parietals,* while men did not. Along with an end to sex discrimination, protesters like those at the University of Kansas wanted administrators to explain how statements that "college students are assumed to have maturity of judgment necessary for adult responsibility" squared with the minute regulation of students' nonacademic lives. One man complained that "a high school dropout selling cabbage in a supermarket" had more rights and freedoms than successful university students.

But it was the war in Vietnam that truly mobilized a national student movement. Believing that

YOUTH AND THE WAR IN VIETNAM

learning and speaking out about issues was their civic duty, university students and faculty held teach-ins about U.S. involvement in Vietnam in 1965. SDS sponsored the first major antiwar march that year, drawing twenty thousand protesters to Washington, D.C. On campuses nationwide, students borrowed from civil rights movement strategies, picketing ROTC buildings and protesting military research and recruiting on their campuses. Despite the antiwar protests' visibility, most students did not yet oppose the war: in 1967 only 30 percent of male college students were antiwar, while 67 percent supported the war. But as the war escalated, more students distrusted the government as well as the seemingly arbitrary authority of university administrations.

During the 1960s, the large baby boom generation would change the nation's culture more than its politics. While many protested the war,

YOUTH CULTURE AND THE COUNTERCULTURE

most did not, and radicalism did not replace fraternities and sororities. And while there was some crossover, black, white, and Latino youth had different cultural styles, clothes, and music. Collectively, as potential consumers, young people exercised tremendous cultural authority and drove American popular culture in the late 1960s.

The most unifying element of youth culture was music. The Beatles electrified American teenagers: 73 million viewers watched their first television appearance on the *Ed Sullivan Show* in 1964. Bob Dylan promised revolutionary answers in "Blowin' in the Wind"; Janis Joplin brought the sexual power of the blues to white youth; James Brown and Aretha Franklin proclaimed black pride; and the psychedelic rock of the Jefferson Airplane and the Grateful Dead—along with hallucinogenic drugs—redefined reality. And at the Woodstock Festival in upstate New York in 1969, over 400,000 people reveled in the power of music, coexisting in rain and mud for four days without shelter and without violence.

Some hoped to turn youth rebellion into a social revolution, rejecting what they saw as hypocritical middle-class values. Instead, they crafted an alternative way of life, or "counterculture," liberated from competitive materialism and celebrating pleasure. "Sex, Drugs, and Rock 'n' Roll" became a mantra of sorts, offering these "hippies," or "freaks," a path to a new consciousness. Many did the hard work of creating communes and intentional communities, whether in cities or in hidden stretches of rural America. Although the New Left criticized the counterculture as apolitical, many hippies did envision revolutionary change through mind-altering drugs, sex, or music.

The nascent counterculture first entered the national consciousness during the summer of 1967, when tens of thousands poured into the Haight-Ashbury district of San Francisco, the heart of America's psychedelic culture, for the "Summer of Love." As an older generation of "straight" (or Establishment) Americans watched with horror, white youth adopted aspects of the counterculture. Coats and ties disappeared, as did stockings—and bras. Young men grew long hair, and parents complained, "You can't tell the boys from the girls." Millions experimented with marijuana or hallucinogenic drugs, read underground newspapers, and thought of themselves as alienated from "straight" culture even though as high-school or college students, they were not completely "dropping out."

Some of the most lasting cultural changes involved sexual attitudes. The mass media were fascinated with "Free Love," and while some enjoyed promiscuous sexuality, most were glad that premarital sex no longer destroyed a woman's "reputation." The birth-control pill, distributed since 1960, greatly lessened the risk of unplanned pregnancy, and venereal diseases were easily cured by a basic course of antibiotics. The number of couples living together increased 900 percent from 1960 to 1970. While many young people no longer hid that they were sexually active, 68 percent of adults disapproved of premarital sex in 1969. The adult generation that grew up in the hard decades of depression and war did not understand how promising young people could risk their futures by having sex without marriage, taking drugs, or opposing the war in Vietnam.

1968

By early 1968, the nation was increasingly fragmented. Divided over the war in Vietnam, disillusioned with the prospect of social change, or angry about racial violence, the nation faced the most serious domestic crisis of the postwar era.

On January 31, 1968, the first day of the Vietnamese New Year (Tet), Vietcong and North Vietnamese forces struck South Vietnam, capturing provincial capitals. During the carefully planned offensive, the Saigon airport, the presidential palace, and the ARVN headquarters were attacked. The American embassy was occupied by Vietcong soldiers for six hours. U.S. and South

THE TET OFFENSIVE

Vietnamese units eventually regained ground, inflicting heavy casualties and devastating numerous villages.

Although the Tet Offensive ultimately counted as a U.S. military victory, the heavy fighting called into question American military leaders' confident predictions in earlier months that the war would soon be won. Had not the Vietcong and North Vietnamese demonstrated that they could strike when and where they wished? If America's airpower, dollars, and half a million troops could not now defeat the Vietcong, could they ever do so?

Top presidential advisers sounded notes of despair. Clark Clifford, the new secretary of defense, told Johnson the war could not be won, even with the 206,000 additional soldiers Westmoreland wanted. Aware that the nation was suffering a financial crisis prompted by rampant deficit spending, they knew that taking the initiative in Vietnam would cost billions more, further derail the budget, panic foreign owners of dollars, and wreck the economy.

Controversy over the war split the Democratic Party, just as a presidential election loomed in November. Senator Eugene McCarthy of Minnesota and Robert F. Kennedy (now a senator from New York), both strong opponents of Johnson's war policies, forcefully challenged the president in early primaries. During a March 31 television address, Johnson changed course: he announced a halt to most of the bombing, asked Hanoi to begin negotiations, and then stunned his listeners by withdrawing from the presidential race. His presidency had become a casualty of the war. Peace talks began in May in Paris, but the war ground on.

JOHNSON'S EXIT

Days after Johnson's shocking announcement, Martin Luther King Jr. was murdered in Memphis. It remains unclear why James Earl Ray, a white forty-year-old drifter and petty criminal, shot King—or whether he acted alone. By 1968 King, the senior statesman of the civil rights movement, had become an outspoken critic of the Vietnam War and of American capitalism. Most Americans mourned his death, even as black rage and grief exploded into riots in 130 cities throughout the nation. The violence provoked a backlash from whites, primarily urban, working-class people who were quickly losing sympathy for black Americans' increasingly

ASSASSINATIONS

The British Invasion

The British invasion began in earnest on February 7, 1964. Three thousand screaming American teenagers were waiting when Pan Am's Yankee Clipper touched down at Kennedy Airport with four British "moptops" aboard. "I Want to Hold Your Hand" was already at the top of the U.S. charts, and 73 million people—the largest television audience in history—watched them on the *Ed Sullivan Show* the following Sunday night.

Although the Beatles led the invasion, they did not conquer America alone. The Rolling Stones' first U.S. hit single also came in 1964. The Dave Clark Five appeared on *Ed Sullivan* eighteen times. And there were many others: Herman's Hermits, the Animals, the Hollies, the Kinks, Gerry and the Pacemakers, Petula Clark.

The British invasion was, at least in part, a triumphant homecoming of American music, a transatlantic exchange that reinvigorated both nations. American rock 'n' roll had lost much of its energy by the early 1960s, and the London-centered popular music industry was pumping out a saccharine version of American pop. But by the late 1950s, young musicians in England's provincial cities were listening to the music of African American bluesmen Muddy Waters and Howlin' Wolf and the early rock 'n' roll of Buddy Holly and Chuck Berry. None of this music had a large following in the United States, where *Billboard* magazine's number one hit for 1960 was Percy Faith's "Theme from *A Summer Place*" (a movie starring Sandra Dee and Troy Donahue).

Young British musicians, including John Lennon, Eric Clapton, and Mick Jagger, re-created American musical forms and reinvented rock 'n' roll. By the mid-1960s, the British invasion bands were at the heart of a youth culture that transcended the boundaries of nations. This music connected not only Britain and America but young people throughout the world.

The Beatles perform on the *Ed Sullivan Show* in February 1964. Although Britain's Queen Mother thought the Beatles "young, fresh, and vital," American parents were appalled when the "long" Beatles haircut swept the nation. (AP/Wide World Photos)

571

radical demands. In Chicago, Mayor Richard Daley ordered police to shoot rioters.

An already shaken nation watched in disbelief only two months later when antiwar Democratic presidential candidate Robert Kennedy was shot and killed after winning the California primary. His assassin, Sirhan Sirhan, an Arab nationalist, targeted Kennedy because of his support for Israel.

Violence erupted again in August at the Democratic National Convention in Chicago. Thousands

CHICAGO DEMOCRATIC NATIONAL CONVENTION

of protesters converged on the city: students who'd gone "Clean for Gene," cutting long hair and donning "respectable" clothes for antiwar candidate Eugene McCarthy; members of the counterculture drawn by the anarchist Yippies' promise of a "Festival of Life" to counter the "Convention of Death"; antiwar groups. Chicago's mayor assigned twelve thousand police to twelve-hour shifts and had twelve thousand army troops with bazookas, rifles, and flamethrowers as backup. Police attacked peaceful antiwar protesters and journalists. "The Whole World Is Watching," chanted the protesters, as police indiscriminately beat people to the ground and Americans gathered around their television sets, despairing over their nation's future.

Upheavals spread around the world that spring and summer. In France, university students protested

GLOBAL PROTEST

rigid academic policies and the Vietnam War. They received support from French workers, who occupied factories and paralyzed public transport; the turmoil contributed to the collapse of Charles de Gaulle's government the following year. In Italy, Germany, England, Ireland, Sweden, Canada, Mexico, Chile, Japan, and South Korea, students held similar protests. In Czechoslovakia, hundreds of thousands of demonstrators flooded Prague streets, demanding democracy and an end to Soviet repression. This so-called Prague Spring developed into a full-scale national rebellion before being crushed by Soviet tanks.

Why so many uprisings occurred simultaneously is unclear. The postwar baby boom produced by the late 1960s a huge mass of teenagers and young adults, many of whom had grown up in relative prosperity with high expectations for the future. Technological advances allowed the nearly instantaneous transmittal of televised images worldwide, so protests in one country could readily inspire similar actions in others.

The 1968 presidential election did little to heal the nation. Democratic nominee Hubert Humphrey,

NIXON'S ELECTION

Johnson's vice president, seemed a continuation of the old politics. Republican candidate Richard Nixon appealed to a nation tired of violence with calls for "law and order." He reached out to those he called "the great, quite forgotten majority—the nonshouters and the nondemonstrators." On Vietnam, Nixon vowed to "end the war and win the peace." Governor George Wallace of Alabama, a vehement segregationist who proposed using nuclear weapons on Vietnam, ran as a third-party candidate. Wallace carried five southern states, drawing almost 14 percent of the popular vote, and Nixon was elected president with the slimmest of margins.

On Christmas Eve 1968, *Apollo 8* entered lunar orbit, in a step toward fulfilling Kennedy's pledge at the start of the tumultuous decade. Looking down on a troubled world, the astronauts read aloud the opening passages of Genesis: "In the beginning, God created the heaven and the earth . . . and God saw that it was good." Many listeners were moved to tears.

Summary ⚙ *Online Study Center* **ACE the Test**

The 1960s began with high hopes for a more democratic America. Civil rights volunteers, often risking their lives, carried the quest for racial equality across the nation. The passage of the Civil Rights Act of 1964 and the Voting Rights Act of 1965 were major milestones. America was shaken by the assassination of President John Kennedy in 1963, but under President Johnson, the liberal vision of government working to improve citizens' lives inspired a flood of legislation designed to create a Great Society.

The Cold War between the United States and the USSR intensified during the 1960s, and a nuclear war nearly happened in the 1962 Cuban missile crisis. Determined not to let Vietnam "fall" to communists, the United States became increasingly involved in the war in Vietnam, sending military forces to prevent communist Vietnamese nationalists led by Ho Chi Minh from succeeding in that nation's civil war. By 1968 there were more than half a million American ground troops in Vietnam, which ultimately divided the country, undermined Great Society domestic programs, and destroyed Lyndon Johnson's presidency.

Despite civil rights gains, many African Americans turned away from the movement, seeking more immediate change. Poor African American neighborhoods burned as riots spread through the nation. Vocal young people—and some of their elders—questioned whether democracy truly existed in the United States. Large numbers of the nation's white youth rebelled by embracing a "counterculture" that rejected white middle-class respectability. With great passion, Americans struggled over the future of their nation.

1968 was a year of crisis, of assassinations and violence in the streets. The decade that started with such promise ended in fierce political polarization.

LEGACY FOR A PEOPLE AND A NATION
The Immigration Act of 1965

When President Johnson signed the 1965 Immigration Act in a ceremony at the foot of the Statue of Liberty, he believed it was important because it "repair[ed] a very deep and painful flaw in the fabric of American justice" by ending national origins quotas that had all but excluded "Polynesians, Orientals, and Negroes" (as Hawai'i's senator Hiram Fong pointed out in 1963). But the president and his advisers mistakenly saw it as primarily symbolic. In fact, this act may have had greater long-term impact on Americans than any other Great Society legislation.

The architects of the Immigration Act did not expect the nature of immigration to change. Attorney General Robert Kennedy argued that abolishing immigration restrictions for Asia and the Pacific would probably produce about five thousand new immigrants before subsiding. But rapid population growth in many poorer nations created a large pool of potential immigrants.

Immigration rates skyrocketed, and by the 1990s, immigration accounted for almost 60 percent of America's population growth. By 2000, more Americans were foreign born than at any time since the 1930s. The majorities came from Mexico, the Philippines, Vietnam, China, the Dominican Republic, Korea, India, the USSR, Jamaica, and Iran.

More than two-thirds of the new immigrants settled in six states: New York, California, Florida, New Jersey, Illinois, and Texas. By the late twentieth century, Spanish-language signs appeared in South Carolina, and Hmong farmers from Southeast Asia offered their produce at the farmers' market in Missoula, Montana. The legacy of the 1965 Immigration Act was unintended but profound: the United States is a more diverse nation today than it otherwise would have been.

CONTINUING DIVISIONS AND NEW LIMITS 1969–1980

*I*n 1969 Daniel Ellsberg was a thirty-eight-year-old former aide to Assistant Secretary of Defense John McNaughton. At the Pentagon, Ellsberg worked on a top-secret study of U.S. decision making in Vietnam. When he left office after Richard Nixon's election, he accessed a copy of the study stored at the Rand Corporation, where he would resume his pregovernment research career. He spent six months poring over the seven thousand pages that made up the so-called Pentagon Papers.

Initially supportive of U.S. intervention in Vietnam, Ellsberg had grown disillusioned. A Harvard-trained Ph.D., former marine officer, and Cold Warrior, he spent 1965 to 1967 in South Vietnam, assessing the war's progress for Washington. He had gone on combat patrols and interviewed military officials, U.S. diplomats, and Vietnamese leaders. The war, he concluded, was in military, political, and moral respects a lost enterprise.

Loyal to the president, Ellsberg was initially reluctant to act. But in 1969 when it became clear that Nixon had no intention of ending the war, Ellsberg boldly decided to risk imprisonment by making the Pentagon Papers public. The study, he believed, showed that presidents had escalated America's presence in Vietnam despite pessimistic estimates from advisers—and that they repeatedly lied to the public about their actions and the results. Ellsberg hoped disclosure would generate sufficient uproar to force a dramatic policy change.

Aided by a Rand colleague, Ellsberg surreptitiously photocopied the study, then spent months pleading with antiwar senators and representatives to release it. When they refused, he went to the press. On June 13, 1971, the *New York Times* published a front-page exposé on the Pentagon Papers. Numerous other newspapers soon published excerpts as well.

Ellsberg's leak became intensely controversial. Nixon tried to stop the papers' publication—the first effort to muzzle the press since the American

The New Politics of Identity

The Women's Movement and Gay Liberation

The End in Vietnam

Nixon, Kissinger, and the World

Presidential Politics and the Crisis of Leadership

LINKS TO THE WORLD
OPEC and the 1973 Oil Embargo

Economic Crisis

An Era of Cultural Transformation

Renewed Cold War and Middle East Crisis

LEGACY FOR A PEOPLE AND A NATION
Human Rights

Online Study Center
This icon will direct you to interactive map and primary source activities on the website
http:college.hmco.com/pic/nortonbrief7e

CHRONOLOGY

- **1966** • National Organization for Women founded

- **1969** • Stonewall Inn uprising begins gay liberation movement
  - *Apollo 11* astronaut Neil Armstrong becomes first person to walk on moon's surface
  - National Chicano Liberation Youth Conference held in Denver
  - "Indians of All Tribes" occupy Alcatraz Island
  - Nixon administration begins affirmative-action plan

- **1970** • United States invades Cambodia
  - Students at Kent State and Jackson State Universities shot by National Guard troops
  - First Earth Day celebrated
  - Environmental Protection Agency created

- **1971** • Pentagon Papers published

- **1972** • Nixon visits China and Soviet Union
  - CREEP stages Watergate break-in
  - Congress approves ERA and passes Title IX, which creates growth in women's athletics

- **1973** • Peace agreement in Paris ends U.S. involvement in Vietnam
  - OPEC increases oil prices, creating U.S. "energy crisis"
  - *Roe v. Wade* legalizes abortion
  - Agnew resigns; Ford named vice president

- **1974** • Nixon resigns under threat of impeachment; Ford becomes president

- **1975** • In deepening economic recession, unemployment hits 8.5 percent
  - New York City saved from bankruptcy by federal loan guarantees
  - Congress passes Indian Self-Determination and Education Assistance Act in response to Native American activists

- **1976** • Carter elected president

- **1978** • *Regents of the University of California v. Bakke* outlaws quotas but upholds affirmative action
  - California voters approve Proposition 13

- **1979** • Three Mile Island nuclear accident raises fears
  - Camp David accords signed by Israel and Egypt
  - American hostages seized in Iran
  - Soviet Union invades Afghanistan
  - Consumer debt doubles from 1975 to hit $315 billion

Revolution—and to discredit Ellsberg and deter other leakers through the illegal actions of a group of petty operatives. Many saw Ellsberg as a hero who acted to shorten an illegitimate war. To others, he was a publicity-seeking traitor.

The 1970s would be a decade of division for Americans. The violence and chaos of 1968 continued in Nixon's early presidency. Antiwar opposition intensified, and as government deceptions were exposed, Americans were increasingly polarized over Vietnam. The movements for racial equality and social justice also became more radical by the 1970s. While some worked for integration, many embraced cultural nationalism, which sought separatist cultures and societies. Even the women's movement, the strongest and most successful movement of the 1970s, had a polarizing effect. Opponents, many of them women, understood feminism as an attack on their way of life and responded with a conservative grassroots movement.

This divided America faced great challenges. Richard Nixon and his national security adviser, Henry Kissinger, understood that the United States and the Soviet Union, weakened by the costs of their competition and challenged by other nations, faced a world where power was diffused. Accordingly, Nixon and

Kissinger sought improved relations with the People's Republic of China and the Soviet Union in an effort to maintain world order and reduce the threat of great-power war.

Ultimately, however, Richard Nixon's illegal acts in the political scandal known as "Watergate" shook the faith of Americans. By the time Nixon, under threat of impeachment, submitted his resignation, Americans were cynical about politics. Neither of Nixon's successors, Gerald Ford or Jimmy Carter, though both honorable men, could restore that lost faith. Carter's presidency was undermined by international events beyond his control. In the Middle East, a region of increasing importance in U.S. foreign policy, Carter helped broker peace between Egypt and Israel but proved powerless to end a hostage crisis in Iran. The Soviet invasion of Afghanistan in 1979 meanwhile revived Cold War tensions.

A deepening economic crisis added to Carter's woes. In the 1970s, middle-class Americans saw unemployment skyrocket and their savings disappearing to double-digit inflation. The downturn was largely triggered by changes in the global economy and international trade, made worse by the oil embargo launched by Arab members of the Organization of Petroleum Exporting Countries in 1973. Americans recognized their vulnerability to decisions made in far-off lands. ▪

The New Politics of Identity

By the end of the 1960s, divisions among Americans deepened. The civil rights movement, begun in a quest for equal rights and integration, splintered as many young African Americans rejected nonviolence and integration for separatism and embraced a distinct African American culture. Mexican Americans and Native Americans, inspired by civil rights, created powerful "Brown Power" and "Red Power" movements by the early 1970s. They too demanded equal rights and cultural recognition. These movements fueled a new "identity politics," which stressed that differences among racial and ethnic groups were critically important foundations for political action.

By 1970, most African American activists no longer sought political power and racial justice by emphasizing the shared humanity of all people. Instead, an emphasis on the distinctiveness of black culture attracted a large following. Many black Americans were disillusioned by the racism that outlasted the end of legal segregation and believed that integration would mean subordination in a white-dominated society.

AFRICAN AMERICAN CULTURAL NATIONALISM

In the early 1970s, though mainstream groups such as the NAACP continued to seek equality through the courts and ballot boxes, many African Americans looked to culture for social change. Rejecting current European American standards of beauty, young people let their hair grow into "naturals" and "Afros." Seeking strength in their own histories, black college students and faculty fought successfully to create black studies departments in American universities. African traditions were reclaimed—or sometimes created. The new holiday Kwanzaa, created in 1966 by Maulana Karenga, professor of black studies at California State University, Long Beach, united African Americans in celebrating a shared heritage.

MEXICAN AMERICAN ACTIVISM

In 1970 the nation's 9 million Mexican Americans (4.3 percent of America's total population) were heavily concentrated in the Southwest and California. Although the U.S. Census classified all Hispanics as white, discrimination in hiring, pay, housing, schools, and the courts was commonplace. In cities, poor Mexican Americans lived in rundown barrios. Almost half of Mexican Americans were functionally illiterate. By the 1970s, although more Mexican Americans were middle class, almost one-quarter of Mexican American families remained below the poverty level. The national Mexican American movement for social justice began with migrant workers. From 1965 through 1970, labor organizers César Chávez and Dolores Huerta led migrant workers in a strike (*huelga*) against grape growers in California's San Joaquin valley. Chávez and the AFL-CIO-affiliated United Farm Workers (UFW) drew national attention to the working conditions of migrant laborers, who received 10 cents an hour (the minimum wage in 1965 was $1.25) and were often housed by employers in squalid conditions without running water or indoor toilets. A national consumer boycott of table grapes brought the growers to the bargaining table, and in 1970 the UFW won better wages and working conditions. The union resembled nineteenth-century Mexican *mutualistas*, or cooperative associations. Its members founded cooperative groceries, a Spanish-language newspaper, and a theater group.

During the same period in northern New Mexico, Reies Tijerina created the Alianza Federal de Mercedes

CHICANO MOVEMENT

(Federal Alliance of Grants). The group wanted the return of land belonging to local *hispano* villagers, whose ancestors occupied the territory before the United States claimed it under the 1848 Treaty of Guadalupe Hidalgo. In Denver, former boxer Rudolfo "Corky" Gonzáles drew more than one thousand Mexican American youth to his "Crusade for Justice" at the National Chicano Liberation Youth Conference in 1969. They adopted a manifesto, *El Plan Espiritual de Aztlán*, condemning the "brutal 'Gringo' invasion of our territories."

These young activists called for the liberation of "La Raza" (from "La Raza de Bronze," the brown people) from oppressive American society, not for equal rights. They also rejected a hyphenated "Mexican-American" identity. The "Mexican American," they explained in *El Plan Espiritual de Aztlán*, "lacks respect for his culture." Instead, they called themselves "Chicanos" or "Chicanas"—barrio slang associated with *pachucos*, hip and sometimes criminal young men who symbolized what "respectable" Mexican Americans despised.

Many middle-class Mexican Americans and members of the older generations never embraced the term *Chicano* or the separatist agenda of *el movimiento*. Younger activists succeeded in introducing Chicano studies into local high-school and college curricula and in creating a unifying cultural identity for Mexican American youth. Politically, La Raza Unida (RUP), a Southwest-based political party, registered thousands of voters and won local elections. Although never as influential as the African American civil rights movement, the Chicano movement effectively challenged discrimination on the local level and created a basis for political action.

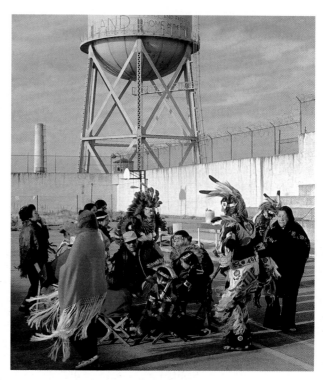

■ Calling their movement "Red Power," these American Indian activists dance in 1969 while "reclaiming" Alcatraz Island in San Francisco Bay. Arguing that an 1868 Sioux treaty entitled them to possession of unused federal lands, the group occupied the island until mid-1971.   (Ralph Crane/Getty Images)

Between 1968 and 1975, Native American activists forced American society to reform U.S. government policies affecting them.

NATIVE AMERICAN ACTIVISM

Young Native American activists were greatly influenced by cultural nationalist beliefs, and seeking a return to the "old ways," they joined with "traditionalists" to challenge tribal leaders advocating assimilation.

In November 1969 a small group of activists, calling themselves "Indians of All Tribes," occupied Alcatraz Island in San Francisco Bay and demanded that the land be returned to native peoples for an Indian cultural center. The protest, which lasted nineteen months and eventually involved more than four hundred people from fifty different tribes, marked the consolidation of a "pan-Indian" approach to activism. Before Alcatraz, protests were reservation based and local. Although the protesters did not reclaim Alcatraz Island, they drew national attention to the growing "Red Power" movement. In 1972 the radical American Indian Movement occupied a Bureau of Indian Affairs office in Washington, D.C., and then in 1973 a trading post at Wounded Knee, South Dakota, where U.S. Army troops had massacred three hundred Sioux men, women, and children in 1890.

Meanwhile, moderate activists, working through pan-tribal organizations such as the National Congress of American Indians and the Native American Rights Fund, lobbied Congress for greater resources to govern themselves. In response, Congress and the federal courts returned millions of acres of land, and in 1975 Congress passed the Indian Self-Determination and Education Assistance Act. Still, during the 1970s and 1980s, American Indians had a higher rate of tuberculosis, alcoholism, and suicide than any other group. Nine of ten lived in substandard housing, with 40 percent unemployment.

As activists made Americans increasingly aware of discrimination and inequality, policymakers struggled to frame remedies. As early as 1965, President Johnson acknowledged the limits of civil rights legislation, calling for "not just legal equality . . . but equality as a fact and equality as a result." Here Johnson joined his belief that the federal government must help individuals attain competitive skills to a new concept: that equality could be measured by group outcomes or results.

AFFIRMATIVE ACTION

Practical issues also contributed to the shift in emphasis from individual opportunity to group outcomes. The 1964 Civil Rights Act had outlawed discrimination but seemingly had stipulated that action could be taken only when an employer "intentionally engaged" in discrimination. The tens of thousands of cases filed suggested a pervasive pattern of racial and sexual discrimination in education and employment, but each required proof of "intentional" actions against an individual before the Equal Employment Opportunity Commission (EEOC) could respond. Consequently, some people argued that it was possible to prove discrimination by "results"—by the relative number of African Americans or women, for example, an employer had hired or promoted.

In 1969 the Nixon administration implemented the first major government affirmative-action programs. The Philadelphia Plan (so called because it targeted government contracts in that city) required businesses contracting with the federal government to show "affirmative action to meet the goals of increasing minority employment" and set specific numerical "goals," or quotas, for employers. Affirmative action for women and racial and ethnic minorities was soon required by all major government contracts, and many corporations and educational institutions launched their own programs.

Supporters saw affirmative action as a remedy for the lasting effects of past discrimination. Critics argued that creating proportional representation for women and minorities meant discrimination against others who had not created past discrimination, and that group-based remedies violated the principle that individuals should be judged on their own merits. As affirmative action affected hiring and university admissions, bringing members of underrepresented groups into college classrooms, law firms, police stations, and companies nationwide, a deepening recession made jobs scarce. Thus, increasing the number of minorities and women hired often meant reducing the number of white men hired, which triggered their resentment.

The Women's Movement and Gay Liberation

During the 1960s, a second wave of the American women's movement emerged, and by the 1970s mainstream and radical activists joined to wage a multifront battle for "women's liberation."

One event that rejuvenated the women's movement was the popularity of Betty Friedan's 1963 book, *The Feminine Mystique*. Writing as a housewife and mother (though she had a long history of political activism), Friedan described "the problem with no name," the dissatisfaction of educated, middle-class wives and mothers like herself, who—looking at their homes and families—wondered guiltily if that was all there was to life. Instead of blaming women for failing to adapt to women's proper role as 1950s magazines often did, Friedan blamed the role itself and the society that created it.

The organized, liberal wing of the women's movement emerged in 1966 with the founding of the National Organization for Women (NOW). Comprising primarily educated women, NOW was a lobbying group seeking to pressure the EEOC into enforcing the 1964 Civil Rights Act. With racial discrimination its priority, sex discrimination fell to the bottom of the EEOC's list. By 1970, NOW had one hundred chapters and over three thousand members nationwide.

LIBERAL AND RADICAL FEMINISM

Another strand of the women's movement developed from the nation's radical social justice movements. In 1968 a group of women protested the Miss America Pageant in Atlantic City as a "degrading mindless-boob girlie symbol." Though nothing was burned, the pejorative 1970s term for feminists, "bra-burners," came from this event, in which women threw items of "enslavement" (girdles, high heels, curlers, and bras) into a "Freedom Trashcan." Many of these women, and others who created a radical feminist movement, had been active in the antiwar or civil rights movements, and those experiences led them to analyze women's roles in American society.

The feminism embraced by these young activists was never a single, coherent set of beliefs. Most radical feminists, however, practiced what they called "personal politics," believing, as feminist author Charlotte Bunch explained, that "there is no private domain of a person's life that is not political, and there is no political issue that is not ultimately personal." In the early 1970s, women throughout the nation came together in suburban kitchens, college dorm rooms, and churches or synagogues to create "consciousness-raising" groups, exploring topics such as power relationships in romance and marriage, sexuality, abortion, healthcare, work, and family.

During the 1970s, the women's movement claimed significant achievements. On March 22, 1972, after massive lobbying by women's organizations, Congress approved the Equal Rights Amendment (ERA) to the Constitution. It stated simply that "equality of rights under the law shall not be denied or abridged by the United States or by any State on account of sex." By the end of the year, twenty-two states (of the thirty-eight necessary to amend the Constitu-

ACCOMPLISHMENTS OF THE WOMEN'S MOVEMENT

tion) had ratified the ERA. Also in 1972, Congress passed Title IX of the Higher Education Act, which prevented federal funds from going to any college or university discriminating against women. As a result, universities began to channel money to women's athletics, and women's participation in sports boomed.

At the state and local levels, women challenged understandings of rape that blamed the victim for the attack. By the end of the decade, activists established rape crisis centers, educated local police and hospital officials about procedures protecting rape survivors, and even changed laws.

Challenging the medical establishment, *Our Bodies, Ourselves* was a book created by the Boston Women's Health Collective in 1971 to help women understand—and take control over—their own sexual and reproductive health. Women who sought the right to safe and legal abortions won a major victory in 1973 when the Supreme Court, in a 7–2 decision on *Roe v. Wade,* ruled that privacy rights protected a woman's choice to end a pregnancy.

Women greatly increased their roles in religious organizations, and some denominations ordained women. In 1970 only 8.4 percent of medical school graduates and 5.4 percent of law school graduates were women; by 1979, those figures had climbed to 23 percent and 28.5 percent, respectively. Colleges and universities also established women's studies departments, with thirty thousand college courses focused on women or gender relations by 1980.

The women's movement was met by opposition, much of it from women. Many had no desire to be "equal" if it meant giving up traditional gender roles in marriage or working at low-wage, exhausting jobs. African American women and Chicanas, many of whom were active in movements for the liberation of their peoples and some of whom helped create second-wave feminism, often regarded feminism as a "white" movement that ignored their cultural traditions and diverted attention from the fight for racial equality.

OPPOSITION TO THE WOMEN'S MOVEMENT

Organized opposition to feminism came primarily from conservative, often religiously motivated men and women. As one conservative Christian writer claimed, "The Bible clearly states that the wife is to submit to her husband's leadership." These beliefs, along with fears about changing gender roles, fueled the

STOP-ERA movement led by Phyllis Schlafly, a lawyer and prominent conservative political activist. Schlafly attacked the women's movement as "a total assault on the role of the American woman as wife and mother." Schlafly's group argued that the ERA would decriminalize rape, force Americans to use unisex toilets, and make women subject to the military draft.

In fighting the ERA, tens of thousands of women became politically experienced and fed a growing grassroots conservative movement that would come into its own in the 1980s. By the mid-1970s, the STOP-ERA movement stalled the Equal Rights Amendment. Despite a congressional deadline extension, the amendment would fall three states short of ratification and expire in 1982.

In the early 1970s, gay men and lesbians faced widespread discrimination. Consensual, same-sex sexual intercourse was illegal in almost every state, and until 1973 homosexuality was labeled a mental disorder by the American Psychiatric Association. Homosexual couples did not receive partnership benefits such as health insurance; they could not marry or adopt children. Gay men and women remained targets of discrimination in hiring and endured public ridicule, harassment, and physical attacks.

GAY LIBERATION

There were small "homophile" organizations, such as the Mattachine Society and the Daughters of Bilitis, that had worked for gay rights since the 1950s. But the symbolic beginning of the gay liberation movement came on June 28, 1969, when New York City police raided the Stonewall Inn, a gay bar in Greenwich Village. (New York City law made it illegal for more than three homosexual patrons to occupy a bar at the same time.) That night, for the first time, patrons stood up to the police. The next morning, a new slogan was spray-painted on neighborhood walls: "Gay Power."

Inspired by the Stonewall riot, some people worked openly and militantly for gay rights. They focused on a dual agenda: legal equality and the promotion of Gay Pride. Some rejected the notion of fitting into straight (heterosexual) culture and helped create distinctive gay communities. By 1973, there were about eight hundred gay organizations in the United States. Centered in big cities and on college campuses, most organizations created supportive environments encouraging gay men and lesbians to come "out of the closet" and push for reform. By decade's end, gay men and lesbians were a public political force in several cities, especially New York, Miami, and San Francisco.

The End in Vietbloqueo

*N*o division pervaded American politics as did the war in Vietnam. Although Richard Nixon said he was going to end the war fast so it would not ruin his political career as it had Johnson's, he did not. Like Johnson, he feared that a precipitous withdrawal would harm American credibility on the world stage. Anxious to get American troops out of Vietnam, Nixon was equally committed to preserving an independent, noncommunist South Vietnam. Hence, he adopted a policy that at once contracted and expanded the war.

INVASION OF CAMBODIA

Nixon's policy centered on "Vietnamization": building up South Vietnamese forces to replace U.S. troops. Accordingly, the president decreased American forces from 543,000 in the spring of 1969 to 156,800 by the end of 1971, and to 60,000 by the fall of 1972. Vietnamization helped quiet domestic dissent—as did the replacement of the military draft with a lottery system, by which only those nineteen-year-olds with low lottery numbers would be subject to conscription—but it did nothing to end the stalemate in the Paris peace talks underway since 1968. Nixon therefore intensified the bombing of North Vietnam and enemy supply depots in neighboring Cambodia, hoping to pound Hanoi into concessions.

The expanded bombing of neutral Cambodia commenced in March 1969 with fourteen months of B-52 pilots flying 3,600 missions and dropping over 100,000 tons of bombs, initially in secret. When the North Vietnamese refused to buckle, Nixon turned up the heat: in April 1970 South Vietnamese and U.S. forces invaded Cambodia. The president publicly said he would not allow "the world's most powerful nation" to act "like a pitiful, helpless giant."

PROTESTS AND COUNTERDEMONSTRATIONS

Instantly, the antiwar movement rose up; students on about 450 college campuses went out on strike, and hundreds of thousands of demonstrators protested the administration's policies in various cities. The crisis atmosphere intensified on May 4 when National Guardsmen in Ohio fired at fleeing students at Kent State University, killing four young people. Ten days later, police armed with automatic weapons blasted a women's dormitory at historically black Jackson State University in Mississippi, killing two and wounding nine others. Police claimed they had been shot at, but no evidence could be found. Nixon's widening of the war sparked congressional outrage, and in June the Senate terminated the 1964 Tonkin Gulf Resolution. After two months, U.S. troops withdrew from Cambodia.

Although a majority of Americans told pollsters they thought the original troop commitment to Vietnam was a mistake, 50 percent said they accepted Nixon's claim that invading Cambodia would shorten the war, and some were angered by demonstrating college students. In New York City, construction workers organized counterdemonstrations against the antiwar protests. Nevertheless, the tumult over the invasion reduced Nixon's options on the war. Henceforth, solid majorities opposed any new missions for U.S. ground troops in Southeast Asia.

Online Study Center   Improve Your Grade
Primary Source: Gayle Smith's Private War

Equally troubling was that morale and discipline among troops had been on the decline before Nixon took office. There were growing re-

MORALE
PROBLEMS IN
MILITARY

ports of drug addiction, desertion, racial discord, even the murder of unpopular officers by enlisted men (a practice called "fragging"). The 1971 court-martial and conviction of Lieutenant William Calley, charged with overseeing the killing of over three hundred unarmed South Vietnamese civilians in My Lai in 1968, got particular attention when an army photographer captured the horror in graphic pictures.

The Nixon administration meanwhile stepped up its efforts to pressure Hanoi into a settlement. When

CEASE-FIRE
AGREEMENT

the North Vietnamese launched a major offensive into South Vietnam in March 1972, Nixon responded with a massive aerial onslaught. In December 1972, after an apparent peace agreement collapsed, the United States launched another air strike on the North—the so-called Christmas bombing.

A diplomatic agreement was close. Kissinger and his North Vietnamese counterpart in the negotiations, Le Duc Tho, resolved many of the outstanding issues. Most notably, Kissinger agreed that North Vietnamese troops could remain in the South after the settlement, while Tho abandoned Hanoi's insistence that the Saigon government of Nguyen Van Thieu be removed. On January 27, 1973, Kissinger and Le Duc Tho signed a cease-fire agreement, and Nixon compelled a reluctant Thieu to accept it by threatening to cut off U.S. aid. The United States promised to withdraw its troops within sixty days. North Vietnamese troops could stay in South Vietnam, and a coalition government that included the Vietcong would be formed in the South.

The United States pulled its troops out of Vietnam, leaving behind some military advisers. Soon, full-scale war erupted again. Just before the South Vietnamese surrendered, hundreds of Americans and Vietnamese advocates were hastily evacuated from Saigon. On April 29, 1975, the South Vietnamese government collapsed, and Vietnam was reunified under a communist government in Hanoi. Saigon was renamed Ho Chi Minh City for the persevering patriot who had died in 1969.

More than 58,000 Americans and between 1.5 and 3 million Vietnamese died in the war. Civilian

COSTS OF THE
VIETNAM WAR

deaths in Cambodia and Laos reached hundreds of thousands. The war cost the United States at least $170 billion, and billions more in subsequent veterans' benefits. With funds shifted from domestic programs, the nation suffered inflation, political schism, and abuses of executive power. The war also delayed accommodation with the Soviet Union and the People's Republic of China, fueled friction with allies, and alienated Third World nations.

In 1975 communists established repressive governments in Vietnam, Cambodia, and Laos, but beyond Indochina, the domino effect once predicted by U.S. officials never occurred. Acute hunger afflicted the people of those devastated lands. Soon refugees—"boat people"—crowded aboard unsafe vessels to escape. Many emigrated to the United States, where they were received with mixed feelings by Americans reluctant to be reminded of defeat and their responsibility for the plight of the Southeast Asian peoples.

As historian William Appleman Williams observed, Americans had had their overseas sphere of influence pushed back for the first time. Hawkish observers claimed that failure in Vietnam undermined the nation's credibility. They pointed to a "Vietnam syndrome"—an American suspicion of foreign entanglements—that they feared would inhibit the future exercise of U.S. power. America lost in Vietnam, they asserted, because Americans had lost their guts at home.

DEBATE OVER THE LESSONS OF VIETNAM

Dovish analysts blamed the war on an imperial presidency that permitted strong-willed men to act without restraint and a weak Congress that conceded too much power to the executive branch. Make the president adhere to the checks-and-balances system— make him go to Congress for a declaration of war— these critics counseled. This view found expression in the War Powers Act of 1973, which limited the president's warmaking freedom and require congressional approval before committing U.S. forces to combat lasting more than sixty days.

Veterans' calls for help in dealing with post-traumatic stress disorder, which afflicted thousands of the 2.8 million Vietnam veterans, also stimulated public discussion. Doctors reported that the disorder, which included nightmares and extreme nervousness, stemmed from soldiers' having seen many children, women, and elderly people killed. Some GIs inadvertently killed these people; some killed them vengefully and later felt guilt. Other veterans publicized their deteriorating health from the defoliant Agent Orange and other herbicides they handled or were accidentally sprayed with in Vietnam.

VIETNAM VETERANS

Nixon, Kissinger, and the World

*T*he difficulties of the Vietnam War signified to Nixon and Kissinger that American power was limited and, in relative terms, in decline. This reality necessitated a new approach to the Cold War. In particular, they believed the United States had to adapt to a new multipolar international system, one no longer defined simply by the Soviet-American rivalry. Western Europe was becoming a major player in its own right, as was Japan. The Middle East loomed increasingly large. Above all, Americans had to come to grips with China by rethinking the policy of hostile isolation.

Nixon and Kissinger were an unlikely duo—the reclusive, ambitious Californian, born of Quaker parents, and the sociable, dynamic Jewish intellectual who fled Nazi Germany as a child. Nixon, ten years older, was a career politician, while Kissinger had made his name as a Harvard professor and foreign policy consultant. What the two men shared was a paranoia about rivals and a capacity to think in large conceptual terms about America's place in the world.

In July 1969 Nixon and Kissinger acknowledged the limits of American power and resources in the Nixon Doctrine. The United States, they said, would provide economic aid to allies, but they should not count on American troops. Washington could no longer afford to sustain its overseas commitments and would have to rely on regional allies, including authoritarian regimes, to maintain an anticommunist world order. Nixon's doctrine partially retreated from the 1947 Truman Doctrine's promise to support noncommunist governments facing threats.

NIXON DOCTRINE

The other pillar of the new foreign policy was détente: measured cooperation with the Soviets through negotiations within an environment of rivalry. Détente's primary purpose, like that of the containment doctrine, was to check Soviet expansion and arms buildup, but through diplomacy and mutual concessions. The second part of the strategy sought to curb revolution and radicalism in the Third World and quash threats to American interests. More specifically, expanded trade with friendlier Soviets and Chinese might reduce the huge U.S. balance-of-payments deficit. And improving relations with both communist giants, at a time when Sino-Soviet tensions were increasing, might weaken communism.

DÉTENTE

The Soviet Union too found that the Cold War drained its resources, with defense and consumer demands increasingly at odds. Improved relations with Washington would also allow the USSR to focus on the threat from China and might generate progress on outstanding European issues, including the status of Germany and Berlin. In May 1972 the two nations agreed to slow the arms race by limiting the construction and deployment of intercontinental ballistic missiles and antiballistic missile defenses.

Meanwhile, the United States took dramatic steps to end two decades of Sino-American hostility. The

OPENING TO CHINA

Chinese wanted to spur trade and hoped that friendlier Sino-American relations would make their one-time ally and now enemy, the Soviet Union, more cautious. In early 1972 Nixon made a historic trip to "Red China," where he and the venerable Chinese leaders Mao Zedong and Zhou Enlai agreed to disagree on many issues, except one: the Soviet Union should not be permitted to make gains in Asia. Sino-American relations improved slightly, and official diplomatic recognition came in 1979.

In the Third World, too, Nixon and Kissinger sought stability, though there they hoped to achieve it by maintaining the status quo. As it happened, events in the Third World would provide the Nixon-Kissinger approach with its greatest test.

In the Middle East the situation had grown more volatile in the aftermath of the Arab-Israeli Six-Day

WARS IN THE MIDDLE EAST

War in 1967. Israel scored victories against Egypt and Syria, seizing the Sinai Peninsula and the Gaza Strip from Egypt, the West Bank and East Jerusalem from Jordan, and the Golan Heights from Syria (see Map 33.1). Instantly, Israel's regional position was transformed as it gained 28,000 square miles and could henceforth defend itself against invading forces. But with Gaza and the West Bank as the ancestral homeland to hundreds of thousands of Palestinians and refugees, Israel found itself governing large numbers of people who wanted to see it destroyed (see Chapter 28). When the Israelis established Jewish settlements in their newly won areas, Arab resentment grew. Terrorists associated with the Palestinian Liberation Organization (PLO) made hit-and-run raids on Jewish settlements, hijacked jetliners, and murdered Israeli athletes at the 1972 Olympic Games in Munich, West Germany. The Israelis retaliated by assassinating PLO leaders.

In October 1973, on the Jewish High Holy Day of Yom Kippur, Egypt and Syria attacked Israel, primarily seeking revenge for the 1967 defeat. Surprised, Israel reeled before launching an effective counteroffensive. To punish Americans for their pro-Israel stance, the Organization of Petroleum Exporting Countries (OPEC), a group of mostly Arab nations that had joined together to raise the price of oil, embargoed oil shipments to the United States and other Israeli supporters. An energy crisis rocked the nation. Kissinger arranged a cease-fire, but OPEC did not lift the embargo until March 1974. The next year Kissinger persuaded Egypt and Israel to accept a U.N. peacekeeping force in the Sinai. But Arabs still vowed to destroy Israel, and Israelis built more Jewish settlements in occupied lands.

In Latin America, the Nixon administration thwarted leftist challenges to authoritarian rule. When

ANTIRADICALISM IN LATIN AMERICA AND AFRICA

voters in Chile elected Marxist president Salvador Allende in 1970, the CIA secretly encouraged military officers to stage a coup. In 1973 a military junta ousted Allende and installed an authoritarian regime under General Augusto Pinochet. (Allende was subsequently murdered.) Washington publicly denied any role.

In Africa, too, Washington preferred the status quo, backing a white-minority regime in Rhodesia (now Zimbabwe), and activated the CIA in a failed effort to defeat a Soviet- and Cuban-backed faction in Angola's civil war. In South Africa, Nixon tolerated the white rulers who imposed segregationist apartheid on blacks and mixed-race "coloureds" (85 percent of the population), keeping them poor, disfranchised, and ghettoized in prisonlike townships. After the leftist government came to power in Angola, however, Washington paid attention to Africa, building economic ties and sending arms to friendly black nations such as Kenya and the Congo, while distancing the United States from the white governments of Rhodesia and South Africa.

Presidential Politics and the Crisis of Leadership

*R*ichard Nixon's foreign policy accomplishments were overshadowed by his domestic failures. He betrayed the public trust and broke laws. That, combined with Americans' belief that leaders had repeatedly lied about the war in Vietnam, shook their faith in government. This new mistrust joined

OPEC and the 1973 Oil Embargo

If one date can mark the decline of American power in the Cold War era and the arrival of the Arab nations as important players on the world stage, it would be October 20, 1973. That day, Arab members of the Organization of Petroleum Exporting Countries (OPEC)—Saudi Arabia, Iraq, Kuwait, Libya, and Algeria—imposed an embargo on oil shipments to the United States and other Israeli allies. The move was in retaliation against U.S. support of Israel in the two-week-old Yom Kippur War. The embargo followed an OPEC price hike days earlier, from $3.01 to $5.12 per barrel. In December, the five Arab countries, joined by Iran, raised prices again, to $11.65 per barrel, almost a fourfold increase from early October.

Gasoline prices surged across America, and some dealers ran low on supplies. Frustrated Americans endured endless lines at the pumps and shivered in underheated homes. When the embargo was lifted in April 1974, oil prices stayed high, and the aftereffects of the embargo would linger through the decade. It confirmed how much America's economic destiny was beyond its control.

In the early 1950s, Americans produced all the oil they needed at home. By the early 1960s the picture changed, as America depended on foreign sources for one out of every six barrels of oil. By 1972, the figure had gone up to about two out of six, or more than 30 percent. But few Americans worried and were shocked by the embargo. As author Daniel Yergin put it, "The shortfall struck at fundamental beliefs in the endless abundance of resources . . . that a large part of the public did not even know, up until October 1973, that the United States imported any oil at all."

When the embargo ended, Americans resumed their wastefulness, but in a changed world: the United States had become a dependent nation, its economic future linked to decisions by Arab sheiks half a world away.

In 1976 OPEC sharply raised the price of oil a second time, prompting this editorial cartoon by Don Wright of the *Miami News.* (Copyright, Tribune Media Services, Inc. All rights reserved. Reprinted with permission)

with conservatives' traditional suspicion of big, activist government to create a crisis of leadership and undermine liberal policies that had governed the nation since the New Deal. Nixon's successors, Gerald Ford and James Earl Carter, were limited by the public's suspicion of government.

Richard Nixon was brilliant, driven, politically cunning, yet also crude, prejudiced against Jews and

NIXON'S DOMESTIC AGENDA

African Americans, happy to use dirty tricks against his enemies, and driven by a resentment that bordered on paranoia. The son of a grocer from an agricultural region of southern California, Nixon loathed the liberal establishment, which loathed him back, and his presidency was driven by that as much as by a philosophical commitment to conservative principles.

Nixon's domestic policy initiatives often appeared oddly liberal, even progressive. The Nixon administration pioneered affirmative action and doubled the budgets of the National Endowment for the Humanities (NEH) and National Endowment for the Arts (NEA). Nixon supported the ERA, signed major environmental legislation, created the Occupational Safety and Health Administration, actively used deficit spending to manage the economy, and even proposed a guaranteed minimum income for all Americans.

At the same time, Nixon pursued a conservative agenda that involved "devolution," or shifting federal government authority to states and localities. He promoted revenue-sharing programs that distributed federal funds back to the states, thus appealing to those who saw high taxes as supporting liberal "giveaway" programs for poor and minority Americans. Nixon worked to equate the Republican Party with law and order and the Democrats with permissiveness, crime, drugs, radicalism, and the "hippie lifestyle." He used his outspoken vice president, Spiro Agnew, to attack protesters and critics as "naughty children." He appointed four conservative justices to the Supreme Court (Chief Justice Warren Burger, Harry Blackmun, Lewis Powell Jr., and William Rehnquist); ironically, Nixon's appointees did not always vote as he would have wished.

But most of Nixon's "liberal" agenda was not so much liberal as tricky—a term commonly applied to Nixon at the time. Instead of attacking liberal programs, Nixon attempted to undermine them while appearing to offer support. For example, when Nixon proposed a guaranteed minimum income for all Americans, his larger goal was to dismantle the federal welfare system and destroy its liberal bureaucracy of social workers.

Nixon additionally sought to attract white southerners to the Republican Party. He nominated two southerners for the Supreme Court—one of whom had a segregationist record. When Congress declined to confirm either nominee, Nixon protested angrily. After the Supreme Court upheld a school desegregation plan requiring a highly segregated North Carolina school system to achieve racial integration by busing both black and white children throughout the county (*Swann v. Charlotte-Mecklenburg,* 1971), Nixon denounced busing.

Nixon was almost sure of reelection in 1972. His Democratic opponent was George McGovern, a pro-

ENEMIES AND DIRTY TRICKS

gressive senator from South Dakota and strong opponent of the Vietnam War who declared, "I am not a centrist candidate." Alabama governor George Wallace, running on a third-party ticket, withdrew from the race after an assassination attempt at a Maryland shopping center left him paralyzed. The Nixon campaign, however, was taking no chances. On June 17, five men from the Committee to Re-elect the President, known as CREEP, were caught breaking into the Democratic National Committee's offices at the Watergate apartment and office complex in Washington, D.C. The break-in got little attention, and Nixon was swept into office in November with 60 percent of the popular vote. McGovern carried only Massachusetts and the District of Columbia. But even as Nixon triumphed, his downfall had begun.

From the beginning of his presidency, Nixon obsessively believed he was surrounded by enemies. He made "enemies lists" that included all black members of Congress and the presidents of most Ivy League universities. On Nixon's order, his aide Charles Colson formed a secret group called the Plumbers. Their first job was to break into the office of the psychiatrist treating Daniel Ellsberg, the former Pentagon employee responsible for making the Pentagon Papers public, looking for material to discredit him. During the 1972 presidential campaign, the Plumbers bugged phones, infiltrated campaign staffs, and wrote anonymous letters falsely accusing Democratic candidates of sexual misconduct. They were going back to plant more surveillance at the Democratic National Committee offices when they were caught by D.C. police at the Watergate complex.

Nixon was not directly involved in the Watergate affair, but instead of distancing himself and firing the people involved, he covered up their connection to the break-ins. He had the CIA stop the FBI's investigation, claiming national security. At this point, Nixon had obstructed justice—a felony and an impeachable crime—but he had also halted the investigation. However, two relatively unknown reporters for the *Washington Post*, Carl Bernstein and Bob Woodward, stayed on the story. Aided by an anonymous, highly placed government official code-named Deep Throat (the title of a notorious 1972 X-rated film), they followed a money trail leading to the White House. (In June 2005, it was revealed that Deep Throat was Mark Felt, a high-ranking FBI official at the time of Watergate.)

WATERGATE COVER-UP AND INVESTIGATION

From May to August 1973, the Senate held televised hearings on the Watergate affair. White House counsel John Dean, fearful that he was becoming the fall guy for the Watergate fiasco, gave damning testimony. On July 13, a White House aide told the Senate Committee that Nixon regularly recorded his conversations in the Oval Office. Nixon refused to turn the tapes over to Congress.

Nixon's problems continued. In October 1973, Vice President Spiro Agnew resigned following charges that he accepted bribes while governor of Maryland. Nixon appointed and Congress approved Michigan's Gerald Ford, the House minority leader, as Agnew's replacement. Meanwhile, Nixon's staff was increasingly concerned about his excessive drinking and seeming mental instability. Then, on October 24, 1973, the House of Representatives began impeachment proceedings.

IMPEACHMENT AND RESIGNATION

Under court order, Nixon released portions of the Oval Office tapes. Though the first tapes revealed nothing criminal, the public was shocked by Nixon's obscenities and racism. In July 1974, the Supreme Court ruled that Nixon must release all the tapes. Despite "mysterious" erasures on two key tapes, the House Judiciary Committee found evidence to im-

■ Resigning in disgrace as impeachment for his role in the Watergate cover-up became a certainty, Richard Nixon flashes the "V for victory" sign as he leaves the White House for the last time.
(Nixon Presidential Materials Project, National Archives and Record Administration)

peach Nixon on three grounds: obstruction of justice, abuse of power, and contempt of Congress. On August 9, 1974, facing certain impeachment and conviction, Richard Nixon became the first president of the United States to resign.

The Watergate scandal shook the confidence of American citizens in their government and prompted Congress to pass several bills aimed at restricting presidential power, including the War Powers Act.

Gerald Ford, the nation's first unelected president, faced a cynical nation. The presidency was discredited; the nation's economy was in decline. Ford was an honorable man who tried to end "the long national nightmare." But when he issued a full pardon to Richard Nixon, his approval ratings plummeted from 71 to 41 percent. Some suggested, though with no evidence, that he had struck a deal with Nixon.

FORD'S
PRESIDENCY

Ford accomplished little domestically during his two and a half years in office. The Democrats gained a large margin in the 1974 congressional elections, and after Watergate, Congress was willing to exercise its power. Ford almost routinely vetoed its bills—thirty-nine in one year—but Congress often overrode his veto. During the course of his brief presidency, Ford was constantly portrayed as a buffoon and klutz in political cartoons, comedy monologues, and especially on the hit television show *Saturday Night Live*. Ford caught the fallout of disdain from Nixon's actions. No longer would respect for the presidency prevent the mass media from reporting presidential stumbles or misconduct.

Jimmy Carter, who was elected in 1976 by a slim margin, initially benefited from Americans' suspicion of politicians. Carter was a one-term governor of Georgia, one of the new southern leaders committed to racial equality. He grew up on his family's peanut farm in rural Plains, Georgia; graduated from the Naval Academy; then served as an engineer in the navy's nuclear submarine program. A born-again Christian, Carter promised America, "I will never lie to you," underscoring his distance from Washington's recent political corruption.

CARTER AS
"OUTSIDER"
PRESIDENT

From his inauguration, when he broke with the conventional motorcade and walked down Pennsylvania Avenue holding hands with his wife and close adviser Rosalynn and their daughter, Amy, Carter emphasized his populist, outsider appeal. But his outsider status proved one of his greatest problems as president. Though an astute policymaker, he scorned the deal making that was necessary to pass legislation in Congress.

Carter faced problems that would have challenged any leader: continued economic downturn, unabated energy shortages, public distrust of government. More than any other postwar American leader, Carter was willing to tell Americans things they did not want to hear. As shortages of natural gas forced schools and businesses to close during the bitterly cold winter of 1977, Carter, wearing a cardigan sweater, called for "sacrifice" and implemented energy conservation at government buildings. In a defining speech, Carter told Americans that the nation suffered from a crisis of the spirit. He talked about the false lures of "self-indulgence and consumption." He called for a "new commitment to the path of common purpose." But he had few solutions for the national malaise.

Carter did ease burdensome government regulations without destroying consumer and worker safeguards, and created the Departments of Energy and Education. He also established a $1.6 billion "Superfund" to clean up abandoned chemical-waste sites and placed over 100 million acres of Alaskan land under federal protection as national parks, forests, and wildlife refuges.

Economic Crisis

Since World War II, except for a few brief downturns, prosperity had dominated American life. Prosperity made possible the great liberal initiatives of the 1960s and improved the lives of America's poor and elderly citizens. But in the early 1970s, that long period of economic expansion ended. In 1974 alone, the gross national product dropped two percentage points. Industrial production fell 9 percent. Inflation—the increase in costs of goods and services—skyrocketed, and unemployment grew.

Throughout the 1970s, the U.S. economy floundered in what economists dubbed "stag-flation": a stagnant economy characterized by high unemployment and out-of-control inflation. Stagflation was almost impossible to manage with traditional economic remedies. When the federal government increased spending to stimulate the economy and so reduce unemployment, inflation grew. When it tried to halt inflation by cutting government spending or tightening the money supply, the recession deepened and unemployment skyrocketed.

STAGFLATION
AND ITS CAUSES

The causes of the economic crisis were complex. President Johnson had created inflationary pressure by waging an expensive war in Vietnam while greatly expanding domestic spending in his Great Society programs. But fundamental problems also came from America's changing role in the global economy. By the early 1970s, both of America's major World War II adversaries, Japan and Germany, had become major economic powers—and competitors in global trade that the United States once exclusively dominated. In 1971, for the first time since the nineteenth century, the United States imported more goods than it exported, beginning an era of American trade deficits.

Corporate decisions also contributed to growing trade imbalances. During the years of global dominance, few American companies improved production techniques or educated workers. Consequently, American productivity—the average output of goods per hour of labor—declined. But wages rarely did. The combination of falling productivity and high labor costs meant that American goods became increasingly expensive. And American companies allowed the quality of their goods to decline. From 1966 to 1973, for example, American car and truck manufacturers recalled almost 30 million vehicles because of serious defects.

America's global economic vulnerability was driven home by the energy crisis in 1973. The country depended on imported oil for almost one-third of its energy. When OPEC cut off oil shipments to the United States, prices rose 350 percent and increased heating costs, shipping costs, and manufacturing costs, as well as the cost of goods and services. Inflation jumped from 3 percent in 1973 to 11 percent in 1974. Sales of gas-guzzling American cars plummeted as people switched to energy-efficient subcompacts from Japan and Europe. General Motors laid off 6 percent of its domestic work force and put larger numbers on rolling unpaid leaves. As the ailing automobile industry quit buying steel, glass, and rubber, manufacturers of these goods laid off workers, too.

American leaders tried desperately to manage the economic crisis, but their actions often exacerbated it instead. As America's rising trade deficit undermined international confidence in the dollar, the Nixon administration ended the dollar's link to the gold standard; free-floating exchange rates increased the price

ATTEMPTS TO FIX THE ECONOMY

of foreign goods and stimulated inflation. Following the monetary theory, which held that with less money available to "chase" the supply of goods, price increases would slow and end the inflationary spiral, Ford curbed federal spending and encouraged the Federal Reserve Board to tighten credit—prompting the worst recession in forty years. In 1975 unemployment climbed to 8.5 percent.

Carter's larger economic policies, including his 1978 deregulation of airline, trucking, banking, and communications industries, would eventually foster economic growth—but not soon enough. After almost a decade of decline, Americans were losing faith in the American economy and the ability of their political leaders to manage it.

The economic crisis of the 1970s accelerated the transition from an industrial to a service economy. During the 1970s, the American economy "deindustrialized," as auto companies laid off workers and steel plant closings left communities devastated. Other manufacturing concerns moved overseas, seeking lower labor costs and fewer government regulations. New jobs were created—27 million of them—overwhelmingly in what economists called the "service sector": retail sales, restaurants, and other service providers. Jobs there, such as warehouse work or retail sales, for example, paid much lower wages than union manufacturing positions and often lacked benefits such as healthcare.

IMPACTS OF THE ECONOMIC CRISIS

Formerly successful blue-collar workers saw their middle-class standards of life slipping away. More married women joined the work force because they had to. High-school and college graduates in the 1970s, raised with high expectations, found limited possibilities—if they found jobs at all.

As the old industrial regions of the North and Midwest went into decline, people headed for the Sunbelt, where the jobs were (see Map 31.1). The federal government had invested heavily in the South and West during the postwar era, especially in military and defense industries. The Sunbelt was primed for the rapid growth of modern industries and services: aerospace, defense, electronics, transportation, research, banking and finance, and leisure. City and state governments competed for business dollars, in part by preventing the growth of unions. Like Atlanta and Houston, many southern cities marketed them-

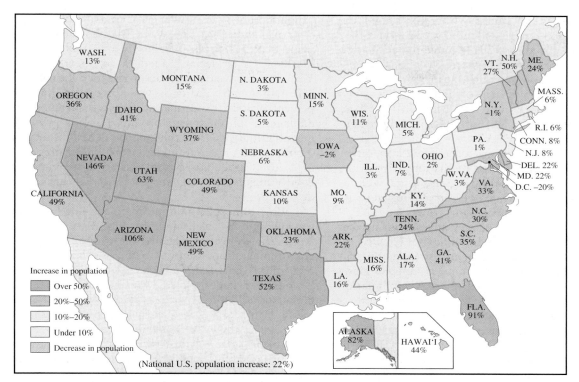

Map 31.1   The Continued Shift to the Sunbelt in the 1970s and 1980s

Throughout the 1970s and 1980s, Americans continued to leave economically declining areas of the North and East in pursuit of opportunity in the Sunbelt. States in the Sunbelt and in the West had the largest population increases.   (Source: "Shift to the Sunbelt," *Newsweek*, September 10, 1990.)

selves as cosmopolitan and racially tolerant; they bought sports teams and built museums.

Online Study Center   **Improve Your Grade**
Interactive Map: Population Increase in the Sunbelt States, 1950–1994

Population shifts created disaster in northern and midwestern cities. New York City, near financial collapse by late 1975, was saved only when the House and Senate Banking Committees approved federal loan guarantees. Cleveland defaulted on its debts in 1978, the first major city to do so since Detroit declared bankruptcy in 1933.

Meanwhile, a "tax revolt" movement grew in the West. In California, inflation had driven property taxes

TAX REVOLTS   up rapidly, hitting middle-class taxpayers hard. Instead of calling for

wealthy citizens and corporations to pay a larger share of taxes, voters rebelled against taxation itself. California's Proposition 13, passed by a landslide in 1978, rolled back property taxes and restricted future increases. Thirty-seven states similarly cut property taxes, and twenty-eight lowered their state income-tax rates.

The impact of Proposition 13 and similar initiatives was originally cushioned by state budget surpluses, but as those surpluses turned to deficits, states cut services—closing fire stations and libraries, ending or limiting mental health services and programs for the disabled. Public schools were hit especially hard.

Before the runaway inflation of the 1970s, home mortgages and auto loans were the only major debt

CREDIT AND INVESTMENT   most Americans had. National credit cards had become common only in the late 1960s, and few

Americans—especially those who remembered the Great Depression—were willing to spend money they did not have. In the 1970s, double-digit inflation rates made it economically smarter to buy goods before prices went up—even if it meant borrowing the money. Since debt was paid off later with devalued dollars, the consumer came out ahead. In 1975 consumer debt hit a high of $167 billion; it almost doubled, to $315 billion, by 1979.

In the 1970s, Americans became investors rather than savers. Because banking regulations capped the interest paid on individual savings accounts, with inflation, an account bearing 5 percent interest actually *lost* more than 20 percent of its value from 1970 through 1980. That same money, invested at market rates, would have grown dramatically. Fidelity Investments, a mutual fund company, saw an opportunity: its money market accounts combined many smaller investments to purchase large-denomination treasury bills and certificates of deposit, thus providing small investors the high interest rates normally available only to major investors. Money market investments grew from $1.7 billion in 1974 to $200 billion in 1982. Deregulation of the New York Stock Exchange spawned discount brokerage houses, whose low commission rates were affordable to middle-class investors.

An Era of Cultural Transformation

*a*s Americans struggled with economic recession, governmental betrayal, and social division, major strands of late-twentieth-century culture were developed. The current environmental movement, a "therapeutic culture" and the growth of born-again Christianity, contemporary forms of sexuality and the family, and America's emphasis on diversity have roots in this decade, sandwiched between the political vibrancy of the 1960s and the conservatism of the 1980s.

A series of ecological crises drove home the fragility of the environment. In 1969 a major oil spill took place off the coast of Santa

ENVIRONMENTALISM

Barbara, California; that same year the polluted Cuyahoga River, flowing through Cleveland,

caught fire. In 1979 human error contributed to a nuclear accident at the Three Mile Island nuclear power plant near Harrisburg, Pennsylvania, and in 1980 President Carter declared a federal emergency at New York State's Love Canal, a dump site for a local chemical manufacturer, after it was discovered that 30 percent of local residents had suffered chromosome damage. Public activism produced major environmental initiatives, from the Environmental Protection Agency (EPA), created (under strong public pressure) in 1970 by the Nixon administration, to eighteen environmental laws enacted by Congress during the decade.

When almost 20 million Americans—half of them schoolchildren—celebrated the first Earth Day on April 22, 1970, they signaled the triumph of a new environmentalism. Central to this movement was a recognition that earth's resources were finite and must be conserved and protected. Many also identified rapid global population growth as a problem, and state public health offices frequently dispensed contraceptives to stem this new "epidemic."

During these years, Americans became increasingly uneasy about the science and technology that had

TECHNOLOGY

been a source of America's might. Americans watched with pride as astronaut Neil Armstrong stepped onto the moon on July 20, 1969, stating, "One small step for man, one giant step for mankind." But technology seemed unable to cope with earthbound problems of poverty, crime, pollution, and urban decay. The failure of technological warfare to deliver victory in Vietnam happened as antiwar protesters were questioning the morality of such technology. But in the 1970s, the foundation was laid for America's computer revolution, with the creation of the integrated circuit in 1970, and mail-order processors later in the decade.

Americans increasingly sought spiritual fulfillment. Methodist, Presbyterian, and Episcopalian churches

RELIGION
AND THE
THERAPEUTIC
CULTURE

lost members during this era, while evangelical and fundamentalist Christian churches grew dramatically. Protestant evangelicals described themselves as "born again" and emphasized the immediate, daily presence of God in their lives. Even some Catholics, such as the Mexican Americans who embraced the *cursillo* movement (a "little course" in faith), sought a more personal relationship with God. Other Americans embraced the New Age movement, which drew from and combined non-Western spiritual and religious practices, including Zen Buddhism, yoga, and shamanism, along with insights from Western psychology and spiritually oriented environmentalism.

Also in the 1970s, America saw the emergence of a "therapeutic" culture. Although some were disgusted with the self-centeredness of the "Me-Decade," best-selling books by therapists and self-help gurus insisted that individual feelings offered the ultimate measure of truth. Self-help titles such as *I'm OK— You're OK* (first published in 1967, it became a best-seller in the mid-1970s) made up 15 percent of all best-selling books.

Sex became far more visible in American culture during the 1970s as network television loosened its

SEXUALITY AND THE FAMILY

regulation of sexual content. At the beginning of the 1960s, married couples in television shows were required to occupy twin beds; in the 1970s, hit shows included *Three's Company,* a comedy based on the then-scandalous premise that a single man shared an apartment with two female roommates—and got away with it by pretending to their suspicious landlord that he was gay. Donna Summers's 1975 disco hit, "Love to Love You Baby," contained sixteen minutes of sexual moaning. And though few Americans participated in heterosexual orgies at New York City's Plato's Retreat, many read about them in *Time* magazine.

Sexual behaviors also changed. The seventies was the era of singles bars and gay bathhouses, but for most Americans, "sexual revolution" meant a broader public acceptance of premarital sex and a limited acceptance of homosexuality, especially among more educated Americans. More heterosexual young people "lived together" without marriage during the 1970s; the Census Bureau even coined the term "POSSLQ" (persons of opposite sex sharing living quarters) to describe the relationship.

Changes in sexual mores and women's roles altered the family structure as well. Men and women married later, and women had fewer children. By the end of the 1970s, the birth rate dropped almost 40 percent from its 1957 peak. Almost a quarter of young single women in 1980 said they did not plan to have children. And a steadily rising percentage of babies were born to unmarried women, as the number of families headed by never-married women rose 400 percent. The divorce rate also rose, in part because states implemented "no-fault" divorce, which did not require evidence of adultery, physical cruelty, abandonment, or other wrongdoing. Americans also developed a greater acceptance of various family forms (the blended family of television's *Brady Bunch,* for example).

The racial justice and identity movements of the late 1960s and 1970s made Americans more aware

DIVERSITY

of differences among the nation's peoples—an awareness strengthened by new immigrants from Latin America and Asia. The challenge was figuring out how to acknowledge the new importance of "difference" in public policy. The solution was the idea of "diversity." Difference was not a problem but a strength; the nation should seek to foster the "diversity" of its schools, workplaces, and public culture.

The 1978 Supreme Court decision *Regents of the University of California v. Bakke* was a crucial early step. Allan Bakke, a thirty-three-year-old white man with a strong academic record, was denied admission to the medical school of the University of California at Davis. Bakke sued, charging that he had been denied "equal protection" because the medical school's affirmative-action program reserved 16 percent of its slots for racial-minority candidates, who were held to lower standards than other applicants. In 1978 the Supreme Court, in a split decision, decided in favor of Bakke. Four justices argued that any race-based decision violated the Civil Rights Act of 1964; four saw affirmative-action programs as constitutionally acceptable. The deciding vote, though for Bakke, contained an important qualification: a "diverse student body," Justice Lewis Powell wrote, is "a constitutionally permissible goal for an institution of higher education." To achieve "diversity," educational institutions could consider race in admissions.

Renewed Cold War and Middle East Crisis

 hen Jimmy Carter took office in 1977, he asked Americans to abandon their "inordinate fear of communism." Carter vowed to reduce the U.S. military presence overseas, cut back arms sales, and slow the nuclear arms race. More than 400,000 American military personnel were stationed abroad, the United States had military links with ninety-two nations, and the CIA was active on every continent. Carter promised to avoid new Vietnams and give more attention to environmental issues. He especially determined to improve human rights abroad—the freedom to vote, worship, travel, speak out, and get a fair trial. Like his predecessors, however, Carter identified revolutionary nationalism as a threat to America's global prominence.

Carter spoke and acted inconsistently, in part because in the post-Vietnam years, no consensus existed

CARTER'S DIVIDED ADMINISTRATION

in foreign policy and in part because his advisers squabbled among themselves. One source of the problem was the stern-faced Zbigniew Brzezinski, a Polish-born political scientist who became Carter's national security adviser. An old-fashioned Cold Warrior, Brzezinski blamed foreign crises on Soviet expansionism. Carter gradually listened more to Brzezinski than to Secretary of State Cyrus Vance, an experienced public servant who advocated quiet diplomacy. Under Carter, détente deteriorated, and the Cold War deepened. Initially, Carter maintained fairly good relations with Moscow and managed some foreign policy successes. The United States signed two treaties with Panama in 1977. One provided for the return of the Canal Zone to Panama in 2000, and the other guaranteed the United States the right to defend the canal after that time (see Chapter 22). With conservatives denouncing a retreat from greatness, the Senate narrowly endorsed both agreements in 1978. The majority agreed with Carter that relinquishing the canal would improve U.S. relations with Latin America.

The crowning accomplishment of Carter's presidency was the Camp David accords, the first mediated peace treaty between Israel and

CAMP DAVID ACCORDS

an Arab nation. In September 1978, the president persuaded Israel and Egypt to agree to a peace treaty, gained Israel's promise to withdraw from the Sinai Peninsula, and forged an agreement that provided for continued negotiations on the future status of Palestinians in the occupied territories of Jordan's West Bank and Egypt's Gaza Strip (see

Map 33.1). Other Arab states denounced the agreement for not requiring Israel to relinquish all occupied territories and not guaranteeing a Palestinian homeland. But the treaty, signed on March 26, 1979, by Israeli prime minister Menachem Begin and Egyptian president Anwar al-Sadat, at least ended warfare along one frontier.

Meanwhile, relations with Moscow deteriorated. U.S. and Soviet officials sparred over the Kremlin's reluctance to lift restrictions on Jew-

SOVIET INVASION OF AFGHANISTAN

ish emigration and over the Soviet decision to deploy new intermediate-range ballistic missiles aimed at western Europe. Then, in December 1979, the Soviets invaded Afghanistan, a remote country whose strategic position made it a source of great-power conflict. Following World War II, Afghanistan struggled with ongoing ethnic and factional squabbling; in the 1970s, it spiraled into anarchy. In late 1979 the Red Army bludgeoned into Afghanistan to shore up a faltering communist government under siege by Muslim rebels. Moscow officials calculated they could be in and out before anyone noticed, including the Americans.

Carter not only noticed but reacted forcefully. He suspended shipments of grain and high-technology equipment to the Soviet Union, withdrew a major arms control treaty from Senate consideration, and initiated an international boycott of the 1980 Summer Olympics in Moscow. He also secretly authorized the CIA to distribute aid, including arms and military support, to the Mujahidin (Islamic guerrillas) fighting the communist government and sanctioned military aid to their backer, Pakistan. Announcing the Carter Doctrine, the president asserted that the United States would intervene, unilaterally and militarily, should Soviet aggression threaten the petroleum-rich Persian Gulf. Carter warned aides that the Soviets, unless checked, would likely attack elsewhere in the Middle East, but declassified documents confirm what contemporary critics said: that the Soviet invasion was largely defensive and did not presage a push to the Persian Gulf.

Carter simultaneously faced a foreign policy test in Iran. The shah, long favored by America, was de-

IRANIAN HOSTAGE CRISIS

throned by a coalition of Iranians who resented the dislocation of their traditional ways by the shah's modernization. Riots led by anti-American Muslim clerics erupted in late 1978. The shah went into exile, and in April 1979 Islamic revolutionaries, led by the Ayatollah Khomeini, an elderly cleric who denounced the United States as the stronghold of capitalism and Western materialism, proclaimed a Shi'ite Islamic Republic. In November, with the exiled shah in the United States for medical treatment, mobs stormed the U.S. embassy in Teheran. They took American personnel as hostages, demanding the return of the shah to stand trial. The Iranians eventually released a few American prisoners, but fifty-two others suffered solitary confinement, beatings, and terrifying mock executions.

Unable to gain the hostages' freedom through diplomatic intermediaries, Carter took steps to isolate Iran economically, freezing Iranian assets in the United States. When the hostage takers paraded their blindfolded captives before television cameras, Americans felt taunted and humiliated. In April 1980, Carter broke diplomatic relations with Iran and ordered a daring rescue mission. But equipment failed and two aircraft collided, killing eight American soldiers. The hostages were not freed until January 1981, just after Carter left office.

The Iranian revolution, together with the rise of the Mujahidin in Afghanistan, signified the emergence of Islamic fundamentalism as a force in world affairs. Socialism and capitalism, the answers that the two superpowers offered to the problems of modernization, failed to solve the problems in Central Asia and the Middle East. Consequently, Islamic orthodoxy found growing support for its message: that secular leaders such as Nasser in Egypt and the shah in Iran had taken their peoples down the wrong path, necessitating a return to conservative Islamic values and Islamic law. The Iranian revolution expressed a complex mixture of discontents within Islamic societies.

U.S. officials took some consolation from the avowedly secular government in Iraq. Ruled by the

RISE OF SADDAM HUSSEIN

Ba'athist Party, Iraq won favor in Washington for its pursuit and execution of Iraqi communists. When a Ba'athist leader named Saddam Hussein took over as president of Iraq in 1979 and threatened the Teheran government, U.S. officials thought Saddam could offset the Iranian danger in the Persian Gulf. As border clashes escalated into war in 1980, Washington policymakers were officially neutral but tilted toward Iraq.

Jimmy Carter earned some diplomatic successes in the Middle East, Africa, and Latin America, but the revived Cold War and prolonged Iranian hostage crisis hurt the administration politically. Contrary to Carter's goals, more American military personnel were stationed overseas in 1980 than in 1976; the defense budget climbed, and arms sales grew to $15.3 billion in 1980. On human rights, the president practiced a double standard, applying the human-rights test to some nations (the Soviet Union, Argentina, and Chile) but not to U.S. allies. Still, Carter's human-rights policy saved the lives of some political prisoners and institutionalized concern for human rights worldwide. But his inability to restore economic and military dominance helped dash his re-election hopes: he lost in 1980 to the hawkish Ronald Reagan, former Hollywood actor and governor of California.

Summary *Online Study Center* ACE the Test

From the crisis year of 1968 on, Americans were extremely polarized—over the war in Vietnam, over the best path to racial equality and equal rights, and over the meaning of America itself. As many activists turned to "cultural nationalism," or group-identity politics, notions of American unity seemed a relic of the past. And while a new women's movement won victories against sex discrimination, powerful opposition arose in response.

During this era, Americans became increasingly disillusioned with politics. Richard Nixon's abuses of power in the Watergate scandal and cover-up, combined with the realization that the administration had lied repeatedly about America's role in Vietnam, produced a profound suspicion of government. A major economic crisis ended the post–World War II expansion, and Americans struggled with the effects of stagflation: rising unemployment rates coupled with high rates of inflation.

Overseas, a string of setbacks—defeat in Vietnam, the oil embargo, and the Iranian hostage crisis—signified the waning of American power. Détente with the Soviet Union flourished for a time; however, by 1980, Cold War tensions escalated. Meanwhile, the Middle East became an increasing focus of U.S. foreign policy.

Plagued by political, economic, and foreign policy crises, America's age of liberalism was over; the elements for a conservative resurgence were in place.

LEGACY FOR A PEOPLE AND A NATION
Human Rights

Human rights—the notion that people worldwide are entitled to life, liberty, and the pursuit of happiness—is not new. It was expressed most famously in the American and French Revolutions.

In the twentieth century, the concept became a consistent theme in U.S. foreign policy, and in the 1970s, a central tenet of American diplomacy. In the wake of the Vietnam War, many Americans yearned to restore America's international moral position. Congress led by restricting economic or military aid to nations that engaged "in a consistent pattern of gross violations of internationally recognized human rights."

Jimmy Carter made human rights a centerpiece of his foreign policy. "Because we are free we can never be indifferent to the fate of freedom elsewhere," he declared in his inaugural address. Carter installed a Bureau of Human Rights in the State Department, monitoring governments worldwide.

The campaign encountered problems, threatening arms control negotiations, alliances, and trade. The United States denounced abuses in nations where it had minimal economic or strategic interests and was almost silent where the interests were greater.

Still, Carter's human-rights emphasis altered the international landscape. It emboldened people around the world to challenge repressive governments and brought the release of political prisoners in many countries. It improved America's image overseas. Although human-rights concerns became less central in the foreign policies of Carter's successors, they remained on the agenda. In June 1993, delegates from 180 countries met in Vienna for the first World Conference on Human Rights, indicating that human rights had established itself firmly on the international map. It proved Carter's greatest legacy, duly noted by the committee awarding him the 2002 Nobel Peace Prize.

CONSERVATISM REVIVED 1980–1992

*N*guyet Thu Ha was twenty-two years old in 1975 when South Vietnam capitulated to North Vietnamese and Vietcong forces. As the fighting neared, Ha fled with her four teenage brothers and sisters and her six-year-old nephew. She found passage on a fishing ship dangerously over-crowded with refugees and arrived in the U.S. territory of Guam, an island over 2,000 miles from Vietnam. From there, they were sent to a refugee camp in Arkansas. Eventually Nguyet Ha and the children settled in Kansas City, Missouri, where they would live throughout the 1980s.

Nguyet Ha worked seven days a week as a hotel housekeeper and wait-ress, saving every possible penny for a house. Ha soon had the down payment for a $16,000 house and worked to pay off the mortgage in three years. She also married and had two daughters. In 1989 the thirty-six-year-old Ha bought a laundromat, five adjoining lots, and a vacant building she hoped would eventually house the family she'd left behind in Vietnam. Pursuing her ambition to become a teacher, Ha earned two associate of arts degrees and was hired as a paraprofessional at Kansas City's Northeast High School.

For ten years, Ha filled out U.S. government forms and visited the offices of the Immigration and Naturalization Service (INS). Finally she received a call from the INS: Ha's mother, two brothers, a sister-in-law, and a niece would be arriving at Kansas City International Airport. By 1997, all eight of Ha's siblings, most with their children, were living in the United States.

Nguyet Thu Ha and her family were part of the "new immigration" be-ginning in the early 1970s and continuing through the 1980s, as record num-bers of immigrants came to the United States from Asia, Mexico, Central and South America, and the Caribbean. But not all immigrants—or Americans—fared as well as Ha in the 1980s, when divisions between rich and poor were increasingly evident. While the urban poor struggled with social problems—drugs, violence, homelessness, the growing AIDS epidemic—those on the other side of the economic divide enjoyed an era of luxury and ostentation.

Reagan and the Conservative Resurgence

"Reaganomics"

Reagan and the World

LINKS TO THE WORLD
CNN

A Polarized People: American Society in the 1980s

The End of the Cold War and Global Disorder

LEGACY FOR A PEOPLE AND A NATION
The Americans with Disabilities Act

Online Study Center

This icon will direct you to interactive map and primary source activities on the website
http:college.hmco.com/ pic/nortonbrief7e

CHRONOLOGY

1980 • Reagan elected president

1981 • AIDS first observed in United States
• Economic problems continue; prime interest rate reaches 21.5 percent
• Reagan breaks air traffic controllers strike
• "Reaganomics" plan of budget and tax cuts approved by Congress

1982 • Unemployment reaches 10.8 percent, highest rate since Great Depression
• ERA dies after STOP-ERA campaign prevents ratification in key states

1983 • Reagan introduces SDI
• Terrorists kill U.S. Marines in Lebanon
• U.S. invasion of Grenada

1984 • Reagan aids contras despite congressional ban
• Economic recovery; unemployment rate drops and economy grows without inflation
• Reagan reelected
• Gorbachev promotes reforms in the USSR

1986 • Iran-contra scandal erupts

1987 • Stock market drops 508 points in one day
• Palestinian *intifada* begins

1988 • George H. W. Bush elected president

1989 • Tiananmen Square massacre in China
• Berlin Wall torn down
• U.S. troops invade Panama
• Gulf between rich and poor at highest point since 1920s

1990 • Americans with Disabilities Act passed
• Communist regimes in eastern Europe collapse
• Iraq invades Kuwait
• South Africa begins to dismantle apartheid

1991 • Persian Gulf War
• USSR dissolves into independent states
• United States enters recession

1992 • Annual federal budget deficit reaches high of $300 billion at end of Bush presidency

The election of Ronald Reagan in 1980 began a twelve-year period of Republican rule, as Reagan was succeeded by his vice president, George Bush, in 1988. Reagan was a popular president who seemed to restore the confidence shaken by the crises of the 1970s. Wealthy people liked Reagan's pro-business policies; the religious New Right embraced his vision of "God's America"; white middle- and working-class Americans were attracted by his charisma and "old-fashioned" values.

Reagan supported New Right social issues: he was anti-abortion, embraced prayer in schools, and reversed the GOP's support of the Equal Rights Amendment. Most important, Reagan appointed Supreme Court and federal judges whose rulings strengthened social-conservative agendas. Reagan's primary focus was on reducing the size and power of the federal gov-

ernment and creating favorable conditions for business and industry. The U.S. economy recovered from 1970s stagflation and rebounded through much of the 1980s. But corruption flourished in financial institutions freed from government oversight. By the end of the Reagan-Bush era, a combination of tax cuts and massive increases in defense spending increased the budget deficit fivefold.

In a single decade, the Cold War intensified and then ended. The key figure in the first development was Reagan, who promised to stand up to the Soviet Union. The central player in ending the conflict was Soviet leader Mikhail Gorbachev, who came to power in 1985 determined to end the USSR's economic decline, which required a more amicable superpower relationship. Gorbachev hoped to reform the Soviet system but lost control of events as revolutions in eastern Europe toppled one communist regime after another. In 1991 the Soviet Union itself disappeared, and the Persian Gulf War demonstrated America's unrivaled world power and the unprecedented importance of the Middle East. ■

Reagan and the Conservative Resurgence

*T*he 1970s were hard for Americans: defeat in Vietnam, the resignation of a president in disgrace, the energy crisis, economic "stagflation," and the Iranian hostage crisis. In 1980 President Carter's approval rating stood at 21 percent, lower than Richard Nixon's during the Watergate crisis. The time was ripe for a challenge to Carter's leadership, the Democratic Party, and the liberalism that had governed the United States since Franklin Roosevelt's New Deal.

In 1980 several conservative Republicans ran for the White House, including Ronald Reagan, former

RONALD REAGAN

movie star and two-term governor of California. In the 1940s, as president of the Screen Actors Guild in Hollywood, Reagan was a New Deal Democrat. But in the 1950s, as a corporate spokesman for General Electric, he became conservative. In 1964 Reagan's televised speech for Republican presidential candidate Barry Goldwater catapulted him to the forefront of conservative politics.

As governor of California two years later, Reagan became known for his right-wing rhetoric: America should "level Vietnam, pave it, paint stripes on it, and make a parking lot out of it." And when student protesters occupied "People's Park" near the University of California in Berkeley, he threatened a "bloodbath," dispatching National Guard troops. But he could be pragmatic: he denounced welfare but presided over reform of the state's social welfare bureaucracy and signed one of the nation's most liberal abortion laws.

In the 1980 election, Reagan offered an optimistic vision for America's future. With his Hollywood charm,

THE NEW CONSERVATIVE COALITION

he succeeded in forging very different kinds of conservatives into a new political coalition. He united political conservatives—strong anticommunists who sought to limit federal power and roll back the liberal social programs of the New Deal and Great Society—with less ideologically oriented economic conservatives, who sought deregulation and tax policies benefiting corporations, wealthy investors, and entrepreneurs.

Reagan united political and economic conservatives with two new constituencies. He tapped into the sentiments that fueled the tax revolt of the 1970s, drawing voters from traditionally Democratic constituencies such as labor unions and urban ethnic groups. These "Reagan Democrats" found the Republican critique of tax-funded social programs and "big government" appealing, even though Reagan's policies would benefit the wealthy at their expense.

Finally, in the largest leap, Reagan attracted the religiously based New Right. "When political conservative leaders began to . . . strike an alliance with social conservatives—the pro-life people, the anti-ERA people, the evangelical and born-again Christians, the people concerned about gay rights, prayer in the schools, sex in the movies or whatever," explained conservative fundraiser Richard Viguerie, "that's when this whole movement began to come alive."

Reagan claimed victory with 51 percent of the popular vote. Jimmy Carter carried only six states.

REAGAN'S CONSERVATIVE AGENDA

Reagan served two terms as president, followed by his vice president, George Bush, who was elected in 1988.

Reagan was not especially focused on the details of governing. When Carter briefed him on foreign and domestic policy issues, Reagan took no notes. Critics argued that his lack of knowledge could prove dangerous— as when he insisted that intercontinental ballistic missiles carrying nuclear warheads could be called back once launched.

But supporters insisted that Reagan focused on the big picture. When he spoke to the American people, he offered what seemed to be simple truths. While even supporters winced at his willingness to reduce complex policy issues to basic (and often misleading) stories, Reagan was to most Americans the "Great Communicator." He won admiration for his courage after he was seriously wounded in an assassination attempt sixty-nine days into his presidency.

Most important, Reagan had a clear vision for America's future. He and his advisers wanted nothing

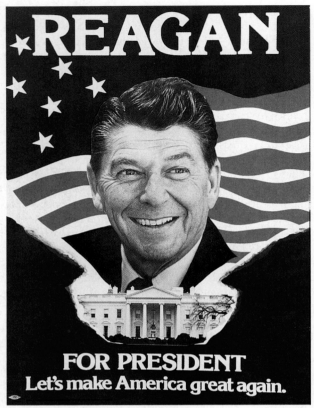

REAGAN

FOR PRESIDENT
Let's make America great again.

■ Ronald Reagan, the Republican presidential candidate in 1980, campaigned for "family values," an aggressive anti-Soviet foreign and military policy, and tax cuts. He also exuded optimism and appealed to Americans' patriotism. This poster, issued by the Republican National Committee, included Reagan's favorite campaign slogan: "Let's make America great again."
(Collection of David J. and Janice L. Frent)

less than to roll back the liberalism of the past fifty years that had made government responsible for the health of the nation's economy and for the social welfare of its citizens.

Reagan, like traditional conservatives, did not think the federal government could solve social prob-

ATTACKS ON SOCIAL WELFARE PROGRAMS

lems. But he drew support from Americans struggling to make ends meet during the economic crises of the 1970s and early 1980s who resented paying taxes that, they be-

lieved, funded government "handouts." Reagan fed a stereotype of welfare recipients as unwed, black, teenage mothers who kept having babies to collect larger checks.

In 1981 the administration cut social welfare funding by $25 billion. But "welfare" (Aid to Families with Dependent Children and food stamp programs) was small compared with Social Security and Medicare—welfare programs benefiting Americans of all income levels. The Reagan administration did shrink the proportion of the federal budget devoted to social welfare programs (including Social Security and Medicare) from 28 to 22 percent by the late 1980s—but a $1.2 trillion increase in defense spending, rather than budget cuts, was responsible for the shift.

Reagan also attacked federal environmental, health, and safety regulations that he believed reduced

PRO-BUSINESS POLICIES AND THE ENVIRONMENT

business profits and discouraged economic growth. Administration officials claimed that removing the stifling hand of government regulation would restore the energy and creativity of America's free-market system. However, removing them did not so much end government's role as deploy government power to aid corporate America. The president even appointed opponents of federal regulations to head agencies charged with enforcing them.

Environmentalists were appalled when Reagan appointed James Watt, a well-known antienvironmentalist, as secretary of the interior. Watt was a leader in the "Sagebrush Rebellion," which sought to return public lands in the West, such as national forests, to state control. The federal government controlled more than half of western lands—including 83 percent in Nevada, 66 percent in Utah, and 50 percent in Wyoming—and many westerners believed eastern policymakers did not understand the realities of western life. But state control was not the only issue: Watt's group wanted to open western public lands to private businesses for logging, mining, and ranching.

Telling Congress, "I don't know how many generations we can count on until the Lord returns," Watt dismissed concerns about protecting resources and public lands for future generations and allowed private corporations to acquire oil, mineral, and timber rights to federal lands for minuscule payments. He was forced to resign in 1983 after he dismissively referred to a federal advisory panel as "a black . . . a woman, two Jews, and a cripple." Even before Watt's resignation, his appointment had backfired as his actions reenergized the nation's environmental movement and even provoked opposition from business leaders who understood that uncontrolled strip-mining and clearcut logging of western lands could destroy lucrative tourism and recreation industries in western states.

The pro-business Reagan administration undercut organized labor's ability to negotiate wages and working conditions. Union power was

ATTACKS ON ORGANIZED LABOR already waning; labor union membership declined in the 1970s as jobs in heavy industry disappeared, and efforts to unionize the high-growth electronics and service sectors of the economy had not succeeded. Reagan intervened in a strike by the Professional Air Traffic Controllers Organization (PATCO) in August 1981. The air traffic controllers—federal employees, for whom striking was illegal—protested working conditions they believed compromised the safety of air travel. Forty-eight hours later, Reagan fired the 11,350 strikers, stipulating that they could never be rehired by the Federal Aviation Administration.

With the support of Reagan appointees to the National Labor Relations Board, businesses took an increasingly hard line with labor during the 1980s, and unions failed to mount an effective opposition. Roughly 44 percent of union families had voted for Reagan in 1980, and despite his anti-union policies, many were still drawn to his espousal of old-fashioned values and vigorous anticommunist rhetoric.

The New Right played an increasingly important role in Reagan's domestic policy, despite the administration's focus on traditional conser-

THE NEW RIGHT vative political and economic goals, and Reagan endorsed New Right social issues including the anti-abortion cause and prayer in public schools.

Reagan's judicial nominations also pleased the religious New Right. While the Senate, in a bipartisan vote, refused to confirm Supreme Court nominee Robert Bork, Reagan added Antonin Scalia and Sandra Day O'Connor (the first woman) to the Court and elevated Nixon appointee William Rehnquist to chief justice.

These appointments made the Court more conservative. In 1986, for example, the Supreme Court upheld a Georgia law that punished consensual anal or oral sex between men with up to twenty years in jail (*Bowers v. Hardwick*); in 1989 justices ruled that a Missouri law restricting the right to an abortion was constitutional (*Webster v. Reproductive Health Services*), thus encouraging further challenges to *Roe v. Wade*. Still, the Reagan administration did not push a conservative social agenda as strongly as some in the new Republican coalition had hoped.

"Reaganomics"

*T*he centerpiece of Reagan's domestic agenda was the economic program that took his name: Reaganomics. The U.S. economy was foundering in the early 1980s. Stagflation proved resistant to traditional remedies: when the government increased spending to stimulate the economy, inflation skyrocketed; when it cut spending or tightened the money supply to reduce inflation, the economy plunged deeper into recession and unemployment rates jumped.

Reagan offered a simple answer. Instead of focusing on the complexities of global competition, deindustrialization, and OPEC's control of oil, Reagan argued that U.S. economic problems were caused by intrusive government regulation of business and industry, expensive social programs giving "handouts" to nonproductive citizens, high taxes, and deficit spending—in short, by government itself. Reagan proposed to "unshackle" the free-enterprise system from government regulation and control, slash social programs, and balance the budget by reducing the role of the federal government.

Reagan's economic policy was based largely on "supply-side economics," the theory that tax cuts (rather than government spending)

"SUPPLY-SIDE ECONOMICS" stimulate growth. Economist Arthur Laffer had proposed one key hypothesis—his soon-to-be famous "Laffer curve." It stated that at some point, rising tax rates discourage people from engaging in taxable activities (such as investing their money): if profits from investments disappear to taxes, what is the incentive to invest? As people invest less, the economy slows and there is less tax revenue to collect. Cutting taxes, in contrast, reverses the cycle.

Although economists at the time accepted the larger principle behind Laffer's curve, almost none believed U.S. tax rates approached the point of disincentive. Even conservative economists were highly suspicious of supply-side principles. Reagan and his staff, however, sought a massive tax cut, arguing that American corporations and individuals would invest funds freed up by lower tax rates, producing new plants, new jobs, and new products. And as prosperity returned, the profits at the top would "trickle down" to the middle classes and even the poor.

David Stockman, head of the Office of Management and Budget, proposed a five-year plan to balance the federal budget through economic growth (created by tax cuts) and deep cuts, primarily in social programs. Congress cooperated with a three-year, $750 billion tax cut, the largest in history. But Stockman's plan required $100 billion in cuts from government programs, including Social Security and Medicare, which Congress rejected. Reagan, meanwhile, canceled out domestic spending cuts by dramatically increasing defense spending.

With major tax cuts, big increases in defense spending, and small cuts in social programs, the federal budget deficit exploded—from $59 billion in 1980, to more than $100 billion in 1982, to almost $300 billion by the end of George H. W. Bush's presidency in 1992. The federal government borrowed to make up the difference, transforming the United States from the world's largest creditor nation to its largest debtor at almost $3 trillion.

Meanwhile, in 1981, the Federal Reserve Bank, an autonomous federal agency, raised interest rates for bank loans to an unprecedented 21.5 percent, battling inflation by tightening the money supply and slowing the economy. The nation plunged into recession. By year's end, the gross national product (GNP) fell 5 percent, and sales of cars and houses dropped sharply. Unemployment soared to 8 percent.

HARSH MEDICINE FOR INFLATION

By late 1982, unemployment reached 10.8 percent, the highest rate since 1940; for African Americans, it was 20 percent. Reagan promised that consumers would lift the economy out of the recession by spending their tax cuts. But as late as April 1983, unemployment remained at 10 percent, and people were angry. Agriculture too was faltering as farmers suffered from falling crop prices, floods and droughts, and burdensome debts at high interest rates. Many lost their property through mortgage foreclosures; others filed for bankruptcy. As the recession deepened, poverty rose to its highest level since 1965.

It was harsh medicine, but the Federal Reserve Bank's plan to end stagflation worked. High interest rates helped drop inflation from 12 percent in 1980 to less than 7 percent in 1982. The economy also benefited from OPEC's 1981 decision to increase oil production, thus lowering prices. In 1984 the GNP rose 7 percent, the sharpest increase since 1951, and midyear unemployment fell to a four-year low of 7 percent.

Reagan got credit for the recovery, though it had little to do with his supply-side policies. Insisting that the escalating budget deficit would have dire consequences for the economy, the 1984 Democratic presidential candidate, former vice president Walter Mondale, said he would raise taxes. Mondale emphasized fairness and compassion: not all Americans, Mondale said, were prospering in Reagan's America. Reagan, in contrast, proclaimed, "It's morning again in America." He won in a landslide, with 59 percent of the vote. Mondale (with running mate Geraldine Ferraro, the first woman vice-presidential candidate) carried only his home state of Minnesota.

"MORNING IN AMERICA"

Deregulation, started by Jimmy Carter and dramatically expanded by Reagan, also transformed America's economy in the 1980s by creating new opportunities for business. The 1978 deregulation of the airline industry lowered ticket prices; airline tickets cost almost 45 percent less in the early twenty-first century (in constant dollars) than in 1978. Deregulation of telecommunications industries created serious competition for the giant AT&T, and long-distance calling became inexpensive.

DEREGULATION

The Reagan administration loosened regulation of American banking and finance industries and purposely cut the enforcement ability of the Securities and Exchange Commission (SEC). In the early 1980s, Congress deregulated the nation's savings-and-loan institutions (S&Ls), organizations previously required to invest depositors' savings in thirty-year, fixed-rate mortgages secured by property within a 50-mile radius of the S&L's main office. The 1980s legislation created conditions for a collapse. By ending government oversight of investment practices, while covering losses from bad S&L investments, Congress left no penalties for failure. S&Ls increasingly put depositors' money into high-risk investments and engaged in shady—even criminal—deals.

Risky investments typified Wall Street as well, as Michael Milken, a reclusive bond trader for the firm Drexel Firestone, pioneered the "junk bond" industry and created lucrative investment possibilities. Milken offered financing to debt-ridden corporations unable to get traditional low-interest bank loans, using bond issues that paid investors high interest rates because they were high risk (thus "junk" bonds). Many of these corporations were attractive targets for takeover by other corporations or investors, who in turn could finance takeovers with junk bonds. Such "predators" could use the first corporation's existing debt as a tax write-off, sell off unprofitable units, and lay off employees to create a more efficient—and thus more profitable—corporation. Investors in the original junk bonds could make huge profits by selling their shares to the corporate raiders.

JUNK BONDS AND "MERGER MANIA"

By the mid-1980s, hundreds of major corporations—including giants Walt Disney and Conoco—fell prey to "merger mania" and "hostile takeovers." Profits for investors were staggering, and by 1987 Milken, the guru of junk bonds, was earning $550 million a year—about $1,046 a minute.

Deregulation helped smaller, often innovative, corporations challenge the virtual monopolies of giants in fields like telecommunications. And the American economy boomed. Although the stock market plunged 508 points on a single day in October 1987—losing 22.6 percent of its value, or almost double that of the 1929 crash—it rebounded quickly. But the high-risk boom of the 1980s had costs. Corporate downsizing meant layoffs for white-collar workers and management personnel, many of whom had difficulty finding comparable positions. The wave of mergers and takeovers left American corporations as a whole increasingly burdened by debt. It also helped to consolidate sectors of the economy—such as media—under the control of an ever smaller number of players.

The 1980s boom, furthermore, was rotten with corruption. By the late 1980s, insider trading scandals—in which people used "inside" information not available to the general public to make huge profits trading stocks—rocked financial markets

THE RICH GET RICHER

and sent some prominent Wall Street figures to jail. Savings and loans lost billions in bad investments, sometimes fraudulently covering them up. Scandal reached the White House: Vice President Bush's son Neil was involved in shady S&L deals. The Reagan-Bush administration's bailout of the S&L industry cost taxpayers half a trillion dollars.

During the 1980s, the rich got richer and the poor got poorer (see Figure 32.1). The number of Americans reporting an annual income of $500,000 increased tenfold between 1980 and 1989, and the salary and benefits of corporate chief executive officers increased from 30 times that of the average factory worker in 1980 to 130 times greater by 1989. In 1987 the United States had forty-nine billionaires—up from one in 1978. Middle-class incomes, however, were stagnant.

Reagan's economic policies benefited the wealthy at the expense of other Americans. Reagan's tax policies decreased the "total effective tax rates"—income taxes plus Social Security taxes—for the top 1 percent of American families by 14.4 percent. But they increased taxes for the poorest 20 percent of families by 16 percent. By 1990, the richest 1 percent controlled 40 percent of the nation's wealth, with 80 percent of wealth controlled by the top 20 percent.

Reagan and the World

a key element in Reagan's winning strategy in the 1980 election was his call for the United States to reassert itself in the world. Although he lacked a firm grasp of world issues, history, and geography, Reagan adhered to a few core principles. One was a deep and abiding anticommunism; a second was an underlying optimism about America's power and ability to positively affect the world. Together, these elements help explain both Reagan's aggressively anticommunist foreign policy and his positive response in his second term to Soviet leader Mikhail Gorbachev's call for "new thinking" in world affairs.

Initially embracing the strident anticommunism of early Cold War U.S. foreign policy, Reagan and his advisers rejected both Nixon's détente and Carter's emphasis on human rights. Where Nixon and Carter saw an increasingly multipolar

SOVIET-AMERICAN TENSION

CNN

When Ted Turner launched CNN, his Cable News Network, on June 1, 1980, few people took it seriously. With a staff of three hundred—mostly young, mostly inexperienced—CNN operated out of the basement of a converted Atlanta country club. CNN was initially known for its on-air errors, as when a cleaning woman emptied anchor Bernard Shaw's trash during a live newscast. But by 1992, CNN was seen in over 150 nations worldwide, and *Time* magazine named Ted Turner its "Man of the Year."

Throughout the 1980s, CNN built relations with local news outlets throughout the world. CNN reported live from Tiananmen Square and from the Berlin Wall in 1989. Millions watched as CNN reporters broadcast live from Baghdad in the early hours of the Gulf War in 1991. When the Soviet Union wanted to denounce the 1989 U.S. invasion of Panama, officials called CNN's Moscow bureau instead of the U.S. embassy. During the Gulf War, Saddam Hussein reportedly kept televisions in his bunker tuned to CNN, and U.S. generals used its broadcasts to judge the effectiveness of missile attacks.

Despite its global mission, CNN's American origins were often apparent. During the U.S. invasion of Panama, CNN cautioned correspondents not to refer to the American military forces as "our" troops. What CNN offered was not international news but a global experience: people throughout the world collectively watching the major moments in contemporary history as they unfolded. But as *Time* magazine noted (while praising Turner as the "Prince of the Global Village"), such connections "did not produce instantaneous brotherhood, just a slowly dawning awareness of the implications of a world transfixed by a single TV image."

The "Boys of Baghdad"—CNN reporters Bernard Shaw, John Holliman, and Peter Arnett—broadcast live by satellite from Suite 906 of the Al Rashid Hotel as Allied bombs fell on Baghdad throughout the night of January 16, 1991. Despite their dramatic reporting on the first night of the war, critics charged that continuing network coverage of Operation Desert Storm, with distant shots of cruise missiles seeking targets and heavy use of animation, graphics, and even theme music, made the war appear more like a video game than a bloody conflict. (CNN)

Percentage Increase in Pretax Income, 1977–1989

Wealthiest 1 Percent	77%
Wealthiest Fifth	29%
Second Wealthiest Fifth	9%
Middle Fifth	4%
Second Poorest Fifth	− 1%
Poorest Fifth	− 9%

Figure 32.1   While the Rich Got Richer in the 1980s, the Poor Got Poorer

Between 1977 and 1989, the richest 1 percent of American families reaped most of the gains from economic growth. In fact, the average pretax income of families in the top percentage rose 77 percent. At the same time, the typical family saw its income edge up only 4 percent. And the bottom 40 percent of families had actual declines in income.   (Source: Data from the *New York Times,* March 5, 1992.)

international system, the Reagan team reverted to a bipolar perspective defined by the Soviet-American relationship. In his first presidential press conference, Reagan described a malevolent Soviet Union. When Poland's pro-Soviet leaders in 1981 cracked down on an independent labor organization, Solidarity, Washington restricted Soviet-American trade and hurled angry words at Moscow. In March 1983, Reagan told evangelical Christians in Florida that the Soviets were "an evil empire." That year Reagan restricted commercial flights to the Soviet Union after a Soviet fighter pilot mistakenly shot down a South Korean commercial jet straying 300 miles off course into Soviet airspace, killing 269 passengers.

Reagan believed that substantial military buildup would thwart the Soviet threat and launched the largest peacetime arms buildup in history. In 1985, when the military budget hit $294.7 billion (double that of 1980), the Pentagon spent an average $28 million an hour. Assigning low priority to arms control talks, Reagan announced in 1983 his desire for a space-based defense shield against incoming ballistic missiles: the Strategic Defense Initiative (SDI). His critics tagged it "Star Wars" and said such a system could never work scientifically—some enemy missiles would get through the shield. Moreover, the critics warned, SDI would elevate the arms race to dangerous new levels. SDI research and development consumed tens of billions of dollars.

Attributing Third World disorders to Soviet intrigue, the president declared the Reagan Doctrine: the United States would openly support anticommunist movements—"freedom fighters" battling the Soviets or Soviet-backed governments. In Afghanistan, Reagan continued providing covert assistance, through Pakistan, to the Mujahidin rebels fighting Soviet occupation. When the Soviets stepped up the war in 1985, the Reagan administration sent more high-tech weapons, particularly anti-aircraft Stinger missiles. Easily transportable and fired by a single soldier, the Stingers turned the tide by making Soviet jets and helicopters vulnerable below fifteen thousand feet.

REAGAN DOCTRINE

Senior White House officials also believed that the Soviets and Castro's Cuba were fomenting disorder in the Caribbean and Central America (see Map 32.1). In October 1983 the president sent troops into the tiny island of Grenada to oust a pro-Marxist government. In El Salvador, he provided military and economic assistance to a military-dominated government struggling with left-wing revolutionaries. The regime used right-wing death squads, which by decade's end killed forty thousand dissidents and citizens as well as several American missionaries. In January 1992 the Salvadoran combatants finally negotiated a U.N.-sponsored peace.

The Reagan administration also meddled in the Nicaraguan civil war. In 1979 leftist insurgents in Nicaragua overthrew Anastasio Somoza, a long-time U.S. ally. The revolutionaries called themselves Sandinistas in honor of César Augusto Sandino—who had headed the anti-imperialist opposition against U.S. occupation in the 1930s and was finally assassinated by Somoza henchmen. When the Sandinistas aided rebels in El Salvador, bought Soviet weapons, and invited Cubans to help reorganize the Nicaraguan army, Reagan officials charged that Nicaragua was becoming a Soviet client. In 1981 the CIA began to train, arm, and direct more than ten thousand counterrevolutionaries, known as contras, to overthrow the Nicaraguan government.

CONTRA WAR IN NICARAGUA

Many Americans, however, including Democratic leaders in Congress, were skeptical about the communist threat and warned that Nicaragua could become another Vietnam. Congress in 1984 voted to stop U.S. military aid to the contras. Secretly, the Reagan administration lined up other countries, including Saudi Arabia, Panama, and South Korea, to funnel money and weapons to the contras, and in 1985 Reagan imposed an economic embargo against Nicaragua. The president rejected a plan by Costa Rica's president, Oscar Arias Sánchez, in 1987 to obtain a cease-fire in Central America through negotiations and cutbacks in military aid to all rebel forces. (Arias won the 1987 Nobel Peace Prize.) Three years later, Central American presidents brokered a settlement; in the national election that followed, the Sandinistas lost to a U.S.-funded party. After nearly a decade of civil war, thirty thousand Nicaraguans had died, and the ravaged economy was one of the poorest in the hemisphere.

Reagan's obsession with defeating the Sandinistas almost caused his political undoing. In November 1986 it became known that the president's national security adviser, John M. Poindexter, and an aide, marine lieutenant colonel Oliver North, in collusion with CIA director William Casey, covertly sold weapons to Iran in an unsuccessful attempt to win the release of Americans held hostage by Islamic fundamentalist groups. Washington condemned Iran as a terrorist nation and demanded that America's allies cease trading there. More damaging was the revelation that money from the Iran arms deal had been illegally diverted to aid the contras. North later admitted that he illegally destroyed government documents and lied to Congress to keep the operation clandestine.

IRAN-CONTRA SCANDAL

Although Reagan survived the scandal, his popularity declined, and Congress reasserted its authority over foreign affairs. In late 1992 outgoing president George Bush pardoned several former government officials convicted of lying to Congress. Critics smelled a cover-up, for Bush himself, as vice president, participated in high-level meetings on Iran-contra deals. As for North, his conviction was overturned on a technicality.

U.S. foreign policy placed increased importance on the Middle East and terrorism. The main U.S. goals in the Middle East were to preserve access to oil and support ally Israel, while checking Soviet influence. In the 1980s, though, American leaders faced new pressures from a deepened Israeli-Palestinian conflict and an anti-American and anti-Israeli Islamic fundamentalist movement that spread after the ouster of the shah of Iran in 1979.

U.S. INTERESTS IN THE MIDDLE EAST

The 1979 Camp David accords between Israel and Egypt raised hopes of a lasting settlement involving self-government for the Palestinian Arabs in the Israeli-occupied Gaza Strip and West Bank. Instead, Israel and the Palestinian Liberation Organization (PLO) remained at odds. In 1982, in retaliation for Palestinian shelling of Israel from Lebanon, Israeli troops invaded Lebanon. The beleaguered PLO and various Lebanese factions called on Syria to contain the Israelis. Soon after Reagan sent U.S. Marines to Lebanon to join a peacekeeping force, American

Map 32.1   The United States in the Caribbean and Central America

The United States often has intervened in the Caribbean and Central America. Geographical proximity, economic stakes, political disputes, security links, trade in illicit drugs, and Cuba's alliance with the Soviet Union and defiance of the United States have kept North American eyes fixed on events in the region.

605

troops became embroiled in a war between Lebanese factions. In October 1983 terrorist bombs demolished a barracks, killing 241 American servicemen. Four months later, Reagan pulled the remaining marines out.

The attack on the marine barracks made the danger of terrorism increasingly real to the United States and other Western countries.

TERRORISM In the 1980s, numerous otherwise powerless groups, many of them associated with the Palestinian cause or with Islamic fundamentalism, relied on terrorism to further their aims. Often they targeted American citizens and property, because of Washington's support of Israel and involvement in the Lebanese civil war. Of the 690 hijackings, kidnappings, bombings, and shootings around the world in 1985, for example, 217 were against Americans, most originating in Iran, Libya, Lebanon, and the Gaza Strip. Three years later, a Pan American passenger plane was destroyed over Scotland, probably by pro-Iranian terrorists.

Washington proposed peace plans persuading the Israelis to give back occupied territories and the Arabs to stop trying to push the Jews out of the Middle East. As the peace process stalled in 1987, Palestinians in the West Bank began an *intifada* (Arabic for "uprising") against Israeli forces. Israel refused to negotiate, but the United States talked with PLO chief Yasir Arafat after he renounced terrorism and accepted Israel's right to live in peace. For the PLO to recognize Israel and the United States to recognize the PLO were major developments in the Arab-Israeli conflict.

In South Africa too, American diplomacy became more aggressive. At first, the Reagan administration

SOUTH AFRICA followed a policy of "constructive engagement"—asking the government to reform its white supremacist apartheid system. But many Americans demanded cutting off imports from South Africa and pressuring 350 American companies to cease operations there. Some American cities and states passed divestment laws, withdrawing investment dollars from American companies active in South Africa. Public protest and congressional legislation forced the Reagan administration in 1986 to impose economic restrictions. Within two years, about half of the American companies in South Africa left.

American conservatives disliked the South Africa sanctions policy. Rabid anticommunists among them also balked when Reagan, his popu-

ENTER GORBACHEV larity declining, entered negotiations with the Soviet Union. At a 1985 Geneva summit meeting between Reagan and new Soviet leader Mikhail Gorbachev, the president agreed in principle with Gorbachev's contention that strategic weapons should be substantially reduced, and at a 1986 Reykjavik, Iceland, meeting, they came close to a major reduction agreement. SDI stood in the way: Gorbachev insisted it should be shelved, and Reagan refused.

But Reagan and Gorbachev got on well. As General Colin Powell commented, while the Soviet leader was far superior to Reagan in mastery of specifics, he recognized that Reagan was, as Powell put it, "the embodiment of his people's down-to-earth character, practicality, and optimism." And Reagan toned down his strident anti-Soviet rhetoric.

The turnaround in Soviet-American relations stemmed more from changes abroad than from Reagan's decisions. Under Gorbachev, a

PERESTROIKA AND GLASNOST younger generation of Soviet leaders came to power in 1985. They modernized the highly bureaucratized, decaying economy through reforms known as *perestroika* ("restructuring") and liberalized the authoritarian political system through *glasnost* ("openness"). For these reforms to work, Soviet military expenditures had to be reduced.

In 1987 Gorbachev and Reagan signed the Intermediate-Range Nuclear Forces (INF) Treaty banning all land-based intermediate-range nuclear missiles in Europe. About 2,800 missiles were destroyed. Gorbachev also unilaterally reduced his nation's armed forces, helped settle regional conflicts, and began the withdrawal of Soviet troops from Afghanistan. The Cold War was coming to an end.

A Polarized People: American Society in the 1980s

 s the Cold War waned, so too did the power of the belief in an America united by shared, middle-class values. By the 1980s, after years of social struggle and division, few Americans believed in the reality of that vision; many rejected it as undesirable. And although the 1980s were never as contentious as the 1960s and early 1970s, deep cultural divides nonetheless prevailed. A newly powerful group of Christian conservatives challenged the secular majority. A growing class of affluent Americans seemed a society apart from the urban poor that sociologists and journalists began calling "the underclass." At the same time, the composition of the American population was changing dramatically as people immigrated to the United States from more nations than ever before.

GROWTH OF THE RELIGIOUS RIGHT

Since the 1960s, America's mainline liberal Protestant churches—Episcopalian, Presbyterian, Methodist—had been losing members, while Southern Baptists and other denominations offering the spiritual experience of being "born again" through belief in Jesus Christ and the literal truth of the Bible (fundamentalism) had grown rapidly. Fundamentalist preachers reached out through television: by the late 1970s, televangelist Oral Roberts drew 3.9 million viewers. Close to 20 percent of Americans identified themselves as fundamentalist Christians in 1980.

Most fundamentalist Christian churches stayed out of the social and political conflicts of the 1960s and early 1970s, concentrating on preaching the gospel instead. But in the late 1970s some influential preachers mobilized their flocks for political struggle. In a "Washington for Jesus" rally in 1980, fundamentalist leader Pat Robertson told crowds, "We have enough votes to run the country." The Moral Majority, founded in 1979 by Jerry Falwell, sought a "Christian America," in part by supporting political candidates. Falwell's defense of socially conservative "family values" and his condemnation of feminism (he called NOW the "National Order of Witches"), homosexuality, pornography, and abortion resonated with many Americans.

Throughout the 1980s, conservative Christians known as the New Right campaigned against America's secular culture. Rejecting multiculturalism—that different cultures and lifestyle choices were equally valid—the New Right wanted what they believed to be "God's law" as the basis for American society. Concerned Women for America, founded by Beverly La-

■ The Reverend Jerry Falwell, an evangelical preacher whose *Old Time Gospel Hour* program reached 15 million Americans, founded the Moral Majority in 1979. This conservative political action group drew support from fundamentalist Christians and played a major role in the political elections of the 1980s.
(Dennis Brack/Black Star/Stockphoto.com)

Hayes in 1979, wanted elementary school readers containing "unacceptable" religious beliefs (including excerpts from *The Diary of Anne Frank* and *The Wizard of Oz*) removed from classrooms. Fundamentalist Christian groups again challenged the teaching of evolution in public schools. The Reagan administration frequently turned to James Dobson, founder of the conservative Focus on the Family, for policy advice. Conservative Christians also joined with Roman Catholics, Mormons, and other groups in the antiabortion or "prolife" movement.

Many Americans vigorously opposed the New Right's seeming intolerance and threat to basic freedoms—including the freedom of religion for those whose beliefs differed from the conservative

"CULTURE WARS"

Christianity of the New Right. In 1982 the politically progressive television producer Norman Lear, influential former congresswoman Barbara Jordan, and other prominent figures in business, religion, politics, and entertainment founded People for the American Way to support American civil liberties, the separation of church and state, and the values of tolerance and diversity. This struggle between the religious right and their opponents for the future of the nation came to be known as the "culture wars."

Many beliefs of Christian fundamentalists ran counter to the ways most Americans lived, especially regarding women's roles. By the 1980s, a generation of girls had grown up with the benefits of the women's movement, expecting freedoms and opportunities their mothers never had. Legislation such as the Civil Rights Act of 1964 and Title IX opened academic and athletic programs to females. In 1960 there were 38 male lawyers for every 1 female lawyer in the United States; by 1983, the ratio was 5.5 to 1. By 1985, more than half of married women with children under age three worked outside the home. The religious right's insistence that women's place was in the home, subordinated to her husband, contradicted the gains made toward sexual equality and the reality of many women's lives.

The racialized nature of poverty also divided the nation. A 1988 national report on race relations looked back to the 1968 Kerner Commission report, claiming, "America is again becoming two separate societies," white and black. Although the majority of America's poor were white and the black middle class was expanding, people of color were much more likely to be poor. In 1980, 33 percent of blacks and 26 percent of Latinos lived in poverty, compared with 10 percent of whites (see Figure 32.2).

THE NEW INEQUALITY

Reasons for poverty varied. The legacies of racism played a role. The changing job structure was partly responsible; the well-paid jobs for unskilled workers disappeared, replaced by lower-paid service jobs. New York alone had 234,000 fewer blue-collar workers in 1980 than in 1970. In addition, families headed by a single mother were five times more likely to be poor than families headed by a married couple. By 1992, 59 percent of African American children and 17 percent of white children lived in female-headed households, and almost half of black children lived in poverty.

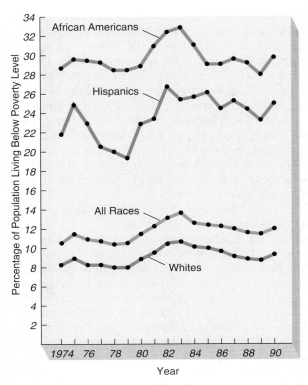

Figure 32.2 Poverty in America by Race, 1974–1990

Poverty in America rose in the early 1980s but subsided afterward. Many people of color, however, experienced little relief during the decade. Notice that the percentage of African Americans living below the poverty level was three times higher than that for whites. It also was much higher for Hispanics.   (Source: Adapted from U.S. Bureau of the Census, *Statistical Abstract of the United States* [Washington, D.C., 1992], p. 461.)

In impoverished inner-city neighborhoods, violent crime—particularly homicides and gang warfare—grew alarmingly, as did school dropout rates, general crime rates, and child abuse. Some poverty-stricken people tried to find escape in hard drugs, especially crack, a derivative of cocaine, which first struck New York City's poorest neighborhoods in 1985. Gang shootouts over drugs were deadly: the toll in Los Angeles in 1987 was 387 deaths, more than half of them innocent bystanders.

SOCIAL CRISES IN AMERICAN CITIES

Many states instituted mandatory prison sentences for possessing small amounts of crack, making penalties for 1 gram of crack equivalent to those for 100 grams of cocaine, the drug favored by more affluent white Americans. Such policies increased America's prison population almost fourfold from 1980 to the mid-1990s, with black and Latino youth arrested in disproportionate numbers. By 2000, young black men were more likely to have been arrested than to have graduated from a four-year college.

Rates of homelessness also grew during the 1980s. Some were impoverished families; many had drug or alcohol problems. About a third of the homeless were former psychiatric patients discharged under "deinstitutionalization." By 1985, 80 percent of the total number of beds in state mental hospitals had been eliminated on the premise that small neighborhood programs would be more responsive to people's needs—though these programs failed to materialize. Consequently, many of America's mentally ill citizens wandered the streets.

Another social crisis in the 1980s was the global spread of autoimmune deficiency syndrome, or AIDS.

THE AIDS EPIDEMIC
Caused by the human immunodeficiency virus (HIV), AIDS leaves its victims susceptible to deadly infections and cancers. The human immunodeficiency virus itself is spread through the exchange of blood or other body fluids, often through sexual intercourse or needle sharing by intravenous drug users.

AIDS was first observed in the United States in 1981. Of the fifty-seven thousand AIDS cases reported between 1981 and 1988, nearly thirty-two thousand resulted in death. Politicians were slow to devote resources to AIDS, in part because it was perceived initially as exclusively a "gay man's disease." "A man reaps what he sows," declared Jerry Falwell of the Moral Majority. AIDS, along with other sexually transmitted diseases such as genital herpes and chlamydia, ended an era defined by penicillin and "the pill," in which sex was freed from the threat of disease or unwanted pregnancy.

For the rich, the 1980s marked an era of ostentation. "Greed is all right," Wall Street financier Ivan

AN ERA OF OSTENTATION
Boesky told students at the University of California, Berkeley, the center of 1960s campus protest, and he was met with cheers and laughter.

New York entrepreneur Donald Trump's $29 million yacht had gold-plated bathroom fixtures. Publisher Malcolm Forbes flew eight hundred guests to Morocco for his seventieth birthday; the party cost $2 million.

Nineteen eighty-four was the "Year of the Yuppie"—Young Urban Professional—proclaimed *Newsweek* magazine. A derogatory term, *Yuppie* (and *Buppie,* for black urban professional) described ambitious and successful young Americans in demanding careers who enjoyed a consumer-driven lifestyle: BMWs, Sub-Zero refrigerators, Armani suits, Häagen-Dazs ice cream. Americans in the 1980s seemed fascinated with tales of the super-rich (making *Dallas* a top-rated television show) and with Yuppie lifestyles (chronicled on the popular show *thirtysomething*). But Yuppies also represented those who got ahead without caring about those left behind. As Yuppies gentrified urban neighborhoods, displacing poorer residents, graffiti appeared in New York: "Die, Yuppie Scum."

America was further polarized by the arrival of new immigrants who did not fit cleanly into old racial categories. Between 1970 and 1990,

NEW IMMIGRANTS FROM ASIA
the United States absorbed more than 13 million arrivals, most from Latin America and Asia. Before the immigration reforms of 1965, Americans of Asian ancestry made up less than 1 percent of the nation's population; by 1990, that figure was 3 percent.

Before 1965, the majority of Asian Americans were of Japanese ancestry (about 52 percent in 1960), followed by Chinese and Filipino. In the 1960s and 1970s, the highest rates of immigration were from nations not previously represented in the United States. There were only 603 Vietnamese residents in 1964. By 1990, the United States had absorbed almost 800,000 refugees from Indochina, many casualties of the Vietnam War. Immigrants flooded in from South Korea, Thailand, India, Pakistan, Bangladesh, Indonesia, Singapore, Laos, Cambodia, and Vietnam. Japanese Americans were now only 15 percent of the Asian American population.

Immigrants from Asia tended to be either highly skilled or unskilled. Unsettled conditions in the Philippines in the 1970s and 1980s created an exodus of well-educated Filipinos to the United States. Korea, Taiwan, India, and China also lost skilled and educated workers to the United States. Other Chinese immigrants, however, had few job skills and spoke little or no English. Large numbers crowded into neighborhoods like New York's Chinatown, where women worked under terrible conditions in the city's nonunion garment industry. Immigrants from Southeast Asia were the most likely to be unskilled and to live in poverty in the United States.

But even highly educated immigrants found their options limited. A 1983 study revealed that Korean Americans owned three-quarters of the approximately twelve hundred greengroceries in New York City. Though often cited as a success story, Korean greengrocers usually had descended the professional ladder: 78 percent of them had college or professional degrees.

Unprecedented immigration rates coupled with a high birth rate made Latinos the fastest-growing group of Americans. In 1970 Latinos made

THE GROWING LATINO POPULATION up 4.5 percent of the nation's population; that percentage jumped to 9 percent by 1990, when one out of three Los Angelenos and Miamians were Hispanic, as was 70 percent of El Paso. Mexican Americans, concentrated in California and the Southwest, made up most of this population, but Puerto Ricans, Cubans, Dominicans, and other Caribbean immigrants also lived in the United States, clustered principally in East Coast cities.

During the 1980s, people from Guatemala and El Salvador fled civil war and government violence for the United States. Although the U.S. government commonly refused them political asylum (about 113,000 Cubans received political refugee status during the 1980s, compared with fewer than 1,400 El Salvadorians), a national "sanctuary movement" of Christian churches defied the law to protect refugees from deportation to places where they risked violence or death. Economic troubles in Mexico and Central and South America also produced a flood of undocumented workers who crossed the poorly guarded 2,000-mile border between the United States and Mexico, seeking economic opportunities. Some moved back and forth across the border; a majority meant to stay.

Many Americans believed new arrivals threatened jobs and economic security, and nativist violence and bigotry increased during the 1980s. In 1982 twenty-seven-year-old Vincent Chin was beaten to death in Detroit by an unemployed auto worker and his uncle. American auto plants were losing to Japanese imports, and the two men seemingly mistook the Chinese

American Chin for Japanese. In New York, Philadelphia, and Los Angeles, African Americans boycotted Korean groceries. Riots broke out in Los Angeles schools between black students and newly arrived Mexicans. In Dade County, Florida, voters passed an "antibilingual" measure that removed Spanish-language signs from public transportation, while at the state and national levels, people debated declaring English the "official" language of the United States.

Concerned about the flow of illegal aliens, Congress passed the Immigration Reform and Control (Simpson-Rodino) Act in 1986. The act's purpose was to discourage illegal immigration by imposing sanctions on employers who hired undocumented workers, but it also provided amnesty to millions who had immigrated illegally before 1982.

Online Study Center
Improve Your Grade
Primary Source: Rosa Maria Urbina and Jose Luis Describe Life as Illegals

The End of the Cold War and Global Disorder

The end of Reagan's presidency coincided with world events that would replace the Cold War with a new international system. Reagan's vice president, George Herbert Walker Bush, would become president and oversee the transition. The son of a Wall Street banker and U.S. senator from Connecticut, Bush had attended an exclusive boarding school and then Yale. He had the advantage in seeking the Republican presidential nomination in having been a loyal vice president. And he possessed a formidable résumé: he had been ambassador to the United Nations, chairman of the Republican Party, special envoy to China, and director of the CIA. He also had been a war hero, flying fifty-eight combat missions in the Pacific in World War II and receiving the Distinguished Flying Cross.

Bush entered the 1988 presidential campaign trailing his Democratic opponent, Massachusetts governor Michael Dukakis, by a wide margin.

1988 PRESIDENTIAL CAMPAIGN Republicans turned that around by waging one of the most negative campaigns in American history. Most notorious, the Bush camp aired a television commercial featuring a black convicted murderer, Willie Horton, who terrorized a Maryland couple, raping the woman, while on weekend furlough—a temporary release program begun under Dukakis's Republican predecessor. The Republicans also falsely suggested that Dukakis had a history of psychiatric problems. Dukakis, though not personally attacking Bush, ran an uninspired campaign. On election day, Bush won by eight percentage points in the popular vote and received 426 electoral votes to Dukakis's 112. The Democrats, however, retained control of both houses of Congress.

Bush focused his attention on foreign policy. He envisioned the United States as the supreme power in a unipolar world. Yet he also knew that the Cold War was drawing to a close. Mikhail Gorbachev's cascading changes in the Soviet Union were now stimulating reforms in eastern Europe that ultimately led to revolution. In 1989 people in East Germany, Poland, Hungary, Czechoslovakia, and Romania startled the world by repudiating their communist governments and staging mass protests against a despised ideology. In November 1989, Germans scaled the Berlin Wall and tore it down; the following October, the two Germanys reunited. By then, other regional communist governments had fallen or were on the verge.

Other communist challenges were less successful. In June 1989 Chinese armed forces stormed into Beijing's

TIANANMEN SQUARE

Tiananmen Square, slaughtering hundreds—perhaps thousands—of unarmed students and citizens who for weeks had held peaceful pro-democracy rallies. The Chinese government emphatically rejected political liberalization; henceforth, the "Chinese solution" came to mean repression in response to popular calls for freedom.

Elsewhere, however, the forces of democratization proved too powerful to resist. In South Africa, a new government under F. W. De Klerk began a cautious retreat from apartheid. In February 1990 De Klerk legalized all political parties in South Africa, including the African National Congress, the chief black party, and released Nelson Mandela, a hero to black South Africans, after a twenty-seven-year imprisonment. Then the government repealed its apartheid laws over several years, allowing all citizens to vote regardless of color. Mandela, who became South Africa's first black president in 1994, called the transformation "a small miracle."

The same phrase could be used to describe what happened in the Soviet Union. In 1990 the Baltic states

COLLAPSE OF SOVIET POWER

of Lithuania, Latvia, and Estonia declared independence from Moscow's rule; the following year, the Soviet Union ceased to exist, disintegrating into independent successor states—Russia, Ukraine, Tajikistan, and many others. Muscled aside by Russian reformers who thought he was moving too slowly toward democracy and free-market economics, Gorbachev lost power. The breakup of the Soviet empire, the dismantling of the Warsaw Pact (the Soviet military alliance formed in 1955 with communist countries of eastern Europe), the repudiation of communism by its own leaders, German reunification, and a significantly reduced risk of nuclear war signaled the end of the Cold War and the Soviet-American rivalry. The United States and its allies had won. The containment policy followed by nine presidents—from Truman through Bush—had had many critics over the years, but it had succeeded at containing communism for four-plus decades without blowing up the world or obliterating freedom at home. Over time, the Soviet socialist economy proved less able to compete with the American free-market one, less able to cope with the demands of the Soviet and eastern European citizenry.

Yet the Soviet empire might have survived longer had it not been for Gorbachev, one of the most influential figures of the twentieth century. Through a series of unexpected overtures and decisions, Gorbachev fundamentally transformed the superpower relationship in a way that could scarcely have been anticipated before. Ronald Reagan's role was less central but vitally important because of his later willingness to negotiate and treat Gorbachev more as a partner than as an adversary. Just as personalities mattered in starting the Cold War, so they mattered in ending it.

Online Study Center **Improve Your Grade**
Interactive Map:
  The End of the Cold War Changes the Map of Europe

The victory in the Cold War elicited little celebration among Americans. The confrontation may never

COSTS OF VICTORY

have become a hot war, but the period after 1945 nevertheless witnessed numerous Cold War–related conflicts claiming millions of lives.

In the Vietnam War alone, at least 1.5 million people died, more than 58,000 of them Americans. Military budgets had eaten up billions of dollars, thereby shortchanging domestic programs. Some Americans wondered whether the communist threat had ever been as grave as officials claimed.

As the Cold War closed, the Bush administration signed important arms reduction treaties with the Soviet Union in 1991, and with the postbreakup Russia in 1993, but the United States sustained a large defense budget and continued to station large numbers of military forces overseas. As a result, Americans were denied the "peace dividend" they hoped would reduce taxes and free up funds for domestic problems.

In Central America, the Bush administration cooled the zeal with which Reagan had meddled, but showed no reluctance to intervene in the region to further U.S. aims. In December 1989, American troops invaded Panama to oust the military leader Manuel Noriega. A long-time drug trafficker, Noriega had stayed in Washington's favor in the mid-1980s by providing logistical support for the Nicaraguan contras. When exposés of Noriega's sordid record provoked protests in Panama, however, Bush decided to dump the dictator. Noriega was captured and taken to Miami, where, in 1992, he was convicted of drug trafficking and imprisoned. Devastated Panama meanwhile became increasingly dependent on the United States.

The strongest test of Bush's foreign policy came in the Middle East. The Iran-Iraq War ended inconclusively in August 1988, after eight years and almost 400,000 dead. The Reagan administration assisted the Iraqis with weapons and intelligence, as had many NATO countries. In mid-1990, Iraqi president Saddam Hussein, facing massive war debts, invaded neighboring Kuwait, hoping to enhance his regional power and his oil revenues. George Bush condemned the invasion and vowed to defend Kuwait, in part fearing that Iraq might threaten U.S. oil supplies in Kuwait and petroleum-rich Saudi Arabia next door.

SADDAM HUSSEIN'S GAMBLE

Within weeks, Bush convinced every important government, including most Arab and Islamic states, to commit to an economic boycott of Iraq. Then, in Operation Desert Shield, Bush dispatched more than 500,000 U.S. forces to the region, joined by over 200,000 from the allies. Likening Saddam to Hitler and declaring the moment the first post–Cold War "test of our mettle," Bush rallied a deeply divided Congress to authorize "all necessary means" to oust Iraq from Kuwait (a vote of 250 to 183 in the House and 52 to 47 in the Senate). Many Americans believed that economic sanctions should be given more time to work, but Bush would not wait. Victory would come swiftly and cleanly.

Operation Desert Storm began on January 16, 1991, with the greatest air armada in history pummeling Iraqi targets. American missiles reinforced around-the-clock bombing raids on Baghdad, Iraq's capital. It was a television war, in which CNN reporters broadcast live from a Baghdad hotel as bombs were falling. In late February, coalition forces launched a ground war that quickly routed the Iraqis from Kuwait. When the war ended on March 1, at least 40,000 Iraqis had been killed; the death toll for allied troops stood at 240 (148 of them Americans).

OPERATION DESERT STORM

Bush rejected a call from advisers to take Baghdad and topple Hussein's regime. Coalition members would not have agreed to such a plan, and it was not clear who would replace the dictator. So Saddam Hussein remained, though with his power curtailed. The U.N. maintained an arms and economic embargo, and the Security Council issued Resolution 687, demanding full disclosure of Iraq's program to develop weapons of mass destruction and ballistic missiles. In Resolution 688, the Security Council condemned a brutal crackdown by the Iraqi regime against Kurds in northern Iraq and Shia Muslims in the south and demanded access for humanitarian groups. The United States, Britain, and France seized on Resolution 688 to create a northern "no-fly zone" prohibiting Iraqi aircraft flights. A similar no-fly zone was set up in southern Iraq in 1992 and expanded in 1996.

Though later many would question Bush's decision to stop short of Baghdad, initially there were few objections. In the wake of Desert Storm, the president's popularity soared to 91 percent, beating the record 89 percent set by Harry Truman in June 1945 after Germany's surrender. Cocky advisers thought Bush could ride his popularity through the 1992 election and beyond. Bush could also claim domestic achievements

DOMESTIC PROBLEMS

that seemed to affirm his pledge to lead a "kinder, gentler nation."

In 1990, for example, Bush signed the Americans with Disabilities Act, banning job discrimination, in companies with twenty-five or more employees, against the blind, deaf, mentally disabled, and physically impaired, as well as against those who are HIV positive or have cancer. The act, which covered 87 percent of all wage earners, also required that "reasonable accommodations," such as wheelchair ramps, be made available to people with disabilities. Also in 1990, the president signed the Clean Air Act, which sought to reduce acid rain by limiting emissions from factories and automobiles.

Yet Bush's poll numbers started falling and kept falling, largely because of his ineffectual response to the weakening economy. He was slow to grasp the implications of the heavy national debt and massive federal deficit. When the nation entered a full-fledged recession after the Gulf War, Bush merely proclaimed that things were not really *that* bad.

Business shrank, despite low interest rates that theoretically should have encouraged investment. Real-estate prices plummeted. American products faced steadily tougher competition from overseas competitors, especially Japan and elsewhere in Asia. As unemployment climbed to 8 percent, consumer confidence sank. By late 1991, fewer than 40 percent of Americans felt comfortable with the way the country was going.

Bush's credibility was diminished further by confirmation hearings for Clarence Thomas, his Supreme

CLARENCE THOMAS NOMINATION

Court nominee, in the fall of 1991. The Bush administration hoped that those who opposed the nomination of another conservative to the high court might nonetheless support an African American justice. But in October, Anita Hill, an African American law professor at the University of Oklahoma, charged that Thomas had sexually harassed her when she worked for him during the early 1980s. The Judiciary Committee hearings, carried on television, turned ugly, and some Republican members suggested that Hill was either lying or mentally ill. Thomas described himself as the "victim" of a "high-tech lynching." However, Hill's testimony focused the nation's attention on issues of power, gender, sex, and the workplace. And the Senate's confirmation of Thomas, along with the attacks on Hill, angered many, further increasing the gender gap in American politics.

Summary *Online Study Center* **ACE the Test**

When Ronald Reagan left the White House in 1988, the *New York Times* wrote: "Ronald Reagan leaves no Vietnam War, no Watergate, no hostage crisis. But he leaves huge question marks—and much to do." George H. W. Bush fulfilled the foreign policy promises of the 1980s, as the Soviet Union collapsed and America won the Cold War. He also led the United States into war with Iraq, which ended in swift victory but left Saddam Hussein in power.

During the 1980s, the United States moved from recession to economic prosperity. However, deep tax cuts and massive increases in defense spending created huge budget deficits, increasing the national debt from $994 billion to more than $2.9 trillion. Pro-business policies, such as deregulation, created opportunities for economic growth but also opened the door to corruption. Policies that benefited the wealthy at the expense of middle-class or poor Americans widened the gulf between the rich and everyone else. Drug addiction, crime, and violence grew, especially in the most impoverished areas.

The 1980s also saw the beginning of the "culture wars" between fundamentalist Christians who sought to "restore America to God" and opponents who championed separation of church and state. The nation shifted to the right politically, though the coalitions of economic and social conservatives that supported Reagan were fragile.

Finally, during the 1980s, the nation's Latino population grew in size and visibility, and new immigrants from Asia arrived in large numbers. During the Reagan-Bush years, America had become both more polarized and more diverse.

LEGACY FOR A PEOPLE AND A NATION
The Americans with Disabilities Act

The Americans with Disabilities Act (ADA), passed by large bipartisan majorities in Congress and signed into law by President George Bush on July 26, 1990, built on the legacy of America's civil rights movement. Beyond banning discrimination, the ADA mandated that public and private entities—schools, stores, restaurants and hotels, government buildings, and public transportation authorities—provide "reasonable accommodations" allowing people with disabilities to participate fully in their communities and the nation.

The equal-access provisions of the ADA have changed the landscape of America. Steep curbs and stairs once blocked access to wheelchair users; now ramps and lifts are common. Buses "kneel" for passengers with limited mobility; crosswalks and elevators use audible signals for those with sight impairments; schools and universities offer qualified students a wide range of assistance. People with a whole spectrum of disabilities have traveled into the Grand Canyon, thanks to National Park Service "accessibility" programs.

At the same time, ADA regulations covering employment have generated difficult legal questions. Which conditions are covered by the ADA? (The Supreme Court has ruled that asymptomatic HIV infection is a covered disability and carpal tunnel syndrome is not.) Employers may not discriminate against qualified people who can, with "reasonable" accommodation, perform the "essential" tasks of a job—but what is "reasonable" and "essential"? The specific provisions of the ADA will likely continue to be contested and redefined in the courts, but as Attorney General Janet Reno noted on the ADA's tenth anniversary, its true legacy is the determination "to find the best in everyone and to give everyone equal opportunity."

GLOBAL BRIDGES IN THE NEW MILLENNIUM
America Since 1992

At 8:46 A.M. on that fateful Tuesday morning, Jan Demczur, a window washer, stepped into an elevator in the North Tower of the World Trade Center in New York City. Before the elevator reached its next landing, one of the six occupants recalled, "We felt a muted thud. The whole building shook. And the elevator swung from side to side like a pendulum." None of the occupants knew it, but American Airlines Flight 175 had just crashed into the building at a speed of 440 miles per hour.

The elevator started plunging. Someone pushed the emergency stop button. Then a voice came over the intercom: there had been an explosion. As smoke seeped through the elevator's doors, several men used the wooden handle of Demczur's squeegee to force open the doors, but discovered they were on the fiftieth floor, where this elevator did not stop. In front of them was a wall.

Demczur, a Polish immigrant who once worked as a builder, saw that the wall was made of Sheetrock, a plasterboard that could be cut. The six men took turns scraping and poking at it, and an hour later burst through to a men's bathroom. Startled firefighters guided them to a stairwell. They reached the street at 10:23 A.M. Five minutes later the tower collapsed.

It was September 11, 2001.

Later that day, Demczur learned that terrorists had hijacked four airliners and turned them into missiles. Two were flown into the World Trade Center, one slammed into the Pentagon in Washington, D.C., and one crashed in a field in Pennsylvania after passengers tried to retake the plane from the hijackers. Both World Trade Center towers collapsed, killing nearly three thousand people.

It was the deadliest attack the United States had ever suffered on its soil, and it would dramatically change American life. The events of the day sent shock waves around the globe, revealing how interconnected the world had become. At the World Trade Center, nearly five hundred foreigners from more

Social Strains and New Political Directions

"The New Economy" and Globalization

Paradoxes of Prosperity

September 11 and the War on Terrorism

Americans in the New Millennium

LINKS TO THE WORLD
The Global AIDS Epidemic

Summary

LEGACY FOR A PEOPLE AND A NATION
The Internet

Online Study Center

This icon will direct you to interactive map and primary source activities on the website http:college.hmco.com/pic/nortonbrief7e

C H R O N O L O G Y

1992 • Violence erupts in Los Angeles over Rodney King verdict
 • Major economic recession
 • Clinton elected president
 • U.S. sends troops to Somalia

1993 • Congress approves North American Free Trade Agreement (NAFTA)
 • U.S. withdraws from Somalia

1994 • Contract with America helps Republicans win majorities in House and Senate
 • Genocide in Rwanda
 • U.S. intervention in Haiti

1995 • Domestic terrorist bombs Oklahoma City federal building
 • U.S. diplomats broker peace for Bosnia

1996 • Welfare reform bill places time limits on welfare payments
 • Clinton reelected

1998 • House votes to impeach Clinton

1999 • Senate acquits Clinton of impeachment charges

 • NATO bombs Serbia over Kosovo crisis
 • Antiglobalization demonstrators disrupt World Trade Organization (WTO) meeting in Seattle

2000 • Nation records longest economic expansion in its history
 • Supreme Court settles contested presidential election in favor of Bush

2001 • Economy dips into recession; begins period of low growth and high unemployment
 • Bush becomes president
 • Al Qaeda terrorists attack World Trade Center and Pentagon
 • PATRIOT Act passed by Congress
 • Enron business scandal results in Justice Department investigation
 • U.S. attacks Al Qaeda positions in Afghanistan, topples ruling Taliban regime

2003 • U.S. invades Iraq, ousts Saddam Hussein regime

than eighty countries lost their lives: sixty-seven Britons, twenty-one Jamaicans, twenty-seven Japanese, seventeen Mexicans, thirty-four Indians, sixteen Canadians, fifteen Australians, and seven Haitians. Many of the victims were, like Demczur, immigrants who sought a better life for themselves and their families; others were on temporary work visas. But all made the World Trade Center a global city within a city, where some 50,000 people worked and another 140,000 visited daily.

An emblem of U.S. financial power, the World Trade Center towers also symbolized the globalization of world trade that marked the 1980s and 1990s. The towers housed the offices of more than four hundred businesses, including some of the world's lead-

ing financial institutions: the Bank of America, Switzerland's Credit Suisse Group, Germany's Deutsche Bank, and Japan's Dai-Ichi Kangyo Bank.

Globalization was a 1990s buzzword and went beyond trade and investment to include connections in commerce, communications, and culture. While the terrorists—the radical Islamic group Al Qaeda—sought to bring down globalization, their attack used the same international technological, economic, and travel infrastructure that had fueled global integration. Cell phones, computers, and intercontinental air travel were crucial in the terrorists' plot to turn four modern jetliners into lethal weapons.

Islamic militants had struck the World Trade Center before, in 1993, bombing its underground parking garage. But Americans at the time paid only fleeting attention. President Bill Clinton took office in 1993 concentrating less on foreign policy and more on domestic issues such as healthcare and deficit reduction. Clinton also sought to harness globalization to America's benefit.

For most Americans, the 1990s offered good times. The stock market soared, unemployment dropped, and more Americans than ever before owned their own homes. But the decade was also marked by violence and cultural conflict: the first multiethnic uprising in Los Angeles, domestic terrorism in Oklahoma City, school shootings, and hate crimes.

These were also politically volatile years. Republicans blocked Democrats' legislative programs. With a conservative agenda of limited government and "family values"—spelled out in his "Contract with America"—House minority whip Newt Gingrich led a "Republican Revolution" that routed Democrats in the 1994 midterm elections. But Republicans alienated voters by shutting down the federal government during the winter of 1995–1996 in a budget standoff, and Clinton was reelected in 1996. However, scandal plagued the Clinton White House, and in 1999 Clinton was impeached by the House of Representatives, alleging he committed perjury and obstructed justice. The Senate failed to convict him, and Clinton's popularity remained high, but his leadership was compromised.

Clinton's successor, George W. Bush, successful in an extremely controversial election, was galvanized by the 9/11 attacks, declaring a "war on terrorism." Bush ordered U.S. forces into large-scale military action, first in Afghanistan where Al Qaeda was headquartered with the blessing of the Taliban regime, then in Iraq to oust Saddam Hussein's government. Militarily, the Taliban and Iraqi government were quickly beaten. Al Qaeda, however, remained a threat, and Iraq endured postwar instability. At home, Bush enjoyed high approval ratings, despite a weak economy and ballooning budget deficit. Bush had declared his a "war presidency," and Americans, following the pattern of many previous wars, rallied around the flag and around the president. ∎

Social Strains and New Political Directions

*a*lthough the 1990s would be remembered for relative peace and prosperity, the decade did not start that way. Scourges of drugs, homelessness, and crime plagued America's cities. Racial tensions had worsened; the gulf between rich and poor had grown more pronounced. The economy tipped into recession. Public disillusion with political leaders ran strong. As the 1992 presidential campaign began, Americans wanted a change.

Racial tensions erupted in Los Angeles in spring 1992. To some, the April 29 violence in South Central L.A. was a riot; to others, a rebellion. The immediate cause: a jury (with no African American members) acquitted four white police officers charged with beating a black man, Rodney King, who had fled pursuing police at over 110 miles per hour. A bystander captured the beating on videotape, and CNN, the new twenty-four-hour news network, replayed it so frequently that the local event became national news.

VIOLENCE IN LOS ANGELES

The roots of this violence, however, went deeper. Well-paid jobs disappeared in the deindustrialization of the 1970s and 1980s, as a hundred manufacturing and industrial plants shut their doors. By the early 1990s, almost a third of South Central residents lived in poverty—a rate 75 percent higher than for the entire city.

Tensions increased as new immigrants arrived: Latinos from Mexico and Central America who competed with African Americans for jobs; Koreans establishing small businesses such as grocery stores. Street gangs struggled over territory in South Central as the crack epidemic further decimated the neighborhood and homicide rates soared. Many African American and Latino residents saw high prices in Korean-owned shops as exploitation, while Korean shopkeepers complained of frequent shoplifting, robberies, even beatings.

The violence in Los Angeles left at least fifty-three people dead. Almost $1 billion in property was destroyed, including twenty-three hundred stores owned by Koreans or Korean Americans. More than sixteen thousand people were arrested, half of them Latinos.

During the administration of George H. W. Bush, the economy had grown slowly or not at all. Thirty

ECONOMIC TROUBLES AND THE 1992 ELECTION

states were in financial trouble in the early 1990s; some local governments faced bankruptcy. In 1978 California's Proposition 13—the first in a series of "tax revolts" nationwide—cut property taxes while the population boomed, and the state government, out of money in mid-1992, paid workers and bills in IOUs. Many businesses closed down or cut back. By 1992, several million Americans were unemployed. In 1991 median household incomes hit the most severe decline since the 1973 recession; in 1992 the number of poor people in America reached the highest level since 1964.

As economic woes continued, President Bush's approval rating fell—to half its high point of 91 percent after the Persian Gulf War. Despite the credit Bush gained for the end of the Cold War and the quick victory in the Gulf War, economic difficulties and a belief that he was out of touch with Americans' problems left him vulnerable in the 1992 presidential election.

Democratic nominee and Arkansas governor Bill Clinton offered a profound contrast to Bush. Clinton's campaign headquarters bore signs with the reminder: "It's the economy, stupid." In a town-hall-format presidential debate, a woman asked how the economic troubles had affected each candidate, and Clinton replied, "Tell me how it's affected you again?" George Bush was caught on camera looking at his watch.

Third-party candidate Ross Perot, a Texas billionaire, was certainly insulated by his vast fortune from the problems of most Americans. Nevertheless, his appeals to common sense and folksy populism attracted many who were fed up with Washington.

On election day, Americans denied George Bush a second term. Ross Perot claimed almost 20 percent of the popular vote but did not carry a single state. Clinton, with 43 percent of the popular vote, swept all of New England, the West Coast, and much of the industrial Midwest, even making inroads into the South and drawing "Reagan Democrats" back to the fold. Although Democrats controlled both houses, incumbents did not fare well. The 103rd Congress had 110 new representatives and 11 new senators. Many were—like Clinton—baby boomers in their forties.

A journalist described the paradoxical Bill Clinton in a 1996 *New York Times* article as "one of the

WILLIAM JEFFERSON CLINTON

biggest, most talented, articulate, intelligent, open, colorful characters ever to inhabit the White House," while also noting that he could be "an undisciplined, fumbling, obtuse, defensive, self-justifying rogue." Clinton was a born politician from a small town called Hope who wanted to be president most of his life. At Georgetown University in Washington, D.C., during the 1960s, he'd protested the Vietnam War and maneuvered to keep himself out of it. Clinton won a Rhodes scholarship to Oxford, earned his law degree from Yale, and returned to his home state of Arkansas, where he was elected governor in 1978 at age thirty-two.

In 1975 Clinton married Hillary Rodham, whom he met when both were law students at Yale. Rodham Clinton was the first First Lady with a significant career of her own, and she spoke of balancing her professional and family life. But Rodham Clinton was attacked by conservatives and antifeminists. After she told a hostile interviewer, "I suppose I could have stayed home and baked cookies and had teas," the *New York Post* called her "an insult to most women."

Politically, Bill Clinton was a "new Democrat," advocating a more centrist—though still socially

A NEW DEMOCRAT'S PROMISE AND PITFALLS

progressive—position for the Democratic Party. Clinton and his colleagues emphasized private-sector economic development rather than public jobs programs, focusing on job training and other policies to promote opportunity, not dependency. Some Democrats found Clinton too conservative. However, the political right vehemently attacked Clinton, making 1990s politics exceptionally partisan and rancorous.

Clinton began his presidency with an ambitious program of reform and revitalization, including appointing a cabinet that "looks like America" in all its diversity. But Republicans, determined not to allow Clinton the traditional "honeymoon" period, maneuvered him into fulfilling his pledge to end the ban on gays in the military before he had secured congressional or military support. Amid great controversy, Clinton accepted a "don't ask, don't tell" compromise that alienated liberals and conservatives, the gay community, and the military.

Clinton's major goal was to make healthcare affordable and accessible for all Americans. But special interests mobilized in opposition: the insurance industry worried about lost profits; the business community feared higher taxes; the medical community worried about more regulation, lower government reimbursement rates, and reduced healthcare quality. The healthcare task force, co-chaired by Hillary Rodham Clinton, could not defeat these forces. Within a year, the centerpiece of Clinton's fledgling presidency had failed.

Scandal also plagued Clinton. Rumors of his past marital infidelities circulated. The suicide of Vincent Foster, deputy White House counsel and Clinton friend, spurred wild theories of murder and conspiracy. By December 1993, Republicans wanted a special prosecutor to investigate the Clintons' involvement in Whitewater, a private Arkansas land deal that figured in one of the savings-and-loan scandals of the 1980s. In January 1994, under political pressure, Attorney General Janet Reno named a special prosecutor.

New-style Republicans challenged the beleaguered "new Democrat." In September 1994, more than

THE "REPUBLICAN REVOLUTION"

three hundred Republican candidates for the House of Representatives endorsed the "Contract with America," ten policy proposals the Republicans pledged to pass. Developed under the leadership of Georgia's conservative representative, Newt Gingrich, the "Contract" promised the "end of [big] government" and "the beginning of a Congress that respects the values and shares the faith of the American family." It included a balanced-budget amendment to the Constitution, reduction of the capital gains tax, a two-year limit on welfare payments (with payments prohibited for unmarried mothers under eighteen), and increased defense spending.

In the midterm elections, the Republican Party mobilized socially conservative voters and took control of both houses of Congress for the first time since 1954. Gingrich was made Speaker of the House, and Bob Dole of Kansas became Senate majority leader. Republicans launched a counterrevolution to reverse

more than sixty years of federal dominance and dismantle the welfare state.

Although many Americans applauded cutting government spending, they opposed cuts to specific programs, including Medicare and Medicaid, education and college loans, highway construction, farm subsidies, veterans' benefits, and Social Security. Republicans angered the public when they issued Clinton an ultimatum on the federal budget and forced the government to suspend all nonessential action during the winter of 1995–1996.

Such struggles led Clinton to make compromises that moved American politics to the right. For exam-

POLITICAL COMPROMISE AND THE ELECTION OF 1996

ple, he signed the 1996 Personal Responsibility and Work Opportunity Act, a welfare reform measure that ended cash assistance to poor children (Aid to Families with Dependent Children) and gave each state a lump sum for its own "welfare-to-work" programs. The law mandated that heads of families on welfare must find work within two years—though states could exempt 20 percent of recipients—and limited welfare benefits to five years over an individual's lifetime. The Telecommunications Act of 1996, signed by Clinton, reduced diversity in America's media by permitting companies to own more television and radio stations.

Clinton and Al Gore were reelected in 1996 (defeating Republican Bob Dole and Reform Party candidate Ross Perot), partly because Clinton stole some of the conservatives' thunder. He declared that "the era of big government is over" and invoked family values, a centerpiece of the Republican campaign. Sometimes Clinton's actions were true compromises; other times he attempted to reclaim issues from the conservatives, as when he redefined family values as "fighting for the family-leave law." The Democrats also benefited from a strong economy and the gender gap: women were more likely to vote Democratic.

"The New Economy" and Globalization

ust how much credit Clinton deserved for the improved economy is debatable. The roots of the 1990s boom were in the 1970s, when

American corporations began investing in new technologies, retooling plants to become energy efficient, and cutting labor costs. Specifically, companies reduced the influence of organized labor by moving operations to the union-weak South and West and to countries such as China and Mexico, where labor was cheap and pollution controls lax.

The rapid development of what came to be called "information technology"—computers, fax machines,

DIGITAL REVOLUTION

cellular phones, and the Internet—had a huge economic impact in the 1980s and 1990s. New companies and industries sprang up, many headquartered in the "Silicon Valley" near San Francisco. By the second half of the 1990s, the *Forbes* list of the Four Hundred Richest People in America featured high-tech leaders such as Bill Gates, who became the wealthiest person in the world with a worth approaching $100 billion, as his company produced the operating software for most personal computers. The high-tech industries had considerable spillover effects, generating improved productivity, new jobs, and sustained economic growth.

The heart of this technological revolution was the microprocessor. Introduced in 1970 by Intel, the microprocessor miniaturized the central processing unit of a computer, meaning small machines could perform calculations previously requiring large machines. Computing chores that took a week in the early 1970s by 2000 took one minute, while the cost of storing 1 megabyte of information, enough for a 320-page book, fell from over $5,000 in 1975 to 17 cents in 1999.

Analysts dubbed this technology-driven sector "The New Economy," and it would have emerged no matter who was in the White House. Yet Clinton and his advisers had some responsibility for the dramatic upturn. With the U.S. budget deficit topping $500 billion, they made the politically risky move of abandoning the middle-class tax cut and making deficit reduction a top priority. White House officials rightly concluded that if the deficit could be brought under control, interest rates would drop and the economy would rebound. The budget deficit decreased (by 1997 it had been erased), leading to lower interest rates, which helped boost investment. Stock prices soared, and the gross national product rose by an average of 3.5 to 4 percent annually.

Clinton perceived early on that the technology revolution would make the world more interconnected.

GLOBALIZATION OF BUSINESS

He was convinced that, with the demise of Soviet communism, capitalism—or at least the introduction of market forces, freer trade, and deregulation—was spreading around the globe.

The journalist Thomas L. Friedman asserted that the post–Cold War world was "the age of globalization," characterized by the integration of markets, finance, and technologies. U.S. officials lowered trade and investment barriers, completing the North American Free Trade Agreement (NAFTA) with Canada and Mexico in 1993, and in 1994 concluding the Uruguay Round of the General Agreement on Tariffs and Trade (GATT), which lowered tariffs for the seventy member nations that accounted for 80 percent of world trade. The administration also endorsed the 1995 creation of the World Trade Organization (WTO) to administer and enforce agreements made at the Uruguay Round. Finally, the president formed a National Economic Council to promote trade missions around the world.

By 2000 there were 63,000 parent companies worldwide and 690,000 foreign affiliates. Some, such as the Nike Corporation and the Gap, subcontracted production of certain merchandise to whichever developing countries had the lowest labor costs. Such arrangements created a "new international division of labor" and generated a boom in world exports, which, at $5.4 trillion in 1998, had doubled in two decades. U.S. exports reached $680 billion in 1998, but imports rose even higher, to $907 billion (for a trade deficit of $227 billion). Sometimes these multinational corporations affected foreign policy, as when Clinton in 1995 extended full diplomatic recognition to Vietnam under pressure from Coca-Cola, Citigroup, General Motors, and United Airlines, all seeking to enter that emerging market.

While the administration promoted open markets, labor unions argued that free-trade agreements

CRITICS OF GLOBALIZATION

exacerbated the trade deficit and often exported American jobs. Average real wages for American workers declined steadily after 1973, from $320 per week to $260 by the mid-1990s. Other critics maintained that globalization widened

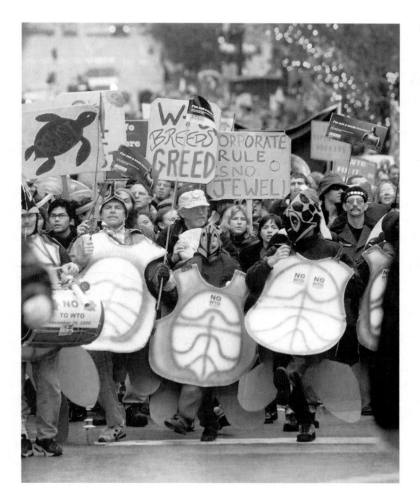

■ Animal protection advocates wear sea turtle costumes while carrying signs to protest what they contend are animal-harming rulings by the World Trade Organization, in Seattle Monday, Nov. 29, 1999. Protests began in earnest Monday against the WTO meetings and the conference schedule was thrown off by a security threat that temporarily closed the meeting's primary venue, the Washington State Trade and Convention Center.   (AP Photo/Beth Keiser)

the gap between rich and poor countries, creating a mass of "slave laborers" in poor countries working under conditions that would never be tolerated in the West. Environmentalists charged that globalization also exported pollution to countries unprepared to deal with it. Still other critics worried about the power of multinational corporations and the global financial markets over traditional cultures.

Antiglobalization fervor reached a peak in fall 1999 when WTO ministers met in Seattle for trade negotiations called the Millennium Round. Hundreds were arrested as thousands of protesters shut down the meeting. In the months that followed, there were smaller protests at meetings of the International Monetary Fund (IMF) and the World Bank. In July 2001, fifty thousand demonstrators protested an IMF and World Bank meeting in Genoa, Italy.

Activists also targeted corporations such as the Gap, Starbucks, Nike, and, especially, McDonald's, which by 1995 was serving 30 million customers daily in twenty thousand franchises in over one hundred countries. Critics assailed the company's slaughterhouse techniques, alleged exploitation of workers, its high-fat menu, and its contributions to creating an increasingly

TARGET:
McDonald's

homogeneous and sterile world culture, a so-called McWorld. For six years starting in 1996, McDonald's endured hundreds of often violent protests, including bombings in Rome, Prague, London, Macao, Rio de Janeiro, and Jakarta.

Others decried the violence and underlying arguments of the antiglobalization campaigners. True, some economists noted, statistics showed that global inequality had grown in recent years. But if one included quality-of-life measurements such as literacy and health, global inequality had actually declined. Some studies found that wage and job losses for U.S. workers were caused not primarily by globalization factors such as imports, production outsourcing, and immigration, but by technological change that made production more efficient. Other researchers saw no evidence that governments' sovereignty had been seriously compromised or that there was a "race to the bottom" in environmental standards.

As for creating a homogeneous global culture, critics noted that McDonald's, supposedly a prime mover of "McWorld," tailored its menu and operating practices to local tastes. And although American movies, TV programs, music, computer software, and other intellectual property often dominated world markets in the 1990s, foreign competition also arrived in America. Millions of American children were gripped by the Japanese fad Pokemon, and satellite television established a worldwide following for European soccer leagues.

Still, it remained true that the United States occupied a uniquely powerful position on the world stage.

CLINTON'S DIPLOMACY

The demise of the Soviet Union created a one-superpower world, in which the United States stood above other powers in terms of political and military might. Yet in his first term, Clinton was more wary in traditional aspects of foreign policy—great-power diplomacy, arms control, regional disputes—than in facilitating American cultural and trade expansion. Recalling the public's impatience in the Vietnam debacle, he was deeply suspicious of foreign military involvements.

Clinton's mistrust was cemented by the difficulties he inherited from Bush in Somalia. In 1992 Bush had sent U.S. Marines to the East African nation as part of a U.N. effort to ensure that humanitarian supplies reached starving Somalis. But in the summer of 1993, when Americans came under deadly attack, Clinton withdrew U.S. troops. And he did not intervene in Rwanda, where in 1994 the majority Hutus butchered 800,000 of the minority Tutsis in a brutal civil war.

Many administration officials argued for using America's power to contain ethnic hatreds, support human rights, and promote democracy around the world. Clinton moved cautiously. In 1991 a military coup in Haiti had overthrown the democratically elected president, Jean-Bertrand Aristide, and imposed a harsh system. Tens of thousands of Haitians fled in boats for U.S. territory, spawning an immigration crisis. In 1994 Clinton sent former president Jimmy Carter to negotiate an arrangement facilitating Aristide's return to power.

CRISIS IN HAITI

Humanitarian intervention faced a real test in the Balkans, which erupted in a series of ethnic wars where Bosnian Muslims, Serbs, and Croats were killing one another. Clinton lashed out against Serbian aggression and atrocities in Bosnia-Herzegovina, especially the Serbs' "ethnic cleansing" of Muslims through massacres and rape camps. He occasionally ordered air strikes, but he primarily emphasized diplomacy. In late 1995, American diplomats brokered a fragile peace.

But Yugoslav president Slobodan Milosevic continued the anti-Muslim and anti-Croat fervor. When Serb forces moved to violently rid Kosovo of its majority ethnic Albanians, Clinton was pressed to intervene. Reports of Serbian atrocities against the Muslim Kosovars and a major refugee crisis stirred world opinion and pushed him to act. In 1999 NATO forces led by the United States launched a massive aerial bombardment of Serbia. Milosevic withdrew his military from Kosovo, where U.S. troops joined a U.N. peacekeeping force.

KOSOVO WAR

In the Middle East, in September 1993 the PLO's Yasir Arafat and Israel's prime minister Yitzhak Rabin signed an agreement for Palestinian self-rule in the Gaza Strip and the West Bank's Jericho. The following year, Israel signed a peace accord with Jordan, further reducing the chances of another full-scale Arab-Israeli war. Radical anti-Arafat Palestinians, however, continued terrorist attacks on Israelis, while extremist Israelis killed Palestinians and, in November 1995, Rabin himself. With American-conducted negotiations and renewed violence in the West Bank, Israel agreed in early 1997 to withdraw troops from the Palestinian city of Hebron. Thereafter, the peace process sagged.

International efforts to protect the environment gathered pace in the 1990s. The Bush administration

ENVIRONMENTAL
DIPLOMACY

opposed many provisions of the 1992 Rio de Janeiro Treaty protecting the diversity of plant and animal species and resisted stricter rules on global warming. Clinton, urged on by environmentalist Vice President Al Gore, signed the 1997 Kyoto Protocol, which aimed to combat emissions of carbon dioxide and other gases. But facing strong congressional opposition, Clinton never submitted it for ratification to the Republican-controlled Senate.

Meanwhile, the administration was privately but increasingly concerned about the threat to U.S. in-

BIN LADEN AND
AL QAEDA

terests by Islamic fundamentalists. Senior officials worried about Al Qaeda (Arabic for "the base"), an international terrorist network led by Osama bin Laden that wanted to purge Muslim countries of what it saw as the profane influence of the West.

The son of a Yemen-born construction tycoon in Saudi Arabia, bin Laden supported the Afghan Mujahidin against Soviet occupation. He then founded Al Qaeda and began financing terrorist projects with his substantial inheritance. U.S. officials grew increasingly concerned, particularly as bin Laden focused on American targets. In 1995 a car bomb in Riyadh killed seven people, five of them Americans. In Yemen in 2000, a small boat laden with explosives hit the destroyer U.S.S. *Cole*, killing seventeen American sailors. Although bin Laden masterminded and financed these attacks, he eluded U.S. attempts to apprehend him. In 1998 Clinton approved a plan to assassinate bin Laden, but it failed.

Paradoxes of Prosperity

For most Americans, the late 1990s marked unprecedented peace and prosperity, fueled by the dizzying rise of the stock market. Between 1991 and 1999, the Dow Jones Industrial Average climbed from 3,169 to a high of 11,497. The booming market benefited the middle class as well as the wealthy, as mutual funds and other new investment vehicles drew a majority of Americans into the stock market. In 1952 only 4 percent of American households owned stocks; by the year 2000 almost 60 percent did.

At the end of the 1990s, the unemployment rate stood at 4.3 percent. Plentiful jobs made it easier for states to implement welfare reform and cut welfare rolls almost in half. Both the richest 5 percent and the least well-off 20 percent of American households saw their incomes rise almost 25 percent. But that meant an average gain of $50,000 for the top 5 percent and only $2,880 for the bottom 20 percent, further widening the gap between rich and poor. Nevertheless, by decade's end, more than two-thirds of Americans were homeowners. Teen pregnancy rates declined, infant mortality dropped, and murder rates hit a thirty-year low.

Still, new crises shook the nation. On April 19, 1995, 168 people were killed in a bomb blast that destroyed the Alfred P. Murrah Federal Building in

OKLAHOMA CITY
BOMBING

downtown Oklahoma City. At first many blamed Middle Eastern terrorists. But a charred piece of truck axle two blocks away, with the vehicle identification number still legible, revealed that the bomber was Timothy McVeigh, a white American and Persian Gulf War veteran. He sought revenge for the deaths of the Branch Davidian religious sect, whom he believed the FBI deliberately slaughtered in a standoff over firearms charges two years earlier in Waco, Texas.

Online Study Center **Improve Your Grade**
Primary Source: Events in Waco

In subsequent months, reporters and investigators discovered networks of militias, tax resisters, and white-supremacist groups nationwide. United by distrust of the federal government, many saw gun control laws as a dangerous usurpation of citizens' right to bear arms. They believed the federal government was controlled by "sinister forces," including Zionists, corrupt politicians, cultural elitists, Queen Elizabeth, the Russians, and the United Nations.

On April 20, 1999, eighteen-year-old Eric Harris and seventeen-year-old Dylan Klebold opened fire

VIOLENCE AND
HATE CRIMES

on classmates and teachers at Columbine High School in Littleton, Colorado, murdering thirteen before

■ On April 20, 1999, students evacuated Columbine High School in Littleton, Colorado, after two schoolmates went on a shooting rampage, killing twelve students and a teacher before killing themselves.   (AP/Wide World Photos)

killing themselves. No clear reason why two academically successful students in a middle-class suburb would commit mass murder ever emerged. Students in Paducah, Kentucky; Springfield, Oregon; and Jonesboro, Arkansas, also massacred classmates. Disgruntled employees opened fire on coworkers; shootings by U.S. Postal Service employees inspired the phrase "going postal" as a synonym for violent outburst.

In the late 1990s, two hate crimes shocked the nation. In 1998 James Byrd Jr., a forty-nine-year-old black man, was murdered by white supremacists who dragged him by a chain from the back of a pickup truck in Jasper, Texas. Later that year, Matthew Shepherd, a gay college student, was beaten and tied to a fence in freezing Laramie, Wyoming. His killers said they were "humiliated" when he flirted with them at a bar. To some, these murders signified that bigotry remained strong in America. Others noted the horror Americans expressed and the growing support for federal legislation against hate crimes as a positive change.

Scandals plagued the Clinton White House. The independent counsel would eventually spend $72 million investigating allegations against Hillary and Bill Clinton. Independent counsel Kenneth Starr, a conservative Republican and former judge, was originally charged with investigating Whitewater, the Arkansas real-estate deal the Clintons participated in during the 1970s, but he never found any evidence against them. Starr did find evidence that the president committed perjury, however.

SCANDAL IN THE CLINTON WHITE HOUSE

Early in Clinton's presidency, former Arkansas state employee Paula Jones brought charges of sexual harassment against the president, which were eventually dropped. But when asked before a grand jury whether he had engaged in sexual relations with twenty-two-year-old White House intern Monica Lewinsky, Clinton said no. Starr discovered evidence proving he had lied. In response, Clinton angrily declared: "I want to say one thing to the American people. . . . I did not have sexual relations with that woman, Miss Lewinsky." In fact, Clinton had at least ten sexual encounters, and fifteen "phone sex" conversations, with Lewinsky. Starr produced phone conversations recorded without Lewinsky's knowledge by her supposed friend Linda Tripp. Most infamously, Starr obtained DNA evidence against the president: a navy blue dress of Lewinsky's, stained with Clinton's semen.

In a 445-page report to Congress, Starr outlined eleven possible grounds for impeachment, including lying under oath, obstruction of justice, witness tampering, and abuse of power. On December 19, 1998, the House voted on four articles of impeachment against Clinton; largely along party lines, the House passed two of the articles, one alleging that the president had committed perjury, the other that he had obstructed justice. Clinton became only the second president to face a trial in the Senate, which has the constitutional responsibility to decide (by two-thirds vote) whether to remove a president from office.

IMPEACHMENT

But the American people did not want Clinton removed from office. Polls showed large majorities approved of the president's job performance, even while condemning his personal behavior. And many did not believe his wrongdoing constituted the "high crimes and misdemeanors" (normally acts such as treason) required by the Constitution for impeachment. The Republican-controlled Senate, responding partly to popular opinion, voted against the charge of perjury 55–45 and voted 50–50 to clear Clinton of obstructing justice. The vote did not approach the two-thirds majority required for conviction. Clinton said he was "profoundly sorry."

Clinton was not the first president to engage in illicit sex. President Kennedy had numerous and well-

POLITICAL
PARTISANSHIP,
THE MEDIA,
AND CELEBRITY
CULTURE

known sexual affairs, including one with a nineteen-year-old intern. But after the Watergate scandals of the early 1970s, the mass media no longer turned a blind eye to presidential misconduct. The fiercely competitive news networks relied on scandal, spectacle, and crisis to lure viewers.

The partisan political wars of the 1990s created a take-no-prisoners climate. Both Republican Speaker of the House Newt Gingrich and his successor, Robert Livingston, resigned when evidence of their extramarital affairs surfaced. Finally, as former Clinton aide Sidney Blumenthal writes, the impeachment struggle was part of the "culture wars": "a monumental battle over . . . cultural mores and the position of women in American society, and about the character of the American people."

Clinton's legislative accomplishments during his two terms in office included the Family and Medical

CLINTON'S
LEGISLATIVE
RECORD

Leave Act, guaranteeing 91 million workers the right to take time off to care for ailing relatives or newborn children. The Health Insurance Portability and Accountability Act ensured that when Americans changed jobs, they would not lose health insurance because of preexisting medical conditions. The federal government operated efficiently with 365,000 fewer employees. Clinton created national parks and monuments that protected 3.2 million acres of American land and made unprecedented progress cleaning up toxic waste dumps.

Vice President Al Gore was initially favored in the 2000 presidential election. The son of a prominent

THE BUSH-GORE
RACE

senator from Tennessee, Gore graduated cum laude from Harvard in 1969, enlisted in the army, and served in Vietnam despite his reservations about the war. He was elected to the House and to the Senate, serving six terms, and wrote a well-received book on global environmental issues. In the Clinton administration, Gore played a greater role than any previous vice president in history, and after eight years of prosperity and relative peace, he had a strong platform. But earnest and intelligent Gore appeared to many as a well-informed policy wonk rather than a charismatic leader.

Gore's Republican opponent was the son of George H. W. Bush, the forty-first president of the United States. An indifferent student, George W. Bush graduated from Yale in 1968 and pulled strings to jump ahead of a one-and-a-half-year waiting list for the Texas Air National Guard, thus avoiding service in Vietnam. After a rocky career in the oil business, Bush gave up alcohol and embraced Christianity at the age of forty. In 1994 he was elected to the first of two terms as governor of Texas.

As a presidential candidate, Bush made up for his limited foreign policy knowledge and often garbled syntax with a confident style that connected with many Americans. He spoke of his relationship with God and his commitment to conservative social values, styling himself a "compassionate conservative." Supported by Republicans and business leaders, Bush amassed the largest campaign war chest in history ($67 million, compared with Gore's $28 million).

Consumer rights activist Ralph Nader ran on the Green Party ticket. Condemning globalization and environmental despoliation, he attacked Bush and Gore, calling them "Tweedledee and Tweedledum." However, Nader drew support from left-liberal voters who might have voted for Gore and so helped tip some districts to Bush.

On election day 2000, Al Gore narrowly won the popular vote but not the presidency. It all came down to

THE CONTESTED
ELECTION OF
2000

Florida (where Bush's brother Jeb was governor) and its twenty-five electoral votes. At first, television coverage declared Gore the winner, giving him the presidency. But by early morning, the election outcome was unclear. When the Florida votes were first tallied, Bush narrowly edged out Gore, but with a close margin that legally required an automatic recount. In several heavily African American counties, tens of thousands of votes went uncounted because voters failed to fully dislodge the "chads," or small perforated squares, when punching the paper ballots. Lawyers struggled over whether "hanging chads" (partially detached) and "pregnant chads" (punched but not detached) were sufficient signs of voter intent. In Palm Beach County, many elderly Jewish residents were confused by a poorly designed ballot and accidentally selected the allegedly anti-Semitic Reform party candidate Pat Buchanan instead of Gore. After thirty-six days, with court cases at the state and federal levels, the Supreme Court voted 5 to 4 along narrowly partisan lines to end the recount process. Florida's electoral votes—and the presidency—went to George Bush.

Online Study Center   **Improve Your Grade**
Interactive Map:
The Election of 2000

Gore won the West Coast, Northeast, and industrial Midwest. The South, Rocky Mountain West (except New Mexico), and heartland went to Bush. More than 90 percent of black voters selected Gore, as did 63 percent of Latinos and 55 percent of Asian Americans. Bush won 60 percent of the white vote, and, overall, 95 percent of his supporters were white. The gender gap was 12 points: 54 percent of women voted for Gore. With such divisions, Bush had no popular mandate and critics referred to him as the "president-select."

September 11 and the War on Terrorism

*W*ith the close election and bitter controversy, many believed Bush would govern from the center. Some also thought he, like his father, moved to the right only to secure conservative evangelical Christian voters. But Bush governed from the right, arguably more so than any modern administration.

The centerpiece of the Bush agenda was a massive tax cut, to be financed by the predicted budget _____ surplus. Critics believed that a mas-
BUSH'S TAX PLAN   sive cut would wipe out the surplus

and that the Bush plan favored the wealthy, but Bush used his party's control of Congress to push through the largest tax cut in U.S. history—$1.3 trillion. To the dismay of environmentalists, he also reiterated his plan to drill for oil in America's last wilderness, the Arctic National Wildlife Refuge.

In international affairs, the administration charted a more unilateralist course. Given America's preponderant power, senior Bush officials reasoned, it did not need the help of other countries. Bush pulled the United States out of the 1972 Anti-Ballistic Missile Treaty with Russia to develop a National Missile Defense system similar to Reagan's "Star Wars." The White House also renounced the 1997 Kyoto protocol on global warming and opposed a carefully negotiated protocol to strengthen the 1972 Biological and Toxin Weapons Convention. These decisions, and the administration's hands-off policy toward the Israeli-Palestinian peace process, caused consternation in Europe.

Then came September 11. On that sunny Tuesday morning, nineteen hijackers seized control of four com-
_____ mercial jets departing from East
9/11   Coast airports. At 8:46 A.M. one
plane crashed into the 110-story
North Tower of the World Trade
Center in New York City. At 9:03 A.M., a second plane flew into the South Tower. In less than two hours, both buildings collapsed, killing thousands of office workers, firefighters, and police officers. At 9:43, the third plane crashed into the Pentagon, leaving a huge hole in its west side. The fourth plane was also headed toward Washington, but several passengers—learning of the World Trade Center attacks through cell phones—stormed the cockpit; in the scuffle, the plane crashed in Somerset County, Pennsylvania, killing all aboard.

More than three thousand people died in the deadliest act of terrorism in history. The hijackers—fifteen Saudi Arabians, two Emiratis, one Lebanese, and, leading them, an Egyptian—had ties to Al Qaeda, Osama bin Laden's radical Islamic organization. Some officials in the Clinton and Bush administrations had warned that an Al Qaeda attack was inevitable, but neither administration made counterterrorism a top foreign policy priority.

In an instant, counterterrorism was priority one. President Bush responded quickly with military force.
_____ Al Qaeda operated out of Afghan-
AFGHANISTAN   istan with the blessing of the ruling
WAR   Taliban, a repressive Islamic funda-

mentalist regime that gained power in 1996. In early October, the United States launched a sustained bombing campaign against Taliban and Al Qaeda positions and sent special operations forces to help resistance groups in northern Afghanistan. Within two months, the Taliban was driven from power, though bin Laden and top Taliban leaders eluded capture.

As administration officials acknowledged, military victory did not end terrorism. Bush spoke of a long and difficult war against evil forces, in which the nations of the world were either with the United States or against it. Some questioned whether a "war on terrorism" could ever be won in a meaningful sense, given that the foe was a nonstate actor with little to lose. Most Americans, however, were ready to believe. Stunned by September 11, they experienced a renewed sense of national pride. Flag sales soared, and Bush's approval ratings skyrocketed.

But the new patriotism had a dark side. Congress passed the USA PATRIOT Act (Uniting and Strengthening America by Providing Appropriate Tools Required to Intercept and Obstruct Terrorism), making it easier for law enforcement to conduct searches, wiretap telephones, and obtain electronic records on individuals. Attorney General John Ashcroft approved giving FBI agents new powers to monitor the Internet, mosques, and rallies. Civil libertarians charged that the Justice Department overstepped, and some judges ruled against the tactics. Yet according to a June 2002 Gallup poll, 80 percent of Americans were willing to give up some freedoms for security.

PATRIOT ACT

In surveys after the attacks, 71 percent said they felt depressed, and a third had trouble sleeping. The discovery of anthrax-laden letters in several East Coast cities heightened fears, particularly after post offices and government buildings were closed and five people died. Investigators found no evidence connecting the letters to the 9/11 hijackings, but also no good clues as to who the perpetrator might be.

Yet continuity was as evident as change. People continued shopping in malls and visiting amusement parks. Although airline bookings dropped significantly in the early weeks (causing severe problems for many airlines), people still took to the skies. In Washington, the partisanship that had disappeared after 9/11 returned, as Democrats and Republicans sparred over judicial appointments, energy policy, and the proposed new Department of Homeland Security. Approved by Congress in November 2002, the department incorporated parts of eight cabinet departments and twenty-two agencies to coordinate intelligence and defense against terrorism.

Economically, the months before September 11 witnessed a collapse of the so-called dot-coms, the Internet companies that were the darlings of Wall Street in the 1990s. In 2001 some five hundred dot-coms declared bankruptcy or closed. There were other economic warning signs as well, notably a meager 0.2 percent growth rate in goods and services for the second quarter of 2001—the slowest growth in eight years. Corporate revenues were also down.

ENRON COLLAPSE

Economic concerns deepened after 9/11 with a four-day closing of Wall Street and a subsequent sharp drop in stock prices. The Dow Jones Industrial Average plunged 14.26 percent. The markets eventually rebounded, but then a corporate scandal made headlines. Enron Corporation, a Houston-based energy company that was one of the largest commodity trading firms in the world, filed for bankruptcy. Enron's twenty thousand employees lost billions in pension plans while many executives—who had advised the White House on energy policies—allegedly raked in profits, selling their shares before the steep fall in prices.

The Enron collapse marked the biggest corporate failure in U.S. history, and it generated a Justice Department criminal investigation. Despite Bush's close relationship with Enron going back to his days as Texas governor, the president seemed largely unscathed, underscoring how 9/11 and his early responses to it strengthened his political position. Notwithstanding growing economic weakness, the general absence of a domestic agenda, and the failure to capture Osama bin Laden and top Taliban leaders, Bush's approval ratings remained high.

GOP MIDTERM GAINS

Bush's clout became clear in the midterm congressional elections. The GOP retook control of the Senate and added to its majority in the House. The Republicans' core message—that a country at war should unite behind the president—resonated with voters. Now the Republicans not only controlled Congress, the White House, and a majority of governorships but also had appointed a majority of Supreme Court justices.

Immediately after September 11, there was an outpouring of support from people everywhere. "We are all Americans now," the French newspaper *Le Monde* wrote the day after the attacks. Governments across the globe announced they would co-operate with Washington in the struggle against terrorism. But by a year later, attitudes had changed dramatically. Bush's good-versus-evil stance had put off many foreign observers from the start, but they initially swallowed their objections. When the president hinted that America might unilaterally strike Saddam Hussein's Iraq or deal forcefully with North Korea or Iran—the three countries of Bush's "axis of evil"—many allied governments strongly objected.

INTERNATIONAL RESPONSES

Bush and other top officials argued that in an age of terrorism, the United States would not wait for a potential security threat to become real; henceforth, it would strike first. "In the world we have entered, the only path to safety is the path of action and this nation will act," Bush declared. Critics, among them many world leaders, called it recklessly aggressive and contrary to international law, and they wondered what would happen if dictators around the world began claiming the same right of preemption.

But Bush was determined, particularly on Iraq. Several of his top advisers, including Secretary of Defense Donald Rumsfeld and Vice President Dick Cheney, had wanted to oust Saddam Hussein since the end of the Gulf War in 1991; they now folded that objective into the larger war on terrorism. Cynics wondered whether the focus on Hussein was intended to deflect attention from the poor economy and failure to capture bin Laden. In September 2002, Bush challenged the United Nations to immediately enforce its resolutions against Iraq or the United States would act on its own. In subsequent weeks, he and his aides offered shifting reasons for getting tough with Iraq. They said Hussein was a major threat to the United States and its allies, a leader who possessed and would use banned biological and chemical "weapons of mass destruction" and who sought to acquire nuclear weapons. They claimed he had ties to Al Qaeda and could be linked to the 9/11 attacks. They said he brutalized his own people.

REGIME CHANGE IN IRAQ

Although Bush claimed he did not need congressional authorization for military action against Iraq, he nevertheless sought it. In early October, the House of Representatives voted 296-133 and the Senate 77–23 to authorize the use of force against Iraq. The vote was misleading: many who voted yes were unwilling to defy a president so close to a midterm election, even though they opposed military action without U.N. sanction. Critics complained that the president had not presented evidence that Saddam Hussein constituted an imminent threat or was connected to the 9/11 attacks. Bush switched to a less hawkish stance, and in early November, the U.N. Security Council unanimously approved Resolution 1441, imposing rigorous new arms inspections on Iraq.

But the Security Council was deeply divided over the next move. In late January 2003, the weapons inspector's report castigated Iraq for failing to carry out "the disarmament that was demanded of it" but also said it was too soon to tell whether the inspections would succeed. While U.S. and British officials said the time for diplomacy was up, France, Russia, and China called for more inspections. As the U.N. debate continued and as massive antiwar demonstrations took place worldwide, Bush sent about 250,000 soldiers to the region. Britain sent about 45,000 troops.

In late February the United States floated a draft resolution to the U.N. that proposed issuing an ultimatum to Iraq, but only three of the fifteen Security Council members affirmed support. Defeated, Bush abandoned the resolution and diplomatic efforts on March 17 when he ordered Saddam Hussein to leave Iraq within forty-eight hours or face an attack. Saddam ignored the ultimatum, and on March 19 the United States and Britain launched an aerial bombardment of Baghdad and other areas. A ground invasion followed days later (see Map 33.1). The Iraqis initially offered stiff resistance, but on April 9, Baghdad fell.

FALL OF BAGHDAD

The military victory was swift and decisive, but stability was slow to return to Iraq, raising concerns that Washington might win the war and lose the peace. U.S. occupying forces faced frequent ambushes and hit-and-run attacks by disaffected Iraqis, indicating that a "guerrilla war" had begun. In December 2003 elite U.S. forces captured Saddam Hussein, raising hopes that the insurgency could be brought under

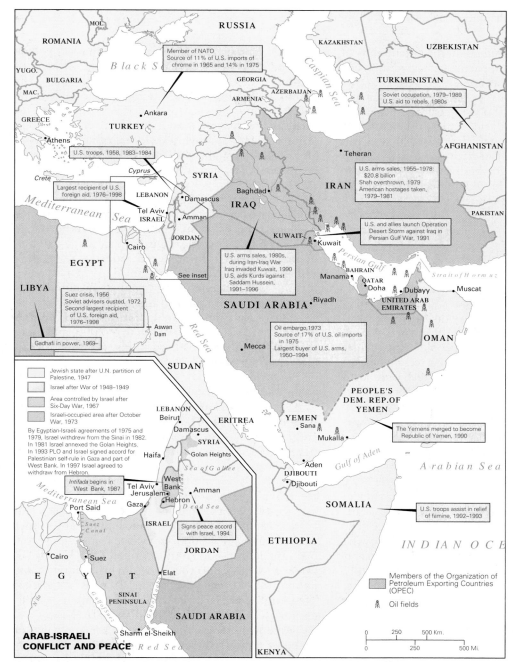

Map 33.1 The Middle East

Extremely volatile and often at war, the nations of the Middle East maintained precarious relations with the United States. To protect its interests, the United States extended large amounts of economic and military aid and sold huge quantities of weapons to the area. At times, Washington ordered U.S. troops to the region. The Arab-Israeli dispute particularly upended order, although the peace process moved forward intermittently.

control. But concerns existed about the potential costs of the postwar occupation, particularly given the uncertain economic climate at home.

Federal, state, and local governments nationwide faced severe budget shortfalls. Education and Medicaid took the brunt of the cuts, but many states also raised taxes. The governor of Missouri ordered every third light bulb unscrewed to save money. In Oklahoma, teachers doubled as janitors.

STATE ECONOMIC WOES

Americans in the New Millennium

*E*arly in the twenty-first century, the United States is a nation of extraordinary diversity. Immigration reform in the mid-1960s opened American borders to large numbers of people from a wider variety of nations than previously. New technologies—the Internet, and cable and satellite television with their proliferation of channels—replaced mass markets with niche markets. Everything from television shows to cosmetics to cars could be targeted at specific groups defined by age, ethnicity, class, gender, or lifestyle choices. These changes helped to make Americans' understandings of identity simultaneously more fluid and more complex.

For the first time in the 2000 U.S. government census, Americans could identify themselves as belonging to more than one race. The change acknowledged the growing number of Americans born to parents of different racial backgrounds. Critics, however, worried that because census data are used to gather information about social conditions in the United States and to allocate resources, the new "multiracial" option would reduce the clout of minority groups. Thus, the federal government counted those who identified both as white and members of a racial or ethnic minority as belonging to the minority group. Consequently, the official population of some groups increased. Others rejected racial and ethnic categories altogether: 20 million people identified themselves simply as "American," up more than 50 percent since 1990.

RACE AND ETHNICITY IN RECENT AMERICA

During the 1990s, the population of people of color grew twelve times as fast as the white population, fueled by immigration and birth rates. The Latino population alone more than doubled. By 2003, Latinos moved past African Americans to become the second largest ethnic or racial group (after non-Hispanic whites). Immigration from Asia also remained high, with people of Asian ancestry comprising 3.6 percent of the U.S. population in 2000.

These rapid demographic changes have altered the face of America. At a Dairy Queen in the far southern suburbs of Atlanta, 6 miles from the "Gone with the Wind Historical District," teenage children of immigrants from India and Pakistan serve Blizzards and Mister Mistys. In the small town of Ligonier, Indiana, the formerly empty main street now boasts three Mexican restaurants and a Mexican western-wear shop. Still, more than half of American counties were still at least 85 percent white in 2000, and more than half of all Latinos lived in just eight metropolitan areas (see Map 33.2).

American popular culture embraced the influences of this new multiethnic population. After all, Latino buying power exceeded $561 billion in 2000, and average income for Asian Americans topped all other groups. But audiences crossed racial and ethnic lines: Jennifer Lopez (of Puerto Rican descent) was the nation's most "bankable" musician/actress; black basketball great Michael Jordan had more commercial endorsements than any other celebrity in history. Suburban white teens took up urban rap and hip-hop culture. Golfer Tiger Woods became a symbol of this new, hybrid, multiethnic nation: of African, European, Native American, Thai, and Chinese descent, he calls himself "Cablinasian" (CAucasian-BLack-INdian-ASIAN).

A MORE DIVERSE CULTURE

Americans were divided over the meaning of changing family structure (see Figure 33.1). The number of people living together without marriage jumped 72 percent during the 1990s, to 5.5 million. Of those, at least 600,000 were same-sex couples—perhaps 1 percent of households nationwide. A third of female-partner households and one-fifth of male-partner households had children, and in 2002 the

THE CHANGING AMERICAN FAMILY

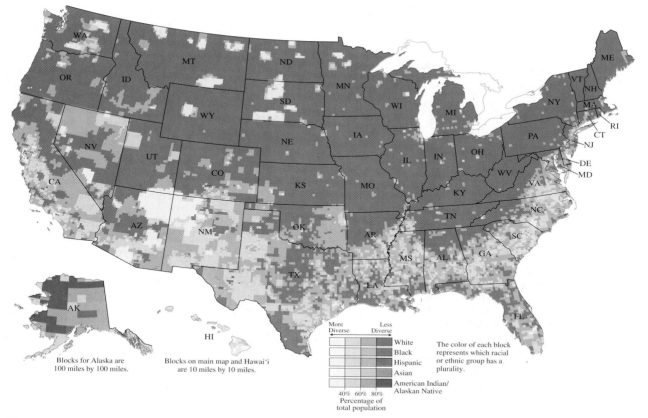

Map 33.2   Mapping America's Diversity

Aggregate figures (more than 12 percent of the U.S. population is African American and about 4 percent is Asian American, for example) convey America's ethnic and racial diversity. However, as this map shows, members of racial and ethnic groups are not distributed evenly throughout the nation.   (Source: Adapted from the *New York Times* National Edition, April 1, 2001, "Portrait of a Nation," p. 18. Copyright © 2001 by The New York Times Co. Reprinted with permission.)

American Academy of Pediatrics endorsed adoption by gay couples. A vocal antigay movement coexisted with support for the legal equality of gay, lesbian, transgendered, and bisexual Americans. While many states and private corporations extended domestic-partner benefits to gay couples, the federal Defense of Marriage Act, passed by Congress in 1996, defined marriage as "only" a union between one man and one woman.

Almost a third of all children and over two-thirds of African American babies were born outside marriage. In the majority of married-couple families with children under age eighteen, both parents held jobs. Statistically, a couple that married in the late 1990s had about a 50–50 chance of divorce. While almost a third of families with children had only one parent present—usually the mother—children also lived in blended families created by second marriages, or

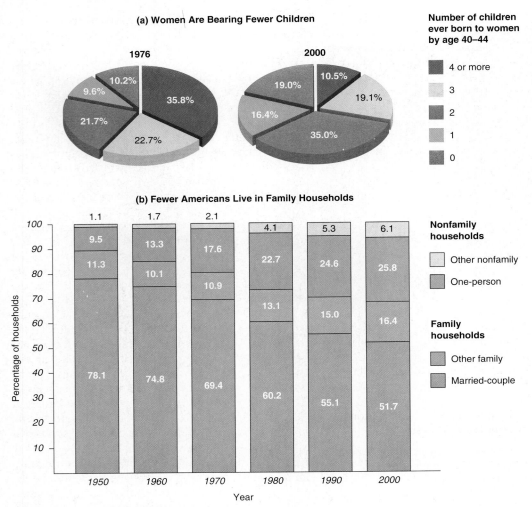

Figure 33.1 **The Changing American Family**

American households became smaller in the latter part of the twentieth century, as more people lived alone and women had, on average, fewer children. (Source: Adapted from U.S. Bureau of the Census: http://www.census.gov/prod/2002pubs/censr-4.pdf and http://www.census.gov/population/pop-profile/2000/chap04.pdf)

moved back and forth between households of parents with joint custody.

Increasingly, new reproductive technologies allowed infertile women or couples to have children. In 2000 more than 100,000 attempted in vitro fertilizations—in which sperm and egg combine in a sterile dish or test tube and the fertilized egg or eggs are then transferred to

New Technologies and New Challenges

the uterus—resulted in the birth of about 35,000 babies. Such techniques raised legal and ethical questions about the rights and responsibilities of sperm and egg donors, the woman who carries the fetus, and male and female prospective parents.

This field of biogenetics offers even knottier philosophical and ethical conundrums. The five- or six-cell blastocytes formed by the initial division of fertilized eggs during in vitro procedures contain stem cells, unspecialized cells that can be induced to become cells with specialized functions. For example, stem cells might become insulin-producing cells of the pancreas—and thus a cure for diabetes. President Bush in 2001 acknowledged the "tremendous hope" of this research but called it "the leading edge of a series of moral hazards," including the possibility of cloning humans for spare body parts. In a highly controversial decision, Bush limited federally funded research to the existing seventy-eight stem cell lines, not all of which are viable.

CENTURY OF CHANGE

The twentieth century had seen momentous changes, some bringing enormous benefits to human beings, others threatening the existence of the human species. Research in the physical and biological sciences provided deep insight into the structure of matter and the universe. Technology—the application of science—made startling advances that benefited people in nearly every aspect of life: better health, more wealth, more mobility, less drudgery, greater access to information.

As a result, Americans at the start of the new century were more connected to the rest of humankind. And the world had shrunk to the size of an airplane ticket. In 1955, 51 million people a year traveled by plane. By the turn of the century, 1.6 billion were airborne every year, and 530 million crossed international borders—about 1.5 million each day. For millions of Americans, this permeability of national boundaries brought many benefits, as did the integration of markets and the global spread of information that occurred alongside it.

On the flip side, the rapid increase in international air travel was a particularly potent force for global

INFECTIOUS DISEASES

disease dissemination, as flying enabled people to reach the other side of the world in less time than the incubation period for many ailments. In early 2003, a respiratory illness known as severe acute respiratory syndrome (SARS) spread from Guangdong Province of China to Hong Kong to various other countries in the world, chiefly via air passengers who unwittingly carried the disease in their lungs. Public health officials also warned that increased human mobility promised more trade in illegal products and contaminated foodstuffs.

Environmental degradation also powerfully contributed to global health threats. In 2003 the World Health Organization (WHO) estimated that nearly a quarter of the global burden of disease and injury was related to environmental disruption and decline. For example, some 90 percent of diarrheal diseases (such as cholera), which were killing 3 million people a year, resulted from contaminated water. WHO also noted that in the final two decades of the twentieth century, more than thirty infectious diseases were identified in humans for the first time—including AIDS, Ebola virus, and hepatitis C and E. Environmentalists meanwhile insisted that the growing global interaction was having a deleterious impact on the ecosystem through climate change, ozone depletion, hazardous waste, and damage to fisheries.

But globalization was also essential in mobilizing the world to find solutions to health crises. Where it

INTERNATIONAL RESPONSE TO DISEASE

took centuries to identify the cause of cholera and two years to identify the virus that caused AIDS, in the case of SARS, thirteen labs in ten countries in a matter of weeks determined that the Coronavirus was responsible. Within a month, laboratories from Vancouver to Atlanta to Singapore had mapped the genome, and efforts to devise a diagnostic test for the virus began. Speed of communication allowed a coordinated international effort at finding the cause of SARS and also enabled individual countries, including the United States, to adopt measures that succeeded early on in keeping the epidemic out.

Even in the interconnected world of the new millennium, then, national borders still mattered. In the wake of 9/11, the United States and other countries imposed tighter security measures on air travelers, imported goods, immigration, and information flows. Some economists predicted these measures would stall the global integration of markets; in the short term, they did, but the long-term outlook was less clear. Trade and investment shrank before September 11 due to economic slowdowns in the world's biggest economies, including the United States, Europe, and Japan. Moreover, the falloff in international economic activity in the months after the attacks was not massive.

In military and diplomatic terms, the 9/11 attacks brought home what Americans had previously only

CONFRONTING TERRORISM

dimly perceived: that globalization had shrunk the natural buffers that distance and two oceans provided the United States. Al Qaeda used the

The Global AIDS Epidemic

AIDS, initially reported in the United States in 1981, has become a global epidemic. Researchers now believe that the first infection with HIV, the human immunodeficiency virus that causes AIDS, may have appeared in West Africa around 1930. HIV/AIDS spread rapidly in the late 1970s, partly as a byproduct of globalization. Increased international travel allowed for sexual transmission of HIV between populations; the international heroin trade stimulated intravenous drug use, another means of transmission; and the international circulation of blood for medical transfusions also contributed to the virus's spread. In 2003 the World Health Organization estimated that 58 million people worldwide were living with HIV/AIDS and that 23 million had died from the disease.

Globally, AIDS claims 350 lives per hour, and while altered behavior and new drug therapies have slowed the disease in North America and western Europe, infection and death rates continue to escalate in sub-Saharan Africa, eastern Europe and the former Soviet Union, and Latin America, especially the Caribbean. In the African nation of Malawi, one in six adults is HIV-positive, and the nation expects to lose almost a quarter of its work force to AIDS in the next decade. Half of current teenagers in the hardest-hit African nations will eventually die of AIDS.

The human suffering is staggering, but U.S. worries about the global spread of AIDS are not solely humanitarian. In 2000 the U.S. National Intelligence Council concluded that "these diseases will endanger U.S. citizens at home and abroad, threaten U.S. armed forces deployed overseas, and exacerbate social and political instability in key countries and regions in which the United States has significant interests." In nations already facing shortages of food and clean water and rife with conflict, AIDS has further undermined the ability to cope with crisis; political instability and social disorder result.

In 2002 U.N. Secretary General Kofi Annan estimated that between $7 billion and $10 billion are needed annually to combat the spread of AIDS—and of tuberculosis and malaria, which have reemerged as threats to world health. President Bush called for increases in U.S. spending to combat AIDS internationally, but many believe the United States should do more. With globalization, diseases do not stop at borders or respect wealth and power. The links between Americans and the rest of the world cannot be denied.

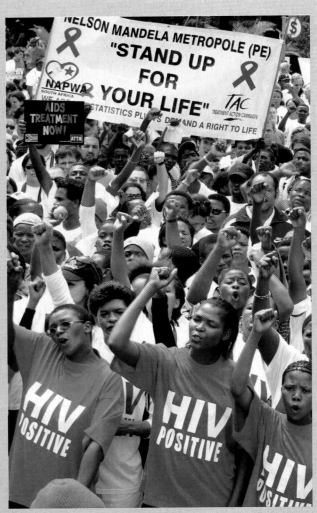

Activists protest outside Parliament in Cape Town, South Africa, calling on South Africa president Thabo Mbeki to make the struggle against AIDS a national priority. An estimated 20 percent of South Africans between the ages of fifteen and forty-nine are HIV-positive. (AP/Wide World Photos)

increasingly open, integrated, globalized world to give themselves new power and reach. They had shown that small terrorist cells could become true transnational threats without a state sponsor or home base. According to American intelligence, Al Qaeda operated in over ninety countries, including the United States.

How would one go about vanquishing such a foe? Was a decisive victory even possible? Questions like this remained open four years after the World Trade Center collapsed. Unchallenged militarily and seeing no rival great power, the United States no longer felt constrained from intervening in sensitive areas

TABLE 33.1			
U.S. Military Personnel on Active Duty in Foreign Countries, 2001[1]			
Region/Country[2]	**Personnel**	**Region/Country**	**Personnel**
United States and Territories		Singapore	160
Continental U.S.	947,955	Thailand	114
Alaska	15,926	**North Africa, Near East, and South Asia**	
Hawai'i	33,191	Bahrain	1,280
Guam	3,398	Diego Garcia	537
Puerto Rico	2,525	Egypt	665
Europe		Israel	38
Belgium*	1,554	Kuwait	4,300
Bosnia and Herzegovina	3,109	Oman	560
France*	70	Qatar	72
Germany*	71,434	Saudi Arabia	4,802
Greece*	526	United Arab Emirates	207
Greenland*	153	**Sub-Saharan Africa**	
Iceland*	1,713	Kenya	50
Italy*	11,854	South Africa	30
Macedonia	346	**Western Hemisphere**	
Netherlands*	696	Brazil	40
Norway*	187	Canada	165
Portugal*	992	Chile	30
Russia	88	Colombia	59
Serbia (includes Kosovo)	5,200	Cuba (Guantánamo)	461
Spain*	1,778	Honduras	426
Turkey*	2,170	Peru	40
United Kingdom*	11,361	Venezuela	30
East Asia and Pacific		**Total foreign countries[2]**	**255,065**
Australia	188	**Ashore**	**212,262**
China (includes Hong Kong)	54	**Afloat**	**42,803**
Indonesia (includes Timor)	48	**Total worldwide[2]**	**1,384,812**
Japan	39,691	**Ashore**	**1,242,524**
Korea, Rep. of	37,972	**Afloat**	**142,288**
Philippines	31		

*NATO countries
[1] Only countries with 30 or more U.S. military personnel are listed.
[2] Includes all regions/countries, not simply those listed.
Source: U.S. Department of Defense, *Selected Manpower Statistics,* Annual.

like the Middle East should national security interests demand it. It continued to spend vast sums on its military. (In 2003 the Pentagon spent about $400 billion, or roughly $50 million per hour.) America had taken on military commitments all over the globe, from the Balkans and Iraq to Afghanistan and Korea (see Table 33.1).

Summary ◯ Online Study Center   ACE the Test

*T*he 1990s were good times for most Americans. A digitized revolution in communications and information was generating prosperity and transforming life in America and around the globe. The longest economic expansion in American history—from 1991 to 2001—meant that most Americans who wanted jobs had them, that the stock market boomed, that the nation had a budget surplus, and that more Americans than ever before owned homes. And with the Soviet Union gone and no other formidable rival, the United States stood as the world's lone superpower.

Yet unsettling events troubled the nation. The Cold War continued to complicate the new world order. Localized and ethnic conflicts in the Balkans, the Middle East, and Africa crowded the international agenda, as did human rights and the environment. At home, violence—the domestic terrorist attack in Oklahoma City in 1995, a rash of school shootings—captured headlines, even as the crime rate dropped. And scandal further undermined Americans' faith in their government, as President Bill Clinton was impeached by the House of Representatives.

Just minutes before midnight on December 31, 1999, President Clinton called on Americans not to fear the future but to "welcome it, create it, and embrace it." The challenges ahead would include a contested presidential election in 2000 that was decided by the Supreme Court in a partisan 5–4 vote and, in 2001, the end of the ten-year economic expansion.

Then, on September 11, 2001, radical Islamic terrorists attacked the World Trade Center and the Pentagon, killing thousands. The new president, George W. Bush, declared a "war on terrorism." While U.S. air and ground forces went after targets in Afghanistan, Congress created the Department of Homeland Security and passed the PATRIOT Act, expanding the federal government's powers of surveillance. To counter a troubled economy, Bush pressed for tax cuts in each of his first three years in office. Congress went along, but the economic impact was uncertain, and the lost revenues added to a ballooning budget deficit.

The world Americans found in the first years of the twenty-first century was much different from the one they'd imagined for the new millennium. The horror of the terror attacks of September 11 shook America to its core. Throughout the nation, people declared that life would never be the same. As Americans coped with the aftermath of 9/11, crafting new foreign and domestic policies, the resilience of the American people was clear, for Americans continued to struggle over the direction of their nation with the passion and commitment that keeps democracy alive.

LEGACY FOR A PEOPLE AND A NATION
The Internet

"Google it." The phrase, essentially unknown before the new century, had within its first years become a household expression. Google was the hugely popular Internet search engine that had gone from obscurity in the mid-1990s to responding, more or less instantly, to 200 million queries per day from around the world—almost 40 percent of all Internet searches. Google's phenomenal rise demonstrates how much the Internet had become an expected part of Americans' daily lives by the twenty-first century.

Yet the widespread use of the Internet was a recent phenomenon, although its history went back four decades. In the mid-1960s, the U.S. military's Advanced Research Projects Agency (ARPA) wanted a communications network for government and university researchers spread across the nation. In 1969 early portions of the experimental system, called ARPANET, went online at UCLA, the University of California at Santa Barbara, Stanford Research Institute, and the University of Utah. By 1971, twenty-three computers were connected, and the numbers reached close to a thousand by 1984. Renamed the Internet in the late 1980s, this system transmitted only words, but in 1990 computer scientists developed the World Wide Web to send graphic and multimedia information. Then in 1993 the first commercial "browser" to aid Web navigation hit the market. It was followed in 1994 and 1995 by two superior browsers: Netscape and Internet Explorer.

By 2003, there were nearly half a billion Internet users worldwide, including 140 million Americans. Thanks to technological advances and the new forms of "broadband" access that provided high-speed connections, these users could send and receive e-mail, join online discussion groups, book vacations, download movies and music, shop, even do their banking—all through a small computer in their home. For Americans in the new globally connected millennium, the Internet was a fitting legacy of the twentieth century.

APPENDIX

Documents

DECLARATION OF INDEPENDENCE IN CONGRESS, JULY 4, 1776

When, in the course of human events, it becomes necessary for one people to dissolve the political bonds which have connected them with another, and to assume, among the powers of the earth, the separate and equal station to which the laws of nature and of nature's God entitle them, a decent respect to the opinions of mankind requires that they should declare the causes which impel them to the separation.

We hold these truths to be self-evident: That all men are created equal; that they are endowed by their Creator with certain unalienable rights; that among these are life, liberty, and the pursuit of happiness; that, to secure these rights, governments are instituted among men, deriving their just powers from the consent of the governed; that whenever any form of government becomes destructive of these ends, it is the right of the people to alter or to abolish it, and to institute new government, laying its foundation on such principles, and organizing its powers in such form, as to them shall seem most likely to effect their safety and happiness. Prudence, indeed, will dictate that governments long established should not be changed for light and transient causes; and accordingly all experience hath shown that mankind are more disposed to suffer, while evils are sufferable, than to right themselves by abolishing the forms to which they are accustomed. But when a long train of abuses and usurpations, pursuing invariably the same object, evinces a design to reduce them under absolute despotism, it is their right, it is their duty, to throw off such government, and to provide new guards for their future security. Such has been the patient sufferance of these colonies; and such is now the necessity which constrains them to alter their former systems of government. The history of the present King of Great Britain is a history of repeated injuries and usurpations, all having in direct object the establishment of an absolute tyranny over these states. To prove this, let facts be submitted to a candid world.

He has refused his assent to laws, the most wholesome and necessary for the public good.

He has forbidden his governors to pass laws of immediate and pressing importance, unless suspended in their oper-

ation till his assent should be obtained; and, when so suspended, he has utterly neglected to attend to them.

He has refused to pass other laws for the accommodation of large districts of people, unless those people would relinquish the right of representation in the legislature, a right inestimable to them, and formidable to tyrants only.

He has called together legislative bodies at places unusual, uncomfortable, and distant from the depository of their public records, for the sole purpose of fatiguing them into compliance with his measures.

He has dissolved representative houses repeatedly, for opposing, with manly firmness, his invasions on the rights of the people.

He has refused for a long time, after such dissolutions, to cause others to be elected; whereby the legislative powers, incapable of annihilation, have returned to the people at large for their exercise; the state remaining, in the mean time, exposed to all the dangers of invasions from without and convulsions within.

He has endeavored to prevent the population of these states; for that purpose obstructing the laws for naturalization of foreigners; refusing to pass others to encourage their migration hither, and raising the conditions of new appropriations of lands.

He has obstructed the administration of justice, by refusing his assent to laws for establishing judiciary powers.

He has made judges dependent on his will alone, for the tenure of their offices, and the amount and payment of their salaries.

He has erected a multitude of new offices, and sent hither swarms of officers to harass our people and eat out their substance.

He has kept among us, in times of peace, standing armies, without the consent of our legislatures.

He has affected to render the military independent of, and superior to, the civil power.

He has combined with others to subject us to a jurisdiction foreign to our constitution, and unacknowledged by our laws, giving his assent to their acts of pretended legislation:

For quartering large bodies of armed troops among us;

For protecting them, by a mock trial, from punishment for any murders which they should commit on the inhabitants of these states;

For cutting off our trade with all parts of the world;

For imposing taxes on us without our consent;

For depriving us, in many cases, of the benefits of trial by jury;

For transporting us beyond seas, to be tried for pretended offenses;

For abolishing the free system of English laws in a neighboring province, establishing therein an arbitrary government, and enlarging its boundaries, so as to render it at once an example and fit instrument for introducing the same absolute rule into these colonies;

For taking away our charters, abolishing our most valuable laws, and altering fundamentally the forms of our governments;

For suspending our own legislatures, and declaring themselves invested with power to legislate for us in all cases whatsoever.

He has abdicated government here, by declaring us out of his protection and waging war against us.

He has plundered our seas, ravaged our coasts, burned our towns, and destroyed the lives of our people.

He is at this time transporting large armies of foreign mercenaries to complete the works of death, desolation, and tyranny already begun with circumstances of cruelty and perfidy scarcely paralleled in the most barbarous ages, and totally unworthy the head of a civilized nation.

He has constrained our fellow-citizens, taken captive on the high seas, to bear arms against their country, to become the executioners of their friends and brethren, or to fall themselves by their hands.

He has excited domestic insurrection among us, and has endeavored to bring on the inhabitants of our frontiers the merciless Indian savages, whose known rule of warfare is an undistinguished destruction of all ages, sexes, and conditions.

In every stage of these oppressions we have petitioned for redress in the most humble terms; our repeated petitions have been answered only by repeated injury. A prince, whose character is thus marked by every act which may define a tyrant, is unfit to be the ruler of a free people.

Nor have we been wanting in our attentions to our British brethren. We have warned them, from time to time, of attempts by their legislature to extend an unwarrantable jurisdiction over us. We have reminded them of the circumstances of our emigration and settlement here. We have appealed to their native justice and magnanimity; and we have conjured them, by the ties of our common kindred, to disavow these usurpations, which would inevitably interrupt our connections and correspondence. They, too, have been deaf to the voice of justice and of consanguinity. We must, therefore, acquiesce in the necessity which denounces our separation, and hold them, as we hold the rest of mankind, enemies in war, in peace friends.

We, therefore, the representatives of the United States of America, in General Congress assembled, appealing to the Supreme Judge of the world for the rectitude of our intentions, do, in the name and by the authority of the good people of these colonies, solemnly publish and declare, that these United Colonies are, and of right ought to be, FREE AND INDEPENDENT STATES; that they are absolved from all allegiance to the British crown, and that all political connection between them and the state of Great Britain is, and ought to be, totally dissolved; and that, as free and independent states, they have full power to levy war, conclude peace, contract alliances, establish commerce, and do all other acts and things which independent states may of right do. And for the support of this declaration, with a firm reliance on the protection of Divine Providence, we mutually pledge to each other our lives, our fortunes, and our sacred honor.

ARTICLES OF CONFEDERATION

(The text of the Articles of Confederation can be found at college.hmco.com.)

CONSTITUTION OF THE UNITED STATES OF AMERICA AND AMENDMENTS*

Preamble

We the people of the United States, in order to form a more perfect union, establish justice, insure domestic tranquillity, provide for the common defense, promote the general welfare, and secure the blessings of liberty to ourselves and our posterity, do ordain and establish this Constitution for the United States of America.

Article I

Section 1 All legislative powers herein granted shall be vested in a Congress of the United States, which shall consist of a Senate and a House of Representatives.

Section 2 The House of Representatives shall be composed of members chosen every second year by the people of the several States, and the electors in each State shall have the qualifications requisite for electors of the most numerous branch of the State Legislature.

---

*Passages no longer in effect are printed in italic type.

No person shall be a Representative who shall not have attained to the age of twenty-five years, and been seven years a citizen of the United States, and who shall not, when elected, be an inhabitant of that State in which he shall be chosen.

Representatives and direct taxes shall be apportioned among the several States which may be included within this Union, according to their respective numbers, *which shall be determined by adding to the whole number of free persons, including those bound to service for a term of years and excluding Indians not taxed, three-fifths of all other persons.* The actual enumeration shall be made within three years after the first meeting of the Congress of the United States, and within every subsequent term of ten years, in such manner as they shall by law direct. The number of Representatives shall not exceed one for every thirty thousand, but each State shall have at least one Representative; *and until such enumeration shall be made, the State of New Hampshire shall be entitled to choose three, Massachusetts eight, Rhode Island and Providence Plantations one, Connecticut five, New York six, New Jersey four, Pennsylvania eight, Delaware one, Maryland six, Virginia ten, North Carolina five, South Carolina five, and Georgia three.*

When vacancies happen in the representation from any State, the Executive authority thereof shall issue writs of election to fill such vacancies.

The House of Representatives shall choose their Speaker and other officers; and shall have the sole power of impeachment.

Section 3 The Senate of the United States shall be composed of two Senators from each State, *chosen by the legislature thereof,* for six years; and each Senator shall have one vote.

Immediately after they shall be assembled in consequence of the first election, they shall be divided as equally as may be into three classes. The seats of the Senators of the first class shall be vacated at the expiration of the second year, of the second class at the expiration of the fourth year, and of the third class at the expiration of the sixth year, so that one-third may be chosen every second year; *and if vacancies happen by resignation or otherwise, during the recess of the legislature of any State, the Executive thereof may make temporary appointments until the next meeting of the legislature, which shall then fill such vacancies.*

No person shall be a Senator who shall not have attained to the age of thirty years, and been nine years a citizen of the United States, and who shall not, when elected, be an inhabitant of that State for which he shall be chosen.

The Vice-President of the United States shall be President of the Senate, but shall have no vote, unless they be equally divided.

The Senate shall choose their other officers, and also a President *pro tempore,* in the absence of the Vice-President,

or when he shall exercise the office of President of the United States.

The Senate shall have the sole power to try all impeachments. When sitting for that purpose, they shall be on oath or affirmation. When the President of the United States is tried, the Chief Justice shall preside: and no person shall be convicted without the concurrence of two-thirds of the members present.

Judgment in cases of impeachment shall not extend further than to removal from the office, and disqualification to hold and enjoy any office of honor, trust or profit under the United States: but the party convicted shall nevertheless be liable and subject to indictment, trial, judgment and punishment, according to law.

Section 4 The times, places and manner of holding elections for Senators and Representatives shall be prescribed in each State by the legislature thereof; but the Congress may at any time by law make or alter such regulations, except as to the places of choosing Senators.

The Congress shall assemble at least once in every year, and such meeting *shall be on the first Monday in December, unless they shall by law appoint a different day.*

Section 5 Each house shall be the judge of the elections, returns and qualifications of its own members, and a majority of each shall constitute a quorum to do business; but a smaller number may adjourn from day to day, and may be authorized to compel the attendance of absent members, in such manner, and under such penalties, as each house may provide.

Each house may determine the rules of its proceedings, punish its members for disorderly behavior, and with the concurrence of two-thirds, expel a member.

Each house shall keep a journal of its proceedings, and from time to time publish the same, excepting such parts as may in their judgment require secrecy; and the yeas and nays of the members of either house on any question shall, at the desire of one-fifth of those present, be entered on the journal.

Neither house, during the session of Congress, shall, without the consent of the other, adjourn for more than three days, nor to any other place than that in which the two houses shall be sitting.

Section 6 The Senators and Representatives shall receive a compensation for their services, to be ascertained by law and paid out of the treasury of the United States. They shall in all cases except treason, felony and breach of the peace, be privileged from arrest during their attendance at the session of their respective houses, and in going to and returning from the same; and for any speech or debate in either house, they shall not be questioned in any other place.

No Senator or Representative shall, during the time for which he was elected, be appointed to any civil office under the authority of the United States, which shall have been created, or the emoluments whereof shall have been increased, during such time; and no person holding any office under the United States shall be a member of either house during his continuance in office.

Section 7 All bills for raising revenue shall originate in the House of Representatives; but the Senate may propose or concur with amendments as on other bills.

Every bill which shall have passed the House of Representatives and the Senate, shall, before it become a law, be presented to the President of the United States; if he approve he shall sign it, but if not he shall return it with objections to that house in which it originated, who shall enter the objections at large on their journal, and proceed to reconsider it. If after such reconsideration two-thirds of that house shall agree to pass the bill, it shall be sent, together with the objections, to the other house, by which it shall likewise be reconsidered, and, if approved by two-thirds of that house, it shall become a law. But in all such cases the votes of both houses shall be determined by yeas and nays, and the names of the persons voting for and against the bill shall be entered on the journal of each house respectively. If any bill shall not be returned by the President within ten days (Sundays excepted) after it shall have been presented to him, the same shall be a law, in like manner as if he had signed it, unless the Congress by their adjournment prevent its return, in which case it shall not be a law.

Every order, resolution, or vote to which the concurrence of the Senate and House of Representatives may be necessary (except on a question of adjournment) shall be presented to the President of the United States; and before the same shall take effect, shall be approved by him, or being disapproved by him, shall be repassed by two-thirds of the Senate and House of Representatives, according to the rules and limitations prescribed in the case of a bill.

Section 8 The Congress shall have power

To lay and collect taxes, duties, imposts, and excises, to pay the debts and provide for the common defense and general welfare of the United States; but all duties, imposts and excises shall be uniform throughout the United States;

To borrow money on the credit of the United States;

To regulate commerce with foreign nations, and among the several States, and with the Indian tribes;

To establish an uniform rule of naturalization, and uniform laws on the subject of bankruptcies throughout the United States;

To coin money, regulate the value thereof, and of foreign coin, and fix the standard of weights and measures;

To provide for the punishment of counterfeiting the securities and current coin of the United States;

To establish post offices and post roads;

To promote the progress of science and useful arts by securing for limited times to authors and inventors the exclusive right to their respective writings and discoveries;

To constitute tribunals inferior to the Supreme Court;

To define and punish piracies and felonies committed on the high seas and offenses against the law of nations;

To declare war, grant letters of marque and reprisal, and make rules concerning captures on land and water;

To raise and support armies, but no appropriation of money to that use shall be for a longer term than two years;

To provide and maintain a navy;

To make rules for the government and regulation of the land and naval forces;

To provide for calling forth the militia to execute the laws of the Union, suppress insurrections, and repel invasions;

To provide for organizing, arming, and disciplining the militia, and for governing such part of them as may be employed in the service of the United States, reserving to the States respectively the appointment of the officers, and the authority of training the militia according to the discipline prescribed by Congress;

To exercise exclusive legislation in all cases whatsoever, over such district (not exceeding ten miles square) as may, by cession of particular States, and the acceptance of Congress, become the seat of government of the United States, and to exercise like authority over all places purchased by the consent of the legislature of the State, in which the same shall be, for erection of forts, magazines, arsenals, dockyards, and other needful buildings; —and

To make all laws which shall be necessary and proper for carrying into execution the foregoing powers, and all other powers vested by this Constitution in the government of the United States, or in any department or officer thereof.

Section 9 *The migration or importation of such persons as any of the States now existing shall think proper to admit shall not be prohibited by the Congress prior to the year 1808; but a tax or duty may be imposed on such importation, not exceeding $10 for each person.*

The privilege of the writ of habeas corpus shall not be suspended, unless when in cases of rebellion or invasion the public safety may require it.

No bill of attainder or ex post facto law shall be passed.

No capitation, or other direct, tax shall be laid, unless in proportion to the census or enumeration herein before directed to be taken.

No tax or duty shall be laid on articles exported from any State.

No preference shall be given by any regulation of commerce or revenue to the ports of one State over those of another; nor shall vessels bound to, or from, one State, be obliged to enter, clear, or pay duties in another.

No money shall be drawn from the treasury, but in consequence of appropriations made by law; and a regular statement and account of the receipts and expenditures of all public money shall be published from time to time.

No title of nobility shall be granted by the United States: and no person holding any office of profit or trust under them, shall, without the consent of the Congress, accept of any present, emolument, office, or title, of any kind whatever, from any king, prince, or foreign state.

Section 10   No State shall enter into any treaty, alliance, or confederation; grant letters of marque and reprisal; coin money; emit bills of credit; make anything but gold and silver coin a tender in payment of debts; pass any bill of attainder, ex post facto law, or law impairing the obligation of contracts, or grant any title of nobility.

No State shall, without the consent of Congress, lay any imposts or duties on imports or exports, except what may be absolutely necessary for executing its inspection laws: and the net produce of all duties and imposts, laid by any State on imports or exports, shall be for the use of the treasury of the United States; and all such laws shall be subject to the revision and control of the Congress.

No State shall, without the consent of Congress, lay any duty of tonnage, keep troops or ships of war in time of peace, enter into any agreement or compact with another State, or with a foreign power, or engage in war, unless actually invaded, or in such imminent danger as will not admit of delay.

Article II

Section 1   The executive power shall be vested in a President of the United States of America. He shall hold his office during the term of four years, and, together with the Vice-President, chosen for the same term, be elected as follows:

Each State shall appoint, in such manner as the legislature thereof may direct, a number of electors, equal to the whole number of Senators and Representatives to which the State may be entitled in the Congress; but no Senator or Representative, or person holding an office of trust or profit under the United States, shall be appointed an elector.

The electors shall meet in their respective States, and vote by ballot for two persons, of whom one at least shall not be an inhabitant of the same State with themselves. And they shall make a list of all the persons voted for, and of the number of votes for each; which list they shall sign and certify, and transmit sealed to the seat of government of the United States, directed to the President of the Senate. The President of the Senate shall, in the presence of the Senate and House of Representatives, open all the certificates, and the votes shall then be counted. The person having the greatest number of votes shall be the President, if such number be a majority of the whole number of electors appointed; and if there be more than one who have such majority, and have an equal number of votes, then the House of Representatives shall immediately choose by ballot one of them for President; and if no person have a majority, then from the five highest on the list said house shall in like manner choose the President. But in choosing the President the votes shall be taken by States, the representation from each State having one vote; a quorum for this purpose shall consist of a member or members from two-thirds of the States, and a majority of all the States shall be necessary to a choice. In every case, after the choice of the President, the person having the greatest number of votes of the electors shall be the Vice-President. But if there should remain two or more who have equal votes, the Senate shall choose from them by ballot the Vice-President.

The Congress may determine the time of choosing the electors and the day on which they shall give their votes; which day shall be the same throughout the United States.

No person except a natural-born citizen, *or a citizen of the United States at the time of the adoption of this Constitution,* shall be eligible to the office of President; neither shall any person be eligible to that office who shall not have attained to the age of thirty-five years, and been fourteen years a resident within the United States.

In cases of the removal of the President from office or of his death, resignation, or inability to discharge the powers and duties of the said office, the same shall devolve on the Vice-President, and the Congress may by law provide for the case of removal, death, resignation, or inability, both of the President and Vice-President, declaring what officer shall then act as President, and such officer shall act accordingly, until the disability be removed, or a President shall be elected.

The President shall, at stated times, receive for his services a compensation, which shall neither be increased nor diminished during the period for which he shall have been elected, and he shall not receive within that period any other emolument from the United States, or any of them.

Before he enter on the execution of his office, he shall take the following oath or affirmation:—"I do solemnly swear (or affirm) that I will faithfully execute the office of President of the United States, and will to the best of my ability preserve, protect and defend the Constitution of the United States."

Section 2   The President shall be commander in chief of the army and navy of the United States, and of the militia of the several States, when called into the actual service of the United States; he may require the opinion, in writing, of the principal officer in each of the executive departments, upon any subject relating to the duties of their respective offices, and he shall have power to grant reprieves and pardons for offenses against the United States, except in cases of impeachment.

He shall have power, by and with the advice and consent of the Senate, to make treaties, provided two-thirds of the Senators present concur; and he shall nominate, and by and with the advice and consent of the Senate, shall appoint ambassadors, other public ministers and consuls, judges of the Supreme Court, and all other officers of the United States, whose appointments are not herein otherwise provided for, and which shall be established by law: but Congress may by law vest the appointment of such inferior officers, as they think proper, in the President alone, in the courts of law, or in the heads of departments.

The President shall have power to fill up all vacancies that may happen during the recess of the Senate, by granting commissions which shall expire at the end of their next session.

Section 3 He shall from time to time give to the Congress information of the state of the Union, and recommend to their consideration such measures as he shall judge necessary and expedient; he may, on extraordinary occasions, convene both houses, or either of them, and in case of disagreement between them, with respect to the time of adjournment, he may adjourn them to such time as he shall think proper; he shall receive ambassadors and other public ministers; he shall take care that the laws be faithfully executed, and shall commission all the officers of the United States.

Section 4 The President, Vice-President and all civil officers of the United States shall be removed from office on impeachment for, and on conviction of, treason, bribery, or other high crimes and misdemeanors.

Article III

Section 1 The judicial power of the United States shall be vested in one Supreme Court, and in such inferior courts as the Congress may from time to time ordain and establish. The judges, both of the Supreme and inferior courts, shall hold their offices during good behavior, and shall, at stated times, receive for their services a compensation which shall not be diminished during their continuance in office.

Section 2 The judicial power shall extend to all cases, in law and equity, arising under this Constitution, the laws of the United States, and treaties made, or which shall be made, under their authority;—to all cases affecting ambassadors, other public ministers and consuls;—to all cases of admiralty and maritime jurisdiction;—to controversies to which the United States shall be a party;—to controversies between two or more States;—*between a State and citizens of another State;*—between citizens of different States;—between citizens of the same State claiming lands under grants of different States, and between a State, or the citizens thereof, and foreign states, citizens or subjects.

In all cases affecting ambassadors, other public ministers and consuls, and those in which a State shall be party, the Supreme Court shall have original jurisdiction. In all the other cases before mentioned, the Supreme Court shall have appellate jurisdiction, both as to law and fact, with such exceptions, and under such regulations, as the Congress shall make.

The trial of all crimes, except in cases of impeachment, shall be by jury; and such trial shall be held in the State where said crimes shall have been committed; but when not committed within any State, the trial shall be at such place or places as the Congress may by law have directed.

Section 3 Treason against the United States shall consist only in levying war against them, or in adhering to their enemies, giving them aid and comfort. No person shall be convicted of treason unless on the testimony of two witnesses to the same overt act, or on confession in open court.

The Congress shall have power to declare the punishment of treason, but no attainder of treason shall work corruption of blood, or forfeiture except during the life of the person attainted.

Article IV

Section 1 Full faith and credit shall be given in each State to the public acts, records, and judicial proceedings of every other State. And the Congress may by general laws prescribe the manner in which such acts, records, and proceedings shall be proved, and the effect thereof.

Section 2 The citizens of each State shall be entitled to all privileges and immunities of citizens in the several States.

A person charged in any State with treason, felony, or other crime, who shall flee from justice, and be found in another State, shall on demand of the executive authority of the State from which he fled, be delivered up, to be removed to the State having jurisdiction of the crime.

No person held to service or labor in one State, under the laws thereof, escaping into another, shall, in consequence of any law or regulation therein, be discharged from such service or labor, but shall be delivered up on claim of the party to whom such service or labor may be due.

Section 3 New States may be admitted by the Congress into this Union; but no new State shall be formed or erected within the jurisdiction of any other State; nor any State be formed by the junction of two or more States, or parts of States, without the consent of the legislatures of the States concerned as well as of the Congress.

The Congress shall have power to dispose of and make all needful rules and regulations respecting the territory or other property belonging to the United States; and nothing in this Constitution shall be so construed as to prejudice any claims of the United States, or of any particular State.

Section 4 The United States shall guarantee to every State in this Union a republican form of government, and shall protect each of them against invasion; and on application of the legislature, or of the executive (when the legislature cannot be convened), against domestic violence.

Article V

The Congress, whenever two-thirds of both houses shall deem it necessary, shall propose amendments to this Constitution, or, on the application of the legislatures of two-thirds of the several States, shall call a convention for proposing amendments, which, in either case, shall be valid to all intents and purposes, as part of this Constitution, when ratified by the legislatures of three-fourths of the several States, or by conventions in three-fourths thereof, as the one or the other mode of ratification may be proposed by the Congress; provided *that no amendments which may be made prior to the year one thousand eight hundred and eight shall in any manner affect the first and fourth clauses in the ninth section of the first article;* and that no State, without its consent, shall be deprived of its equal suffrage in the Senate.

Article VI

All debts contracted and engagements entered into, before the adoption of this Constitution, shall be as valid against the United States under this Constitution, as under the Confederation.

This Constitution, and the laws of the United States which shall be made in pursuance thereof; and all treaties made, or which shall be made, under the authority of the United States, shall be the supreme law of the land; and the judges in every State shall be bound thereby, anything in the Constitution or laws of any State to the contrary notwithstanding.

The Senators and Representatives before mentioned, and the members of the several State legislatures, and all executive and judicial officers, both of the United States and of the several States, shall be bound by oath or affirmation to support this Constitution; but no religious test shall ever be required as a qualification to any office or public trust under the United States.

Article VII

The ratification of the conventions of nine States shall be sufficient for the establishment of this Constitution between the States so ratifying the same.

Done in Convention by the unanimous consent of the States present, the seventeenth day of September in the year of our Lord one thousand seven hundred and eighty-seven and of the Independence of the United States of America the twelfth. In witness whereof we have hereunto subscribed our names.

AMENDMENTS TO THE CONSTITUTION*

Amendment I

Congress shall make no law respecting an establishment of religion, or prohibiting the free exercise thereof; or abridging the freedom of speech, or of the press; or the right of the people peaceably to assemble, and to petition the government for a redress of grievances.

Amendment II

A well-regulated militia being necessary to the security of a free State, the right of the people to keep and bear arms shall not be infringed.

Amendment III

No soldier shall, in time of peace, be quartered in any house without the consent of the owner, nor in time of war, but in a manner to be prescribed by law.

Amendment IV

The right of the people to be secure in their persons, houses, papers, and effects, against unreasonable searches and seizures, shall not be violated, and no warrants shall issue but upon probable cause, supported by oath or affirmation, and particularly describing the place to be searched, and the persons or things to be seized.

Amendment V

No person shall be held to answer for a capital, or otherwise infamous crime, unless on a presentment or indictment of a grand jury, except in cases arising in the land or naval forces, or in the militia, when in actual service in time of war or public danger; nor shall any person be subject for the same of-

---

*The first ten Amendments (the Bill of Rights) were adopted in 1791.

fense to be twice put in jeopardy of life or limb; nor shall be compelled in any criminal case to be a witness against himself, nor be deprived of life, liberty, or property, without due process of law; nor shall private property be taken for public use without just compensation.

Amendment VI

In all criminal prosecutions, the accused shall enjoy the right to a speedy and public trial, by an impartial jury of the State and district wherein the crime shall have been committed, which district shall have been previously ascertained by law, and to be informed of the nature and cause of the accusation; to be confronted with the witnesses against him; to have compulsory process for obtaining witnesses in his favor, and to have the assistance of counsel for his defense.

Amendment VII

In suits at common law, where the value in controversy shall exceed twenty dollars, the right of trial by jury shall be preserved, and no fact tried by a jury shall be otherwise reexamined in any court of the United States, than according to the rules of the common law.

Amendment VIII

Excessive bail shall not be required, nor excessive fines imposed, nor cruel and unusual punishments inflicted.

Amendment IX

The enumeration in the Constitution, of certain rights, shall not be construed to deny or disparage others retained by the people.

Amendment X

The powers not delegated to the United States by the Constitution, nor prohibited by it to the States, are reserved to the States respectively, or to the people.

Amendment XI

[Adopted 1798]

The judicial power of the United States shall not be construed to extend to any suit in law or equity, commenced or prosecuted against one of the United States by citizens of another State, or by citizens or subjects of any foreign state.

Amendment XII

[Adopted 1804]

The electors shall meet in their respective States, and vote by ballot for President and Vice-President, one of whom, at least,

shall not be an inhabitant of the same State with themselves; they shall name in their ballots the person voted for as President, and in distinct ballots the person voted for as Vice-President, and they shall make distinct lists of all persons voted for as President, and of all persons voted for as Vice-President, and of the number of votes for each, which lists they shall sign and certify, and transmit sealed to the seat of government of the United States, directed to the President of the Senate;—the President of the Senate shall, in the presence of the Senate and House of Representatives, open all the certificates and the votes shall then be counted;—the person having the greatest number of votes for President shall be the President, if such number be a majority of the whole number of electors appointed; and if no person have such majority, then from the persons having the highest numbers not exceeding three on the list of those voted for as President, the House of Representatives shall choose immediately, by ballot, the President. But in choosing the President, the votes shall be taken by States, the representation from each State having one vote; a quorum for this purpose shall consist of a member or members from two-thirds of the States, and a majority of all the States shall be necessary to a choice. And if the House of Representatives shall not choose a President whenever the right of choice shall devolve upon them, before *the fourth day of March* next following, then the Vice-President shall act as President, as in the case of the death or other constitutional disability of the President.

The person having the greatest number of votes as Vice-President shall be the Vice-President, if such number be a majority of the whole number of electors appointed; and if no person have a majority, then from the two highest numbers on the list the Senate shall choose the Vice-President; a quorum for the purpose shall consist of two-thirds of the whole number of Senators, and a majority of the whole number shall be necessary to a choice. But no person constitutionally ineligible to the office of President shall be eligible to that of Vice-President of the United States.

Amendment XIII

[Adopted 1865]

Section 1 Neither slavery nor involuntary servitude, except as a punishment for crime whereof the party shall have been duly convicted, shall exist within the United States, or any place subject to their jurisdiction.

Section 2 Congress shall have power to enforce this article by appropriate legislation.

Amendment XIV

[Adopted 1868]

Section 1 All persons born or naturalized in the United States, and subject to the jurisdiction thereof, are citizens of the United States and of the State wherein they reside. No State shall make or enforce any law which shall abridge the privileges or immunities of citizens of the United States; nor shall any State deprive any person of life, liberty, or property, without due process of law; nor deny to any person within its jurisdiction the equal protection of the laws.

Section 2 Representatives shall be apportioned among the several States according to their respective numbers, counting the whole number of persons in each State, excluding Indians not taxed. But when the right to vote at any election for the choice of Electors for President and Vice-President of the United States, Representatives in Congress, the executive and judicial officers of a State, or the members of the legislature thereof, is denied to any of the male inhabitants of such State, being twenty-one years of age and citizens of the United States, or in any way abridged, except for participation in rebellion, or other crime, the basis of representation therein shall be reduced in the proportion which the number of such male citizens shall bear to the whole number of male citizens twenty-one years of age in such State.

Section 3 No person shall be a Senator or Representative in Congress, or Elector of President and Vice-President, or hold any office, civil or military, under the United States, or under any State, who, having previously taken an oath, as a member of Congress, or as an officer of the United States, or as a member of any State legislature, or as an executive or judicial officer of any State, to support the Constitution of the United States, shall have engaged in insurrection or rebellion against the same, or given aid or comfort to the enemies thereof. Congress may, by a vote of two-thirds of each house, remove such disability.

Section 4 The validity of the public debt of the United States, authorized by law, including debts incurred for payment of pensions and bounties for services in suppressing insurrection or rebellion, shall not be questioned. But neither the United States nor any State shall assume or pay any debt or obligation incurred in aid of insurrection or rebellion against the United States, or any claim for the loss of emancipation of any slave; but all such debts, obligations, and claims shall be held illegal and void.

Section 5 The Congress shall have power to enforce, by appropriate legislation, the provisions of this article.

Amendment XV

[Adopted 1870]

Section 1 The right of citizens of the United States to vote shall not be denied or abridged by the United States or by any State on account of race, color, or previous condition of servitude.

Section 2 The Congress shall have power to enforce this article by appropriate legislation.

Amendment XVI

[Adopted 1913]

The Congress shall have power to lay and collect taxes on incomes, from whatever source derived, without apportionment among the several States, and without regard to any census or enumeration.

Amendment XVII

[Adopted 1913]

Section 1 The Senate of the United States shall be composed of two Senators from each State, elected by the people thereof, for six years; and each Senator shall have one vote. The electors in each State shall have the qualifications requisite for electors of [voters for] the most numerous branch of the State legislatures.

Section 2 When vacancies happen in the representation of any State in the Senate, the executive authority of such State shall issue writs of election to fill such vacancies: Provided, that the Legislature of any State may empower the executive thereof to make temporary appointments until the people fill the vacancies by election as the Legislature may direct.

Section 3 This amendment shall not be so construed as to affect the election or term of any Senator chosen before it becomes valid as part of the Constitution.

Amendment XVIII

[Adopted 1919; Repealed 1933]

Section 1 After one year from the ratification of this article the manufacture, sale, or transportation of intoxicating liquors within, the importation thereof into, or the exportation thereof from the United States and all territory subject to the jurisdiction thereof, for beverage purposes, is hereby prohibited.

Section 2 The Congress and the several States shall have concurrent power to enforce this article by appropriate legislation.

Section 3 This article shall be inoperative unless it shall have been ratified as an amendment to the Constitution by the legislatures of the several States, as provided by the Constitution, within seven years from the date of the submission thereof to the States by the Congress.

Amendment XIX

[Adopted 1920]

Section 1 The right of citizens of the United States to vote shall not be denied or abridged by the United States or by any State on account of sex.

Section 2 The Congress shall have power to enforce this article by appropriate legislation.

Amendment XX

[Adopted 1933]

Section 1 The terms of the President and Vice-President shall end at noon on the 20th day of January, and the terms of Senators and Representatives at noon on the 3rd day of January, of the years in which such terms would have ended if this article had not been ratified; and the terms of their successors shall then begin.

Section 2 The Congress shall assemble at least once in every year, and such meeting shall begin at noon on the 3d day of January, unless they shall by law appoint a different day.

Section 3 If, at the time fixed for the beginning of the term of the President, the President-elect shall have died, the Vice-President–elect shall become President. If a President shall not have been chosen before the time fixed for the beginning of his term, or if the President-elect shall have failed to qualify, then the Vice-President–elect shall act as President until a President shall have qualified; and the Congress may by law provide for the case wherein neither a President-elect nor a Vice-President–elect shall have qualified, declaring who shall then act as President, or the manner in which one who is to act shall be selected, and such persons shall act accordingly until a President or Vice-President shall have qualified.

Section 4 The Congress may by law provide for the case of the death of any of the persons from whom the House of Representatives may choose a President whenever the right of choice shall have devolved upon them, and for the case of the death of any of the persons from whom the Senate may choose a Vice-President whenever the right of choice shall have devolved upon them.

Section 5 Sections 1 and 2 shall take effect on the 15th day of October following the ratification of this article.

Section 6 This article shall be inoperative unless it shall have been ratified as an amendment to the Constitution by the Legislatures of three-fourths of the several States within seven years from the date of its submission.

Amendment XXI

[Adopted 1933]

Section 1 The eighteenth article of amendment to the Constitution of the United States is hereby repealed.

Section 2 The transportation or importation into any State, Territory, or Possession of the United States for delivery or use therein of intoxicating liquors, in violation of the laws thereof, is hereby prohibited.

Section 3 This article shall be inoperative unless it shall have been ratified as an amendment to the Constitution by conventions in the several States, as provided in the Constitution, within seven years from the date of submission thereof to the States by the Congress.

Amendment XXII

[Adopted 1951]

Section 1 No person shall be elected to the office of President more than twice, and no person who has held the office of President, or acted as President, for more than two years of a term to which some other person was elected President shall be elected to the office of President more than once. But this article shall not apply to any person holding the office of President when this article was proposed by the Congress, and shall not prevent any person who may be holding the office of President, or acting as President, during the term within which this article becomes operative from holding the office of President or acting as President during the remainder of such term.

Section 2 This article shall be inoperative unless it shall have been ratified as an amendment to the Constitution by the legislatures of three-fourths of the several States within seven years from the date of its submission to the States by the Congress.

Amendment XXIII

[Adopted 1961]

Section 1 The District constituting the seat of Government of the United States shall appoint in such manner as the Congress may direct:

A number of electors of President and Vice-President equal to the whole number of Senators and Representatives in Congress to which the District would be entitled if it were a State, but in no event more than the least populous State; they shall be in addition to those appointed by the States, but they shall be considered for the purposes of the election of President and Vice-President, to be electors appointed by a State; and they shall meet in the District and perform such duties as provided by the twelfth article of amendment.

Section 2 The Congress shall have the power to enforce this article by appropriate legislation.

Amendment XXIV

[Adopted 1964]

Section 1   The right of citizens of the United States to vote in any primary or other election for President or Vice-President, for electors for President or Vice-President, or for Senator or Representative in Congress, shall not be denied or abridged by the United States or any State by reason of failure to pay any poll tax or other tax.

Section 2   The Congress shall have the power to enforce this article by appropriate legislation.

Amendment XXV

[Adopted 1967]

Section 1   In case of the removal of the President from office or of his death or resignation, the Vice-President shall become President.

Section 2   Whenever there is a vacancy in the office of the Vice-President, the President shall nominate a Vice-President who shall take office upon confirmation by a majority vote of both Houses of Congress.

Section 3   Whenever the President transmits to the President pro tempore of the Senate and the Speaker of the House of Representatives his written declaration that he is unable to discharge the powers and duties of his office, and until he transmits to them a written declaration to the contrary, such powers and duties shall be discharged by the Vice-President as Acting President.

Section 4   Whenever the Vice-President and a majority of either the principal officers of the executive departments or of such other body as Congress may by law provide, transmit to the President pro tempore of the Senate and the Speaker of the House of Representatives their written declaration that the President is unable to discharge the powers and duties of his office, the Vice-President shall immediately assume the powers and duties of the office as Acting President.

Thereafter, when the President transmits to the President pro tempore of the Senate and the Speaker of the House of Representatives his written declaration that no inability exists, he shall resume the powers and duties of his office unless the Vice-President and a majority of either the principal officers of the executive department[s] or of such other body as Congress may by law provide, transmit within four days to the President pro tempore of the Senate and the Speaker of the House of Representatives their written declaration that the President is unable to discharge the powers and duties of his office. Thereupon Congress shall decide the issue, assembling within forty-eight hours for that purpose if not in session. If the Congress, within twenty-one days after receipt of the latter written declaration, or, if Congress is not in session, within twenty-one days after Congress is required to assemble, determines by two-thirds vote of both Houses that the President is unable to discharge the powers and duties of his office, the Vice-President shall continue to discharge the same as Acting President; otherwise, the President shall resume the powers and duties of his office.

Amendment XXVI

[Adopted 1971]

Section 1   The right of citizens of the United States, who are eighteen years of age or older, to vote shall not be denied or abridged by the United States or by any State on account of age.

Section 2   The Congress shall have power to enforce this article by appropriate legislation.

Amendment XXVII

[Adopted 1992]

No law, varying the compensation for the services of the Senators and Representatives, shall take effect, until an election of Representatives shall have intervened.

Presidential Elections

Year	Number of States	Candidates	Parties	Popular Vote	% of Popular Vote	Electoral Vote	% Voter Participation[a]
1789	10	**George Washington**	No party			69	
		John Adams	designations			34	
		Other candidates				35	
1792	15	**George Washington**	No party			132	
		John Adams	designations			77	
		George Clinton				50	
		Other candidates				5	
1796	16	**John Adams**	Federalist			71	
		Thomas Jefferson	Democratic-Republican			68	
		Thomas Pinckney	Federalist			59	
		Aaron Burr	Democratic-Republican			30	
		Other candidates				48	
1800	16	**Thomas Jefferson**	Democratic-Republican			73	
		Aaron Burr	Democratic-Republican			73	
		John Adams	Federalist			65	
		Charles C. Pinckney	Federalist			64	
		John Jay	Federalist			1	
1804	17	**Thomas Jefferson**	Democratic-Republican			162	
		Charles C. Pinckney	Federalist			14	
1808	17	**James Madison**	Democratic-Republican			122	
		Charles C. Pinckney	Federalist			47	
		George Clinton	Democratic-Republican			6	
1812	18	**James Madison**	Democratic-Republican			128	
		DeWitt Clinton	Federalist			89	
1816	19	**James Monroe**	Democratic-Republican			183	
		Rufus King	Federalist			34	
1820	24	**James Monroe**	Democratic-Republican			231	

Presidential Elections (continued)

Year	Number of States	Candidates	Parties	Popular Vote	% of Popular Vote	Electoral Vote	% Voter Participation[a]
		John Quincy Adams	Independent Republican			1	
1824	24	**John Quincy Adams**	Democratic-Republican	108,740	30.5	84	26.9
		Andrew Jackson	Democratic-Republican	153,544	43.1	99	
		Henry Clay	Democratic-Republican	47,136	13.2	37	
		William H. Crawford	Democratic-Republican	46,618	13.1	41	
1828	24	**Andrew Jackson**	Democratic	647,286	56.0	178	57.6
		John Quincy Adams	National Republican	508,064	44.0	83	
1832	24	**Andrew Jackson**	Democratic	701,780	54.2	219	55.4
		Henry Clay	National Republican	484,205	37.4	49	
		Other candidates		107,988	8.0	18	
1836	26	**Martin Van Buren**	Democratic	764,176	50.8	170	57.8
		William H. Harrison	Whig	550,816	36.6	73	
		Hugh L. White	Whig	146,107	9.7	26	
1840	26	**William H. Harrison**	Whig	1,274,624	53.1	234	80.2
		Martin Van Buren	Democratic	1,127,781	46.9	60	
1844	26	**James K. Polk**	Democratic	1,338,464	49.6	170	78.9
		Henry Clay	Whig	1,300,097	48.1	105	
		James G. Birney	Liberty	62,300	2.3		
1848	30	**Zachary Taylor**	Whig	1,360,967	47.4	163	72.7
		Lewis Cass	Democratic	1,222,342	42.5	127	
		Martin Van Buren	Free Soil	291,263	10.1		
1852	31	**Franklin Pierce**	Democratic	1,601,117	50.9	254	69.6
		Winfield Scott	Whig	1,385,453	44.1	42	
		John P. Hale	Free Soil	155,825	5.0		
1856	31	**James Buchanan**	Democratic	1,832,955	45.3	174	78.9
		John C. Frémont	Republican	1,339,932	33.1	114	
		Millard Fillmore	American	871,731	21.6	8	
1860	33	**Abraham Lincoln**	Republican	1,865,593	39.8	180	81.2
		Stephen A. Douglas	Democratic	1,382,713	29.5	12	
		John C. Breckinridge	Democratic	848,356	18.1	72	
		John Bell	Constitutional Union	592,906	12.6	39	
1864	36	**Abraham Lincoln**	Republican	2,206,938	55.0	212	73.8
		George B. McClellan	Democratic	1,803,787	45.0	21	

Presidential Elections (continued)

Year	Number of States	Candidates	Parties	Popular Vote	% of Popular Vote	Electoral Vote	% Voter Participation[a]
1868	37	**Ulysses S. Grant**	Republican	3,013,421	52.7	214	78.1
		Horatio Seymour	Democratic	2,706,829	47.3	80	
1872	37	**Ulysses S. Grant**	Republican	3,596,745	55.6	286	71.3
		Horace Greeley	Democratic	2,843,446	43.9	b	
1876	38	**Rutherford B. Hayes**	Republican	4,036,572	48.0	185	81.8
		Samuel J. Tilden	Democratic	4,284,020	51.0	184	
1880	38	**James A. Garfield**	Republican	4,453,295	48.5	214	79.4
		Winfield S. Hancock	Democratic	4,414,082	48.1	155	
		James B. Weaver	Greenback-Labor	308,578	3.4		
1884	38	**Grover Cleveland**	Democratic	4,879,507	48.5	219	77.5
		James G. Blaine	Republican	4,850,293	48.2	182	
		Benjamin F. Butler	Greenback-Labor	175,370	1.8		
		John P. St. John	Prohibition	150,369	1.5		
1888	38	**Benjamin Harrison**	Republican	5,447,129	47.9	233	79.3
		Grover Cleveland	Democratic	5,537,857	48.6	168	
		Clinton B. Fisk	Prohibition	249,506	2.2		
		Anson J. Streeter	Union Labor	146,935	1.3		
1892	44	**Grover Cleveland**	Democratic	5,555,426	46.1	277	74.7
		Benjamin Harrison	Republican	5,182,690	43.0	145	
		James B. Weaver	People's	1,029,846	8.5	22	
		John Bidwell	Prohibition	264,133	2.2		
1896	45	**William McKinley**	Republican	7,102,246	51.1	271	79.3
		William J. Bryan	Democratic	6,492,559	47.7	176	
1900	45	**William McKinley**	Republican	7,218,491	51.7	292	73.2
		William J. Bryan	Democratic; Populist	6,356,734	45.5	155	
		John C. Wooley	Prohibition	208,914	1.5		
1904	45	**Theodore Roosevelt**	Republican	7,628,461	57.4	336	65.2
		Alton B. Parker	Democratic	5,084,223	37.6	140	
		Eugene V. Debs	Socialist	402,283	3.0		
		Silas C. Swallow	Prohibition	258,536	1.9		
1908	46	**William H. Taft**	Republican	7,675,320	51.6	321	65.4
		William J. Bryan	Democratic	6,412,294	43.1	162	
		Eugene V. Debs	Socialist	420,793	2.8		
		Eugene W. Chafin	Prohibition	253,840	1.7		
1912	48	**Woodrow Wilson**	Democratic	6,296,547	41.9	435	58.8
		Theodore Roosevelt	Progressive	4,118,571	27.4	88	
		William H. Taft	Republican	3,486,720	23.2	8	
		Eugene V. Debs	Socialist	900,672	6.0		

Presidential Elections (continued)

Year	Number of States	Candidates	Parties	Popular Vote	% of Popular Vote	Electoral Vote	% Voter Participationa
		Eugene W. Chafin	Prohibition	206,275	1.4		
1916	48	**Woodrow Wilson**	Democratic	9,127,695	49.4	277	61.6
		Charles E. Hughes	Republican	8,533,507	46.2	254	
		A. L. Benson	Socialist	585,113	3.2		
		J. Frank Hanly	Prohibition	220,506	1.2		
1920	48	**Warren G. Harding**	Republican	16,143,407	60.4	404	49.2
		James M. Cox	Democratic	9,130,328	34.2	127	
		Eugene V. Debs	Socialist	919,799	3.4		
		P. P. Christensen	Farmer-Labor	265,411	1.0		
1924	48	**Calvin Coolidge**	Republican	15,718,211	54.0	382	48.9
		John W. Davis	Democratic	8,385,283	28.8	136	
		Robert M. La Follette	Progressive	4,831,289	16.6	13	
1928	48	**Herbert C. Hoover**	Republican	21,391,993	58.2	444	56.9
		Alfred E. Smith	Democratic	15,016,169	40.9	87	
1932	48	**Franklin D. Roosevelt**	Democratic	22,809,638	57.4	472	56.9
		Herbert C. Hoover	Republican	15,758,901	39.7	59	
		Norman Thomas	Socialist	881,951	2.2		
1936	48	**Franklin D. Roosevelt**	Democratic	27,752,869	60.8	523	61.0
		Alfred M. Landon	Republican	16,674,665	36.5	8	
		William Lemke	Union	882,479	1.9		
1940	48	**Franklin D. Roosevelt**	Democratic	27,307,819	54.8	449	62.5
		Wendell L. Willkie	Republican	22,321,018	44.8	82	
1944	48	**Franklin D. Roosevelt**	Democratic	25,606,585	53.5	432	55.9
		Thomas E. Dewey	Republican	22,014,745	46.0	99	
1948	48	**Harry S Truman**	Democratic	24,179,345	49.6	303	53.0
		Thomas E. Dewey	Republican	21,991,291	45.1	189	
		J. Strom Thurmond	States' Rights	1,176,125	2.4	39	
		Henry A. Wallace	Progressive	1,157,326	2.4		
1952	48	**Dwight D. Eisenhower**	Republican	33,936,234	55.1	442	63.3
		Adlai E. Stevenson	Democratic	27,314,992	44.4	89	
1956	48	**Dwight D. Eisenhower**	Republican	35,590,472	57.6	457	60.6
		Adlai E. Stevenson	Democratic	26,022,752	42.1	73	
1960	50	**John F. Kennedy**	Democratic	34,226,731	49.7	303	62.8
		Richard M. Nixon	Republican	34,108,157	49.5	219	
1964	50	**Lyndon B. Johnson**	Democratic	43,129,566	61.1	486	61.7
		Barry M. Goldwater	Republican	27,178,188	38.5	52	
1968	50	**Richard M. Nixon**	Republican	31,785,480	43.4	301	60.6
		Hubert H. Humphrey	Democratic	31,275,166	42.7	191	

Presidential Elections (continued)

Year	Number of States	Candidates	Parties	Popular Vote	% of Popular Vote	Electoral Vote	% Voter Participation[a]
		George C. Wallace	American Independent	9,906,473	13.5	46	
1972	50	**Richard M. Nixon**	Republican	47,169,911	60.7	520	55.2
		George S. McGovern	Democratic	29,170,383	37.5	17	
		John G. Schmitz	American	1,099,482	1.4		
1976	50	**James E. Carter**	Democratic	40,830,763	50.1	297	53.5
		Gerald R. Ford	Republican	39,147,793	48.0	240	
1980	50	**Ronald W. Reagan**	Republican	43,904,153	50.7	489	52.6
		James E. Carter	Democratic	35,483,883	41.0	49	
		John B. Anderson	Independent	5,720,060	6.6		
		Ed Clark	Libertarian	921,299	1.1		
1984	50	**Ronald W. Reagan**	Republican	54,455,075	58.8	525	53.3
		Walter F. Mondale	Democratic	37,577,185	40.6	13	
1988	50	**George H. W. Bush**	Republican	48,886,097	53.4	426	50.1
		Michael S. Dukakis	Democratic	41,809,074	45.6	111[c]	
1992	50	**William J. Clinton**	Democratic	44,909,326	43.0	370	55.2
		George H. W. Bush	Republican	39,103,882	37.4	168	
		H. Ross Perot	Independent	19,741,048	18.9		
1996	50	**William J. Clinton**	Democratic	47,402,357	49.2	379	49.1
		Robert J. Dole	Republican	39,196,755	40.7	159	
		H. Ross Perot	Reform	8,085,402	8.4		
		Ralph Nader	Green	684,902	0.7		
2000	50	**George W. Bush**	Republican	50,455,156	47.9	271	51.2
		Albert Gore	Democratic	50,992,335	48.4	266	
		Ralph Nader	Green	2,882,955	2.7		
2004	50	**George W. Bush**	Republican	62,039,073	50.7	286	55.3
		John F. Kerry	Democratic	59,027,478	48.2	251	
		Ralph Nader	Independent	240,896	0.2		

Candidates receiving less than 1 percent of the popular vote have been omitted. Thus the percentage of popular vote given for any election year may not total 100 percent.

Before the passage of the Twelfth Amendment in 1804, the electoral college voted for two presidential candidates; the runner-up became vice president.

Before 1824, most presidential electors were chosen by state legislatures, not by popular vote.

[a]Percent of voting-age population casting ballots.

[b]Greeley died shortly after the election; the electors supporting him then divided their votes among minor candidates.

[c]One elector from West Virginia cast her electoral college presidential ballot for Lloyd Bentsen, the Democratic Party's vice-presidential candidate.

Presidents and Vice Presidents

1. President	**George Washington**	1789–1797	
Vice President	John Adams	1789–1797	
2. President	**John Adams**	1797–1801	
Vice President	Thomas Jefferson	1797–1801	
3. President	**Thomas Jefferson**	1801–1809	
Vice President	Aaron Burr	1801–1805	
Vice President	George Clinton	1805–1809	
4. President	**James Madison**	1809–1817	
Vice President	George Clinton	1809–1813	
Vice President	Elbridge Gerry	1813–1817	
5. President	**James Monroe**	1817–1825	
Vice President	Daniel Tompkins	1817–1825	
6. President	**John Quincy Adams**	1825–1829	
Vice President	John C. Calhoun	1825–1829	
7. President	**Andrew Jackson**	1829–1837	
Vice President	John C. Calhoun	1829–1833	
Vice President	Martin Van Buren	1833–1837	
8. President	**Martin Van Buren**	1837–1841	
Vice President	Richard M. Johnson	1837–1841	
9. President	**William H. Harrison**	1841	
Vice President	John Tyler	1841	
10. President	**John Tyler**	1841–1845	
Vice President	None		
11. President	**James K. Polk**	1845–1849	
Vice President	George M. Dallas	1845–1849	
12. President	**Zachary Taylor**	1849–1850	
Vice President	Millard Fillmore	1849–1850	
13. President	**Millard Fillmore**	1850–1853	
Vice President	None		
14. President	**Franklin Pierce**	1853–1857	
Vice President	William R. King	1853–1857	
15. President	**James Buchanan**	1857–1861	
Vice President	John C. Breckinridge	1857–1861	
16. President	**Abraham Lincoln**	1861–1865	
Vice President	Hannibal Hamlin	1861–1865	
Vice President	Andrew Johnson	1865	
17. President	**Andrew Johnson**	1865–1869	
Vice President	None		
18. President	**Ulysses S. Grant**	1869–1877	
Vice President	Schuyler Colfax	1869–1873	
Vice President	Henry Wilson	1873–1877	
19. President	**Rutherford B. Hayes**	1877–1881	
Vice President	William A. Wheeler	1877–1881	
20. President	**James A. Garfield**	1881	
Vice President	Chester A. Arthur	1881	
21. President	**Chester A. Arthur**	1881–1885	
Vice President	None		
22. President	**Grover Cleveland**	1885–1889	
Vice President	Thomas A. Hendricks	1885–1889	
23. President	**Benjamin Harrison**	1889–1893	
Vice President	Levi P. Morton	1889–1893	
24. President	**Grover Cleveland**	1893–1897	
Vice President	Adlai E. Stevenson	1893–1897	
25. President	**William McKinley**	1897–1901	
Vice President	Garret A. Hobart	1897–1901	
Vice President	Theodore Roosevelt	1901	
26. President	**Theodore Roosevelt**	1901–1909	
Vice President	Charles Fairbanks	1905–1909	
27. President	**William H. Taft**	1909–1913	
Vice President	James S. Sherman	1909–1913	
28. President	**Woodrow Wilson**	1913–1921	
Vice President	Thomas R. Marshall	1913–1921	
29. President	**Warren G. Harding**	1921–1923	
Vice President	Calvin Coolidge	1921–1923	
30. President	**Calvin Coolidge**	1923–1929	
Vice President	Charles G. Dawes	1925–1929	
31. President	**Herbert C. Hoover**	1929–1933	
Vice President	Charles Curtis	1929–1933	
32. President	**Franklin D. Roosevelt**	1933–1945	
Vice President	John N. Garner	1933–1941	
Vice President	Henry A. Wallace	1941–1945	
Vice President	Harry S Truman	1945	
33. President	**Harry S Truman**	1945–1953	
Vice President	Alben W. Barkley	1949–1953	
34. President	**Dwight D. Eisenhower**	1953–1961	
Vice President	Richard M. Nixon	1953–1961	

Presidents and Vice Presidents (continued)

35. President	**John F. Kennedy**	1961–1963	
Vice President	Lyndon B. Johnson	1961–1963	
36. President	**Lyndon B. Johnson**	1963–1969	
Vice President	Hubert H. Humphrey	1965–1969	
37. President	**Richard M. Nixon**	1969–1974	
Vice President	Spiro T. Agnew	1969–1973	
Vice President	Gerald R. Ford	1973–1974	
38. President	**Gerald R. Ford**	1974–1977	
Vice President	Nelson A. Rockefeller	1974–1977	
39. President	**James E. Carter**	1977–1981	
Vice President	Walter F. Mondale	1977–1981	
40. President	**Ronald W. Reagan**	1981–1989	
Vice President	George H. W. Bush	1981–1989	
41. President	**George H. W. Bush**	1989–1993	
Vice President	J. Danforth Quayle	1989–1993	
42. President	**William J. Clinton**	1993–2001	
Vice President	Albert Gore	1993–2001	
43. President	**George W. Bush**	2001–2009	
Vice President	Richard Cheney	2001–2009	

For a complete list of Presidents, Vice Presidents, and Cabinet Members, go to college.hmco.com.

Justices of the Supreme Court

	Term of Service	Years of Service	Life Span		Term of Service	Years of Service	Life Span
John Jay	1789–1795	5	1745–1829	Joseph P. Bradley	1870–1892	22	1813–1892
John Rutledge	1789–1791	1	1739–1800	Ward Hunt	1873–1882	9	1810–1886
William Cushing	1789–1810	20	1732–1810	*Morrison R. Waite*	1874–1888	14	1816–1888
James Wilson	1789–1798	8	1742–1798	John M. Harlan	1877–1911	34	1833–1911
John Blair	1789–1796	6	1732–1800	William B. Woods	1880–1887	7	1824–1887
Robert H. Harrison	1789–1790	—	1745–1790	Stanley Mathews	1881–1889	7	1824–1889
James Iredell	1790–1799	9	1751–1799	Horace Gray	1882–1902	20	1828–1902
Thomas Johnson	1791–1793	1	1732–1819	Samuel Blatchford	1882–1893	11	1820–1893
William Paterson	1793–1806	13	1745–1806	Lucius Q. C. Lamar	1888–1893	5	1825–1893
*John Rutledge**	1795	—	1739–1800	*Melville W. Fuller*	1888–1910	21	1833–1910
Samuel Chase	1796–1811	15	1741–1811	David J. Brewer	1890–1910	20	1837–1910
Oliver Ellsworth	1796–1800	4	1745–1807	Henry B. Brown	1890–1906	16	1836–1913
Bushrod Washington	1798–1829	31	1762–1829	George Shiras Jr.	1892–1903	10	1832–1924
Alfred Moore	1799–1804	4	1755–1810	Howell E. Jackson	1893–1895	2	1832–1895
John Marshall	1801–1835	34	1755–1835	Edward D. White	1894–1910	16	1845–1921
William Johnson	1804–1834	30	1771–1834	Rufus W. Peckham	1895–1909	14	1838–1909
H. Brockholst Livingston	1806–1823	16	1757–1823	Joseph McKenna	1898–1925	26	1843–1926
Thomas Todd	1807–1826	18	1765–1826	Oliver W. Holmes	1902–1932	30	1841–1935
Joseph Story	1811–1845	33	1779–1845	William D. Day	1903–1922	19	1849–1923
Gabriel Duval	1811–1835	24	1752–1844	William H. Moody	1906–1910	3	1853–1917
Smith Thompson	1823–1843	20	1768–1843	Horace H. Lurton	1910–1914	4	1844–1914
Robert Trimble	1826–1828	2	1777–1828	Charles E. Hughes	1910–1916	5	1862–1948
John McLean	1829–1861	32	1785–1861	Willis Van Devanter	1911–1937	26	1859–1941
Henry Baldwin	1830–1844	14	1780–1844	Joseph R. Lamar	1911–1916	5	1857–1916
James M. Wayne	1835–1867	32	1790–1867	*Edward D. White*	1910–1921	11	1845–1921
Roger B. Taney	1836–1864	28	1777–1864	Mahlon Pitney	1912–1922	10	1858–1924
Philip P. Barbour	1836–1841	4	1783–1841	James C. McReynolds	1914–1941	26	1862–1946
John Catron	1837–1865	28	1786–1865	Louis D. Brandeis	1916–1939	22	1856–1941
John McKinley	1837–1852	15	1780–1852	John H. Clarke	1916–1922	6	1857–1945
Peter V. Daniel	1841–1860	19	1784–1860	*William H. Taft*	1921–1930	8	1857–1930
Samuel Nelson	1845–1872	27	1792–1873	George Sutherland	1922–1938	15	1862–1942
Levi Woodbury	1845–1851	5	1789–1851	Pierce Butler	1922–1939	16	1866–1939
Robert C. Grier	1846–1870	23	1794–1870	Edward T. Sanford	1923–1930	7	1865–1930
Benjamin R. Curtis	1851–1857	6	1809–1874	Harlan F. Stone	1925–1941	16	1872–1946
John A. Campbell	1853–1861	8	1811–1889	*Charles E. Hughes*	1930–1941	11	1862–1948
Nathan Clifford	1858–1881	23	1803–1881	Owen J. Roberts	1930–1945	15	1875–1955
Noah H. Swayne	1862–1881	18	1804–1884	Benjamin N. Cardozo	1932–1938	6	1870–1938
Samuel F. Miller	1862–1890	28	1816–1890	Hugo L. Black	1937–1971	34	1886–1971
David Davis	1862–1877	14	1815–1886	Stanley F. Reed	1938–1957	19	1884–1980
Stephen J. Field	1863–1897	34	1816–1899	Felix Frankfurter	1939–1962	23	1882–1965
Salmon P. Chase	1864–1873	8	1808–1873	William O. Douglas	1939–1975	36	1898–1980
William Strong	1870–1880	10	1808–1895	Frank Murphy	1940–1949	9	1890–1949

Justices of the Supreme Court (continued)

	Term of Service	Years of Service	Life Span		Term of Service	Years of Service	Life Span
Harlan F. Stone	1941–1946	5	1872–1946	Abe Fortas	1965–1969	4	1910–1982
James F. Byrnes	1941–1942	1	1879–1972	Thurgood Marshall	1967–1991	24	1908–1993
Robert H. Jackson	1941–1954	13	1892–1954	*Warren C. Burger*	1969–1986	17	1907–1995
Wiley B. Rutledge	1943–1949	6	1894–1949	Harry A. Blackmun	1970–1994	24	1908–1998
Harold H. Burton	1945–1958	13	1888–1964	Lewis F. Powell Jr.	1972–1987	15	1907–1998
Fred M. Vinson	1946–1953	7	1890–1953	*William H. Rehnquist*	1972–2005	33	1924–2005
Tom C. Clark	1949–1967	18	1899–1977	John P. Stevens III	1975–	—	1920–
Sherman Minton	1949–1956	7	1890–1965	Sandra Day O'Connor	1981–	—	1930–
Earl Warren	1953–1969	16	1891–1974	Antonin Scalia	1986–	—	1936–
John Marshall Harlan	1955–1971	16	1899–1971	Anthony M. Kennedy	1988–	—	1936–
William J. Brennan Jr.	1956–1990	34	1906–1997	David H. Souter	1990–	—	1939–
Charles E. Whittaker	1957–1962	5	1901–1973	Clarence Thomas	1991–	—	1948–
Potter Stewart	1958–1981	23	1915–1985	Ruth Bader Ginsburg	1993–	—	1933–
Byron R. White	1962–1993	31	1917–	Stephen Breyer	1994–	—	1938–
Arthur J. Goldberg	1962–1965	3	1908–1990	John G. Roberts	2005–	—	1955–

Note: Chief justices are in italics.

*Appointed and served one term, but not confirmed by the Senate.

AAA, *see* Agricultural Adjustment Act

A&P stores, 332

Aborigines (Australia), 311, 311(illus.)

Abortion, 351, 395, 579, 599

Abraham Lincoln Brigade, 482

Accommodation policy: of Booker T. Washington, 386, 387

Acheson, Dean, 522

ACLU, *see* American Civil Liberties Union

Activism: by blacks, 366; federal, 467–468. *See also* Protest(s); Revolts and rebellions

Adams, Henry, 399

Adamson Act (1916), 393

Addams, Jane, 349, 406, 419, 432; woman suffrage and, 387; peace efforts of, 476

Adding machines, 323, 324

Adkins v. Children's Hospital, 436

Adolescence, 352

Adoption: by gay couples, 631

Advanced Research Projects Agency (ARPA), 636

Advertising, 332–333, 332(illus.), 439

Aerospace industry, 543

Affirmative action, 578, 591

Affluence, 329–330, 607

Afghanistan: Soviet Union and, 576, 592, 606; U.S. and, 617, 626–627

AFL, *see* American Federation of Labor (AFL)

Africa: American missionaries in, 361; black emigration to, 385; imperialism in, 398; independence of, 525; Nixon policy toward, 583. *See also* Slaves and slavery

African Americans, 284; family and, 283; religion and, 284; and 1868 election, 289; equality of, 291; "Negro Rule" myth and, 291; as Exodusters, 296, 307; Reconstruction and, 296–297; in West, 307; as cowboys, 315(illus.); unions and, 327, 328; migration by, 341, 426, 440; culture of, 344; settlement houses and, 349–350; vaudeville and, 355; as missionaries, 361; Jim Crow laws and, 366; women and, 366, 388, 438, 457, 498; Farmers' Alliance and, 368; associations of, 378; in Progressive era, 385–387; Niagara movement and, 386–387; in Spanish-American War, 406; First World War and, 421, 429; Harlem Renaissance and, 449; jazz and, 449–450; unemployment of, 457; at 1936 Olympics,

469; New Deal and, 471; Second World War and, 485, 497, 503, 540–543; illiteracy among, 504; in postwar period, 534, 536; population of, 544, 630; on television, 545; poverty of, 550, 608; sit-ins by, 553–554; King assassination and, 570–572; cultural nationalism of, 576; affirmative action and, 578; Korean immigrants and, 610; Rodney King riots and, 617–618; and 2000 election, 626. *See also* Civil rights; Civil rights movement; Freedpeople (Civil War); Race and racism; Segregation; Slaves and slavery; Voting and voting rights

African Methodist Episcopal (AME) Church, 344, 388

African National Congress, 611

Afrika Korps, 496

Age and ageism, *see* Older Americans

Agency for International Development (AID), 527

Agent Orange, 582

Age of Innocence, The (Wharton), 449

Agnew, Spiro, 585, 586

Agrarian protest, 367–369

Agribusiness, 543, 550

Agricultural Adjustment Act, 460, 461, 462, 470

Agricultural colleges, 368

Agriculture: immigrant labor for, 307; in West, 309–310; in late 1800s, 313–314; exports of, 399; in First World War, 425; in 1920s, 436; after Second World War, 535. *See also* Farms and farming

Aguinaldo, Emilio, 407

AIDS (autoimmune deficiency syndrome), 609, 633, 634

Aid to Families with Dependent Children (AFDC), 465, 562, 598

Air force, 483, 503

Airline industry, 442, 442(illus.), 600

Airplanes, 434; in First World War, 422; in Second World War, 496

Air pollution, 336, 510

Air traffic controllers: Reagan and, 599

Alabama, 559

Alabama (ship), 402

Alabama Midlands case, 362

Alaska, 295, 402

Alcatraz: Indian occupation of, 577, 577(illus.)

Alcohol and alcoholism, 382, 383, 449. *See also* Temperance

Aldrich, Nelson W., 380, 391

Alfalfa, 314

Algeciras, Spain: Moroccan settlement at, 413

Alianza Federal de Mercedes, 577

Alienation, literature of, 449

Alien Registration (Smith) Act (1940), 500–502

Allende, Salvador, 583

Alliance(s): in First World War, 417; in Second World War, 488; NATO as, 519; with Japan, 522. *See also* specific alliances

Alliance for Progress, 556

Allies (First World War), 417, 430, 451, 479

Allies (Second World War), 493, 494, 496, 506(map); D-Day and, 505; end of, 508; Cold War and, 516–517

Al Qaeda, 616, 617, 623, 633–635; September 11, 2001, attacks and, 626

Alternating current system, 319

Altgeld, John P., 327

Amalgamated Association of Iron and Steelworkers, 328

Amendments to Constitution: listing of, A7–A11

America First Committee, 485

American Airlines Flight 175, 615

American Association for Old Age Security, 381

American Bar Association, 378

American Birth Control League, 388, 395

American Century (Luce), 490

American Civil Liberties Union, 432–433

American Council on Education: collegiate athletics and, 452

American Dilemma, An (Myrdal), 541

American Expeditionary Forces (AEF), 421

American Federation of Labor (AFL), 327–328, 426, 466

American Friends Service Committee, 455, 477, 567

American Indian Defense Agency, 467

American Indian Movement (AIM), 578

American Indians: containment policy against, 293–295; cultures of, 301, 302–305; economic activities of, 301–302; "civilizing" of, 303, 304; treaties with, 303; Dawes Severalty Act and, 305; resistance

I-1

American Indians (*cont.*)
by, 305; in West, 307; in Progressive era, 387; in 1920s, 438; in New Deal, 461, 467; Navajo code-talkers and, 492–493; population of, 544; poverty of, 550–551; in 1970s, 576; Red Power and, 577–578, 577(illus.). *See also* Land
Americanization, 413, 474, 477–479, 517, 622; of Philippines, 407; of Vietnam War, 564, 566
American League (baseball), 352
American Legion, 428, 485
American Liberty League, 462
American Missionary Association, 284
American Peace Commission, 430
American Psychiatric Association: on homosexuality, 580
American Railway Union, 371, 379
American Relief Administration, 476
American Samoa, 398
Americans with Disabilities Act (1990), 613, 614
American Tobacco Company, 323, 333
American Union Against Militarism, 419
American University (Beirut), 361
American Woman Suffrage Association, 366
Amnesty Act (1872), 293
Amusement centers, 353(illus.)
Anaconda Copper Company, 307
Anarchism, 327, 428, 446
Ancestry, 544
Anderson, Marian, 472
Anglo-American relations, 413
Anglos: White Hats and, 368; Mexican labor and, 441
Angola, 583
Animals, 301
Annan, Kofi, 634
Annexation: Dominican Republic and, 295; by cities, 339; of Virgin Islands, 402; Hawai'i and, 403–404, 406; of Samoa, 406; of Wake Island, 406
Anthony, Susan B., 282, 287, 366
Anti-Americanism, 557
Antiballistic missile defenses, 583
Anti-Ballistic Missile Treaty, 626
Anti-Bookerites, 386
Anti-Comintern Pact, 482
Anticommunism, 522–523, 538–540, 601
Anticoolie clubs, 295
Antigay movement, 631
Antiglobalization, 621–622
Anti-imperialism, 402, 406–407
Anti-Imperialist League, 407
Anti-Klan laws, 293
Antilynching newspaper, 365
Anti-Saloon League, 383
Anti-Semitism: Brandeis and, 393; of Coughlin, 464; in United States, 469; immigration and, 483. *See also* Jews and Judaism
Antitrust laws, 335, 390
Antiwar protests: in First World War, 419; in Vietnam War, 567, 569, 572, 580–581; in Iraq War (2003–), 628

ANZUS Treaty, 522
Apartheid, 583, 611
Apollo 8, 572
Appeasement: at Munich, 482, 483
Appliances, 436, 438, 443
Apprentice laws, 290
Arabic (ship), 418
Arab-Israeli disputes, 528–529, 629(map); Six-Day War and, 583; Yom Kippur War (1973), 583
Arab world, 513, 576, 606. *See also* Arab-Israeli disputes; Oil and oil industry
Arafat, Yasir, 606, 622
Arapaho Indians, 300
Arbenz Guzmán, Jacobo, 528
Arbitration, 391
Architecture: skyscrapers, 346
Arctic National Wildlife Refuge, 626
Ardennes Forest, battle in, 505
Argentina, 593
Argentina (ship), 501
Argonne Forest, battle in, 422
Aristide, Jean-Bertrand, 622
Arizona, 308
Arizona (ship), 489
Armed forces: African Americans in, 406, 420–421, 503, 540; First World War and, 420, 422; Second World War and, 494, 504–505; Japanese Americans in, 503; in Vietnam War, 566; AIDS and, 634. *See also* Military; Soldiers
Armed neutrality policy, 420
Armed Slave, The (Sprang), 283(illus.)
Armistice: Spanish-American War and, 404, 406; in First World War, 422
Arms and armaments: First World War and, 425; Washington Naval Conference and, 477; shipments of, 482, 488; Second World War and, 483, 486, 488, 496, 498; for China, 484. *See also* Weapons
Arms race, 477, 515, 522, 556, 592; missiles and, 583; INF Treaty and, 606; reduction of, 612
Armstrong, Louis, 449
Armstrong, Neil, 590
Army Industrial College, 432
Army-McCarthy hearings, 540
Army of the Republic of Vietnam (ARVN), 563
Arnett, Peter, 602(illus.)
Around the World with General Grant (Young), 294
ARPANET, 636–637
"Arsenal of democracy," 494, 496
Art(s): in 1920s, 449
Arthur, Chester, 362, 364
Articles of Constitution: Article I, A2–A5; Article II, A5–A6; Article III, A6; Article IV, A6–A7; Article V, A7; Article VI, A7; Article VII, A7
Article 10: of League of Nations, 430, 431
Artisans, 324
Ashcroft, John, 627

Asia: immigrants from, 341, 609–610, 630; imperialism in, 398, 407–410, 409(map); Second World War and, 483–484, 513; Cold War in, 519–520. *See also* Southeast Asia
Asian Americans, 343, 344, 536
Asians: in West, 307; in cities, 344; segregation of, 400–401
Assassinations: of McKinley, 389, 410; of King, 555, 570–572; attempts against Castro, 557; of John F. Kennedy, 560, 572
Assembly lines, 319–322, 322(illus.), 324, 352
Assimilation: urban neighborhoods and, 343; religion and, 344–345; by African Americans, 385; of Indians, 387, 467
Associated Press (AP), 479
Associationalism: of Hoover, 450, 461
Aswan Dam, 529
Athletics, *see* Sports
Atlanta Compromise, 386, 387
Atlanta Exposition (1895), 386
Atlanta Journal, 558
Atlanta University, 284
Atlantic Charter, 488
Atlantic Ocean region: telegraph cable in, 321, 321(illus.); Second World War in, 494
Atomic bomb, 494, 497, 508; at Hiroshima and Nagasaki, 509; environmental damage from, 510; after Second World War, 515; Soviet, 519
Atomic diplomacy, 515
Atomic Energy Act (1954), 538
Atomic waste, 510
Australia, 311, 522
Austria, 422, 482
Austria-Hungary, 341, 417, 420, 423
Automobiles, 318, 438–439, 440(illus.), 545; Ford and, 319–322; strike in, 466; Second World War and, 497, 535; Nader on, 561; in 1970s, 588; Japan and, 610
Axis powers, 482, 488, 494, 505
Ayer, N. W., & Son, 332

Ba'athist Party (Iraq), 593
Baby and Child Care (Spock), 546
Baby boom, 535–536, 547; Social Security and, 473
Baghdad, 602(illus.), 628
Bailey v. Drexel Furniture Company, 436
Baker, Josephine, 449
Bakke, Allan, 591
Balanced-budget amendment, 619
Balance-of-payments deficit, 582
Balance of power, 359, 417–418
Balch, Emily Greene, 427, 476
Baldwin, Roger, 432
Balfour Declaration, 430
Balkan region, 417, 622
Ball, George W., 564
Ballots: in 2000 election, 626
Baltic region, 422, 483, 514, 611
Bank(s) and banking: investments and, 334; property ownership and, 343; 1890s de-

pression and, 370; regulation of, 393; stock market crash and, 450–451; in Great Depression, 455, 459–460; foreign branches and, 479; in Germany, 481; Reagan and, 600

Bankruptcy: of governments, 618

Bao Dai, 520, 529, 530

Baptists, 284, 344; black, 388

Barbed wire, 314–315

Barbie dolls, 548, 548(illus.)

Barone, Michael, 467

Barrios, 344, 441

Baruch, Bernard, 425, 515

Baruch Plan, 515

Baseball, 352, 354, 354(illus.), 448, 541

Bataan Death March, 495

Batista, Fulgencio, 481, 528

Battles, *see* Wars and warfare

Baum, L. Frank, 374–375

Bayard, Thomas E., 400

Bay of Pigs invasion, 556–557

Beals, Jessie Tarbox, 401(illus.)

Beard, Charles A., 384, 427

Beatles, 569, 571, 571(illus.)

Begin, Menachem, 592

Belgium, 417, 485

Bellamy, Francis, 551

Belleau Wood, battle at, 422

Bemis, Edward, 335

Benefits: in postwar period, 536

Berenson, Senda, 355

Berkeley: Free Speech Movement in, 568–569

Berlin: Khrushchev and, 525

Berlin airlift, 519

Berlin Wall, 556, 611

Bernstein, Carl, 585

Bethlehem Steel Company, 323

Bethune, Mary McLeod, 464

Biardot, Alphonse, 356

Bible, 579–580, 607

Bicycles, 353

Big business, 335, 381; in South, 291; cattle industry and, 315; in Gilded Age, 358; Theodore Roosevelt and, 391; Taft and, 392; in 1920s, 435–436. *See also* Business; Corporations

Big Four: after First World War, 430

Big government, 597, 619

Big Three: in Second World War, 507

Bilingualism: in Puerto Rico, 414; Florida and, 610

Billboards, 332

Billionaires, 601

Bill of Rights, *See* Amendments to Constitution; specific amendments

Bin Laden, Osama, 623, 626, 627, 628

Biogenetics, 632–633

Biological and Toxin Weapons Convention (1972), 626

Birmingham, Alabama, 558, 560

Birth control, 351, 358; movement, 388; Sanger and, 388, 394–395; clinics,

394–395; in 1920s, 443; in 1950s, 546; population growth and, 590. *See also* Pill, the

Birth Control Clinical Research Bureau, 395

Birth Control Federation of America, 395

Birth of a Nation, The (film), 356, 429

Birth rate: decline in, 350–351; in Great Depression, 455; in Second World War, 500; from 1945 to 1964, 535(illus.); in 1970s, 591; of Hispanics, 610

Black, Hugo, 471

Black Boy (Wright), 541

"Black cabinet," 464

Black codes, 285–286

Black Kettle (chief), 303

Blacklists: of union members, 327

Black market: in Second World War, 499

Blackmun, Harry, 585

Black Muslims, 568

Black Panthers, 568

Black Power movement, 568

Blacks, *see* African Americans

Black Shirts (fascists): in United States, 457

Black Star line, 441

Black Thursday, 450

Black Tuesday, 451

Blaine, James G., 360, 364, 403

Blair, Ezell, 553

Blake, Eubie, 449

Bland-Allison Act (1878), 363

Blatch, Harriot Stanton, 388

Blended families, 591, 631

Blitzkrieg (lightning war), 483

Blockades: in Spanish-American War, 406; in First World War, 417; of Berlin, 519; of Cuba, 557

Blue-collar workers, 543–544, 588

Blues (music), 571

Blumenthal, Sidney, 625

Bly, Nellie (Elizabeth Cochrane), 356, 402

B'nai B'rith, 329

Board games, 352

Boarding process, 351

"Boat people" (Southeast Asians), 581

Bodegas, 441

Boesky, Ivan, 609

Boiardi, Hector (Chef Boyardee), 356

Bolshevik Revolution (1917), 422, 423, 515

Bolshevism, 382, 428–429, 430

Bombings: Haymarket Riot and, 327; in Second World War, 494; of Japan, 508; hydrogen bomb, 519, 523; of Vietnam, 564. *See also* Atomic bomb

Bond, Julian, 558

Bonds: risky, 601

Bonsack, James, 323

Bonus Army, 459

Books, 356; fundamentalists on, 607

Boom-and-bust cycles, 333

Boone, Pat, 549

Borah, William, 480

Borden, Gail, 331

Border(s): between North and South Korea, 522; illegal immigrants and, 610; international, 633

Bork, Robert, 599

Born-again Christians, 590, 597, 607

Borrowing: by United States, 600

Bosnia: First World War and, 417

Bosnia-Herzegovina, 622

Bosnian Muslims, 622

Bosses (political), 348–349, 360, 379, 381, 393

Boston: police strike in, 437

Boston (ship), 403

Boston marriages, 351

Boston Red Sox, 352, 449

Boston Women's Health Collective, 579

Boulder Dam (Hoover Dam), 467

Boundaries: Venezuelan dispute and, 404. *See also* Border(s)

Bow, Clara, 445

Bowers v. Hardwick, 599

Boxer Rebellion, 396, 410

Boycotts, 366; of Montgomery buses, 541; of table grapes, 577; of Iraq, 612

Bracero program, 550

Braddock, James, 468

Bradwell, Myra, 295

Bradwell v. Illinois, 295–296

Brain Trust, 460

Branch Davidians, 623

Brandeis, Louis D., 384, 393

Brand names, 332

Bread-and-butter reforms, 379

Brest-Litovsk, Treaty of, 422

Bretton Woods Conference (1945), 514

Brice, Fanny, 355

Bridges, 346

Britain, *see* England (Britain)

British Guiana, 404

British Trans-Indian railroad, 398

Briton, Nan, 437

Brooklyn Bridge, 346

Brotherhood of Sleeping Car Porters, 472, 497, 559

Brown, James, 569

Brown Power movement, 576

Brown v. Board of Education of Topeka, 298, 366, 433, 527, 534, 541

Bruce, Blanche K., 284

Brundage, Avery, 469

Bryan, William Jennings, 373, 374, 391, 406; First World War and, 415, 416; Scopes trial and, 446–447

Brzezinski, Zbigniew, 592

Buchanan, James, 364

Buchanan, Pat, 626

Buck, Pearl, 483

Buckley, William F., 568

Bud Dajo, Battle of, 407

Budget, *see* Federal budget; Spending

Budget and Accounting Act (1921), 437

Buffalo (American bison), 301, 302, 305, 314

"Buffalo Bill," 299

Bulge, Battle of the, 505

Bull Moose Party, 392
Bunch, Charlotte, 579
Bundy, McGeorge, 555
Buppies (black urban professionals), 609
Bureaucracy: in First World War, 423; Homeland Security and, 531
Bureau of Corporations, 390
Bureau of Human Rights, 594
Bureau of Indian Affairs (BIA), 438, 467, 578
Bureau of Public Roads, 439
Bureau of Reclamation, 467
Bureau of Refugees, Freedmen, and Abandoned Lands, *see* Freedmen's Bureau
Burger, Warren, 585
Burlingame Treaty (1868), 400
Burma, 513
Burnham, Daniel, 407
Bus boycott: in Montgomery, 534, 541, 542
Bush, George H. W., 596, 597, 611–613, 618; budget and, 600; Iran-contra and, 604; Operation Desert Storm and, 612; ADA and, 613, 614; Somalia and, 622; environment and, 623
Bush, George W., 414, 531, 617; Social Security and, 473; 2000 election and, 625–626; tax plan of, 626; antiterrorism and, 626–627; stem-cell research and, 633
Bush, Neil: S&L scandal and, 601
Business: organization of, 318, 333–334; government and, 334–335, 425, 436–437; urban sprawl and, 339; silver vs. gold issue and, 363; African Americans in, 366; in 1920s, 435–436; Great Depression and, 451, 457; New Deal and, 462; in Second World War, 496–497; productivity and, 588; Reaganomics and, 599; globalization of, 620; Enron collapse and, 627. *See also* Corporations
Business cycle: in Great Depression, 457
Busing, 585
Byrd, James, Jr., 624
Byrnes, James F., 515

Cabinet: women in, 464
Cable Act (1922), 438
Cable cars, 339
California, 295, 300, 543; gold in, 307; oil in, 307; irrigation in, 309; in 1920s, 440; Proposition 13 in, 589, 618
Calley, William, 581
Cambodia, 565(map), 580, 581
Camp David accords (1979), 592, 604
Camp Fire Girls, 524
Canada: Indians in, 304; immigrants from, 341
Canals, 399
Canal Zone, 412, 592
Cannon, Joseph ("Uncle Joe"), 380
Cantigny, battle at, 422
Capital (financial), 323
Capital gains tax, 619
Capitalism, 399, 479; Progressives and, 379; foreign trade and, 399; Lenin on, 422;

Great Depression and, 455; Third World and, 527
Capone, Al, 449
Cárdenas, Lázaro, 481
Cardozo, Francis, 284
Caribbean region: immigrants from, 342(illus.), 610; U.S. hegemony in, 411(map), 412; intervention in, 604, 605(map)
Carlisle School, 305
Carmichael, Stokely, 568
Carnegie, Andrew, 334, 406, 419
Carnegie Foundation, 527
Carnegie Steel: Homestead strike and, 328, 371
Carpentier, Georges, 448
Carpetbaggers, 291, 292
Cars, *see* Automobiles
Carson, Rachel, 550
Cartels: in New Deal, 461
Carter, James Earl ("Jimmy"), 576, 585, 587, 597; Cold War and, 591–592, 601–603; Camp David accords and, 592; Iran hostage crisis and, 592–593; human rights and, 593, 594; in Haiti, 622
Carter, Rosalynn and Amy, 587
Carter Doctrine, 592
Carver, George Washington, 314
Casey, William, 604
Cash-and-carry arms sales, 483
Cash registers, 323, 324
Cassatt, Alexander, 379
Castro, Fidel, 481, 523, 528, 556–557. *See also* Cuba
Catcher in the Rye, The (Salinger), 549
Catell, J. M., 427
Catholicism, *see* Roman Catholicism
Catt, Carrie Chapman, 388, 419, 476
Cattle and cattle industry, 314–315. *See also* Ranching
Cavalry: in Spanish-American War, 388
CCC, *see* Civilian Conservation Corps (CCC)
Censorship: in First World War, 427
Census: Hispanics on, 576; POSSLQ and, 591; in 2000, 630
Central America: United Fruit and, 410–411; intervention in, 605(map); refugees from, 610; drug trade and, 612. *See also* Latin America
Central banking system, 393
Central High School, Little Rock, 541
Central Intelligence Agency (CIA), 517–519, 527, 528, 531; foreign policy and, 523; Vietnam and, 529–530; Bay of Pigs and, 556–557; in Africa, 583; Islamic guerrillas and, 592; Nicaragua and, 604
Central Pacific Railroad, 310
Central Powers, 417
Century of Dishonor, A (Jackson), 304
Cermak, Anton, 458
Chain stores, 332
Chamberlain, Neville, 482
Chaplin, Charlie, 356

Charity Organization Societies, 346–347
Charleston, 279
Charter(s): of League of Nations, 430, 431
Château-Thierry, battle at, 422
Chávez, César, 576
Chemical industry, 318, 322–323
Cheney, Dick, 628
Cheney, James, 558
Cheyenne Indians, 299–300
Chicago: Columbian Exposition in, 299, 350; Haymarket Riot in, 327, 371; real estate in (1890–1920), 339; Hull House in, 349; African Americans in, 426, 541; race riot in (1919), 429; suburbs of, 441; postwar housing in, 536; Democratic National Convention (1968) in, 572
Chicago Vice Commission, 383
Chicago White Sox, 448
Chicanos/Chicanas, 577. *See also* Mexicans and Mexican Americans
Childbearing: in 1950s, 546; by infertile women, 632
Childbirth: in 1920s, 443
Childcare, 498, 546
Childhood, 351
Child labor, 324–325, 436, 443–444; in textile mills, 323; regulation of, 325, 376, 381, 393
Children: of freedpeople, 290; family size and, 350–351; in 1920s, 443–444; Barbie dolls and, 548, 548(illus.); born outside marriage, 631
Chile, 480, 583
Chin, Vincent, 610
China, 519; baseball in, 354; missionaries in, 361, 396–397, 401; Japan and, 398, 413, 417, 476, 485(map); communications with, 402; and Open Door policy, 407–410, 409(map); dollar diplomacy and, 413; sovereignty of, 477; Second World War and, 483–484, 513; Mao Zedong and, 519; communism in, 520; Korean War and, 521; Nixon and, 583; Tiananmen Square slaughter in, 611. *See also* Open Door policy
China lobby, 520
Chinatowns, 344, 610
Chinese Exclusion Act (1882), 344, 507
Chinese immigrants, 295, 307, 308, 400; as railroad labor, 310; in Australia, 311
Chinese people: segregation of, 344, 400–401
Chinese Revolution (1911), 483
Chivington, John, 303
Chlorine gas, 421
Christianity: in China, 396–397; fundamentalist, 446–447, 590, 607–608; in 1950s, 545; born-again, 590, 597, 607; conservative, 607. *See also* Evangelicalism; Missions and missionaries; Religion
Chrysler: UAW and, 466
Churches: African Americans in, 284, 344. *See also* Religion

Churchill, Winston, 487, 496, 507(illus.); Atlantic Charter and, 488; at Teheran, 505; on "iron curtain," 515, 516(illus.)
Church of Jesus Christ of Latter-Day Saints, *see* Mormons
CIA, *see* Central Intelligence Agency (CIA)
Cigarettes, 323, 330. *See also* Tobacco and tobacco industry
Cigar Makers' Union, 327
Cigars, 404
Cimarron (film), 316
CIO, *see* Committee for Industrial Organization (CIO)
Circuses, 355
Cities and towns, 377–378; railroads and, 310; pollution in, 336; society and, 337–338; growth of, 338–343; work zone in, 339; geographic mobility and, 341; occupational mobility in, 342; neighborhoods in, 343–345; sanitation in, 345; poverty in, 346–347, 550; crime and violence in, 347; management of, 347–350; family life and, 350–352; leisure, mass culture, and, 352–356; ethnicity in, 356, 357; government for, 380, 381; African Americans in, 440; in 1920s, 440–441; in Second World War, 499; in Sunbelt, 543; in South, 588–589; in North and Midwest, 589; social crises in, 608–609
Citizens and citizenship: African American, 287, 366; Supreme Court on, 295; for Indians, 303, 305, 438; for Asians, 344; for Hawaiians, 404; for Puerto Ricans, 414
Citizens Committee (New Orleans), 366
City Beautiful movement, 350, 407
City commission plan, 380, 381
City manager plan, 380, 381
City planning, 378
Civic organizations, 378, 448
Civic reform, 349
Civilian Conservation Corps (CCC), 461
"Civilizing": of Indians, 303, 304
Civil liberties: First World War and, 417, 427–428; ACLU and, 432–433; in Soviet Union, 515; in 1980s, 608
Civil rights: Fourteenth Amendment and, 297–298; Du Bois and, 387; after Second World War, 540–543; J. Edgar Hoover and, 541; Supreme Court on, 541; affirmative action and, 578. *See also* Civil rights movement
Civil Rights Acts: of 1875, 293, 366; of 1964, 298, 560–561, 567, 578, 579, 591, 608; of 1957, 542
Civil rights bills: of 1866, 286; Kennedy and, 559
Civil rights movement, 541–543; Kennedy and, 544; in 1960s, 557–560, 567–568; March on Washington and, 559–560, 559(illus.)
Civil service, 350, 360–362, 364, 379, 381
Civil Service Commission, 362

Civil war(s): in Latin America and Caribbean region, 412; in Mexico, 412–413; in Russia, 430; in Spain, 482; in China (1920s), 484; in Greece, 516; in China (1949), 519; Korean War as, 521; in Rwanda, 622
Civil War (U.S.): Reconstruction and, 281–282; pensions for veterans of, 360, 364
Civil Works Administration, 461
Clanton family, 308, 309
Clarke, Edward, 445
Classes (social and economic): in postwar period, 534. *See also* Elites; specific classes
Clayton Anti-Trust Act (1914), 393
Clayton-Bulwer Treaty (1850), 412
Clean Air Act: of 1970, 336; of 1990, 613
"Clear and present danger," 428
Clemenceau, Georges, 421, 430
Clergy: in 1920s, 448
Clerical positions: women in, 324
Cleveland, 426, 441, 589
Cleveland, Grover, 328, 364, 372, 373, 403; 1890s depression and, 370
Clifford, Clark, 570
Clinton, Bill, 618, 619, 622–623; globalization and, 617; impeachment of, 617, 624–625; healthcare and, 619; New Economy and, 620; on future, 636
Clinton, Hillary Rodham, 618, 619, 624
Closed shop, 436, 498, 534
Clothing: ready-made, 319, 323, 332; cultural adaptation and, 344; in 1920s, 445; in Second World War, 498
CNN, 602, 612
Coal and coal industry, 336, 390–391, 498
Coaling stations, 402
Coalitions: in Gilded Age, 360. *See also* Democratic Party; Republican Party
Coca-Cola, 477
Cocaine, 608–609
Codes: in Second World War, 492–493, 496
Cody, "Buffalo Bill," 299
Coeducational colleges, 384
Coeur d'Alene, Idaho: miners' strike at, 371
Cohan, George M., 355
COLAs (cost-of-living adjustments), 543
Cold War, 513, 514–520; use of term, 516–517; Eisenhower and, 522–525, 538; People-to-People campaign in, 524; national security state and, 531; domestic politics in, 536–538; anticommunism and, 538–540; in 1960s, 554–555; Kennedy and, 555–557; Nixon, Kissinger, and, 582–583; Carter and, 591–592; Reagan and, 596, 601–603; end of, 611; costs of, 611–612
Cold War, The (Lippmann), 517
Cole (ship): attack on, 623
Cole, Nat ("King"), 545
Collar Laundry Union, 329
Collective bargaining, 326, 394
Collective security, 431, 476, 488
Colleges, *see* Universities and colleges

Collier, John, 467
Colombia, 412
Colonies and colonization, 399; navalism and, 403; after First World War, 430; Vietnam and, 512; Third World nations as, 513
Colorado, 307, 309
Colored Farmers' National Alliance, 368
Colored Women's Federation, 388
Color line: in baseball, 352, 541
Colson, Charles, 585
Columbian Exposition (1893), 299, 350
Columbia University: in First World War, 427
Columbine High School: murders at, 623–624, 624(illus.)
Comic operas, 355
Comics, 356
Commerce: Wilson and, 393; foreign, 399. *See also* Trade
Commercial farming, 314, 368
Commission on Civil Rights, 542–543
Commission plan, *see* City commission plan
Committee for Industrial Organization (CIO), 466
Committee on Public Information (CPI), 427
Committee to Defend America by Aiding the Allies, 485
Committee to Re-elect the President (CREEP), 585
Commons, John R., 335
Commonwealth: Puerto Rico as, 414
Communications, 356, 402; industry, 535
Communism: Marx and, 371; Red Scare (1919–1920) and, 428–429; in China, 484, 520; of Ho Chi Minh, 511, 512; policy toward, 512–513; in Greece, 516; McCarthy and, 522–523; in Vietnam, 529–530; in Southeast Asia, 581; Reagan and, 601; in eastern Europe, 611
Communist Control Act, 539
Communist Party of the United States of America, 428, 458–459, 464, 539
Communities: "dry," 383
Community Action Programs, 562
Commuter railroads, 339
Compulsory school-attendance laws, 325, 331, 352, 383
Computer(s), 636–637, 637
Computer revolution, 543, 590, 620
Comstock laws, 388
Concerned Women for America, 607
Coney Island, 353(illus.)
Confederacy (Civil War South), *see* Reconstruction; South
Congo, 583
Congress (U.S.): Lincoln's 10 percent plan and, 281; ex-Confederates in, 285; and Andrew Johnson, 286; and 1876 election, 296; foreign affairs and, 530; 103rd, 618; Clinton and, 619

Congressional Reconstruction, 286–289, 290, 291

Congress of Racial Equality (CORE), 503, 558, 559, 568

Conkling, Roscoe, 360, 364

Conner, Howard, 492

Connor, Eugene ("Bull"), 558

Conscientious objectors (COs): in First World War, 421

Conscription, *see* Draft (military)

Conservation, 308, 391

Conservatives and conservatism, 406, 427, 537, 585, 597–601, 625; on War on Poverty, 562; in 1960s, 568; on Supreme Court, 599; in 1994 elections, 619

Constitution(s): in Reconstruction, 290; Cuban, 411–412

Constitution (U.S.): document, A2–A7

Constitutional conventions: during Reconstruction, 285, 290

Constitutional doctrines, 394

Construction, 345, 346

Consumer goods, 329–330, 545

Consumers and consumerism, 434, 435–436, 549; stores and, 332; protection measures, 385, 561; in 1920s, 441; Great Depression and, 451; debt of, 545, 590; in 1980s, 609. *See also* Materialism

Consumer society, 313, 318–319, 329–330

Containment doctrine, 512, 517, 519; in Asia, 519–520, 567; CIA and, 528; Kennedy and, 555

Contraception, *see* Birth control

Contract with America, 617, 619

Contras, 604

Coolidge, Calvin, 434, 436, 437

Cooney, Joseph, 317

Copland, Aaron, 450

Copper: in West, 307

Coral Sea, Battle of the, 495(map)

Cordon sanitaire (buffer zone), 430

CORE, *see* Congress of Racial Equality (CORE)

Corn (maize), 301, 314

Coronado Coal Company v. United Mine Workers, 436

Coronavirus, 633

Corporations: consolidation of, 333–334, 371; taxation of, 425; international, 479; ties with Nazi Germany, 482; in Second World War, 497; mergers by, 601; protest against, 621–622. *See also* Business

Corruption: in Reconstruction, 292; in Grant administration, 293; political machines, bosses, and, 348–349; spoils system and, 360–362; Progressives and, 381; in 1980s, 596

Costa Rica: Oscar Arias Sánchez in, 604

Cotton and cotton industry: Civil War and, 367, 368. *See also* Textile industry

Coughlin, Charles (Father), 464

Council of Economic Advisors, 534

Counterculture, 569–570

Counterinsurgency, 556

Counterterrorism, 626–627

Court-packing scheme, 470–471

Courts, *see* Judiciary; Supreme Court (U.S.)

Courtship: automobiles and, 439

Covenant: of League of Nations, 430, 431

Covert operations: by CIA, 519, 523, 527, 528, 604

Cowboys, 308, 314, 315, 315(illus.)

Cowell, Henry, 450

Cox, James M., 437

Coxey, Jacob S., 372

Coxey's army, 372

Crack cocaine, 608–609

Craft unions, 327, 466

Crazy Horse (Oglala Sioux), 303–304

Credit, 440(illus.); for farmers, 393; in 1920s, 439; in 1930s, 471; in 1970s, 588; in 1960s and 1970s, 589–590

Creditors: gold vs. silver issue and, 363

Creel, George, 427

Crime and criminals: urban, 347; after Second World War, 549

Croats, 622

Croker, Richard, 348

Cronkite, Walter, 560

Crop-lien system, 367–368

Crops: Indian, 301; southern, 367, 368; exporting of, 399; in 1920s, 440. *See also* Farms and farming

Croquet, 352

Cross of gold speech (Bryan), 373

Crow Indians, 303

Crusade for Justice: by Mexican Americans, 577

Cruz, Oswaldo, 474

Cryptanalysts: in Second World War, 488, 489

Cuba, 528; in Spanish-American War, 389; immigrants from, 404, 610; revolutions in, 404, 481; independence for, 406; U.S. hegemony in, 411–412, 411(map); Reagan and, 603–604

Cuban immigrants, 404

Cuban missile crisis, 554, 557

Cullen, Countee, 449

Cultural adaptation: by immigrants, 344–345

Cultural imperialism, 398

Cultural nationalism, 575; Puerto Rico and, 414; of African Americans, 576

Culture(s): Indian, 301, 302–305, 438; retention in neighborhoods, 343; African American, 344; diversity in cities, 345; national holidays and, 352; mass, 352–356; missionaries and, 361; Americanization of, 397, 399, 401, 413, 474, 477–479, 517; media and, 439, 544–545; in 1920s, 443–444, 449–450; WPA programs and, 464; in Great Depression, 468–470; middle-class, 543–545, 549–551; whiteness and, 545–546; youth, 547; Mexican American, 577; transformation in 1970s, 590–593; therapeutic, 591; global, 622;

population diversity and, 630. *See also* Popular culture

Culture wars, 608, 625

Cummins v. County Board of Education, 366

Currency: gold vs. silver, 363; 1890s depression and, 370

Cursillo movement, 590–591

Custer, George A., 304, 304(illus.), 305

Cuyahoga River: pollution of, 590

Cycling, 353

Czechoslovakia: German invasion of, 482; Franklin D. Roosevelt and, 483; after Second World War, 515; Stalin and, 519; Prague Spring in, 572; revolution in (1989), 611

Czolgosz, Leon, 389

Daimler, Gottlieb, 319

Dairy farming, 313

Dakotas, 308

Daley, Richard J.: 1968 riots and, 572

Dams: in West, 467

Darrow, Clarence: Scopes trial and, 446–447

Darwin, Charles, 334, 383, 385, 446

Daughters of Bilitis, 580

Daughters of the American Revolution (DAR): Marian Anderson and, 472

Davis, Henry W., 281

Davis, Jefferson, 280

Davis, John W., 437

Dawes Act (1887), 305, 438

Dawes Plan (1924), 479

D-Day, 505

DDT, 549, 550

Dean, James, 547

Dean, John, 586

Death camps: Nazi, 503

Death rates, *see* Mortality

Debs, Eugene V., 328, 371–372, 379, 392, 393, 419; First World War and, 427

Debt: silver vs. gold issue and, 363; farming and, 368; First World War, 479; Russian, 479–480; consumer, 545; in 1960s and 1970s, 589–590

Declaration of Independence: document, A1–A2

Decolonization: of Third World, 525–526

Decoration Day, 279

Deep South: in 1964 election, 561

Deep Throat, 586

Defense (national), 517–519, 522; spending on, 598, 600, 603, 612, 619

Defense Department, 531

Defense industry, 497, 498, 532, 543

Defense of Marriage Act (1996), 631

Deferments: in Second World War, 504

Deficits: in First World War, 423–424; in Second World War, 499; under Eisenhower, 538; in balance of payments, 582; trade, 588, 620; state, 589; in Reagan-Bush era, 596; federal, 600; Clinton and, 620

Defoliants: in Vietnam War, 567, 582

De Gaulle, Charles, 572
Deindustrialization, 588, 617
De Klerk, F. W., 611
DeLeon, Daniel, 373
Demagogues: in New Deal, 462–463
Demczur, Jan, 615–616
Democracy and Education (Dewey), 383
Democratic National Committee: break-in at, 585
Democratic National Convention: in 1964, 561; in 1968, 572
Democratic Party: Klan and, 292; in South, 293; coalitions in, 360; factions in, 360; Populists and, 372, 373; 1896 election and, 372–374; voting base of, 450; voter coalition of, 465–466, 537; in 1960s, 554; Reagan and, 597; in 1990s, 617. *See also* Elections
Demographics: in 21st century, 630; of diversity, 631(map)
Demonstrations: against Vietnam War, 580–581; against WTO, 621–622, 621(illus.). *See also* Protest(s)
Dempsey, Jack, 448
Denmark, 402, 485
Department stores, 324, 332
Dependents' Pension Act, 364, 365
Deportation: of radicals, 428, 429; in Great Depression, 457
Depressions: of 1890s, 370–372, 399. *See also* Great Depression (1930s)
Deregulation, 600–601
Desegregation: foreign policy and, 527; of military, 540; of schools, 541–542, 542(illus.); Nixon and, 585. *See also Brown v. Board of Education of Topeka*
Desert Storm, *see* Operation Desert Storm (1991)
Destroyers: trade of, 486
Détente policy, 582–583, 592
Detroit: black population of, 426; bankruptcy of, 589
Developing nations: use of term, 513; foreign aid to, 527; labor costs in, 620
Dewey, Alice, 383
Dewey, George, 406
Dewey, John, 383
Dewey, Thomas, 537
Díaz, Porfirio, 412
Dictatorships: in Latin America, 481; in 1930s, 481–482
Diem, Ngo Dinh, 530, 563–564
Dienbienphu, battle at, 529
Diet (food): refrigeration and, 323, 331; reform in, 331–332; in 1920s, 443
Diné language, 492
Dingley Tariff (1897), 363, 373
Diplomacy: racism and, 401; *Alabama* claims and, 402; status of U.S. in, 402; before Spanish-American War, 404–405; Open Door policy, 407–410, 409(map); dollar, 413; in Fourteen Points, 422; atomic, 515; Third World and, 527; human rights and,

594; Clinton and, 622; September 11, 2001, and, 633–635
Direct election: of senators, 360, 381, 392
Direct investments: American, 399
Direct primaries, 379, 381
Disabled Americans, 613, 614
Discount rate, 393
Discrimination: in cities, 344; in voting, 365; and segregation, 365–366; against women, 384, 547; against African Americans, 385, 440, 541; in war industries, 497; during Second World War, 503; end of legal, 560–561; in employment, 578; against disabled, 613, 614
Diseases: among Indians, 303; germ theory of, 331, 345, 347; industrialization and, 331; pollution and, 336, 347; in Spanish-American War, 406; yellow fever and, 412; First World War and, 421, 422–423, 424, 424(illus.); AIDS and, 609; in 21st century, 633
Disfranchisement: of blacks, 365, 380
Disinformation: by CIA, 523
District banks, 393
District of Columbia, *see* Washington, D.C.
Diversity, 631(map); in 1970s, 591; in 21st century, 630
Divine, Father (George Baker), 448
Divorce, 352, 631; in 1920s, 443; during Second World War, 500; "no-fault," 591
Dobson, James, 607
Dodd, Samuel, 333
Dole, Bob, 619
Dole, Sanford B., 403
Dollar (U.S.): gold standard and, 588
Dollar diplomacy, 413
Domestic service, 324, 365
Dominican Republic, 295, 402, 412, 480; intervention in, 418; immigrants from, 610
Domino theory, 523, 581
Donnell, Ed, 313
Donnelly, Ignatius, 369
Doolittle raid, 495
Double V campaign, 503
Douglas, Aaron, 449
Douglas, William O., 471
Douglass, Frederick: on white supremacy, 297; on assimilation, 385
Doves: in Vietnam War, 582
Dow Jones Industrial Average, 623, 627
Draft (military): in First World War, 420–421; in Second World War, 488, 494; in Vietnam War, 566
Drama, 355, 449
Dred Scott decision, 295
Dresden: firebombings of, 509
Drinking, *see* Alcohol and alcoholism
Drugs: patent, 390; malaria and, 398; mind control and, 523; hallucinogenic, 569; trade in, 608–609; Noriega and, 612
"Dry" communities, 383
Dry farming, 314
Du Bois, W. E. B., 387, 421, 429, 441

Dukakis, Michael, 610–611
Duke, James B., 323
Dulles, John Foster, 522, 527
Dumbarton Oaks meeting, 505
Dunkirk, 486
Dunne, Edward F., 379
Du Pont de Nemours, E. I., and Company, 322
Du Pont family, 322–323
Dupuy de Lôme, Enrique, 404
Dust Bowl, 451, 453–454, 455, 462, 467
Duties: increase in, 458. *See also* Protective tariffs; Tariffs; Taxation
Dylan, Bob, 569
Dynamic conservatism: of Eisenhower, 538
Dynamic Sociology (Ward), 335

Earp brothers, 308, 309
Earth Day (1970), 590
"East" (communist countries), 513
East Asia: Japanese hegemony in, 413
Eastern Europe: immigrants from, 385; Nazi-Soviet pact and, 483; after Second World War, 505, 507; Soviets and, 515; revolutions in (1989), 611
Easter Rebellion (Ireland), 419
East Germany, 519, 556, 611
Eastman, Crystal, 388
Eastman, George, 356
East St. Louis, Illinois: race riot in, 347, 429
Ebola virus, 633
Ecology: in 1970s, 590. *See also* Environment
Economic boom: of 1980s, 601
Economic Interpretation of the Constitution (Beard), 384
Economic power: of U.S., 400(illus.)
Economics: laissez faire, 334, 335; Progressives and, 384
Economies of scale, 323
Economy: Indian, 301–302; western irrigation and, 309–310; boom-and-bust cycles and, 333; from sectional to national, 371; regulation of, 393–394; foreign trade and, 399; Cuba and, 404; of Philippines, 407; First World War and, 417–418, 425–426, 477–479; in 1920s, 435–436; materialism and, 438–439; New Deal and, 460–461, 463(illus.); Second World War and, 472, 494; U.S. role in worldwide, 477–479, 478(illus.); in Third World, 527; postwar, 534; in 1950s, 543; middle-class culture and, 549–550; Kennedy and, 560; in 1970s, 587–590; Reagan and, 596, 598, 599–601; George H. W. Bush and, 613, 618; Clinton and, 618; globalization and, 619–622. *See also* Boom-and-bust cycles; Panics (financial)
Ecosystem: global interaction and, 633
Ederle, Gertrude, 448
Edge Act, 479
Edison, Thomas A., 319, 355
Edison Electric Light Company, 319

Ed Sullivan Show, 547–549, 569, 571, 571(illus.)
Education, 443–444; for blacks, 284, 366, 367(illus.), 385; for Indians, 305; reform in, 349; compulsory school-attendance laws, 352, 383; American missionaries and, 361; in Progressive era, 383–384; U.S. system in Philippines, 408; in 1930s, 470; after Second World War, 535; NDEA and, 538; for women, 547; of new immigrants, 609–610. *See also* Public schools; Schools
Educational Amendments Act (1972): Title IX of, 452, 608
Education Department, 587
EEOC, *see* Equal Employment Opportunity Commission (EEOC)
Efficiency: Taylor and, 323–324; in Progressive era, 379
Egypt, 527; Suez crisis and, 525; Camp David accords and, 592
Eighteenth Amendment, 382, 383, 449, A9
Eighth Amendment, A8
Eight-hour workday, 352
Eisenhower, Dwight D., 505; Korean War and, 522; Cold War and, 522–525; military and, 523; Cuba and, 528; Suez crisis and, 529; Vietnam and, 529–530; on "military-industrial complex," 531, 538; 1952 election and, 538; domestic policy of, 538; on racial segregation, 541; Pledge of Allegiance and, 551–552
Eisenhower Doctrine, 529
Elections: of **1866**, 285, 287; of **1868**, 289; of **1872**, 293; of **1874**, 293; of **1876**, 296, 296(map), 364; of **1896**, 359, 363, 365, 370, 372–374; **1876 to 1897**, 360; of senators, 360, 381, 392; of **1880**, 364, 365; of **1884**, 364; of **1888**, 364; of **1890**, 364; of **1892**, 369–370; of **1900**, 374, 379; voter participation in, 378; nonpartisan, 379, 381; Progressive reforms for, 379; of **1912**, 392; of **1916**, 393; of **1918**, 430; of **1920**, 436–437; of **1924**, 437; of **1928**, 450–451; of **1932**, 459; of **1936**, 465, 483; of **1952**, 522, 538; of **1948**, 537; of **1960**, 555; of **1964**, 561; of **1968**, 572; of **1972**, 585; of **1974**, 587; of **1980**, 593, 596; of **1988**, 596, 597, 610–611; of **1984**, 600; of **1992**, 618; of **1996**, 619; of **2000**, 625–626; of **2002**, 627; list of presidential, A12–A16
Electoral commission: in 1876, 296
Electricity, 318, 435–436, 438; electrical industry and, 319; in textile industry, 323; nuclear power for, 538
Electric-powered streetcars, 339
Electric sewing machine, 323
Electric signs, 332
Electronics, 535
Elevated railroads, 339
Elevators, 346
Eleventh Amendment, A8

Eliot, Charles W., 383
Eliot, T. S., 449
Elites: industrialization and, 330; foreign policy and, 399; in Philippines, 408; Hispanic, 441
Ellsberg, Daniel, 574–575, 585
El movimiento, 577
El Paso: Hispanics in, 610
El Salvador, 604, 610
Ely, Richard, 335
Emancipation: Fourteenth Amendment and, 287
Embargo: by OPEC, 576, 583, 584; against Nicaragua, 604
Embassies: in Teheran, 593
Emergency Banking Relief Bill, 460
Emergency Fleet Corporation, 426
Emergency Quota Act (1921), 446
Emerging markets, 620
Empires: U.S., 398; benefits of, 401; anti-imperialists and, 402; after First World War, 423; after Second World War, 513
Employees: working class as, 324
Employers: control over workers, 324
Employment: sex discrimination in, 324; trends in, 325(illus.); in government, 360–362; minimum age of, 381; in First World War, 425–426; in Second World War, 497; by Defense Department, 531; of women, 546; discrimination in, 578; Los Angeles riots and, 617. *See also* Labor
Employment Board: of Civil Service Commission, 540
"Enemies lists": of Nixon, 585
Enemy Alien Camps, 502
Energy crisis: in 1970s, 576, 583, 584; Carter and, 587; economy and, 588
Energy Department, 587
Enforcement Acts, 293
Engineering: railroads and, 310; urban, 348; advances in, 398
England (Britain), 398; transatlantic cable and, 321, 321(illus.); immigrants from, 341; models for reform from, 378; economic power of, 400(illus.); *Alabama* claims and, 402; Samoa and, 402–403; Venezuela dispute and, 404; in China, 407, 409(map); Panama Canal and, 412; Anglo-American cooperation and, 413; in First World War, 417, 418; Irish and, 419; Munich Conference and, 482; Second World War and, 483, 486(map), 490, 513; Dunkirk withdrawal and, 486; Operation War Bride in, 501(illus.); Cold War and, 515; Palestine and, 528; Suez crisis and, 529
English language, 344; as "official" language, 610
Enola Gay (airplane), 509
Enron: collapse of, 627
Entertainment: in 1920s, 439

Entrepreneurs: in Machine Age, 319
Environment: Southwestern Indians and, 302; ranching and, 315; atomic bomb and, 510; degradation of, 549; Nixon and, 585; Reagan and, 598–599; WTO and, 621(illus.); in 1990s, 623; George W. Bush and, 626; global interaction and, 633; health and, 633
Environmentalism: in 1970s, 590
Epidemics: typhoid, 406; influenza, 422–423, 424, 424(illus.); AIDS, 609. *See also* Diseases
Epstein, Abraham, 443
Equal Employment Opportunity Commission (EEOC), 561, 578, 579
Equality: southern Republican Party and, 291; cultural nationalism and, 576; for women, 579–580
Equal opportunity: ADA and, 614
Equal-protection clause, 297–298
Equal rights: Second World War and, 503
Equal rights amendment (ERA): of 1920s, 438; of 1970s, 579–580, 585, 596
Espionage Act (1917), 427
Estonia, 430, 483, 514, 611
Ethics: biogenetics and, 632–633
Ethiopia: Italian invasion of, 482
Ethnic cleansing, 622
Ethnic groups: foods of, 356; immigration quotas on, 446; in postwar period, 534; in 1950s, 550; identity politics and, 576; affirmative action for, 578; hatreds among, 622
Eugenics, 385
Europe and Europeans: immigration from, 307, 341; imperialism of, 398; Latin America and, 413; Monroe Doctrine and, 413; after First World War, 476–477, 479; Second World War and, 481–483, 506(map), 507–508, 513, 518(map); Nazi invasions of, 486(map); student protests in, 572
"Europe First" strategy, 496, 506(map)
Evangelicalism: in 1970s, 590
Evans, Hiram Wesley, 445
Evers, Medgar, 559
"Evil empire": Reagan on, 603
Evolution: theory of, 383, 446–447; fundamentalist Christians on, 607
Exceptionalism, 398–399
Exchange rates: in 1970s, 588
Exclusion: in Gilded Age, 359
Executive and executive branch, *see* President and presidency
Executive Orders: No. 8802, 497; on racial discrimination, 540
Exodusters, 296, 307
Expansion and expansionism: after Civil War, 295, 398; foreign policy and, 398–399; of foreign trade, 399, 400(illus.); racism and, 399–401; navalism and, 403; Hawai'i and, 403–404; Cuban crisis and, 404; Venezuelan boundary dispute and, 404; by Japan, 485(map)
Ex parte Milligan, 295

Export-Import Bank, 479, 480, 481
Exports, 477, 479, 620; increase in, 399, 400(illus.); of U.S. surpluses, 399; to Latin America, 410
Extinction: of buffalo, 305
Extraterritoriality: in China, 484

Factions: in party politics, 360
Factor, Max, 439
Factories: women in, 324, 426; child labor in, 325; in Second World War, 497, 498
Fads: in 1920s, 441
Fair employment, 540
Falwell, Jerry, 607, 607(illus.), 609
Families: slavery and, 283; Navajo, 302; incomes of, 330; of immigrants, 341; home-ownership by, 343; inner-city housing for, 345, 346(illus.); sizes of, 350; structure of, 350; in urban areas, 350–352; boarding and, 351; stages of, 352; women's employment and, 444; in Great Depression, 457; during Second World War, 500; in 1950s, 546; single-parent and blended, 591, 631; in 21st century, 630–631; changes in, 632(illus.)
Family and Medical Leave Act, 625
Family planning, 395
Family values: Reagan on, 598(illus.)
Farewell Address: of Eisenhower, 538
Farmers' Alliances, 358, 367, 368–369; sub-treasury scheme of, 437
Farmers' Holiday Association, 458
Farms and farming: sharecropping and, 284, 367–368; irrigation for, 309; in Great Plains, 310–314; debt, silver coinage, and, 363; crop-lien system, 367–368; tenant farming, 367–368; commercial, 368; in Midwest, 368; in Southwest, 368; in West, 368; global marketplace and, 371; credit for, 393; price supports for, 394; exportation of agricultural goods and, 399; in 1920s, 436; Coolidge and, 437; large-scale, 440; Great Depression and, 451, 455; in Dust Bowl, 453–454; AAA and, 461; agribusiness and, 550. See also Agriculture; Ranching
Farm Security Administration (FSA), 453–454
Farm workers: Mexican, 441
Far West, see West
Fascists: in United States, 457; Popular Front against, 464; in 1930s, 470; in Italy, 481; in Spanish Civil War, 482. See also Nazi Germany
Faubus, Orval E., 541, 542
Fauset, Jessie, 449
FBI, see Federal Bureau of Investigation (FBI)
Federal Arts Project: of WPA, 464
Federal Aviation Administration, 599
Federal budget: tariff revenues and, 362; in 1890, 364; deficit in, 600; Clinton and deficit, 620

Federal Bureau of Investigation (FBI): anti-communism and, 539; antiterrorism efforts of, 627
Federal Emergency Relief Agency, 471
Federal Farm Loan Act (1916), 393
Federal government, see Government (U.S.)
Federal Highway Act (1921), 439
Federal Housing Administration (FHA), 536
Federal police power, 384
Federal Reserve Act (1913), 393
Federal Reserve Board, 393, 588; in 1930s, 471; stagflation controlled by, 600
Federal Theater Project, 464
Federal Trade Commission (FTC), 393, 436
Federal Writers Project (FWP), 465
Felt, Mark, 586
Female-headed households: poverty in, 563
Feminine Mystique, The (Friedan), 578
Femininity: in 1920s, 445
Feminism and feminists, 388, 578–580, 579; abortion and, 395; Moral Majority and, 607. See also Women; Women's movement
Fences: barbed wire and, 314–315
Ferraro, Geraldine, 600
Fiction: after Second World War, 549
Field, Cyrus, 321, 402
Fifteenth Amendment, 281, 289, 293, 296, 365, A9; citizenship rights in, 303; voting rights and, 366
Fifth Amendment, A7–A8
Filene, E. A., 379
Filibuster: over antilynching bill, 471
Filipinos: in Second World War, 495. See also Philippines
Film industry, see Movies and movie industry
Finances: of railroads, 310
Financiers, 334
Financing: by cities, 349; of Social Security, 473; Reagan and, 600. See also Economy
Finland, 422, 430, 485
Finlay, Carlos Juan, 412, 474
Fireside Chats, 460, 487
Firestorms, 508, 509
First Amendment, A7
First Hundred Days: of Franklin D. Roosevelt, 460, 461
First New Deal, 459–461
"First World," 513
First World War, 393–394; women in, 388; Japan and, 413; American attitude toward, 415–417; United States in, 416, 420; alliances in, 417; economy in, 417–418; neutrality during, 417–418; draft in, 420–421; soldiers in, 420–423; casualties in, 422–423; end of, 422–423; home front in, 423–426; civil liberties and, 427–428; Red Scare after, 428–429; Great Depression and, 451; Europe after, 476–477
Fish, Hamilton, 402
Fisk University, 284
Fitzgerald, F. Scott, 449
Five-Dollar-Day plan, 322, 324

Five-Power Treaty, 477
Florida: 2000 election and, 625–626
Flu, see Influenza pandemic
Flynn, Elizabeth Gurley, 328
Focus on the Family, 607
Foner, Eric, 292
Fong, Hiram, 573
Fongs (Chinese associations), 343
Food(s): production of, 318; canned, 319, 331; refrigeration and, 323, 331; processed, 331; purity of, 390; in 1920s, 443. See also Agriculture; Crops; Diet (food)
Food Administration, 425
Food stamps, 562, 598
Football, 353–355
Forbes, Charles, 437
Forbes, Malcolm, 609
Ford, Gerald, 576, 585, 586, 587
Ford, Henry, 319–322, 419, 477; Five-Dollar-Day plan of, 322, 324; in Second World War, 498
Ford Foundation, 527
Ford Motor Company, 322, 324; Model T and, 438; UAW and, 466; in Soviet Union, 480
Fordney-McCumber Tariff Act (1922), 436, 479
Foreign affairs: gendered imagery in, 400; presidential control over, 530; world response after September 11, 2001, 628
Foreign Affairs: Kennan article in, 517
Foreign aid, 522
Foreign-born Americans, 573
Foreign-branch banks, 479
Foreign investment: in U.S. companies, 334; by United States, 399; in Latin America, 410, 411; in Mexico, 412; in Britain, 413
Foreign policy: in late 19th century, 398–399; elite, 399; anti-imperialists and, 406; Theodore Roosevelt and, 410–413; Taft and, 413; League of Nations and, 431; toward Latin America, 480–481; after Second World War, 513–517; CIA and, 523; racism and, 527; toward Israel, 528–529; of Truman, 538; Kennedy and, 555; Peace Corps and, 556; of Lyndon Johnson, 563–567; Kissinger and, 575–576; of Nixon, 575–576, 582–583; Carter and, 592; Reagan and, 601–606. See also Annexation
Foreign Relations Committee, 399
Foreign service, 399, 523
Foreign trade, see Trade
Forest reserves, 308
Formosa, 407, 522. See also Jiang Jieshi (Chiang Kai-shek)
Formosa Resolution, 525
Foster, Vincent, 619
442nd Regimental Combat Team, 503
"Four-Minute Men," 427
Fourteen Points, 422

Fourteenth Amendment, 281, 286–287, 293, 326, 333, 366, 384, A8–A9; Supreme Court and, 295, 296, 297; equal-protection clause of, 297–298; citizenship rights in, 303

Fourth Amendment, A7

Fragging, 581

France, 398; in Mexico, 402; China and, 407, 409(map); Morocco and, 413; First World War and, 417, 421–422, 430; black soldiers in, 421; Munich Conference and, 482; Second World War and, 483, 485–486, 513; Vietnam and, 511, 512, 520, 529; Indochina and, 520; Suez crisis and, 529; student protests in, 572

Franco, Francisco, 482

Frankfurter, Felix, 471

Franklin, Aretha, 569

Franz Ferdinand (Austria-Hungary), 417

Fraternal societies, 329

Free blacks, *see* African Americans; Slaves and slavery

Freedmen's Bureau, 282, 284, 286

Freedom(s): of speech, 428, 432–433; during Second World War, 500; New Right and, 607–608

Freedom Riders, 558

Freedom Schools, 558

Freedom Summer (1964), 558

Freedpeople (Civil War), 282–284; black codes for, 285–286; land redistribution and, 288; male voting and, 290; economic progress and, 291; failure of Reconstruction and, 292

Free enterprise: Progressivism and, 380, 381; Reagan and, 599

"Free love," 570

Free-market system: Reagan and, 598; in former Soviet Union, 611

Free people of color, 284

Free silver, 372

Free Speech and Headlight, The, 365

Free Speech Movement (FSM), 568–569

Free trade, 362, 514, 620–621

French Communist Party, 520

French Indochina, 488

Frey, John, 317

Frick, Henry C., 328

Friedan, Betty, 578

Friedman, Thomas L., 620

Friendship Seven (space capsule), 560

Frontier: closing of, 299, 301; Turner and, 299, 403; end of, 306(map); Australian, 311, 311(illus.); ranching, 314–315

FTC cease-and-desist orders, 393

Fuel Administration, 425

Fulbright, J. William, 491, 567

Full Employment Act (1946), 534, 537

Fundamentalism: in 1920s, 446–447; Christian, 446–447, 590, 607–608; Islamic, 615–616, 623

Gabaccia, Donna, 356

Gadsden Purchase, 398

Galton, Francis, 385

Gandhi, Mohandas K., 432, 542

Gangsters, 449

Garbage, 348

Garfield, James A., 321, 362, 364

Garment industry: labor in, 610

Garvey, Marcus, 429, 441

Gas warfare, 421

Gates, Bill, 620

Gates, Frederick, 401

GATT, *see* General Agreement on Tariffs and Trade (GATT)

Gay liberation, 580. See also Homosexuals and homosexuality

Gay Power and Gay Pride, 580

Gays, *see* Homosexuals and homosexuality

Gaza Strip, 583, 592, 604, 622

Geary Act (1892), 344

Gebhardt, William, 356

Gender and gender roles: for Indian children, 305; in West, 307; employment discrimination and, 324; during Second World War, 500; postwar benefits and, 536; roles in 1950s, 546; Civil Rights Act of 1964 and, 560–561; courses in, 579. *See also* Men; Women

Gender gap, 613, 626

General Agreement on Tariffs and Trade (GATT), 620

General Electric Company, 319, 333, 436, 439, 480

General Federation of Women's Clubs, 438

General Motors (GM), 466, 497, 543, 588

Generation gap: in 1960s, 554

Geneva Accords (1954), 529

Geneva Prisoners of War Convention (1949), 521–522

Genome mapping, 633

"Gentleman's agreement": with Japan, 401

Geography: of Soviet Union, 514

George, Henry, 335

Georgia: homosexual sex in, 599

German Americans, 417, 427

Germany, 398; immigrants from, 341; Samoa and, 402–403; China and, 407, 409(map); Morocco and, 413; *Lusitania* and, 415; First World War and, 417–418, 423, 430, 431; submarine warfare by, 419–420; reparations from, 451, 479; Great Depression (1930s) in, 481; after Second World War, 513; Soviets and, 515; zones in, 515; Berlin Wall in, 556; economy of, 588; reunification of, 611. See also East Germany; Nazi Germany; Second World War; West Germany

Germ theory of disease, 331, 345, 347

Gershwin, George, 450

Ghana, 527

Ghettos, 440

Ghost Dance, 305

GI Bill of Rights, 503, 534, 535

Gilbert Islands, 403

Gilded Age, 358–374, 388

Gilded Age, The (Twain and Warner), 358

Gilman, Charlotte Perkins, 388

Gingrich, Newt, 617, 619, 625

Ginsburg, Ruth Bader, 547

Gish, Lillian, 356

Gitlow, Benjamin, 428

Glackens, William, 405(illus.)

Gladden, Washington, 385

Glasnost (openness), 606

Glenn, John, 560

Glidden, Joseph F., 314

Global economy: United States in, 588

Globalization, 619–622, 633–636; use of term, 616; Clinton and, 617

Global marketplace: in 1890s, 371

Global telecommunications: transatlantic telegraph cable and, 321

GNP, *see* Gross national product (GNP)

Godkin, E. L., 402

Gold: in West, 307; 1890s depression and reserves of, 370; discoveries of, 373

Gold Democrats, 372, 373

Goldman, Emma, 428

Gold rush, 307, 363

Gold standard, 363, 372, 373, 588

Gold Standard Act (1900), 373

Goldwater, Barry, 561, 564, 597

Gollop, Rahel, 337, 351

Gompers, Samuel, 327, 373, 407, 426

Gonorrhea: among Indians, 303

Gonzáles, Rudolfo ("Corky"), 577

Good Earth, The (Buck), 483

Goodman, Andrew, 558

Good Neighbor policy, 480–481

Google, 636

GOP ("Grand Old Party," Republican Party), 516

Gorbachev, Mikhail, 596, 601, 606, 611

Gore, Al, 619, 623, 625–626

Gospel of Wealth, 334

Gould, Jay, 327

Government: Reconstruction, 290–292; urban, 347; civic reform and, 349; Progressives and, 379, 381; business cooperation with, 436–437; bankruptcy of local, 618. See also Government (U.S.)

Government (U.S.): Indian policy of, 303; West and, 316; business and, 334–335, 425, 436; employment in, 360–362; in First World War, 423–425; New Deal and, 455; in Great Depression, 458; power of, 467–468; South and, 468; Franklin D. Roosevelt and, 472; military contracts and, 497; fair employment by, 540; school integration and, 541–542; Nixon and, 585; Reagan and, 596, 598; under Clinton, 625. *See also* New Deal

Government agencies: in First World War, 425

Governors: during Reconstruction, 285; Progressive, 380, 381

Graduated income tax, 393

Graft, 348

Graham, Billy, 545

Grand Alliance, 494

Grand Army of the Republic, 360

Grand Canyon, 391

Grand Coulee Dam, 458, 461, 467

Grange movement, 367, 368

Granger laws, 368

Grant, Julia, 294

Grant, Madison, 385, 446

Grant, Ulysses S., 288, 402; Reconstruction and, 289; corruption and, 293; world tour by, 294, 294(illus.); civil service and, 362

Grape growers: Mexican American strike against, 576–577

Grateful Dead, 569

Great Atlantic and Pacific Tea Company (A&P), 332

Great Britain, *see* England (Britain)

Great Communicator: Reagan as, 597

Great Depression (1930s): activism during, 432; causes of, 451; Hoover and, 455–459; bank crisis in, 459–460; labor during, 466–467; federal power in, 467–468; international debt default in, 479; in Germany, 481. *See also* Unemployment

Greater East Asia Co-Prosperity Sphere, 485(map), 488

Great Gatsby, The (Fitzgerald), 449

Great Lakes Naval Training Station, 327

Great Migration: of African Americans, 440

Great Plains, 300; farming in, 310–314; Farmers' Alliances in, 368–369; Dust Bowl in, 453–454

Great powers: in U.N., 515

Great Society, 554, 560–563, 562(illus.), 567–570

Great War, The, *see* First World War

"Great White Fleet," 413

Greece, 513, 516

Greeley, Horace, 293

Greenbacks, 370

Green Corn Rebellion, 427

Green Party, 625

Greensboro, North Carolina, 553–554

Greenville, Treaty of, 303

Greer (ship), 488, 490–491

Grenada: invasion of, 604

Gresham, Walter Q., 399

Griffith, D. W., 356, 429

Grocery chains, 332

Gross national product (GNP): after First World War, 425; in Great Depression, 454; decline in, 600; in 1990s, 620

Guadalcanal, battle at, 492

Guadalupe Hidalgo, Treaty of, 577

Guadeloupe: immigrants from, 342(illus.)

Guam, 406, 490, 496

Guantánamo Bay: naval base at, 412

Guardianship laws, 290

Guatemala: CIA and, 523; Arbenz Guzmán in, 528; immigrants from, 610

Guerrilla warfare: in Philippines, 407

Guiteau, Charles, 364

Gulflight (ship), 418

Gulf of Tonkin Resolution, 564

Gulf War, *see* Persian Gulf War (1991)

Guomindang Party, 484

Gypsies: Nazis and, 503

Ha, Nguyet Thu, 595–596

Habeas corpus, writ of, 293

Hague peace conferences (1899, 1907), 413

Haight-Ashbury district (San Francisco), 570

Haiti, 418, 480, 622

Halberstam, David, 555

Half Breeds, 360

Hall, G. Stanley, 383

Hallucinogenic drugs, 569

Hamer, Fannie Lou, 561

Hamilton, Alexander, 381

Hampton, Fred, 568

Hampton Institute, 305

Handler, Ruth, 548

Hanna, Marcus A., 372

Hanoi, *see* North Vietnam

Haole (foreigners), 403

Harding, Warren G., 436–437

Harlem: violence in, 567

Harlem Renaissance, 449

Harper's magazine, 405(illus.)

Harris, Eric, 623–624

Harrison, Benjamin, 308, 364, 403

Harrison, William Henry, 364

Harte, Bret, 309

Harvard University, 383

Hate crimes: in 1990s, 623–624

Havana, 481, 528; Inter-American conference in, 480

Hawai'i, 295, 398, 495(map); annexation and, 403–404, 406; Pearl Harbor attack in, 488–489, 489(illus.)

Hawks: in Vietnam War, 582

Hawley-Smoot Tariff (1930), 458, 479

Hay, John, 399, 410

Hayes, Rutherford B., 296, 296(map), 326, 364

Haymarket Riot, 327, 371

Hay-Pauncefote Treaty (1901), 412, 413

Haywood, William D. (Big Bill), 328

H-bomb, *see* Hydrogen bomb (H-bomb)

Head Start program, 561

Head tax: in First World War, 426

Health: dietary reform and, 331–332; air pollution and, 336; in 21st century, 633. *See also* Diseases

Healthcare: costs of, 563; Clinton and, 619

Health Insurance Portability and Accounting Act, 625

Hearst, William Randolph, 356, 404

Hefner, Hugh, 547

Hegemony: of U.S. in Caribbean and Latin America, 411(map), 413; of Japan in East Asia, 413; of United States, 517

"Hello girls," 421

Hemingway, Ernest, 449

Henry, Guy V., 412

Hepatitis C and E, 633

Hepburn Act (1906), 390

Herbert, Victor, 355

Herbicides: in Vietnam War, 582

Higginson, Thomas Wentworth, 366

Higher education, *see* Universities and colleges

Higher Education Act, 452, 579, 608

High schools, 383

High-tech industries, 620

Highway Act (1956), 536

Highways, *see* Roads and highways

Hijackings: on September 11, 2001, 626, 627

Hill, Anita, 613

Hill, David, 372

Hiraoka, Hiroshi, 354

Hiroshima: bombing of, 494, 509

Hispanics: racism against, 295; in West, 307; migration by, 341; immigration of, 441; in postwar period, 536; percentage of, 544; Census classification of, 576; poverty of, 608; birth rate of, 610; Los Angeles riots and, 617–618; 2000 election and, 626; population growth of, 630

Hiss, Alger, 539

Hitler, Adolf, 454, 470, 476, 481–482, 505; 1936 Olympics and, 469; Franklin D. Roosevelt and, 471; automobile production and, 477–479; radio use by, 487; suicide by, 493, 508. *See also* Nazi Germany

HIV (human immunodeficiency virus), 609, 614

Hmong immigrants, 573

Hobos, 471

Ho Chi Minh, 432, 511–512, 520, 529–530, 563

Ho Chi Minh City, 565(map), 581

Hoffman, Elizabeth Cobbs, 556

Holden v. Hardy, 326, 384

Holding company, 334

Holidays: celebrations of, 352; Kwanzaa, 576

Holliday, John Henry ("Doc"), 309

Holliman, John, 602(illus.)

Hollywood, *see* Movies and movie industry

"Hollywood Ten," 539

Holmes, Oliver Wendell, Jr., 384, 428

Holocaust, 503–504

Home front: in First World War, 423–426; in Second World War, 494, 498–500

Homeland Security Department, 531

Homelessness: in 1890s depression, 370; in Great Depression, 455; in 1980s, 609

Homeownership, 343

Homestead Act (1862), 313

Homestead strike, 328, 371

Homosexuals and homosexuality: subculture in cities, 351; in 1920s, 445; Nazis and, 503; Kinsey on, 547; gay liberation and, 580; in 1970s, 591; Supreme Court and, 599; AIDS and, 609; in military, 619; same-sex couples and, 630–631; antigay movement and, 631

Honduras, 528

Hong Kong, 407, 490

Hoover, Herbert, 425, 437, 438; business and, 436; 1928 election and, 450; Great Depression and, 454, 455, 457–458; 1932 election and, 459

Hoover, J. Edgar, 428, 429, 541, 559

Hoovervilles, 455, 459

Hope, John, 366

Horizontal integration, 333

Horton, Willie, 611

Hostage crisis (Iran), 592–593, 597, 604

Hostile takeovers, 601

Hot line: with Soviet Union, 557

House, Edward, 422

Households: structure of, 350; appliances for, 436; in 1920s, 443; poverty in, 550; in late 20th century, 632(illus.)

House Judiciary Committee: Andrew Johnson and, 289

House Un-American Activities Committee (HUAC), 539

Housework: in 1920s, 443

Housing: on Great Plains, 312, 313(illus.); for middle class, 330; suburban, 339, 441, 532; inner-city, 345, 346(illus.); reforms in, 345, 349; subsidized workers', 378; in First World War, 426; for blacks, 440; Levitt and, 536; redlining and, 536; after Second World War, 536; Model Cities program and, 561; rent subsidies and, 561

Houston, Charles Hamilton, 298, 540

Howard University, 284

Howe, Elias, Jr., 332

HUAC, see House Un-American Activities Committee (HUAC)

Huerta, Victoriano, 412

Huerto, Dolores, 576

Hughes, Charles Evans, 393, 437, 476, 477, 484

Hughes, Langston, 449

Hull, Cordell, 477, 479

Hull House, 349, 376

Humanitarian interventions, 622

Human rights, 593, 594

Humphrey, Hubert H., 539, 564, 572

Hungary: after Second World War, 515; revolt in, 525, 611

Hunger: during Great Depression, 455

Hunter, Jane, 350

Hurston, Zora Neale, 449

Hussein (Jordan): CIA and, 523

Hutus: in Rwanda, 622

Hydroelectricity, 391, 467

Hydrogen bomb (H-bomb), 519, 523

Hygiene: in 1920s, 443

Ibn Saud (Saudi Arabia), 529

ICBM, see Intercontinental ballistic missile (ICBM)

Ickes, Harold, 464

Idaho, 307, 308

Idealism: in U.S. foreign policy, 527

Identity, 387–388

Identity politics, 576–578

"If We Must Die" (McKay), 429

Igorot people, 401(illus.)

"I Have a Dream" speech (King), 559–560, 559(illus.)

Illegal immigrants, 610

Illinois Central Railroad, 459

Illness: from pollution, 590. See also Diseases

Imbrie, William, 354

IMF, see International Monetary Fund (IMF)

Immigrants and immigration, 378; Civil War and, 293; Chinese, 307; Mexican, 307, 341, 441; to Australia, 311; as workers, 324; unions and, 327, 328; urban areas and, 339, 350; old and new, 341, 573, 595–596; mobility of, 341–343; culture and, 343, 344–345; machine politics and, 349; kinship obligations and, 351; show business and, 355; party politics and, 360; socialism of, 371; eugenics and, 385; in First World War, 426, 427; labor and, 436; Klan and, 445–446, 447; national origin and, 446, 573; quotas on, 446; sources of (1907 and 1927), 447(illus.); in Great Depression, 457; by German Jews, 483; Japanese, 484; Hungarian, 525; population characteristics and, 544; Latin American, 550; in 1980s, 609–610; to Los Angeles, 617–618; in 21st century, 630; from Asia, 630. See also Migration

Immigration Act (1965), 561, 573

Immigration Reform and Control Act (1986), 610

I'm OK—You're OK, 591

Impeachment: of Andrew Johnson, 289; Nixon and, 585, 585(illus.); of Clinton, 617, 624–625

Imperialism: of McKinley, 373–374; cultural, 398; of European nations, 398; of foreign policy elite, 399; formal and informal, 406; Spanish-American War and, 406; arguments for, 407; in Asia, 407–410, 409(map); in Latin America, 480. See also Anti-imperialism

"Imperial presidency," 491, 530

Imports: tariffs and, 393; duties on, 458

Inauguration: of Franklin D. Roosevelt, 459–460; of Carter, 587

Incandescent bulb, 319

Inchon, battle at, 521

Income: industrialization and, 330; in 1920s, 451; during Second World War, 499; in 1990s, 623

Income tax, 392, 393, 425, 437

Incorporation laws, 333

Independence: of Vietnam, 511–512; of Philippines, 513; after Second World War, 513; in Third World, 525; in Cold War, 526(map); of Balkan states, 611

India, 527; after First World War, 432; after Second World War, 513

Indian Defense Association, 438

Indian policy, 303; containment policy, 293–295; in 1920s, 438

Indian Reorganization Act (1934), 467, 550

Indian Rights Association (IRA), 304–305, 438

Indians, see American Indians

Indian Self-Determination and Education Assistance Act (1975), 578

"Indians of All Tribes," 577

Individualism: in West, 316; socialism and, 371

Indochina, 520; after First World War, 432; Japan and, 488; crisis in (1954), 529; immigrants from, 609. See also Vietnam

Indonesia, 527

Industrial accidents, 325–326, 381

Industrial capitalism, 377

Industrialization, 317–333, 378; in South, 291, 323; after Civil War, 293; pollution and, 336; growth of cities and, 338–339

Industrial unions, 466

Industrial Workers of the World (IWW, Wobblies), 328, 426, 427, 428

Industry: railroads and, 310; production by, 320(map); 1890s depression and, 370, 371; electricity and, 435–436; in 1920s, 436; urbanization and, 440; in suburbs, 441; Great Depression and, 451, 455–457; postwar, 535; Eisenhower and, 538; deindustrialization and, 588; in South and West, 588–589; Reaganomics and, 599; high-tech, 620. See also specific industries

Inequality of wealth, 335

Infant mortality, 350–351; in 1920s, 443

Infectious diseases, see Diseases

Inflation: postwar, 534; after Second World War, 537; in 1970s, 576, 587, 588, 590; control of, 600

Influence of Sea Power upon History, The (Mahan), 403

Influenza pandemic: after First World War, 422–423, 424, 424(illus.)

Information technology, 620

Initiative, 379, 381

Injunctions: strikes and, 328

"In loco parentis" doctrine, 569

Inner cities, 345–347, 550

Insider trading scandals, 601

Insull, Samuel, 319

Insurance: old-age, 443

Integrated circuit, 590

Integration: of armed forces, 503, 540; of schools, 541–542, 542(illus.). See also Desegregation; Segregation

Intel, 620

Intellectual thought: Social Darwinism and, 334; on industrialization, 335; Marx and, 371; Progressives and, 384; expansionism and, 399. See also Art(s); Literature

Intelligence operations, 523. See also Spies and spying

Inter-Allied government debts: after World War I, 479

Inter-American conference: in Havana, 480

Intercollegiate Athletic Association, 353–355
Intercollegiate sports, 384, 452
Intercontinental ballistic missile (ICBM), 523, 583
Interest groups, 356
Interlocking directorates, 393
Intermediate-Range Nuclear Forces (INF) Treaty, 606
Internal combustion engine, 318, 319, 322
Internal Security (McCarran) Act, 539
International Brigades: in Spanish Civil War, 482
International Harvester, 480
International Ladies Garment Workers Union (ILGWU), 329
International Monetary Fund (IMF), 514, 621
International order: after First World War, 432, 474–475; after Second World War, 513–517
International Telephone and Telegraph (IT&T), 479
Internet, 636–637
Internet Explorer, 637
Internment: of Japanese Americans, 494, 502–503, 502(illus.); of suspected spies, 502
Interstate commerce: labor strikes and, 328; Sherman Anti-Trust Act and, 335; public welfare and, 384; Congress's power over, 470–471
Interstate Commerce Act (1887), 333, 362
Interstate Commerce Commission (ICC), 362, 390, 391, 436
Interstate highway system, 536
Interventions: and U.S. hegemony in Caribbean and Latin America, 411(map); humanitarian, 622
Intifada (uprising), 606
Inventions: by Edison, 319; of Granville T. Woods, 319. *See also* Technology
Investments, 620; in railroads, 310; in southern industry, 323; foreign, 399; in Latin America, 410, 411, 480; in Third World, 525–527; in 1970s, 590; economy and, 599; risky, 600–601; in South Africa, 606; September 11, 2001, and, 633. *See also* Foreign investment
In vitro fertilization, 632
Involuntary sterilization laws, 385
Iran: Soviets and, 514; U.S. vs. Soviets and, 515; CIA and, 523; hostage crisis in, 592–593, 597, 604
Iran-contra scandal, 433, 604
Iran-Iraq War, 612
Iraq, 513; Saddam Hussein in, 593; war in (2003–), 617, 628–630; weapons inspections in, 628
Ireland: in First World War, 419. *See also* Irish people
Irish people, 341, 417
Iron curtain, 515
Iron industry, 323

"Iron law of wages," 326
Irrigation, 440; in West, 309–310; Newlands Act and, 391
Islam: orthodoxy in, 593. *See also* Muslims
Islamic fundamentalism, 623; in Iran, 604; terrorism and, 615–616. *See also* September 11, 2001, terrorist attacks; Terrorism
Island-hopping: in Pacific War, 495(map), 508
Isolationism, 475, 482
Israel: Arab conflict with, 528–529; creation of, 528–529; 1972 Olympics and, 583; Six-Day War and, 583; terrorism against, 583, 622–623; Yom Kippur War (1973), 583, 584; Camp David accords and, 592; Lebanon invasion by, 604; *intifada* against, 606
Issei, 344
Italian immigrants, 341
Italy: First World War and, 417; in 1930s, 481; Ethiopia invaded by, 482; Second World War and, 490, 505, 513, 515
Iwo Jima, 495(map); Navajo code-talkers and, 492; battle at, 508
IWW, *see* Industrial Workers of the World (IWW, Wobblies)

Jackson, Helen Hunt, 304
Jackson State University: students killed at, 581
Jails, *see* Prisons
Japan: immigrants from, 307, 341; baseball in, 354, 354(illus.); expansion by, 398, 413, 485(map); communications with, 402; in China, 407, 409(map), 410; in East Asia, 413; First World War and, 417, 430; Second World War and, 476, 483–484, 494, 513; Soviet-American relations and, 480; Anti-Comintern Pact and, 482; aggression by, 484; in French Indochina, 488; Pearl Harbor attack by, 488–489, 489(illus.); in Second World War, 494, 495(map), 507–508, 509; in Cold War, 520; Indochina and, 520; alliance with, 522; economy of, 588; automobiles from, 610
Japanese Americans: employed women among, 444–445; internment of, 494, 502–503, 502(illus.); in 442nd Regimental Combat Team, 503
Japanese immigrants, 308, 344, 380, 400–401
Jarvis, Anna, 352
Jazz Age: in 1920s, 449–450
Jazz Singer, The (film), 448
Jefferson, Thomas, 381
Jefferson Airplane, 569
Jewish homeland, *see* Israel
Jews and Judaism: immigration by, 337; pogroms against, 341; Orthodox, 343; religious assimilation and, 344–345; Democratic Party and, 360; on Supreme Court, 393; Balfour Declaration and, 430; 1936 Olympics and, 469; Nazi Germany and, 481, 482, 483; in Second World War,

503–504; in Soviet Union, 592. *See also* Arab-Israeli disputes; Israel
Jiang Jieshi (Chiang Kai-shek), 484, 507–508, 520
Jim Crow, 503, 558; laws, 297, 366, 385
Jinmen (Quemoy), 525
Job Corps, 562
Johnson, Andrew, 280, 284–285; Reconstruction plan of, 281; vs. Congress, 286–287; impeachment of, 289
Johnson, Hiram, 380
Johnson, James Weldon, 429
Johnson, Lyndon B.: Tonkin Gulf crisis and, 491; Vietnam and, 529, 563–567, 570; civil rights and, 554; Kennedy assassination and, 560; Great Society and, 560–563; 1964 election and, 561; War on Poverty and, 561–563; Immigration Act and, 573; affirmative action and, 578; inflation and, 588
Johnson, Tom, 349
Johnson Act (1934), 479
Joint Chiefs of Staff, 531
Jones, Bobby, 448
Jones, Mary Harris ("Mother"), 328
Jones, Paula, 624
Jones, Samuel ("Golden Rule"), 349
Jones Act (1916), 407, 414
Jonesboro: school shootings in, 624
Joplin, Janis, 569
Jordan, 513; Israel peace accord with, 622
Jordan, Barbara, 608
Jordan, Michael, 630
Journalism: yellow, 356; muckrakers in, 379, 383
Judaism, *see* Jews and Judaism
Judiciary: in Gilded Age, 358–359. *See also* Supreme Court (U.S.)
Jungle, The (Sinclair), 379, 390
Junk bonds, 601
Jupiter missiles: in Turkey, 557
Justice Department, 428, 627
Juvenile delinquency, 500, 547, 549

Kaiser, William, 498
Kaiser shipyards, 498
Kamikaze attacks, 508
Kansas Alliance: Populist party and, 369
Kansas and Kansas territory, 310; African American migration to, 296–297; black communities in, 385
Karenga, Maulana, 576
KDKA (radio station), 439
Kearney, Dennis, 344
Keller, Helen, 432
Kelley, Florence, 349, 376, 378, 379, 384
Kelley, Oliver H., 368
Kellogg, John H., 331
Kellogg, William K., 331
Kellogg-Briand Pact (1928), 477, 484
Kennan, George F., 515, 517; on Southeast Asia, 567
Kennedy, Jacqueline, 560

Kennedy, John F.: CIA and, 523; Cuba and, 528; civil rights and, 554, 558–559; Cold War and, 554–557; health of, 555; assassination of, 560; Vietnam and, 563, 564
Kennedy, Robert F., 555, 556, 570, 572, 573
Ken societies, 343
Kent State University: students killed at, 581
Kenya, 583
Kerensky, Aleksander, 422
Kerner, Otto, 567
Kerner Commission report (1968), 567, 608
Khomeini (Ayatollah), 593
Khrushchev, Nikita, 523–525; Cuban missile crisis and, 554, 557; Kennedy and, 556
Kim Il Sung (North Korea), 521
King, Martin Luther, Jr., 541–542, 558, 559; assassination of, 555, 570–572; "I Have a Dream" speech by, 559–560, 559(illus.); March on Washington and, 559–560, 559(illus.)
King, Rodney, 617
Kinsey, Alfred, 547
Kinship: urbanization and, 351, 352
Kipling, Rudyard, 407
Kissinger, Henry, 575–576, 582–583; Vietnam cease-fire and, 581
"Kitchen debate," 525
Klamath Indians, 551
Klan, see Ku Klux Klan
Klebold, Dylan, 623
Knickerbocker Club, 352
Knight Foundation Commission on Intercollegiate Athletics, 452
Knights of Labor, 327
Knox, Frank, 486
Konoye (Japan), 488
Korea, 407; Japan and, 413, 484; split of, 520–521. See also North Korea; South Korea
Korean immigrants, 610; segregation of, 400–401; Los Angeles riots and, 617–618
Korean War, 520–522, 537–538; consequences of, 522; desegregated military in, 540
Kosovo War, 622
Kristallnacht, 483
Ku Klux Klan, 281, 292, 293, 369, 541; after First World War, 429; 1924 election and, 437; in 1920s, 445–446, 447; in Great Depression, 459; civil rights workers and, 558
Kuwait, 612
Kwanzaa holiday, 576
Kyoto protocol (1997), 623, 626

Labor: immigrant, 307, 441, 446, 610; in West, 308; for railroads, 310; in textile industry, 323; in tobacco industry, 323; mechanization and, 324–326; increase in wage, 330–331; reforms in, 381, 391–392; in First World War, 425–426; African American, 426; public opinion on, 436; of women, 444, 444(illus.); in Great Depression, 454, 466–467; in 1970s, 588; international, 620. See also Slaves and slavery; Strikes (labor)

Labor and Commerce Department, 390
Laboratory School (University of Chicago), 383
Labor Department: in First World War, 426
Labor unions, 379; Knights of Labor as, 327; AFL as, 327–328; IWW as, 328; membership of, 329; women and, 329; Sherman Anti-Trust Act and, 335; Theodore Roosevelt and, 390–391; anti-imperialism and, 407; in First World War, 426; prosecution of, 436; craft vs. industrial workers and, 466; in Great Depression, 466; in Second World War, 498; Taft-Hartley Act and, 534–535, 537; in 1950s, 543, 550; Reagan and, 599; free-trade agreements and, 620–621. See also Trade unions
Laffer, Arthur, 599
Laffer curve, 599
La Follette, Philip, 464
La Follette, Robert M. ("Battling Bob"), 381, 390, 392; First World War and, 420
La Follette, Robert M., Jr., 464
LaHayes, Beverly, 607
Laissez faire, 334, 335, 381
Lakota Indians, 301, 303–304, 305
Land: freedpeople and, 283; redistribution of, 288; in West, 301, 307; Dawes Severalty Act and, 305; Indians and, 305, 467, 551, 578; preservation of public, 308; reclamation and irrigation for, 309; in Great Plains, 313; for cattle industry, 314; Mexican American, 577; private acquisition of, 598–599
Land-grant colleges, 383, 384
Landlords: in inner city, 345
Landon, Alf, 465
Lange, Dorothea, 456(illus.)
Language(s): Indian, 303; English as "official," 610
Laos, 565(map), 581
La Raza Unida (RUP), 577
Las Gorras Blancas (White Hats), 368
Latin America, 374; immigrants from, 341, 550; U.S. power in, 398, 410, 411(map), 480–481; intervention in, 410–411, 411(map), 412, 477; Roosevelt Corollary and, 411(map), 412; air travel to, 442; American business in, 477; Franklin D. Roosevelt and, 480–481; Soviet Union and, 515; nationalism in, 525; United Fruit Company in, 528; Alliance for Progress and, 556; Nixon, Kissinger, and, 583; Carter and, 592. See also Central America; South America
Latinos, see Hispanics
Latvia, 430, 483, 514, 611
Law(s): in West, 308; Progressives and, 379, 384
Law enforcement: in cities, 348
Leach, William R., 375
League of Nations, 417, 422, 430–431, 475, 476; German withdrawal from, 482; Japanese aggression and, 484

League of Women Voters, 438, 485
Lear, Norman, 608
Lease, Mary Elizabeth, 358, 369, 374
Lebanon, 430, 513, 529; Israeli invasion of, 604; U.S. marines in, 604–606
Le Duc Tho, 581
Left (political), 464, 562. See also Liberals and liberalism
Legal Defense and Education Fund, 540
Legal thought: Progressive, 384
Legislation: for working conditions, 326; antitrust, 335; pollution, 336; in Gilded Age, 358, 360–363; in New Deal, 460–461, 462; under Clinton, 625. See also Law(s)
Leisure, 352–356, 436; party politics and, 360; in 1920s, 448–449
Le Monde: on September 11, 2001, attacks, 628
Lend-Lease Act (1941), 488
Lenin, V. I., 422, 430
Leningrad, see St. Petersburg
Lennon, John, 571
Lesbians: gay liberation movement and, 580. See also Homosexuals and homosexuality
Levitt, William, 536
Lewinsky, Monica, 624
Lewis, John (civil rights activist), 558
Lewis, John L. (labor leader), 466
Liberal Republicans, 293
Liberals and liberalism, 379, 560–563, 568, 585
Liberator bombers, 498
Liberty League, 462, 466
Liberty Loans, 427
Liberty-of-contract doctrines, 394
Liberty ships, 498
Life expectancy, 331, 351
Lifespan: in 1920s, 443; Social Security and, 473
Life stages: in late 19th century, 351–352
Lifestyle: on Great Plains, 312; of wage workers, 329; industrialization and, 329–333, 330(illus.); of immigrants, 337; spread of American, 399; automobiles and, 438–439; of working class, 439; of Mexican workers, 441; in 1920s, 441–445; in Second World War, 498–500, 504–505; suburban, 532–534; in 1950s, 543–545; of Indians, 578; after September 11, 2001, 627. See also Culture(s)
Light bulb, 319
Lili'uokalani (Hawai'i), 403
Lilli doll, 548, 548(illus.)
Lincoln, Abraham: 10 percent plan of, 281; Wade-Davis bill and, 282
Lindbergh, Charles A., 434, 442, 468
Lindsey, Ben, 378
Lippmann, Walter, 564
Literacy: growth in, 356; of soldiers, 504
Literacy requirements, 365, 380; in First World War, 426

Literature: about West, 309, 316; Arabic, 361; muckrakers and, 379; in 1920s, 449; after Second World War, 549
Lithuania, 430, 483, 514, 611
Little Big Horn, battle at, 304, 304(illus.)
Littlefield, Henry M., 374
Little Rock, Arkansas: school integration in, 541–542, 542(illus.)
"Little Rock Nine," 541–542
Livestock: of Indians, 301. *See also* Cattle and cattle industry
Livingston, Robert, 625
Livingstone College, 367(illus.)
Lloyd George, David, 430
Loans: business and, 334; in First World War, 418; in Great Depression, 458; to Germany, 479; to Latin America, 480
Lobbying: in 1920s, 436
Local government(s): bankruptcies of, 618
Locarno Pact (1925), 477
Lochner v. New York, 326, 384
Locke, Alain, 449
Lodge, Henry Cabot, 398, 399, 403, 431, 476
London: Nazi blitz in, 487, 494
Lonely Crowd, The (Riesman), 549
Long, Huey, 464
Lopez, Jennifer, 630
Los Alamos, New Mexico, 497
Los Angeles: railroads in, 310; suburbs of, 441; Hispanics in, 550, 610; drug-related deaths in, 608; Rodney King riot in, 617; immigrants in, 617–618
Lost Generation: in 1920s, 449
Louis, Joe, 468, 470(illus.)
Love Canal: pollution of, 590
Loyalists (Spanish Civil War), 482
Loyalty oaths: for white southerners, 285, 287
Loyalty risk: in 1950s, 539
Luce, Henry, 490
Luftwaffe (German air force), 486
Lumber industry, 306(map), 307, 323
Luna Park, 353(illus.)
Lusitania (ship), 415, 418
Luxuries, 329–330
Lynch, James, 291
Lynchings, 365, 385, 429, 459

MacArthur, Douglas, 459, 495, 508, 520, 521
Machine Age, *see* Industrialization; Industry
Machine guns, 398
Machinery: farm, 313; productivity and, 318
Machines (political), *see* Political machines
Machine-tool industry, 322
Macune, Charles W., 369
Macy's, 332
Magazines, 356; muckraker journalism in, 379; women's, 545; mass, 549
Magee, Christopher, 348
Mahan, Alfred Thayer, 403
Mail, 356
Mailer, Norman, 549
Mail-order companies, 313

Maine (battleship), 404, 405
Malaria: drugs for, 398
Malaya, 490
Malcolm X, 568
Mammoth Oil Company, 437
Managed economy, 556
Management: of cities, 347–350; in Great Depression, 466. *See also* Scientific management
Manchuria, 407, 413, 484
Mandela, Nelson, 611
Manhattan Project, 497, 509
Manila, 407; Dewey in, 406
Mann Act (1910), 383, 384
Mann-Elkins Act (1910), 391
Manufacturing: in South, 291; growth of, 318; production and, 324, 399, 400(illus.); women in, 324; depression of 1890s and, 370; in Second World War, 497
Manypenny, George, 304
Mao Zedong, 484, 508, 519, 520, 583
Maple Floor Association v. U.S., 436
March on Washington: in Second World War, 497; in 1963, 559–560, 559(illus.)
Margin buying: in Great Depression, 451
Marin, John, 450
Marine Corps, 421; in Cuba, 412; in Latin America, 480; blacks in, 503; in Lebanon, 604–606; in Somalia, 622
Market(s): in West, 300; farmers and, 399; foreign, 399; emerging, 620; integration of, 620, 633
Marketing, 318; of cigarettes, 323
Marne River: battles at, 422
Marriages: Boston marriage, 351; in Great Depression, 455; in Second World War, 500, 501, 501(illus.); in 1950s, 545–546; of female labor force, 546(illus.); in 1970s, 591; age at, 591; defined, 631
Marshall, George C., 503, 517
Marshall, Thurgood, 298, 503, 540–541
Marshall Plan (1948), 517, 518(map)
Martí, José, 404
Martial law: Enforcement Acts and, 293
Marx, Karl, 371
Marxism-Leninism: of Stalin, 514
Masculinity: crisis of, 547
Massacres: at Sand Creek, 303; at Wounded Knee, 305; at My Lai, 581
Mass culture, 468–470; criticisms of, 549. *See also* Popular culture
Massive retaliation policy, 523
Mass marketing: radio and, 439
Mass media, *see* Media
Mass production, 477; in auto industry, 319–322, 322(illus.); of cigarettes, 323; of clothing, 323, 332; in cities, 339
Mass transportation, 339, 343
Masterson, William ("Bat"), 308–309
Materialism: in 1920s, 438–439
Mattachine Society, 580
Mattel, 548

Maximilian (Mexico), 402
Maximum Freight Rate case, 362
May Day, 372, 380(illus.)
Mazu (Matsu), 525
McAdoo, William G., 437
McCain, Franklin, 553
McCarran Act, *see* Internal Security (McCarran) Act
McCarthy, Eugene, 570, 572
McCarthy, Joseph R., 522–523, 539
McClure's (magazine), 379
McCormick farm machinery factories, 327, 370
McDonald's: protests against, 622
McGovern, George, 585
McKay, Claude, 429
McKinley, William, 364, 373–374, 403–404; 1896 election and, 372, 373; assassination of, 389, 410; Cuba and, 404–405; Spanish-American War and, 405–406; Open Door policy and, 407, 410
McKinley Tariff (1890), 362, 373, 403
McLaughlin, Hugh, 348
McMurtry, Larry, 316
McNamara, Robert, 555, 557, 567
McNary-Haugen bills (1927, 1928), 437
McNaughton, John, 574
McNeil, Joe, 553
McPherson, Aimee Semple, 448
McVeigh, Timothy, 623
"McWorld," 622
Meat Inspection Act (1906), 390
Meatpacking industry, 315, 334, 379, 390
Mechanization, 317–318, 441–443; labor and, 324–326; mobility and, 331; of mass transportation, 339; leisure and, 352; of agriculture, 367, 368, 440, 550
Me-Decade (1970s), 591
Media, 602; cultural impact of, 439, 545–546; consolidation of, 601; diversity in, 619
Medical schools, 384
Medicare, 563; Reagan and, 598, 600
Medicine: in 1920s, 443; in Second World War, 504
Mehta, G. L., 527
Mellon, Andrew, 437
Melodramas, 355
Memorial Day, 279
Men: Indian, 305; in West, 307; employment trends and, 325(illus.); clothing for, 332; occupational mobility and, 342–343; in homosexual subculture, 351; unmarried, 351; gender roles and, 546; in 1950s, 547
Menlo Park, New Jersey, 319
Mennonites: as COs, 421
Meredith, James, 559
Mergers, 334; corporate, 601
Merrick, Dwight, 317
Mestizos, 307
Methodists, 284
Metropolitan Club, 399
Meuse-Argonne offensive, 422

Mexicans and Mexican Americans, 295, 343–344, 610; in West, 308; agrarian protest by, 368; employed women among, 444–445; in Great Depression, 457, 471; in Second World War, 497; zoot suit riots and, 500; in postwar period, 536; *bracero* program and, 550; in Los Angeles–Long Beach area, 550; in 1970s, 576–577; Chicano movement and, 577; *cursillo* movement and, 590–591. *See also* Hispanics

Mexico: immigrants from, 307, 341, 441; French in, 402; relations with, 412–413; intervention in, 418; First World War and, 420; workers from, 426; U.S. relations with, 481

Miami: Hispanics in, 610

Microprocessor, 620

Middle class: industrialization and, 330; mass transit, 339; housing in, 345; in Progressive era, 378; Indians in, 387; women in, 387–388; in Great Depression, 457; black, 541; in 1950s, 543–545, 549–551; television and, 545; in 1970s, 576

Middle East, 513, 622–623, 629(map); missionaries in, 361; Cold War and, 516; Arab-Israeli conflict in, 528–529; U.S. interests in, 604–606; terrorism in, 606; national security and, 636

Midway, Battle of, 495(map), 496, 508

Midway Islands, 295, 402, 490

Midwest, 368; cities in, 440, 589; industrial decline in, 588

Migrant workers, 456(illus.); Mexican American activism and, 576–577

Migration, 534; African American, 296–297, 385, 426, 497; in West, 300, 312; urban population growth and, 339–341; families and, 350, 352; in Great Depression, 453–454; in Second World War, 499; to suburbs, 536. *See also* Immigrants and immigration; Slaves and slavery

Militarism: economics and, 477

Military: labor unrest and, 326, 328; women in, 420–421, 504; U.S., in foreign countries, 480–481, 635; production for, 496; science and, 497; segregation of, 503; growth of, 519; aid to Vietnam and, 520; spending on, 522, 531, 636; Eisenhower, Dulles, and, 523; highways and, 536; desegregation of, 540; Reagan and, 603; gays in, 619; September 11, 2001, and, 633–635; AIDS and, 634. *See also* Armed forces; Soldiers

Military bases: in Second World War, 486; on Okinawa, 520

Military districts: in South, 287, 288(map)

Military-industrial complex, 531, 538

Military technology: in Vietnam War, 567

Militias: in 1990s, 623

Milken, Michael, 601

Millennium Round, 621

Milligan, Lambdin P., 295

Millman, Zelma, 524(illus.)

Milosevic, Slobodan, 622

Minerals: in West, 307; in Australia, 311

Minimum wage, 537, 577

Mining, 306(map), 307, 392; strikes against, 328, 371, 390–391; gold vs. silver issue, 363. *See also* Gold; Silver

Minor, Rufus, 347

Minorities, 308, 349, 378, 578. *See also* specific groups

Minstrel shows, 355

Miscegenation, 308

Miss America Pageant: protests at, 579

Missiles, 523; limiting, 583; Reagan and, 603; INF Treaty and, 606

Missions and missionaries: Protestant, 308; world expansion of, 361; in China, 396–397, 410, 484; cultural imperialism and, 398; American culture and, 401

Mississippi: Freedom Summer in, 558; African American voting in, 561

Mississippi Freedom Democratic Party (MFDP), 558, 561

Mississippi Plan (1890), 365

MKULTRA program, 523

Mobility: industrialization and, 331; of immigrants, 341–343; in urban borderlands, 343

Mobilization: for First World War, 394

Model Cities program, 561

"Model tenements," 345

Model T Ford, 322, 322(illus.), 438

Modern Woman: The Lost Sex, 547

Molotov, V. M., 514

Mondale, Walter: 1984 election and, 600

Monetary policy: gold vs. silver, 363

Money, *see* Currency

Money supply: in 1890s depression, 370; under Reagan, 600

"Monkey trial," 433

Monopolies, 334, 335

Monroe Doctrine, 402, 413; Venezuelan dispute and, 404; Roosevelt Corollary to, 411(map), 412

Montana, 307, 308

Montgomery, Marvin, 453–454

Montgomery bus boycott, 534, 541, 542

Montgomery Ward (store), 313

Moon, Charlotte Diggs (Lottie), 396–397

Moon landing (1969), 590

Moral Majority, 607, 607(illus.), 609

Moral reform: societies for, 324. *See also* Reform and reform movements

Morgan, J. P., 319, 334, 370, 390, 391, 402

Morgan v. Virginia, 541

Morgenthau, Henry, Jr., 504

Mormons, 308, 309

"Morning in America," 600

Morocco, 413

Moro Province, Philippines, 407

Morrill Act (1890), 314

Morrill Land Grant Act (1862), 313–314

Mortality: rates of, 331

Mortgages, 536

Moscow: in Second World War, 496

"Mother and Child on the Road" (Lange), 456(illus.)

Mothers: unmarried, 591. *See also* Women

Mother's Day, 352

Mountains: in West, 300

Movies and movie industry, 355–356, 528; westerns in, 316; in First World War, 426, 427; in 1920s, 448, 449; in 1930s, 468; in Second World War, 499; for teenagers, 547

"Mr. X": Kennan as, 517

Muckrakers, 379, 383

Mugwumps, 360

Muir, John, 308

Mujahidin (Islamic guerrillas), 592, 603, 623

Mulattos: education of, 284

Muller v. Oregon, 326, 381, 384

Multiculturalism: New Right on, 607

Multiethnicity, 630

Multiethnic neighborhoods, 343–344

Multiracial categories: on Census, 630

Multiracial society, 403; in West, 307

Munich Conference, 482

Municipal bonds, 349

Municipal Voters League, 379

Munn v. Illinois, 362

Murrah Federal Building: bombing of, 623

Murrow, Edward R., 487, 487(illus.)

Music, 352; jazz, 449–450; in 1920s, 450; of youth culture, 547–548; rock 'n' roll, 549; in 1960s, 569; "British invasion" in, 571

Musical comedy, 355, 449

Muslims: in Philippines, 407; in Afghanistan, 592; Iran hostage crisis and, 593; in Bosnia, 622. *See also* Islam

Mussolini, Benito, 470, 481, 482

Mutual aid societies, 343

Mutual defense agreement: ANZUS as, 522

Mutual Defense Assistance Act, 519

Mutualistas (cooperative associations), 577

Mutual Security Treaty: with Japan, 520

My Lai massacre, 581

Myrdal, Gunnar, 541

NAACP, *see* National Association for the Advancement of Colored People (NAACP)

Nader, Ralph, 561; 2000 election and, 625

NAFTA, *see* North American Free Trade Agreement (NAFTA)

Nagasaki: bombing of, 494, 509

Naked and the Dead, The (Mailer), 549

Napalm, 567

Napoleon III (France), 402

NASA, *see* National Aeronautics and Space Administration (NASA)

Nash, Diane, 558

Nasser, Gamal Abdel, 529, 593

Nast, Alice, 524(illus.)

Nast, Thomas, 290(illus.)

Nation, The, 402, 455

National Advisory Commission on Civil Disorders, *see* Kerner Commission report (1968)

National Aeronautics and Space Administration (NASA), 523, 560

National American Woman Suffrage Association, 366, 378, 388

National Association for the Advancement of Colored People (NAACP), 298, 356, 387, 421, 429, 503, 540, 541, 559

National Association of Colored Women, 388, 438

National Chicano Liberation Youth Conference (1969), 577

National Child Labor Committee, 381

National Civil Service Reform League, 362

National College Athletic Association (NCAA), 355, 452

National Committee for Organizing Iron and Steel Workers, 428

National Conference on the Cure and Cause of War, 476

National Congress of American Indians, 578

National Consumers League (NCL), 378, 384–385, 438

National Cordage Company, 370

National Council of Churches, 541

National Defense Act (1916), 420

National Defense Education Act (NDEA), 538

National Economic Council, 620

National Endowment for the Arts (NEA), 561, 585

National Endowment for the Humanities (NEH), 561, 585

National forests, 391

National Geographic, 400

National Guard: First World War and, 420; at Central High School, Little Rock, 541; Kent State University killings by, 581

National Housing Act (1949), 550

National Industrial Recovery Act (NIRA), 460, 461, 462, 470

Nationalism, 399; Hawaiian, 403; after First World War, 432; in Latin America, 480, 525; in Mexico, 481; in China, 484; in Vietnam, 512; after Second World War, 513; in Africa, 525; cultural, 575

Nationalist Chinese, 522

Nationalities: in Europe, 422; immigration quotas on, 446

National Labor Relations (Wagner) Act (1935), 466, 470

National Labor Relations Board (NLRB), 462, 466, 467, 599

National Labor Union, 326

National League (baseball), 352

National Liberation Front (NFL), *see* Vietcong

National Military Establishment, 531

National Missile Defense system, 626

National Municipal League, 378

National Negro Business League, 378

National Organization for Women (NOW), 579, 607

National origins: immigration quotas by, 573

National Origins Act (1924), 446

National parks, 308, 391

National Progressive Republican League, 391

National Recovery Administration (NRA), 460–461, 471

National Research Council, 432

National security, 531

National Security Act (1947), 517–519

National Security Council: NSC-68 and, 519, 531

National Socialism, *see* Nazi Germany

National Traffic and Motor Vehicle Safety Act (1966), 561

National War Labor Board (NWLB), 426, 498

National Woman's Party, 388, 438

National Woman Suffrage Association (NWSA), 366

National Youth Administration, 464

Nation of Islam, 568

Native American Rights Fund, 578

Native Americans, *see* American Indians

Native Son (Wright), 541

Nativism: urban crime and, 347; in First World War, 427; in 1920s, 446

Nat King Cole Show, 545

NATO, *see* North Atlantic Treaty Organization (NATO, 1949)

Naturalization, 344

Natural resources, 301, 306–309, 306(map); Newlands Reclamation Act and, 309–310; government management of, 381, 391; Reagan and, 598–599

Navajo Indians, 301–302, 467; trade with, 303; "code-talkers" and, 492–493

Navalism, 403

Navy(ies): steel for, 398; of Japan, 413; in First World War, 418; Washington Naval Conference and, 477. *See also* Navy (U.S.); Submarines

Navy (U.S.), 420; modernization of, 403; in Spanish-American War, 406; "Great White Fleet" of, 413; Theodore Roosevelt and, 413; before Second World War, 488; Pearl Harbor attack and, 489, 489(illus.); Second World War battles by, 495(map)

Navy Act (1916), 420

Nazi Germany, 476, 481–482; 1936 Olympics and, 469, 469(illus.); Munich Conference and, 482; U.S. business ties with, 482; Jews in, 483; Poland and, 483; Soviet nonaggression pact with, 483; invasions by, 485–486, 486(map); in Second World War, 490; surrender of, 493, 508

Nazi-Soviet nonaggression pact, 488

NCAA, *see* National College Athletic Association (NCAA)

NDEA, *see* National Defense Education Act (NDEA)

Nebraska, 310

Negro Business Men's League, 366

"Negro Rule" myth, 291

Negro World (newspaper), 441

Neighborhoods, 339, 343–345

Nestor, Agnes, 329

Netherlands, 485

Netscape, 637

Networks: television, 545

Neutrality, 476; in First World War, 417–418, 419–420; before Second World War, 485; Dulles on, 522, 527

Neutrality Acts (1935, 1936, 1937), 482, 484, 490

Nevada, 307

Nevada (ship), 489

New Age movement, 591

Newark, New Jersey: riot in, 567

New Deal, 455, 463(illus.); First, 459–461; legislation in, 460–461, 462; Second, 461–466; federal power in, 467; limits of, 470–472. *See also* Social Security

"New Democrat": Clinton as, 618

New Economy, 620

"New Freedom," 392, 393

New Frontier: of John F. Kennedy, 560

New immigrants, 341, 573, 595–596, 609–610

New Jersey, 334

Newlands Reclamation Act (1902), 309–310, 391

New Left, 568, 569

Newly independent nations: since 1943, 526(map)

New Nationalism, 392, 393, 425

New Navy, 403, 404

"New Order": in Asia, 484

New Orleans: general strike in, 371

New Right, 596, 597, 599, 607

News, 356, 487, 602. *See also* Media; Newspapers; Television

New South, 323

Newspapers: advertising in, 332; yellow journalism and, 356

"New woman": in 1920s, 445

New York (city): Triangle Shirtwaist Company fire in, 326; "Great White Way" in, 332; growth of, 339; population density in, 345; drug trade in, 608; Chinatown in, 610; Korean immigrants in, 610

New York (state): housing reform in, 345

New York Herald, 294

New York Journal, 356, 404

New York Stock Exchange, 334

New York Times: Pentagon Papers and, 574–575; on Reagan, 613

New York Tribune, 293

New York World, 356, 402

New York Yankees, 448–449

New Zealand: in ANZUS, 522

Nez Percé Indians, 303

Niagara movement, 386–387

Nicaragua, 480, 604

Nicholas II (Russia), 382

Nicodemus, Kansas, 307

Nine-Power Treaty, 477, 484

Nineteenth Amendment, 388, 426, 429, 438, A9–A10

Ninth Amendment, A8

NIRA, *see* National Industrial Recovery Act (NIRA)

Nitze, Paul, 519

Nixon, Richard, 523–525; as vice president, 522; Red Scare and, 539–540; 1960 election and, 555; 1968 election and, 572; foreign policy and, 575–576; affirmative action and, 578; Vietnam War and, 580; Cold War and, 582–583, 601–603; 1972 election and, 585; impeachment, resignation, and, 585, 585(illus.); Watergate and, 585–587

Nixon Doctrine, 582

NLF, *see* Vietcong

NLRB, *see* National Labor Relations Board (NLRB)

NLRB v. Jones & Laughlin Steel Corp., 470

"No-fault" divorce, 591

"No-fly zone": in Iraq, 612

Nonaggression pact: Nazi-Soviet, 483

Nonpartisan elections, 381

Non-Partisan League, 427

Nonrecognition: of China, 520

Nonviolence, 503, 542, 558

Noriega, Manuel, 612

Normandy invasion, 493, 505

Norris, George, 420

North: Reconstruction and, 292–293; African American migration to, 341, 385, 426; desegregation in, 541; industrial decline in, 588; cities in, 589

North, Oliver, 433, 604

North Africa: in Second World War, 496, 506(map)

North American Free Trade Agreement (NAFTA), 620

North Atlantic Treaty Organization (NATO, 1949), 518(map), 519, 622

North Carolina, 585

North Carolina Agricultural and Technical College, 553–554

North Dakota, 308

Northern Securities case, 390

Northern Securities Company, 390

North Korea, 520–521. *See also* Korea; Korean War

North Vietnam, 529–530, 563. *See also* Vietnam War

Northwest: Indian treaties in, 303

Norway, 485

NOW, *see* National Organization for Women (NOW)

NSC-68, 519, 531

Nuclear arms race, 515

Nuclear household, 350

Nuclear power, 538, 590. *See also* Atomic bomb

Nuclear weapons: cancers from testing, 510; after Second World War, 515; hydrogen bomb and, 519, 523; Soviets and, 519;

Korean War and, 521; under Eisenhower, 523; in China, 525; anticommunism and, 539; wastes from, 549; Kennedy and, 556; in Cuba, 557

Nuremberg Laws (1935), 481

Nurse Corps: in First World War, 420

Nutrition: in 1920s, 443. *See also* Diet (food)

NWLB, *see* National War Labor Board (NWLB)

Nye Committee, 482

Occupational Safety and Health Administration (OSHA), 585

Occupations (jobs), 341–342

Oceania: imperialism in, 398

O'Connor, Sandra Day, 599

Officeholders: African Americans as, 290–291, 365

Office of Management and Budget (OMB), 600

Office of Price Administration (OPA), 498–499

Office of Strategic Services (OSS): in Vietnam, 511

Office of War Information (OWI), 499

Oil and oil industry, 307, 439, 543; trusts and, 333–334, 390; Arab-Israeli conflict and, 528–529; in 1970s, 576, 583, 584, 588; OPEC production and, 600; Persian Gulf War (1991) and, 612; Arctic drilling and, 626. *See also* Energy crisis

Oil spills, 590

Ojibwa Indians, 305

OK Corral, shootout at, 309

O'Keeffe, Georgia, 449

Okies, 453

Okinawa, 495(map), 520; battle at, 508

Oklahoma and Oklahoma Territory, 385

Old-age assistance, 378, 381, 437. *See also* Pensions; Social Security

Older Americans, 351, 381; age bias and, 399; in 1920s, 443; poverty among, 550, 562

Old immigrants, 341

Old Man Hat (Navajo), 301

Oligarchy: in Hawai'i, 403

Oligopolies, 436

Olney, Richard, 328, 404

Olympia (ship), 406

Olympic Games: of 1904, 401(illus.); of 1936, 469, 469(illus.); of 1972, 583; of 1980, 592

Omaha platform: of Populists, 369

O'Neill, Eugene, 449

OPEC, *see* Organization of Petroleum Exporting Countries (OPEC)

Open Door policy, 407–410, 409(map), 476–477, 483, 484; Japan and, 413; before Second World War, 488

Open markets, 620

Open-range ranching, 314

Open shops, 436, 498

Operation Desert Shield, 612

Operation Desert Storm (1991), 602(illus.), 612. *See also* Persian Gulf War (1991)

Operation Mongoose, 557

Operation Overlord, 505

Operation Rolling Thunder, 564

Operation War Bride, 501(illus.)

Oregon, 307

Organic Act (1900), 404

Organization Man, The (Whyte), 549

Organization of Petroleum Exporting Countries (OPEC), 576, 583, 584, 600

Organizations: of Progressive era, 378

Organized labor, 534, 620. *See also* Labor; Labor unions

Orinoco River, 404

Orlando, Vittorio, 430

OSHA, *see* Occupational Safety and Health Administration (OSHA)

OSS, *see* Office of Strategic Services (OSS)

Oswald, Lee Harvey, 560

Ottoman Empire, 417, 423, 430

Our Bodies, Ourselves, 579

Our Country (Strong), 400

Our Indian Wards (Manypenny), 304

Outdoor billboards, 332

Overtime pay, 393

Owens, Jesse, 469, 469(illus.)

Ownership: of utilities, 381

Pachucos (gang members), 500, 577

Pacification, 405, 411

Pacific Ocean region, 300, 374; U.S. empire in, 398; U.S. claims in, 402; Japan and, 430; fortifications in, 477; islands in, 483; Second World War in, 494–496, 495(map), 508

Pacifism: First World War and, 419, 477; in Vietnam War, 567

Padrone (boss), 343

Paducah, Kentucky: school shootings in, 624

Pago Pago, 402

Painting, 449

Pakistan, 513, 603

Palestine and Palestinians, 430, 513, 528–529, 592, 622–623

Palestinian Liberation Organization (PLO), 583, 604, 606, 622

Palmer, A. Mitchell, 428, 429

Palmer Raids, 429

Panama, 412, 442, 480; Canal Zone and, 592; invasion of, 602, 612

Panama Canal, 412, 474, 480

Pan American Airways, 442, 442(illus.), 606

Pan-Americanism, 480

Pan-Arabic movement, 529

Panay (gunboat), 484

Panics (financial): of 1873, 293, 326; in late nineteenth century, 333; of 1907, 391

Pardons: for Confederates, 280, 281, 285; of Nixon, 587

Parietals, 569

Paris: summit in (1960), 525

Paris, treaties of: in 1898, 406, 407, 412

Paris Peace Conference: after First World War, 417, 430

Parks, Rosa, 542

Parrington, Vernon L., 384

Party caucuses, 379

Party politics: in Gilded Age, 359; alignments in, 360

Passchendaele, battle at, 421

Passing of the Great Race, The (Grant), 385, 446

Patent(s), 319

Patent medicine industry, 390

Paternalism: toward foreigners, 399

PATRIOT Act, 627

Patriotism: First World War and, 417, 426, 427; Second World War and, 496; after September 11, 2001, 627

Patronage, 364

Patterson, Floyd, 528

Patti, Archimedes, 511–512

Paul, Alice, 388

Paulucci, Jeno, 356

Pawnee Indians, 299, 301, 303

Payne-Aldrich Tariff (1909), 391

Peace accord: Israel-Jordan, 622

Peace Corps, 556

"Peace dividend," 612

Peaceful coexistence policy, 525

Peace groups: after First World War, 476–477

Peacekeeping: in Lebanon, 604–606; in Kosovo, 622

Pearl Harbor, 403, 488–489, 489(illus.)

Peer groups, 443

Pendergast, Tom, 348

Pendleton Civil Service Act (1883), 362, 364

Penitentiaries, *see* Prisons

Pennsylvania: September 11, 2001, and, 615, 626

Pensions: for Civil War veterans, 360, 364; old-age, 381, 437, 443, 465, 473; Townsend plan for, 464; judicial, 471

Pentagon: attack on, 615, 626

Pentagon Papers, 574

Pentecostal churches, 448

People for the American Way, 608

People of color: free, 284; in urban borderlands, 344; eugenics movement and, 385; stereotypes of, 400, 401(illus.); New Deal and, 471; women and, 547; poverty of, 550; population of, 630

People's Party, *see* Populist party

People's Republic of China (PRC), 520, 521, 525, 576. *See also* China

People-to-people campaign, 524, 524(illus.)

Perestroika (restructuring), 606

Perkins, Frances, 464

Permanent Court of International Justice, *see* World Court

Perot, Ross, 618, 619

Pershing, John J. ("Black Jack"), 412–413, 421

Persian Gulf region: Carter and, 592; Saddam Hussein in, 593

Persian Gulf War (1991), 597, 612, 613, 618

Persico, Joseph, 487

Personal Responsibility and Work Opportunity Act (1996), 619

Pesticides, 549

Petroleum, *see* Oil and oil industry

Pharmaceutical industry, 323

Phelps-Stokes Fund, 479

Philadelphia Plan: for affirmative action, 578

Philanthropy, 334, 346–347

Philippines, 398, 401, 401(illus.), 413, 477, 483, 488, 490, 494–495, 496; communications with, 402; Spanish-American War in, 406; Republic of, 407; independence for, 513; immigrants from, 609

Phonograph, 356

Physicians: as missionaries to China, 361; birth control and, 394–395. *See also* Medicine

Pickford, Mary, 356

Piecework rates, 324

Pill, the, 570, 609

Pinchot, Gifford, 391

Pine Ridge, South Dakota, 305

Pingree, Hazen S., 349

Pinkerton Detective Agency, 328

Pinochet, Augusto, 583

Pittsburgh: railroad strike in, 326

Pittsburgh Pirates, 352

Plains Indians, 299–300, 301, 304(illus.)

Plains states, *see* Great Plains

Plan Espiritual de Aztlán, El, 577

Planned Parenthood Federation of America (PPFA), 395

Planning and zoning commissions, 437–438

Platt Amendment, 411–412, 481

Playboy magazine, 547

Pledge of Allegiance, The, 551–552

Plessy, Homer, 366

Plessy v. Ferguson, 366, 541

PLO, *see* Palestinian Liberation Organization (PLO)

Plumbers group (Watergate), 585–586

Plunkitt, George Washington, 348

Pluralism, 356

Plutonium, 510

Pocket-veto: of Wade-Davis bill, 282

Poets and poetry: in 1920s, 449

Pogroms, 337, 341

Poindexter, John M., 604

Poland: Russia and, 422; Hitler and, 483; after Second World War, 507, 514; revolt in, 525, 611; Solidarity in, 603

Polaris missiles, 523

Police: in cities, 348; in Boston, 437; in 1968 Chicago riots, 572

Polish Roman Catholic Union, 329

Political cartoons, 290(illus.), 363(illus.)

Political conventions, *see* Elections

Political geography: engineering and, 398

Political machines, 348–349; Progressives and, 379; Tammany Hall as, 450

Political parties, *see* Factions; specific parties

Politics: in South, 289–292; machine, 348–349; pluralism, interest groups, and, 356; in Gilded Age, 358–374; Farmers' Alliances in, 369; Progressives and, 381; world, 398; in 1920s, 436–438; women and, 438; radio and, 439; Second New Deal and, 461–466; identity politics and, 576–578; AIDS and, 609

Polk, Leonidas, 369

Poll taxes, 365, 380

Pollution: from cattle processing, 315; industrialization and, 336; of water, 347; from wartime industry, 510; in 1950s, 549–550; in 1970s, 590; controls of, 623

Polygamy: among Mormons, 308

Pools (business), 333, 362

Poorhouses, 443

Poor people: diet of, 331–332; Progressives and, 378. *See also* Poverty

Popular culture: in 1930s, 468–470; in Second World War, 499; population diversity and, 630. *See also* Mass culture

Popular Front, 464, 465

Population: of West, 301; in cities, 339–341, 340(map), 440; age of (1880–1920), 350; of southern black voters, 365; in schools, 384; in 1920s, 443; baby boom and, 535–536; distribution of (1930–1970), 536(illus.); of Sunbelt and Southwest, 543; ancestry of, 544; ethnic and racial groups in, 550; poverty in, 563; immigrants in, 573; shift to Sunbelt, 588–589, 589(map); environmentalism and, 590; Hispanic, 610; of people of color, 630

Populism (political doctrine), 369

Populist demagogues: in New Deal, 462–463

Populist party, 327, 358, 369–370, 378; free silver and election of 1896, 372–374

Porter, Roy, 424

Porter, Sylvia F., 535

Port Huron Statement, 568

Portsmouth Conference (1905), 413

POSSLQ, 591

Post, Charles W., 331

Post, Louis, 429

Postal service, 360; Rural Free Delivery (RFD) and, 313; employee shootings and, 624

Posttraumatic stress disorder, 582

Postwar era, 532–536

Potsdam Conference, 508

Potsdam Declaration, 509

Pound, Ezra, 449

Poverty: relief for, 346–347; causes of, 347, 562–563; in 1920s, 443; rural, 534; in 1950s, 550; War on Poverty and, 561–563; 1959–1974, 563(illus.); in 1980s, 595, 608; taxation and, 601; of underclass, 607; reasons for, 608; homelessness and, 609; Los Angeles riots and, 617

Powderly, Terence V., 327

Powell, Colin, 606

Powell, Lewis, Jr., 585, 591

Power (energy): hydroelectricity and, 467. *See also* Electricity; Energy crisis; Oil and oil industry

Power (political): of political machines, 348; Progressives and, 377; of Franklin D. Roosevelt, 460; federal, 467–468

Power plants, 319

Powers, Francis Gary, 525

POWs, *see* Prisoners of war (POWs)

Prague Spring, 572

PRC, *see* People's Republic of China (PRC)

Precision machine tools, 322

Premarital sex, 547, 591. *See also* Sex and sexuality

Preservation: vs. conservation, 391

President and presidency: in Gilded Age, 359, 364–365; expansion of power, 391, 392; Theodore Roosevelt and, 391; Franklin D. Roosevelt and, 472, 491; foreign affairs and, 530; after Nixon, 587; list of elections, A12–A16; list of, A17–A18. *See also* Elections; specific presidents

President's Organization on Unemployment Relief (POUR), 458

Presley, Elvis, 547–549

Price discrimination, 393

Prices: in 1970s, 590

Princeton University, 393

Printing, 356

Prisoners of war (POWs): in Korean War, 521–522

Prisons: in Civil War, 279

Privacy rights: abortion and, 579

Private enterprise, 556

"Proclamation of Amnesty and Reconstruction," 281

Production: machines and, 318; mass, 319–322, 322(illus.); industrial (1919), 320(map); standardization of, 323; efficiency in, 323–324; in First World War, 425; in Second World War, 496–498

Productivity, 441–443, 588

Professional Air Traffic Controllers Organization (PATCO), 599

Professionalization: of foreign service, 399

Professional organizations, 378; in 1920s, 436

Professions and professionals, 378; women and, 343, 349, 358, 408, 444, 547, 579, 608; in 1950s, 543

Profiles in Courage (Kennedy), 555

Profiteering: in First World War, 425

Profits: production organization and, 323; from foreign sales, 399

Progress and Poverty (George), 335

Progressive era, 376–395; poverty relief and, 347; reforms and reformers in, 376, 378–379, 380, 381; associations during, 378; foreign influences on, 378; goals of, 378, 394; Socialists in, 379; in South,

379–380; temperance, prohibition, and, 382, 383; prostitution and white slavery in, 383; education in, 383–384; social institutions in, 383–385; legal thought in, 384; social science and, 384–385; African Americans in, 385–387; Indians in, 387; women during, 387–388; Margaret Sanger and birth control in, 388, 394–395; presidency in, 388–392; trustbusting in, 390; pure food and drug laws in, 390–391; conservation in, 391; business regulation in, 393; tariff and tax reform in, 393

Progressive Party, 377; of 1912 (Bull Moose Party), 392; of 1920s, 437–438; in 1934, 464; in 1948, 537

Progressives and progressivism: use of term, 377; and First World War, 419, 425, 427; in New Deal, 464

Prohibition, 358, 379, 383, 449; in Russia, 382; support for, 448

Project C, 558

Prolife movement, 607

Propaganda: in First World War, 427; in Second World War, 500; in Cold War, 523–525

Property: social mobility and, 343. *See also* Land

Property rights: for women, 290

Proposition 13 (California), 589, 618

Prosperity: under Coolidge, 437; during Second World War, 499; in 1950s, 543; in 1970s, 587; in 1990s, 623

Prostitution: white slavery and, 383; in First World War, 421

Protective tariffs, 458. *See also* Tariffs

Protest(s): against lynchings, 365; agrarian, 367–369; in 1890s depression, 371, 372; against Vietnam War, 567, 580–581; in universities, 568–569; in Chicago, 572; by Indians, 577–578. *See also* Demonstrations

Protestants and Protestantism: missionaries and, 308; Republican Party and, 360; evangelicals and, 590; religious right and, 607

Provisional governors: in Reconstruction, 285

Psychedelic drug culture, 569–570

Publications: mass-market, 356

Public education: accessibility of, 331. *See also* Education; Schools

Public health and safety, 474, 476; Progressives and, 381, 384–385; regulatory measures for, 384

Public housing, 562

Public lands, 308

Public opinion: on labor, 436

Public ownership: of utilities, 381

Public schools: educational reform and, 349

Public works: in Great Depression, 458, 461; in West, 467

Public Works Administration (PWA), 461

Puck (magazine), 363(illus.)

Puerto Ricans, 610

Puerto Rico, 406, 412; status of, 414; immigrants from, 441, 550

Pulitzer, Joseph, 356

Pullman, George, 328

Pullman Palace Car Company, 328

Pullman strike, 328, 365, 371

Punishment: for drug possession, 609

Pure Food and Drug Act (1906), 384, 390

PWA, *see* Public Works Administration (PWA)

Qing (Manchu) dynasty, 407

Quakers: as COs, 421; peace efforts by, 477

Quality-of-life issues: global, 622

Quotas: on immigration, 446, 561, 573

Rabin, Yitzhak, 622

Race and racism: Andrew Johnson and, 285; in West, 293–295, 307–308; Reconstruction and, 295; segregation in cities, 344; in Farmers' Alliance movement, 369; in Progressive era, 380, 385; southern Progressivism and, 380; classification by race, 399; expansionism and, 399–401; of anti-imperialists, 402; in Spanish-American War, 406; First World War and, 417, 421; Klan and, 445–446; in 1930s, 457, 459, 471; Second World War and, 499–500, 502–504, 540–543; Japanese American internment and, 502–503, 502(illus.); Third World relations and, 527; in postwar period, 534, 536; in 1950s, 550; immigrants and, 561; identity politics and, 576; discrimination and, 578; in college admissions, 591; 1988 report on, 608; poverty and, 608, 608(illus.). *See also* Minorities

Race Course prison camp, 279

Race riots: against immigrant labor, 308; in late 19th century, 347; anti-Chinese, 400; after First World War, 429; in Second World War, 494, 499–500; in Los Angeles, 610; Rodney King and, 617

Racial segregation, *see* Segregation

Radical feminism, 579

Radical Reconstruction, 288(map), 292. *See also* Congressional Reconstruction

Radical Republicans, 281, 284, 285, 286, 289

Radicals and radicalism: after First World War, 428–429; Wilson and, 429–430; labor and, 436; Sacco-Vanzetti case and, 446; in New Deal, 462

Radio, 439; baseball on, 448; Franklin D. Roosevelt and, 460; Coughlin on, 464; in 1930s, 468, 470(illus.); news reporting on, 487, 487(illus.)

Radioactive waste, 510

Radio Corporation of America (RCA), 479

Railroad Administration, 425

Railroads: in South, 291; Chinese workers on, 295; Indians and, 302; time zones and, 310; in West, 310; western settlement and, 312; mechanization and, 318; inventions for, 319; strikes against, 326, 364, 371;

Pullman strike and, 328; pools and, 333; government assistance to, 334–335; commuter, 339; elevated, 339; regulation of, 362, 381; farming and, 368; depression of 1890s and, 370; ICC, freight and storage rates, and, 390; trusts and, 390; Adamson Act and, 393; hobos on, 471
Rain-in-the-Face (chief), 303–304
Ranching, 306, 314–315
Randolph, A. Philip, 472, 497, 559
Rankin, Jeannette, 420, 490
Rape: by Klan, 292; Scottsboro Boys and, 471; women's movement and, 579
Rate wars: among railroads, 362
Rationing system: in Second World War, 498–499
Rauschenbusch, Walter, 385
Raw materials: for Japan, 484
Ray, James Earl, 570
Raza Unida, La (RUP), *see* La Raza Unida (RUP)
Reading, *see* Literacy; Literature
Ready-made clothing, 332
Reagan, Ronald, 597–598, 598(illus.); 1950s anticommunism and, 539; 1980 election and, 593, 596; conservatism of, 597–601; business, 598–599; New Right and, 599; 1984 election and, 600; foreign relations and, 601–606; Soviet Union and, 606, 611; *New York Times* on, 613
Reagan Democrats, 597, 618
Reaganomics, 599–601
Real-estate covenants: discrimination and, 344
Real-estate development, 339, 543
Rearmament: of Germany, 482
Rebellions, *see* Revolts and rebellions
Recall, 379, 381
Recessions: of 1937–1939, 471; under Eisenhower, 538; in 1970s, 588. *See also* Depressions
Reciprocal Trade Agreements Act (1934), 479
Reconcentration policy: in Cuba, 404, 405
Reconstruction, 279–298; freedpeople during, 282–284; presidential, 285; congressional plan for, 286–289, 290; military districts during, 288(map); Grant and, 289; reversal of, 292–297; and 1876 election, 296, 296(map); Compromise of 1877 and, 296; end to, 296, 296(map)
Reconstruction Acts (1867–1868), 287, 289
Reconstruction era amendments, *see* Fifteenth Amendment; Fourteenth Amendment; Thirteenth Amendment
Reconstruction Finance Corporation (RFC), 458
Recreation: in 1920s, 448–449; in Sunbelt, 543
Red Army, *see* Soviet Union
Red China, *see* China; People's Republic of China (PRC)
Red Cross, 421, 426, 503

Redlining, 536
Red Power movement, 576, 577–578, 577(illus.)
Red Record, A (Wells), 365
Red Scare: in 1919–1920, 428–429; immigrant labor and, 436; in 1950s, 538–540
Reed, John, 428
Reed, Walter, 412, 474
Referendum, 379, 381
Reform and reform movements: progressive reformers and, 297; housing, 349; social problems and, 349–350; civil service, 360–362; African American female reformers, 366; Populist goals and, 374; sources of, 377–378; bread-and-butter reforms, 379; Social Gospel and, 385; in 1930s, 464, 471; in Soviet Union, 606; of welfare system, 623. *See also* Progressive era; Progressive Party
Reform Judaism, 345
Reform party, 619; in 2000 election, 626
Refrigeration, 323, 331
Refugee camps: for Jews, 504
Refugees: Jewish, 483; from Southeast Asia, 581, 609; from Central America, 610. *See also* Immigrants and immigration
Regents of the University of California v. Bakke, 591
Region(s): in West, 300
Regionalism: in Farmers' Alliance and, 369
Regulation: of child labor, 325; of business, 335; of air pollution, 336; of railroads, 362; of trusts, 390; economic, 393–394; in 1920s, 436; Reagan and, 598. *See also* Deregulation
Rehnquist, William, 585, 599
Relief programs: in late 19th century, 346–347; in Great Depression, 458–459, 461
Religion: immigrants and, 343; cultural adaptation and, 344–345; Progressive reform and, 385; Klan and, 445; in 1950s, 545; Pledge of Allegiance and, 551–552; women and, 579; in 1970s, 590–591; New Right and, 597
Religious fundamentalism: in 1920s, 446–447; in 1980s, 607
Religious right, *see* New Right; Religious fundamentalism
Relocation camps: for Japanese Americans, 502–503, 503(illus.)
Removal: of Indians, 303
Renaissance: Harlem, 449
Reno, Janet, 614, 619
Reparations: from Germany, 451, 482; after First World War, 479; after Second World War, 505
Representation: Fourteenth Amendment and, 287
Reproduction, *see* Birth control
Reproductive technologies, 632
Republican Party: Reconstruction and, 290–292; Klan violence against, 292; and 1876 election, 296(map); coalitions in,

360; factions in, 360; in Progressive era, 391; split of, 392; African Americans and, 466; Nixon and, 585; Contract with America of, 617, 619. *See also* Elections; Liberal Republicans; Radical Republicans
Republic Steel plant (Chicago), 466–467
Research: agricultural, 313–314; military, 497; spending on, 543; into sexual habits, 547; stem-cell, 633
Research laboratories: for electrical products, 319; Du Pont, 322–323
Reservations: policy of, 303; for Australian Aborigines, 311; termination policy and, 550–551
Reserve Officers Training Corps (ROTC), 431
Resettlement Administration, 464
Resistance, 305. *See also* Protest(s); Revolts and rebellions
Resolutions of U.N. Security Council: Resolution 688, 612; Resolution 1441, 628
Restraint of trade, 335, 436
Restrictive covenants: illegality of, 541
Retailing: mail-order companies and, 313; women in, 324
Retirement, 351–352; in 1920s, 443; Social Security and, 473
Reuben James (ship), 488
Reunification: of Germany, 611
Revels, Hiram, 284
Revenue Acts: of 1916, 425
Revenue-sharing programs, 585
Revivalism: in 1920s, 448
Revolts and rebellions: Boxer, 396; in Poland and Hungary, 525; in Czechoslovakia, 572; against taxes, 589, 618
Revolution(s): in Cuba, 404, 481; Bolshevik, 422, 423, 515; in China (1911), 483; U.S. hostility toward, 527; in Iran, 592–593; in eastern Europe, 611
Reykjavik, Iceland: summit meeting in, 606
Reynolds, David, 514
Rhee, Syngman (South Korea), 521
Rhodesia (Zimbabwe), 583
Rhythm and blues music, 549
Rice and rice industry, 314
Richmond, David, 553
Rich's (store), 332
Rickenbacker, Eddie, 422
Riesman, David, 549
Right (political), 562, 597. *See also* Conservatives and conservatism
Rights: individual, 379; for women, 438; for gays, 580. *See also* Human rights; Protest(s)
Right-to-work laws, 534–535
Riis, Jacob, 345
Ringgold, John ("Johnny Ringo"), 308
Rio de Janeiro Treaty (1992), 623
Riots: Haymarket Riot, 327; in 1890s depression, 371; in 1960s, 567; in Watts, 567; in Chicago, 572; Stonewall, 580. *See also* Race riots; Revolts and rebellions

Riparian rights, 309
Roads and highways, 439; suburbs and, 536
Roberts, Oral, 607
Robertson, Pat, 607
Robinson, Jackie, 503, 541
Robinson, Sugar Ray, 528
Rockefeller, John D., 333
Rockefeller Foundation, 474, 476, 479, 527
Rock 'n' roll music, 549, 571, 571(illus.)
Rock Springs, Wyoming: violence in, 308, 400
Roebling, John A., 346
Roe v. Wade, 395, 579, 599
Roman Catholicism: assimilation and, 344–345; Democratic Party and, 360; of Alfred E. Smith, 450; John F. Kennedy and, 555; *cursillo* movement and, 590–591
Romania: revolution in (1989), 611
Rome-Berlin Axis, 482
Rommel, Erwin, 496
Roosevelt, Eleanor, 459, 460, 464, 472, 499
Roosevelt, Franklin D., 455, 507(illus.); power of, 459; youth culture and, 468–470; court-packing plan of, 470–471; scholarly assessment of, 472; Social Security and, 473; Second World War and, 476; Soviet recognition by, 479–480; Good Neighbor policy of, 480–481; Mexico and, 481; events leading to Second World War and, 482; Neutrality Acts and, 482; on neutrality, 484–485; military sales by, 486; radio and, 487; Atlantic Charter and, 488; Pearl Harbor attack and, 489–490; *Greer* attack and, 490–491; Japanese Americans and, 502–503, 502(illus.); at Yalta, 505; Vietnam policy of, 512; Truman and, 538
Roosevelt, Theodore, 316, 353, 376, 379, 389–390, 398, 399, 403; pure food and drugs and, 390; trusts and, 390; labor and, 390–391; conservation and, 391; Panic of 1907 and, 391; election of 1912 and, 392; people of color and, 400; "gentleman's agreement" with Japan and, 401; Spanish-American War and, 405(illus.), 406; foreign policy and, 410–413; Panama Canal and, 412; government-business cooperation and, 436
Roosevelt Corollary, 411(map), 412, 413
Root, Elihu, 399
Root-Takahira Agreement (1908), 413
Rosenberg, Ethel and Julius, 539–540
Rosie the Riveter, 497
Ross, Edward A., 384
ROTC, *see* Reserve Officers Training Corps (ROTC)
Rough Riders, 389, 405(illus.), 406, 410
Rubinow, Isaac Max, 443
Ruby, Jack, 560
"Rugged individualism," 316
Rumsfeld, Donald, 628
Rural areas: lifestyle in, 313; population in, 339, 340(map); migration from, 339–341; discontent in, 359; poverty in, 534

Rural Electrification Administration, 464
Rural Free Delivery (RFD), 313
Rusk, Dean, 555
Russell, Lillian, 355
Russia, 398; Alaska and, 295, 402; immigrants from, 341; temperance in, 382; Japan and, 398, 413; Trans-Siberian Railway of, 398; in China, 407, 409(map); communist revolution in, 417; First World War and, 417, 423; Bolshevik Revolution in, 422; U.S. troops in, 429–430; after Soviet Union, 611. *See also* Soviet Union
Russo-Japanese War, 413, 507
Ruth, George Herman ("Babe"), 439, 448–449
Rwanda, 622

Sacco, Nicola, 446
al-Sadat, Anwar, 592
Saddam Hussein, 617; in 1970s, 593; CNN and, 602; Kuwait invasion by, 612; capture of, 628; George W. Bush and, 628
Safety bicycles, 353
"Sagebrush Rebellion," 598
Saigon, *see* Ho Chi Minh City; South Vietnam
Sailors: black, 503. *See also* Ships and shipping
St. Domingue, *see* Haiti
St. Louis: World's Fair in, 400, 401(illus.)
St. Louis (ship), 483
St. Mihiel, battle at, 422
St. Petersburg, 496
Salinger, J. D., 549
Salmon: Northwest Indians and, 301
Saloons, 383
Same-sex couples, 630. *See also* Homosexuals and homosexuality
Samoa, 398, 402–403, 406
Sánchez, Oscar Arias, 604
Sanctuary movement, 610
Sand Creek Massacre, 303
Sandinistas (Nicaragua), 604
Sandino, Augusto, 604
San Francisco: Chinese in, 344; counterculture in, 570
San Francisco School Board: segregation of Asians by, 400–401
Sanger, Margaret, 388, 394–395, 443
Sanitary engineers, 348
Sanitation, 345; flush toilets, 331, 347; in 1920s, 443. *See also* Hygiene
San Juan Hill, 405(illus.)
Santiago, Cuba: siege of, 405(illus.), 406
SARS (severe acute respiratory syndrome), 633
Saturday Evening Post, 499
Saudi Arabia, 529
Savages: image of Indians as, 302
Savings-and-loan institutions (S&Ls), 343, 600–601
Savings banks, 334
Savio, Mario, 569

Scalawags, 291–292
Scalia, Antonin, 599
Scandals: in Harding administration, 437; Clinton and, 624; media coverage of, 625
Scandinavia, 341
Schenck v. U.S., 427–428
Schiff, Jacob, 334
Schlafly, Phyllis, 580
Schlesinger, Arthur, Jr., 530
Schmelling, Max, 470(illus.)
Schneiderman, Rose, 329
School and Society, The (Dewey), 383
Schools: for Indians, 305; compulsory attendance laws for, 325, 331; legal segregation in, 366; high schools, 383; population in, 384; in 1930s, 470; budget deficits and, 589; shootings in, 623–624. *See also Brown v. Board of Education of Topeka*; Education; Universities and colleges
Schurz, Carl, 360, 364, 402
Schwerner, Michael, 558
Science: agricultural research and, 313–314; military and, 497; in 1970s, 590
Scientific agriculture, 436
Scientific management, 317, 323–324
Scientific method, 378
SCLC, *see* Southern Christian Leadership Conference (SCLC)
Scopes, John Thomas, 446
Scopes trial, 433, 446–447
Scott, Edward and Clarence, 331
Scottsboro Boys, 471
Screen Actors Guild, 539, 597
Scrymser, James A., 402
SDI, *see* Strategic Defense Initiative (SDI, "Star Wars")
Sea Islands: land for freedpeople on, 283
Sears, Roebuck, 313
Seattle: WTO meeting in, 621
Second Amendment, A7
Second Battle of the Marne, 422
Second Bill of Rights (1944), 538
Second front: in Second World War, 496
Second New Deal, 461–466
"Second World," 513
Second World War, 476, 484–490, 492–494; events leading to, 481–484; opening of, 483; U.S. entry into, 490; Navajo code-talkers and, 492–493; in Pacific region, 494–496, 495(map); Battle of Midway in, 496; Europe First strategy in, 496; home front in, 498–500; cost of, 499; combat in, 504; winning of, 505–509; end of, 506(map), 509; recovery after, 509–510; international system after, 513–517; Europe after, 518(map)
Securities and Exchange Commission (SEC), 600
Security: of United States, 514; National Security Act and, 517–519; in 1950s, 539; after September 11, 2001, attacks, 627
Security Council (U.N.), 515; Resolution 1441 on Iraq and, 628

Sedition acts: of 1918, 427
Segregation, 540; in cities, 344; in settlement-house movement, 349–349; legal, 365–366; of northern blacks, 385; of Asians in San Francisco schools, 400–401; *Brown* case and, 433; of armed forces, 503; foreign policy and, 527–528; in northern cities, 541; in 1950s, 550; sit-ins and, 553–554; in 1960s, 557–558; Kennedy and, 558–559; in Alabama, 559
Selective Service Act (1917), 420
Selective Training and Service Act (1940), 488, 504
Self-determination, 422; anti-imperialism and, 406; Puerto Rico and, 414; for Latin America, 480; after Second World War, 505
Self-help books: in 1970s, 591
Self-help movements: for blacks, 472
Self-help strategy: of Booker T. Washington, 386
Senate (U.S.): Andrew Johnson's trial in, 289; League of Nations and, 417; Treaty of Versailles and, 431
Senators: direct election of, 360, 381, 392; as state bosses, 360; in Gilded Age, 363
Seoul, South Korea, 521
Separate-but-equal doctrine, 366, 541
Separation of church and state: Pledge of Allegiance and, 552
Separatist cultures, 575
September 11, 2001, terrorist attacks, 615–616; war on terrorism and, 626–627; international responses to, 628
Serbia: First World War and, 417
Serbs, 622
Servicemen's Readjustment Act, *see* GI Bill of Rights
Service sector: African Americans in, 341; in 1970s, 588
Settlement(s): in Great Plains, 310–313. *See also* Colonies and colonization
Settlement houses, 349–350, 378, 380
Seventeenth Amendment, 360, 381, 392, A9
Seventh Amendment, A8
Severalty policy, 438
Sewage disposal: in cities, 347–348
Sewall, Arthur, 373
Seward, William H., 295, 402
Sewing machine, 323, 332
Sex and sexuality: Progressives and, 383, 388; Margaret Sanger and, 394; automobiles and, 439; in 1920s, 443, 445; after Second World War, 545–546, 547; counterculture and, 570; in 1970s, 591; Clinton and, 624–625; John F. Kennedy and, 625
Sex roles, *see* Gender and gender roles
Sex typing, 388
Sexual Behavior in the Human Female (Kinsey), 547
Sexual Behavior in the Human Male (Kinsey), 547
Sexual discrimination, 578

Sexual division of labor, 305
Sexual harassment: Thomas-Hill hearings and, 613; charges against Clinton, 624
Sexually transmitted diseases, 609
Sexual revolution, 591
Sexual violence, 383
Seymour, Horatio, 289
Shah of Iran, 592–593
Shamans and shamanism, 591
Shame of the Cities, The (Steffens), 379
Shandong, China, 407, 413, 417, 484
Shanghai: Japanese bombing of, 484
Shantytowns, 455, 459
Sharecropping, 284, 367–368, 461, 468, 472
Share Our Wealth Society (Long), 464
Shaw, Bernard, 602, 602(illus.)
Sheep: Southwestern Indians and, 301
Sheepherders: cattle and, 314
Sheldon, Charles, 385
Shelley v. Kramer, 541
Shell shock, 421
Shepherd, Matthew: murder of, 624
Sheppard-Towner Act (1921), 438
Sheridan, Fort, 327
Sherman, John, 335
Sherman, William Tecumseh, 283, 532
Sherman Anti-Trust Act (1890), 335, 393
Sherman Silver Purchase Act (1890), 363, 370
Shi'ite Islamic Republic: in Iran, 593
Ships and shipping: steamships, 398; steel-hulled warships, 403; in First World War, 415, 418; military, 477; in Second World War, 496
Shopping centers, 339
Show business: in late 19th century, 355–356
Shuffle Along (musical comedy), 449
Siberia, 514
Sierra Club, 308
Signal Corps, 421
"Significance of the Frontier in American History, The" (Turner), 299
Silent majority, 572
Silent Spring (Carson), 550
Silicon Valley, 620
Silver: in West, 307; coinage of, 363, 363(illus.), 372–374; 1890s depression and, 370
Silver Republicans, 373
Simmons, William J., 445
Simpson, "Sockless Jerry," 369
Simpson-Rodino Act, *see* Immigration Reform and Control Act (1986)
Sinai Peninsula, 583
Sinclair, Upton, 379, 390, 464
Sin fronteras (without borders), 441
Singer, Isaac M., 332
"Single tax" proposal, 335
Sino-American relations, 520, 522, 583
Sino-Japanese War (1937), 484
Sino-Soviet relations, 520
Sirhan, Sirhan, 572
Sit-down strike: in automobile industry, 466

Sit-in movement, 553–554, 557
Six-Day War (1967), 583
Sixteenth Amendment, 392, A9
Sixteenth Street Baptist Church (Birmingham): bombing of, 560
Sixth Amendment, A8
Skilled labor, 466; AFL and, 327, 328; women as, 497
Skyscrapers, 346
Slaughter-House cases, 295
"Slave laborers" (workers), 621
"Slave narratives": WPA and, 465
Slaves and slavery: families and, 283. *See also* Africa; African Americans; Revolts and rebellions
Slavic nationalism, 417
Slums: in 1920s, 443; in 1950s, 550
Small, Albion, 384
Smith, Alfred E., 379, 437, 450, 462
Smith, Bessie, 449
Smith Act, *see* Alien Registration (Smith) Act (1940)
Smith College, 384
Smith-Connally Act, *see* War Labor Disputes (Smith-Connally) Act
Smith v. Allwright, 541
Smoke: industrialization, pollution control, and, 336
Smyrna, Georgia: housing in, 532
Soccer: European, 622
Social Darwinism, 334, 335, 385, 399, 400
Social Evil in Chicago, The, 383
Social Gospel, 385, 477
Social institutions: in Progressive era, 378, 383–385
Socialism: in Russia, 422; in eastern Europe, 611
Socialist Labor Party, 371
Socialist Party of America, 372, 379, 392, 393, 426, 427, 428, 429, 459
Socialists and socialism, 371–372, 373, 379, 380(illus.)
Social mobility, 371
Social science, 384
Social Security, 473; Reagan and, 598, 600
Social Security Act, 465, 471; amendments to (1954), 538
Social service, 376
Social welfare, *see* Welfare and welfare programs
Society: in Civil War, 280; in West, 307–308; industrialization and, 329–333; cities and, 337–338, 608–609; multiracial, 403; First World War and, 417; in 1920s, 451–452; Second World War and, 509–510; after Second World War, 532–534; divisions in, 567–570, 575–576; in 1980s, 606–610; in 1990s, 617–623; in 21st century, 630–636
Society of American Indians (SAI), 387
Society of Friends, *see* Quakers
Sociologists: Progressive, 384
Sod houses: on Great Plains, 312, 313(illus.)
Soil: efficient use of, 314

Soldiers: pensions for Union, 360; in Span-ish-American War, 406; in First World War, 420–423; in Vietnam War, 563, 564, 581; in Iraq (2003–), 628. *See also* Armed forces; Military
Solidarity (Poland), 603
Solid South, 465
Solomon Islands, 403
Somalia, 622
Somme, Battle of the, 421
Somoza, Anastasio, 604
Soong Meiling (Madame Jiang, China), 484
Sorensen, Theodore, 555
Sound money policies, 293
South: black codes in, 285–286; military districts in, 287, 288(map); "military rule" myth in, 289; Reconstruction in, 289–292; Republican Party and, 290–291; "Negro Rule" myth and, 291; carpetbaggers and scalawags in, 291–292; Klan in, 292, 293; Amnesty Act and, 293; technology and industry and, 323; child labor in, 324–325; segregation in, 328, 384; black migration to cities in, 341; pensions for soldiers in, 360; African Americans in, 365–366, 385; farming in, 367–368; Farmers' Alliances in, 368–369; Progressive reform in, 379–380; in Great Depression, 468; TVA and, 468; New Deal in, 471; desegregation in, 541; economy of, 543; Freedom Riders in, 558; Nixon and, 585; growth of, 588. *See also* Reconstruction
South Africa, 583, 606, 611
South America, 610
South Dakota, 308
Southeast Asia: Vietnam War and, 565(map); Kennan on, 567; communism in, 581; im-migrants from, 609–610
Southern Baptist Foreign Mission Board, 397
Southern Christian Leadership Conference (SCLC), 541, 558, 559
Southern Europe: immigrants from, 385
Southern Pacific Railroad, 310
Southern Tenant Farmers' Union, 472
South Korea, 520, 522, 603. *See also* Korea; Korean War
South Vietnam, 529, 563. *See also* Vietnam War
Southwest, 301, 543, 544(map); Indians in, 301; oil in, 307; Las Gorras Blancas (White Hats) in, 368; Mexican Americans in, 610
Southwest Railroad, 327
Sovereignty: Chinese, 484
Soviet Union: U.S. policy toward, 479–480, 512; Nazi nonaggression pact with, 483; in-vasion of Finland by, 485; Lend-Lease aid to, 488; Second World War and, 496, 505, 514; Truman Doctrine and, 516; atomic bomb and, 519; China and, 520; North Korea and, 521; Third World and, 525; Cuba and, 528; Kennedy and, 556; détente with, 582–583; Afghanistan and, 592; Carter and, 592; collapse of, 596–597, 611;

Reagan and, 603–604, 606; arms reduction treaties with, 612. *See also* Cold War; Russia
Space exploration, 523, 538; spending for, 543; Kennedy and, 560; *Apollo 8* and, 572; moon landing and, 590
Spain, 398; Cuba and, 404–405
Spanish-American War, 374, 389–390, 405–407, 413; Hawaiian annexation and, 403–404; casualties in, 405(illus.), 406; in Philippines, 406
Spanish Civil War (1936), 482
Spanish language: bilingualism and, 610
Special interests, 362, 381
Spectator amusements, 448
Speculation: land, 305; Panic of 1907 and, 391; Great Depression and, 451
Speech, freedom of, 428, 432–433
Spending: in First World War, 423–424; consumer, 438–439; in Second World War, 499; defense, 519, 531, 600, 603, 612, 619; on Korean War, 522; military, 522, 636; under Eisenhower, 538; by teens, 547; on social programs, 562; in Reagan-Bush era, 596, 598; cutting, 619
Spheres of influence: in China, 407, 409(map), 410; Second World War and, 490; Soviet, 505
Spies and spying: in Second World War, 502; in 1950s, 538–540. *See also* Intelligence operations
Spirit of St. Louis, The, 434
Spock, Benjamin, 546
Spoils system, 360–362, 364
Sports: organized, 352–355; intercollegiate, 384, 452; in universities, 384; in 1920s, 448–449, 452; women in, 579
Sprang, William, 283(illus.)
Springfield, Oregon: school shootings in, 624
Sputnik, 523, 538
Sri Lanka (Ceylon), 513
Stagflation, 587, 597, 599, 600
Stalin, Joseph, 470, 496, 505, 507(illus.); after Second World War, 514; Czechoslovakia and, 519; Korean War and, 521
Stalwarts, 360
Standard-gauge rails, 310
Standardization, 322, 329
Standard of living: in 1950s, 543–544; for immigrants, 550. *See also* Lifestyle
Standard Oil Company: trusts, holding companies, and, 333–334; Tarbell's history of, 379; in Latin America, 477; in Mexico, 481
Standard time zones, 310
Stanton, Edwin M., 288, 289
Stanton, Elizabeth Cady, 282, 287, 366, 388
Starr, Kenneth, 624
Starvation: in Great Depression, 455
State(s): business regulation by, 335; disfran-chisement of blacks by, 365; segregation in, 366; woman suffrage in, 366–367, 388, 389(map); elderly in, 443; new immigrants

in, 573; revenue-sharing programs with, 585; deficits in, 589; tax increases in, 630
State Department: in Cold War, 522–523; McCarthy and, 539
Statehood: in West, 308; Puerto Rico and, 414
State legislatures: election of senators and, 360, 381
States' rights, 285, 293
State universities: agricultural research at, 313–314
Steamboats, 398
Steam engines, 318
Stearns, Harold, 450
Steel and steel industry, 310, 323, 436; pools in, 333; mergers in, 334; construction with, 346; strike in, 428
Steffens, Lincoln, 379
Steinbeck, John, 465
Stem cells: ethics of use, 632–633
Stephenson, David, 445
Stereotypes, 355, 399–400
Sterilization statutes, 385
Stevens, John L., 403
Stevens, Thaddeus, 281, 287–288
Stimson, Henry L., 486, 515
Stimson Doctrine, 484
Stinger missiles, 603
Stock(s), 333, 334
Stock and bond exchanges, 334
Stockman, David, 600
Stock market, 479; 1929 crash of, 450–451; in 1987, 601; in 1990s, 623; after Septem-ber 11, 2001, 627
Stone, Lucy, 366
Stonewall riot, 580
STOP-ERA movement, 580
Strategic Defense Initiative (SDI, "Star Wars"), 603, 606
Strike(s): in Panic of 1873, 293; at Water-town Arsenal, 317; against railroads, 326, 327, 365, 371; Haymarket Riot and, 327, 371; Knights of Labor and, 327; Home-stead strike, 328, 371; IWW and, 328; by miners, 328, 371, 390–391; Pullman strike, 328, 365, 371; by ILGWU, 329; by telephone operators, 329; in 1890s depression, 371; in First World War, 426; after First World War, 428; in automobile industry, 466; in Great Depression, 466; at Republic Steel, 466–467; by coal miners, 498; in Second World War, 498; postwar, 534; after Second World War, 537; against grape growers, 576–577
Strikebreakers, 326, 327, 347
Strip-mining, 599
Strong, Josiah, 400
Student Nonviolent Coordinating Commit-tee (SNCC), 557–558, 559, 568
Students: Vietnam deferments for, 566; 1960s student movement, 568–569;

protests in France by, 572. *See also* Antiwar protests

Students for a Democratic Society (SDS), 568

Subcultures: of homosexuals and unmarried people, 351

Submarines: in First World War, 415, 418, 419–420, 419(illus.), 422; in Second World War, 488, 494; nuclear, 523

Subsidies: to railroads, 310; to corporations, 334; for workers' housing, 378; to farmers, 461, 467; for rents, 562

Subtreasury plan: of Farmers' Alliances, 369, 437

Suburbs, 441; annexation of, 339; mass transit and, 339; after Second World War, 532, 536; norms of, 545–546; lifestyle in, 546

Subversives: fears of, 539

Subways, 339

Sudeten region: German invasion of, 482

Suez Canal, 398, 412, 496; crisis over (1956), 525, 529

Suffrage: Fourteenth Amendment and, 287. *See also* Voting and voting rights; Woman suffrage

Suffragists, 388

Sugar industry: in Hawai'i, 403; McKinley Tariff and, 403; in Cuba, 404, 481, 528

Sugar Trust, 335

Sullivan, "Big Tim," 379

"Summer of Love," 570

Summit meetings: in Paris (1960), 525; in Reykjavik, 606

Sumner, Charles, 281, 402

Sunbelt, 533, 543, 544(map), 588; in 1970s and 1980s, 589(map)

Sunday, Billy, 448

Sunday closing laws, 360, 379

Superfund, 587

Superpowers: arms race and, 556; U.S. as, 622

Supply-side economics, 599–600

Supreme Court (U.S.): Reconstruction and, 295–296; on Indian affairs, 303; on working conditions, 326; on interstate commerce and labor strikes, 328; on corporations, 333; on restraint of trade, 335; Chinese and, 344; railroads and, 362; blacks and, 365; segregation and, 366; Granger laws and, 368; labor reforms and, 381; Progressive legal thinking and, 384; on trusts, 390; Taft and, 392; Jews on, 393; on abortion, 395; civil liberties and, 427–428; business and, 436; AAA and, 461; NRA and, 461; Franklin D. Roosevelt and, 470–471; civil rights and, 541; Nixon and, 585; Reagan and, 599; Clarence Thomas nomination to, 613; 2000 election and, 626; list of justices, A19–A20

Suribachi, Mount, 508

Surplus: exportation of, 399

Sussex (ship), 419

Swann v. Charlotte-Mecklenburg, 585

Swanson, Gloria, 445

Sweatshops, 329, 376

Swift, Gustavus, 334

Syphilis, 303

Syria, 513, 604

Taft, Robert A., 519

Taft, William Howard, 391–392, 413; on expansionism, 401; as Chief Justice, 436

Taft-Hartley Act (1947), 534–535, 537

Taft-Katsura Agreement (1905), 413

Taiwan, *see* Formosa

Takeovers: corporate, 601

Taliban, 617, 626–627

Tammany Hall, 349, 379, 450

Tanguay, Eva, 355

Tanks: in Second World War, 496

Tarbell, Ida M., 379

Tariffs, 364, 436; as government assistance to business, 335; of McKinley, 362, 373; in Gilded Age, 362–363; Taft and, 391; reform, 393; Cuba and, 404; in Great Depression, 479. *See also* Protective tariffs

Taxation, 394; by Reconstruction governments, 292; income tax, 392, 393; in First World War, 425; Coolidge and, 437; Huey Long on, 464; for Social Security, 473; in Second World War, 499; Nixon and, 585; resistance to, 589, 618; Reagan and, 596, 597, 599, 601; cuts in, 600; George W. Bush and, 626; state increases in, 630

Tax relief: for business, 334

Taylor, Frederick W., 323–324

Taylor, Major, 353

Taylor Grazing Act (1934), 467

Teachers: Klan violence against, 292; in Philippines, 408

Teach-ins, 567, 569

Teamster's Union, 466

Teapot Dome scandal, 437

Technology, 377; railroads and, 310; agriculture and, 314; for meatpacking industry, 315; industrialization and, 317–318, 319–324; consequences of, 323; southern industry and, 323; for housing, 345–346; for movies, 355–356; international communications and, 402; road building and, 439; in 1950s, 550; in 1970s, 590; revolution in, 620; worldwide quality of life and, 622; reproductive, 632; in 20th century, 633

Teenagers: in 1950s, 547. *See also* Youth; Youth culture

Teheran: U.S. embassy in, 593

Teheran meeting (1943), 505

Tejanos, 341

Telecommunications: global, 321; deregulation of, 600, 601

Telecommunications Act (1996), 619

Telegraph, 321, 321(illus.), 398, 402

Telephone, 323, 356

Telephone Operators' Department of the International Brotherhood of Electrical Workers, 329

Televangelists, 607

Television, 545; preachers on, 545; youth culture and, 547; Vietnam War and, 567; sex, sexuality, and, 591; CNN and, 602

Teller, Henry M., 373

Teller Amendment (1898), 405, 411

Temperance, 324, 350, 383

Temple, Shirley, 539

10 percent plan, 281

Tenant farming, 367–368, 436; in New Deal, 461, 468; in 1930s, 472; in 1950s, 550

Tenements, 345, 346(illus.)

Tennessee Iron and Coal Company, 391

Tennessee Valley Authority (TVA, 1933), 468

Tenth Amendment, 366, A8

Tenure of Office Act, 288–289

Termination policy: for Native Americans, 550–551

Terrorism: by Klan, 281, 292, 293; PLO and, 583, 606; in Middle East, 604–606; by Islamic fundamentalists, 615–616; on September 11, 2001, 615–616; against Israel, 622–623; counterterrorism and, 626–627; confronting, 633–635

Tet Offensive, 570

Texas, 310; oil in, 307

Textile industry, 318; electricity and, 323; in South, 323; women in, 324

Thailand, 490

Thanksgiving (holiday), 352

Thayer, Webster, 446

Theater, *see* Drama

Therapeutic culture, 591

Thieu, Nguyen Van, 581

Third Amendment, A7

Third parties, 374, 618, 619

Third World, 513; CIA covert operations in, 523; struggle for, 525–530; newly independent nations in, 526(illus.); Kennedy and, 556; Nixon, Kissinger, and, 583

Thirteenth Amendment, 282, 293, A8

This Side of Paradise (Fitzgerald), 449

Thomas (ship), 408

Thomas, Allison, 511

Thomas, Clarence: nomination of, 613

Thomas, Norman, 432, 459

369th Infantry Regiment, 421

Three Mile Island nuclear plant, 590

Tiananmen Square, 611

Tijerina, Reies, 577

Tilden, Bill, 448

Tilden, Samuel J., 296, 296(map)

Till, Emmett: murder of, 541

Timber and Stone Act (1878), 307

Time magazine, 602

Time zones, 310

Title IX, *see* Higher Education Act

Tito, Josip Broz, 515

Tobacco and tobacco industry: industrialization and, 323; after Civil War, 367

Tokyo: Doolittle bombing of, 495
Tolstoy, Leo, 382
Tombstone, 308
Tongs (Chinese associations), 343
Tonkin Gulf crisis, 491
Tonkin Gulf Resolution (1964), 581
Towns, *see* Cities and towns
Townsend, Francis E., 464
Toynbee Hall (London), 349
Trade: Indian-white, 303; expansion of foreign, 399; navalism and, 403; Open Door policy and, 410; Mexico and, 412; in First World War, 417–418; Great Depression and, 476, 479; Chinese- and Japanese-American, 484; free trade, 514; promotion of, 620; September 11, 2001, and, 633
Trade barriers, 620
Trade deficits, 588, 620
Trademark law (1881), 332
Trade unions, 326, 328, 329
Transatlantic telegraph cable, 321, 321(illus.), 402
Transistors, 543
Transportation, 402; in West, 310; growth of, 318; engineering advances in, 398; desegregation in, 541. *See also* Mass transportation; Roads and highways
Trans-Siberian Railway (Russia), 398
Travel: transatlantic air, 434; by 21st century, 633
Treaties, *see* specific treaties
Trench warfare: in First World War, 421
Triangle Shirtwaist Company fire, 326
Tribal government, 467
Triborough Bridge, 461
"Trickle-down" economics, 600
Tripartite Pact, 488, 490
Triple Alliance, 417
Triple Entente, 417
Tripp, Linda, 624
Trippe, Juan, 442
Truman, Harry S, 508; Vietnam policy of, 512; Stalin and, 514; iron curtain and, 516(illus.); MacArthur and, 520, 521; Korean War and, 521, 537–538; Taft-Hartley Act and, 528; domestic policy of, 536–537; 1948 election and, 537; as vice president, 538; loyalty oaths and, 539
Truman Doctrine, 516
Trump, Donald, 609
Trusts, 333–334, 335; Theodore Roosevelt and, 390; Taft and, 391; Wilson and, 393; antitrust prosecution and, 479
Turkey, 417, 422; Soviets and, 514; Cold War and, 516; U.S. missiles in, 557
Turner, Frederick Jackson, 299, 384, 403
Turner, Ted, 602
Tuskegee Airmen, 503
Tuskegee Institute, 314, 386, 386(illus.), 479
Tutsis: in Rwanda, 622
TVA, *see* Tennessee Valley Authority (TVA, 1933)

Twain, Mark, 309, 358, 406
Twelfth Amendment, A8
Twentieth Amendment, 459, A10
Twenty-fifth Amendment, A11
Twenty-first Amendment, 382, A10
Twenty-first U.S. Colored Regiment, 279
Twenty-fourth Amendment, A10–A11
Twenty-One Demands, 413
Twenty-second Amendment, A10
Twenty-seventh Amendment, A11
Twenty-sixth Amendment, A11
Twenty-third Amendment, A10
Tyler, Elizabeth, 445
Typewriters, 323, 324
Typhoid, 347, 348, 406

UAW, *see* United Auto Workers (UAW)
U-boats, *see* Submarines
Ukraine, 382(illus.), 422
U.N., *see* United Nations (U.N.)
Underclass, 607
Underwood Tariff (1913), 393
Undocumented workers, 610
Unemployed Councils, 458–459
Unemployment: in Panic of 1873, 293; in 1890s depression, 370; after First World War, 435; in Great Depression, 454, 461; African American, 457; of women, 457; in New Deal, 463, 471; in 1939, 472; in Germany, 481; after Second World War, 534; under Reagan, 600; in 1990s, 623
Unemployment compensation, 465, 534
Unification: of Germany, 611
Unilateralism: of George W. Bush, 626
Union League clubs, 292
Union of Soviet Socialist Republics (USSR), *see* Soviet Union
Union Pacific Railroad, 308, 310
Unions, *see* Labor unions
United Auto Workers (UAW), 466, 543
United Farm Workers (UFW), 576–577
United Fruit Company, 410–411, 477, 528
United Mine Workers, 390–391, 436, 466, 498
United Nations (U.N.), 505; Cold War and, 515; China and, 521; Palestine partition and, 528; Persian Gulf War (1991) and, 612; Kosovo peacekeeping by, 622; Iraq war (2003–) and, 628
United States: in world economy, 477–479, 478(illus.); after Second World War, 514
U.S. Agency for International Development (USAID), 527
U.S. Chamber of Commerce, 379
U.S. Commission on Civil Rights, 541
U.S. Employment Service, 426
U.S. Forest Service, 391
U.S. Housing Corporation, 426
U.S. Information Agency (USIA), 524
U.S. Patent Office, 319
U.S. Steel Corporation, 334, 391, 428, 436
U.S. v. Cruikshank, 296
U.S. v. E. C. Knight Co., 335
U.S. v. Reese, 365

Universal Negro Improvement Association (UNIA), 441
Universities and colleges, 408; for black students, 284, 314, 384; Morrill Acts and, 313, 314; state schools as, 313–314; football in, 353–355; for African Americans, 366, 367(illus.), 384; agricultural, 368; land-grant colleges, 383, 384; curriculum expansion in, 383–384; growth of, 383–384; women in, 384, 579; after Second World War, 535; *Bakke* case and, 591
University of Alabama, 559
University of California (Berkeley): Free Speech Movement in, 568–569; People's Park in, 597
University of Chicago: Laboratory School at, 383; nuclear chain reaction at, 497
University of Mississippi, 559
University of Philippines, 408
Unmarried people, 351, 591
Unsafe at Any Speed (Nader), 561
Unskilled labor, 328, 341, 347
Upper class: in Progressive era, 379
"Uprising of the 20,000," 329
Upward Bound program, 561
Urban areas: growth of, 313; mass transportation and, 339; in First World War, 426; in 1920s, 440–441; suburbs and, 441; riots in 1960s, 567; crises in, 608–609; Hispanics in, 630. *See also* Cities and towns
Urban borderlands, 343–344
Urban engineers, 348
Urbanization: industrialization, technology and, 338; 1870–1920, 338–343, 340(map); family life and, 350–352
Urban League, 559
Uruguay Round: of GATT, 620
USA PATRIOT Act, *see* PATRIOT Act
USSR, *see* Soviet Union
Utah, 307, 308; irrigation in, 309
Utilities, 319, 345, 379, 381
U-2 spy plane, 525, 555

Valentino, Rudolph, 449
Values: in 1920s, 448
Vance, Cyrus, 592
Vanzetti, Bartolomeo, 446
Vaqueros, 314
Vare, "Duke," 348
Vaudeville, 355
V-E Day, 506(map)
Veiller, Lawrence, 345
Venereal disease, 421, 570
Venezuela: boundary dispute of, 404
Venona Project, 538–539, 540
Veracruz, 412
Verdun, battle at, 421
Versailles Treaty, 417, 481, 482
Vertical integration, 334
Veterans: Civil War pensions for, 360, 364; as Bonus Army, 459; racism toward, 536; universities and, 536; after Vietnam War, 582

Vetoes, 286, 289, 364, 587
Vice president: list of, A17–A18
Vichy government, 486
Victoria (England), 294
Victory gardens, 494
Vieques Island, 414
Vietcong, 530, 563, 564
Vietminh, 511, 520, 529
Vietnam, 565(map); OSS in, 511–512; independence of, 512; Cold War and, 513; France and, 520; division of, 529; Eisenhower and, 529; bombings of, 564; wounded in, 566(illus.); immigrants from, 595–596, 609; diplomatic recognition to, 620. *See also* Indochina
Vietnamization policy, 580
"Vietnam syndrome," 582
Vietnam War, 555, 563–567; Southeast Asia and, 565(map); Tet Offensive in, 570; Pentagon Papers and, 574; end of, 580–582. *See also* Antiwar protests
Vigilantism: First World War and, 427, 428–429
Viguerie, Richard, 597
Villa, Francisco "Pancho," 413
Villages, *see* Cities and towns
Villard, Henry, 319
Violence: against blacks, 286, 292, 365, 459, 567; against Indians, 295; against Planned Parenthood clinics, 395; in labor strikes, 466; in civil rights movement, 558. *See also* Riots
Virginian, The (book), 316
Virgin Islands: annexation of, 402
Vitamins, 443
V-J Day, 495(map)
Voice of America, 527
Volkswagen, 479
Volunteerism: in Great Depression, 458
Voting and voting rights: Fourteenth Amendment and, 287; African Americans and, 290, 365, 466, 558; Klan and, 292; for women, 308, 426, 429, 438; political machines and, 348; 1870–1896, 360; in Progressive era, 378; in Cuba, 411
Voting Rights Act (1965), 561

Wabash case, 362, 368
WACs (Women's Army Corps), 504
Wade, Benjamin, 281
Wade-Davis bill (1864), 281–282
Wage labor, 329, 330–331
Wages: for women, 324, 444; iron law of, 326; vs. living costs, 329; industrialization and, 330; minimum, 537, 577; in 1950s, 543
Wagner, Robert F., 379
Wagner Act, see National Labor Relations (Wagner) Act (1935)
Wake Island, 406, 490
Walker, C. J., 439
Wallace, George, 559; 1968 election and, 572; 1972 election and, 585

Wallace, Henry A., 516, 537; as vice president, 508
Wallace, Henry C., 437
Walsh, David I., 379
Wanamaker's, 332
War brides: in Second World War, 501
Ward, Lester, 335, 384
War industries: wastes from, 510
War Industries Board (WIB), 394, 425
War Labor Disputes (Smith-Connally) Act, 498
Warner, Charles Dudley, 358
War on Poverty, 561–563
War on terrorism, 617, 626–627; invasion of Iraq (2003) and, 628
War Powers Act (1973), 582, 586
War Production Board, 496
War Refugee Board, 504
Warren, Earl, 541, 560
Warren Commission, 560
War Revenue Act (1917), 425
Wars and warfare: Indians and, 303–304; condemnation of, 477; technology and, 590; ethnic, 622. *See also* specific battles and wars
Warsaw Pact (1955), 518, 525, 611
War Shipping Board, 425
Warships, 403; in Second World War, 488
Washington (state), 307, 308
Washington, Booker T., 386–387, 386(illus.), 479
Washington, D.C.: Coxey's march on, 372; women's abortion rights march on, 395
Washington Naval Conference, 477
Washington Post: Watergate and, 585
Washington Treaty (1871), 402
Waste: atomic, 510. *See also* Sewage disposal
Water: for West, 309–310; in Great Plains, 312; purification of, 347–348; diseases and, 633
Water closets, 331
Watergate scandal, 576, 585–587
Water pollution, 347
Water power: sites, 391
Watertown Arsenal, 317
Watson, Tom, 369, 373
Watt, James, 598
Watts (Los Angeles): riots in, 567
Wealth and wealthy, 607; from natural resources, 306; industrialization and, 330; Social Darwinism and, 334; intellectual thought on, 335; in 1980s, 596, 601, 603(illus.), 609; taxation of, 601; in 1990s, 623
Wealth gap: worldwide, 620–621
Weapons: in Vietnam War, 567; for contras, 604. *See also* Arms and armaments
Weapons of mass destruction: Iraq war and, 628
Weaver, James B., 369, 370
Web, *see* World Wide Web
Webb-Pomerene Act (1918), 479
Webster v. Reproductive Health Services, 599
Welch, Joseph, 540

Welfare and welfare programs, 364, 448, 619; AFDC and, 465, 562; Reagan and, 597, 598; cuts in, 600; reform of, 619, 623. *See also* Relief programs
Wellesley College, 427
Wells, Ida B., 365, 366
West: Turner's frontier theory and, 299; regions of, 300; Indians in, 301–305; resources of, 306–309, 306(map); development of, 306(map), 316; mining in, 307; society in, 307–308; conservation in, 308, 391; states in, 308; water in, 309–310; Theodore Roosevelt and, 316; Hispanics in, 341; farming in, 368; anti-Chinese riots in, 400; in New Deal, 467; growth of, 588
"West" (capitalist countries), 513
West Bank, 583, 592, 604, 622
West Coast, 543, 544(map). *See also* Pacific Ocean region
Western Europe, 517. *See also* Eastern Europe; Europe and Europeans
Western Federation of Miners, 328
Western Health Reform Institute, 331
Westerns (movies), 316
Western Samoa, 402
West Germany, 519
West Indies: immigrants from, 341
Westinghouse Electric, 319
Westmoreland, William, 566, 570
West Virginia (ship), 489(illus.)
Weyler, Valeriano, 404
Wharton, Edith, 449
"What Every Girl Should Know" (Sanger), 394
Wheat, 314
Whey (Chinese loan associations), 343
Whiskey, 333
White, Theodore A., 523
White, William Allen, 373
White Citizens' Councils, 541
White-collar workers, 352, 543–544
White Hats (Las Gorras Blancas), 368
Whites: Reconstruction and, 290; racism against Indians, 293–295; West and, 300, 306–309; migration of, 301; Indians and, 302, 303–304; in Australia, 311; African Americans and, 365; in Hawai'i, 403; employed women among, 444; desegregation and, 541; national culture and, 545–546; in 1950s, 550; poverty of, 608; 2000 election and, 626
White slavery, 383
White Slave Traffic Act (Mann Act, 1910), 383, 384
White supremacy, 295, 366, 624; Douglass on, 297; Progressives and, 380; in 1990s, 623
Whitewater scandal, 619, 624
WHO, *see* World Health Organization (WHO)
Whyte, William H., 547, 549
Wildlife: conservation and, 308
Wild West, 299, 308

Williams, Burt, 355
Williams, William Appleman, 582
Wilmington, North Carolina: race riot in, 347
Wilson, Horace, 354
Wilson, William Dean, 492–493
Wilson, Woodrow, 294, 352, 376, 380, 392–393, 399, 413, 476; racism of, 387; First World War and, 393–394, 415, 416, 417, 420, 429–431; Mexico and, 412–413, 481; Fourteen Points of, 422; civil liberties under, 427–428; League of Nations and, 430–431; Haiti and, 480
Wilson-Gorman Tariff (1894), 362–363, 404
Wire telegraphy, 402
Wisconsin, 381
"Wise use" policy: of conservation, 391
Witch hunt: in 1950s, 539
Withholding taxes, 499
Wobblies, see Industrial Workers of the World (IWW, Wobblies)
Woman Rebel, The (Sanger), 394
Woman's Christian Temperance Union (WCTU), 358, 379, 382, 383
Woman's Peace Party, 419
Woman suffrage, 358, 387, 388, 426; Fourteenth Amendment and, 287; movement, 366–367; before 1920, 389(map)
Women: Thirteenth Amendment and, 282; Fourteenth Amendment and, 287; property rights for, 290; Supreme Court and, 295–296; Indian, 304–305; in West, 307; voting rights for, 308, 426, 429, 438; in textile industry, 323; in tobacco production, 323; in work force, 324, 330, 444, 444(illus.), 457, 588; employment trends and, 325(illus.); work reforms and, 326, 381, 384; unions and, 327, 328, 329; clothing and, 332; black women in service sector, 341; social mobility and, 343; in professions, 349; settlement-house movement and, 349–350; Boston marriages of, 351; unmarried, 351; in sports, 353, 355; in show business, 355; as missionaries, 361, 361(illus.), 396–397, 401; black female reformers, 366; Farmers' Alliance and, 368; as reformers, 376, 379; organizations of, 378; as southern Progressives, 380; Russian temperance and, 382; prostitution and, 383; higher education for, 384; feminism and, 388; birth-control controversy and, 394–395; education of, 408; antiwar protests by, 419; in First World War, 420–421, 426; in 1920s, 443; in Great Depression workplace, 457; during Second World War, 494, 497–498, 500, 504; magazines for, 545; gender roles and, 546; in 1950s, 546–547; Civil Rights Act of 1964 and, 560–561; poverty among, 563; affirmative action for, 578; opposition to women's movement by, 579–580; roles

in 1970s, 591; sexual revolution and, 591; Christian fundamentalists and, 608; 2000 election and, 626
Women and Economics (Gilman), 388
Women of color, see People of color
Women's clubs, 387–388
Women's Committee: of Council of National Defense, 426
Women's Era Club, 366
Women's International League for Peace and Freedom (WILPF), 419, 476–477, 567
"Women's jobs": in Great Depression, 457
Women's Loyal National League, 282
Women's Medical College, 384
Women's movement, 387–388, 575; labor and, 329; of 1960s and 1970s, 578–580
Women's National Indian Association (WNIA), 304–305
Women's Peace Union, 477
Women's rights: advocates for, 387; missionaries and, 397
Women's Trade Union League (WTUL), 329, 438
Wonderful Wizard of Oz, The (Baum): as Populist parable, 374–375
Wong, Albert and Helen Chia, 501
Woodall, Kate, 361(illus.)
Woods, Granville T.: inventions of, 319
Woods, Tiger, 630
Woodstock Festival, 569
Woodward, Bob, 585
Woolworth's: sit-ins at, 553–554
Work: change in nature of, 330–331; compensation for injuries or illness and, 393. See also Labor
Workday, 326, 352, 376, 381, 384, 392, 393, 438
Workers: mass production and, 324; industrial accidents and, 325–326; First World War and, 425–426, 428; in 1920s, 441–443; in Great Depression, 454, 455–457; layoffs of, 457, 588; marginal, 457; craft vs. industrial, 466; in Second World War, 496–498; incomes of, 601; illegal, 610; immigrant, 610. See also Labor; Women
Workers' compensation, 393, 437
Work force: restructuring of, 324; women in, 324, 330, 444; increase in, 330–331
Working class: as employees vs. producers, 324; industrialization and, 330; diet of, 331–332; mass transit and, 339; housing for, 345; political machines and, 348; civil service and, 350; boarders and, 351; leisure and, 356; in Progressive era, 379; lifestyle of, 439
Workplace: conditions in, 326; gender segregation in, 444; women in, 457
Work relief, 461, 464
Works Progress [Projects] Administration (WPA), 464–465
Workweek, 352; in 1920s, 443

World Bank, 514
World Conference on Human Rights, 594
World Court, 430, 476
World Health Organization (WHO), 633
World order: after First World War, 474–476
World power: United States as, 416
World Series, 352
World Trade Center, 615–616, 626
World Trade Organization (WTO), 621–622, 621(illus.)
World War I, see First World War
World War II, see Second World War
World Wide Web, 637
Wounded Knee: battle at, 305; AIM occupation of, 578
WPA, see Works Progress [Projects] Administration (WPA)
Wright, Don, 584
Wright, Richard, 465, 541
WTO, see World Trade Organization (WTO)
Wyoming, 308, 309

Yalta meeting (1945), 505–507, 507(illus.), 514
Yamamoto, Isoroku, 495, 496, 508
Yellow fever, 347, 412, 474
Yellow journalism, 356
Yellowstone River region, 308
Yeoman farmers: as scalawags, 292; after Civil War, 368
Yergin, Daniel, 584
Yippies, 572
Yoga, 591
Yom Kippur War (1973), 583, 584
Yosemite Valley: preservation of, 308
Young, John Russell, 294
Young Americans for Freedom (YAF), 568
Young Joseph (Nez Percé Indians), 303
Young Men's Christian Association (YMCA), 351, 477
Young Plan (1929), 479
Young Women's Christian Association (YWCA), 351, 379
Youth: migrations to cities, 341; subdivisions of, 351
Youth culture: in 1930s, 468–470; in 1950s, 547–548; in 1960s, 568–570
Youth in Crisis (newsreel), 500
Yugoslavia, 515
Yuppies (young urban professionals), 609

Zen Buddhism, 591
Zhou Enlai, 583
Ziegfeld, Florenz, and Ziegfield Follies, 355
Zimmermann telegram, 420
Zionism, 513, 528
Zones: in eastern Europe, 507; in Germany, 515, 519
Zoning commissions, 438
Zoot suit riots, 500